FIREWALL

FIREWALL

The Iran-Contra Conspiracy and Cover-up

Lawrence E. Walsh

THE INDEPENDENT COUNSEL
IN THE IRAN-CONTRA
INVESTIGATION

W. W. NORTON & COMPANY

NEW YORK   LONDON

Copyright © 1997 by Lawrence E. Walsh

All rights reserved
Printed in the United States of America
First published as a Norton paperback 1998

For information about permission to reproduce selections from this book, write to Permissions, W. W. Norton & Company, Inc., 500 Fifth Avenue, New York, NY 10110.

The text of this book is composed in ITC Legacy Serif Book with the display set in Berthold City Medium and Bold.
Composition by Innodata.
Manufacturing by the Haddon Craftsmen, Inc.
Book design by Charlotte Staub.

Library of Congress Cataloging-in-Publication Data

Walsh, Lawrence E.
    Firewall: the Iran-Contra conspiracy and cover-up /
    Lawrence E. Walsh.
    p.   cm.
    Includes index.
    ISBN 978-0-393-31860-9
    1. Iran-Contra Affair, 1985–1990. I. Title.
    E876.W33   1997
    955.05'42—dc21   96-48443   CIP
    ISBN 978-0-393-31860-9

W. W. Norton & Company, Inc., 500 Fifth Avenue,
New York, N.Y. 10110
http://www.wwnorton.com

W. W. Norton & Company Ltd., 10 Coptic Street,
London WC1A 1PU
1 2 3 4 5 6 7 8 9 0

To my wife, Mary,
partner and
best friend

CONTENTS

List of Illustrations   ix

Preface   xiii

PART I

ROGUE CONSPIRACY:

THE CONGRESS AGAINST THE COURTS   1

1. From Stonewall to Firewall   3

2. The Private War   16

3. Call to Counsel   23

4. Opening View   34

5. The Bramble Bush   48

6. First Convictions   72

7. Close Pursuit   96

8. Crossroads   115

9. The Basic Indictment   138

PART II

LITIGATION:

THE COURTS AGAINST THE CONGRESS   161

10. Half a League Onward   163

11. The Trial of Oliver North   182

12. Deniability Triumphant   210

13. The Trial of John Poindexter   222

14. Reversal and Revival   247

15. The CIA Cracks   263

16. Roller Coaster   291

PART III

BEHIND THE FIREWALL   315

17. What the Secretary of State Knew   317

18. The Note-Taker   336

19. The Chief of Staff   355

20. The President's Protector   371

21. Like Brushing His Teeth   387

PART IV

POLITICAL COUNTERATTACK   411

22. Nuclear War   413

23. An Unusual Proposal   434

24. Boomerang: The Character Issue   451

25. Bob Dole, Pardon Advocate   467

26. The Last Card in the Cover-up   490

Reflections   517

Index   533

LIST OF ILLUSTRATIONS

Between pp. 208 and 209:

Ronald Reagan, Oliver North, and Adolfo Calero

Vice President George Bush with Alfonso Robelo, Arturo Cruz, and Adolfo Calero

Adnan Khashoggi with arms broker Manucher Ghorbanifar

Michael Ledeen, McFarlane's consultant-intermediary

David Kimche, director general of the Israeli foreign ministry

Robert "Bud" McFarlane, President Reagan's national security advisor, 1984–85.

McFarlane and Howard Teicher report to President Reagan, Vice President Bush, and Chief of Staff Donald Regan

A closed National Security Planning Group meeting in the White House situation room

Attorney General Edwin Meese takes over from President Reagan in press conference

Vice Admiral John Poindexter

Lieutenant Colonel Oliver North

Retired United States Air Force major general Richard Secord

Secord's partner, Albert Hakim

William Casey, director of central intelligence

Clair George, CIA deputy director for operations

Duane "Dewey" Clarridge, chief of the CIA's Latin American division until 1984 and then chief of the West European division

Alan Fiers, chief of the Central American task force

Judge George MacKinnon, presiding judge of the panel that appoints me independent counsel

Judge Walter Mansfield, a member of the appointing panel

Photographers surprise my German shepherd, Bertie

The "luxurious" office of the independent counsel

Guy Struve, my closest associate counsel

Early team leaders in the investigation

Chief Judge Aubrey Robinson, Jr., who impaneled the grand jury

Fawn Hall, our reluctant informant

Carl "Spitz" Channell, who conspired with North to violate tax laws in their Contra fundraising

Richard Miller, who pleaded guilty to the same crime as Channell

North testifies before the joint select committees

Joint committee leaders take a break during North's immunized testimony

Between pp. 368 and 369:

Joint committee leaders posing with Weinberger

Caspar Weinberger fends off the joint committee's inquiries

Projecting the course of the grand jury's investigation

United States Judge Gerhard Gesell, in charge of the North trial proceedings

With Mike Bromwich and David Zornow, I explain the twenty-three-count indictment of Poindexter, North, Secord, and Hakim

Former judge Abraham Sofaer, legal advisor to the State Department

Attorney General Richard Thornburgh

About to accept the dismissal of the conspiracy and the diversion counts

Our North trial team, John Keker, David Zornow, and Mike Bromwich, after North's conviction

CIA station chief Joseph Fernandez

Judge Claude M. Hilton, who dismissed the Fernandez case because the CIA refused to release nonsecret classified information

President Bush, CIA Director William Webster, and Deputy Director Richard Kerr

U.S. District Judge Harold Greene, who presided over the Poindexter trial proceedings

Vice Admiral John Poindexter after his sentencing

Associate counsel Dan Webb and our Poindexter trial team after Poindexter's conviction

U.S. Court of Appeals Judge Laurence H. Silberman

Chief Judge Patricia Wald, U.S. Court of Appeals for the District of Columbia Circuit

Assistant Secretary of State Elliot Abrams

Charles Allen, North's liaison with the intelligence community

President Bush announces the nomination of Robert Gates for director of the CIA

President Bush criticizes the continuation of my investigation

Attorney General Edwin Meese

Secretary of State George Shultz

Chief of Staff Donald Regan

Deputy independent counsel Craig Gillen explains the Weinberger indictment

Weinberger leaves press conference without taking questions

Senate Republican Leader Bob Dole, opposed to making deals with terrorists

Counsel to the president Boyden Gray with George Bush

Jim Brosnahan takes over the Weinberger trial

Judge William Clark, one of Weinberger's advisors and President Reagan's former national security advisor

William Barr, President Bush's last attorney general

Weinberger and his lawyers react to the pardon by President Bush

Mary Belcher and I leave the press conference after the release of my final report

PREFACE

This is a story of willfulness, a trait shared by many who will read this book as well as by the independent counsel who wrote it. The line between willfulness and independence is often hard to draw. Even harder to draw is the line between willfulness and leadership, the essential attribute of a president.

This is also the story of a serious constitutional confrontation that pitted the executive, legislative, and judicial branches of government against one another. The conflict, which desecrated the rule of law, reached into the White House itself, as two presidents deeply involved in illegal clandestine activities attempted to thwart investigations by Congress and the courts.

The story began in 1984, as President Ronald Reagan's first term in office was ending. At his urging, Congress had for three years supported covert activity by the Central Intelligence Agency to aid the military and paramilitary activities of Nicaraguan insurgents known as the Contras. The president and his foreign policy advisors saw the group's survival as a necessity: The Contras offered the only hope for bringing the communist-leaning government of Nicaragua into the diplomatic framework of the rest of Central America and, more immediately, for stopping the flow of weapons from Cuba through Nicaragua to communist insurgents in El Salvador.

When excesses by the CIA led Congress to terminate the agency's authority to help the Contras, the president and his advisors were unwilling to abandon those whose insurgency they had encouraged. It was an election year, however, and polls showed that public support for the Contras was weak. Unable to make a winning campaign issue of the congressional ban on aid to the Contras, the president decided to evade the ban. To replace the funds formerly appropriated by Congress, he and his national security advisor, Robert C. McFarlane, turned to a wealthy and dependent ally: Saudi Arabia, which contributed the equivalent of more than $1 million a month to the Contras for two years.

Because Congress had prohibited any intelligence agency from assisting the Contras, the president ordered McFarlane—the president's liaison to the national security community—to hold the Contras together. McFarlane selected a member of his staff, Marine Lieutenant Colonel Oliver L. North, to coordinate the administration's effort. North directly advised the Contra leaders on military strategy and tactics, raised money for the Contras, and recruited retired U.S. military officers to procure weapons for them. North and his colleagues ultimately organized a supply network with funds in Swiss banks, arms sources in Portugal, and a small fleet of aircraft for transporting the weapons to Nicaragua.

North's success led to publicity, which sparked congressional inquiries. Fearing that their efforts to persuade Congress to reauthorize and fund the CIA to assist the Contras might be jeopardized by the truth, several high-level Reagan administration officials concealed North's activities by lying to congressional oversight committees. Deceit became essential for North and those who supported him.

After winning reelection, President Reagan undertook another covert program, an effort to release seven American hostages who were being held captive in Lebanon by the radical Shiite Islamic group Hezbollah. Acting against the advice of his principal foreign policy advisors, Secretary of State George P. Shultz and Secretary of Defense Caspar W. Weinberger, as well as his own stated policy against negotiating with terrorists, the president agreed to deal indirectly with the kidnappers: The United States would sell arms to Iran, which was then at war with Iraq, and the Iranian leaders would induce the kidnappers to release the hostages. At the time, the United States was vigorously urging its allies to present a united front in refusing to traffic with terrorists and hostage takers and to refrain from shipping arms to either Iraq or Iran.

For the first half year of the initiative, the American weapons were relayed through Israel. Israel delivered weapons from its own stockpile, with the assurance that it would be replenished by the United States. This secret arrangement violated the Arms Export Control Act, which prohibited the transfer of U.S. arms by any recipient without the express permission of the president and notice to Congress. President Reagan authorized the transfers to Iran, but he deliberately did not notify Congress.

In 1986, President Reagan authorized the CIA to sell arms directly to Iran. Oliver North coordinated this activity for the president. As foreign funding for the Contras ran out, North and his colleagues inflated the price of the weapons sold to Iran and secretly diverted the excess proceeds from the United States to private Swiss bank accounts. They used this money to support the Contras and to fund other covert activities.

In November 1986, after several shipments of arms to Iran, the release of three hostages, and the kidnapping of two more, a Lebanese periodical published an article exposing the arms sales. This led to a new round of deception by high-ranking officials who lied to Congress in a concerted effort to protect President Reagan from disgrace and possible impeachment.

For more than six years, I was responsible for investigating what became known as the Iran-Contra affair and for prosecuting the crimes committed by the individuals who had participated in it. In the process of conducting a criminal investigation of the most complex and difficult sort, I found myself at the center of a constitutional maelstrom: the conflict between the rule of law, as administered by the courts and prosecutors, and the system of political checks and balances, as exercised by the president and the Congress. While struggling to learn the truth and unravel a willful cover-up that extended all the way to the Oval Office, my staff and I had to fend off attacks from members of Congress and the president's cabinet and to break through the barriers erected by the national security community.

In the years since I finished my work as independent counsel, I have been invited to address many groups. The continuing interest in Iran-Contra, not only among lawyers and scholars but also among concerned citizens, has surprised me. On more than one occasion, an audience has sat through a longer than usual speech and then kept me at the podium answering questions for more time than that taken by the speech itself.

As a result, I have been forced to rethink my achievements and mistakes. Did I try to accomplish too much? Was I excessive? Was I obsessive? Were my objectives frustrated by judicial, congressional, or political excesses, or simply by my own errors? Despite many defeats, did I ultimately win? And if I won, was it the war I thought I was fighting or one quite different? Will the effort, however evaluated, deter future comparable misconduct?

Several scholarly works about Iran-Contra have already been written, and the *Report of President's Special Review Board* (the Tower Commission report), *Report of the Congressional Committees Investigating the Iran-Contra Affair*, and my own three-volume *Final Report of the Independent Counsel for Iran/Contra Matters* provide detailed information about the activities of those who participated in the affair. Volume 3 of my report contains 1,150 pages of criticism by subjects of my investigation who disagree with some of the views and statements I have expressed.

This book is intended to provide a relatively simple, straightforward narrative of what happened (although the nature of the investigation makes some repetition inevitable) and to enable readers to evaluate for themselves the performances of the independent counsel and the three branches of government in one of the most serious constitutional confrontations in recent history.

ACKNOWLEDGMENT

I gratefully acknowledge the invaluable editorial contribution of author Anne Meadows, the administrative assistance of Brenda Carman, and the wise counsel and ultimate editorial review by my publisher, Donald Lamm.

To my wife, Mary, and my family and to my associates in the Office of Independent Counsel, Iran-Contra, their spouses and families, I acknowledge my everlasting debt for their loyalty, forbearance, and commitment.

Lawrence E. Walsh
January 20, 1997

PART ONE

Rogue Conspiracy: The Congress Against the Courts

CHAPTER ONE

From Stonewall
to Firewall

On Monday, November 24, 1986, Ronald Reagan left his handsome Oval Office, passed the bright cabinet room, and descended to the situation room in the White House basement. The low-ceilinged, tightly shuttered conference room looked nothing like the bustling wartime military command post its name suggested. The President sat at the end of a long conference table, between Vice President George Bush, Secretary of Defense Caspar Weinberger, Director of Central Intelligence William Casey, and National Security Advisor John Poindexter on his right and Secretary of State George Shultz, Attorney General Edwin Meese, and Chief of Staff Donald Regan on his left. The chairs along the walls, where subordinate staff members usually sat, were empty. A single CIA official had made a report and then left. The taping equipment that sometimes recorded presidential meetings was shut off. The cabinet members took their own notes.

Reagan was within range of impeachment for his secret authorization of the sale of American weapons to Iran in exchange for American hostages, which had violated not only the Arms Export Control Act and the National Security Act but also his own stated policy against dealing with terrorists. Moreover, breaking the cardinal rule of covert operatives, he had begun to believe his own cover: He had persuaded himself that he had not been trading arms for hostages; he had merely tried to establish a friendly relationship with Iranian moderates.

Sitting next to the president, the secretary of state was weighing resignation against the danger of dismissal. Weinberger and Casey, angered by Shultz's unwillingness to support the arms sales publicly, were eager to see him go. As the meeting began, Shultz and Poindexter battled for the president's ear over control of negotiations with Iran. After they wore each other down, Donald Regan turned the discussion to Meese, who, perhaps more than anyone else in the room, felt a personal responsibility for the president's political safety. Regan had that official responsibility, but Meese was the president's most devoted troubleshooter. He had been counselor to the president before becoming attorney general, and he had long served under Reagan in California and in political campaigns.

The sequence of events that necessitated this meeting had begun in 1979, with the overthrow of the shah of Iran and the seizure of the U.S. embassy in Tehran by radical Iranians loyal to an aged Islamic leader, the Ayatollah Ruhollah Khomeini. With its embassy's staff held hostage, the United States had broken diplomatic relations and embargoed trade with Iran. After the hostages were released, the United States made some concessions to Iran but continued to embargo arms shipments. In the meantime, Iraq had opened war on Iran. The United States remained neutral and refused to ship arms to either side.

On January 20, 1984, the secretary of state designated Iran a sponsor of international terrorism. Thereafter, in what was called "Operation Staunch," the United States actively urged its allies not to ship arms to Iran.

Beginning in March 1984, members of Hezbollah, a fundamentalist Shiite group sympathetic to the government of the Ayatollah Khomeini, kidnapped seven Americans—including William Buckley, the CIA chief of station—in Beirut, Lebanon. The United States and, in particular, President Reagan adamantly opposed dealing with hostage takers. "America will never make concessions to terrorists—to do so would only invite more terrorism," he stated to the press on June 18, 1985. "Once we head down that path, there would be no end to it." Three weeks later, I heard him say much the same thing in a speech to the annual meeting of the American Bar Association. The members responded with cheers and a standing ovation.

Not all American foreign policy experts favored the isolation of Iran. Poindexter's predecessor as national security advisor, Robert "Bud" McFarlane, had been concerned with a possible Soviet move after the death of the Ayatollah Khomeini. With support from the CIA, McFarlane had analyzed the feasibility of establishing better relations with moderate Iranians and relaxing the arms embargo to reduce the danger of Iran's being proselytized by the Soviet Union. This tampering with the embargo had been vehemently rejected by Shultz and Weinberger. Iran was desperate for weapons to use in its war with Iraq, however, and various Iranians approached U.S. officials with offers to help free the hostages in Lebanon in exchange for arms. In the summer of 1985, an offer from an Iranian arms broker, Manucher Ghorbanifar, found its way to McFarlane through Israeli intermediaries.

Despite the strong views of Shultz and Weinberger, the high-level Israelis persuaded McFarlane to explore with the president the possibility of discussions with the Iranians. The weapons were said to be merely a token of the administration's good faith to establish the credibility of the Iranian negotiators in their own country. If they succeeded in freeing the hostages, Israel would sell the Iranians missiles that Israel had previously obtained from the United States; the Israelis would then buy replacements from the United States. Casey supported McFarlane. Shultz and Weinberger questioned the likelihood of any favorable changes in our relations with Iran, and they vigorously opposed arms sales to Iran by any nation. Nonetheless, after reflection, the president approved the transaction. Israel, through Ghorbanifar and its private intermediaries shipped ninety-six wire-guided antitank (TOW) missiles to Iran on August 30 and another 408 on September 14. One hostage was released.

In mid-November, McFarlane and Poindexter learned from Lieutenant Colonel Oliver North, the National Security Council counterterrorism expert who kept them abreast of the Israeli arms shipments, that a much larger Israeli arms sale was in train. They informed the president, the vice president, Regan, Casey, and Shultz. Israel was to sell as many as five hundred large Hawk antiaircraft missiles to Iran, with replacements to be supplied by the United States. At least four hostages were to be released.

To locate enough Hawks to replenish Israel's arsenal, McFarlane telephoned Weinberger. The defense secretary protested that the shipment would be illegal, but McFarlane told him that the president had decided the matter. Shultz disapproved of the operation but agreed not to stand in the way.

There were logistical problems, however, because Israeli aircraft carrying weapons could not fly directly to Iran. After the privately chartered aircraft carrying the first shipment had lifted off from Israel, officials in the European country where the Hawks were to be transferred to planes of a different nationality for delivery to Iran unexpectedly denied permission for the cargo to land. The Israeli defense minister telephoned McFarlane for help. He turned to Oliver North, who drew in the CIA, arranging for one of the agency's proprietary air fleets to carry the first installment of the shipment to Iran.

The shipment was a disaster on all counts. Only about eighty Hawks had been available, and when the first eighteen were delivered on November 24, the Iranians were outraged to find that the shipment consisted of outdated Israeli castoffs with the Star of David stenciled on them. At the CIA, John McMahon, the acting director (in Casey's absence), was dumbfounded and then furious to learn of the agency's participation. To provide political and legal cover for the agency, McMahon and Casey promptly obtained a retroactive finding from the president approving the CIA's action.

Fearing for the hostages' safety, the president urgently convened a Saturday-morning session of the National Security Planning Group, the high-level core of the National Security Council. The NSC consisted of four statutory members: the president, the vice president, the secretary of state, and the secretary of defense. Additional invited members had traditionally included the head of the CIA and the chairman of the Joint Chiefs of Staff, but President Reagan had invited so many others to NSC meetings over the years that the NSPG was established to deal with the most sensitive and important issues.

When the group met in the president's residential quarters, Weinberger explicitly warned that the U.S. arms embargo imposed against Iran in 1979 and strengthened in 1983 made the sale of any weapons illegal, even if it was carried out through the Israelis. Moreover, the Arms Export Control Act provided that the resale of so large a quantity of arms by a foreign recipient had to be authorized by the president with notice to Congress.

Dismissing Weinberger's objections, the president declared that "he could answer charges of illegality but he couldn't answer [the] charge that 'big strong President Reagan passed up a chance to free hostages.' " Jokingly, he remarked that if he went to jail, "visiting hours are Thursday."

Weinberger rejoined that Reagan would not be alone.

The consensus of the meeting had been to stop the arms sales and, for the time being, to limit discussions to the improvement of U.S.-Iranian relations. McFarlane delivered this message to Ghorbanifar and the Israeli representatives, but Ghorbanifar refused to relay it to his principals, arguing that the message would be tantamount to a death warrant for the hostages. Although McFarlane advised Reagan to end the negotiations, other Israeli proposals were pressed on the president.

After two more NSPG meetings in January 1986, the president ordered Poindexter and the CIA to drop the Israelis as middlemen and to negotiate a direct sale of arms from the United States to Iran. Reagan signed a presidential finding, which he kept secret from Congress, authorizing the sale. "I agreed to sell TOWs to Iran," he noted in his diary for January 17.

This new covert action was undertaken by Poindexter and North, with the CIA in a supporting role. The financial negotiations and the arms deliveries were handled by North and retired Air Force major general Richard Secord, who was also working with North to resupply the Contras in Nicaragua. North and Secord dealt with Ghorbanifar and midlevel Iranian officials.

Secord delivered a thousand U.S. TOW missiles to Iran in February. Ghorbanifar had paid Secord in advance. Secord had paid the CIA in advance. The CIA had bought the weapons from the Department of Defense at cost. With Poindexter's approval, North and Secord had marked up the price almost threefold—from $3.7 million to $10 million—and kept the extra proceeds to pay for arms for the Contras and for other purposes unauthorized by Congress. No hostages were freed.

In May, at President Reagan's request, McFarlane led a secret mission with North and others to Tehran to deliver two planeloads of spare parts for Hawk missiles and to recover the hostages. After three and a half frustrating days, McFarlane reported failure. He had delivered one planeload of parts, but when this failed to win the release of any more hostages, he held back the second planeload. On his return, he repeated his previous advice to the president: Quit.

Still Ronald Reagan pressed on. After six more weeks, a second hostage was released, so the president authorized the delivery of the second load of Hawk spare parts. North had marked the prices up by 370 percent, and Ghorbanifar had added a markup of his own. The Iranians discovered the markups, however, and refused to pay. Ghorbanifar, as an intermediary, had borrowed to prepay Secord for the U.S. matériel. Secord had already used part of the payment to buy arms for the Contras. While Ghorbanifar haggled with the Iranians for reimbursement, another Iranian intermediary negotiated the sale of five hundred more TOW missiles. Hezbollah then played a cynical hand: As one group of kidnappers was about to release a third hostage, another group kidnapped two more.

On November 3, the plot unraveled. A Lebanese periodical, *Al Shiraa*, published a story revealing that the United States had sold arms to Iran. The article also detailed McFarlane's failed mission to Tehran, portraying McFarlane as a supplicant and North as a naive amateur carrying a

Bible and a chocolate cake. Picked up by the news media in the United States and abroad, and confirmed by the speaker of the Iranian parliament, Ali Akbar Rafsanjani, the story could not be ignored.

From the beginning, the White House had looked for ways to suppress the truth. The story had "no foundation," President Reagan assured reporters on November 6, and publicity about it was "making it more difficult for us in our effort to get the other hostages free." In his diary the next day, he sketched his approach: "We can't and won't answer [questions] because [to do so] would endanger those we are trying to help."

Vice President George Bush, who had just begun keeping a diary, also understood the need for secrecy. "I'm one of the few people that know fully the details," he wrote on November 5, "and there is a lot of flack and misinformation out there. It is not a subject we can talk about."

Poindexter and Casey argued forcefully against any disclosure. Both encouraged North to continue his secret negotiations with emissaries from Tehran.

Meanwhile, journalists energetically pursued the story. Rafsanjani supplied additional details of McFarlane's visit. Don Regan fingered McFarlane, in anonymous comments to magazine reporters, as the central culprit in humiliating the nation.

McFarlane had at first brushed off the story as "fanciful." On hearing that Regan was blaming him, however, he exploded in an angry computer message to Poindexter, threatening to sue Regan for singling him out for a policy that had received collective, though not unanimous, top-level endorsement from the start. Poindexter reported back that Regan "would keep his mouth shut."

On November 8, McFarlane sent a message to North concerning the records of the National Security Agency, an intelligence agency that had been monitoring the arms deals: "I hope to daylights that someone has been purging the NSA's files on this episode." North was already shredding and altering documents from his office and from the permanent files of the National Security Council.

Secretary of Defense Weinberger complained to Poindexter that the secretary of state had "suggested 'telling all' on attempts to deal with Iran to get their help." According to his notes, Weinberger had "strongly objected. I said we should simply say nothing—John [Poindexter] agrees."

This division deepened in a meeting of the National Security Planning Group on November 10. In a ninety-minute session at the

White House, Reagan, Bush, Regan, Poindexter, Casey, Shultz, Weinberger, and Meese discussed the administration's dealings with Iran but could not reach a consensus about what to acknowledge publicly. Only Shultz wanted to concede the failure and try to defend it.

Donald Regan preferred a response more forthcoming than "no comment," as he noted on November 10: "We must get a statement out now, we are being attacked, and we are being hurt."

The president put the issue more colorfully: "We must say something but not much. I'm being held out to dry."

Admiral Poindexter, still hoping the stonewall would hold, warned that any acknowledgment of the arms deals would "end our Iranian contacts." If there had to be a statement, he thought, it should "say less about what we are doing and more about what we are not doing."

Poindexter drew the line at exposing the 1985 Israeli transactions, which the president had approved without notifying Congress. In briefing the NSPG, Poindexter falsely claimed that Israel had sold U.S. arms in 1985 without our permission; that we had only accidentally discovered the arms en route to Iran in a European warehouse; and that the presidentially approved sales had begun only after January 1986, when the president had signed a finding formally authorizing direct sales to Iran. Poindexter made no mention of the Hawks delivered in November 1985.

Shultz pressed Reagan for a commitment that no more arms would go to Iran, but his proposal drew no support. After the meeting, a White House press release stressed concern for the safety of the hostages and pledged that "no U.S. laws have been or will be violated and . . . [that] our policy of not making concessions to terrorists remains intact." President Reagan "asked his advisors to ensure that their departments refrain from making comments or speculating about these matters." Before being released, the statement had to be revised because Shultz rejected a proposed reference to the "unanimous support for the president's policies." At his insistence, the final version recited only "unanimous support for the president."

To his aides, Shultz fumed that the press release showed that the president's advisors were "trying to get me to lie." Whatever they were "trying to pull on me," he added, the maneuver was "taking the president down the drain." The way to halt that slide, he believed, was to make a clean breast of the errors, restore the authority to deal with Iran to his department, and end the freelance operations of the National Security Council's staff.

While presidential aides worried about impeachment, Ronald Reagan considered the public reaction excessive. "This whole irresponsible press bilge about hostages and Iran has gotten totally out of hand," he noted in his diary for November 12. "The media looks like it's trying to create another Watergate. . . . I want to go public personally and tell the people the truth." In an address to the nation broadcast from the Oval Office the next day, the president declared that the dealings with Iran had been aimed primarily at restoring normal relations and only secondarily at freeing Americans held captive in the Middle East. True, Iran had acquired some defensive U.S. weaponry, but the charge that America had been "trafficking with terrorists," he said, was "utterly false."

His audience did not believe him. Polls by the news media and the White House found that for every American who accepted the president's version of events, six others doubted it and him. Ronald Reagan seemed to be deceiving himself. He *had* traded arms for hostages. He had pushed eager aides to keep bargaining when more seasoned officers had advised against it. In his own mind, he had arranged the facts into the context of McFarlane's original proposal of an "Iran initiative"—a secretive effort to open lines of communication and support to factions in Tehran that might someday replace the Ayatollah Khomeini's radical regime with pro-Western policies, and that might, as a gesture of goodwill, persuade their Lebanese followers to release the hostages. In fact, the dialogue had never gone beyond bartering missiles for prisoners. The hidden trade and the diversion of part of the proceeds to the Contras had violated American policy and law.

Two days later, in the situation room, the president and his top advisors fed congressional leaders the false account that had been developed for public consumption. Ronald Reagan described the activity as "principally a covert intelligence operation" that had involved "no negotiations with terrorists" and had been designed "to enhance [America's] position in the Middle East."

Poindexter began his report with the direct sales to Iran authorized by the president's January 1986 finding. Senate Majority Leader Robert Byrd asked when the first contact with Iran had occurred, and Poindexter admitted that the process had begun in 1985, but he claimed that "no transfer of material" had taken place until after the presidential finding had been signed.

The journalists were more aggressive than the congressional leaders had been. The day after misleading Senator Byrd, Poindexter had to acknowledge to a reporter that a "small amount of stuff" had gone to Iran in connection with the first release of a hostage, the Reverend Benjamin Weir.

McFarlane feared that by lack of candor, the administration might find itself caught up in a scandal on the order of Watergate. In the earlier debacle, he warned Poindexter, "well-meaning people who were in on the early planning of the communications strategy didn't intend to lie but ultimately came around to it." The Reagan White House had to choose, he urged, between ducking and accepting the blame. If the policy was to be defended "on its merits," the manner "must not be confrontational but open and candid."

Calls for congressional inquiries multiplied. After President Reagan's televised speech of November 13, the pressure for a public accounting heightened. The House and Senate intelligence committees scheduled hearings and asked Casey, Shultz, and Poindexter to testify.

Within the administration, concern centered on what to say about the illegal November 1985 Hawk shipment, which exposed the president to the most danger. Both the CIA and Oliver North compiled chronological accounts, which conflicted with each other and with the truth. The narrowly self-protective CIA version said that no one in the agency had known at the time that its proprietary aircraft had carried Hawk missiles rather than oil-drilling equipment. North broadened the claim to say that "no one in the government" had been aware of the cargo's true nature.

Richard Secord, who had arranged with the CIA proprietary for the delivery of the Hawks, was dismayed to read that the president had been upset and that those involved in the transport had thought they were carrying oil-drilling equipment. "The new, phony version would stand," Secord realized. Having believed that his activities had been authorized by the president, he told North, "I guess I get the picture, now. I'll get out of your hair. I'm not going to be a part of this anymore."

Appearing on a Sunday-morning television news show, George Shultz stated that he opposed any further arms transactions with Iran. Asked whether he, as secretary of state, spoke for the whole administration on this policy, Shultz candidly answered that he did not.

Ignoring a direct warning from Shultz that he was being deceived, the president repeated at a news conference on November 19 that he had not traded arms for hostages. He went on to deny that the Israeli shipments had occurred. The White House press office hastily issued a clarifying statement conceding that a "third country" had taken part in "our secret project."

On the evening of November 20, George Shultz and Don Regan visited the president in the family quarters in the White House. For forty-five minutes, Shultz tried without success to get the president to face the truth. Reagan insisted that because he had never *intended* to bargain arms for hostages, he had never done so. Shultz reminded him that McFarlane had told them both about the planned Israeli Hawk shipment during the November 1985 summit conference with Soviet leader Mikhail Gorbachev in Geneva.

"Oh, I knew about that," replied Reagan, "but that wasn't arms for hostages."

Shultz later told an aide, "I didn't shake him one bit. . . . He refuses to see that we have a problem. So I never got to what should be done."

Casey's prepared testimony to the House intelligence committee the next day simply omitted the Hawks, but in answering questions, he fell back on the canard about the oil equipment. Having denied knowledge that weapons were carried, he could not then reveal that at his request the president had signed a retroactive finding approving the CIA's carrying them.

Just before noon on Friday, November 21, Poindexter, Regan, and Meese met with the president in the Oval Office. Reagan agreed that someone should develop a coherent position for the administration. The assignment went to Meese.

When North and Poindexter learned about the attorney general's mission, they stepped up their efforts to purge their files. North and his secretary, Fawn Hall, shredded a pile of documents, including North's telephone records and copies of his memoranda to McFarlane and Poindexter. They also altered documents taken from the permanent files of the National Security Council. As North and the NSC staff counsel watched, Poindexter calmly tore up the original presidential finding that Ronald Reagan had signed on December 5, 1985, retroactively authorizing the CIA to assist the shipment of the Hawk weapons and specifying that the shipment's purpose was to obtain the release of Americans held hostage in the Middle East.

Over the weekend, the attorney general questioned cabinet officers. He exchanged many telephone calls with Casey and Regan but, departing from his usual practice, took no notes. Meese later claimed that he could not remember what was said. Casey and Regan suffered memory lapses, as well. In an early-Saturday-morning meeting in Shultz's office, Shultz told Meese that the president had admitted knowing about the Hawk shipment. Meese bridled, warning Shultz that if what he said was true and if the president had failed to notify Congress, the law might have been violated. Meese asked whether Shultz knew of any other writings except the notes he had himself dictated. Shultz knew of none.

The attorney general then left to meet with McFarlane, who said that he had told President Reagan about the planned Hawk shipment but that he had nothing in writing. Meese next telephoned Weinberger and concluded that he had little information about the transaction. In reality, Weinberger had preserved notes of his conversations with McFarlane, warning him in advance that the Hawk transaction would be illegal, whether carried out through Israel or not.

While Meese talked to the cabinet officers, his assistants found in North's office a draft copy of an April 1986 memorandum in which North explained for Poindexter the diversion of $12 million from the proceeds of the Iran arms sales to rearm the Nicaraguan insurgents known as the Contras. Not only had President Reagan flouted the National Security Act and the Arms Export Control law, but North's illegal use of the proceeds to finance the Contras had usurped Congress's constitutional authority over government appropriations. Because the proceeds should have gone to the U.S. Treasury, the diversion had amounted to theft. The next day, Meese and his assistants questioned North for four hours in what Meese later testified was "a chat among colleagues." North assured Meese that the memorandum had not gone to the president.

Shultz spent that Sunday considering resignation, and others were eager to hurry his departure. Before the weekend was out, William Casey had written to President Reagan to attack "the public pouting of George Shultz" and to recommend that he be replaced by Senator Paul Laxalt of Nevada or by Jeane Kirkpatrick, the U.S. ambassador to the United Nations.

Tension filled the situation room on November 24, as President Reagan pounded the table and insisted that he had not traded arms for hostages, that the sale of missiles was meant to restore normal relations with Iran, that the hostage release was only incidental to it. His undeniable prior knowledge of the Hawk shipment—which had been expressly intended to free the hostages—frustrated any honest effort to develop a coherent position that would exculpate him.

Finally, Regan turned to Meese for the answer to the critical question: Had the president approved the November 1985 Hawk shipment? Everyone in the room already knew the true answer. Regan had heard the president admit knowledge of the shipment to Shultz on Thursday.

Shultz had confirmed this to Meese on Saturday. What was needed now was a political answer.

Before Meese could speak, Poindexter said that McFarlane had handled the Israeli–Iran sales all alone, with no documentation. Meese then fabricated the president's defense. He told the group that although McFarlane had informed Shultz of the planned shipment, McFarlane had not informed the president. Meese warned the group that the shipment might have been a violation of law because the arms had been shipped without notice to Congress. Meese suggested that even after the Hawk shipment, the president had been told only that the hostages would be out in short order.

Regan, who had heard McFarlane inform the president and who had heard the president admit to Shultz that he knew of the shipment of Hawk missiles, said nothing. Shultz and Weinberger, who had protested the shipment before it took place, said nothing. Bush, who had been told of the shipment in advance by McFarlane, said nothing. Casey, who had also known about the shipment ahead of time and had later requested that the president sign the retroactive finding to authorize the CIA-facilitated delivery, said nothing. Poindexter, who had torn up the finding, said nothing. Meese asked whether anyone knew anything else that hadn't been revealed. No one spoke.

Shultz left the meeting early. As always, he immediately dictated notes of the meeting to his executive assistant, Charles Hill. Poindexter's claim that McFarlane had run the operation by himself and that no one had known what he did, Shultz told Hill, was inconsistent with what Shultz knew. They were, he said, "rearranging the record." The president was "now saying he didn't know anything about [McFarlane's] November 1985 activities." The White House was employing, through Meese, a "carefully thought out strategy" to insulate the president and "blame it on Bud" McFarlane.

During the meeting, Meese and Regan had not mentioned the discovery of North's candid outline of the diversion of the arms sales proceeds to the Contras. The simple message they wished to convey to their colleagues was that the president needed to be insulated from the November 1985 Hawk shipment. After the meeting, Meese and Regan followed the president to the Oval Office and told him about the diversion of funds. Reagan seemed genuinely surprised—"as though he had been hit in the stomach," in Regan's words.

Regan, Meese, and Casey then embarked on a desperate gambit, which Regan laid out that day in a memorandum entitled "Plan of

Action." "Tough as it seems," he wrote, "blame must be put at NSC's door—rogue operation, going on without president's knowledge or sanction." The goal would be to "try to make the best of a sensational story."

The authors of the plan concluded that it would not be enough to fire North. They needed more than a scapegoat; they needed a firewall. Poindexter had to go. The next day, he resigned at a meeting in which Reagan and Bush expressed their regrets. North, who would be summarily returned to the Marine Corps, received no advance warning of his dismissal; he learned about it on a live television broadcast from the White House.

At noon on November 25, the president and the attorney general went before the White House press corps. The president said he had not been "fully informed on the nature of one of the activities undertaken," which raised "serious questions of propriety." He announced the departures of Poindexter and North, then hurriedly left the podium without taking questions. The job of explaining was left to Meese.

The attorney general had already told his tale that morning, once to cabinet officers and then to congressional leaders, in meetings at the White House. In each case, he omitted reference to the Hawk shipment. He said that the Israelis had handled the arms sales, overcharging the Iranians and depositing the excess funds in Calero's Swiss bank accounts. He said North knew this and Poindexter suspected it. He repeated the falsehood that the president had not learned of the November 1985 Hawk shipment until months afterward.

Shortly before the press conference, an agitated Secord got through to Poindexter on the telephone and asked about rumors that he was resigning. Poindexter confirmed them.

"Stay at your post, admiral," the feisty Secord entreated. "Force the president to step up to the plate and take responsibility for his actions. . . ."

Poindexter replied that time had run out. The attorney general, he said, was about to hold a press conference. The game was over.

Secord felt as if smoke were coming out of his ears. "I would like to talk to the president," he told Poindexter.

"It's too late," said Poindexter. "They're building a wall around him."

CHAPTER TWO

The Private War

Nicaragua, the largest Central American republic, had been of strategic importance to the United States since the construction of the Panama Canal, which opened in August 1914. A treaty signed in 1911 gave the United States, in return for a financial reorganization, the right to intervene in the government of Nicaragua. At the request of the Nicaraguan president, U.S. Marine Corps forces were dispatched to protect the property and safety of Americans in 1912. The marines remained for twenty years. After training the Nicaraguan national guard, the Americans turned the command over to General Anastasio Somoza García and withdrew. Somoza supported the government of President Adolfo Díaz, who was backed by the United States, against the efforts of General Augusto César Sandino to rid Nicaragua of "U.S. imperialists."

Sandino was assassinated in 1934. Two years later, Somoza seized power as a military dictator. He remained in charge until 1956, when he was assassinated; he was succeeded by his son, Anastasio Somoza Debayle. Both men were greedy, and the latter's administration was corrupt. During the late 1970s, strikes and street protests met with harsh retaliation. Leftist rebels calling themselves Sandinistas, after the murdered General Sandino, launched guerrilla raids against Somoza's government, and the repression escalated.

In 1977, President Jimmy Carter reduced U.S. military and economic aid to Nicaragua. In January 1978, Pedro Joaquín Chamorro, the editor of opposition newspaper *La Prensa*, was assassinated. Afterward, otherwise conservative groups—ranging from professionals and business leaders to the church—ignored the Sandinistas' Marxist rhetoric and joined the rebellion. The United States negotiated a settlement with the rebels, but Somoza refused to accept the terms. The United States then dropped its support for Somoza, and the Sandinistas took over the government in 1979.

The Sandinistas initially elected a five-person directorate, which consisted of the moderate Violeta Chamorro (widow of the murdered editor), two other moderates, and two radical militants, including Daniel Ortega. Not long afterward, Chamorro and another moderate were forced to resign, and the Sandinistas seized control of the television and radio stations and censored *La Prensa*. They refused to hold national elections.

In addition to breaking their promise of a democratic government, the Sandinistas permitted weapons from Cuba to be transported through Nicaragua to rebels in neighboring El Salvador. As the number of resident Cuban advisors increased, the Sandinistas signed agreements with the Soviet Union and eastern-bloc countries, inviting their advice and military and intelligence assistance. President Carter, who had previously resumed economic aid to Nicaragua, responded by suspending that aid shortly before leaving office. Ronald Reagan, who had campaigned on his opposition to support for the Sandinistas, withheld aid to the Nicaraguan government throughout his presidency.

Meanwhile, the Contra movement, which opposed the Sandinistas, was growing from a nucleus of a few hundred former national guardsmen to include former Somoza supporters and former Sandinistas who felt betrayed. The largest and most active group of Contras was the Nicaraguan Democratic Force (FDN). Its fighters were based in the jungles near the Honduran border in northern Nicaragua. They were supported by Indians along the Atlantic Caribbean coast. Another anti-Sandinista group, led by Eden Pastora, spread along the southern border with Costa Rica.

The leader of the FDN was former businessman Adolfo Calero Portocarrero. After supporting the movement to oust Somoza, Calero had been disillusioned by the Sandinistas and had become the coordinator of the Conservative Democratic Party. His criticism of the government prompted raids on his office and home, and he was forced into exile. As moderates were pushed out of the Nicaraguan government, many other Contra leaders—including Alfonso Robelo Callejas and Arturo J. Cruz—also fled to the United States and, from their headquarters in Miami, began a campaign to win support from the U.S. Congress.

Congress was almost evenly divided on the question of whether to support the Contras or not. The majority of Americans, remembering what had happened in Vietnam, opposed intervention in Nicaragua. In December 1981, President Reagan authorized the CIA to undertake a covert program of support for the Contras, and Congress funded the program. Duane "Dewey" Clarridge, a daring and resourceful organizer, was transferred from his CIA station in Rome to assume leadership of the operation as chief of the agency's Latin American division.

On Capitol Hill, some legislators supported the CIA's effort as a check on the spread of communism, while others feared that the Contras' activities would supply a convenient pretext for the Sandinistas to impose martial law and suppress all civil liberties. The conflict resolved into a question of whether the CIA, in the guise of inhibiting arms traffic and inducing Ortega to negotiate with other Central American countries, was in reality trying to undermine and overthrow the Sandinista government.

To prevent such a broadened undertaking, Representative Edward P. Boland of Massachusetts introduced a series of legislative limits on the use of government appropriations. The first of these "Boland amendments," as they came to be known, restricted U.S. activity to the interdiction of arms transfers to rebel guerrillas in El Salvador. As the CIA's efforts expanded, investigating congressmen concluded that the agency had exceeded the authority intended by Congress. Concerned that Congress would cut the funding or terminate the program altogether, the CIA—aided by the Department of Defense—began to stockpile arms for the Contras.

In the 1984 budget, congressional opponents of paramilitary activity obtained a cap of $24 million on the CIA's spending for the Contras. That amount was soon exhausted, as Clarridge guided the Contras to make speedboat assaults on Sandinista patrol craft and to attack fuel tanks and fuel transmission lines. The Pacific ports that served Nicaragua's population centers and also provided the shortest route to El Salvador were targeted. CIA agents planted magnetic mines in Sandino harbor. An air attack destroyed a Sandinista naval arms depot and communications center. More mines were placed in Corinto harbor. In the south, the CIA supported Eden Pastora's effort to establish a base for a provisional government.

Damage to a neutral vessel resulted in a suit against the United States in the World Court. For the first time, the United States denied that the court had jurisdiction over its activities. At the same time, Congress learned of the *Tayacan Manual*, a counterrevolutionary handbook that advocated the assassination of government leaders. Sponsorship of the manual was attributed to the CIA.

Against a backdrop of negative publicity, the Reagan administration vainly sought to increase funding for the Contras. Congress responded by enacting the most severe of the Boland amendments, which barred The CIA and the Defense Department as well as any "entity engaged in intelligence activities" from assisting the Contras. The generalized prohibition included the National Security Council, which was responsible for coordinating intelligence activities.

Backed by a unanimous National Security Planning Group, President Reagan was determined that the Contras should be supported to prevent the spread of communism in Central America. His political advisors, however, persuaded him to refrain from raising this generally unpopular issue in the 1984 presidential election. Accordingly, Reagan signed the appropriation acts containing the Boland amendments, but he had no intention of abiding by the restrictions.

First, he directed Robert McFarlane to "keep the Contras together body and soul," ignoring the fact that McFarlane could not do so without breaking the law. McFarlane then invited the Saudi Arabian ambassador, Prince Bandar bin Sultan, to replace part of the funds withheld by Congress. Bandar arranged a contribution of $1 million a month to the Contras, beginning in mid-1984. At a breakfast meeting with Reagan in early 1985, King Fahd bin Abdul Aziz volunteered to double that amount. In all, the Saudis contributed $32 million to the Nicaraguan insurgents.

When the CIA was forced to stop assisting the Contras, Director William Casey reassured the Contra leaders that U.S. support would continue. He and Clarridge introduced Oliver North in July 1984 as the Contras' future government contact. Thereafter, North reported directly to Casey as well as to McFarlane.

By 1985, Adolfo Calero had become the head of United Nicaraguan Opposition (UNO), a new organization that coordinated the Contras' activities; he remained the head of FDN, which had become UNO's military operating unit. North supplied Calero with intelligence information and assisted him in selecting and obtaining the arms best suited for the Contras' operation. At Casey's suggestion, North introduced Calero to Richard Secord, who arranged three shipments of arms that arrived in early 1985 and were paid for by funds the Contras had received from the Saudis. With the support of others on the National Security Council's staff, North raised additional funds for the Contras from

Taiwan and tried to raise funds from Korea. Through McFarlane, North also helped the Contras obtain logistic assistance from other Central American countries.

McFarlane understood that the prohibitions of the Boland amendments applied to actions taken by his staff. He tried to walk a tightrope of ostensible compliance, whereas North was determined to do whatever was necessary to succeed. McFarlane instructed his staff not to raise money for the Contras. He told North that "no one could solicit, encourage, coerce, or broker the transmission of money . . . to the Contras." North nevertheless continued to participate actively in fundraising operations carried out by professional fund-raisers. North kept McFarlane informed of many of his activities, and McFarlane kept the president informed, reporting to Reagan almost daily on the growth of the Contras and developments in the military situation in Nicaragua.

In the summer of 1985, as the president pressed Congress for a resumption of CIA funding for the Contras, reports of North's accomplishments published by the *Miami Herald* and other newspapers prompted inquiries from Capitol Hill. If the truth came out, it would anger many members of Congress and jeopardize the possibility of favorable legislation. Therefore, in letters to the congressional committees, McFarlane denied that North had engaged in the forbidden activities.

In spite of this close call, North and Secord accelerated and formalized their control of the operation to resupply the Contras. After the Saudi funds were exhausted, North and Secord unified the supply effort to ensure the most effective arsenal and to eliminate their competition. Rather than go directly to Calero for the purchase of arms, the funds raised by North went into the Swiss bank accounts controlled by Secord, and he selected the arms and made the purchases and deliveries.

In 1986, when their other funding sources dried up, North and Secord—with John Poindexter's approval—turned to the proceeds of the Iranian arms sales. North negotiated low purchase prices with the Department of Defense and marked them up for the sales to Iran. The surplus funds, minus substantial personal payments for Secord and his partner Albert Hakim, were then available for the Contras. North thus replaced the Saudis as the principal source of the Contras' funds.

North and Secord kept the arms deliveries to the Contras moving. Chartered jets flew the weapons from Europe to the Salvadoran air base at Ilopango; from there, a small fleet of aircraft purchased by Secord with North's authorization distributed the arms to Contra drop zones in Nicaragua. North referred to this activity as "the operation" and later as "Project Democracy." Secord called it "the Enterprise." In the CIA and the State Department, the individuals who delivered the lethal supplies were referred to as "private benefactors."

In the summer of 1986, President Reagan persuaded Congress to authorize the renewal of CIA support for the Contras. With an appropriation of $100 million for such support pending in Congress, new reports of North's activities surfaced. A resolution of inquiry that would have required the president to provide information and documents regarding the pro-Contra activities of the National Security Council's staff was referred to three House committees for approval. Responding for the president, Poindexter wrote to the committees and repeated McFarlane's false assurances from a year earlier. Dissatisfied, the House intelligence committee requested a meeting with North.

On August 6, testifying from the president's chair in the White House situation room, North assured eleven members of the committee that he had not violated the spirit or the letter of the Boland amendments. He denied that he had raised funds for the Contras, offered them military advice, or communicated with their military operatives. The committee was satisfied and killed the resolution of inquiry.

The $100 million appropriation passed the House and Senate in slightly different forms. As the legislation awaited reconciliation by a conference committee, a C-123K plane loaded with lethal supplies was shot down over Nicaragua by Sandinista antiaircraft fire. The pilot and copilot were killed, but the cargo kicker, forty-five-year-old Eugene Hasenfus, parachuted safely and was taken prisoner. Hasenfus, a former marine who had worked for a CIA front in Southeast Asia, told his captors that he worked under "Max Gomez," the "CIA's overseer" of operations at Ilopango, where the flight had originated.

In the wreckage, the Nicaraguans found a variety of documents identifying the plane as the property of Corporate Air Services, a Pennsylvania company, and the crew as its American employees. Telephone records showing frequent calls from the pilots and others based at Ilopango to CIA safe houses in El Salvador seemed to reinforce Hasenfus's claim that he worked for the CIA.

In reality, Corporate Air Services was not a CIA front. The real proprietor of the small air fleet, through several dummy corporations, was Richard Secord. Behind Secord stood not the CIA but Oliver North. Max Gomez was the alias of a retired CIA officer whom North had recruited to coordinate the Ilopango operation. Gomez was actually

Felix Rodriguez, a friend and former colleague of Vice President George Bush's national security advisor, Donald Gregg.

Aroused by the shootdown, Congress convened another round of hearings, at which CIA and State Department officers falsely denied knowledge of Max Gomez and the identities of the individuals who were running the operation to resupply the Contras. On October 17, 1986, Congress passed the new appropriation for the CIA, and the need for North's operation came to an end.

Seventeen days later, *Al Shiraa* published the story of the arms sales to Iran. When the diversion of the proceeds to the Contras was revealed, it became apparent that the Reagan administration had deceived Congress regarding two major international operations, both of which had been illegal.

CHAPTER THREE

Call to Counsel

Long before the Iran-Contra scandal broke, Ronald Reagan's reputation for indifference to detail and aloofness from daily operations had become firmly established in Washington lore. Not surprisingly, the conventional wisdom quickly pegged Iran-Contra as a runaway conspiracy, with Oliver North as the antihero. His bosses were seen as lesser characters in the drama—Robert McFarlane and John Poindexter having sinned mostly by omission and President Reagan having merely blessed the policies without taking any part or interest in their implementation.

Poindexter told the FBI that he had consciously chosen not to learn the details of North's diversion of the proceeds from the Iranian arms sales to the Contras. Donald Regan reported that the president, on learning about the activity from his attorney general on November 24, had "blanched. . . . The color drained from his face. . . . He was the picture of a man to whom the inconceivable had happened."

By contrast, Oliver North emerged as a can-do, gung-ho lone warrior fending off Middle Eastern terrorists with one hand and Nicaraguan communists with the other. Portrayed as a Gulliver among bureaucrats, the Marine officer won the dual role of superstar and scapegoat. A few hours after being fired, North received a telephone call from Reagan, who declared him a hero. But within two days, White House sources were planting press stories about his destruction of documents in the midst of Attorney General Edwin Meese's weekend inquiry. Unnamed insiders told reporters for the *Los Angeles Times* that the diversion of funds, a "brilliant if twisted" concept, "was Ollie's idea. . . . He tried to do the driving."

The image of the junior officer at the steering wheel with the commander in chief dozing in the rear seat remains fixed in popular history. This picture reflects not only the evidence put before the public when attention was highest but also the political strategy to preserve Ronald Reagan and the national security establishment from damaging scrutiny. Given a choice of evils, the administration chose to present the president as ignorant. To depict him otherwise, as a central figure in executing two policies he heartily endorsed, might have set in motion a drive for impeachment.

Occasionally, Reagan seemed to chafe at the passive role he had been assigned. "As a matter of fact," he told newspaper editors in May 1987, "I was very definitely involved in the decisions about support to the freedom fighters. It was my idea to begin with." At the same time, he consistently maintained that the financial support derived from overcharging Iran for U.S. missiles had been kept secret from him. Other than Oliver North's self-serving contention that he believed the "profit-taking" had been fully authorized and McFarlane's testimony to a similar belief, nothing in the record contradicted Reagan's claim.

Nonetheless, the president must have, however subtly, understood and authorized the transformation of Iranian payments into Contra-support funds. Leaving aside the question of whether such a consummate staff officer as Poindexter would have short-circuited the chain of command, even the most credulous observer would surely wonder why the White House would have persisted throughout 1986 in humiliating dealings with Iran unless the president understood that this otherwise losing proposition had the highly desirable by-product of funding for the secret war in Nicaragua. Except for financing the Contras, the policy produced rewards too small and entailed risks too high to justify its continuation.

The diversion was no fringe detail. It was the lifeline for the Contras. How could Poindexter, in his daily briefings for the president, have avoided all mention of this vital link between Reagan's two highest personal priorities? Would William Casey, who met privately with Reagan from time to time, have kept him in the dark? The secret would have seemed too good to withhold.

When the diversion was disclosed publicly, it riveted the nation's attention, shifting the focus from the president's deceit of Congress to his staff's performance. The revelation of the diversion abetted the cover-up. A reporter in the White House press room on the afternoon of November 25 apparently spotted the maneuver. "What's to prevent an increasingly cynical public from thinking that you went looking for a scapegoat and came up with this whopper," the journalist asked Meese, "but it doesn't have a lot to do with the original controversy?"

The attorney general brushed the reporter off with a nonresponse. The president's priority was "to lay out the facts . . . just as rapidly as we've gotten them," Meese said, ". . . to be sure that there is no hint that anything is trying to be concealed." As for having a special prosecutor look into the matter, Meese saw no need for outside help.

The question about scapegoating was an intelligent one. It should have been pursued. Although I didn't know it yet, I would be the one to undertake that pursuit.

I had disapproved strongly of Ronald Reagan's failure to support President Gerald Ford in the 1976 election, when Reagan believed that Ford's defeat would leave the road open for him four years later. Nevertheless, I had come to admire his performance in the office that Ford had lost. I supported Reagan's determined fight against communist expansion in Central America. And as a Republican of fifty years' standing, I did not want to see the Iran-Contra furor undo the respect he had restored to the presidency.

On several counts, then, I found the news from Washington in November 1986 dismaying. Five years after retiring from a demanding corporate-law practice in New York to a firm in Oklahoma City, the hometown of my wife, Mary, I was a mere spectator of national politics. I may have been an interested and even partisan onlooker, but my seat was in the bleachers.

From that distance, I saw the beleaguered president and his aides in a favorable light. Abrupt vacillation in foreign affairs or economic policy was abhorrent to me. I saw the cause the administration supported in Nicaragua as necessary and the president's discretion in the conduct of foreign policy as wide. Congress had used its power irresponsibly, leaving our allies, the Contras, at the mercy of our enemies.

One December morning, I approvingly read aloud to Mary a newspaper article that applauded North's patriotism and initiative. I even thought briefly of the arguments I could make in his defense. But personal involvement in the controversy seemed out of the question.

One month short of my seventy-fifth birthday, I was content to be far from the center of action. Oklahoma City had proved to be a congenial place to live, and the firm of Crowe & Dunlevy a hospitable place to work. I had been busy defending a product-liability suit for an old client, Richardson-Merrell, a major pharmaceutical company, and sitting on a special litigation committee appointed by Kansas Gas and Electric Company (KGE), a utility company that had suffered gigantic cost overruns associated with its efforts to build a nuclear power plant.

My responsibility, shared with two other members of the committee, was to analyze what had happened, evaluate blame, and recommend action. Toward the end of 1986, the committee members were moving toward decisions, but we had not reached a final agreement, and the task required a great deal of preparation, tact, and time.

I was enjoying life. Mary had turned an ordinary suburban house into a beautiful home, with all the convenience and privacy we had wanted in retirement. The swimming pool invited my daily regimen of laps, and the library shelves held the books I wanted to read or reread and the music I longed to hear and hear again. If I missed the high-powered partnership I had held for twenty years at Davis Polk & Wardwell in New York, I felt no nostalgia for the long hours of air travel and stays in impersonal hotel rooms that had been my lot as an itinerant litigator.

And yet, a single telephone call on Saturday, December 6, was all it took to turn me into a frequent flier again and to put me back on a diet of room-service meals. The caller was Walter Mansfield from the U.S. court of appeals in New York. He was one of three judges on the panel charged with appointing an independent counsel to investigate possible criminal aspects of the Iran-Contra affair. Four days earlier, at the direction of the White House, the attorney general had finally asked the court to designate an outsider to take over the inquiry begun by the Department of Justice.

I had thought that the job would go to Robert Fiske, a Davis Polk partner and former U.S. attorney, who had exactly the right mix of prosecutorial experience and judiciousness for the task. Former judge Harold Tyler, who had been deputy attorney general under President Ford, also struck me as an excellent and likely choice. The idea that I might be considered seemed too remote to entertain. But here was Walter Mansfield asking if I would take a call later that day from George MacKinnon, a senior judge on the U.S. court of appeals in Washington and the presiding judge of the appointing panel. Mansfield did not say what MacKinnon would be calling about. He didn't need to. I was thrilled, as always, at the prospect of having a new client.

I cut through the niceties and urged Judge Mansfield to give the independent counsel broad investigative authority. I reminded him of the problems we had encountered while working together on the staff of the special prosecutor in the Drukman murder case during the New York corruption scandals of the 1930s. The order appointing our boss as a special assistant attorney general had been too narrowly drawn, and we had lacked the jurisdiction to deal with closely related crimes that would have implicated reluctant witnesses. You never know where a break might come in a case, so I urged Judge Mansfield to make sure to give the independent counsel all the points of entry he might need, because there would probably be no friendly witnesses.

Suddenly the prospect was real. Mary urged me on, but I hardly needed persuasion. When Judge MacKinnon called at seven that evening to say I was under consideration, I promised an answer by Monday as to whether my firm had any conflicts of interest that might disqualify me. On Wednesday, the judge called me to Washington and initiated an FBI investigation for my clearance to handle top-secret information.

That night, I went to Philadelphia for a meeting of the Council of the American Law Institute. Philip Shenon of the *New York Times* tracked me to my hotel room to ask whether I had the job. I could not comment. He seemed to be betting on Harold Tyler. Other reporters also called, and I was able to put them off until Nina Totenberg of National Public Radio reached me at home a week after Judge Mansfield's first call. I had known Nina too long and held her in too high regard to deceive her even if I could have, and she saw through one of my evasive answers. The story she immediately broadcast set my telephone ringing as never before. If I hung it up, it immediately rang again. The next day, when I took my German shepherd Bertie for a walk, we had television crews and photographers for company. His picture made page one in newspapers around the country.

Despite the excitement, I had immediately and grimly begun to sort out the extra dimensions of the legal challenge I had so readily accepted. Whatever criminal acts I might uncover, the core of the scandal was political, and politicians—rather than lawyers—would decide what direction events would take. My title would confer the appearance of independence, but in reality it would mean isolation. I would need a lot of help.

The first place I turned to for advice and assistance was Davis Polk, the firm that had given me my start in private practice in 1941 and, after an interruption of eighteen years in public office, had again been my home for more than two decades. My first telephone call went to Bob Fiske. I wanted him as my deputy for a year or so, after which I would cede full authority to him. Although Fiske ultimately declined, he quickly suggested a group of young lawyer-prosecutors for my staff. Leon Silverman, the managing partner of a leading New York law firm, also joined the recruiting drive. Not only had Silverman been an independent counsel himself, but he had been my assistant deputy attorney general during President Dwight D. Eisenhower's administration. He was one whose help I sought for any important personal problem.

The first person to agree to become an associate counsel was forty-three-year-old Guy Miller Struve, who had been my closest colleague at Davis Polk since the day he had walked through its doors, fresh from brilliant academic careers at Yale University and Harvard Law School. In our work together, he had been the incisive legal scholar who made up for my own shortcomings in that department and the keen analyst who could bolster or check my intuitive approach to problems. As my right hand on the independent counsel's staff, he became the counselor on whom I relied the most for professional acumen and personal advice. Other lawyers soon found that if they could persuade Struve to take their side, they would have little trouble bringing me around.

He and Fiske and Silverman felt, as I did, that a staff of ten associate counsel should see me through. To Silverman, even that number seemed high. If we had been thinking like politicians instead of lawyers, however, we would have realized that the investigation and prosecution of Oliver North and his associates would be only one of many bitter battles that our little team would have to fight.

In mid-December, my assignment appeared comfortably limited. Every public indication pointed to the "rogue operation" on which the administration had decided to pin all blame. Robert McFarlane's testimony to the Senate intelligence committee, along with North's and Poindexter's refusals to testify, intensified that impression. William Casey, hospitalized with a massive brain tumor, was not available to clarify the record. Other cabinet officers and White House officials distanced themselves from the arms sales profits and their diversion. Caspar Weinberger said he had been "horrified" to learn of the scheme, about which George Shultz declared he had "zero" knowledge to go with only "fragmentary" information about the arms shipments to Iran. "No role in it," said Vice President George Bush. "Ridiculous," said Donald Regan, when a news service reported that North had briefed him. "Does the bank president know whether a teller in the bank is fiddling around with the books? No."

Although we were always skeptical of such denials, the natural course at the beginning of the Iran-Contra investigation was to follow the trail that was already open. North and Poindexter might eventually lead us to other actors in other agencies, but the two central figures' conduct, their associates, and their vulnerabilities were the logical places to begin. With the help of several seasoned prosecutors as well as sharp legal analysts, I felt reasonably confident of my prospects.

There was no shortage of eager applicants. A high-profile Washington investigation could make the reputation of a young lawyer. None of the younger lawyers whom I approached with a job offer turned me down, and many actively sought a chance to come on board. I sought lawyers with prosecutorial experience in cases involving corruption and organized crime as well as lawyers experienced in complex litigation in other fields. Our work would entail not only evaluating individuals and cases but also using criminal procedures to develop testimony against higher-ups from unwilling witnesses.

Of the mix of recruits and volunteers, the final selection gave me a high-level team of full-time and part-time lawyers. My senior appointments included two lawyers contributed by U.S. Attorney Rudolph Guiliani in New York as well as a former prosecutor from that office and another from Washington who was then the president of the District of Columbia Bar Association. They led a group of able assistants who had been judicial law clerks or litigators for top law firms.

Of unique value from the outset was John Douglass, a tall, soft-spoken prosecutor who had just successfully tried an espionage case in Baltimore. He brought us especially valuable experience related to the use of classified documents. Perhaps the most seasoned member of the group was John Keker, a former public defender who came recommended as the best criminal trial lawyer in San Francisco. Like Oliver North, Keker had been wounded as a marine fighting in Vietnam. During our first meeting, I began to think of Keker as the perfect man to put up against North if a case ever came to trial. Rick Ford, whom I esteemed as a Crowe & Dunlevy colleague, took on the thankless job of overseeing the office administration for the first three months. Ford remained a trusted but unpaid personal confidant, a no-nonsense sounding board for my ideas and worries throughout the seven years of my service.

When I arrived to take the formal oath of office on December 19, Washington already teemed with Iran-Contra investigators. I inherited the FBI agents who had been mobilized initially by the attorney general and who outnumbered and, at first, seemed to dominate my legal staff.

The topflight press corps was also going all out after the story, and excellent reporters were uncovering fresh details almost daily. A three-member blue-ribbon panel appointed by the president and headed by former senator John Tower was reviewing the operations of the National Security Council and its staff. On Capitol Hill, the Senate intelligence committee's hearings continued, and both houses of Congress were establishing select committees of inquiry.

Full-scale public hearings by Congress had the power to destroy us. Six years after Reagan's first election victory, Democrats had recaptured a majority in the Senate. Firmly in control of Congress again, they saw Iran-Contra as a political windfall potentially as damaging to the Republicans as the Watergate scandal had been. The overconfident leadership gave the Republicans almost equal representation on both select committees, a move that let conservative members often call the shots.

Beyond partisan motives, the legislative branch had a clear constitutional grievance against the executive branch. Congress had used its strongest card, its control of appropriations, to cut off U.S. military and intelligence support to the Contra forces, but the White House had staged an end run to keep funds and guidance flowing. Moreover, by failing to notify Congress of the dealings with Iran, the administration had frustrated the clear intent of the statutes that required "timely notification" to Congress of intelligence activities.

In the constant jockeying for influence between the two elected branches of government, a contest the drafters of the Constitution foresaw as a healthy check on efforts to concentrate power, legislators now had ample justification to call the executive to account. Certainly their hearings would embarrass an already profoundly shaken president. Conceivably they could topple him. And there could be no stopping the process. My primary concern was to prevent the Capitol Hill steamroller from flattening the criminal investigation I had been appointed to conduct.

I quickly realized that the greatest danger lay in the possibility of the congressional committees' taking testimony from reluctant witnesses under grants of immunity that could place my targets beyond prosecutory reach. John Poindexter and Oliver North had already asserted their Fifth Amendment rights not to answer questions before the Senate intelligence committee. So long as they risked criminal charges, they would be unlikely to waive those rights in any setting.

Congress, however, could force them or any other prospective witness to testify by guaranteeing that nothing they revealed could be used against them in court. Such "use immunity" would not only put a likely defendant's actual words off limit, but also bar a prosecutor from following up leads derived from the immunized testimony and require him to show that all the evidence produced at a trial came from other, untainted sources.

Immunizing witnesses is a standard procedure when prosecutors need the help of minor miscreants to indict and convict higher-ups. As my staff and I developed an understanding of the players and the illegal actions taken in the Iran-Contra affair, we agreed not to prosecute many lower-ranking public and private figures whose candid disclosures we counted on to lead us toward the truth. Before giving them immunity—or, in several instances, negotiating guilty pleas—we had to be satisfied that the bargains would produce useful evidence and forthcoming witnesses in proceedings against other individuals.

Congress had different priorities. Its first responsibility, it believed, was to put the full Iran-Contra story before the public and then to allot blame in political terms, rather than to decide legal guilt or innocence. Above all, I thought, Congress wanted to hold the president and his highest aides to account and would see Poindexter and North as the most direct sources of information about the actions of their superiors. Having these former National Security Council officials publicly reveal Ronald Reagan's participation was an obvious political imperative.

But Poindexter and North were also my prime targets. If any crimes had been committed—a question still revolving in my mind in the first weeks of my assignment—these two men had played central roles. The fact that they had lost their White House jobs after Meese's hasty inquiry was one strike against them. That those jobs had carried the responsibility for coordinating policy toward Iran and Nicaragua was enough to make them suspect. And that both Poindexter and North had retreated into silence compounded the impression that they had important, and very probably guilty, knowledge.

On that premise, formed by what was already a matter of public record and supported by our hurried preliminary investigation and analysis, I recognized in Congress a rival operation that could undo my work before it produced any results. My mandate was to prosecute wrongdoing, not just uncover it. If Poindexter and North had broken the law, I would have to take them to court and prove their crimes beyond a reasonable doubt. Only after trial could they be compelled to testify about others who might have given them their orders or supported their activities.

To build a convincing and comprehensive case and get it before a jury would clearly take weeks, possibly months. I wanted to do the job quickly, but I could fix no time limit. Congress, however, was working against a self-imposed deadline, initially set for the end of August and then postponed by two months. That schedule was the result of a compromise between Democrats who hoped for a thorough inquiry and Republicans who demanded that the process not spill over into the 1988 presidential campaign season.

The bargain created problems for the committees' investigators. Two members of the Senate panel, for instance, noted the slowness with which the administration delivered documents and issued security clearances for the staff. "The Committee's deadline provided a convenient stratagem for those who were determined not to cooperate," Senators William S. Cohen and George J. Mitchell, both of Maine, wrote later, as well as "critical leverage for the attorneys" of reluctant witnesses.

Congress's arbitrary time frame put me under fierce pressure to move quickly. Unless I could persuade the investigators on Capitol Hill to let Poindexter and North keep silent, I would have to gather as much evidence against them as I could before they were questioned in public. This would ensure that my leads did not come from immunized testimony. If the congressional committees insisted on having Poindexter and North testify, I would need to delay their testimony as long as possible. To buy time, I needed to offer something in return. I soon discovered, however, that in the local currency I was little more than a pauper.

I had none of the standard ingredients of political capital in Washington—no elective office, no backing from a powerful constituency, no control over federal funds or regulations, and no access to decision-makers. My team of lawyers, talented as it was, contained no veteran skirmishers in capital politics. And those who might have been able to help us were not about to do so: The administration, having been forced to retain me, regarded itself as an adversary rather than a client. Even our offices were makeshift. We operated temporarily out of a pair of three-room suites usually assigned to federal judges in the U.S. district courthouse and, several blocks away, some cubicles in the basement of the FBI headquarters.

The one valuable commodity I was presumed to possess was secret information, but I could not disclose the results of the early investigation without violating laws that restricted premature disclosures by prosecutors. On Christmas Eve, Danny Coulson, who headed the FBI team, had given me a briefing in Oklahoma City on the agents' work to date. After being held back by Attorney General Meese, while hundreds of documents were destroyed, the FBI had conducted a remarkably wide sweep. The agents had already pinned down the opening positions of scores of administration officials, all of whom had denied having been significantly involved in the relevant policies or knowing much about their execution. The FBI had begun gathering records to challenge or verify these claims, which would prove a massive undertaking.

To help me get up to speed, Coulson had brought a binder containing the summaries of the FBI reports and had installed a heavy safe in my kitchen in Oklahoma City so that I could keep secret material at home. Every time I had to work the complex combination lock, which was so delicate that the slightest tremor of my hand would necessitate my starting over, I wondered when I would have enough in the safe to justify the effort.

CHAPTER FOUR

Opening View

On the first Sunday of 1987, I moved into room 609 of the Watergate Hotel, my home for months to come. Facing inward over the central grounds of the Watergate complex, the room was filled with light in the morning and shadowed in the afternoon and evening by the balconies projecting from the rooms above. Sunday evenings away from home had always seemed lonely, and as I emptied my overtraveled bag and briefcase, the loneliness deepened. I had so little to unpack.

I did not even have the FBI briefing book. Although nothing that would imperil the national security was in the book, it was classified top secret because its contents could anger Central American officials and embarrass high-ranking Americans. As a result, I could not read it on the airplane or keep it in my unsecured hotel room. I did not even have a secure office. In fact, I had no office. It took two months for the General Services Administration to find me one that the intelligence agencies would accept as a depository for their documents.

In the past, when I had taken on a new case out of town for a large corporation, I would begin by getting a view from the inside, a picture from which to plan. As an independent counsel, I had no comparable client. There was no high-ranking officer to supply me with the information I needed. The court that had appointed me did not know the facts. I would have to start from scratch.

The FBI had been held back while Attorney General Edwin Meese conducted his personal investigation of the arms sales. During this delay, the scores of officials who would be questioned by the FBI had had time to think, to coordinate their stories, and to hide or destroy documents. When the agents eventually moved in, they had not yet had time to assimilate the available records or to obtain any evidence with which to confront those being questioned. Nevertheless, the agents had conducted a remarkably wide sweep and interviewed many important witnesses.

In terms of a potential prosecution, no ready-made case sprang from the FBI report. Oliver North and Richard Secord, who could have supplied the most useful information, had refused to talk. William Casey, silenced by cancer, was now dying. Albert Hakim, Secord's Iranian-born business partner, had fled to Europe. Robert McFarlane and Donald Regan were talking to the press and disputing each other's statements about the president's authorization of the arms shipments to Iran. McFarlane was in trouble: In his December congressional testimony, he had initially withheld the fact that he and Ronald Reagan had invited Saudi Arabia to fund the Contras after Congress had cut them off.

After pointing the finger at Oliver North and John Poindexter, the president had called on Congress to grant them immunity, which would block their criminal prosecution and allow them to deny his participation in the theft of the proceeds from the direct sales of American arms to Iran. North and Poindexter were the obvious immediate targets for possible prosecution. If convicted, they might be tempted to tell the entire truth in exchange for lenient sentences. Immunity, however, would obviate their need for leniency.

Conducting a complex investigation would require us to alternate between the one-piece-at-a-time gathering of facts and periodic consolidations and reconsolidations of the facts into a coherent history. This narrative attempts to limit the repetition of facts to that which is necessary to an evaluation of my developing views and the actions of others as well as myself, but even so, extensive repetition is at times inevitable.

Aided by the work of other investigators, beginning with the briefing I received from the FBI in late December and concluding with the report issued by the Tower Commission in late February, we assimilated a preliminary understanding of the facts underlying the Iranian aspects of our investigation. Our understanding of the Nicaraguan aspects of the affair would take time, because neither the FBI, before my appointment, nor the Tower Commission had been authorized to investigate issues concerning the Contras. Moreover, although our independence was absolute, our sophistication and knowledge of covert activities was almost nil. In the meantime, we were bombarded with new reports by the FBI, newspaper stories by investigative reporters, and ultimately the flow of documents from the National

Security Council. Our evaluation of what crimes might have been committed and what evidence was available to prove them had to await the completion of an overview.

The Iranian initiative, our early sources indicated, seemed to have been little more than a confidence game on an international scale. American officials, from the president on down, had played the part of suckers to a changing cast of Iranians and Israelis who had been pursuing their own ends. This picture, however, grossly oversimplified the position of the Reagan administration as it attempted to deal with fundamentalist Islamic terrorists in Lebanon who blamed the United States for the Israeli invasion of Lebanon. On March 18, 1984, after murderous attacks on the U.S. embassy and Marine barracks in Lebanon, members of the Shiite Islamic group Hezbollah had kidnapped the CIA's local chief of station, William Buckley. He was reportedly being tortured in an attempt to compel him to reveal CIA operations and operatives. Another six Americans had been kidnapped and were being held. Two others had been murdered.

These events had coincided with McFarlane's effort to prompt a rethinking of U.S. relations with Iran, which had been a valuable U.S. ally before the overthrow of the shah. Hoping to assist supposedly pro-Western politicians in Tehran before and—crucially—after the anticipated death of the Ayatollah Ruhollah Khomeini, McFarlane had asked the CIA to prepare a Special National Intelligence Estimate for interagency review, the first step toward a possible change in U.S. policy on Iran. The foreign policy experts who reviewed the CIA study had rejected its recommendations for a new National Security Decision Directive—which would have formalized a policy change—and had decided to stand pat, retaining the ban on weapons sales to Iran and the denunciation of the Khomeini regime as a supporter of terrorism.

The embargo had stood in the way of the potentially immense profits that drew together some of the individuals who would become the targets of my investigation. Desperate for weapons to use in the war with Iraq, Iranians claiming to speak for their government (or for factions within it) had regularly approached American officials with offers to exchange inside intelligence for antitank missiles. Some had hinted that a relaxation of the arms embargo could lead to Iranian intercession with the Lebanese who were holding the American captives in Beirut.

Among the first to offer such a trade was Manucher Ghorbanifar, who had approached retired CIA officer Theodore Shackley in Hamburg, Germany, in November 1984. Ghorbanifar was, to some extent, a mystery man. He had managed an Iranian shipping company and may have been an informant for SAVAK (the shah's intelligence service) before fleeing to Paris when the shah was overthrown. Now a proprietor of an export-import business built in part on his purported ties to Iran's intelligence services and its armed forces, Ghorbanifar had proposed to serve as the middleman to negotiate the release of the hostages. Having found him to be a "fabricator" in the past, however, the CIA had classified him as unreliable—so unreliable that it had issued a rare "burn notice" warning all personnel against him. The State Department had rebuffed his proposal, but Ghorbanifar had not given up.

With the help of Roy Furmark, a New York financial venturer and former client of William Casey, Ghorbanifar had gained the backing of Furmark's former employer, Saudi Arabian financier Adnan Khashoggi, in 1985. Khashoggi had urged Ghorbanifar to proceed through Israeli arms merchant Adolf "Al" Schwimmer, a confidant and advisor of Israel's prime minister, Shimon Peres.

In the complex politics of the Middle East, Israel had had an interest in preventing Iraq from defeating Iran, and Israeli arms merchants had had an interest in selling weapons from the Israeli arsenal at a profit. In May 1985, Michael Ledeen, a scholar-activist and freelance policy analyst who worked as a consultant to McFarlane, had persuaded McFarlane to permit him to approach Peres, ostensibly to take advantage of Israeli intelligence in formulating a policy for dealing with Iran after Khomeini's death. Peres and Ledeen, who were both interested in international labor activities, were friends. Expressing interest in Ledeen's project, Peres had set up an unofficial group to study the issue and share ideas with the Americans. The members of the group, in addition to Israeli defense officials, had included Al Schwimmer and Yaacov Nimrodi, a businessman and former government official. Schwimmer and Nimrodi, who were interested in selling weapons, had become a conduit for proposals for the sale of U.S. weapons through Israel in exchange for the release of the hostages. The group had become Ghorbanifar's sponsor and used Ledeen and Israeli diplomats to draw McFarlane into the scheme.

Unlike the CIA, Israel had apparently accepted Ghorbanifar as a reliable source of intelligence on Iranian politics and as someone with access to influential figures in Tehran. In early July 1985, Schwimmer and David Kimche, the senior career officer in the Israeli foreign ministry, had come to Washington to relay a new feeler from Ghorbanifar to Ledeen and McFarlane.

According to the Israelis, Ghorbanifar had reported that high-level Iranians were offering—as a way of demonstrating their political clout and good faith—to help free the seven American hostages. What the Iranians wanted in return, Ghorbanifar had said, was dialogue. Kimche had told McFarlane that weapons would enter the picture only later, if at all, and that Israel would hold no further discussions on the matter without a go-ahead from the United States.

McFarlane had briefed President Reagan on Kimche's proposal, including the possibility of arms transfers. Reagan had seemed interested, and McFarlane had raised the matter with him again at the Bethesda Naval Hospital on July 18, five days after the president had undergone successful surgery for cancer. In Donald Regan's presence, McFarlane had asked for the authority to explore the contact with Iran through Israel. According to Regan, the president had replied, "Yes, go ahead. Open it up."

From the beginning, the president had been interested less in a political dialogue with Iran than in liberating the seven hostages, whose families' pleas for action had stirred his emotions at a meeting earlier that month. As the summer wore on, he had submitted McFarlane to "recurrent, virtually daily questioning" about the hostages' welfare and whether there was "anything new" on freeing them.

David Kimche had soon returned to Washington to press for an answer to the question of arms transfers and to advise McFarlane that if the White House approved, Schwimmer and Nimrodi would sell the Iranians military equipment, including antitank missiles, that Israel had previously obtained from the United States. Israel would then expect to purchase replacements from the United States. On August 6, McFarlane had taken Kimche's proposition to a meeting of the National Security Planning Group in the White House family quarters, where Reagan was convalescing in pajamas. As the president, vice president, Casey, and Regan listened, George Shultz and Caspar Weinberger had vigorously objected to the sale of arms to Iran by any nation. Reagan had announced no immediate decision. According to McFarlane, the president had called him a few days later to approve the Israeli proposal and had granted permission for Israel to replenish its arsenal with U.S. equipment.

McFarlane had passed the word to Kimche, and a shipment of ninety-six wire-guided antitank missiles (TOWs) had left Israel for Iran on August 30. A second consignment had followed two weeks later, bringing the total to 504. The next day, the Reverend Benjamin Weir, a Presbyterian missionary who had been held hostage for more than a year, had been released in Lebanon.

No other hostages had been freed. McFarlane had requested that CIA station chief William Buckley be released first, but in October an Islamic group had announced that Buckley had been executed in retaliation for an Israeli air force attack on the Tunis headquarters of the Palestine Liberation Organization. As the Americans later learned, however, Buckley had actually died of his torture in June, before Kimche delivered Ghorbanifar's summer 1985 proposal. Unaware of the deception, Ledeen had continued to meet with Ghorbanifar, Kimche, Schwimmer, and Nimrodi during September, October, and November, but nothing had come of their conversations. McFarlane had suspected bad faith and seriously considered ending all negotiations.

According to our early information, Israel had believed it had an open-ended authorization to continue to sell arms for hostages. In mid-November, Israeli Defense Minister Yitzhak Rabin, who was then in New York, had telephoned McFarlane in Geneva, Switzerland, where President Reagan and Soviet leader Mikhail Gorbachev were about to meet for the first time. Rabin had asked for help in arranging for an Israeli shipment of Hawk missiles to pass through a third country and be transferred to non-Israeli planes for delivery to Iran. McFarlane had directed Oliver North, who was in Washington, to attend to the matter.

At the same time, McFarlane had alerted George Shultz, who was in Geneva, and had told the president and Donald Regan about the plan: Israeli aircraft chartered by Schwimmer and Nimrodi were about to fly a hundred Hawk antiaircraft missiles to a West European country, where the cargo would be transferred to other aircraft; these planes would take the missiles on to Iran as soon as four hostages had been released; Israel would then buy replacement Hawks from the United States. Shultz had protested the operation and his last-minute notification but agreed not to ask the president to block the effort.

North had advised McFarlane's then deputy, John Poindexter, that the swap would take place on November 22 and that eighty Hawks, for which $18 million had already been paid, would be traded for the remaining five American hostages. Forty more missiles, North had said, would be delivered later. He had added that the Iranians would pledge not to condone more kidnappings. He had warned that the Defense Department would need to move quickly to replenish Israeli stocks. North had concluded that it wasn't "that bad a deal."

It had turned out to be no deal at all. No hostages had been set free, and only eighteen Hawks had been delivered to Iran, which had promptly rejected them with an angry protest that the missiles were obsolete and useless against high-flying aircraft, not to mention stenciled with the Star of David.

To make matters worse, the Israeli arms merchants had not properly cleared the transshipment of missiles with the authorities of the European country, and the Israeli aircraft had been turned back in midflight. North had sent Secord to Europe, but Secord had been unable to reach the appropriate officials. North had then involved the CIA in the operation, turning to Duane "Dewey" Clarridge, who had been transferred from the agency's Latin American division to head the West European division of the operations directorate. But Clarridge, through agency contacts, had had no more success than Secord. He had then given North the name of a commercial air charter company that secretly belonged to the CIA, making it what is known in the trade as a CIA proprietary. Secord, using funds deposited by Schwimmer in the Swiss bank account that had been set up for arming the Contras, had chartered the aircraft to take over the delivery for Israel.

In Clarridge and Secord, Oliver North's two covert activities had abruptly joined. Clarridge had been the CIA official responsible for supporting the Contras. Secord had been the central figure in the Contra-supply operation after the CIA had been forced to bow out. To North, Secord was an admired and trusted colleague. In an early evening message to Poindexter on the day scheduled for the Hawk shipment, North had reported that Secord would "charter two 707s in the name of LAKE Resources (our Swiss Co.) and have them [pick up] the cargo and deliver it. . . ." Lake Resources was one of the Swiss dummy corporations used to finance arms purchases for the Contras. An hour later, North had told Poindexter that one of the Lake Resources aircraft that was to have flown ammunition to the Contras was being hastily repainted for use in delivering Hawks to Iran. "One hell of an operation," North had concluded.

At the time, William Casey had been away from the CIA. When Deputy Director John McMahon learned of Clarridge's weekend collaboration with North, McMahon had "hit the overhead," according to his associates. Recognizing that the agency had been dragged into the kind of operational activity that by law required formal presidential approval, a written finding, and notification to Congress, McMahon had instructed Stanley Sporkin, the CIA's general counsel, to draft a finding that the president could sign to sanction the operation retroactively.

The finding drafted by Sporkin and signed by President Reagan on December 5, 1985, had authorized the agency to assist "private parties" trying to free American hostages in the Middle East and, in furtherance of those efforts, to provide "certain foreign material and munitions . . . to the government of Iran, which is taking steps to facilitate the release of American hostages." The draft finding had also specified that Congress was not to be informed of the operation until the president gave permission to relax secrecy.

On November 26, after Casey returned, he had sent the proposed draft to Poindexter at the White House. There, the finding had disappeared. Reports circulated that it had been signed, but—unlike other presidential findings—this one had not been returned to the CIA to be filed as authority for its action.

On December 5, in the wake of the fiasco, Poindexter had relayed President Reagan's call for a secret Saturday-morning meeting of the National Security Planning Group in the White House residence. Poindexter had told Shultz to make no entry on his calendar. The meeting had been stormy. John McMahon had substituted for William Casey. George Bush had been at the Army-Navy football game. Shultz and Weinberger had argued against further involvement in trading arms for hostages and had challenged the legality of the proposals. They believed that they had carried the day. McFarlane, too, saw the group as having been "unanimous" in thinking that the Iranian negotiations "had gone badly off course" and that any future conversations with Iranians should start with a declaration that the United States would neither sell weapons nor permit others to do so.

Although McFarlane had just resigned, he had agreed to go immediately to London, where Ghorbanifar, Nimrodi, Schwimmer, and Kimche were meeting with North to consider ways to put the operation back on track. McFarlane had told them that the arms aspect of the deal was off, but Ghorbanifar—professing concern for the safety of the hostages—had refused to transmit the message to his principals.

After returning to Washington, McFarlane had met in the Oval Office with the president, Regan, Casey, Weinberger, and Poindexter to report that Ghorbanifar had seemed primarily interested in weapons. McFarlane had recommended an end to the dealings with Iran and particularly with Ghorbanifar, whom he judged "not a trustworthy person and ... an unsatisfactory intermediary." The effort to apply Iranian influence on the hostage takers seemed to have come to a dead end.

One person, however, had refused to accept that verdict. The lone, silent dissenter was Ronald Reagan. Consequently, the Iranian initiative had been resurrected by new promises from Ghorbanifar; new proposals from the Israelis through Amiram Nir, Shimon Peres's advisor on terrorism; and repeated warnings from Oliver North that the hostages would probably be murdered if the administration failed to act.

President Reagan's determination to help the hostages had made him vulnerable, and Ghorbanifar had continued to exploit the president's weakness.

When Poindexter became the national security advisor, he had dismissed Ledeen as an NSC consultant, but Ledeen had continued to sponsor Ghorbanifar. To CIA intelligence officer Charles Allen, Ledeen had described Ghorbanifar as "a good fellow who is a lot of fun." Ledeen had told the CIA chief of the Iran branch that Ghorbanifar was "a wonderful man ... almost too good to be true." In connection with other matters preceding the arms sales, the CIA had given Ghorbanifar a polygraph test, which he had flunked. Now, supported by North, Ledeen had persuaded Casey to have the CIA give Ghorbanifar a new polygraph test in the hope that he could win over the CIA professionals who distrusted him. But the new test had not worked out as Ledeen had hoped: The polygraph instrument had dispassionately revealed Ghorbanifar to be telling one lie after another.

Hundreds of consultants glide in and out of federal office buildings every day. With specialized skills, the consultants serve high-ranking officials whose broad responsibilities call for generalized judgments. Although these part-time operators are necessary, and many of them are able and devoted, their loyalties are sometimes divided. Whether they are providing impartial advice or using the officials to serve private interests is sometimes in question.

Ledeen was more than a messenger. He had pressed McFarlane for permission to open discussions with Peres and had become the Washington spokesman for the Israeli arms merchants and Ghorbanifar. Until he was replaced by North after the Hawk debacle, Ledeen had actually been the principal negotiator for the United States. It was Ledeen to whom Ghorbanifar had made his demands for one exotic weapons system after another, and it was Ledeen who had relayed Ghorbanifar's promises.

Ledeen's actions invited questions, but whether they had been criminal was something we would have to decide. Had he been simply an amateur welcoming a chance to help formulate presidential policy, while the professional diplomats were excluded from the process? Had he been a cat's-paw for McFarlane's ambition for a historic breakthrough to Iran? Had he been paid off by Ghorbanifar or the Israeli arms merchants?

We did not have access to the Israeli and Swiss bank records that might have answered the last question, but Ledeen eventually supplied us with his financial records, including his income tax returns. A net-worth study by our Internal Revenue Service agents uncovered no unexplained income or wealth.

As for whether Ledeen had been using the officials he advised, he had not carried messages to babes in the woods: He had been dealing with William Casey, who not only was the director of central intelligence but also was personally skilled in conducting covert activities. Despite the strongly worded warnings of his professional staff, the CIA director had seemed convinced that Ghorbanifar offered the best hope for freeing the hostages. Casey had said as much to Reagan in a December 23, 1985, letter, which also warned the president that questions had been raised about Ghorbanifar's reliability. Casey had probably recognized that, as an intermediary trying to negotiate arms deals between two countries whose public dogma called for hatred, Ghorbanifar was unlikely to be as clean as an archbishop.

We had no direct means of ascertaining Casey's perspective on Iran-Contra. He apparently had neither kept notes nor confided in anyone. He was said to have walked out of conferences when notes were taken, and he had once told North that if he had to take notes, he was in the wrong business. I hypothesized that Casey had probably been drawn into the hostage-rescue activities by his concern for the recovery of William Buckley; that even after learning that Buckley was dead, Casey had felt he could not reverse the course he had set; and that he had already felt committed to this precarious course when Ledeen appealed to him to keep Ghorbanifar in the action.

Such questions and speculations necessarily accompanied our accumulation and integration of the facts that were pouring in not only from the FBI, the Tower Commission, and my own lawyers but also from the Washington press corps. After working all day with my staff and the FBI contingent, I carefully read the newspaper coverage for hours in my hotel room every night. Each day began with more questions than answers. If we couldn't answer the questions, we formed temporary, limited hypotheses to decide whether persons about to be questioned were likely to be witnesses, immunized witnesses, or targets of our investigation.

According to our early investigation, North and Sporkin had drafted a new presidential finding at the beginning of 1986. For the first time, an objective broader than the recovery of the hostages had been cited. The finding had authorized intelligence support by the CIA and arms sales through third parties and countries to "moderate elements within and outside" the Iranian government who were capable of "establishing a more moderate government in Iran," providing valuable insights into official Iranian policy, and "furthering the release of the American hostages held in Beirut." The finding had directed that no notice be given to Congress. In a covering memorandum explaining the draft finding, North had reported that the Iranians wanted to acquire four thousand TOW missiles in a hurry, and that Israel was prepared to sell the weapons if it could restock from U.S. supplies within thirty days.

Ordinarily, a finding authorizing a new covert action would have been reviewed within the CIA and circulated to members of the National Security Planning Group. Perhaps by accident, however, the president had signed the draft finding when it was given him to study on January 6. He had not mentioned it the next day when, after an NSPG meeting, Casey, Regan, Meese, Shultz, Weinberger, and Vice President George Bush had joined him in the Oval Office to consider the proposal that the finding had been intended to authorize. The undisclosed finding had permitted the sale of arms to Iran by the CIA through "third persons" as well as "third countries," but except for Poindexter, the conferees had been unaware of this change. They had assumed that the transfer would be made through the Israelis, as before. Only Shultz and Weinberger had opposed the sale, and their arguments had failed to persuade Ronald Reagan.

On January 17, Poindexter had had the president re-sign the finding, because the authorization to sell through "third persons" had been inadvertently omitted from one of the authorization paragraphs. Also present at this signing were Bush, Regan, and Poindexter's deputy, Donald Fortier. In a meeting the day before, Poindexter, Weinberger, Meese, Casey, and Sporkin had decided to drop the Israelis and have the CIA sell directly to Iran, using Secord as an intermediary. By this time, they had concluded that sales to Israel for resale to Iran would require notice to Congress under the Arms Export Control Act but that notice of direct sales by the CIA could be delayed. (Weinberger had dissented, saying that notice was required regardless of who made the sales.) A cover memo for the finding had stated that the program would end if the American hostages were not released after Iran received the first thousand TOW missiles. According to the members of the NSPG, they had never seen either version of the finding.

In a series of organizational meetings beginning on January 20, Poindexter and North had introduced Secord to the CIA officials who were to take over for Casey—Clair George, the director of operations, and Thomas Twetten, the deputy chief of the Near Eastern division. North was to be Poindexter's operational counterpart, and Twetten was to be George's. George had viewed the effort as an NSC operation with the CIA in support. North and Twetten had quickly obtained low prices for a thousand TOWs from the Defense Department. With Poindexter's approval, North had then persuaded Ghorbanifar to buy the missiles at three times their cost. According to Ghorbanifar, even with the markup these TOWs had been cheaper than those he had bought from the Israelis.

Secord had delivered the U.S. TOWs to Iran in two equal consignments on February 18 and 27. "Operation Recovery," as North called the mission, had recovered no hostages, but it had brought Richard Secord and Albert Hakim to the fore. At a February meeting in Germany, Ghorbanifar had produced an Iranian official from the prime minister's staff, and North, using the alias "Goode," had introduced Secord and Hakim, who were also using aliases, as officers of the U.S. Defense Intelligence Agency. Over the following months, Secord and Hakim had acted more and more as if those roles were real, as though— with North's blessing and guidance—they represented the American government in matters Iranian. In vain, Twetten had warned North against linking two covert actions by using Secord for both selling arms to Iran and supplying arms to the Contras.

The dealings with Iran had brought no quick results. The Iranian official had promised to arrange a high-level meeting and, in connection with it, to secure the release of all the hostages, but March had passed without action. Hoping for the profits that could be expected if the embargo on arms sales to Iran ended, Secord and Hakim had nevertheless continued to negotiate with Ghorbanifar. After arriving in Washington in early April, Ghorbanifar claimed to have broken the logjam. He had proposed that an official American party travel to Tehran for talks with an Iranian delegation headed by Ali Akbar Rafsanjani, who was the speaker of Iran's Majlis, or parliament, and a reputed moderate. To bring off the meeting, Ghorbanifar had said, the Americans would have to supply Iran with a specified variety of spare parts for the Hawk missiles that had been acquired by the shah.

As North had explained the arrangement in a lengthy draft memorandum that he expected Poindexter to pass along to the president, the spare parts would be held at an Israeli airfield and would be delivered only after the U.S. emissaries had reached Tehran and all of the American hostages had been released in Beirut. Noting that the Iranians were to pay $17 million for Defense Department matériel that would cost the CIA only $3.6 million, North had also spelled out his plans for "the residual funds from this transaction." Israel would get $2 million with which to buy replacements for the TOWs it had sold in 1985 "to Iran for the release of Benjamin Weir." The remainder, rounded upward to $12 million in North's accounting, would "be used to purchase critically needed supplies for the Nicaraguan Democratic Resistance Forces"—the Contras. North had set down this plan as matter-of-factly as he had reported the Iranians' willingness to discuss ending their assistance to the Sandinista regime in Nicaragua and beefing up their help to anticommunist forces in Afghanistan.

Seven months later, when the attorney general's aides read the draft memorandum in North's office, they had understood that the financial arrangements it spelled out could mean profound trouble for the Reagan administration. This was the first documentary evidence that the covert activities in Iran and Nicaragua had been linked at all, much less linked improperly. The memorandum had sought the president's approval not only for the Tehran meeting and trading arms for hostages but also for channeling U.S. funds from the illegal trade into a secret war Congress had specifically refused to finance.

McFarlane's mission to Iran had received the full attention of the Reagan administration. The State Department had prepared talking points. The Israelis had repainted and disguised an airplane usually reserved for its highest officials. False Irish passports were given to the members of the party. But the mission had failed: The U.S. delegation was kept waiting at the airport, then confined to a hotel, and finally confronted with junior officials who had made ridiculous assertions and excessive demands that differed from those relayed by Ghorbanifar through North.

Only one pallet of Hawk parts had accompanied the delegation. Most had been left on a second aircraft in Israel to be delivered after the hostages had been released. Ghorbanifar had borrowed from Adnan Khashoggi to pay for them in advance, but he would not be repaid by Iran until they were delivered. The negotiations had broken down when it became clear that the Iranians had not arranged for the release of any hostages. McFarlane had given orders for his team to leave. Without McFarlane's permission, North had ordered the second aircraft to deliver its cargo. McFarlane had found out and angrily countermanded the order, turning the flight back in midair. The Iranians had proposed that the weapons be delivered in exchange for the release of two hostages. McFarlane had rejected the proposal, and the U.S. delegation had returned to Israel and then to Washington.

For the next six weeks, North and his Israeli counterpart, Amiram Nir, had sought permission for the delivery of the spare parts. On July 26, an additional hostage had been released. Three days later, Vice President Bush had met in Israel with Nir, who had briefed him on the concept of sequential hostage releases followed by deliveries of weapons, rather than the release of all hostages in advance. On July 30, President Reagan had ordered the delivery of the second planeload of Hawk parts.

After this shipment, the U.S. officials had dropped Ghorbanifar. Another Iranian had negotiated the release of one more hostage, who was freed on November 2, 1986, two days before election day and six days after the delivery of five hundred TOWs. On November 3, the Lebanese magazine *Al Shiraa* had published its exposé of the arms sales.

The next day, Rafsanjani had confirmed the story in an address to the Iranian parliament. Meanwhile, the Iranians had found that they were being grossly overcharged; they had paid only part of the purchase price to Ghorbanifar, who had begun spreading rumors that Iranian funds were being diverted to the Contras.

While both North and the Iranians attempted to continue their meetings, the Reagan administration had been divided over how to proceed. Then, when North's memorandum describing the diversion of the arms sales proceeds to Nicaragua came to light, President Reagan had terminated the operation.

Almost before my team could begin to sort through this information to identify possible crimes and appropriate lines of investigation, we found ourselves between the hammer and the anvil: Congress was trying to rush us to a superficial conclusion, while the national security community tried to delay our progress.

CHAPTER FIVE

The Bramble Bush

Dick Moe, Davis Polk's Washington counsel and a former advisor to both Senator Edmund S. Muskie of Maine and Vice President Walter Mondale, had urged me to make the rounds of Capitol Hill to show the appropriate respect for those who would be responsible for the congressional investigation. Congress was out of session in December, so I arranged a January meeting with the speaker of the House of Representatives. I then telephoned Senator Daniel Inouye, the Hawaii Democrat who had been named to head the Senate select committee investigating Iran-Contra. Senator Inouye was leaving for Hawaii, so our exchange of courtesies, although pleasant, was too brief to build rapport.

On January 5, 1987, Guy Struve and I went to the Capitol to meet the new speaker of the House, Jim Wright of Texas. A shrewd parliamentary leader and political moderate, Wright had just replaced Massachusetts Democrat Thomas P. "Tip" O'Neill, Jr., a New Deal liberal, in the second most powerful elected post in the government. As we passed through the security barriers and walked down the marble corridors into the speaker's ornate outer office, I was prepared for a superficial conversation that, at best, would help me to gauge the mood of the House of Representatives and to sketch out the independent counsel's mandate.

The speaker had other plans. There to meet me and take my measure were Minority Leader Robert H. Michel of Illinois and Majority Leader Thomas P. Foley of Washington. Foley was a member of the House select committee, whose Democratic chairman, Lee H. Hamilton of Indiana, and ranking Republican, Dick Cheney of Wyoming, were also present.

---

1. Respectfully taken from *The Bramble Bush*, an introduction to the study of law, by a favorite professor, the late Karl N. Llewellyn.

(The House and Senate select committees on Iran-Contra at first proceeded separately. They later held joint hearings and filed a joint report.)

Wright and Michel cordially welcomed me, then quickly detached themselves from the discussion. With Hamilton taking a temperate but very firm line and Cheney coldly radiating dissatisfaction, the conversation took the form of a polite but determined inquisition: How much information did the independent counsel have? How much would he share with congressional investigators? How soon could the cooperation begin?

Hamilton had been a long-standing opponent of support for the Contras and a recognized congressional expert on the Middle East. As chairman of the permanent House intelligence committee he had already made a first effort to unravel some of the Iran-Contra mysteries. But despite the closed-door hearings that he had held in December, he remained in the dark about how much money the arms sales to Iran had generated and how the proceeds had been shared.

Hamilton put his questions to me courteously but with measured intensity. He suggested that his new committee and my office, which were seeking the same ends and information, should find ways to work together. I agreed but had to point out the difference between our roles. As searchers for the facts, we ran parallel courses. Our goals, however, were far apart. The primary purpose of legislative oversight was to identify abuses of executive power so that tighter legal restraints could be written to prevent future misconduct. Unless abusive conduct reached the level of an impeachable offense by the president or other top official, congressional interest in the criminality of the conduct was less exacting than that of an independent counsel. I had to determine whether crimes had been committed and to prosecute the individuals who had perpetrated them. As an outsider, a surrogate for the attorney general in a matter where political interests made the impartiality of the Justice Department suspect, I was appointed not simply to disclose wrongdoing but to enforce the law.

Despite my readiness to cooperate, I could not agree to share everything my office learned or to share information as soon as we learned it. We were legally bound, for instance, to maintain the secrecy of evidence presented to a grand jury. Disclosing such evidence before trial could amount to prosecutorial misconduct.

The Swiss bank records of Albert Hakim and Richard Secord raised a critical problem. The treaty under which the Department of Justice had already persuaded Switzerland to freeze their accounts and to consider permitting the production of their records had created only a narrowly drawn exception to the famed secrecy of Swiss banks. The treaty allowed the release of documents only to law-enforcement officials, only for use in criminal investigations, and only after a number of procedural reviews that frequently enabled the account holders to delay or block the delivery of the records. Even if I ultimately obtained the records for the accounts of Secord and Hakim, I would not be able to transmit the records to Congress without some special and unlikely dispensation from the Swiss authorities. Hamilton appeared genuinely troubled by the possibility of conflict. He intimated that to obtain information the committees would probably have to grant immunity to someone who had access to the accounts.

Representative Cheney, who had been Gerald Ford's White House chief of staff in 1975 and 1976, was less sensitive to our position. Speed was not only essential, he contended, it was also justified. He acidly characterized our position as a desire for a "one-way street," in which they would share information with us and get nothing in return. Struve and I promised memoranda explaining the extent of our possible assistance to the committees.

Obviously, my priorities were not political. Nor were they subordinate, even though Congress—through its unrestricted power to grant immunity—could jeopardize my prosecutions. The new select committees on Iran-Contra had one immediate job: to provide a full, public accounting of the Iran-Contra affair. The independent counsel had another job: to uncover violations of the law and, if warranted, to punish the individuals who had committed them. I had to get on with my duties, cooperating where cooperation was possible but colliding where collision was unavoidable. As I left the Capitol, I saw no way to avoid the conflict and little likelihood that it could be long postponed.

Returning to my temporary office in the federal courthouse, I looked up at Capitol Hill to the left and down the sweep of federal office buildings to the right—the edifices of the most powerful government in the world. I sensed the enormous power lodged in those buildings, the power of my opposition. I wondered where I would find the client who wanted me to do what the law required that I do. What support I had would come from the courthouse in which I was standing, but it would come only if I could mobilize it. At best, it would be the support of neutral judges.

In the congressional office buildings flanking the Capitol served the rarely seen staffs of the committees that oversaw the agencies of government. These specialists produced the information necessary for policy decisions and constantly studied the agencies they oversaw. They had already evaluated the key officials and determined whom to believe and whom to disbelieve. The more controversial the agency, the more intense had been the oversight.

If I had overlooked the invisible forces on Capitol Hill, I had also underestimated the power of the formidable departments and agencies responsible for national security. The national security community comprised the largest and the most protected government entities, each with its own legal staff. The Defense Department and the CIA had scores of lawyers. Headed by former federal judge Abraham Sofaer, the State Department's legal team always seemed to excel in its highly specialized field.

For the first time, I fully recognized the nature of the awesome, three-sided conflict in which I found myself. My team and I could be crushed when the political forces of government, the national security community, and the courts collided. Struve and I, who were still recruiting lawyers, knew that we would have to double our staff.

On the morning of January 7, the first recruits of my staff met with the team leaders of the FBI detail assigned to me. When my lawyers and I entered my borrowed chambers, we found no empty chairs—the FBI team leaders had crowded both sides of the large conference table opposite the big double desk of the absent judge. We brought in additional chairs and arranged them around the stale room, encircling the desk and conference table. As the FBI leaders sized us up, my associate counsel and I must have resembled a pickup team about to engage the varsity.

Danny Coulson, the special agent in charge, had already been marked for leadership at the FBI. Having led a hit team that had shot the tires out from under hijacked aircraft, he had the fearless forthrightness to lead an investigation into very high levels of government. Neil Divers, his chief of staff, was a wise and sober counselor. The team leaders showed a range of competence and commitment, as they briefed the lawyers and profiled the principal participants and government agencies that we would study. Much we already knew from the deluge of news reports but we were beginning the collective process of deciding what was or was not evidence and who would be the individual subjects of our investigation.

Oliver North was described as a Marine lieutenant colonel who had been decorated for valor in Vietnam and detailed to the National

Security Council as deputy head of the office of political-military affairs. An expert on counterterrorism, he had been a staff member of Vice President George Bush's committee to study the problem. Ruthless both in personal ambition and in determination to accomplish his goals, he had known how to use the appearance of presidential support. People who shared his right-wing views liked him. Some of his colleagues did not.

The White House team leader described John Poindexter. First in his class at Annapolis, he had later earned a doctorate in nuclear physics. He had risen through important commands and had been under observation for possible eventual promotion to chief of naval operations. He had been detailed to serve as military aide and then deputy to the president's national security advisor, before becoming the national security advisor himself. The information gathered by the FBI and the press showed Poindexter to have little apparent regard for Congress and the public's right to know. He seemed to believe that disinformation was appropriate if it served his view of the public interest.

Robert C. "Bud" McFarlane, we were told, had a more varied career. He had commanded the first American unit to land in Vietnam. Between two tours in the heaviest of fighting, he had been trained as an expert in foreign affairs. After leaving the Marines as a lieutenant colonel, he had held important posts on congressional staffs and in the State Department. He then had been appointed President Reagan's deputy national security advisor and, finally, national security advisor. In that post, he had attempted to reconcile the sometimes harshly conflicting views of Casey, Weinberger, and Shultz. According to some observers, McFarlane's pursuit of the opening to Iran reflected his ambition to match Henry Kissinger's successful bridge to the Republic of China in 1971.

Another FBI team leader described Richard Secord as a retired Air Force major general (one of the youngest to reach that rank) who had served with distinction in Vietnam and Iran. The team leader said that a former commanding officer had once evaluated Secord as the most abrasive, yet ablest, officer with whom he had served. After leaving the Air Force, Secord had been appointed as the deputy assistant secretary of defense for international affairs and had been the key coordinator of the sale of airborne warning and control system (AWACS) aircraft to Saudi Arabia. Touched by scandal in an arms transaction with former CIA colleagues from Vietnam days, he had left the government and become a partner of Albert Hakim in a venture called Stanford

Technology Trading International. When North replaced the CIA as the U.S. government's liaison with the Contras, Casey had recommended Secord to aid him in the continued supply of the Contras.

The team leader in charge of tracing funds described Albert Hakim as a former Iranian businessman who had become a naturalized U.S. citizen after the fall of the shah of Iran. As Secord's financial partner, Hakim had assisted him in creating the financial structure used to supply the Contras. Hakim was accustomed to an environment where monetary rewards were expected for many kinds of government service. As he once explained during a federal court proceeding, "In Iran, this skill is learned in boyhood." We were told of the efforts, unsuccessful to date, to obtain records from Switzerland and Israel.

The Defense Department team had traced the weapons for Iran through that department to the CIA. The team was then following up charges that the weapons had been underpriced. Caspar Weinberger claimed to have little knowledge of the arms sales. Assistant Secretary Richard Armitage admitted that he had been concerned when he read intelligence reports pointing to someone in the White House as the coordinator of the sales. He had invited North to lunch and advised him to "get the elephants together" and cover his backside. This had led to the meeting of the National Security Planning Group in the White House family quarters on the morning of December 7, 1985.

The Justice Department team had established Attorney General Edwin Meese's exclusion of the FBI and the department's criminal division from his November 1986 "fact-finding" investigation until two days after he had discovered the diversion of the Iranian arms sales proceeds to the Contras and after the extensive destruction of NSC documents. The team was also investigating the possible influence on Justice Department officials in gunrunning cases pending in Miami as well as the investigation of customs violations by Secord's charter carrier, Southern Air Transport.

The FBI team leaders believed that proceeds of the direct shipments from the United States to Iran were probably the only funds that had been diverted to the Contras. The diversion had begun after President Reagan signed the finding authorizing direct arms sales from the Defense Department through the CIA to Iran. Charles Allen, a CIA intelligence officer who had assisted North in using U.S. intelligence to monitor the arms sales, had suspected the diversion when, in the summer of 1986, the Iranians complained of having been overcharged. When Allen asked about the markup, North had blamed Manucher

Ghorbanifar. Allen had informed William Casey and his deputy, Robert Gates. In October 1986, they had informed Poindexter, who had said he would have the NSC counsel look into the matter.

Although the CIA team leader held back because some members of my staff had not yet been cleared for highly classified information, the State Department team was more forthcoming. Because of the embarrassment the NSC and the CIA had suffered when one of the CIA's proprietary air carriers was drawn into the November 1985 Hawk shipment, North and the CIA staff had later made conflicting false disclaimers of responsibility and prior knowledge that the flight had carried weapons. The false chronology prepared for Casey's congressional testimony, which had stated that "no one in the government" had known that the shipment contained weapons, had caused the State Department's legal advisor to warn the president's counsel that Shultz had known about the shipment in advance.

When this was reported to Meese, he had returned from an out-of-town speaking engagement to meet with Reagan, Poindexter, and Donald Regan—to begin the weekend investigation that exposed North's memorandum describing the diversion. Questioned by Meese, North had admitted the diversion but attributed it to the Israelis. He had concealed the activities of Secord and Hakim. That night, a security officer had discovered North locked in his office. Later, the officer had found in North's office a bulging shredder bag and a broken shredder.

After the FBI briefing, we braced for four major responsibilities: first, to conduct an investigation that was broad enough to ascertain and prove the extensive, complex activities underlying our mandate; second, to prosecute the individual crimes revealed in the course of this work, without interrupting our broader investigation; third, to minimize congressional interference; and fourth, to fend off collateral litigation, so that it would not disrupt our basic investigation. We had not begun to address our greatest vulnerability, which derived from the national security community's power to overclassify information to prevent the full exposure of its misconduct.

Guy Struve and a New York team of lawyers who could not move to Washington took responsibility for our basic legal research and pre-indictment litigation. Supporting them in Washington was Paul Friedman, who was a partner of the New York firm of White & Case, the president of the District of Columbia Bar Association, a former prosecutor, and a former law clerk to the chief judge of the district court.

Robert Shwartz, a former prosecutor and partner in the New York firm of Debevoise & Plimpton, agreed to prove the flow of funds, which entailed interviewing witnesses and recovering financial records from Switzerland, Germany, Great Britain, the Cayman Islands, Panama, Costa Rica, Bermuda, Monte Carlo, and, if possible, Israel. Former public defender John Keker and former prosecutors Randy Bellows, Michael Bromwich, and David Zornow took on the CIA, the State Department, and the Contras. Zornow had been U.S. Attorney Rudolph Giuliani's principal assistant in a major political corruption case, Bromwich had headed Giuliani's narcotics division and had tried conspiracy cases, and Bellows had handled complex criminal cases for the Justice Department. Former prosecutor John Douglass headed the team investigating the White House and the National Security Council.

This subdivision of our small group drove home the extent to which I had underestimated our mission. Assigning two or three young lawyers to deal with agencies like the CIA would have seemed laughable without my preconception that the questionable activities centered on Oliver North.

Our underlying need was for documents with which to confront witnesses who ranged from reluctant to hostile. We had to know the facts better than they did. Unfortunately, these records were in the hands of senior members of the national security community. We expanded Attorney General Edwin Meese's earlier document requests to cover the Contra-supply operation. By February, the CIA had produced a mere handful of records. The White House was doing better but was still withholding many of the documents we needed. Production from private organizations, such as American banks and service organizations, moved more quickly.

In relying on written document requests rather than subpoenas, I probably made a basic mistake. I was acting like a government lawyer who could expect honest compliance by a government agency. Although the threat to use subpoenas could be effective, I believed that issuing them would invite litigation as to the scope of our demands, which would delay me at a time when I was racing with Congress. Such litigation would disperse my limited legal staff and pit it against the large legal staffs of the Justice Department and other agencies. Nevertheless, in the long run, the delays in document production would probably have been better fought in court at the outset.

Former senator John Tower invited me to meet with him and members of his staff in the New Executive Office Building, and I went there with Struve and Douglass on a cold, unpleasant January 20. Tower kept us standing in the seemingly unheated building lobby for a half hour, waiting to be escorted past the security barrier. Finally, as we were about to leave, a staff assistant rescued us.

Tower's message was brief: He wanted us to use our power to grant immunity and the power of our grand jury to subpoena witnesses and documents to get information for him so that he could publish the information in his report. My answer was even briefer. What he proposed was contrary to law, and we would not do it. After exploring the possibility of sharing other information and, particularly, a joint appeal for cooperation by the government of Israel, we both saw clearly that we were pursuing different issues. He believed that as chairman of a presidential commission out to reform the NSC, he could obtain more help by working alone than by working with my team, whose goal was to prosecute crimes.

Brief as our meeting was, it helped me to grasp that senators and former senators believed that they were the ones to learn the facts. In their view, the role of an independent counsel was just to prosecute the crimes that they exposed. But I was not that kind of prosecutor.

After leaving Tower's office, we called on David Abshire and his counsel, Charles Brower, in the Old Executive Office Building. President Reagan had recalled Abshire, a highly regarded career diplomat serving as ambassador to NATO, to coordinate the administration's responses to the investigations by the Tower Commission, Congress, and my office. Abshire helped us by serving as an intermediary with the recalcitrant CIA, and he later succeeded in getting the president to provide me with critical support, which might not have been available if I had begun by using subpoenas.

Lawyers for witnesses began to propose testimony in return for immunity. Willard I. Zucker—who had managed the Swiss financial transactions for Secord, Hakim, and North through the Compagnie de Services Fiduciaires—was among the first. Because he and CSF were located in Geneva, Swiss financial restrictions prevented him from talking directly to us until after the bank documents and CSF documents had been released by the Swiss courts. He submitted his proffer of testimony through his American lawyers, who relayed the facts to which he would testify. He was an American, trained as a staff lawyer of the Internal Revenue Service. Operating from Switzerland, he had used dummy corporations in several countries and various money-laundering techniques to help Americans evade their taxes. Hakim had recruited him to establish and disguise the financial framework to support the Contra-supply effort and later to handle the proceeds of the arms sales. We agreed to give immunity to Zucker on the basis of his proposed testimony.

Edward T. DeGaray, president of Amalgamated Commercial Enterprises, Inc. (ACE), which through its subsidiary Corporate Air Services had employed the Central American pilots delivering supplies to the Contras and managed other on-site activities in Nicaragua, also gave us his records and a satisfactory proffer in return for immunity.

Others gave us the runaround. Contra leader Adolfo Calero agreed to be interviewed in Miami but changed his mind after two associate counsel had flown down to question him. Fearing that he would claim his privilege against self-incrimination, we decided to negotiate with him rather than serve him with a grand jury subpoena. It was March before he would talk to us. This pattern became typical. Few important witnesses talked willingly. Fewer told their full stories in their initial interviews.

We had to find new quarters. My staff was becoming too large to stay in the courthouse. Most previous independent counsel had remained in their private offices while taking on the additional work; some had also maintained small offices in the District of Columbia courthouse. The scope of our assignment, like Watergate, however, necessitated a new government mini-agency, but hurrying the General Services Administration, which rents all government space, seemed impossible. Space was then tight in Washington. For two months, GSA and Rick Ford, who was overseeing our administration, tried to find space that was secure enough to satisfy the agencies whose records we would hold.

I also needed a press officer. I had been taking all the press inquiries but could only explain our procedures, not discuss any substantive facts. Several reporters nevertheless persisted in seeking "guidance," which they elicited with expert cross-examination. Because press deadlines came at mealtimes, dinner in my hotel room was always cold. In late January, the American Bar Association lent me Gail Alexander, its outstanding Washington press officer.

Arthur Liman had been appointed counsel to the Senate select committee. A former assistant U.S. attorney in New York and later a partner and protégé of former federal judge Simon H. Rifkind in a leading New York firm, Liman had established his public reputation as chief counsel to the special New York commission investigating riots in the Attica state prison.

On January 27, he came to meet with Struve, Friedman, and me. Liman had traveled from New York, met his new clients at the Capitol, and, unable to find a taxi, walked all the way to the courthouse as a heavy snow turned to slush. Lanky and slightly stooped, with his overcoat collar turned up, his curly hair sprinkled with droplets and his shoes whitened by melting snow, he resembled a preoccupied professor. But preoccupation quickly gave way to intensity.

He wasted no time. He had already been warned of our "one-way-street" approach. He knew that we could not furnish grand jury information or share the Swiss financial records. Nonetheless, to the extent that the committees could not get the documents they needed, he said, there would be enormous pressure to immunize central figures in the scandal. The committees had to be able to trace the flow of money.

Confidently, almost arrogantly, he predicted that by carefully insulating ourselves, we would be able to prosecute individuals who had received congressional immunity. Struve and I were skeptical. Someone had misinformed the congressional committees that persons given immunity in the Watergate investigation had been convicted. Actually, the only immunized Watergate defendants who were convicted were two who had pleaded guilty.

As Liman knew, the Supreme Court had laid a heavy burden on prosecutions after a grant of immunity in the landmark *Kastigar* decision in 1972. Subsequent lower-court decisions had added obstacles, among them the requirement that prosecutors prove that even the *leads* they followed in obtaining their evidence were untainted.

We both recognized that we would ultimately be in conflict. Congress, by law, had the upper hand, because it was free to grant immunity. By doing so, it could destroy my investigation. We agreed to minimize the damage as much as possible.

The next day, Chief Judge Aubrey Robinson empaneled a grand jury exclusively for our investigation. As I introduced myself to the jurors, our investigation was barely beginning to take shape. The experienced prosecutors in the office, with no witnesses lined up, thought I was moving too quickly. I used the time to present noncontroversial witnesses from the National Security Council's staff and the State Department to explain how the NSC operated and the history of U.S. policy in Iran and Central America.

With the grand jury activated, some of the tension eased. We had retained Swiss lawyers in Bern and Geneva. John Douglass had received a proffer of testimony from Fawn Hall, North's secretary. In return for

immunity from the charge of destroying federal records, she was prepared to testify about North's destruction of documents and to provide
an inside view of his day-to-day contacts and activities.

Then, without warning, I received a formal letter from Lee Hamilton,
chairman of the House select committee, advising me to hurry because
the congressional committees would have to grant immunity to some
of the persons we were investigating. Even though I had known this
would happen, I felt like the last fellow in the showers in a drafty locker
room with no hot water left after a crew workout on a freezing day: I
knew it would be unpleasant, but I gasped when it hit. I had not
expected this decision so soon. I had not expected it to be so blunt.

Two days later, John W. Nields, Jr., who had just been appointed
counsel to the House select committee, and his deputy, Neil Eggleston,
visited Struve, Friedman, and me. Though younger than Liman, Nields
had an impressive record. After acquiring substantial prosecutorial
experience in the U.S. attorney's office in New York and serving as a law
clerk to Supreme Court Justice Byron White, Nields had been the counsel to an important congressional investigating committee. Nields said
that he understood we could not divulge grand jury testimony but that
if we hoped to avoid premature grants of immunity, we must find some
way to let the committee know what evidence warranted indictments.

Clearly the time for generalized education was running out. I gave
Struve ten days to analyze the information then available to us and to
summarize the crimes we were likely to pursue. Half my staff had not
yet been cleared for top-secret information. We were going to make
decisions that ordinarily would have been weeks away. Struve would
respond on schedule.

Fawn Hall had already given Douglass enough information to prosecute North for destroying federal records, if we were willing to depend
primarily on the testimony of a person so devoted to North. Even that
seemingly simple crime had not been fully investigated. The destruction
was undeniable, but we had to corroborate Hall and to develop evidence
of criminal intent to rebut any claim by North that he had acted out of
concern for the hostages' safety. If we had indicted him for this crime
before our investigation into other possible crimes was well underway,
our strength would have been sapped by the intensity of trial preparation and the need to respond to the remorseless discovery demands and
defense motions for which North's lawyer, Brendan Sullivan, was noted.
Douglass did not recommend indicting North then, nor did anyone

else. Theoretically, North could have been indicted again and again as new evidence came to us, but too many indictments would have invited a defense claim of persecution and an early acquittal would have been a serious embarrassment.

In February, our staff doubled as we were joined by young lawyers finishing judicial clerkships and young associates from several firms, including two from Shwartz's firm and two from Davis Polk. Because our office was already jammed, the FBI lent us space in the basement of its Washington headquarters and in the federal office building in New York.

As we began to investigate North's Contra-supply effort, all of Secord's operational assistants and office staff refused to testify. Before deciding whether to grant immunity to any of them, we needed to know enough to evaluate each potential witness. Even under the apprehension of oncoming congressional immunity, we had to take some time to make these decisions.

Albert Hakim refused to give us a proffer. His lawyer felt confident that Hakim would certainly receive immunity, because Congress needed him for access to the Swiss records.

We got a significant break, however, when Jane McLaughlin, the executive assistant of an early fund-raiser for the Contras, left her job and came to John Douglass with an offer to cooperate. She exposed the inside of North's private fund-raising operation, headed by Carl R. "Spitz" Channell.

Channell had organized a tax-exempt foundation, the National Endowment for the Preservation of Liberty, through which he had solicited supposedly tax-exempt donations from wealthy American citizens sympathetic to President Reagan's Contra policy and for other conservative causes. Channell had teamed with Richard R. Miller, a public relations consultant, who arranged White House briefings to impress the donors.

In June 1985, despite the Boland amendments, North had joined Channell and Miller in giving individual and group briefings to potential contributors. North had been extraordinarily effective as he explained what the Contras needed. He would describe the necessity for specific weapons and their cost. Channell would then take the contributors to lunch in the Hay-Adams Hotel, across Lafayette Park from the White House, and ask them to contribute the amount specified by North. They had usually done so. President Reagan had met personally with the largest donors and been photographed with them. He later said he had thought they were simply raising funds for propaganda.

By February, we had settled into a weekly routine of team and staff conferences. The conferences consumed time, but our individual investigations were interlocked. With such a broad investigation, this was the only practical way for all of us to keep abreast of the information that was coming in. Moreover, inasmuch as we had begun as strangers, the conferences gave us a chance to evaluate one another. As our decisions became more difficult and our disagreements sharper, we never lacked team unity. There were no resignations and no protests.

Having watched Governor Thomas E. Dewey challenge groups of advisors, I often became the devil's advocate. By presenting an extreme or challenging position, I could usually provoke unanimous disagreement, which—with luck—would lead to unanimous agreement on a more moderate and appropriate course. At an early staff conference, I startled my associates by arguing as an advocate for Ronald Reagan and Oliver North. The response confirmed the determination of my group. With help from others, John Keker stood my argument on its head. Before his days as a public defender and top-notch criminal trial lawyer in San Francisco, he had been a law clerk to Chief Justice Earl Warren. Politically more liberal than most of us, Keker normally had a breezy, unbuttoned style, but on this occasion he spoke with force and eloquence.

The fund-raising for the Contras, he declared, was not an improvisation; it was a conspiracy to undo laws that Congress had enacted. Even if Representative Edward Boland's riders to two appropriations bills spelled out no penalties for violations, the will of Congress was clear, and the effort to frustrate its will was an effort to defraud the government and the citizens of the United States of their due: the faithful execution of the law. Keker's was an impressive analysis, but much more the first word than the last. Although everyone united against me, Robert Shwartz, David Zornow, and Michael Bromwich were openly skeptical that violations of the less-than-lucid Boland amendments could be successfully presented to a jury as crimes. Danny Coulson, the head of our FBI team, had the same reaction as these former prosecutors. Follow the money, he advised. Stick to simple, straightforward charges.

At that point, we did not have enough evidence to support an indictment on any count, but we were beginning to get a few breaks. Willard Zucker, for example, expanded his proffer to include an account of the way Albert Hakim had ordered him in February 1986 to set up a trust fund for Oliver North's children. The purpose had been to quiet Betsy North's complaints about her husband's long hours and low pay. If North had bowed to his wife and taken another job, Hakim and Secord would have lost their White House conduit into the lucrative arms trade and would not have been so well positioned if normal relations with Iran were restored.

Hakim had arranged for Zucker and Betsy North to meet in Philadelphia in March 1986. After she described the educational needs of her children, Zucker made a series of transfers from the cluster of Swiss accounts to open a $200,000 investment account in the name "B. Button." The fund was calculated to provide, with accrued income, for the education of the Norths' four children. At Hakim's instruction, Zucker also attempted to persuade a Washington lawyer to arrange a real estate or other business arrangement that would allow Betsy North to receive commissions without having to do any work.

Fawn Hall began to supply additional, colorful evidence of the underside of the cover-up. Hall was no eager informant, but John Douglass's ever courteous, continuing interrogation paid off. She reluctantly told him that when Attorney General Meese began his investigation, she had been engaged in altering original NSC memoranda from North to McFarlane outlining some of North's Contra-supply activities. Simultaneously, she and North had been shredding his personal office files.

When NSC counsel Paul Thompson warned North that Meese's investigation had begun, North had left to visit McFarlane, Michael Ledeen, and North's then lawyer, Tom Green. While North was gone, NSC security officer Brenda Reger, tired of waiting for instructions from Meese or Thompson, had simply secured North's office. Nothing was to be removed. Those leaving had been subject to inspection.

Meanwhile, Hall had noticed the original documents from the NSC's permanent files, replete with North's handwritten alterations, lying on North's desk. She had urgently telephoned him. When he returned, accompanied by Green, Hall had hidden the incriminating documents in her boots and under her blouse. After asking North if anything showed, she had left with the two men. Twice she had tried to give the documents to them, but they had insisted that she wait until they were in Green's car. When she pulled them out, they had laughed. Green had asked her what she would say about the shredding. She had replied that she would simply say that they shredded every day. "Good," he had said.

North had already taken the notebooks in which he had methodically and cryptically recorded most of his activities. He now claimed that they were personal documents, not office records. The courts would not compel him to produce them for us unless he took the stand in his own trial.

Our staff spread overseas from Washington. We had lawyers and FBI agents traveling to Europe to trace Secord's arms purchases through Thomas Clines, a seasoned, hard-boiled former CIA agent who had known Secord in Vietnam and done business with him later. We identified nine arms shipments sold through Clines to the Contras. In Denmark, we found the evidence of Secord's purchase of a small cargo ship he used for carrying arms to the Contras and for other missions requested by North.

On February 10, I again met with Congressmen Hamilton and Cheney and their counsel, John Nields. Hamilton warned that the pressure to grant immunity to North would rise. Two-thirds of the House committee's members had not yet approved immunity for him, and they were sensitive to our problem, but they could not wait much longer. As to Hakim, Hamilton was explicit: The committee could not wait nine months for us to obtain the Swiss bank records through the Swiss courts.

Twenty-four hours later, Paul Friedman, Guy Struve, John Douglass, Neil Divers, and I listened as Senate committee counsel Arthur Liman and his assistant, Paul Barbadoro, assured us again that if Congress did not get the Swiss records, the pressure to immunize Secord and Hakim would be irresistible. He believed that unless their crimes were venal, involving personal enrichment, the committee would vote for immunity. I argued that such a conclusion would be premature. Neither he nor we were in a position to know whether some of the crimes were venal. I argued that I could serve the committees best by getting all the facts. I asked for four weeks and promised an interim report to Congress.

Liman expected to make his decision by March. He said the committees did not want to have the hearings hanging over the president. He explained that the committees were anxious to work out new understandings with the executive branch to prevent another Iran-Contra from happening. He urged us to turn up the fires.

Our gloom at the prospect of immunity was temporarily lifted when our FBI team discovered a trove of computerized messages, known as PROF notes, that Poindexter and North thought they had destroyed. These messages, sent electronically through the National Security

Council's computer system, had been preserved by being automatically copied into a "dump" on a fortnightly basis. When Poindexter and North wiped out the contents of their own computers, they had actually destroyed only the messages for the preceding two weeks. Duplicates of the older messages had remained in the dump. The White House provided copies not only to us, but also to Congress and the Tower Commission.

The hundreds of surviving messages starkly exposed North's communications with Poindexter and McFarlane. Poindexter had programmed his computer to create a secret channel directly to North, a continuing message captioned "private blank check." If either of them began a message with those words, the message went directly and only to the recipient. Bypassing the NSC secretariat allowed North and Poindexter to be spontaneous and candid, which proved invaluable to our investigation.

Meanwhile, behind my back in mid-February, the congressional committees had agreed to allow the Israelis to produce a historical chronology and a financial chronology instead of live witnesses. On learning of this arrangement, I wrote the Israeli ambassador to say that I disavowed the agreement and would proceed without regard for it. On February 24, Eli Rubenstein, who had succeeded David Kimche as the director of the Israeli foreign service, called on me with the Israeli ambassador. Rubenstein accused me of chutzpah and asked if I knew what it meant. I gave him the classic example: A person kills his parents and asks for mercy because he is an orphan. The conversation in this and a subsequent meeting were pleasant and businesslike but led nowhere. I would not agree to forgo live testimony. He would not agree to permit it. My team issued subpoenas for the necessary Israeli witnesses and arranged a watch for them at the principal ports of entry to the United States.

The first to arrive was David Kimche, who had come to visit his grandchildren in Florida. He was outraged by the subpoena. Claiming that he had diplomatic immunity even though he had retired, the Israelis moved to quash the subpoena. I was surprised when our State Department agreed with Kimche, saying that it did not want a precedent by which our former diplomats could be subpoenaed in foreign countries. This position seemed farfetched to me, but it was beyond my control. I assumed that most judges would follow the State Department's position in so sensitive a matter. After weeks of negotiations and exchanging briefs, I finally agreed to accept extended Israeli chronologies, with some helpful supporting documents. Meanwhile, Bob Shwartz and Bruce Yannett, a young associate counsel recruited from his firm, had visited Israel in a vain attempt to examine records and question witnesses; the Israeli government had prevented them from interviewing any prospective witness—even individuals who were willing to be questioned.

On February 17, the first full blueprint of our investigation—Guy Struve's memorandum of probable crimes—was presented to my staff. The most likely charges were for crimes arising out of the unauthorized conduct of covert hostilities in Nicaragua, the use of a tax-exempt foundation to fund covert hostilities in Nicaragua, and the diversion of proceeds from the Iranian arms sales. Struve believed that even without the Swiss records, we could prove a conspiracy to use CIA and other government personnel and assets to carry out illegal covert hostilities in Nicaragua at a time when these activities were prohibited by the Boland amendments. The deceitful misuse of government personnel and funds could support a charge of conspiracy to defraud the government, even though the Boland amendments carried no criminal penalties.

Other charges could include spending government funds without appropriation, theft of government property (the proceeds of the Iranian arms sales), and mail fraud. Struve calculated that we would need four to six months to investigate most of these crimes. He estimated that we would need nine to twelve months to look into the charge of diversion and theft of government funds, for which we would probably need the Swiss records. Another possible charge was personal enrichment from the diverted proceeds, which would also require nine to twelve months of investigation and the Swiss records, unless our IRS team's net-worth studies of North and other likely targets yielded proof sooner than that.

We could probably also bring charges of obstruction of justice and obstruction of congressional investigations against the persons who, by giving or preparing false testimony or destroying records, had blocked congressional inquiries or our own investigation.

The Iranian arms sales themselves probably were not criminal, even though the 1985 sales violated the Arms Export Control Act. That statute, like the Boland amendments, did not provide for criminal penalties. Unlike the supposed runaway conspiracy to supply the Contras, the arms sales had been approved by the president. Accordingly, the sale of arms fell along the hazy boundary of constitutional conflict between the chief executive and Congress over control of foreign transactions, and prosecution simply for the sales was uninviting.

Almost without discussion, however, we decided to simultaneously investigate both of President Reagan's intertwined covert activities, because crimes related to the arms sales were connected with and perhaps motivated by Contra resupply. Thus, sixty days after my appointment, we had committed ourselves to many hundreds of witness interviews and broad document searches. We expanded our legal staff to twenty-eight lawyers (some of whom worked part-time) and requested the assignment of agents from the Internal Revenue Service and more FBI agents.

For the next eighteen months, our investigation would follow the course laid out by Struve's singularly unerring predictions. Our teams regrouped around these charges and moved with remarkable speed to collect evidence and leads before they could be tainted by immunized congressional testimony. Keker continued to lead the team investigating the CIA, the Contras, and the Contra-supply operation. Randy Bellows and a pair of FBI agents moved into the CIA headquarters basement and, except at staff meetings, were not seen for weeks. Bill Hassler, a former assistant to FBI Director Bill Webster, pursued evidence of Secord's supply organization in Central America and, to the extent necessary, information about the individual leaders of the Contras. Mike Bromwich and David Zornow closed in on the fund-raising operation run by Channell and Miller. Bob Shwartz, with associate counsel Vicki Been and Bruce Yannett, both former judicial law clerks recruited from his New York firm, and a top-notch team of FBI and IRS agents, pursued financial records and witnesses across a dozen foreign countries as well as the United States. Shwartz was also in persistent negotiation with the Israeli and Swiss governments.

The White House and National Security Council investigation suffered from shifting, part-time leadership as first Douglass and then Paul Friedman could not give it their full attention. The investigation was taken over by Chris Todd, another former assistant U.S. attorney from New York; Chris Mixter and Louise Radin, former Davis Polk associates; Judith Hetherton, a former D.C. prosecutor; and an excellent group of FBI agents. This team pursued records and questioned reluctant witnesses again and again as we reconstructed the activities of Poindexter, North, and their associates.

Bit by bit, with much repetition and with frequent disappointment, the disjointed evidence accumulated. We learned, for example, that the

Guatemalan government had given Secord's organization false end-user certificates for arms-exporting countries in order to conceal the Nicaraguan destination, and that, despite the Boland amendments, CIA personnel had illegally facilitated these deliveries. CIA personnel had also been manipulating the Contra forces in southern Nicaragua—supplying weapons to leaders deemed aggressive and withholding weapons from others deemed less useful.

Necessary recapitulation of piecemeal disclosures by reluctant witnesses extended our staff meetings. On February 17, John Douglass again presented the expanded case against Oliver North for his destruction of documents and obstruction of justice and congressional investigations: North had attempted to falsify Casey's congressional testimony, had shredded the transcriptions of PROF notes, had erased PROF notes, had stolen documents, and had altered permanent NSC records. Douglass thought that we could prove these charges beyond a reasonable doubt, but he did not recommend prosecution. Unanimously, right or wrong, the staff again rejected the notion of prosecuting North solely for the crimes of destroying records and obstructing justice or the congressional investigation.

Later, when the *Los Angeles Times* broke the story of North's destruction of records, Arthur Liman warned Struve to indict quickly, if at all, so that the committees could do whatever they had to do in response. At our next weekly meeting with Liman, Nields, and their associates, Liman warned us that once the Tower Commission issued its report, the pressure to expedite the congressional hearings would be irresistible. He expected them to begin within less than a month. The committees would then have to consider immunity for North and Poindexter. Liman emphasized that to a person, the Senate committee wanted to get the hearings over with. Public statements by committee members supported this view. See-no-evil conservative Republican Senator Orrin Hatch of Utah had been urging grants of immunity to North and Poindexter since mid-December. "It's ridiculous on the part of some of my colleagues," Hatch asserted, "to drag this out for a long period of time just for political purposes."

By mid-February, we seemed to be making progress. Our team had been given space and filing cabinets in the basement of the CIA's headquarters in Langley, Virginia. Our lawyers and FBI agents were permitted to look at unredacted documents, so that we could know what the CIA had blacked out as irrelevant before giving copies to us. The IRS, with the approval of Treasury Secretary James Baker, gave us eleven agents expert in the reconstruction of hidden financial transactions and the exposure of hidden income. A half-dozen customs agents joined us to help trace and analyze the movement of equipment and funds between countries.

Then, just as we thought the CIA was being less obstructive, Acting Director Robert Gates ordered the agency's inspector general to conduct an internal investigation of CIA officials. No longer would we be able to question CIA witnesses while they were fresh. They would already have run their stories by the inspector general. The CIA high command—Gates and his director of operations, Clair George—would learn where the agency was vulnerable before we had a chance to uncover the truth.

I felt frustrated. I might represent the government of the United States, but I had no control over my client. I doubted that a court could or would prevent the agencies from intruding in my investigation. Even an honest management would understandably want to clean up its act without awaiting a criminal prosecution. The question was: Where should the priority be? Correction or prosecution? Cover-up or prosecution? If the correction could not be made without risking a cover-up, could not internal discipline have waited?

While the CIA was preceding our investigation with its own, the House select committee was dogging our tracks from behind. Counsel John Nields had instructed the CIA to give him a copy of every document the agency gave us. He had extended this request to all departments so that Congress would know not only what those under investigation had done but also what we, as prosecutors, were doing. Vainly, we insisted that the committees seek their information through us, the proper channel, as they would if the Department of Justice were conducting the investigation. Traditionally, except in very-high-profile cases, Congress had not intruded into criminal investigations; it awaited the results. But the public's interest was too intense to ignore. Given conflicting demands by Congress and the independent counsel, the agencies deferred to Congress. Congress could retaliate. The independent counsel was a more uncertain threat.

On February 24, North challenged the constitutionality of the Independent Counsel Act (formally the Independent Counsel Chapter of the Ethics in Government Act). We had foreseen the move. On North's behalf, attorney Brendan Sullivan argued that the act violated the constitutional requirement for the separation of powers between the executive and judicial branches. He argued that a panel of judges could not constitutionally appoint a person to carry out the law-enforcement functions of the executive branch, that prosecution was the job of the executive, and that the judiciary's function was to decide cases, not to decide who should bring the cases to court.

Congress had first authorized the court appointment of an outside prosecutor in the wake of the Watergate scandal, during which Richard Nixon had forced the dismissal of an independent counsel appointed by the attorney general. In what came to be known as the "Saturday Night Massacre," Nixon had ordered Attorney General Elliot Richardson to fire independent counsel Archibald Cox. Richardson had refused and resigned. His deputy, William Ruckelshaus, had then refused and resigned. Finally, the solicitor general, Robert Bork, had carried out the order.

We saw little immediate danger to our office from North's suit. He had no standing to complain of my activities when I had not brought charges against him. But that point would be moot once I lodged charges. At the moment, we had more to fear from a different direction. Michael Deaver, a confidant of President Reagan's and former White House deputy chief of staff, was about to be indicted for perjury regarding lobbying activities. With a word-for-word adaptation of North's complaint, Deaver's lawyers had moved to enjoin the independent counsel in his case, Whitney North Seymour, Jr., from proceeding. The judge concluded that the legal question raised by Deaver's claim that he was being prosecuted by a usurper required a stay in the proceedings to avoid irreparable damage while Deaver sought a ruling from the court of appeals.

The Deaver case, I feared, might not be resolved short of a Supreme Court ruling. As long as the stay was outstanding, my own status would be under a cloud. And if the ultimate decision went against independent counsel, all our work would be in jeopardy.

While Guy Struve and his New York team mustered the legal arguments to dismiss North's suit, I called up a political reserve: President Reagan. He had declared full cooperation and openness as his administration's policy toward the Iran-Contra investigations. Earlier, after I had told David Abshire, the president's liaison to the investigation, that unless the CIA became more cooperative, I would denounce it and proceed by grand jury, the flow of CIA files had changed from drought to flood. I now called Abshire's counsel, Charles Brower, to suggest that

President Reagan request a backup appointment for me from the attorney general. Having the attorney general appoint me as independent counsel would ensure continuity while the legal challenges to Seymour's and my court appointments worked their way through the courts. Such action would show the president's sincerity in supporting the investigation. Brower responded favorably. I followed with a polite letter outlining our discussion. If our request had been denied, the administration's claim of full cooperation would have suffered. Abshire approved of the request. The president supported it. Meese agreed. After we met with him twice and engaged in some tough negotiations over the terms of the appointment, Meese signed an order that guaranteed both my continuity and my independence.

My new appointment was announced on March 5. The court of appeals vacated the stay in Deaver's case, but the backup appointment proved a godsend when, in another case a few months later, the court of appeals, led by Judge Laurence H. Silberman, a hard-line Reagan loyalist, struck down the Independent Counsel Act as unconstitutional. Only the attorney general's appointment kept my investigation alive during the critical period until the Supreme Court, voting seven to one, reversed this erroneous decision.

On February 26, the Tower Commission released its report, which essentially accepted the concept of a runaway conspiracy. McFarlane and Poindexter, said the report, had thrust the staff of the National Security Council into a line operation, a covert activity. This had been a misuse of the staff, which was intended primarily to coordinate the views and activities of other relevant government agencies into a presidential policy on national security.

The Tower Commission's report provided the public with its first coherent narrative history of the arms sales to Iran. The report also provided new information about the diversion and contained information about the NSC's efforts to provide arms to the Contras. By meeting the public's need to know what had happened, the report should have obviated the need for haste by Congress. Having had a six-week advantage over the congressional committees and me in accumulating facts, the Tower Commission was able to broaden the information we were each obtaining for ourselves and to integrate the evidence that we were still assimilating.

Nonetheless, the report hurt us. It inevitably stimulated the crystallization of political judgment, particularly by members of the select committees, and reinforced the notion that Iran-Contra had been a limited conspiracy that flourished in the misuse and misconduct of the NSC staff. Accordingly, the report fueled the clamor of those who, for political purposes, wanted to put an end to further investigation.

The commission had tried to ascertain President Reagan's advance knowledge of the November 1985 Hawk shipment. Tower and his colleagues had questioned the president but had come away frustrated. Reagan's testimony regarding his authorization of the Israeli arms sales had vacillated. First, he had said that he had authorized them. Later, after talking with Donald Regan, the president had told the commission that he and Regan could not remember any conversation authorizing the shipment. Finally, Reagan's counsel, Peter Wallison, had sent the commission a letter saying the truth was that the president had no recollection; he just plain did not remember.

CHAPTER SIX

First Convictions

With the Tower Commission's report now a matter of record, our persistence in conducting a comprehensive investigation annoyed many Republicans and some Democrats. The Republicans did not want Iran-Contra disclosures impinging on the upcoming presidential campaign. Neither party wanted the 1988 campaign, presidential or congressional, to serve as a postmortem on America's Nicaraguan policy. Nor did anyone on Capitol Hill really want to impeach or even imperil a very popular president.

No doubt about it, everyone conceded, Oliver North had destroyed government records. Prosecute him if you must, then go home. The most stubborn Republicans doubted that even North should be prosecuted. With the Senate select committee evenly divided between the two parties, the Democrats could not ignore these views if they hoped to avoid separate party-line committee reports. Chairman Daniel Inouye, who had had little prosecutorial or litigation experience, became increasingly dependent on Senator Warren Rudman, the committee's Republican vice chairman, who had been the attorney general of New Hampshire.

We had already decided not to limit our focus to North's document-shredding activities. We did, however, try to accommodate Congress's political need for haste without narrowing the scope of our investigation, working ten-to-twelve-hour days from March through June.

During the first weekend in March, we finally moved into an office of our own at the corner of 13th and F, within walking distance of the courthouse, in the heart of downtown Washington. It was a sublet; we were not planning on a long stay. Construction was still in progress, and the coffee we spilled at night had already stained the carpets before the last of the builder's dirt was swept away. The lawyers' working files were stacked on the floors of their small offices along the outer walls. More files, subpoenaed records, computers, and copiers filled the central core area. We were inundated with documents awaiting processing; the piles never seemed to shrink. The passageway between the core and the lawyers' offices was jammed with the secretaries' cluttered workstations. Paralegals were penned into tiny private offices carved out between the document-storage rooms.

The partitions between the offices were steel and opaque glass. The steel venetian blinds on the outside windows were always closed. The black furniture came from prison workshops. There were no curtains or decorations. A few of the lawyers did have family photographs, and John Keker hung a print of a scene in a nineteenth-century coffee auction house. As construction progressed, we expanded our space, establishing a working library and trebling the area set aside for documents and for high-speed copying equipment. More lawyers arrived, and our FBI contingent moved in with us, as did the IRS agents and the Customs Service agents.

Day and night, security guards from the General Services Administration were posted outside our door, but they did not have the combination of the lock. To get into the office on weekends or evenings, we had to have two security officers. Strangers could enter only with escorts. To talk with the press, I would leave the office and use an outer room.

Our conference room in the heart of the office was specially soundproofed and protected from eavesdropping. Chairs, close together, surrounded the long oblong table and lined the walls. In here, we fought out our differences. I ran the office the way I would have run a law firm. All the lawyers were partners. One of the few times I overruled the group was when the former prosecutors objected to the presence of Gail Alexander, my press officer, during the discussion of grand jury testimony. For us to survive the public attacks, she needed to be fully informed. I told the lawyers to list her with the court as one of the nonlawyers to whom it was necessary to expose the testimony. For the most part, our early discussions were less disputes than mutual interrogations, as we all tried to keep abreast of the accumulating information. Later, as it came time to take action, the disputes sharpened.

Robert Shwartz was remarkably able and well organized. In many ways the senior full-time lawyer, he drew to him the other full-time former prosecutors and many of the young lawyers. He also had the admiring loyalty of his own team of attorneys, accountants, FBI agents, and IRS agents. As the individual lawyers and teams developed their own witnesses, our three interview rooms, just inside the office entrance, were always busy. Competition for grand jury time arose as we needed to build our record for future indictments. Michael Bromwich was designated traffic cop to regulate the flow of witnesses and also to act as liaison with the court and the grand jurors.

Our immediate goal was to indict and convict a guilty person who might turn into a valuable witness in the hope of receiving a lenient sentence. We knew that the sentences meted out by Chief Judge John Sirica in the Watergate trials had jolted more than one witness into revealing the truth. Oliver North would clearly make the best witness for these purposes, but he was represented by a lawyer who had a reputation for never cooperating with the prosecution. John Poindexter, the personification of stolidity, was not likely to succumb to pressure. We would have to look elsewhere.

Our early investigation had to emphasize the Contra-supply activities coordinated by North. Like those of most business or government organizations, these activities had fallen into the categories of funding and operations. But North's project had had a third dimension—covering up the activities related to funding and operations. The cover-up made it more difficult to trace the activities but helped us dramatize them after they had been exposed.

Lacking access to the Swiss and Israeli financial records, we had to reconstruct them from the information available in other countries about each transaction. After Congress cut off appropriations for the Contras, the funding had come first from Saudi Arabia, then from the contributions solicited by North and Spitz Channell, and finally from the diverted proceeds of the arms sales to Iran.

With witnesses unwilling to talk, we found it equally difficult to discern the operational pattern. Richard Secord had begun as one of several suppliers procuring and delivering arms to the Contras. His first deliveries, through a Canadian arms supplier, had taken months. He had then turned to former CIA agent Thomas Clines and his source, Defex, Inc., a Portuguese arms supplier. The arms had been delivered to Central America by ship and by aircraft chartered from a former CIA proprietary which had been bought from the CIA by its operatives, Southern Air Transport, Inc. The arms had then been redistributed in Nicaragua by smaller aircraft flown by pilots employed by Edward

DeGaray's Corporate Air Services and supervised by Secord's assistants Richard Gadd and, later, Robert C. Dutton.

Selecting the right witnesses for grants of immunity required a basic understanding of what crimes might have been committed; we needed to evaluate the proffered testimony and the culpability of each person seeking immunity. To make these evaluations, we set up a committee of former prosecutors headed by Audrey Strauss.

Getting the full story from a willing witness who had been immunized usually took several interviews; our questions improved as we learned more and knew what details to develop and what a jury would find convincing if a case came to trial. With so many witnesses reluctant and hostile, we often had to confront them with documents or the testimony of other individuals as we questioned them. A major witness like Fawn Hall, for example, was interviewed many times. Instead of being repetitive exercises, subsequent interviews usually produced new information, which led to new areas of investigation or required confirmation.

Once we had gathered the facts, we had to determine whether they amounted to crimes. If the Contra-supply operation had been in private hands, for instance, it probably would not have been criminal; certainly it would not have been within my mandate. The Boland amendments had prohibited only the expenditure of government funds appropriated to an "entity engaged in intelligence activities." Thus, to prove that North's participation in the operation had been illegal, we planned to show that he had acted in his capacity as a government official subject to the Boland amendments. Because he had been paid from Defense Department appropriations and detailed to the National Security Council, an "entity engaged in intelligence activities," we expected to prove that he had been subject to the same restrictions as the CIA officers he replaced.

By early March, we had reviewed the PROF notes and the surviving written memoranda North had sent during the first half of 1985 to Robert McFarlane and thereafter to Poindexter. These documents clearly showed that North had participated in the decisions regarding military activities undertaken by the Contras, that he had been involved in the Contra-supply effort, and that he had kept McFarlane and Poindexter informed of his accomplishments. Having been set aside for alteration in 1985, when Congress first inquired about North's activities, the memoranda had escaped the shredder. They were part of the case we were building not only against North but also against

McFarlane and Poindexter, who had concealed North's operational and fund-raising activities in their answers to congressional inquiries.

The Tower Commission had copies of the same memoranda and PROF notes that we had. Uninhibited by prosecutorial restraints, the commission had published much of this evidence as an appendix to its report, which made the information available both to Congress and to every potential witness. Each would know what the others had said. In these documents, for example, North had said his own role was "to oversee" deliveries to the Contras. He had described Albert Hakim as vice president of one of the European companies set up to handle aid to resistance movements and had characterized him as an American citizen who ran the European end of "our" operation to support the Nicaraguan resistance.

In his Contra-support activities, North had created a private communication system linking him to Secord and his assistants and also to CIA chief of station Joseph Fernandez and his assistants in Costa Rica. For secrecy, North had used fifteen National Security Agency KL-43 encryption devices. Secord's secretary and Fawn Hall had arranged the monthly code changes in the encryption devices. Unknown to Fernandez and some others, the devices had recorded the communications they transmitted. These communications included three dozen messages from North to members of his resupply network, as well as messages in which Secord and others had asked North for instructions on munitions drops, told him of the Contras' arms requirements, and apprised him of payments, balances, and deficits. A CIA field officer, for example, had told North of a plane loaded for delivery and had asked, "When and where do you want this stuff?"

Nine drops of weapons had been coordinated through this channel between March and June 1986. These included one drop by an L-100, a Southern Air Transport aircraft that North had commandeered at the Ilopango air base, diverting it from a legal chartered delivery of humanitarian supplies for the State Department to a delivery of weapons from Ilopango to southern Nicaragua.

We learned from copies of a series of encrypted messages that Fernandez had told North that the CIA's objective was the creation of a 2,500-man force in southern Nicaragua. After the arms supplies were flowing, North had invited Fernandez to meet with President Ronald Reagan for three minutes for a photo session in the Oval Office. Also present had been Costa Rica's minister of public security, his wife, Don Regan, Poindexter, and North.

As time passed, North's PROF messages within the White House had taken on an exuberant tone. In messages to McFarlane, who by then had resigned, North had described his efforts to obtain British Blowpipe antiaircraft missiles and launchers for the Contras. He had begun calling his network of operatives, aircraft, and secret bank accounts "Project Democracy." During the summer of 1986, North had sent Poindexter a note claiming that the assets of Project Democracy exceeded $4.5 million and included six aircraft, warehouses, supplies, maintenance facilities, ships, boats, leased houses, vehicles, ordnance, munitions, and communications equipment as well as a secret 6,520-foot runway in Costa Rica. In another 1986 PROF message to Poindexter, North had said that "the president obviously knows why he has been meeting with several select people to thank them for their 'support for democracy' in Cent[ral] Am[erica]." Fearing that North's PROF notes had become too flamboyant, Poindexter and McFarlane both had expressed concern, to North and to each other, about his vulnerability.

According to Lewis Tambs, the U.S. ambassador to Costa Rica, North had reported to (and at times had professed to speak for) a "restricted interagency group" (RIG) composed of Elliott Abrams, an assistant secretary of state; Alan Fiers, the chief of the CIA's Central American task force; Richard Armitage, an assistant secretary of defense; and representatives of the Joint Chiefs of Staff.

We needed a witness to guide us through the cascade of documents and to help us integrate the information, and McFarlane seemed to be our best bet. Having attempted suicide with an overdose of Valium, he had clearly been shaken by the various investigations. I happened to see him on television following his recovery, and he appeared to be suffering from remorse. After discussions with his lawyer, we conducted a series of interviews with McFarlane. I had thought that Keker, as a former marine, would be able to gain his confidence, but they never trusted each other. Keker did not believe that McFarlane would ever tell the whole truth; he might accept *responsibility* for the misconduct but would never quite admit his *role* in it.

Nonetheless, I thought that McFarlane was trying to do his best, considering the public battering he had been through. Chris Mixter, an associate counsel on the team investigating the White House and the National Security Council, took over many of the interviews. McFarlane was still reserved, but he gave Mixter valuable background information and testimony that would contradict North's inevitable claim that he had been carrying out the orders of a superior.

Donald Regan resigned after the Tower Commission report was released. So did Peter Wallison and David Abshire. They were replaced by former Senate leader Howard Baker and a lawyer of his selection, A. V. Culvahouse, Jr. Not having been involved in the transactions under investigation, the new team was less vulnerable and somewhat more resistant to our requests. Some NSC staff witnesses were also grudging. A document supervisor refused to give us copies of National Security Council documents that even the White House counsel did not object to our having. These witnesses acknowledged whatever our documentary evidence compelled them to acknowledge, but some gave us little else. Consequently, as we assimilated documents, we had to repeat many of the interviews.

Kenneth deGraffenreid, who headed the National Security Council's unit on intelligence and shared North's right-wing views, had to be questioned more than once. On the eve of Attorney General Edwin Meese's fact-finding investigation, deGraffenreid had, without making copies, given North the original NSC documents that North had then altered. In one of several interviews, deGraffenreid claimed not to remember this breach of protective procedures. He did not remember having given the documents to North but did not deny having done so.

NSC counsel Paul Thompson, a career naval officer who had studied law while in the service and should have been the person most concerned with misconduct by the NSC's staff, had lacked the independent stature of most agency counsel. His primary role had been administrative. Papers coming to McFarlane or Poindexter had often been routed through Thompson, who had set aside those deemed too sensitive to be placed in the NSC's files. He had referred matters that required serious legal study to the Justice Department or to the CIA's lawyers—with a singular exception: To interpret the restrictions of the Boland amendments, Thompson had turned to Bretton G. Sciaronni, counsel to the president's intelligence oversight board, an entity created to advise not on the law, but on policy.

Thompson had reviewed North's memoranda when McFarlane was answering the questions raised by Congress, and Thompson had identified for McFarlane the "problem documents" that North and Fawn Hall had later altered. We continuously balanced the thought of prosecuting Thompson against our hope of additional assistance from him, but we never felt that he was forthcoming.

In early March, we granted immunity to Robert C. Dutton, who had run the Contra-supply operation for Secord from May to December 1986. In sixteen hours of interviews, Dutton related the details of the operation during its most effective period. Arms shipped by sea had been delivered to Guatemala and trucked across Honduras to the Nicaraguan border. Arms shipped by air had been flown into the large Salvadoran military base at Ilopango and then redistributed along the Honduras-Nicaragua border or flown south to the Nicaragua–Costa Rica border. The round trip from Ilopango to the southern front had been at the limit of the range of the supply aircraft. To avoid crossing Nicaragua, the pilots had flown along the Pacific coast to the border of Costa Rica, then inland, and had returned by the same route. The secret Costa Rican airstrip, built by a dummy corporation controlled by Secord, had provided a refuge for damaged aircraft and for planes that needed refueling. Dutton confirmed North's hands-on participation in and coordination of the Contra-supply effort.

Dutton's predecessor had been Richard Gadd, a retired Air Force lieutenant colonel. Negotiations with his lawyer took more time, but we wanted Gadd's proffer before North testified. In late 1985, at the request of North and Secord, Gadd had organized the small fleet of aircraft to distribute the arms flown into Ilopango from Portugal. His written plan of operation had been approved first by Secord and then by North. North had had the last word on controversial questions.

The surviving pilots who had flown these planes gave us their views of the operation. They described maintenance and performance problems. One pilot, who had made five or six flights a day to Contra sites, said that two CIA sources had furnished him the location of the Sandinistas' positions so that he could avoid them. Another pilot said he believed that, after it was learned from the CIA that the Nicaraguans had antiaircraft weapons ready for a C-123 flight, William Cooper and Wallace Sawyer were nonetheless ordered to fly the C-123 mission in which they had died and Eugene Hasenfus had been captured.

The pilots told us that the North-Secord group and the CIA had had adjoining hangars at Ilopango, with a common parking lot, and that the delivery of lethal supplies had at times been mingled with the delivery of legal humanitarian supplies provided by a State Department program. As their rule of thumb, up to 10 percent of the cargo would be lethal, but that proportion had routinely been exceeded. At North's insistence, the contract for providing the humanitarian supplies had been given to Richard Gadd.

Other evidence implicated Alan Fiers, the chief of the CIA's Central American task force and a key member of the RIG. With Fiers's knowledge, his subordinate Joseph Fernandez had been instrumental in the construction of the airstrip for Secord's supply operation. Fiers had also known that Fernandez had coordinated with North and Secord, via KL-43 coded communications equipment, to supply the Contras in the south. As we raised these issues before the grand jury, Fiers refused to continue his testimony, claiming his constitutional privilege against self-incrimination.

Most of the U.S. ambassadors to Central American countries had realized that North was a major player in supplying arms to the Contras, but they denied having known the details of the operation. One or two said that they had met North. Edwin G. Corr, the ambassador to El Salvador, admitted having known that arms had been shipped to Ilopango for the Contras, that Felix Rodriguez had acted as liaison between the Salvadoran air force and North's private supply groups, and that Rodriguez had claimed the backing of Vice President Bush. Corr claimed, however, that he could not recall ever having reported any of this to his immediate superior, Elliott Abrams, until after Hasenfus's plane was shot down.

The tracing of funds never stopped. All the relevant countries other than Switzerland and Israel were forthcoming. Carefully tracing each transaction through the bank-account records we obtained from the other countries, Bob Shwartz, the IRS agents, and one of the FBI teams reconstructed the missing Swiss accounts. We identified the principal Swiss dummy corporate accounts used by Secord and Hakim as Energy Resources, which had disbursed $9,349,838 between 1984 and September 1985; Lake Resources, which had disbursed $30,833,000 after July 1985; and Hyde Park, which had made intercompany transfers of $4 million and received $4,837,000 from outside sources. Other dummy overseas corporations had been used to break the trail left by the disbursements.

The records of Adolfo Calero's five Contra bank accounts confirmed that Saudi payments of $1 million a month had begun in the second half of 1984, followed by a much larger infusion in March 1985. We found some of Calero's accounts in the names of other Contras.

We followed the flow of arms through dealers Trans World Arms in Montreal and Defex in Portugal. We traced the origins and payments for the aircraft in Secord's Contra-supply fleet. After receiving immu-

nity, members of Secord's staff testified to cash deliveries from Willard
Zucker to Secord's wife and Fawn Hall. Southern Air Transport pilots
regularly carried cash to Nicaragua from Miami after couriers had
brought it from Zucker-controlled U.S. accounts or from money laun-
derers. Zucker would make payments in Switzerland to an associate of a
person in the United States who would supply cash to one of North's
couriers. Albert Hakim was personally implicated in an illegal transaction in which he had simultaneously cashed checks for $8,000 and
$7,000 in an attempt to avoid the law requiring the reporting of trans-
fers of more than $10,000 in cash. We also obtained the records of the
Canadian investors who had helped Adnan Khashoggi finance the
"bridge" payments to Ghorbanifar.

Zucker continued to expand his proffered testimony. He told us that
Hakim and Secord had created a false Swiss account in which to secrete
their personal profits from the Contras. The account was that of a
Liberian dummy corporation that had borrowed the name Defex. The
Portuguese arms supplier received nothing from this misnamed
account. Instead, 40 percent of the funds belonged to Hakim, 40 percent to Secord, and 20 percent to former CIA officer Thomas Clines,
who had acted as the purchasing agent for Secord and Hakim.

In addition to tracing the arms purchases and other financial
transactions, we also traced the arms deliveries and all the movements of the two small cargo ships, the *Erria* and the *Iceland Saga*,
that had been operated by the Enterprise. The ships' captains said
that they had followed the sometimes bizarre orders of Secord, delivering weapons to Central America (once to the United States), vainly
awaiting the release of hostages from Lebanon as well as a Soviet tank
captured by the Iranians in their war with Iraq, and, at times, circling
in the mid-Atlantic while Secord and North decided what to tell them
to do next.

North's most vulnerable co-conspirators were the fund-raisers Spitz
Channell and Richard Miller, who had paid themselves handsome compensation from funds solicited as tax-exempt contributions to the Contra
cause. Because John Douglass's time was limited, Michael Bromwich and
David Zornow had taken over the case against Channell and Miller.
Within three months, Bromwich and Zornow had obtained guilty pleas
to felonies as well as commitments by both defendants and their staffs to
testify against North for his role in the fund-raising tax dodge.

The evidence of North's personal involvement in soliciting and
distributing private funds to support and arm the Contras was

convincing. North and Channell had begun to collaborate in the spring of 1985, after Channell and Miller agreed to pool their contacts and energies to help finance the Nicaraguan resistance. Using the National Endowment for the Preservation of Liberty, purportedly an educational foundation, as their vehicle and North as their pitchman, Channell and Miller had in 1985 and 1986 arranged five White House briefings on Nicaragua for groups of potential contributors and six private sessions with the president for the most generous donors. The funds raised by NEPL had been transferred to Miller's International Business Communications bank accounts in the United States and the Cayman Islands and from there to the Swiss accounts of the Enterprise and to a variety of payees.

The Contra-related funds raised by NEPL had come to $6,323,000; a little more than half—$3.3 million—had actually gone to aid the Contras. Payments of more than $1.7 million had gone to the Swiss dummy corporation Lake Resources. Adolfo Calero had received more than $1 million, and $488,882 had funded other Contra-related activities. Channell had paid himself a total of $345,000 from NEPL funds in 1985 and 1986. Richard Miller, his associate Frank Gomez, and IBC had grossed approximately $1.7 million. And the donors who had supplied these funds had deducted their contributions from their taxable incomes as charitable expenses.

Had the money actually gone into educational work in "support of democracy," those deductions might have been legitimate, but both the fund-raisers and the donors had known that a different game was being played. The contributions had followed briefings by Oliver North on weapons and armament, not education. At an August 1985 meeting in his office next to the White House, for example, North had explained to Channell and a wealthy Connecticut widow, Ellen Garwood, that the forces in the field needed a $75,000 Maule airplane. Mrs. Garwood had later given Channell a check for that amount. She had admired North and befriended him. He and his wife had visited her home.

In September 1985, North had flown to Dallas in a private plane with Channell and NEPL's executive director, Daniel Conrad, to dine with Texas oilman Bunker Hunt at the Petroleum Club. North had brought along a budget for military supplies costing between $5 million and $6 million. He had carefully explained the budget to Hunt, then withdrawn, whereupon Channell had stepped in and obtained $475,000 in gifts and loans from the Texan. Channell had heard North tell Hunt that he was willing to go to jail for his efforts in support of the Contras and to lie to Congress, if necessary.

Our investigation continued at a tooth-pulling pace. McFarlane told us what he knew about the diversion: He had heard about it, or spoken of it, four times. First, on the tarmac at Tel Aviv when he and his colleagues were returning from Iran, North had tried to console him for the failure of his mission by boasting that the Iranians were supporting the Contras. Second, as an NSC meeting broke up on November 19, 1986, after the arms sales had been publicly exposed, McFarlane had mentioned to North and Poindexter that he saw the diversion as their most difficult problem in preparing for their congressional testimony. North, noticing that Howard Teicher, the NSC's director for political-military affairs, was still in the room, had pulled McFarlane aside and whispered, "My God, Bud, Howard doesn't know about that." Third, on the day Meese's fact-finding investigation began, North, North's lawyer Tom Green, and Secord had discussed the diversion with McFarlane at his office; North had told them that the diversion had been approved and that they did not have to worry about it. Fourth, Meese had asked McFarlane whether he knew about the diversion. In addition, when questioned by the Senate intelligence committee in December 1986, McFarlane had speculated that President Reagan must have known about it and that this would "surely become a matter of record" when Poindexter testified.

In mid-March, after being asked the right, precise question, Fawn Hall gave us additional information incriminating Robert Earl, North's principal assistant, in the removal and destruction of NSC documents. This information led us to open negotiations in which Earl would receive immunity and testify against North. Equally important, Hall also assured us that she had given Poindexter the memorandum in which North had described the diversion of the arms sales proceeds to the Contras.

When Fawn Hall told us that North's very explicit diversion memorandum had definitely reached Poindexter, I found it increasingly hard to believe that Ronald Reagan had been so scrupulously protected from at least a generalized understanding of the operational details that North's reports to McFarlane and Poindexter had continually spelled out. As North himself once acknowledged to a friend, the Marine Corps had long ago trained him to CYA—"cover your ass." In his lengthy communications to McFarlane and Poindexter, North had consistently insinuated recitals of activity that were less necessary to decision than to his own ratification and protection. I came to believe that this had been one of North's purposes when he submitted to Poindexter—and, with luck, the president—such an explicit and incriminating memorandum about the diversion.

What still puzzled me was President Reagan's single-minded pursuit of Iran's help in freeing the hostages when only one captive had been released between the first arms shipment at the end of August 1985 and McFarlane's mission in May 1986. It seemed uncharacteristically naive. In addition to swallowing one broken Iranian promise after another, the president had disregarded the strong opposition of his principal foreign policy advisors, George Shultz and Caspar Weinberger, and the informed skepticism of the initiative's original proponent, Robert McFarlane.

What, then, had made Ronald Reagan, who had dealt so successfully with Gorbachev, such an easy dupe for Manucher Ghorbanifar? Had it been a combination of ignorance, emotion, and faith in happy endings? Or had it been, at least from 1986 onward, the knowledge that the arms trade with Iran was providing essential funds for the secret war in Nicaragua? We had no proof with which to turn the second question into an answer. But my mind could not accept the implausibility that the president, who had insisted on daily briefings regarding the hostages, would have known nothing of the interrelationship of his two personal priorities—North's pair of covert operations.

Moreover, the Tower Commission had authenticated reports of President Reagan's personal intrusions into the hostage negotiations. The media had ridiculed North for having delivered a Bible and a chocolate cake to his Iranian counterparts, but the Tower Commission had revealed the president's acknowledgment that he had personally inscribed the Bible for North so that the Iranian recipient would know that North was "getting through."

Once given this imprimatur, North had grossly exaggerated his relationship with the president. George Cave, a retired CIA expert on Iran assigned to North's operation in March 1986, had written chilling notes about the mission to Tehran. According to Cave, North had told the Iranians that unless it came through him, "there is no official message from the United States." As he presented the Bible, North had said, "We inside our government had an enormous debate, a very angry debate inside our government, over whether or not my president would authorize me to say 'We accept the Islamic Revolution of Iran as a fact.' . . .

[The president] went off one whole weekend and prayed about what the answer should be, and he came back almost a year ago with that passage I gave you that he wrote in the front of the Bible I gave you. And he said to me, 'This is a promise that God gave to Abraham. Who am I to say that we should not do this?' "

In the Bible, Reagan had written the following: "And the Scripture, foreseeing that God would justify the Gentiles by faith, preached the gospel beforehand to Abraham, saying, 'All the nations shall be blessed in you.' Galatians 3:8, Ronald Reagan Oct. 3, 1986." President Reagan had testified before the Tower Commission that he had indeed inscribed the Bible for North and that Poindexter had approved the inscription, saying that it was a favorite passage of one of the negotiators.

Was it possible that Poindexter would have exposed the president so directly to Iranians without credentials and yet would not have let him know that the principal value of the arms transactions was that they supported the Contras? We attempted to obtain the briefing books that had been supplied each day to President Reagan. We were told they had been routinely disassembled after use. If this was so, there was no permanent record of what the national security advisor had told the president.

At the beginning of March, as our investigation gathered steam, I had to face the reality of being undercut by Congress. Having developed generally good working relationships with the counsel to the select committees on Iran-Contra, I awaited the political judgment of their principals, the final arbiters on immunity for their most dramatic witnesses, our chief targets.

I met first with the House select committee. All fifteen members were in attendance, including Edward Boland. Judging by their perceptive questions, I believed them to be prepared to give the conflict between legislative oversight and criminal prosecution serious consideration. Most members had read the memorandum in which I had outlined in very general terms the prospects of our investigation. I had asked for at least ninety more days before the committees acted to compel North and Poindexter to testify. The congressmen exhibited little partisanship and no hostility; I felt as though I were arguing before a well-prepared appellate court.

I acknowledged that the issue was political in the broad and best sense of the word, and that the Constitution and our statutes left this issue to our most experienced political bodies—the houses of Congress. Independent counsel, my brief said, "recognizes the primacy of

Congress" and its right to exercise "seasoned political wisdom in establishing national priorities." All parties sought the same primary goal: the truth. "The more complete the investigation that can be conducted before immunity is granted," I maintained, "the more likely it is that the truth will emerge."

Chairman Lee Hamilton and his colleagues seemed sympathetic. Most members had questions or observations. Their questions were professional and directed to the merits, without any meanness. I left the session buoyed by the sense that I had received a fair hearing and that I could expect a reasonable result. Whatever the outcome, I would have no complaint. I felt that the committee, within the limits of its own needs, would do the best it could for me.

My encounter the next day with the Senate select committee made a dismal contrast. The meeting was supposed to begin at four in the afternoon, but when Guy Struve, John Keker, and I reached the anteroom of the soundproof chamber on the fourth floor of the Capitol where chairman Daniel Inouye and his ten colleagues were already in session, a staff member told us that the committee was running behind schedule.

Although I seldom minded waiting in court to be heard, I was uneasy as we were led to a closetlike cubicle where we were to remain until the committee was ready for us. I argue extemporaneously and often don't have more than skeletal notes. Sometimes I use waiting time to work on an argument I already have in mind. But I had made a good presentation the day before, and I assumed that I would be able to repeat it in substance. I decided to use the time trying to relax. As time passed, however—thirty minutes, sixty minutes, nearly an hour and a half—relaxation turned to a mix of anger and foreboding. I sensed that the committee was discussing immunity with its own counsel, that its decisions about immunizing North and Poindexter were already being made, and that I would have, at best, a slim chance to persuade the committee members to delay or change these decisions.

Once inside the small hearing room, built years earlier for a committee on atomic energy, I observed that the patience of many committee members had already been exhausted. Some faces were flushed. Senators were drifting in and out of the room. I wondered whether Arthur Liman had set me up. Had he already argued for immunity, without my knowing what arguments he had made?

An apologetic, impassive, and weary Inouye explained that the committee wanted to hear anything I had to say, but that in view of how late in the day it was, the committee would be grateful for brevity. A more seasoned lobbyist might have persisted in giving a full presentation. Believing the odds were against me, however, I gambled on brevity and on my ability to condense my argument without losing too much. It was a mistake. Either the facts and the law were too complicated, or I was too tired: The presentation was jumbled, one of my worst.

Senators seem always to be overscheduled. Each represents a statewide constituency of voters who expect personal access. The large number of Senate committees and subcommittees means many meetings that often conflict. As a result, senators often seem impatient and reliant on quick, intuitive decisions rather than on extended argument and reasoning. With dinnertime crowding us, senators continued to drift in and out of the room. Some listened attentively; a few addressed the immunity problem on the merits; but others consumed more than half of my time complaining about the "slowness" of my investigation in a nitpicking way. The junior member, Senator Paul S. Trible, Jr., of Virginia, who later became friendly, used his time—and mine—in an essentially irrelevant and abusive lecture.

Confidently, I reported that most of my staff were now cleared for classified information and working full-time, which to me represented progress. Many senators, however, took this report as confirmation that I was moving too slowly; they believed that they were moving into the home stretch. No one advocated a comprehensive investigation. Seizing on my supposed delay, some Republicans brushed off the need for a broad inquiry. Their approach reflected an oversimplified concept of the nature of the crimes most likely to have been committed. The one crime the critical senators understood was the destruction of records. Put Fawn Hall before the grand jury and get on with it, they argued. If the Iran-Contra prosecutions could be deflated to a case against North for destroying records, the independent counsel's investigation, like Congress's, would be concluded long before George Bush faced New Hampshire's voters in the first presidential primary.

After the session, I made a conciliatory statement to waiting reporters and then drove back to the courthouse. The Capitol's magnificent dome, beautifully illuminated, stood out against the gathering darkness. I was tired, physically and mentally, but that feeling was nothing new. The weekly trips between Oklahoma City, Wichita, Topeka, and Washington since January had taken their toll. I had been given a hearing, but a majority of those who were listening seemed to know already what they wanted and to be merely looking for some vulnerability of mine that would excuse their actions.

I knew that I had been unconvincing, and I was disgruntled by my unimpressive performance, but I was much more concerned about the lack of support for a broad investigation. I had dealt frequently with the Senate when I was deputy attorney general and when I represented the American Bar Association concerning federal judicial appointments. I respected the Senate's power and instinctive political shrewdness. We were on a collision course, not only as to immunity but as to the scope of my investigation.

This assessment seemed all too well founded when I read the comments Inouye made to reporters two days after my appearance before his committee. "At times," the chairman remarked, "we find it a bit difficult to appreciate [Walsh's] need for five, six, seven weeks to question a witness. Most respectfully, I believe that it could be done with more expedition."

Warren Rudman, the vice chairman, was more abrupt. The Senate committee, he said, does not "need anyone's approval to do what we're doing, and we don't intend to seek it."

The day after the hearing, Senator David Boren of Oklahoma told Struve, his Yale classmate and friend, that the committee thought that I had been moving slowly and would want to go on moving slowly. Some already wanted to vote for immunizing North and Poindexter. Boren predicted that if negotiations broke off, the committee would vote for immunity the following week. He said that the hearings had to begin in May at the latest, and he expected that the immunized witnesses would be called during the last week in May. If we would agree to withhold any indictment of North, the committee might delay the hearings until May 7 and call the witnesses in mid-June.

Because the select committees felt bound by their political commitment to finish their work before the beginning of 1988, the next presidential campaign year, they could not risk having to take North to court to compel his testimony. If we indicted North, it would be weeks or months before we could try him. In the meantime, he might refuse to testify even with congressional immunity, claiming that so long as he was under indictment the Fifth Amendment protected him from being compelled to say anything—even though his statements technically could not be used against him. Although the grant of immunity would be voted by Congress, the order compelling the witness to testify would have to be obtained from the courts. Congress might ultimately prevail, but the litigation including appeals could take months.

Liman told Struve that he was planning to begin the public hearings on May 4 or later and to postpone the public testimony of North or

Poindexter until June 15. The senators felt the need for a few principal witnesses. He apologized for our "getting beat up": While we were waiting to be heard, the committee had been debating a grant of immunity to Hakim.

John Nields also talked to Struve. The House select committee overwhelmingly favored acceding to our request that it defer any grant of immunity to North and Poindexter, but Nields urged us not to indict them on the eve of the hearings.

The following week, Liman proposed to Struve that the Senate select committee begin taking North's testimony privately on June 15, and that we agree not to seek the twenty-day delay the statute would allow us. (The statute provided that a government prosecutor could automatically stay testimony pursuant to a grant of immunity for twenty days.) Liman predicted that North would not be called to testify in public before June 21; if we needed another week, said Liman, it could be arranged. He said that Poindexter would be deposed three days before the hearings began, probably on May 2, but that the testimony would be in private, with only two committee members, one counsel, and the official recorder in attendance. Poindexter's public testimony would not begin before June 15.

A few days after receiving this proposal, we accepted it and thanked the committees for agreeing to wait ninety days before acting to compel the testimony of North and Poindexter. We agreed not to use our power to force a twenty-day further delay, but we did not agree not to indict. There had been little likelihood that the committees would forgo their star witnesses; the extra time would give us a fighting chance to compile most of our evidence before North and Poindexter testified publicly.

Congress immunized Albert Hakim on March 23. He was a necessary witness for the select committees if they were to keep their schedule: Only he could provide the Swiss financial records in time for public hearings beginning in May.

Meanwhile, in Wichita, my last private-practice responsibility was finally completed. The Kansas Gas and Electric Company special litigation committee unanimously agreed on its final report; the board of directors approved it on March 17. My relief was tremendous, and the outcome was excellent: Our report generated plenty of praise and, so far as I know, not a single complaint.

At a staff conference on March 24, we confronted the timetable fixed by the congressional committees. We decided against trying to rush partial indictments of North and Poindexter. It was a decision I would reassess many times, but never did I believe in settling for anything less than a full prosecution. I could not have discharged my mandate simply by prosecuting North for destroying documents. I attributed Senator Rudman's public effort to force that outcome to political concern for Ronald Reagan and particularly for presidential candidate George Bush.

Neither North nor Poindexter could have been tried before they were scheduled to testify on Capitol Hill, and the effect of their immunized testimony on a trial conducted afterward would have been much the same no matter when they were indicted. If we had indicted them and they had then refused to testify before Congress, even with immunity, litigation would have been certain; its outcome would have been unpredictable, its premature rulings possibly disastrous to our investigation. My goal was to delay a court ruling on the effect of immunity until after we had acted so that the judge could assess the actual outcome rather than to have a judge, on the basis of speculation, try to tell us in advance how he thought we should act or how he would permit us to act.

With this decision behind us, we moved to protect our ability to try North and Poindexter even after they had given immunized congressional testimony. First, there was the matter of collecting as much evidence as possible before the immunized testimony became public, so that we could demonstrate, if necessary, that we had not relied on immunized material for leads to our own evidence. Next, we had to take steps to shield ourselves from the immunized testimony and to instruct grand jurors to do the same. This left the problem of what to do about our witnesses. Many would be mentioned in the immunized testimony. They would certainly listen to it despite our requests that they refrain from doing so. We finally decided simply to rely on instructing them to avoid disclosing to us anything they learned from the testimony of immunized witnesses.

We accelerated our rush to accumulate and seal evidence in court-controlled depositories, a tactic known as "canning." Every document or memorandum of interview was deposited in a closet by the clerk of the court. When the closet overflowed, our security officer began keeping material in sealed cabinets, where it would be available to the judge if he should wish to check the date on which we had learned some fact or if it became necessary for us to disprove a claim that we had learned a fact from immunized testimony.

Item by item, record by record, interview by interview, disconnected information accumulated. In a further interview, NSC intelligence officer Kenneth deGraffenreid disclosed that he had not seen any presidential findings related to Iran-Contra, although NSC procedures provided for all findings to be deposited with him or transmitted through him to the CIA. After deGraffenreid read a newspaper story that mentioned the January 17, 1986, finding, NSC counsel Paul Thompson reassured him that it had been only a contingency finding, not an official one. Bryan Merchant, who regularly logged in presidential findings, had never seen this finding either. Thus, no contemporaneous government record supported President Reagan's claim that the finding had, in fact, been signed before the direct sales from the United States to Iran had begun.

We confirmed that Betsy North had met with Willard Zucker in the Philadelphia office of the accounting firm Touche Ross on June 5, 1986. The testimony of Zucker, probably a co-conspirator, required confirmation. Telephone records documented Zucker's telephone call to her on June 4. Bob Shwartz had even subpoenaed Amtrak for all the tickets collected from passengers between Washington and Philadelphia on June 5, 1986. The tickets were then checked for Mrs. North's fingerprints. Although her prints were not found on any of the tickets, the fact of her trip was confirmed by her sister, who took care of the Norths' children that day; Betsy North had said that Ollie wanted her to meet someone in Philadelphia.

The individuals who were maneuvering with the congressional committees included not only our principal targets, but also probable witnesses with whom we were negotiating proffers of testimony. On March 30, Congress granted immunity to the CIA's Joseph Fernandez, North's courier Robert Owen, North's assistant Robert Earl, and Secord's assistant Richard Gadd. Exercising our statutory power to briefly delay immunized testimony, we stayed the grants for twenty days. Our problem was minimized because the testimony would be taken in private, without publicity. Also, most of the witnesses still wanted immunity from us; they shared our uncertainty about how complete the protection of congressional immunity would prove to be.

On April 6, I met with our senior counsel to discuss a draft indictment of North and others, to test our ability to prove the charges by the end of sixty days. We were still focusing on McFarlane, Poindexter, North, Secord, and Hakim. Unhappily, we concluded that the only way to surmount the delays caused by the Swiss secrecy laws might be to grant immunity to Albert Hakim.

He was still hiding in Europe, insisting that in addition to his immunity from Congress, he be given immunity from us. When John Nields and Arthur Liman continued to press us to immunize Hakim, we replied that we would certainly consider a proffer from his lawyer but that, to date, he had refused to make one. Liman reported that Hakim's lawyer thought that he could "hang tough" because Hakim, as the nominal owner of the Swiss bank accounts, controlled the Swiss records. Without an impressive proffer, however, none of my staff was willing to let Hakim escape in order to convict North.

As Lincoln Steffens related in his autobiography, investigators of government corruption, at least since the muck-raking days of the turn of the century, have often prosecuted government employees while permitting bribe-givers to go free in return for their testimony. Having worked as a government official for half of my professional life, I was not going to follow that pattern. And even if I had been willing to do so, I was not ready to trust Hakim without a written agreement to cooperate on the basis of which we could set aside immunity if he welched on his commitment.

On April 10, the Swiss Federal Office for Police Matters approved the release of the Swiss financial records to us. Hakim appealed to the courts and stayed delivery. A decision on his appeal was expected in four to six months.

By mid-April, we had cleared our backlog of White House records and were keeping pace with the new documents that were coming in. During this period, we obtained relevant notes taken by Paul Thompson, including notes from the meeting of President Reagan with the congressional leaders on November 12, 1986, after the arms sales to Iran had been publicly exposed, showing that Poindexter had concealed the 1985 arms shipments by Israel.

We began negotiations for a proffer of testimony from Robert Earl. A Rhodes scholar who had been number one in his class at Annapolis, Earl had become a friend of North's at an amphibious-warfare training school. Earl had assisted the vice president's task force on terrorism before being assigned to the National Security Council's staff. When preparing to travel to Tehran with McFarlane, North had briefed Earl on the arms sales to Iran and told him of the diversion of funds to the Contras.

Our Channell-Miller team reported that Bunker Hunt had given North $700,000 for military weapons. Hunt denied that he had known the money was for weapons. Joseph Coors, the beer magnate, had deposited $65,000 in the Lake Resources account to pay for a small airplane. Channell and Miller had paid David Fischer, a former member of Reagan's White House staff, a $50,000 retainer plus $20,000 a month to use his White House contacts to set up meetings between contributors and the president.

We began extensive interviews with Felix Rodriguez, also known as Max Gomez, who had overseen the Ilopango operation and had acted as liaison with the Salvadoran base commander. Rodriguez was a former CIA operative who had served under Donald Gregg, Vice President George Bush's national security advisor. Having significantly aided the Salvadoran air force's efforts to hunt down leftist guerrillas, Rodriguez was admired by the Salvadoran base commander. He had been essential to the North-Secord operation's maintaining a good relationship with the base commander. In his interviews with us, Rodriguez was candid about the activities of North and Secord but very protective of Gregg and Bush. He outlined the operational scheme of the Contra-supply effort through Ilopango. He described meetings North and Secord had held with Contra leaders at Ilopango. In addition to giving us his personal logs of chartered flights to and from the Ilopango air base, he also surrendered the NSA encryption device that he had received from North.

On April 22, I appeared before the House select committee and successfully opposed immunity for Thomas Clines, the former CIA officer who had purchased arms for Secord and Hakim. As at my previous appearance before the committee, the members were attentive and considerate. I argued that Clines certainly appeared to deserve prosecution and that the committee did not really need his testimony. The committee agreed and withheld immunity.

The next day, George Bush's ally from New Hampshire, Senator Rudman, blasted me. "There are too many important issues facing the country for the American people," he told an audience of editors, "to wait while [Walsh's] investigation goes on ad nauseam." Insisting once more that the only Iran-Contra crime worth prosecuting was North's possible destruction of government documents, Rudman derided the notion that more complex crimes had been committed: "If they go with some grand, wild conspiracy case, you're going to have a hell of a time proving it. . . . The Congress has really got to get on with this."

Up to this point, I had put my arguments against immunity to the Senate and House select committees behind closed doors and in written memoranda reserved for them. Now it was time to state my case to a larger audience. As independent counsel, I was charged with reporting periodically to Congress. Even before Senator Rudman's blast, I had begun working on a public interim report to dispel the accusation that our investigation was moving too slowly or in the wrong direction. I released my report on April 28.

The report summarized our progress in quantitative terms—eight hundred witness interviews conducted, hundreds of boxes of White House and NSC documents examined, roughly 200,000 pages from CIA files scrutinized, some thirty full days of grand jury sessions held. Our investigation had reached beyond the White House and the National Security Council to the vice president's office; to the departments of State, Defense, Justice, Transportation, and the Treasury; to the CIA; and to thirteen foreign countries. The interim report forecast that our efforts to gather and evaluate evidence of crimes by "a combination of certain government officers, former government officers, and other individuals" involved in arming Nicaraguans and Iranians would require "extensive" investigation.

"Most lines of inquiry are proving fruitful," I wrote. "None has yet been abandoned." The greatest danger to the work of the independent counsel arose not from the considered pace of the investigation, but from the hasty decisions on Capitol Hill to grant immunity to witnesses who might then escape prosecution.

The Iran-Contra affair had involved "possible violations of public trust and possible misuse of position by high government officials," the interim report continued. "Large sums of public money are unaccounted for. . . . In such matters, the public is entitled to a fair and deliberate prosecutive judgment. Additional grants of congressional immunity to central figures may frustrate the evenhanded application of justice."

As we continued to piece together the story of the actions taken by North and Secord to supply the Contras, Secord decided to forgo immunity and become the first witness to testify before the congressional committees. At the same time, he consented to be debriefed by us in what is known as a "queen for a day" arrangement: We did not agree not to prosecute him, but we did agree that we would not use his testimony against him unless it became necessary to impeach his future testimony. In exchange, Secord agreed to give us a true account of his activities.

During this period, we also began to work with Glenn Robinette, a former CIA employee who had worked for Secord on various investigative assignments. An important witness who could prove that North had personally benefited from the arms sales, Robinette had installed an expensive security system at North's home. As we pierced Robinette's initial lies, he admitted that Secord had paid him and that his correspondence with North regarding payment by North had been a false cover proposed by North and approved by Secord after the arms-for-hostages deals had been exposed. Obtaining the proof for these statements took a few more weeks.

As major witnesses began to respond, Spitz Channell and Richard Miller decided to plead guilty and to cooperate with us against North, in hopes of receiving lenient sentences. On April 29, Channell pleaded guilty to a felony charge that he had conspired to defraud the United States by violating the Internal Revenue laws. A week later, Miller pleaded guilty to the same crime. When they were arraigned, both men identified Oliver North as their co-conspirator.

Our progress was now unmistakable and objectively measurable. We still needed the Swiss records, and it looked as though we would receive them in about four months. We also needed freedom from congressional interference, but that was less assured.

Reporters were covering us almost daily. The interim report, followed a day later by Channell's plea of guilty, produced page-one stories, editorials, and columns—almost all favorable. In his May 1 column in the *New York Times*, for example, Anthony Lewis wrote, "The independent counsel for the Iran-Contra affair . . . is evidently following a standard prosecutorial strategy. That is to focus first on lower-level wrongdoers, get them to cooperate and gradually build a case against higher-ups. . . . The big question is whether the charges of conspiracy . . . will reach President Reagan."

While we were receiving favorable notices, public attention shifted to Capitol Hill. The Iran-Contra hearings—a pageant in which I would have no part, not even a spectator's role—were to start on May 5. Neither I nor most of my associate counsel could listen to the testimony of immunized witnesses. We entered a unique limbo, a world where everyone we knew was assiduously following Iran-Contra developments, but we had to be like Ulysses' crew, with our ears stopped against the song of the sirens.

CHAPTER SEVEN

Close Pursuit

As the congressional hearings moved into the spotlight in early May 1987, our investigation assumed the rhythms of a varsity crew pulling together with mutual confidence, almost out of sight of the spectators. In my team, I saw excellence, diligence, imagination, and fairness—qualities that would be needed to prove beyond a reasonable doubt that government power had been criminally misused.

On Capitol Hill, a less-disciplined group of the people's elected representatives was impatient to tear into the same subject matter. Congress has many investigative procedures through which it discharges its oversight responsibilities. It may conduct inquiries formally or informally, in private or in public. A public hearing is not necessary to learn the facts; it is designed and directed to reveal facts to the public. A congressional hearing lacks the long-established rules, the structure, and the tight control by a presiding officer that a court trial has.

A public hearing may seem easy to conduct because it is so one-sided. Having chaired a commission appointed by Governor Nelson Rockefeller to investigate a scandal in the administration of New York's alcoholic beverage control law, however, I knew that hastily prepared public hearings could be woeful disasters. This is what I feared as the select committees rushed to present their incomplete information to the public. Once the committees began holding televised proceedings, the chances of their losing control of the hearings greatly increased. Television can be devastating to the imperfectly prepared, and the committee members would subject themselves to the mercy of the public before whom they performed. Every facial expression, every hesitation, every inflection, and every hint of unfairness in the patently artificial proceedings would take on significance when beamed into millions of living rooms. Rushing into televised hearings would be like opening on Broadway without rehearsals, a mistake that Oliver North's lawyer surely would not make.

On May 2, shortly before the public hearings began, Congress had given immunity to John Poindexter. We did not try to stay the grant of immunity for the twenty days available to us by law. Poindexter's initial testimony was taken in private and under very secure conditions. From his earlier statement to the FBI, we assumed that Poindexter would admit having known that the proceeds from the arms sales to Iran had been diverted to the Contras, but would deny having ever told the president about the diversion. If Poindexter *did* describe what Ronald Reagan had known about the affair, North's testimony might not be essential to Congress.

From the outset, however, North had been the colorful focus not only of the Contra-supply operation and the arms sales to Iran, but also of the public's curiosity. Although he had not been the most seasoned operator, North somehow personified the U.S. government. More than Poindexter, more than anyone else, North was the face of presidential authorization, real or spurious. It was North who had called on the great agencies of government for assistance—and had gotten it. It was North who had assured his confederates that they were doing what President Reagan wanted. Accordingly, although North probably could not claim a link to the president comparable to Poindexter's, the public desire to see the colonel and hear his testimony was a force that even responsible and concerned members of the committees would find difficult to disregard.

Racing against Congress, we were scooping up every possible scrap of evidence related to North and Poindexter, without enough time to absorb all that was significant. Everything had to be "canned." Too little could be digested. Already focused on the idea of a five-man conspiracy—with Oliver North as the central figure, Robert McFarlane and John Poindexter as aiders and abetters, and Richard Secord and Albert Hakim as principal agents—our investigation was further constrained by our need for haste. If we were to have our proof fully assembled before North and Poindexter testified on Capitol Hill, we would have to put other issues and other individuals aside. We would get back to them later, I told myself, as I heard about officers of the CIA and the State Department who had flown or fallen into North's web. First, we had to nail down our primary case.

Our narrowed preoccupation was probably inevitable. We would have concentrated on North in any event. He was a logical target and, if he could be compelled to talk, the most useful witness. He knew more about the affair than anyone else. In PROF notes and in conversations with witnesses, he had shown an increasing urge to talk about his activities. And, having destroyed government records and other evidence, North was vulnerable.

Venality also was emerging as an issue. North had received personal benefits from the Swiss account in which the Iranian arms proceeds were deposited. We had confirmed Willard Zucker's account of his meeting Betsy North and then establishing a $200,000 "B. Button" fund. When an excited John Nields telephoned Guy Struve to say that Hakim could give "cataclysmic" testimony that would merit our granting him immunity, we assumed that Nields was referring to the $200,000. We thanked him but were noncommittal. I was not eager to let Hakim or any bribe-giver buy his way out of prosecution. Nor would I gamble on his testimony without a full proffer, which his lawyer still refused to give.

Similarly, when associate counsel Bob Shwartz and Bill Hassler reported that Glenn Robinette had finally admitted that Richard Secord had paid him some $14,000 to install the security system at North's Virginia home, we had unquestioned proof that North had accepted an illegal gratuity—a gratuity that we expected to show had been paid from the illegally diverted proceeds of the arms sales to Iran. We had colorful, undisputable confirmation of criminal intent in the form of backdated letters in which North had pretended that Robinette had billed him $8,000 for the work. Shwartz was also developing proof that of the more than $90,000 in traveler's checks entrusted to him by Adolfo Calero for Contra expenses and the recovery of hostages, North had used some $4,000 for personal expenses.

Provable though these crimes might be, I did not want to reduce our case to indicting North as a common scrounger. He had been more than that. Iran-Contra had been more than profiteering. I had been appointed to investigate an intricate and dangerous conspiracy, a high-level breach of trust and contempt for the Constitution. To indict the central conspirator only for incidental misconduct might produce a relatively quick conviction, but I distrusted that route. I had long since learned the dangers of distorting an investigation just to reach a short-term conclusion to an apparently easy case. Neither North's attorney Brendan Sullivan nor Congress could be expected to allow me the time I would need to supplement a fragmentary indictment, once I had filed it. I was not ready to reduce the grave abuse of power that I knew to have occurred to an incident of petty personal culpability.

The broad outline of an indictment for conspiracy to defraud the United States was now constantly in my mind. The components included the diversion, the misuse of tax-exempt foundations, the destruction of official records, the lying to Congress, and the obstruction of justice.

The comprehensive case was developing, as one unwilling witness followed another. In May, when we confronted Robert Earl, North's closest associate at the National Security Council, with the charge of document destruction, he gave us an acceptable proffer of testimony in return for immunity.

In many ways, Earl had acted as North's deputy for both the arms sales to Iran and the last months of the Contra-supply operation. Among other assignments, Earl had assisted North in determining the prices of the equipment sold to the Iranians. Earl had calculated that the February 1986 TOW shipments had been marked up 370 percent, and he had applied this markup to subsequent sales, including the sale of Hawk parts in May of that year. After the arms sales had been exposed and North had learned that Attorney General Edwin Meese was going to investigate, North had asked Earl for the contents of his working files on Iran. Earl had given the folders to North, who had later returned them empty. Earl had then gone through his own remaining files and destroyed his copies of documents and computer notes regarding the arms sales to Iran. He had seen North and Fawn Hall feeding documents from North's files to the shredder. When North returned from a White House meeting later that day, he had spoken of himself in the third person, telling Earl "that it was time for North to be the scapegoat." North had reported that he had asked the attorney general for another twenty-four or forty-eight hours but that Meese had replied that he didn't know if he could wait that long.

The next day, the shredder in North's suite had broken. North and Earl had decided to use the one in the White House situation room. Earl had seen North take from the suite a large pile of documents that he intended to shred. Earl had been present when the attorney general's assistants, William Bradford Reynolds and John Richardson, began to review the documents that North had placed on the table for them in his office. While Meese's assistants were at lunch, North had removed another stack of documents from his suite as NSC counsel Paul Thompson looked on.

After document-security officer Brenda Reger had sealed off North's suite, Fawn Hall had told Earl that she needed to take some documents out of the suite. Earl had volunteered to put them in the pockets of his suit coat, but Hall had hidden them under her clothes instead. She had asked Earl if he could see the documents under her clothes, and he had told her no. They had agreed not to disclose each other's activities to the FBI.

On the evening after North was fired, Earl, Hall and another staff member had met North on the stairway between their offices. North had told them that he had received a telephone call from President Reagan. According to Earl, North had turned to him and said "in substance that the president had told him that it was important that he [the president] not know; that he [North] was told that it was important that he [the president] not know." Earl had inferred that North was to take the blame for an unauthorized diversion of funds from the arms sales. Until then, Earl had believed that the Iranian initiative and the diversion of funds to the Contras had been approved clandestine policies of the Reagan administration.

By June, we had a fairly full picture of the administration's dealings with Iran, although the CIA witnesses answered questions narrowly, requiring multiple interviews. Charles Allen had been assigned to work with North in the fall of 1985, during the Israeli arms sales to Iran. After President Reagan had signed the January 1986 finding authorizing direct sales to Iran, the CIA's operations directorate had taken over the responsibilities from Allen, but he had continued to assist North in monitoring the Iranians. The National Security Agency had delivered concurrent intelligence reports to William Casey, his deputy director Robert Gates, John Poindexter, Caspar Weinberger, and the Joint Chiefs of Staff.

In interviews with my staff, the CIA's director of operations, Clair George, described the organizational meeting in Poindexter's office at which Secord had been introduced to George and Thomas Twetten and North had outlined the new undertaking, the day after the finding was signed. Twetten, who then had taken over for the CIA, reviewed the negotiations between his agency and the Defense Department to lower the prices for the arms. He did not know that Manucher Ghorbanifar and North had agreed on a sales price almost three times that charged by the Defense Department. Twetten had accompanied North to the February meeting in Germany with Secord, Hakim, Ghorbanifar, and an Iranian official. Upon realizing that North was using Secord as his operations officer in two different covert activities, which was contrary to CIA procedures, Twetten had warned North against that practice.

Twetten had then essentially replaced himself with George Cave, a retired CIA agent who had served in the operations directorate. Fluent in Farsi, Cave had acted as the interpreter in subsequent meetings with the Iranians and had been North's intermediary in telephone conversations with the Iranians. Cave had accompanied McFarlane and North to Tehran in May 1986 and been the note-taker for the meeting. Clair George claimed that Cave, who had been assigned by the CIA to keep tabs on North, had instead become a North devotee.

In interviews with my staff, Cave and Allen described the tension when, in June 1986, the Iranians discovered the overpricing of the arms. In an effort to continue to deceive the Iranians, North had had the CIA produce a false price list, which he had then given the Iranians. His trick had been counterproductive.

In view of the scale of the overcharge exacted from Iran, Allen had suspected North of using the excess proceeds to finance the Contras. Allen had passed his suspicions along to his boss, Richard Kerr, the deputy director for intelligence. Kerr, in turn, had warned Gates in August 1986, just as Congress was about to pass the $100 million appropriation to permit the CIA to renew its Nicaraguan activities. Later, Allen had directly warned Gates about the diversion and had been told to write a memorandum for Casey. But the memorandum had not been submitted to Casey until early October. At the same time, New York financial venturer Roy Furmark had expressed similar suspicions to Casey and told him that Ghorbanifar had not been paid for the Hawk spare parts.

Matters had come to a head the day after Hasenfus's aircraft was shot down in Nicaragua. North had flown back from a meeting with the Iranians in Germany and had eaten lunch with Casey. Gates, whose office adjoined Casey's, claimed he had been in and out of the meeting and had heard North making cryptic remarks about Swiss bank accounts. Gates said that he had subsequently asked Casey about the remarks but that Casey had simply ignored his question.

In interviews by my staff, Gates professed not to remember having been warned by Kerr and Allen during the summer of 1986. The first warning he acknowledged having received had come on the day in October when he had told Allen to pass the information on to Casey. We did not believe Gates. It simply was not credible that the second-highest officer of the CIA would forget a warning of an illegal activity linking President Reagan's two favorite programs. We decided against prosecuting Gates for making a false statement, however, because there had been only one witness to each of the conversations he claimed to have forgotten. Kerr and Allen had each been alone with Gates when they gave him the information, so we could not corroborate their testimony as to either incident.

Gates's problems epitomized those of the administration. At a time when negotiations with the Soviets for arms control were especially promising, Gates was perhaps our most accomplished intelligence analyst on Soviet matters. Reagan needed his help. The president nominated him to succeed Casey as director of central intelligence, but the Senate intelligence committee questioned the truthfulness of Gates's claim that he did not remember the early warnings of the diversion. He asked to have his nomination withdrawn. President Reagan then appointed Gates as his deputy national security advisor, a personal staff appointment that did not require Senate confirmation but kept Gates in a position to assist in dealing with the Soviets. FBI Director William Webster was then nominated to head the CIA. After Webster's nomination was confirmed, Richard Kerr became his deputy.

Another CIA witness, Duane "Dewey" Clarridge, at first answered our questions, adhering to the false claim that he had not realized that the November 1985 Hawk shipment comprised weapons. After giving a deposition to Congress, however, he claimed his privilege against self-incrimination and refused to answer further questions. Both Clarridge and Alan Fiers left the agency following an unfavorable internal review of their activities.

We were also piecing together the final details of the Contra-supply operation, developing through witnesses the hundreds of individual incidents that had made up the guerrilla war in Nicaragua—the secret war that appeared to have given the administration a motive for continuing the secret trade with Tehran. CIA field agents had actively helped supply and advise the Contras while senior State Department officials studiously looked the other way. High-level officials had deceived members of Congress about the National Security Council's support of the Contras in defiance of the congressional prohibitions.

Witnesses put into narrative form the documents that told us that as early as September 1984, just before the Boland amendments' ban on support went into effect, North had begun to meet with Adolfo Calero and to replace the CIA's Duane Clarridge as the Contras' liaison.

Vincent N. Cannistraro, a CIA officer who had been detailed to the NSC as director of intelligence programs, told us that in late spring

1984, Calero had met with Clarridge, North, and Cannistraro at a Virginia motel to discuss how to continue support for the Contras if congressional funding was cut off. They had discussed private fund-raising. According to Cannistraro, North not only had been the principal person keeping the Contra resistance alive but also had claimed to be getting his authority directly from the president.

Other members of the NSC's staff noted that North had regularly reported directly to McFarlane and Poindexter, disregarding the usual staff procedures. McFarlane had supported North's tactical needs at the highest levels. At North's insistence, for example, McFarlane had requested—albeit unsuccessfully—that his opposite number on Prime Minister Margaret Thatcher's staff help to get her government's approval for the purchase of British Blowpipe missiles for the Contras.

By 1986, North had become boastful about his work with the Contras. To Bretton G. Sciaronni, counsel to the president's intelligence oversight board, North had claimed to have operated and managed the Contras' war effort from his office in the Old Executive Office Building for approximately two years before it became public knowledge. To Spitz Channell's assistant, North had bragged that when he obtained money from foreign countries, President Reagan had contacted the heads of the countries beforehand. North had characterized the president as his "advance man."

Not only had North raised funds himself, but he also had used top-ranking associates from the National Security Council's staff. The head of the NSC's East Asia section, Gaston Sigur, told us of having arranged a meeting between North and General Zhang Wtang of the People's Republic of China to expedite Secord's first arms shipment from China to the Contras in late 1985. Sigur had also set up a 1986 meeting between North and Fred Chien, director of the Coordinating Council for North American Affairs of the Taiwan Republic of China. In that meeting, North had negotiated a $1 million gift for the Contras.

North had fully understood the Boland amendments. He had participated in the White House lobbying effort to liberalize the restrictions. The White House director of legislative and legal affairs told us of having specifically cautioned North on several occasions about the Boland amendments' applicability to his involvement with the Contras.

Associate counsel and FBI agents questioned dozens of Central American witnesses. According to CIA Central American personnel and the agency's inspector general, CIA helicopter pilots assigned to Honduras had transported whatever type of cargo was necessary, lethal or humane, to the Contras' jungle bases along the Coco River, the Nicaragua-Honduras border, at Bocay, Yamales, Kisan, and RusRus.

In 1985, it had become clear to North and the CIA officials monitoring the Contras that an active southern front was needed to divide the Sandinista forces. Alfonso Robello, one of the three principals of United Nicaraguan Opposition (UNO), the top Contra organization, told us that he'd had thirty or forty meetings with Joseph Fernandez, the CIA's chief of station in Costa Rica, and a significant number with Fernandez's superior, Alan Fiers, while the Boland amendments were in effect. Robello identified Fernandez as having been responsible for establishing a southern front and for the eventual resumption of American aid. Fernandez's secretary testified that Fernandez had been in regular contact with North, and that Fernandez had worked in concert with Ambassador Lewis Tambs in Costa Rica to open a southern front.

One CIA officer told us that Fernandez had persuaded *comanderos* to defect from Eden Pastora, the original anti-Sandinista leader in the south, to Pedro "Blackie" Chamorro, who had been more aggressive and more responsive to the CIA. CIA officers had trained the *comanderos* in reading maps, selecting drop zones, and marking and reporting drop locations. Another CIA official testified about Fernandez's participation in selecting the site for the clandestine airstrip to supply the southern front and about his dealings with both the Americans who had built it and the Costa Rican officials who had permitted its construction.

Rob Owen, North's principal courier to the Contras and others in Central America, finally gave us a satisfactory proffer and received immunity. He described having delivered Contra requests to North and transported cash and intelligence information to Contra leaders and those in North's supply organization.

Rafael Quintero, a retired CIA officer whom Secord described as his eyes and ears in Central America, explained to us that he had been linked to North, Secord, and Fernandez by a KL-43 communication system supplied by the National Security Agency. Through Quintero and North, Fernandez had relayed the needs of the Contras to Secord and Thomas Clines, who had bought weapons in Europe and arranged their delivery through the Ilopango air base in El Salvador.

Ambassador Tambs told us that when he was appointed, North had informed him that a southern front was to be opened for the Contras and had asked him to obtain Costa Rica's permission to build a supporting airstrip at Santa Elena. North's instructions had been confirmed by Assistant Secretary of State Elliott Abrams.

Casey's supervision of North was apparent from the information provided by Clair George, the CIA's director of operations. He told us that Casey had felt personally responsible for convincing Reagan to commit funds and intelligence support for Central America. Casey's top priority had been the Contra resistance. George believed that Casey had known about North's activities and had participated in discussions with the "private benefactors," the CIA's euphemism for the North-Secord group, regarding contributions to support the Contras with arms. George denied that he himself had known of the relationship between Fernandez and North, of Fernandez's assistance to North, or of Fernandez's encrypted KL-43 communications with North. George said that the CIA and many government officials had been aware of North's activities but had tried to distance themselves from the operation.

Through Felix Rodriguez (Max Gomez), Vice President George Bush's office had been drawn into North's activities. Donald Gregg, the vice president's national security advisor and Rodriguez's former CIA supervisor, told us that he had recommended to the U.S. embassy in El Salvador that Rodriguez be assigned to assist the Salvadoran air force in antiguerrilla helicopter tactics. By sharing his expertise, Rodriguez had earned the respect and support of the Ilopango base commander. North had then used this relationship to maintain his Contra-supply station at the base. Rodriguez had kept Bush informed of his helicopter activities but, according to Gregg, had not discussed his Contra-supply activities until August 8, 1986, when Rodriguez told Gregg that he was concerned about Secord's operation. Rodriguez had said that he believed Secord and Clines to be profiteering. Gregg had called a meeting in the vice president's office on August 12 to discuss Rodriguez's complaints. Gregg claimed that Fiers, Abrams, and Earl (in North's absence) had attended the meeting but that Bush had not been informed about it.

Gregg's claims conflicted with information provided by the vice president's former deputy assistant in charge of scheduling, Deborah J. Hutton, who told us that she recalled having set up a meeting between Rodriguez and Bush in May 1986. The scheduling memorandum specified two subjects. One was Contra resupply. The memorandum had been dictated by Colonel Samuel J. Watson III, Gregg's deputy, who had already known that Rodriguez was involved with North in supplying the Contras. (Rodriguez's May visit had indeed taken place, but all the parties claimed that too many persons had been present to permit him to discuss Contra resupply. Instead, he had shown photographs of his helicopter activities.)

It was Watson whom Rodriguez had telephoned on October 6, 1986, to report the downing of the C-123 in Nicaragua, describing it as "one of Ollie's planes." When Watson then tried to question North, Earl had denied knowledge of the C-123, said that it was not Watson's concern, and told him to stop asking questions. Gregg had been out of town. Watson claimed that he had decided not to tell Bush. According to Watson, the vice president had known of Rodriguez only through his helicopter activities against guerrilla rebels in El Salvador.

The State Department officials in El Salvador had known that Rodriguez was Max Gomez. David Passage, the U.S. chargé d'affaires, told us that Rodriguez had introduced himself to the embassy staff before beginning work at Ilopango. Passage had known that Rodriguez worked in North's Contra-supply operation. Rodriguez had communicated directly to North by public telephone. Passage had been told by Ambassador Edwin Corr not to interfere; CIA staff members had been told by their superiors to stay away from the "private benefactors."

John Ferch, the U.S. ambassador to Honduras, had been concerned about North's activities and had been relieved of his post in 1986 after requesting that his instructions regarding North be put in writing. In his testimony, Ferch told us that Undersecretary of State Michael Armacost had explained to him that the "seventh floor [State's top officials] doesn't do Central American policy anymore." He further said that job had been taken over in the summer of 1985 by a group under the direction of Elliott Abrams. Ferch regarded Abrams as having been in charge of Central American policy politically and North as having been in charge operationally, with Fiers participating both in political planning and in operations.

Assistant Secretary of State Robert Duemling, who was responsible for the Nicaraguan Humanitarian Assistance Office, the State Department's legal humanitarian aid program for the Contras, had been pressed by Abrams to hire Rob Owen, North's courier to the Contra leaders, as an on-the-scene specialist. Duemling had resisted; he did not want his legal humanitarian operation to be tainted by North's activities. In the end, he had been given no choice. After North had complained at a restricted interagency group meeting about Duemling's operation, Abrams had said, "I guess, Bob, you'd better hire Rob."

In 1986, word of North's cache of funds for secret activities had begun to spread beyond those supplying the Contras with weapons. Robert Kagan, Abrams's special assistant for the State Department's office of public diplomacy, for example, had obtained a $25,000 contribution from North to continue the operation of the Contras' political office in Washington. And the State Department had referred to North an ambassadorial request to supply the head of a West Indian nation with certain radio broadcasting equipment. At North's direction, the equipment had been paid for out of the Crédit Suisse account in which Secord had deposited the excess proceeds of the Iranian arms sales. North had become a recognized funding source for irregular, off-the-books activities.

This accumulation of facts was swept into place unexpectedly by the man who had set up North's two covert actions: Richard Secord. In return for waiving his Fifth Amendment rights, he had secured the position of leadoff witness at the congressional hearings. He had also agreed to talk with us.

Determined to show that his motives had been honorable, his activities authorized, and his earnings legitimate, Secord had axes to grind. As he saw it, the administration had used and then deserted him. More than once, he claimed, Oliver North had said that "all [his] bosses" knew what he was doing and appreciated it. Secord was not about to be a commander who hid behind the Fifth Amendment while his subordinates took the rap. He wanted to clear his name and restore the honor he felt he had earned as a combat aviator in Vietnam and a military diplomat in Iran during the shah's last years.

Secord had met North in 1981, when Secord was a deputy assistant secretary of defense working on a major aircraft sale to Saudi Arabia. The two men had not become close until mid-1984, after Casey recommended that North ask Secord to lend the Contras a helping hand. Secord had been selling security systems in partnership with Albert Hakim. The Contras had exhausted the funds appropriated by the United States, and the only thing keeping them in action had been their $1-million-a-month contribution from Saudi Arabia.

North had first asked Secord to help Calero improve the Contras' weapons procurement process. Secord had begun as a broker, then had expanded his role significantly in 1985, when the Saudi gift doubled and funds raised by North began to flow through the tax-exempt National Endowment for the Preservation of Liberty. During the first five months of 1985, Secord had arranged arms deals worth nearly $10 million for the Contras. Of that total, profits of $2,586,079 had gone to Secord and his partners, principally Albert Hakim and Thomas Clines.

On June 28, 1985, North had convened a meeting in Miami with Secord, Clines, Quintero, Calero, and the Contras' military chief, Enrique Bermúdez. At the meeting, North had announced that Secord's operation would thenceforth handle all arms purchases and receive the outside funds for them. Until then, contributed funds had gone first to Calero and then to the arms suppliers. After mid-1985, the funds from North's solicited contributions and the proceeds of the arms sales to Iran had gone directly to Secord's Enterprise accounts and had been used not just to buy supplies for the Contras but also to equip and operate the supply network.

Within thirteen months, this mini-conglomerate, referred to variously as the operation, Project Democracy, and the Enterprise, had acquired assets it valued at more than $4 million: eight aircraft of different sizes and capabilities, a small freighter, the airstrip and adjacent land at Santa Elena, spare aircraft parts, and a variety of munitions and military supplies. Through various corporate covers, North and Secord's network had included a force of twenty-five salaried pilots and other personnel in El Salvador, Honduras, Costa Rica, Miami, and Washington.

In mid-1986, as the Reagan administration moved Congress toward approving a resumption of CIA support for the Contras, Secord and Hakim had seen their function coming to an end. Their proposal, enthusiastically endorsed by Oliver North, had been to sell the whole operation to the CIA for somewhat less than $4 million. But when Eugene Hasenfus went on display as a Nicaraguan prisoner in early October, the assets had lost almost all their market value.

When North's operation in Central America collapsed, the Swiss-based Enterprise had still been going strong in the even more lucrative business of selling U.S. arms to Iran. Secord described how, while he was operating the secret Contra-supply network, his logistical skills had been sought to help North untangle the November 1985 Hawk shipment for Iran. Violating the basic rule against merging two covert operations, North had coordinated and manipulated the process that had transformed Secord and Hakim into America's commercial and diplomatic interlocutors with Iran, beginning in January 1986.

To Congress and to us, Secord presented that metamorphosis as a logical development of his success with the Contras. As a provider of full-service logistical support, Project Democracy had brought a signal measure of order to the often chaotic workings of the guerrilla effort. The project had linked fund-raising with arms-purchasing and, through Secord, had established an integrated operation that bought and delivered military supplies and even medical care. The achievement had been impressive, and Secord was proud of it.

He felt the same about the arms trade with Tehran. The shipments of missiles and spare parts that he and North had arranged in 1986 were, in Secord's view, the unavoidable currency of a diplomatic dialogue that had been showing genuine promise when disclosure wrecked it in November. Nor did he seem to regret that the currency had been debased by the practice of overcharging Iran's broker for Defense Department weapons. He said that Manucher Ghorbanifar had actually set the prices. The extra earnings, Secord insisted, had gone not to himself but to Project Democracy.

Thus, Secord had become a key player on two fronts. Planes he chartered had carried the two shipments of TOW missiles delivered in February 1986. His Lake Resources bank account, into which Contra-support funds solicited by North also flowed, had been used to receive the $10 million Iranian payment for the TOWs and to reimburse the CIA for the official price of $3.7 million.

In May 1986, Secord had undertaken the delivery of 240 sets of spare parts for Hawk missiles to Iran. Their official U.S. price had been $4,337,000 plus shipping and handling, but Ghorbanifar, with funds borrowed from Adnan Khashoggi, had paid nearly $15 million in advance for them. Before expenses, Secord's Enterprise had withheld about $6.3 million from the markups on the TOWs in February and more than $10 million from the Hawk transaction in May.

In continuing interviews with us and in sworn testimony to the select committees, Robert McFarlane filled in the details of the shipment of the spare parts and his own mission to Iran. Flown to Israel from the United States, the spare parts had been stored under Secord's supervision. On May 24, one pallet had been loaded onto the unmarked aircraft carrying the five Americans—Robert McFarlane, Oliver North, George Cave, NSC staffer Howard Teicher, and a CIA communications specialist—to Tehran. Amiram Nir, the Israeli expert on counterterrorism who had helped restore U.S. dealings with Iran after the botched Hawk shipment in November 1985, had accompanied them disguised as an American.

The secret mission had been postponed from April to enable Ghorbanifar to produce a high-level reception that would turn the arms trade into a more elevated, substantive political discourse. But even a month later, he had been unable to make good on his pledge. McFarlane's party had found no one to welcome them at the airport; they had been installed incommunicado on the top floor of the erstwhile Tehran Hilton, where they had waited until five in the afternoon for the arrival of an Iranian official.

The meetings that followed had been fruitless. The Iranians had given only false names and had possessed no real negotiating authority. They had repeatedly spoken of their country's need for more weaponry; they had harped on their disappointment with America's proclaimed neutrality in the Iran-Iraq conflict; and they had refused to give specific assurances about the release of the hostages.

In April, North had laid out for Poindexter, Casey, and his CIA support group a timetable predicting that the American captives in Lebanon would be freed seven hours after the arrival of McFarlane's team in Tehran. In a May 19 note, North had moved the timing of the release back by seventeen hours to the morning of Monday, May 26. Once the hostages had been freed, a second 707 would fly the bulk of the Hawk spare parts to Tehran.

North's forecasts had proved wildly unreliable. During the delegation's stay, the Iranians had taken the pallet of spare parts but released no hostages. Nor had any new understanding been achieved. Neither the prime minister nor any other minister had acknowledged the Americans' presence. The highest Iranian official to meet them had been a senior foreign affairs advisor. McFarlane had wanted to discuss the Soviet threat to Iran and the possibility of strategic cooperation once the hostage issue was out of the way; the Iranians had seemed interested only, and urgently, in acquiring more weapons.

McFarlane had cut off the conversations and had angrily left Tehran on the morning of May 28, after abruptly countermanding North's unauthorized order to bring the second load of Hawk parts to Tehran. On the way home, at the Tel Aviv airfield where they changed planes, North had told McFarlane that there was a silver lining. "It's not a total loss," North had said. "At least some of the money from this deal is going to Central America." McFarlane had thought, "Oh, shit." The next day, after being briefed by McFarlane, the president had described the outcome of the mission in his diary as "a heart-breaking disappointment for all of us."

Meanwhile, said Secord in his congressional testimony and interviews with us, Ghorbanifar had feared assassination. The Iranians had refused to pay him anything for the Hawk spare parts, so he had possessed nothing with which to repay Khashoggi. Worse, the Iranians had obtained a U.S. Defense Department price list through their London representatives and had discovered that they were being overcharged by 600 percent. As senior U.S. officials learned from intelligence sources, Ghorbanifar had added his own markup of approximately $10 million to the Americans' markup of more than $10 million.

After weeks of unproductive discussion, Amiram Nir had, on July 24, obtained the release of one more hostage, the Reverend Lawrence Martin Jenco, who had directed Catholic Relief Services in Beirut. Israeli Prime Minister Shimon Peres had asked Vice President Bush, who was visiting the Middle East, to meet Nir. Bush had done so. His chief of staff and, later, Bush himself testified that the discussion had been very general. Nir, however, said that he had explained to Bush the need to alternate individual hostage releases with arms deliveries. The Iranians could not release all the hostages in advance, as North had promised and Poindexter and McFarlane had insisted. Unable to reach Poindexter, Bush had reported this conversation to North. On July 30, the day after Bush's meeting with Nir and six days after Jenco's release, President Reagan had approved the second shipment of Hawk parts, which had been held in Israel since May. This had led the Iranians to pay Ghorbanifar part of the purchase price, so that he could partially pay his angry bankers.

The shipment had also marked a radical change from the previous U.S. position that weapons sales would stop unless all the American hostages were released. A new round of secret talks between the Iranians and North, Secord, and Hakim had ensued. Meetings in Brussels, Washington, and Frankfurt between August and October 1986 had opened a fresh negotiating effort with a new Iranian intermediary developed by Hakim. Secord explained that North, aided and occasionally replaced in these negotiations by Secord and Hakim, had agreed to another arms deal, the third for that year: an October sale to Iran of five hundred TOWs. North and Secord had reimbursed the CIA a little more than $2 million for the TOWs, which had then been sold for $3.6 million. Although the Americans had hoped that two hostages would be released, only David P. Jacobsen, the director of the American University hospital in Beirut, had been set free. While the first half of the TOW shipment was being delivered to Iran, however, two other Americans had been taken hostage in Lebanon.

North, Secord, and Quintero had flown to Beirut to pick up Jacobsen and had taken him to Cyprus for a press conference on November 3, the eve of the midterm elections in the United States. Overly optimistic as ever, North had returned to the United States with Jacobsen and had left Secord behind to handle the release of two more hostages. But the hostages had remained in captivity, and Secord had left the Middle East empty-handed. As Jacobsen was answering journalists' questions, the edition of *Al Shiraa* that contained the account of McFarlane's mission to Tehran was appearing on Beirut newsstands.

Throughout May and June 1987, our haste in accumulating documents deprived us of an adequate opportunity to evaluate those that did not apply directly to North and Poindexter, which meant that the agencies and individuals producing the documents could withhold some of the most sensitive ones without our realizing it. We accepted Caspar Weinberger's denial that he had relevant notes, for example, and we accepted the assurance of George Shultz's executive assistant, Charles Hill, that he had given us all of Shultz's relevant notes. The CIA, which produced thousands of documents, withheld for months the working files of Charles Allen, the intelligence officer who had worked most closely with North. Notes of the two critical restricted interagency group meetings in August and September 1986, at which North had disclosed his activities, were also kept from us, and we were misled about the substance of these meetings by Elliott Abrams and his deputies.

Judge Abraham Sofaer, the State Department's legal advisor, told us that he had raised questions, at a White House meeting with the president's counsel Peter Wallison, about William Casey's proposed congressional testimony on the arms sales to Iran. NSC counsel Paul Thompson had refused to divulge the facts to Wallison, Sofaer, and several other government attorneys. Poindexter had then invited Sofaer and Michael Armacost to his office for a briefing, but would not give Sofaer a copy of the chronology that was being developed. Sofaer felt certain that he had not been told the full story.

According to John Richardson, Meese's chief of staff, the attorney general's fact-finding exercise in November 1986 had been precipitated by Sofaer's dissatisfaction. Richardson characterized the undertaking as a review designed to assess the president's political liability, not as a criminal investigation.

During the spring of 1987, I had concluded that Meese might have been a major player, not as the attorney general but as the president's former counselor. We had thought of Meese's November 1986 activities as professionally sloppy, but not until almost five years later—when we

finally obtained the cabinet officers' notes discussing his investigation—
did we have evidence that his activities might have been criminal.
Instead, our investigation of the Justice Department's actions had
focused on the delay of certain FBI investigations into gunrunning and
other matters at the request of North or Poindexter.

We had by now developed most of the facts needed to assure us that
Secord, in delivering arms to Iran, had been a government agent, not an
independent middleman entitled to profits. The inflated arms proceeds
constituted U.S. government funds. As a private cutout used to mask
U.S. government activity, Secord had formally bought from the government and sold to Ghorbanifar, who in turn had sold to Iran, but Secord
had never really owned the arms; he had not been free to sell the arms,
except at the direction of the president and those representing him.
When McFarlane held back the second planeload of Hawk spare parts,
for example, Secord could not deliver them even though he had already
received payment from Ghorbanifar and had paid the CIA for them.
The delivery of the arms had been conditioned on the hostages' release,
not on Secord's independent action. Clair George had thought that
Secord was a consultant to NSC; a CIA logistics officer had regarded
Secord as "North's truck driver."

In a June staff conference, we moved from North to Poindexter.
Would we have a case against him as part of the runaway conspiracy?
Chris Mixter and Louise Radin summed up a possible case against him:
First, Poindexter's authorization and supervision of North's activities
was part of a conspiracy to violate the Boland amendments; second,
Poindexter had deceived Congress to conceal North's support of the
Contras and the diversion of proceeds from the arms sales; third,
Poindexter had approved the diversion; fourth, he had lied to Congress
in November 1986 in response to inquiries about the sale of arms to
Iran; and fifth, he had interfered with the Justice Department's investi-
gations into gunrunning and other matters.

As we turned our attention back to the pressure on Capitol Hill, our
knowledge of the facts was substantial enough to frame a comprehensive indictment, but our evidence was still incomplete. To support
charges of embezzlement, for example, we needed the Swiss records and
Swiss authorization for the use of Willard Zucker's testimony, which we
expected to have by September. Technically, a grand jury—unlike a trial
jury—can act on hearsay evidence, but in a case of this public promi-
nence, especially in a case so saturated with deviousness, I was not will-

ing to take a chance on proceeding with hearsay evidence. Moreover, we still had not received all the U.S. government records we had requested, nor had we fully assimilated those in our possession.

Nonetheless, the Boland amendments had clearly been violated. North had not acted alone but in concert with others. A conspiracy to defraud the United States was chargeable, and we had drafts of an indictment ready for presentation. In addition, we had several individual charges against North and some of the people who had acted with him. But if we indicted North now, preventing the congressional committees from taking his testimony, could our investigation survive the inevitable political fracas? If we did not act now and Congress granted immunity to North, could we indict him later? Could the indictment survive? Our dilemma was obvious. The resolution was murky. I thought ruefully of the advice J. Edgar Hoover had given me thirty years earlier when I was the deputy attorney general: "Don't take responsibility unless you can control the situation."

CHAPTER EIGHT

Crossroads

The stage for the Iran-Contra hearings was the cavernous, marble-walled caucus room in the Russell Senate Office Building. In 1954, the chamber was the setting for the hearings that exposed anticommunist Senator Joseph McCarthy as a demagogue. In 1973, it was the backdrop for the Watergate investigation that ended the presidency of Richard Nixon. Although the 1987 production was expected to be less explosive, it required some new props. A single table could not accommodate the eleven senators and fifteen House members on the joint select committees, so a two-tiered dais was built. From its lower level, a pair of short extensions reached toward the witness table.

This design unintentionally created a kind of pit in which witnesses appeared at a disadvantage, almost as victims. The committee members and their aides showed up on television as overbearing rather than dispassionate. Interpreting the scene as it came into their homes, Americans characteristically sided with the people who seemed to be getting less than a fair shake. From the start, the caucus room was an arena for upset victories by underdogs.

The committees' strategists had not foreseen any such role reversal. Most of them were intent on using the hearings to prove a two-pronged theory: first, that members of Ronald Reagan's administration had practiced systematic deception in order to conduct improper (Contra) and unwise (Iran) covert operations; and, second, that the chief offenders had been Oliver North and John Poindexter. This was the rogue-operation analysis promulgated by the White House, endorsed by the Tower Commission, and initially followed by my office.

Some committee members and staff had advocated taking a different tack. They had recommended opening the hearings with presentations by recognized authorities on the history and ground rules of covert operations. An orderly chronological exposition of Iran-Contra would follow, moving from the evasion of the Boland amendments' restrictions against support for the Contras through the arms sales to Iran to the intersection of the two schemes. Underlying this approach was the hypothesis that the need for Contra funds had become the motivating force that had propelled the arms sales well past the point of diminishing human and political returns.

A preliminary staff memorandum outlining this case had won few supporters. Republicans saw it as dangerous conjecture. If it were proved or even made plausible, it could drag the president into the diversion either as a party to the scam or as a hapless pawn, who had been easily manipulated by his advisors. In private and in public, Reagan's defenders countered with the argument that the Democratic majorities in Congress had to share the responsibility for the scandal. The Boland amendments, these observers said, had deprived the president of his rightful control over foreign policy in Central America, thereby endangering national security and forcing the White House to adopt its devious but, under the circumstances, defensible support of the Contras. By abruptly terminating its support, Congress had left the Contras and their families to defend themselves from retaliation by the Sandinistas. Whatever North, Secord, and their colleagues had done, good or bad, had prevented a massacre.

The muffled internal argument about the hearings' approach had become moot when Richard Secord agreed that if he could be the lead-off witness, he would testify without a grant of immunity. Persuaded that the hearings needed a dramatic start that would capture public attention, the committees opted to open with a headline act—Secord followed by Robert McFarlane. Although the decision served to paper over the partisan differences among the committee members, the committees lost the chance to tell the complicated Iran-Contra tale in a coherent manner. It was as though a criminal trial were commenced by hearing the defendant's case before the prosecution offered any proof of guilt. In a trial, jurors must promise to withhold judgment until they have heard the entire case. The public audience watching the hearings on television made no such commitment.

I did not watch or listen to the hearings during the day, but I watched the evening reruns of testimony by witnesses who had not been granted immunity. Knowing that I would not be able to listen to much of the proceedings, I had thought out what would be likely to happen and the effect it would have on our work. The elementary problem both for a trial and for the hearings would be the devotion that many of the witnesses felt for North. They would become his character witnesses.

Only hints of the internal tension emerged in the public statements each member of the select committee made at the opening session on the morning of May 5. Far more apparent was the degree to which most seemed to have already reached firm judgments on the nature and meaning of the Iran-Contra affair. Senate committee chairman Daniel Inouye, for instance, led off with a condemnation of "secret policymaking" that used "irregular channels and private parties accountable to no one on matters of national security." Vice chairman Warren Rudman called the scandal "an inexcusable fiasco of the first order." House committee chairman Lee Hamilton, echoing the Tower Commission's report, spoke of actions taken "without authority," of "checks and balances . . . ignored," and of "established procedures circumvented."

Only House Republicans raised the issue of the Boland amendments as having induced executive misconduct. "One important question to be asked," said ranking minority member Dick Cheney, "is to what extent did the lack of a clear-cut policy by the Congress contribute to the events we will be exploring." Illinois conservative Henry Hyde took up the same theme more bluntly, characterizing the Boland amendments as an unconstitutional effort to "bind and gag" the executive branch. Republican Senator William S. Cohen came closer to defining a bipartisan consensus. Predicting that the hearings would not serve "as a brass band parade or a funeral march," he said they "will help determine whether the administration's moral zeal obscured its collective judgment and . . . led some individuals into the zone of lawlessness."

These essentially ceremonial statements amounted to a polite and politic cover for the one strategy on which most committee members could agree: to discredit Oliver North well before he took the stand and thus ensure that he would bear the lion's share of blame. Instead of calling senior officials to explain the policy rationales for the sub rosa funding of the Contras and the secret negotiations with Iran, the committees followed Secord and McFarlane with a parade of witnesses, many of them minor figures, whose testimony would impeach the probity of Oliver North. The plan reflected the conventional wisdom. It ruffled no partisan feathers. It would yield a detailed explanation of what had gone wrong and—the crucial point—would give the American people an identifiable villain to blame.

The plan ran into immediate trouble. Richard Secord dominated the afternoon session and the next two days, painting a rosy self-portrait of a patriot who had been summoned to arduous duty and was proud of the service he had rendered. In civilian clothes, he nevertheless was commanding. Admitting that he, Albert Hakim, and Thomas Clines had profited from their work as arms brokers to the Contras, Secord defended their markups as legitimate business practices. "This was a strictly commercial kind of transaction," he testified. "There was nothing spooky about it, . . . just a normal brokering deal."

Secord also strongly denied having taken any profits at all from the dealings with Iran, and the committees lacked sufficient familiarity with the detailed financial documentation to disprove him. From the beginning of his involvement, Secord insisted, he had seen his actions as honorable, authorized, and advantageous to the United States; only at the end, when he confronted North over the drafting of a false narrative of the 1985 Hawk shipment, had Secord perceived impropriety.

Supporting Secord's claims was the message North had sent him over McFarlane's signature (but without McFarlane's knowledge) on November 19, 1985, asking for Secord's "discrete [sic] assistance . . . in support of our national interests" to help arrange the transshipment of "sensitive matériel being shipped from Israel." Secord told the committees that North had described the problem of moving the Hawk missiles through a West European country as an operation "sanctioned by the United States." It had been an assurance Secord said he had had no reason to doubt, particularly after Poindexter called Secord to the White House in mid-January 1986 to ask him to be the U.S. agent for the presidentially approved sale of TOW missiles to Iran.

As for the overpricing of those arms and the use of the surplus funds in Central America, Secord testified that he had had good grounds for believing that the diversion had been approved at the highest level. On one occasion, Oliver North had confided that the president had savored the irony of using the Ayatollah Ruhollah Khomeini's money to support the Contras. According to Secord, North had not told this story of a supposed conversation with Reagan "in a way that I took it as a joke."

The leadoff witness proved to be tougher than the committees had expected. Guided through his account by neutral questioning from John Nields and then harshly challenged on his financial dealings by Arthur Liman, Secord was generally confident and forceful in both phases of his testimony. His military bearing and assurance impressed television viewers favorably, whereas Liman's confrontational manner drew thousands of messages of protest, some of them anti-Semitic and laced with mean-spirited references to Liman's New York City background.

One key issue in dispute was the ownership of the funds generated by the arms sales to Iran. On that point, Secord was obdurate in his assertion that the money belonged to his and Hakim's Enterprise. The decision to spend some of it on behalf of the Contras had amounted, he claimed, to a charitable gesture by Hakim.

This basic contention, which Liman failed to shake, seemed to enrage Warren Rudman. When Secord suggested on his last day of testimony that most of the approximately $8 million frozen in Switzerland could be converted into a fund honoring William Casey for the benefit of Nicaraguan insurgents, the New Hampshire Republican angrily told Secord that he had no "right to send that money anywhere. That money belongs to the people of the United States." In comments to reporters, Rudman added a condemnation of people who "wrapped themselves in the flag and go around spitting on the Constitution."

If Rudman saw Secord in that light, however, the public did not. Deceived in part by Hakim, who had withheld some of his own financial documents, and lacking some of the Swiss bank records that might have served to show up Secord as a profiteer, the committees appeared to the television audience as "hostile, belligerent, pompous, patronizing, or unpatriotic." Secord not only scored a personal public relations victory, he forced the investigators to begin the Iran-Contra story in the middle. The narrative never really got back on track.

As the next witness, Robert McFarlane might have restored a measure of coherence, but his testimony was already well known from his public appearance before the House foreign affairs committee in December and from extensive published excerpts of his discussions with the Tower Commission. Perhaps because he had told his story so many times, McFarlane's performance in the caucus room was notably undramatic. Nevertheless, he presented the accepted portrayal of Ronald Reagan as remote and uninvolved.

Sometime in the spring or summer of 1984, as Congress was moving to cut all official ties to the Nicaraguan exiles, the president had directed McFarlane to mount a rescue effort with the staff of the National Security Council. In McFarlane's telling, he was to gain "the good graces of Congress and the American people" for the Contras and, until funding was restored, "to help them hold body and soul together." McFarlane said that although he had believed that the Boland amendments ruled out the NSC's playing an active role in supporting the Contras, the president had "had a far more liberal interpretation" of the law.

Slowly reading his opening statement, McFarlane went on: "The president had made clear that he wanted the job done. The net result was that the job fell to the National Security Council staff. I think it is fair to say that this occurrence was not an example of an NSC staff eagerly grabbing power from other departments and agencies. In the case of the Contra operations, it was the NSC that was the agency of last resort."

Asked later why he had not tried to dissuade Reagan, McFarlane admitted "not having the guts to stand up and tell the president that. To tell you the truth," he continued, "probably the reason I didn't is because if I had done that, Bill Casey, Jeane Kirkpatrick, and Cap Weinberger would have said I was some kind of commie."

McFarlane had kept the president informed and had sometimes turned to him for help. When the Honduran military seized a shipment of Chinese-made ground-to-air missiles meant for Contra stockpiles, for example, McFarlane had persuaded Reagan to call President Roberto Suazo in Tegucigalpa and ask that the arms be released. After Suazo's successful intervention, McFarlane had recommended a $75 million program of economic assistance to Honduras.

Discussing the early stages of the arms trade with Iran, McFarlane portrayed a decisive and determined president. In August 1985, said McFarlane, a few days after Weinberger and Shultz told the president that they opposed breaching the weapons embargo, Reagan had called McFarlane to authorize a modest Israeli sale of TOW missiles. The president had hedged his instructions with remarkable precision: The purchases must not tip the scales in the conflict between Iran and Iraq or fall into the hands of terrorists.

McFarlane recalled Reagan's frustration and disappointment at having to suspend the sales in early December 1985 and his unwillingness to abandon the effort for good. Asking "why couldn't we let Israel manage the program," the president had been, according to McFarlane, "searching for . . . ways to keep alive the hope for getting the hostages back." Reagan "was profoundly concerned for the hostages."

Other than these glimpses of the president's commitment to the two elements of the Iran-Contra operation, McFarlane's testimony consisted largely of admiring descriptions of the central role played by Oliver North. The witness's warmest encomium to his junior had come in an exchange of PROF messages on February 27, 1986. With typical overconfidence, North had forecast "that we may well be on the verge of a major breakthrough—not only on the hostages/terrorism but on the relationship as a whole." He had asked McFarlane to hold himself ready for an imminent meeting in Iran. (This was the meeting that had finally occurred in May, producing more of a breakdown than a breakthrough.)

"Roger Ollie. Well done," McFarlane had promptly replied to North's message. "If the world only knew how many times you have kept a semblance of integrity and gumption to U.S. policy, they would make you secretary of state." In response to questions from committee members, McFarlane stepped back from that praise, but not far. Without condemning any of North's actions, McFarlane admitted that North had exceeded orders and the Boland amendments' limits by transmitting CIA intelligence about the location of Sandinista helicopters to the Contras. McFarlane also said that, while in Tehran, North had actually violated an order of McFarlane's by directing that the plane carrying the second shipment of Hawk parts fly to the Iranian capital before any agreement on the release of hostages had been reached. Angrily countermanding North's instructions, McFarlane had been "upset" with his subordinate, "very abrupt with him, and short."

For most of their professional relationship, however, McFarlane had treated North with fond respect for his energy and dedication. Like many of North's associates who appeared in the caucus room, or in the Rayburn House Office Building hearing room where the select committees sat on alternate weeks, McFarlane saw flaws in his aide's conduct but none in his character.

As the committees discovered, even those witnesses who testified to North's disregard for legal restraints were ready to defend his actions as having been justified by a higher cause. Gaston Sigur, who had been recruited to help in the search for Contra-support funds from Asian governments, for example, said that North had assured him that the activity was legal. "I had no reason to doubt Ollie at all," Sigur told the committees' lawyers. "Everybody knew, at least I thought, that on matters involving this area Ollie spoke for McFarlane."

Robert Owen, North's secret liaison to the Contra leaders, had given himself the code name "TC" ("The Courier") and had taken to addressing North as "The Hammer," "Steelhammer," or "Blood and Guts." Owen conceded that working for North had involved "walking a very thin line" between legitimate and suspect conduct. Still, he told the committees, he had felt protected from a fall, because he had been "working for—or working with . . . someone who had access to the president of the United States."

Following Owen in the witness chair, Adolfo Calero was also ready to give Oliver North the benefit of every doubt. Full of gratitude for North's help to the Contras, Calero said he had responded willingly when North later asked for funds to be used to win the release of U.S. hostages in Lebanon. Over time, Calero had provided North with blank traveler's checks worth more than $90,000. "I gave the money," Calero explained, "for a worthy effort which I considered was one and the same with our own effort."

His judgment was not shaken when committee counsel used a set of outsize charts—a graphic aid for the television audience—to show him some of the uses to which North had put $4,300 of the Contras' donation. Among the expenditures had been a $1,000 wedding gift to Robert Owen, $50 for groceries at Giant Food, $60 to Fawn Hall, and other payments for dry cleaning, clothing, and snow tires. Calero replied with assurance that North would be able to explain these outlays.

I could not watch any of the testimony of the next witness, Albert Hakim, because he had been compelled to testify under a grant of immunity. As I learned much later, however, his testimony was about what I would have expected. He added to the chorus of praise with his tribute to North as a man who "works around the clock . . . [and] doesn't care about when he eats or he does eat or he doesn't." His "love" for North, for North's "love for his country," and for "so much sincerity," Hakim claimed, was what had impelled him to transfer $200,000 on May 20, 1986, into the "B. Button" account over which Willard Zucker had held fiduciary power. Conceding that he had only met North once before setting up this "insurance coverage," and that Secord had persuaded him to lower the amount from $500,000, Hakim scorned Liman's description of the transaction as a kickback. After all, Hakim countered, he had never told North about the fund, and North had never received any of the money.

Hakim did confirm that he had sent Zucker to meet Betsy North in Philadelphia, and that Zucker, at his urging, had later explored the possibility of getting a Washington-area real estate developer to give Mrs. North a job for which Hakim would provide the compensation. Hakim said that, speaking for himself and Secord, he had once promised Oliver North that "as long as one of us is alive, you need not worry about your family." But, Hakim added, the money had never been touched. "I put a wheel in motion," he said, "and then if North's family wanted to open the door . . . they could." According to Hakim, however, they had not done so.

Hakim's early-June testimony on the finances of the Enterprise and the share in them that he had set aside for Oliver North did serve to deepen the impression that North had fallen in with some very shady operators. More egregious, but less remarked, was the disclosure that when Eugene Hasenfus was captured in Nicaragua, North had left a negotiating session with the Iranians in Frankfurt and had given Hakim and Secord his proxy to speak for the United States. Secord had then had to go to Brussels for a business meeting, and George Cave had also departed, leaving Hakim to deal with the Iranians on his own.

"Did you feel like you had been the secretary of state for a day?" Arthur Liman asked.

"I would not accept that position for any money in the world, sir," Hakim answered. "I have it better than the secretary. . . . I can achieve more, too." Among the things he had hoped to achieve, Hakim acknowledged, were "many millions" of dollars in earnings for the arms-brokerage business he and Secord had contemplated. "I had enough imagination and self-confidence," he testified, "that somewhere along the line . . . I would be making a bundle of money."

Whatever his motive, Hakim had made extraordinary concessions to the Iranians. He had dropped the U.S. demand that all hostages be released and had settled for a promise that one captive would definitely be freed and that "all effective possible effort" would be made to liberate a second.

Hakim had also unilaterally reversed proclaimed U.S. antiterrorism policy. Bowing to a demand that the Iranians had been pressing in vain from their earliest indirect overtures to U.S. officials, Hakim had pledged to "provide a plan for the release" of seventeen terrorists held in Kuwaiti prisons since December 1983. These members of al-Da'wa al-Islamiya (the Islamic Call), an extremist group based in Lebanon and backed by Iran, had been convicted of setting off six bombs in Kuwait City over a ninety-minute period, killing five people and injuring eighty-six more. Among their targets had been the U.S. embassy in Kuwait. American diplomats, praising Kuwait for its tough stand against terror-ism, had always refused to consider swapping the freedom of innocent U.S. citizens in Lebanon for the release of the Da'wa bombers.

North, Hakim testified, had endorsed the agreement and advised him that President Reagan had given his approval as well. According to Hakim, North had particularly liked the deadline that the accord had set for the arms-for-hostages swap: If the timetable was met, a U.S. hostage would be freed by election day, a date that North said was important to the president.

Committee members found Hakim's insensitivity appalling. Some wondered how North could have trusted him with such authority, much less backed his abuse of it. Some of them jokingly called North the first five-star lieutenant colonel in military history.

The next public revelation came from one of North's most devoted admirers, Fawn Hall, who described the shredding party that had begun on the day in November 1986 when North learned of the attorney general's inquiry. North had first asked her to retype five NSC documents written in 1984 and 1985 dealing with his Contra-support activities and to incorporate his handwritten changes into new versions that would then be filed in place of the originals. The request had made her uneasy, but she had assumed "there was a solid and very valid reason.... Sometimes," she told House Majority Leader Thomas Foley, "you have to go above the written law."

Early that evening, she said, she had put aside her retyping work to help North remove a large stack of documents from his safe and feed them into the office shredder. Four days later, after NSC officials ordered that the contents of North's office not be disturbed, she had spotted the originals of the documents on his desk. She described how she had smuggled them out of the building in the company of North and his attorney.

"Just what were you trying to protect?" Senator Rudman asked.

"I was protecting the initiative," Hall replied.

"From whom?"

"From everyone, because I felt that I knew that we were trying to get back the hostages, and I knew we were dealing with Iranian moderates, and if this is exposed, there would be people whose lives would be lost...."

"Did you know," the senator pressed on, "that it was the White House personnel ... standing in the office barring people from leaving? You did know that?"

"I knew it was an NSC official, yes."

"It wasn't the KGB that was coming, Ms. Hall," Rudman concluded. "It was the FBI."

Instead of shocking the television audience into a realization that North had attempted to conceal and distort the record, Fawn Hall's testimony earned her public sympathy. Rudman and his colleagues, in contrast, earned angry letters and telephone calls rebuking them for browbeating a young woman who had just been doing her job.

Working in the Manhattan office that the FBI had lent us, Audrey Strauss had meticulously reviewed the history of criminal cases brought against defendants who had testified under grants of use immunity. She had convinced me that we had only one hope of trying Iran-Contra figures who had been given such immunity. At the very outset of the proceedings against them, we would have to convince a judge that the grand jury had not been tainted; that our case would make no use of immunized testimony either as direct evidence or as leads to evidence; and that the judge could safely proceed without questioning our witnesses before trial to ensure that their testimony would not be tainted.

As proof, we had continued putting the information we had gathered under seal before the immunized witnesses testified at the congressional hearings; this would let us show the court that we had independently gathered our facts. For the twenty-three grand jurors, the blackout had to be almost total. During the hearings, they had to give up all electronic news and read only the newspaper sections covering local news, sports, and features—unless family members had excised all the Iran-Contra articles from the national sections.

We would also have to prove that no prosecutor had knowledge of the testimony. Associate counsel and I could read Iran-Contra stories once they had been censored to blot out references to immunized testimony. We could listen to radio or television newscasts, but the moment they touched on a forbidden subject—a subject that might reflect the testimony of an immunized witness—we were to turn the sound off. The phrase "Swiss bank records" or any reference to the financial activities of Secord and Hakim, for instance, was a verbal fire alarm, because Hakim, as part of his bargain with Congress, was under a grant of immunity to hand over Enterprise records. This meant listening with the volume control or mute button always in hand.

If we did accidentally expose ourselves, we were to report the incident by memorandum to John Douglass, either in Richmond or during one of his visits to Washington. No longer able to give us much of his time, John would be our confessor and our judge, with the authority to decide whether the taint was serious enough to disqualify a lawyer from further participation in an investigation. Although there were some close calls, no one was sidelined. I appointed a New York attorney who had no connection with our work to follow the hearings, immunized testimony included, to let me know whether our investigation had been discredited or whether it was critical that I taint myself in order to hear some testimony.

On May 29, I sent another memorandum on congressional immunity to the House and Senate select committees. On June 3, Bob Shwartz and I had lunch with the committee members in the Capitol. As they started on their sandwiches, I urged that they deny immunity to North and offer him an opportunity to give a public explanation of his activities. This would give North a forum to address the public and would discharge the committees' obligation to let the public hear North if he was willing to talk. I asked the committees to defer any decision about immunity for North until after John Poindexter had testified and, if North was given immunity, to defer his public testimony until after the committees had reviewed his private testimony. Senator Rudman assured me that the committees always withheld their decisions on taking public testimony until after they had been briefed on witnesses' private testimony.

Senator George Mitchell asked me whether I really thought the committees could conclude their work without calling North. I acknowledged the pressure the committee members were under, but I expressed the hope that they would defer their decisions on immunity and public testimony as I had requested. The public wanted to hear from North but did not necessarily want the committees to destroy my prosecution.

On June 8, Liman telephoned to recommend that I give Hakim immunity. Hakim would contradict Secord's claim of lack of profit. He would give us the Swiss records and release Zucker as a witness to testify immediately. I did not trust Hakim. Neither Hakim nor his lawyer, Richard Janis, would give us a proffer of testimony on which we could condition the grant of immunity. We did not need Hakim as a witness against Secord. The only question was whether, to accommodate Congress's self-imposed schedule, we would give Hakim immunity to expedite the production of the financial records that we expected to receive from the Swiss courts in September.

The committees by divided vote granted North immunity and then subpoenaed him on June 15.

I could not imagine that the committees would let North come before them on his terms rather than theirs. Yet when Brendan Sullivan, his able and combative attorney, threatened to keep his client off the stand unless Congress agreed that North would testify only once—in private or in public, but not both—the committees capitulated.

Sullivan's June 17 twenty-seven-page letter outlining his demands worked. "Eyeball to eyeball" with Oliver North, Senators Cohen and Mitchell later wrote, the committees "blinked" and "caved in."

Disastrously, they agreed to let North testify without having been first interviewed in private. Although the chairmen accepted other conditions that Sullivan had devised—a thirty-hour limit on the duration of North's testimony, for instance, and a promise not to recall him later—the worst of the self-inflicted damage came from letting North take his chair at the witness table without his having given the committees any commitment, or even any information, about what he would say. Even the greenest trial attorney knows to avoid, if at all possible, calling a witness without knowing what he or she is going to say. Not only did the committees lack prior testimony as a basis for impeachment, but they had given North immunity without any proffer of testimony by which to judge his truthfulness as a witness. The committees had backed away from a court test of Sullivan's demands because the delay of litigation would have thrown off their schedule.

This abject surrender to Sullivan diminished my respect for the committees as a serious investigative force. The scorn my staff and I felt sharpened and embittered the central question I meant to resolve at a staff conference on June 29: whether to indict North and Poindexter and others before they testified. I had made no promise to the committees not to indict before they had heard the testimony of these men, but in light of the committees' willingness to delay North's congressional appearance for ninety days, I had not wanted to be unnecessarily destructive. The chief considerations, however, were our readiness to prosecute and our confidence in the outcome.

We could, of course, prove beyond a reasonable doubt that North had destroyed and altered records during his final hectic days at the National Security Council. We could prove that he had lied to the House intelligence committee. With Glenn Robinette's testimony and documents from Richard Secord's U.S. bank account, we could also show that North had received an illegal gratuity, the $14,000 security system, and had tried to conceal it. And with testimony from McFarlane, Secord, Calero, Spitz Channell, Richard Miller, and others, as well as the copious PROF messages, we had a compelling case showing a conspiracy to conduct a covert action that had defied the will of Congress and had enriched a handful of inside operators. Most of the basic facts were not in dispute. The question was whether there had been criminal intent.

Ours was a house divided. All agreed that we could not charge the theft of government funds—the diversion of the arms sales proceeds—without the Swiss bank records and Zucker's sworn testimony. We were unwilling to proceed on the hearsay statements of his lawyers. The veteran prosecutors (Bob Shwartz, Michael Bromwich, and David Zornow) and the FBI's Danny Coulson continued to oppose any indictment that did not concentrate on the theft of government funds and, if possible, on personal corruption. Those charges, they believed, were the kind that juries could understand. They considered political arguments, the fruit of policy disputes between the president and Congress, to be too confusing for clear presentation in the courtroom. Without the Swiss records, they opposed any indictment. A second faction of former prosecutors (Audrey Strauss and Chris Todd) favored an immediate indictment limited to charges of false statements and obstruction of congressional investigations.

The third faction was headed by Guy Struve and John Keker. Following Struve's blueprint, they favored charging a conspiracy to violate the Boland amendments' prohibitions: a conspiracy to defraud the U.S. government by putting misappropriated government funds, personnel, and property to forbidden use in a secret Central American war. They would add counts charging false statements to congressional committees and the destruction of records.

Because the Boland amendments had barred "entities engaged in intelligence activities" from assisting the Contras, North's management of Project Democracy from his NSC office had violated the law. So had Joseph Fernandez's active participation in the operation while serving as CIA station chief in Costa Rica. And so had the deceptions and other activities practiced by McFarlane and Poindexter. Secord and Hakim had conspired with them.

Struve's theory of the case pulled the separate strands and chief actors together. It was elegant and sophisticated. But as we argued throughout the day about our options, the majority swung against invoking the broad conspiracy charge and favored waiting until the Swiss authorities permitted us to talk directly to Zucker and to use the Swiss financial records as proof of the disposition of the U.S. arms proceeds and of the $200,000 gratuity from Hakim to North.

In our crowded conference room, some of the advocates for delay argued that the Boland amendments were unclear, and that North had obtained an in-house opinion, albeit from an inappropriate lawyer, that NSC activities were exempt. Against a defense that all his activities had been authorized by superior officers, it might be difficult to prove that North's intent had been criminal. Besides, several argued, more evidence was constantly coming in; we had not even been able to absorb what we already had. We should not be stampeded to an indictment we were not ready to try on the assumption that Brendan Sullivan and the courts would let us patch it up later.

Struve's approach had great appeal for me. I respected juries and had been successful in other complex cases. I had never liked the bare obstruction-of-justice charges that some of the attorneys favored. I felt that they had to be appended to some basic charge.

An indictment of North before he testified would be free from immunity problems, but if North, in spite of such an indictment, gave testimony under immunity, we would still have immunity problems at trial, because our trial witnesses would be tainted. If, as a result of indictment, North refused to testify, the committees would be required to proceed in court by charging him with contempt of Congress. That might lead to judicial decisions that expanded the concept of immunity to our disadvantage.

I was also concerned that starting a case now, particularly in the wild political climate I feared would develop from the hearings, might foreclose our progress to a more comprehensive indictment after we received the Swiss records. Although superseding indictments would be permissible, once an indictment had been returned, the grand jury could not be used simply to bolster proof of the crimes already charged. Continued activity by a grand jury exploring further charges is always subject to challenge, specious or otherwise, by a defendant and to review by the courts. Once we put ourselves in the hands of the courts, we would be responding to defense motions and demands that could lead to premature rulings on immunity as well as divert us from completing our investigation. At the same time, our indictment would be under attack in the continuing congressional hearings to which we could not even listen.

Except for Struve, Keker, and two younger lawyers, associate counsel recommended delay. The deciding vote was mine. Ours was, in many ways, a democratic office in which we all spoke our minds, but ultimate authority rested with me. And I reluctantly concluded that we should wait at least until we could question Zucker face to face and see the Swiss bank records.

During college and law-school summer vacations, I had worked as a seaman on oceangoing ships. To qualify for lifeboat certificates, those of us who worked on deck (as distinguished from the "black gang" in the engine room and the stewards) had learned how to beach a loaded lifeboat in heavy surf. Before reaching the breakers, the lifeboat's bow was to be turned to the sea. The oarsmen backed down toward the beach but rowed toward the sea to mount each beach-bound, cresting swell before it broke. The sooner the swell was crossed, the less the danger of swamping or capsizing. The swells carried the boat toward the beach. Now, I found myself instinctively reacting the same way. I could not control the political surf. Although *Time* reporters and photographers gathered material for a "Man of the Week" story about me, I was not about to do anything dazzling or foolhardy. I was going to keep the office afloat and let the seas carry us to what I hoped would be a safe landing.

I recognized that my choice was a fateful one. It meant that North and Poindexter would give their immunized testimony and, in doing so, would win exaggerated protection against *any* use of it for prosecution. But it seemed wiser to accept that setback than to offer to the courts and to the public only fragments of our best case in a political storm that I could not accurately evaluate and certainly could not control. I did not agree with Congress's hurry-up mode. If the select committees destroyed our case, let their responsibility be clear-cut.

In my office, the decision left a bitter taste. "You will regret this day," Struve warned us as he left to fly home to New York. Our grand jurors were similarly disappointed when I told them that the decision toward which we and they had been driving so hard was to be postponed. And I felt a sense of shame in holding off. I have had to ask myself ever since whether I was right. The moment was a crucial one in our investigation, a tide we might well have "taken at the flood" and ridden "on to fortune."

As it was, we continued to prepare our case. We had obtained our minimum objective. We had canned enough evidence, except for the missing Swiss records, to support a comprehensive indictment. As for the Swiss records, we could easily demonstrate that we had already had independent leads and that we had not learned about them for the first time from immunized testimony. We looked to what else we might do to secure our position: Was there anything else we could put in the can? I decided to draft an indictment, based on the evidence as I then knew it, prior to North's testimony. I also drew up an outline of what I thought North's testimony would be, to minimize any claim that the actual testimony had provided new information for us. We decided how to instruct the grand jury.

Then I sent the jurors home for two weeks; my associates also took a breather, a short vacation during which I hoped we could consciously seal ourselves off from the show in the caucus room.

There was, however, no avoiding what became known as Olliemania. In a bravura performance, abetted by aggressive interventions from Brendan Sullivan, a uniformed Oliver North, his chest decorated with six rows of military ribbons, turned the tables on his congressional inquisitors. Overnight, he became what Ronald Reagan had called him eight months before, a national hero.

I had to wait nearly two years before reading his testimony. The core of his defense, as of Fawn Hall's explanation of her actions, was the familiar and discredited philosophy that the end justifies the means. The way North saw it, Congress had deserted the cause of democracy in Central America, and until the senators and representatives came to their senses, the administration had kept the Contras alive and fighting. Rescuing Americans from Middle Eastern terrorists had amounted to a sacred duty, which excused anything the administration might have done, including telling lies, paying ransom, and making secret commitments to those with influence over the kidnappers.

Making a melodrama of this rationale, North argued that in "a dangerous world" he had been required "to weigh in the balance the difference between lives and lies." Repeatedly, he had judged that it was not just necessary, but proper, to lie to Congress, which could not keep secrets; to other executive branch officials, who had to be shielded from the details of covert operations in which they could not or should not take part; and to Iranian negotiators. Any trick that would get the hostages released had been warranted, he said. "I lied every time I met the Iranians."

As a second explanation, North claimed that his actions had been authorized. "I sought approval of my superiors for every one of my actions," he testified. He said he had "assumed" that approval from national security advisors meant "that they had indeed solicited and obtained the approval of the president." McFarlane, North claimed, had known of his fund-raising for the Contras and had worked with him to hide it from Congress. Poindexter had known of the diversion of funds from the arms sales to Contra support and had given the diversion a specific go-ahead three times, leading North to believe that Poindexter "had received authority from the president." Not until November 21,

1986, when North asked Poindexter directly if Reagan had known of the diversion, had the national security advisor suggested that the president had been kept in the dark.

Within a few days, the committee heard Poindexter confirm the thrust, if not all the details, of North's testimony on the diversion. McFarlane, however, took the stand a second time to deny ever having authorized North to ignore the Boland amendments, ever having told North to alter official records, and ever having instructed North to cover up the November 1985 Hawk missile shipment with a fabricated reference to oil-drilling machinery.

The charge North made public against William Casey, who had just died, was electrifying: The old spymaster, a veteran of the World War II Office of Strategic Services, had encouraged North to establish a hidden, privately held fund, financed by proceeds from U.S. arms sales, to support various covert operations that the CIA could not mount. North said that he and Casey had engaged in "several discussions about making what he called off-the-shelf, self-generating activities . . . an ongoing operation" that could provide anticommunist groups the kind of support the Enterprise had delivered to the Contras.

"Why don't you give us a description of what [Casey] . . . meant by pulling something off the shelf?" asked Arthur Liman.

"Director Casey had in mind, as I understood it," North answered, "an overseas entity that was capable of conducting operations or activities of assistance to U.S. foreign policy goals that was a stand-alone."

"Self-financed?"

"That was self-financing, independent of appropriated monies, and capable of conducting activities similar to the ones we had conducted here."

Such a fund available to a few select government officials would give them unaccountable power over some of the most sensitive aspects of national policy. North argued that the executive branch needed to have something of the sort on hand against the day when Congress next failed to measure up in defense of democracy. "We cannot be seen . . . in the world today as walking away and leaving failure in our wake," North testified.

He, Casey, and others had stepped in only because Congress had acted irresponsibly. "I suggest to you," North declared, "that it is the Congress which must accept the blame in the Nicaraguan freedom-fighting matter, plain and simple. You are to blame because of the fickle, vacillating, unpredictable, on-again, off-again policy toward the resistance."

At another moment in the hearings, he put his argument in emotional, personal terms. "Hang whatever you want around the neck of Oliver North. . . . But for the love of God and the love of this nation, don't hang around Ollie North's neck the cutoff of funds to the Nicaraguan resistance again."

Responding, Senator Mitchell remarked on North's "deep devotion to this country" but said, "Please remember that others share that devotion, and recognize that it is possible for an American to disagree with you on aid to the Contras and still love God and still love this country just as much as you do. . . . Although he's regularly asked to do so, God does not take sides in American politics. And in America, disagreement with the policies of the government is not evidence of lack of patriotism."

But Mitchell's eloquence, even he admitted, did not dent "Ollie North's image a bit." By the time Mitchell made his point, the marine and his image had achieved overwhelming popularity. North's military bearing, the look of sincere conviction in his frequently moist gray eyes, the apparent candor of his admissions—all these factors and more—evoked a near tidal wave of public support. Tens of thousands of telegrams poured onto Capitol Hill. Brendan Sullivan began to stack piles of them on the witness table, challenging the committee members "to listen to the American people. . . . Two thousand telegrams . . . came in this morning. The American people have spoken."

Sullivan, who had taken a bellicose stance from the start, drew some of that support to himself. At one point during Arthur Liman's questioning, Sullivan challenged chairman Inouye to accord his client "plain fairness" and rule a hypothetical question out of order. "Let the witness object, if he wants to," Inouye at length replied. "Well, sir," said Sullivan, "I'm not a potted plant. I'm here as the lawyer. That's my job." After that exchange, Sullivan's law firm received dozens of potted plants.

The witness had a well-prepared response to every question. Hakim's "B. Button" fund? North knew nothing about it. His personal use of the traveler's checks? They were just his way of reimbursing himself for outlays he had made from his monthly paycheck for the Contras. Asked whether he knew that Secord had paid for the security system at the Norths' home, North ignored the question and asserted that his life had been threatened by Abu Nidal, "the principal, foremost assassin in the world today . . . a brutal murderer." Abu Nidal's terrorists, he added, were the ones who had gunned down "eleven-year-old American Natasha Simpson" in the Rome airport, "deliberately zeroed in and fired an extra burst at her head, just in case. Gentlemen, I have an eleven-year-old daughter, not perhaps a whole lot different than Natasha Simpson."

North went on to say, "If it was General Secord who paid the bill, . . . you guys ought to write him a check, because the government should have done it to begin with." As to the backdated correspondence with Robinette, North admitted to "probably the grossest misjudgment that I have made in my life," but justified his lapse on the grounds that the actual record of the transaction "just didn't look right."

Committee counsel and members did not inquire further. Indeed, after his third day of testimony, North heard more speeches than questions. The House committee's Republican counsel used some of his time, for instance, to ask about North's combat record in Vietnam, his two Purple Hearts, his Bronze Star, and his Silver Star for "conspicuous gallantry and intrepidity in battle."

Two weeks before North's apotheosis, Representative Bill McCollum, a Florida Republican, had said that North, Casey, McFarlane, and Poindexter "may well" have committed a crime and "certainly one of the highest acts of insubordination and one of the most treacherous things that has ever occurred to a president." By North's seventh day in the caucus room, McCollum had apparently changed his mind. "You have been a dedicated, patriotic soldier," he told North, "and . . . you've gone above and beyond—on many occasions—the call of duty. For that, . . . I know the country is grateful."

Briefly interrupting the chorus of praise, Warren Rudman, who had supported the Reagan administration's policy in Central America, offered a mild rebuke of North's attack on the fickleness of Congress. By an opinion-poll margin of 74 percent to 22 percent, Rudman noted, Americans opposed aid to the Contras. "This Congress represents the people," he said. "The American people have the constitutional right to be wrong."

More typical of the committee Republicans was Utah's Orrin Hatch. He managed to applaud the diversion of funds as a "neat idea," using North's own words; to admit that the diversion had been improper; and to credit North with having been "at least well motivated" in wanting to help the Contras, whom Congress had let down. Finally, Hatch came to the point. "I don't want you prosecuted," he proclaimed. "I don't. I don't think many people in America do. And I think there's going to be one lot of hell raised if you are. That doesn't mean they won't. It doesn't mean that sticklers in the law won't pursue the last pound of flesh, but I'll tell you, I don't want you prosecuted."

I neither saw nor heard North's performance, but even home in Oklahoma, I could not escape its impact. As I walked Bertie one afternoon, a car pulled to a halt next to us. The lady behind the driver's wheel rolled down her window to say, "I think of you every day. You are having such a run of bad luck." That evening or the next, my daughter Sara, then practicing law in Washington, called to say that she had just begun to realize what a difficult job I had.

Mary reported that a friend had overheard a woman asking their hairdresser for a "Betsy North" cut. Slightly confused about my position, a boyfriend of our teenage daughter, Elizabeth, boasted to me that he had bought the first "North for President" bumper sticker in Oklahoma City. And back in Washington, on a downtown street corner near our office, I found tourists posing for photographs next to a cardboard cutout of Oliver North. A poll of Americans listing the ten most admirable persons in the world placed North in the middle, between President Reagan and the pope.

After North's star turn, the concluding sessions of the congressional hearings could only be anticlimactic. It was left to Poindexter to close the one politically critical question that North had left open: Ronald Reagan's role, if any, in using the Iranians' overpayments to support the Contras' operations. The president, Poindexter said, had been innocent because ignorant. Puffing stolidly on his pipe, the former national security advisor claimed that he had "understood the president's thinking on this. . . . [I]f I had taken it to him, . . . he would have approved it." But Poindexter had recognized that this irregular financing of the fighting in Central America was "a politically volatile issue." Accordingly, he asserted, "I made a very deliberate decision not to ask the president, so that I could insulate him from the decision and provide some future deniability for the president if it ever leaked out."

Delivered in a matter-of-fact tone, his testimony on this point came as no surprise. It simply added explanatory detail to the line that administration officials had taken since Attorney General Edwin Meese had disclosed the diversion eight months before. Nevertheless, the sworn confirmation of the president's noninvolvement seemed to many Washington opinion-makers to close the books on the Iran-Contra investigation and the scandal. As a banner headline in the *Washington Post* proclaimed on July 16, "Poindexter: 'The Buck Stops Here.'"

I should not and would not have seen those words if a hotel waiter had not delivered the paper to my room along with my breakfast. Barely awake, I did not realize what he had put down next to the check that I picked up to sign until after I had read the oversize type. I promptly reported my exposure to immunized testimony to John Douglass, who was keeping the office record of all such incidents, mine being the fourth. Because I had not read beyond the headline, which had simply repeated Poindexter's previous denials, we were able to treat the matter as a close call, not a disqualifying taint.

I may have suffered a private moment of alarm, but the public received Poindexter's embrace of sole responsibility for the diversion with apparent relief. Even though Americans were not convinced that he was telling the truth—a poll published by *U.S. News & World Report* in July found that 57 percent of the people surveyed believed that Reagan had known of the scheme—most seemed ready to let the issue drop. Neither the public nor members of Congress wanted Iran-Contra, like the Watergate scandal, to bring down a president.

As I learned much later, few of the committee members had challenged Poindexter's credibility. On 184 occasions he claimed that he could not remember events or conversations in which he had taken part. He even said he could not recall what he and William Casey had discussed during a two-hour lunch on Saturday, November 22, 1986, the day after both men had given misleading testimony on Capitol Hill and the second day of the attorney general's effort to assemble the facts about the arms sales to Iran.

An admiring superior in the U.S. Navy had once praised Poindexter's "spectacular mental capacity" and ability to "retain fully" and "recall accurately" everything he read. On Capitol Hill, however, Poindexter could not recollect a single one of the five or six memoranda that Oliver North claimed to have sent him in 1986 to spell out the way the funds from the Iranian arms sales were being channeled to the Contras and other covert operations.

Low-key and uncontrite about his deception in concealing North's Contra-support role, Poindexter took the last bit of suspense out of the committees' proceedings when he admitted, "My objective all along was to withhold from the Congress exactly what the NSC staff was doing." Once he left the stand, the major television networks ended their live coverage. George Shultz, Edwin Meese, Donald Regan, and Caspar Weinberger testified, but they revealed nothing they had not already made public. Meese struggled to explain his delay of an FBI investigation after he learned of the conflicting statements of cabinet officers and even after he learned of the diversion. Shultz and Weinberger repeated their opposition to the arms sales and their denials of having participated in them. Shultz was emphatic. Weinberger showed a memory loss almost equal to Poindexter's when answering key questions. Regan essentially reprised his already publicized testimony to the Tower Commission.

One of the notes Shultz had provided to the committees described the November 22, 1986 meeting at which he had told Meese that President Reagan had admitted having known of the November 1985 Hawk shipment in advance. Meese had tried to override Shultz. Although Shultz's staff had prepared him to answer questions about this meeting, nobody at the hearings asked him about it.

Meese's explanation of his three-day fact-finding investigation was so unconvincing that Senator Rudman characterized it as "a case of gross incompetence." Added Rudman, "I guess it's better to be dumb than crooked." In a way, that judgment summed up the capital's thinking, or wishful thinking, about all of Iran-Contra. The president had committed not a crime but a regrettable lapse or, in NBC commentator John Chancellor's words, a "sin of inattention."

CHAPTER NINE

The Basic Indictment

Once Oliver North and John Poindexter had testified at the congressional hearings on Iran-Contra, the pressure to rush our work subsided. In July 1987, when we returned to the office after our two-week break, we commenced a two-year artificially cloistered existence in which we had to avoid discussing the hearings and, for all practical purposes, discussing our work with anybody but one another. Even sympathetic outsiders could inadvertently taint us. This deepened the isolation inevitable in our strange prosecutorial position and bound us closer together. Associate counsel began having lunches together, now that we had time for lunch. I usually had a sandwich at my desk. I was always available to my associates, but I did not fraternize with them. That had never been my way of working, not even in the days when I was not separated from my colleagues by a generation or more. In fact, I did not socialize at all in Washington, and I spent the weekend back in Oklahoma whenever possible.

Congress's grant of immunity to North and the groundswell of public support for him forced me briefly to consider quitting. For two weeks in Oklahoma and again after the staff reunited in Washington, I pondered whether the likelihood of a sustainable conviction was now so remote that we should quit. No one on the staff suggested this to me. All wanted to continue. I concluded that we had to see the case through. From the beginning, we had assumed that Congress would grant immunity to North. We were satisfied that we had done everything we could to minimize the damage.

No precedent dealt with the public exposure of immunized witnesses, because never before had immunized testimony been broadcast on this scale. The previous cases had involved prosecutorial exposure to testimony given in secret grand jury proceedings or in closed administrative hearings. My deepest concern was that the extraordinary degree to which the public had been exposed to North's testimony might cause the Supreme Court to modify its basic *Kastigar* holding by expanding the scope of the immunity North had received. In federal courts, the immunity granted to individual witnesses in exchange for their testimony prevents only the use of that testimony against them. In many states, witnesses who are forced to testify about particular transactions receive "transactional immunity"—blanket protection for those transactions. In *Kastigar*, the Supreme Court had held that testimonial immunity was an adequate substitute for the constitutional right to remain silent, but that case had dealt with secret testimony, not with testimony that had been heard by millions, including probably every prospective witness in the case and many who would be on the panel from which the jury was to be selected.

Nevertheless, I could not drop a prosecution for fear that the Supreme Court would change a precedent. I had to follow the decided cases as best I could and favor the prosecution when I had no decision to guide me. If my judgment was faulty and the courts reversed a conviction, the law would be clarified and the defendant set free. If I failed to prosecute, there would be no decision; the law would be left in doubt, and I would have backed away from a fair test.

I expected the courts to hold that the effect of exposure to immunized testimony would be a question of fact for evaluation with respect to each witness, rather than that the scale on which the testimony had been broadcast had, in itself, made all the witnesses who had heard North's congressional testimony ineligible to testify against him at trial. We directed the witnesses we interviewed not to tell us anything they had learned from the hearings. Witnesses who felt unable to distinguish what they learned from the immunized testimony and what they had previously known were told not to not answer any question that put them in doubt. Any more complicated effort to probe a witness's mind, we thought, would only heighten the effect of the immunized testimony. Even if the influence of North's testimony on a witness was probed by a tainted lawyer like John Douglass, who would not participate in the subsequent trial, the danger of emphasizing the testimony and making a bad situation worse would be too great. We hoped that the courts would be realistic in applying the doctrine of harmless error, which recognizes that perfection in a trial, as in most human affairs, is rarely attainable, and that technical errors that do not significantly affect the trial may be disregarded.

This left the question whether we could use a witness who, in the course of voluntarily listening to immunized testimony, had revived his own temporarily forgotten recollection. Ordinarily, the law permits a witness who has temporarily forgotten an event or a detail to have his or her memory refreshed by another witness's testimony or by viewing a document. The document—for example, a telephone book—does not itself become evidence, because the witness's refreshed memory exists independently of what refreshed it. But would our calling a witness whose memory had been refreshed during the congressional hearings constitute a forbidden use of the immunized testimony?

We concluded that if, independently of any action by us, listening to immunized testimony refreshed a witness's recollection so that he or she then had an independent recall of an event, the witness could testify to this independent recollection without informing us of any element of the immunized testimony. The witness would simply give his or her own restored recollection and not tell us what North or Poindexter had said. We, of course, would not deliberately use the immunized testimony to refresh recollection.

We knew that the immunization of North, Poindexter, and Albert Hakim would handicap almost every hour of our work. It would hamper our interrogation of witnesses and would be raised repeatedly during pretrial proceedings and at the trial itself. A trial judge who decided in our favor on motions related to the issue of immunity would inevitably worry about the possibility that the rulings would be grounds for reversal on appeal. In an effort to avoid increasing the danger of reversal, a judge might be particularly cautious in these or other rulings.

The congressional immunizations also hindered our ability to deal with an array of hostile witnesses. A prosecutor always hopes to have information that witnesses do not have, to impress on them that the prosecutor's knowledge is broad and deep and that, therefore, they had better not lie. In our case, the witnesses had the advantage. Most of them had heard North's testimony and knew that we had not.

During July, five members of my staff were accidentally exposed to immunized testimony. Only one incident was serious. Paul Thompson, who had falsely denied knowing what had happened to the finding that had retroactively authorized the CIA's assisting the November 1985 Israeli Hawk shipment, rushed in to clear his skirts after Poindexter admitted to the congressional committees that he had destroyed the finding in Thompson's presence. Claiming that his recollection had been refreshed, Thompson insisted on giving one of my associate counsel, Judy Hetherton, information that was based on what he had heard about the deposition Poindexter had given the committees before testifying in public. Hetherton did not relay this information to me or to any member of the staff except Douglass, although she discussed the problem in general terms with Chris Mixter in seeking his advice. She did not work directly on the case against Poindexter. Douglass concluded that she could continue as an associate counsel on other matters and recorded the incident for future disclosure to the trial court.

To some extent, we benefited from the public's disapproval of the congressional committees and their counsel. The public had expected to see blood, but the inflated expectations had not been fulfilled; as often happens, public opinion then turned in favor of the underdog. After the collapse of the congressional committees, the difficulties we faced in dealing with North had become apparent to everyone: Congress had made *us* the underdog.

Opinion actually shifted faster than I had expected. A Harris Survey conducted in mid-August found that although Americans had split evenly a month before over the propriety of North's actions, nearly two-thirds had come to see them as "more wrong than right." A slightly higher proportion (68 percent) said they wanted our investigation to continue, and three-quarters of those polled viewed both North and Poindexter as certainly or probably guilty of lawbreaking.

I again considered becoming tainted to better gauge public reaction and to have the advantage of the congressional testimony in plotting our course. At the time, however, it seemed more important for me to be able to try North and Poindexter or at least to be consulted about these prosecutions, so I decided to avoid taint as long as possible. Davis Polk partner Lowell Gordon Harris, who had no other connection with our office, continued to read the transcript of the congressional hearings and to follow the public reaction in order to warn me if in some way unknown to me our investigation was so jeopardized that I had to taint myself to protect it.

Having decided to continue, I needed to make some sort of public announcement. I had to explain why, despite North's immunity and his apparent public vindication, my work should go on. I considered an interim report to Congress but decided in favor of a speech to the

American Bar Association, which was about to meet. Eugene Thomas, the president of the association, offered me a forum. The opening address to the assembly, the most prominent spot in the program, had already been committed to the chief justice of the United States. The next best spot was the prayer breakfast on Sunday, which marked the midpoint between the meetings of smaller components, such as the board of governors, and the meetings of the larger groups, such as the sections (which dealt with legal specialties) and the house of delegates. That day had usually drawn the highest attendance. It would also offer the best timing for news coverage: On a Sunday in August, I would have little competition for headlines.

Traditionally, addresses made at the prayer breakfast were not sectarian, but they had usually been devoted to serious subjects with moral overtones and had followed readings from the Old Testament and the New Testament. In considering how to approach my address, I thought back to the speeches of the Reverend Robert I. Gannon, S.J., the former president of Fordham University and one of the most eloquent and persuasive advocates of the 1940s. He had always relaxed his audience and had it laughing just before driving home his most important point. I would try to do the same.

At the prayer breakfast, I opened my address by citing the advice Dr. Donald Read, minister of the Madison Avenue Presbyterian Church in New York, had provided at a Law Day sermon: He had urged us to be more like Moses and less like Machiavelli.

My audience laughed.

I moved quickly to the towering figure of Moses—how impossible it was for any of us to be like him; we might as well try to be like Mount Everest. Moses, with his people surrounded by hardship and engulfed in danger, had retreated to a mountain and returned with commandments so simple that every schoolchild could learn them, and yet so profound that they had formed the essence of the legal codes of the Western world.

One of those commandments demanded truth: Thou shalt not bear false witness against thy neighbor. Deep in uncertainties, without even a permanent place to live, Moses and his people had worried about truth: truth, the bridge between faith and knowledge, the basis of all scientific learning; truth, the basis of our system of law for centuries; truth, the basis for the checks and balances prescribed by the Constitution.

I explained that we would proceed in spite of the immunity grants from Congress, and that the popularity of a person would not prevent his prosecution any more than unpopularity would cause us to prose-

cute him. The rule of law was not to be defeated. I recalled for my listeners the Supreme Court's opinion in *United States v. Lee.*[1] During the
bitterest period of the Civil War, the federal government had seized
General Robert E. Lee's estate in Arlington to use as a soldiers' cemetery.
The government had paid no compensation and had denied the Lee
family a hearing. The Supreme Court held that the seizure had been
contrary to law and could not be justified even by the exigencies of the
Civil War. The Court said:

> No man in this country is so high that he is above the law. No officer
> of the law may set that law at defiance, with impunity. All the officers
> of the government, from the highest to the lowest, are creatures of the
> law and are bound to obey it.
>
> It is the only supreme power in our system of government, and every
> man who, by accepting office, participates in its functions, is only the
> more strongly bound to submit to that supremacy, and to observe the
> limitations which it imposes upon the exercise of the authority which
> it gives.

I received a standing ovation, and many came up to congratulate me
on the talk and wish me well in the work I had described to them. The
speech was widely and favorably covered; it was carried on page one in
the major newspapers, sometimes as the lead story. But as I returned to
my hotel shortly after the prayer breakfast, I had run into Supreme
Court Justice Lewis Powell on the steps. He had been in my audience
and had kind words for my speech, but he seemed to want to say something more. I waited, hoping for a bit of wisdom from a lawyer I greatly
admired and the judge who had written the *Kastigar* opinion. But Justice
Powell merely shook his head a little, smiled, and said, "Oh, Ed," before
walking away in silence.

On Wednesday, August 12, Ronald Reagan responded to the congressional hearings in a nationwide television broadcast. I watched with the
remote control in hand to mute any reference to immunized testimony.
The president assumed responsibility for having "let my preoccupation
with the hostages intrude into areas where it didn't belong" and having
been "stubborn in my pursuit of a policy that went astray." He declined
to make excuses: "There's nothing I can say that will make the situation

---

[1] 106 U.S. (16 Otto) 196, 220 (1882).

right." George Shultz and Caspar Weinberger, the president said, had been correct to predict that the plan would be seen as "an arms-for-hostages deal and nothing more."

But North and Poindexter had also been right in "believ[ing] they were doing what I would've wanted done, keeping the democratic resistance alive in Nicaragua." Their mistake, Reagan said, had been to keep the diversion of Iranian payments a secret from him. "Let me put this in capital letters. I did not know about the diversion of funds. Indeed, I didn't know there were excess funds." He implied that the wrongdoing had been Poindexter's: "No president should ever be protected from the truth. No operation is so secret that it must be kept from the commander in chief. I had the right, the obligation, to make my own decision." Reagan said that the biggest "lesson" was that the White House and Congress must regain trust in each other.

Although he professed to have been as "mad as a hornet," he did not look angry; he looked rueful. I woke up in the middle of the night, as I sometimes did, picked up my pen and notebook, and moved to a coffee table in front of the living-room sofa to outline my thoughts. I believed that the president had been transparently insincere and had attempted to brush off the American people. I had been skeptical that neither Poindexter nor William Casey had disclosed the diversion to the president. My skepticism now deepened to conviction. When claiming not to have known about the excess proceeds from the arms sales, Reagan had flashed a wry smile, with no hint of indignation. Earlier, he had said that Poindexter had withheld the fact of the diversion to protect him. He had then stated that Poindexter was an "honorable man," in spite of his deceit and excesses.

I thought about Donald Regan's early statement to the FBI that Poindexter had claimed to have failed to stop North's diversion "because he felt sorry for the Contras." That did not sound like Poindexter. He did not do anything because he felt sorry for people. The president's "acknowledgment" of a "stubborn" adherence to erroneous policy treated the diversion as a mere unknown detail of a known policy, not as a crime. I concluded that Poindexter or Casey must have informed the president of the interrelationship in some way, however veiled. After Robert McFarlane's humiliation and the failure of his mission to Tehran, after nine months had passed without the release of a single hostage, Poindexter had recommended that the president authorize the resumption of the delivery of Hawk spare parts. What reason could Poindexter have given the president except that the operation somehow supported the Contras?

This simply confirmed my opposition to a fragmentary indictment and my determination to seek a comprehensive indictment based on the inter-locked conspiracies to resupply the Contras, trade arms for hostages, and deceive Congress. Our ongoing investigation consistently strengthened this position. There was no longer any point in rushing to a partial indict-ment. North had overpowered the congressional committees in their haste. He had apparently defused the venal personal charges—his accep-tance of the home-security system and the misuse of Adolfo Calero's trav-eler's checks—with which I assumed the congressional committees had confronted him. I felt certain that we could get a conviction from a jury on these counts, but only if we could append them to a broader charge that would give the jury a full picture of his misconduct.

The weakness of our case was the lack of a true central figure other than North. The two possible lines of evidence against President Reagan had both been blocked, one by Casey's death and the other by Poindexter's denials. Accordingly, the case that I thought best fit the facts would be against not just one person but a group of conspirators. Poindexter and possibly McFarlane would appear as the senior figures, North as the most exposed government official, and Richard Secord and Albert Hakim as the principal financial beneficiaries. Others on the staffs of the National Security Council, the CIA, and the State Department appeared to have played supporting roles.

The lawyers who had been with me longest and on whom I had relied the most were assigned to this case, divided by subject matter: the Contra-supply operation, the diversion, and the obstruction of congres-sional inquiry. The team would have to convey to a lay jury an exact understanding of the procedural limitations on the president's power to launch covert activities, whether to supply the Contras or to ransom the hostages.

We expected the defendants, particularly North, to claim authoriza-tion and lack of criminal intent. Our legal research and factual investi-gation had to focus on both. I was concerned that, even from the grave, Casey might prove a central figure in the defense. Because he was no longer around to speak for himself, North and other defendants could easily claim that Casey had authorized what they had done. The ques-tion would become whether, as director of central intelligence, Casey had had the power to authorize the activities of North and others in furtherance of what they believed to be the president's wishes.

Tactically, we needed a credible, storytelling witness. At the moment, we had none. North would have been ideal, but he had refused to give a proffer even in return for immunity. Riding high after his congressional testimony, he seemed out of reach. Secord would not be an attractive witness against North because he had heavily shared in the proceeds of the sale of arms to Iran and had then lied to Congress about it. Poindexter would never talk. McFarlane might be available, but using him would present the unattractive picture of a superior testifying against a junior officer whom he had permitted or invited to get out of hand.

Like a storm gathering on the horizon—a storm I did not want to look at—the near hopelessness of conducting a prosecution so heavily dependent on classified secret information was for the moment brushed aside. We had not worried much about it because there was little we could do to avoid it. There were no satisfactory alternate routes of evidence. The immunity problem was much more immediate and had been a live issue.

With that issue already framed, classified information problems now drew our attention and over the next year almost took control of our progress. That summer, Lord Rawlinson, a former attorney general of England and Wales who had been the chairman of the Bar Council of England and Wales when I was the president of the American Bar Association, had lunch with me in Washington. With the directness of an English barrister, he put his finger on the issue: How could we hope to prosecute high-ranking individuals in the national security area? When I explained that we simply intended to do the best we could, he just shook his head, very much as Justice Powell had done.

The departments and agencies concerned with national security had absolute control over the classified information we needed. One of the two powers of the attorney general that had been withheld by statute from independent counsel was the power to reject the agencies' claims of the necessity of continued secrecy. Attorney General Edwin Meese and his successor, Richard Thornburgh, were the only ones who could protect my prosecution from the excessive, self-protective classification of information. The law did not provide for court review, even though these agencies were, in a very real sense, subjects of our investigation.

On August 19, 1987, we learned that the highest Swiss court had affirmed the Swiss Federal Office for Police Matters decision to release the financial documents of the Secord-Hakim corporations, their banks, and Willard Zucker's Compagnie de Services Fiduciaires. The court characterized Hakim's appeal as "frivolous." On September 1, we were told that all the Swiss documents had been collected by the magistrate in Geneva.

Meanwhile, Hakim and Manucher Ghorbanifar had also filed independent, parallel appeals in the cantonal court (roughly comparable to a state court). Theoretically, though it was unlikely, the cantonal court could assert jurisdiction and reach a different decision from that of the federal court. We were told to expect a decision by September 14. Hakim had also requested that an advisory commission, a temporary national agency, be appointed by the Swiss governing body to consider the national policy aspects of the release of the financial records. This request was unlikely to be granted, but if it was, the commission could take several months to reach a decision.

On September 21, the cantonal appeals were decided in our favor. Associate counsel Vicki Been was on her way to Switzerland to collect the records. On September 29, she reported that the Geneva magistrate, a protégé of Hakim's Swiss lawyer, was holding back the Swiss bank documents. The magistrate continued to withhold the records through the month of October. He then decided to permit Hakim and his attorney to review all the documents before giving them to the Federal Office for Police Matters for transfer to us.

Our collection of records from the U.S. government was now steadily progressing, but we had some troubles, centered in the CIA. By September 1, the CIA had produced fifty thousand documents, only about a quarter of what we had requested. We knew, for example, that as chief of the CIA's Central American task force, Alan Fiers had prepared a basic policy paper in 1984, but the CIA had not produced it. The CIA's legal staff was partly decentralized, in that its various units had their own lawyers. This weakened the control of the agency's general counsel. It also meant that lawyers loyal to Clair George and other subjects of our investigation were sifting the documents to be sent to us. Some twenty or thirty document requests had not been filled. Counsel had slowed down in responding to new requests. There were heavy redactions as well as gaps in production.

I considered serving interrogatories on the CIA and other agencies to require them to specify their procedures to assure the completeness of their production of documents. In the end, however, I decided not to use interrogatories, because they could have been answered on an exculpatory, best-efforts basis, and because the preparation of answers would undoubtedly have been used as an excuse for further delay.

I also considered making a presentation to CIA Director William Webster regarding his agency's dilatory production of documents. We had been friends for thirty years, going back to the day I persuaded him to leave private practice and join Dwight D. Eisenhower's administration as the U.S. attorney in St. Louis. After serving as a federal court of appeals judge, Webster had resigned to become the director of the FBI in the wake of the Watergate scandal. With the exposure of the Iran-Contra activities, President Reagan had appointed him to head the CIA.

Before I had a chance to contact Webster, the CIA replaced its most obstructive lawyer and committed itself to filling all our document requests by February 10, 1988. We hoped to have the material indexed on our computers by March. Webster helpfully agreed to treat our office as a CIA annex and deliver documents to us as though they were still in CIA custody. This reduced the need for the time-consuming preliminary redaction.

The Justice Department turned over a total of 68,494 pages of documents. The department had flooded us with irrelevant documents but had also produced some important records, such as Meese's notebooks from his days as counselor to the president. In addition to documents related to gunrunning investigations, they included the notes of Meese's assistants regarding his November 1986 investigation.

We had already reviewed 75 percent of the four thousand documents provided by the National Security Council. Ralph Sigler, the deputy director of the White House situation room, assured us that he had reviewed all the tape-recorded conversations and that none concerned Iran-Contra. (Presidential conversations were recorded on audiotape only when notes were not taken.) Nor, said Sigler, did any of the tapes contain the voices of McFarlane, Poindexter, or North.

In September and October, while the Geneva magistrate withheld the Swiss financial records, our office was like a becalmed ship. We were doing useful work, but the ship was not sailing, and the crew was restless. The lawyers on my staff had interrupted promising careers for what they perceived as not only an important public service but also an opportunity for litigation experience in a major case. The delay grew increasingly irksome to them, as the weeks passed and the personal cost of their contributions increased. Guy Struve was now unable to give us more than 10 percent of his time. When John Keker had to spend more time in California, Michael Bromwich replaced him as head of the team investigating the role of the CIA.

We used part of this time reviewing and trying to assimilate the CIA documents that we already had, sorting out those that we would probably introduce as exhibits at trial, those that provided leads for further investigation, those that the defense might request as exculpatory, and those that were useless. First, each document had to be read, primarily by lawyers, and color-tagged according to its category. Then, in order of apparent significance, documents were scanned into our computers for quick recall. Using more than a dozen individuals who had not previously been assigned to CIA matters to read the documents, I was reconciled to our doing an imperfect job; dividing the responsibility among so many readers might allow the absence of a critical document to slip by unnoticed, whereas having two or three people do the job would have allowed us to catch gaps in continuity. The coded wording of CIA documents increased the difficulty. A superficial reading would miss the true content of many of the documents. But we had no alternative, if we were to digest the voluminous material we had accumulated. Although this approach would probably be adequate to prepare us for North's trial, it was far from a thorough investigation of the CIA hierarchy.

During this period, I again considered granting immunity to Hakim. Not only was he the impediment to our getting the Swiss records, but we would run into difficulty prosecuting him if he did not receive top security clearance to examine the classified documents that would constitute much of the evidence surrounding his activities. As a defendant, he would be entitled to review all the documents relevant to his trial; without the proper security clearance, he would be denied this right. Review by his attorney probably would not be an adequate substitute. I asked Bob Shwartz to evaluate once more the strength of our case against Hakim and present his conclusions on November 3. By coincidence, most of the Swiss records we had requested finally became available to us that day. They were delivered to the U.S. embassy in Paris. Shwartz flew there to pick them up and began his interviews with Willard Zucker on November 6.

In five days of interviews, Zucker delivered somewhat less than his attorneys had led us to expect. He confirmed that he had met with Betsy North in Philadelphia; that she had given him the names and birth dates of her four children and talked about their schooling; and that on May 20, 1986, pursuant to Hakim's orders and out of Hakim's share of the Swiss funds, he had established a $200,000 "B. Button" account for the benefit of North's family. But Zucker could not demonstrate that North, whom he had never met, had known the purpose or details of the financial arrangement. On that point, all we had was the text of an April 21 message from Secord to North listing a $200,000 "insurance fund" among a number of the Enterprise's near-term obligations. The bank records showed only that the Button account had been funded and had accrued interest undisturbed. Zucker's notes, though, listed the Norths' home telephone number as that of the fictitious Mrs. Button.

Without question, Hakim had engineered a $200,000 payoff for North, but beyond the fact of North's having sent his wife to meet Zucker in Philadelphia, the evidence provided no compelling proof that North had been a party to the transaction. The long-awaited clincher—proof in simple terms that North had knowingly received a substantial cash payment from the Iranian arms sales proceeds—could not be charged. We could not risk such a prejudicial charge without absolute certainty that we could prove it beyond a reasonable doubt. We could not call Betsy North as a witness, because as Oliver North's spouse she did not have to testify against him. Hakim and Secord, as codefendants, could not be forced to testify, and Zucker, having disappointed us, seemed unlikely to carry the charge under cross-examination. Any suggestion of our having tried to blacken North with such an unproven charge could jeopardize his conviction on the other counts, through an adverse reaction by the jury or an adverse holding by an appellate court.

Although Zucker's answers to some questions disappointed us, he gave us a good deal of insight into the financial manipulations of the Enterprise and its principals. He guided Shwartz through a maze of eleven corporate accounts and ten investment accounts and, with the records as documentation, tracked the distribution of more than $3.1 million that had gone, in equal shares, to Secord and Hakim. Zucker also confirmed the purpose of the account that belonged to a shell company registered in Liberia and called Defex S.A., almost identical to the name of Secord's principal arms supplier in Portugal. Zucker acknowledged that the account's name had been intended to deceive the Contras and any government auditor, who would be led to believe that the transfer of funds to Defex S.A. represented expenses related to the purchase of arms for the Contras although the transfers had actually been profits for Hakim, Secord, and Thomas Clines, their partner in the Contra-supply operation.

The dealings with Iran had been even more lucrative. Gross sales to Iran and Israel had amounted to $30.3 million. Of these proceeds, repayments to the CIA had taken $12.2 million, and transport and related expenses had taken another $2.1 million. Of the remaining $16 million, $7.8 million had still been in Enterprise accounts when the Swiss authorities froze them. The rest of the funds had been spent, with at least $3.6 million going directly to supplies for the Contras and $1.1 million to related activities. Distributions already made to Secord and Hakim in 1986 had come to more than $1.7 million.

The diversion of these proceeds from the U.S. Treasury, as proved by the Swiss accounts and Zucker's testimony, would be the heart of our criminal accusation against the Iran-Contra conspirators. The most comprehensive charge would be that of conspiracy to defraud the United States by using government officials and assets to support the Contras in an unauthorized foreign covert action, at a time when such conduct was forbidden by the Boland amendments and when no government funds had been appropriated for that purpose. A second, slightly narrower set of charges would be the theft of the proceeds of the arms sales to Iran and their diversion from the U.S. Treasury to the Contras and other unauthorized recipients, including Secord and Hakim. (Clines had not been involved in the Iranian deals.) The next narrower unifying charge would be the obstruction of congressional investigations by Poindexter, McFarlane, North, and possibly others. Other charges against individual defendants would include North's acceptance of a gratuity (the home security system) and the giving of it by Hakim and Secord, North's income tax violations through the National Endowment for the Preservation of Liberty, and the individual false statements Poindexter and North had made to congressional committees. Because the Treaty for Mutual Assistance in Criminal Matters between the United States and Switzerland did not permit the use of Swiss financial records in criminal tax prosecutions, tax prosecutions against Secord and Hakim were unlikely.

The charge of obstruction of congressional investigations linked McFarlane, North, and Poindexter, although not all of them had participated in each act of obstruction. During the summer of 1985, McFarlane had twice answered congressional inquiries by denying North's activities in support of the Contras. In part, McFarlane claimed to have relied on North's statements that he had not raised funds. McFarlane, however, had also denied activities that had been included in North's memoranda to him. In the summer of 1986, when two congressional committees, responding to a pending resolution of inquiry, more pointedly raised questions about North's activities, Poindexter had deliberately repeated McFarlane's false disclaimers. North had appeared in person before the House intelligence committee and had falsely denied many of his activities. In November 1986, after the arms sales to Iran were exposed, North, Poindexter, and McFarlane had participated in the preparation of a false chronology to be used as a basis for congressional testimony by Poindexter and William Casey. And McFarlane had withheld information when answering the inquiries on Contra funding by the House foreign affairs committee in December 1986.

The basic question about the diversion charge was whether North, Secord, and Hakim had stolen from the Iranians or from the United States. If only the Iranians had been the victims of a crime, it would certainly not be a crime we wanted to try. We were satisfied that to prove that North and Secord and their co-conspirators had stolen from the United States, we could establish as a matter of law that the arms had been U.S. government property when sold and that the proceeds had therefore been government funds. We would prove that Secord had acted as a government agent and disprove Secord's claim that he had bought and sold the weapons in actuality, as well as in form.

The documents supporting the presidential finding authorizing the sale had described Secord as an agent of the CIA. The CIA was to buy the arms from the Defense Department at cost. Secord was to collect the purchase price from the Iranian broker Ghorbanifar and transmit the funds to the CIA, which was to pay the Defense Department before receiving the arms for delivery. Ordinarily the CIA's review of a prospective new finding before submitting it to the president would have specified the details of the financing, but that procedure had been bypassed. Nevertheless, in meetings convened by Poindexter after the president had signed the finding, Secord had been introduced as a private intermediary who would insulate our government from direct transactions with the Iranians, making him what is known in the trade as a cutout.

Paul Thompson, who had attended part of the organizational meeting, stated that everyone had regarded Secord as just a transporter. Zucker had believed North to be directing the operation from the White House. When the ultimate test of ownership came—the delivery of the second planeload of Hawk spare parts after McFarlane's mission to Iran—Secord, even though he had transmitted Ghorbanifar's payment to the CIA, could not make the delivery until it was released by the U.S. government. This evidence convinced us that Secord had been no more than an agent of the U.S. government and that the proceeds of the Iranian arms sales, less the transportation charges, had been government funds.

The president's finding had authorized only the CIA to carry out the covert operation. There had been no written presidential authorization for the National Security Council's staff to take over the project, as would have been required by the president's standing executive orders. The CIA's Clair George had had the operational responsibility, but he had delegated it to Thomas Twetten, then deputy chief of the CIA's Near Eastern division. Twetten had dealt with, and deferred to, North. Twetten had made no agreement with Secord. North had acted for both the government and the Enterprise.

With CIA officers and Secord helping him, North had coordinated the details of the shipments with U.S. agencies. In 1986, he had been in practical control of the Iranian operation. He had arranged for all funds deposited in the Enterprise accounts, although he had not been a signatory to the accounts. Hakim and Zucker had simply been stakeholders for Secord and North. By not informing the U.S. government officials who had supplied the arms about his secret purpose to accumulate surplus funds for the Enterprise, North had had a conflict of interest as he negotiated with the CIA and the Defense Department for the lowest possible prices.

We also had overwhelming evidence of North's control over the Contra-supply operation. Secord had been the operating officer, the logistics expert, but major decisions had been left to North. Secord and Hakim had been required to check back with North on large purchases and on the movements of their freighter, the *Erria*. Except for the Saudi money, North had been the principal source of funds—both from the private contributions through Spitz Channell and Richard Miller and from the diversion of the proceeds of the sale of arms to Iran. North had dominated the meetings with Calero and the other Contra leaders in Ilopango and Miami to resolve controversies related to the supply operation. North had linked the support of the CIA and the State Department. He had had access to William Casey and Alan Fiers at the CIA and to Elliott Abrams, who had dominated the State Department's policy on Central America.

Our preliminary investigation of the CIA divided into two parts—the CIA headquarters at Langley and the CIA agents in the field in Costa Rica and Honduras. Of the half-dozen major components of the CIA at Langley, we were concerned primarily with the directorate of operations (covert action) and to a lesser extent with the directorate of intelligence. Our two most-hoped-for witnesses, Joseph Fernandez, the station chief in Costa Rica, and Alan Fiers, the chief of the Central American task force (at Langley), refused to testify or give a proffer as a basis for immunity. Without their help, we did not have the evidence to penetrate CIA headquarters.

When we reluctantly gave up our efforts to persuade Fernandez to cooperate, we had no choice but to prosecute him for conspiring with North and Secord and lying about his activities. Fernandez's violations of the Boland prohibitions had been flagrant. He had in fact been a day-in, day-out participant in North's operation. Connected to the secret KL-43 communications system, he had served as the principal intermediary between the Contras' military forces and North's supply group. Fernandez's superiors had warned him to stop working with North and the "private benefactors." Fernandez had lied to the Tower Commission on two occasions. Confronted with KL-43 printouts, he had then admitted having lied to the commission and to the CIA's deputy inspector general.

Because Fernandez had not been involved in activities in Washington or Switzerland or in the sale of arms to Iran, we concluded that he should not be included with North and Poindexter in the central conspiracy case, but should instead be indicted separately after the return of the basic conspiracy indictment.

Our preliminary investigation did not establish an adequate case against anyone in other government agencies for inclusion in our basic indictment of the central conspirators. Investigations of these agencies were subordinated to our work on the central conspiracy, and persons who had from time to time assisted North were better dealt with in individual cases rather than as peripheral participants in the major case.

The joint select committees on Iran-Contra released their report on November 13, but we could not read it, for fear of becoming tainted.

In seeking testimony from Ronald Reagan, we had to decide between sending him written interrogatories and questioning him in an oral deposition. The answers to interrogatories would, of course, be prepared by the president's counsel. The answers to questions in a deposition would be the president's own, but they would depend on his uncertain memory. We were primarily interested, just then, in cutting off any claims by North and Poindexter that their actions had been authorized by the president. Interrogatory answers could be expected to do that. A deposition could come later as a follow-up or as a final effort to elicit the details of the president's recollection.

We began by drafting the interrogatories as the comprehensive set of questions a lawyer would ask an opposing party: general questions backed up by more detailed and specific questions that might be lengthy and overly refined in an effort to cover every possible ambiguity.

I then rewrote them in simple, straightforward language. We knew that the questions we asked the president would become public; we wanted them to be understandable by the average citizen and not to seem over-bearing, hostile, or disrespectful. President Reagan answered the inter-rogatories in January 1988. As we had expected, he denied having known of the diversion of funds or having authorized Poindexter or North to violate the Boland amendments or to deceive Congress.

By this time, Vice President George Bush was already deep in his pres-idential primary campaigns. Constrained by his busy schedule, we took his deposition, narrowing our questions to what we needed as protec-tion against his possible testimony as a witness for North and Poindexter. We expected to return for a broader deposition when our investigation was complete. Bush frequently claimed to be unable to recall details. While acknowledging that McFarlane had told him about receiving money for the Contras from the Saudis, Bush denied having known the nature of North's Contra-supply activities. The vice presi-dent admitted having known about the arms sales to Iran but not about the diversion of the proceeds. Bush acknowledged that the Iranian ini-tiative had been discussed in the president's intelligence briefings more often than once a month but less often than once a week.

At the request of Prime Minister Shimon Peres, Bush told us, he had met at the King David Hotel in Jerusalem with Amiram Nir, who had reported on the hostage negotiations that had broken down when the Iranians discovered they were being overcharged. Bush said that Nir's report, which he had later described to North, had been general and had not mentioned the diversion or the overcharges. A hostage had been released just before the meeting. After the meeting, President Reagan had authorized the completion of the delivery of the Hawk spare parts.

No issue split my staff more severely or for a longer time than the for-mulation of the conspiracy charge based on North's coordination of the effort to resupply the Contras. For a long time, only a minority of the lawyers would support the concept. I delayed making a final decision until I had a consensus. It would have been reckless to obtain an indict-ment that neither the staff nor I could support wholeheartedly.

As we pieced together our evidence with the Swiss records and the information supplied by Zucker, the resulting unity of the Contra-supply activities, the arms sales to Iran, and the diversion of funds brought my staff together. This had not been a naked conspiracy to vio-late the Boland amendments. It had been a conspiracy to conduct an unauthorized covert action in Nicaragua and finance it by the theft of government funds. Some of the conspirators were government officials. Not only had they committed U.S. resources to the Contras in violation of the Boland amendments, but by overcharging the Iranians they had jeopardized the possibility of obtaining the release of the hostages. Moreover, Casey, North, and Secord had had the even broader objective of setting up a privately controlled slush fund to finance other unauthorized covert activities, bypassing congressional oversight and the need for congressional appropriations. The entire staff could commit itself to this broadened indictment.

During the early weeks of 1988, we drafted the major count of the indictment. This count described a conspiracy of deceit with a triple objective: supporting an illegal covert action in Nicaragua in defiance of congressional controls; stealing proceeds of the Iranian arms sales to build a fund to be spent at the discretion of the conspirators rather than the U.S. government; and endangering the effort to rescue Americans held hostage in Lebanon by pursuing a conflicting objective that was both illegal and inconsistent with the goal of releasing the hostages. One subdivided paragraph spelled out the objectives of the conspiracy; thirty-six more paragraphs explained the methods of the conspiracy—supported by the specification of seventy well-established and essentially indisputable overt acts.

The broadening of the indictment gave impetus to the negotiations we were already conducting with McFarlane's lawyer. McFarlane had been a party to some violations of the Boland amendments, but he had not participated in the conspiracy's other two components. Naming him as a defendant in the major indictment would have increased the likelihood that the court would conclude that forcing him to stand trial with others who were charged with more flagrant crimes involving the theft of government funds was unfair. The court might then sever some of the charges, order separate trials for some or all of the defendants, or sever both the charges and the defendants. Once this process began, the unity of the indictment as to the other defendants would be in danger.

Accordingly, we intensified our effort to obtain a plea bargain from McFarlane, even though we recognized the incongruity of extending leniency to North's former supervisor while continuing the case against North. We thought a felony plea would be appropriate. McFarlane's attorney sought exculpation because of McFarlane's cooperation, albeit after exposure, with Congress and with us. Statements from physicians who described McFarlane's then-fragile mental state supported his effort. We reluctantly compromised, accepting a plea of guilty to four misdemeanors, each of which charged the withholding of information from Congress. An agreement of cooperation was a condition of the plea. We unwisely agreed to McFarlane's insistence that he be sentenced before he testified, so that it could not be claimed at trial that he was motivated by fear of a prison sentence. I was satisfied with the plea because McFarlane had always been willing to testify and had never asserted his constitutional privilege against self-incrimination. President Reagan had put McFarlane in an impossible position. His crimes had been the inevitable result of his having undertaken to carry out a willful presidential policy. McFarlane pleaded guilty before Chief Judge Aubrey Robinson on March 11, 1988.

During the first ten days of March, I conferred with counsel for North, Poindexter, Secord, and Hakim and invited proffers. I told the attorneys that an indictment was forthcoming and that I would welcome negotiations. None was willing to make a proffer. Indeed, on the day of McFarlane's arraignment, North announced his defiance. "*This* marine," he said, "will never cop a plea."

Brendan Sullivan called on me and urged that I forgo prosecuting his client. In a presentation made all the more telling by the absence of rhetoric, he offered three basic arguments. First, as a wounded, decorated Vietnam veteran and a dedicated public servant, North deserved America's gratitude, not its condemnation. Second, North had been carrying out two presidential mandates; he had not invented his tasks and had not hidden his actions from his superiors; and he had had every reason to think that his conduct had been fully authorized. Third, there were practical legal obstacles to successful prosecution. North's immunized testimony had been too widely broadcast to be kept out of the courtroom. Sullivan argued that I would never be able to meet the *Kastigar* standard of untainted evidence. And he predicted that the issue of classified information would outweigh even our immunity burden. Without secret documents from government files, the prosecution would not have a case and North would not have a defense. But the keepers of official secrets would fight any release, and the law—the Classified Information Procedures Act (CIPA)—left them, not the prosecutor or the judge, in complete control.

Prosecuting North under such circumstances, Sullivan concluded, was a losing proposition. An indictment would expose me to "national ridicule," he declared, and a trial would leave my "reputation destroyed." I found Sullivan's arguments sobering, although neither novel nor persuasive. He was a forceful advocate. He left the impression that his candor was a means of showing his respect for my integrity. With similar respect for his, I advanced an argument that would have been hopeless against a shallow lawyer. I suggested that we could find a way to resolve the case without taking five years out of everyone's life. An "honorable disposition," a negotiated plea admitting guilt, I said, would serve the national interest.

Sullivan responded sharply, "I can't substitute the national interest for my client's interest."

"No," I agreed, "but your client can." If North was the patriot Sullivan described, he would forthrightly take responsibility for his actions and assist in the cleanup.

Sullivan was doubtful, but he did not dismiss my suggestion out of hand. Warning me that the likelihood of a plea was remote, he agreed to consult two of his partners and let me know their decision. I promised to discuss the idea with only two of my associates. On the afternoon of McFarlane's arraignment, Sullivan telephoned to turn down the idea of a plea bargain. By then, in any case, our course was set: We would bring a comprehensive indictment for the conspiracy to defraud the United States.

On March 16, 1988, the grand jury returned a twenty-three-count indictment charging Poindexter, North, Secord, and Hakim with the conspiracy and with the theft of government funds. North and Poindexter were individually charged with lying to Congress and obstructing its investigation. North was also charged with lying to the attorney general in November 1986 and obstructing his investigation. In addition, North was charged with accepting a gratuity (the home-security system), and Secord and Hakim were charged with conspiring to give a gratuity to a government officer. North was also charged with conspiring to violate the Internal Revenue Code by misusing a charitable organization.

In his lawyer's office, North told the press, "I have now been caught in a bitter dispute between the Congress and the president over the control of foreign policy. . . . I did not commit any crime."

Brendan Sullivan backed his client up. "A criminal court," he declared, "is not the proper place to resolve foreign policy disputes." The indictment, he held, constituted an "abuse of the criminal process" premised on "novel and sometimes ridiculous legal theories."

As the defendants appeared in court on March 24 to plead their innocence, Republican leaders were pressing Ronald Reagan to pardon

North and Poindexter. The president, at a White House meeting with college students, ducked a question about his intentions regarding pardons. Instead of addressing the issue, Reagan lashed out at the prosecutors. "The whole so-called Iran scandal," said the president, "I find it hard to think of 'scandal' in connection with it.... I still think Ollie North is a hero, I just have to believe that they're going to be found innocent, because I don't believe they were guilty of any lawbreaking or any crime."

At speaking engagements in Syracuse and New York City, Vice President Bush stated publicly that he hoped North and Poindexter would be "found innocent." He declared, however, that pardons should not be discussed, "way too premature to discuss pardon—you know why? Pardoning imputes guilt ... let the system work all this out."

The possibility of pardons had surfaced briefly the previous November, when former national security advisor William Clark, one of Ronald Reagan's oldest political friends, had urged him to pardon Poindexter and North because "the story has been told" and the chief actors "have suffered enough." Clark was supported by North's admirers, who were numerous and vocal. In the two weeks after North testified at the congressional hearings, they had contributed more than $1 million to his legal defense. My detractors also supported pardons. Not least among them was the editorial page of the *Wall Street Journal*: "The American people already have made clear they don't want Ollie North or John Poindexter charged with anything."

We had prepared a thorough report on our year-long investigation and on the effect of a pardon, so that it would be ready if the White House asked for advice. If the president had acted without requesting our views, the report would have gone to Congress. Fortunately, Ronald Reagan did not use his pardon power. He viewed pardons as no substitute for a court determination after a public trial.

Three weeks into the new year, the United States Court of Appeals for the District of Columbia Circuit had thrown a new shadow of uncertainty over our work and our future. In a case brought against Alexia Morrison, another independent counsel, the court held by a two-to-one vote that the office of independent counsel "so deeply invades the president's executive prerogatives and responsibilities [for law enforcement] and so jeopardizes individual liberty as to be unconstitutional.... A statute that vests the appointment of an officer who prosecutes the criminal law in some branch other than the executive," wrote Judge

Laurence H. Silberman for the majority, "obstructs the president's ability to execute the law." And violating the Constitution's separation of powers to create a prosecutor free of the usual restraints, he reasoned, "has troubling consequences for those who find themselves the target of the independent counsel."

Although the suit had been brought against another independent counsel who was investigating the possible obstruction of a congressional investigation by a former assistant attorney general, the decision jeopardized all independent counsel. In practical terms, the backup appointment I had secured the previous March from the attorney general protected our office. Its validity had been upheld by Chief Judge Aubrey Robinson of the U.S. district court on July 10, and his decision had been affirmed by the court of appeals on August 10. But problems would arise from activities that had preceded the backup appointment. Moreover, what an attorney general had given, an attorney general could also take away.

In most cases, there is no automatic right of appeal to the Supreme Court. Review is sought by the ancient writ of certiorari asking the Court to review the lower court's decision. In this case, the Supreme Court granted certiorari and expedited argument. The solicitor general, Charles Fried, the government's counsel in Supreme Court proceedings, argued that the Independent Counsel Act was unconstitutional. We retained Professor Laurence Tribe of the Harvard Law School as special counsel to support Morrison's position. Several months later, the Supreme Court reversed the court of appeals and, by a vote of seven to one, upheld the constitutionality of the Independent Counsel Act and thus my original appointment.[2]

In February, on the eve of asking the grand jury to indict, I retained former federal judge Herbert Stern of Newark as our *Kastigar* counsel. I knew that I could not respond to defense motions based on North's and Poindexter's immunized testimony without tainting myself. I needed an able advocate who was detached from the decisions I had made and the measures I had put in place to deal with the immunity problems. He had to be ready before the indictment was returned. The defendants' attack would not be long in coming.

[2.] *Morrison v. Olson*, 487 U.S. 654, 101 L. Ed 569 (1988).

PART TWO

Litigation:
The Courts Against
the Congress

CHAPTER TEN

Half a League
Onward

As a reward for continuing my lease in the Watergate Hotel during large-scale renovations, I was moved to a fourteenth-floor room-and-a-half suite overlooking the Potomac River. This would be my Washington home and private office for the next four years. After rising between six and seven in the morning, I would prepare my arguments, rewrite briefs, and study memoranda until I went to the independent counsel's office for my first appointment, usually at ten-thirty. There I met with staff members and outsiders until six or seven. I usually had dinner in my hotel room while watching news broadcasts. I worked during the evening.

I spent one day a week giving interviews to the reporters who were covering our investigation. Because of the secrecy of the grand jury proceedings, I did not discuss the witnesses' testimony or targets of our investigation. I did not have to, because reporters often staked out the corridor leading to the grand jury room and could figure in what direction the investigation headed by observing whom we called as witnesses. Instead, I used the interviews as opportunities to explain why our investigation was taking so long and costing so much and, to some extent, to guide the reporters away from unsound speculation that could damage our credibility. Furthermore, in a crucial sense, these reporters were my principal constituency: Only their informed reporting protected my office from annihilation by the powerful government agencies and the even more powerful political forces in the White House and Congress.

We prepared for a speedy trial. Rightly or wrongly, I sacrificed the management of the ongoing investigation to supervise the trial preparation. I was not one of those gifted lawyers who could delegate pretrial proceedings. After our case was assigned to U.S. District Judge Gerhard Gesell, I felt that, as an outsider to the Washington courts, I ought to appear early in the proceedings.

The judge had been one of Washington's best-known lawyers. As a partner of Dean Acheson in the Washington firm of Covington & Burling, Gesell had specialized in complex litigation. Brilliant, mercurial, hardworking, and demanding, he dominated his courtroom with assurance and with the deference and respect of the bar, although at seventy-eight (two years older than I), he sometimes seemed to tire at the end of long court sessions.

Brendan Sullivan was by all measurements the leading lawyer for the defense. He was in his forties but, as he once said, "going on eighty." His tense, slim build personified near-perfect preparation, devotion to his client, and uncompromising confrontation. Already known and respected by Gesell, Sullivan wisely avoided most of the pretrial bickering, leaving it to his partner, Barry Simon, a former law clerk to Supreme Court Justice William Brennan. Simon had instant recall not only of every Supreme Court criminal law decision but seemingly of every word in every opinion, and each opinion became the basis for a pretrial motion. He filed more than a hundred, which we had to study, brief, and argue and the judge had to decide, while the onerous work of trial preparation went on. With three or four important exceptions, every motion was denied, but they took their toll on us and the judge.

Sullivan's firm, Williams & Connally, had a reputation for overpowering government counsel, who were frequently understaffed in ordinary prosecutions. Having successfully defended a private client against this firm while a Davis Polk partner, I was determined to match Sullivan's resources. Doing so did not come cheaply, however, and news stories soon began appearing about our expenses. Bypassing me, Sullivan first asked the Justice Department for data on our travel expenses; he then used the Freedom of Information Act to obtain the data.

Other defense counsel played less prominent roles. John Poindexter's counsel, Richard Beckler, had a short temper and frequently clashed with Gesell. Richard Secord's counsel, Tom Green, avoided most of the skirmishing. Albert Hakim's counsel, Richard Janis, concentrated his efforts on exploiting his client's need for classified information, knowing that Hakim's foreign intelligence contacts and travel caused concern that he might be a security risk.

Immediately after the defendants were arraigned on March 24, Judge Gesell addressed the three issues that were to dominate the rest of the year: discovery for the defendants; the consequences of the congressional grants of immunity; and the declassification of secret documents.

We volunteered to provide open discovery, agreeing to produce copies of our relevant files to the defendants as fast as the documents could be duplicated and cleared by counsel for the intelligence agencies. By the end of May, we had produced copies of virtually all our relevant documents except those still under review by the agencies.

The court held that each of the defendants should have an office suite as secure as our own—a secure compartmented information facility (SCIF) in which to work with classified material. While defense counsel complained of being uprooted from their own offices, we supplied each of them, at our expense, a separate office, more roomy than our own, with all the necessities, from round-the-clock security officers and secure word processors (at $10,000 each) to telephone service and parking spaces. Of our total expenditures, more than 20 percent was directly attributable to security measures for the defendants and ourselves. After the defendants' SCIFs were constructed, we delivered hundreds of thousands of documents to them.

An interagency group of lawyers, representing the State and Defense departments, the CIA, the National Security Council, the National Security Agency, and other entities, met steadily in our office and cleared documents for delivery to the defendants and their counsel. (This process did not declassify them for use at trial.) The group cleared 100,000 pages of nongovernment documents by the end of April. (Even private, previously unclassified documents had to be reviewed and were subject to reclassification to prevent publication.) Next, records classified up to the level of secret were cleared and delivered. Meanwhile, the interagency group studied the more sensitive government documents line by line. By May 2, we had turned over 82,820 pages of classified government documents and 22,965 pages of classified nongovernment documents, a total of 105,785 pages. We also delivered 192,475 pages of unclassified documents. By June 15, we had specified for the defendants all the documents we intended to offer in evidence at trial. Each defendant received an index of our probable trial exhibits and a list of our proposed witnesses. We convinced the judge that we were forthcoming.

On his own motion, Judge Gesell addressed the question of the defendants' congressional grants of immunity. The defense counsel insisted that the judge hold a full pretrial hearing at which the prosecution would produce all its intended testimony and other proof, item by item, witness by witness, so that any possible taint from the immunized congressional testimony could be assessed. We urged the judge to delay the hearing until after the trial, so that he could rule on the evidence actually used. This would avoid the equivalent of two trials. The judge could retrospectively deal with any use we had made of immunized testimony; he could, for example, order a new trial or dismiss the indictment or individual counts. We were ready to risk dismissal after trial, but we did not want to give the defendants a full preview of our case, which would subject all our witnesses to double cross-examination.

The court ordered a partial preliminary hearing on our insulation procedures. I was to be the first witness. Just as doctors dislike being patients, lawyers do not enjoy being witnesses, so I prepared myself thoroughly, reviewing office memoranda and checking with my staff for details. Then, for two days, defense counsel cross-examined me on the effectiveness of our procedures and the incidents of accidental exposure. Brendan Sullivan took the lead. He wasn't very effective; he asked no questions I could not answer, and he gave me openings for some very strong responses that, it seemed to me, impressed the judge with my credibility and sincerity and the effectiveness of our procedures.

Richard Beckler infuriated Gesell by being repetitive, and Richard Janis also aroused the court by attempting to cover areas that Sullivan had already covered. Inasmuch as Secord had not received immunity from Congress, Tom Green did not question me. At the end of my testimony, Judge Gesell, speaking within the limits of impartiality, congratulated me. He became friendly and cordial. His restrained words were solidly complimentary. I had crossed the bridge from out-of-town counsel to one in whom the court had confidence.

The judge also reviewed the summary of our leads to all of our evidence, and he read the entire grand jury transcript. On that basis, he satisfied himself that we had leads to the evidence necessary for indictment before North testified, and that it did not appear that we had made use of the immunized testimony. He deferred a more extensive hearing until after the trial. Defense counsel requested the D.C. circuit court of appeals to order a more extensive pretrial hearing. The request was denied.

The defendants next moved for severance, seeking to break up the indictment by separating the charges of individual misconduct not common to all defendants from the charges of conspiratorial and common misconduct. More important was their request that each of the immunized defendants be tried separately. They argued that it might be necessary for one defendant to use the immunized congressional testimony of another and that this would be prejudicial to the defendant whose immunized testimony was so used.

At a court hearing on June 8, Simon argued the motion. Although Judge Gesell left undisturbed the charges of the indictment, individual and common, he ordered that each defendant be tried separately. He was concerned that the congressional testimony of one immunized defendant might be admissible, as an exception to the hearsay rule, in the defense of a second immunized defendant. In my argument, I had concentrated on holding the charges together, because I thought that our brief had clearly demonstrated that testimony before a congressional committee was not within any exception to the hearsay exclusion; it was not comparable to testimony in a previous trial or administrative proceeding, in which the government prosecutor had had a chance to ask questions. Committee counsel or committee members were in no sense allied with the prosecution. I had strenuously urged the court to proceed with a common trial, or at least to wait until we were confronted with more than speculation about what a defendant *might* try to do. The judge, however, thought it better to sever the cases at the beginning than to risk even a speculative danger of a mistrial as the trial proceeded.

This was my first defeat, and it was a major one. Michael Bromwich and David Zornow, who were with me in court, could not hide their despair. I felt worse than they looked, because I realized that my oral argument had not adequately addressed the point on which the judge had decided. I congratulated Simon and then broke the news to the staff back at our office. For my associate counsel, whose regular careers and personal lives would be largely suspended until our work was done, the decision was like doubling a prison sentence.

I eventually concluded that Judge Gesell's approach was probably sound, although, as he later agreed, his reason might have been wrong. The problem of policing a trial of one immunized person proved so demanding that I came to believe that the judge's instinct for simplification had probably made it possible to complete each trial.

The judge instructed us to try a government official, Oliver North or John Poindexter, first. We chose North. The judge then postponed all proceedings related to the trials of the others. Desperately, we asked that he permit the joint trial of North and Poindexter, with a separate jury for each; if one defendant sought to use the immunized testimony of the other, the appropriate jury could be sent out of the courtroom and not prejudiced by the disclosure. Gesell denied the request, declaring that a joint trial would be too complicated.

Having been forced into separate trials, we lost the advantage of having the jurors view the defendants as a group while evaluating their finger-pointing at each other. Our principal witnesses would be cross-examined not once, but two or three times, increasing the risk of their making inconsistent statements that might, even if trivial, supply a basis for hostile cross-examination and disparagement. North's trial would also provide a full preview for the subsequent trials. The pretrial proceedings for each case could take months, and each trial could take weeks. We were unlikely to be able to try more than one case a year, which meant that we were stuck for at least two years. The additional expense, in the millions of dollars, was staggering.

In staff conferences, we considered the consequences of severance, particularly the need for members of the team trying North to become familiar with Poindexter's immunized testimony, which would make them ineligible to try Poindexter. We would probably have to field two or more separate trial teams.

On July 8, Judge Gesell scheduled North's trial to begin on September 20. I decided not to ask the court to reassign the Poindexter case to another judge for simultaneous trial, because the publicity from one trial would probably affect the jurors of the other. For the time being, I decided to concern myself only with North's trial and to defer consideration of our use of the immunized congressional testimony of Poindexter or Hakim.

In April, we had begun serious discussions with the government intelligence agencies about the declassification of documents for use in a public trial. Judge Gesell would not conduct any part of the trial in private. The interagency group was extraordinarily cooperative in meeting the demanding production schedule set by the court. Understandably, some members of the group were angered by the unreasonableness of some of North's demands, including the quantity of documents he requested and his reaching for documents of little relevance but utmost sensitivity. We showed our respect for the group's concerns by reducing our own demands for the declassification of documents and by vigorously presenting the group's position in court.

In the past, defendants in national security cases had been able to force the dismissal of criminal charges by waiting until trial to demand disclosure of information that needed to be kept secret to protect the national security. The Classified Information Procedures Act (CIPA), which was enacted to prevent such maneuvers, required pretrial notice to the government of the need for such information. The procedural outline was simple. The prosecution and the defense notified the intelligence agencies of their intent to use specific classified information. The intelligence agencies then had a range of alternatives: declassify the information; declassify part of the information and redact other parts; give the defendant the information that was material to his or her defense but in a substitute artificial form that protected sources; or refuse to declassify the information. If the intelligence agencies refused to declassify information that the court held to be material, the attorney general or a designated assistant attorney general could overrule the agencies and release the information. But if the attorney general supported the agencies' refusal and filed an affidavit with the court to this effect, the court could not itself order production but would impose sanctions on the prosecution. The sanctions could entail requiring the prosecutor to make concessions or dismissing the indictment or individual counts of the indictment.

Previous cases had concerned only a small number of documents. Never had a court been confronted with the need to thread its way through thousands of classified documents. Moreover, the statute contemplated that each side would be willing to explain before trial why some piece of evidence was material. To this extent, the parties would have to disclose their strategy. The government had no choice. North, however, claimed that this requirement deprived him of his constitutional right not to disclose his position in advance.

We were afraid that North's counsel might simply refuse to comply with the statute, but Judge Gesell perceptively invited them to file a motion challenging the constitutionality of the statute as applied to the facts in our case. After hearing full argument, the judge reserved a final determination and decided to proceed under the statute, adapting it to the case's unusual needs. To minimize the chance that the court would declare the statute unconstitutional, I had offered to permit the defendants to explain their defense in an ex parte conference with the court—a conference at which no representative of the prosecution would be present. Although a private conversation between defense counsel and the court would put us at an enormous disadvantage, it would enable the judge to assess the defendant's claim of the materiality of the information that he wanted declassified.

On May 23, shortly before Judge Gesell ordered separate trials for each defendant, Poindexter and North had moved for a supplemental discovery of classified material. Specifying documents that the agencies had not previously produced for us, this extraordinarily sweeping motion called for documents of the utmost sensitivity. Only someone who knew the most telling points of the government's most secret activities—someone like Poindexter—could have specified so frightening a list. It called for thousands of documents that had not been disclosed even to us. Just the listing of this parade of documents in a single document was said to endanger national security. We were told that some activities were unknown to the lawyers in the interagency group; some were unknown even to agency heads.

"Graymail" is the term used for a defendant's effort to force the termination of a prosecution by threatening exposure of secrets vital to the security of the United States. Never before had such a scheme been directed by such ruthless and skilled experts as Poindexter, the president's former national security advisor, and North, a meticulously record-conscious expert who knew exactly what sensitive or embarrassing records were likely to exist, not only regarding Iran-Contra but also in other fields he claimed were analogous. Some documents might embarrass friendly foreign countries. Others would expose human sources and secret intelligence-gathering and analytical capabilities.

At the request of the shocked agencies and with their assistance, we opposed the discovery. Judge Gesell spent more than four hours in an ex parte conference with North's counsel on July 6, then ordered the production of twenty of the 140 groups of documents that North and Poindexter had requested. These documents significantly affected the forthcoming trial. They also exposed the fact that the White House, the National Security Council, the CIA, and the State Department had withheld thousands of documents that should have been turned over to us.

North's counsel impressed the judge with his claim that the fact that we had not had these documents demonstrated the incompleteness of our inquiry. He argued that their absence distorted the remaining documentary evidence and obscured the true nature and effect of certain critical events. During the ex parte conference, according to the opinion issued by the judge, defense counsel illustrated how some of the with-held material tended to exonerate North, as did redacted portions of documents that the defense had already received.

Although North's counsel conceded that the money from the sale of missiles to Iran had been combined in private accounts with gifts from foreign governments and private donations, and that the funds had then been used to carry out several covert operations, including support of the Contras, he claimed not only that North's activities had generally been known to North's superior, but also that they had been approved at or near the cabinet level and that their execution had been closely followed at the cabinet level by intelligence surveillance introduced at North's request. To permit North to reinforce these claims, the court granted his request for discovery of many of the doc-uments and strongly intimated that their public release might be nec-essary at trial.

Because the conspiracy and diversion counts were in jeopardy, the court ordered me to indicate by August 1 how the documents from our case in chief related to the other counts. The court concluded that "at a minimum," substantive charges of cover-up, falsification, and North's alleged receipt of personal benefits derived from his activities as a gov-ernment employee would proceed to trial.

Despite the burdens the order put upon us, our position was so diffi-cult that we actually regarded the order as favorable, because it dimin-ished the danger that Judge Gesell would throw the statute out as unconstitutional. At our next staff conference, some associate counsel suggested trying the case without the conspiracy and diversion counts. I predicted that we would end up without those counts, but I decided to stand pat as long as possible. Only the conspiracy count explained the true object of all the other crimes—to support the Contras no matter what law was broken. That was why the funds had been diverted from the Iranian arms sales and why North had lied. If we left out the true axis, the case would be skewed.

On July 19, CIA Director William Webster, his counsel Russell Bruemmer, and William Landers, associate counsel to the president, requested a meeting in Webster's Washington office in the Old Executive Office Building. Webster claimed that the production of the supplemental material would be giving the defendants the "crown jew-els." The others added that searching for and producing this material would take months. A few days later, I met with the agencies' general counsel in the White House situation room. I urged them to separate their concerns about the scale of the task from their concerns for national security. They decided to comply with the order but warned that it would take all summer.

On July 20, North's counsel moved for a continuance of the trial date, citing the need to review more than one million documents and claiming that it would be impossible to be ready by September 20, when the trial was supposed to begin. We moved to narrow the new discovery, arguing that there was no evidence that anyone other than co-conspirators Poindexter and Robert McFarlane had authorized North's acts, and that he should have been able to narrow his demands by identifying the persons whose files had to be searched. We reported that the intelligence community could not meet the court's schedule for the production of the additional discovery. Desperately trying to preserve the court's September trial date, we moved that the conspiracy and diversion counts be severed and tried later because this new discovery related primarily to those counts. Embarrassed that apparently relevant documents had been concealed from my own office, as well as the defendants, I was afraid that no less drastic measure could save these counts and preserve the early trial date that the judge had fixed.

On August 5, Judge Gesell, deferring to Sullivan's request, canceled the September trial date. He ordered the government to fulfill its discovery obligations by October 10. He denied our motion to sever the conspiracy and diversion counts as moot. Again, I shared my associates' disappointment at the delay but I welcomed one more chance to save the basic counts. I was moving instinctively to try the counts or force the intelligence agencies to take full public responsibility for their dismissal. By October, we had produced the additional documents collected by the intelligence agencies.

While the agencies gathered the thousands of additional documents they had been ordered to give North, we prepared for the defense motions to dismiss the indictment as legally insufficient. The judge had directed that they be filed by October 10. We expected Brendan Sullivan and Barry Simon to file as many motions as possible to force us to ask for time to answer them. In anticipation, we roughed out draft responses to all the likely motions so that we would not have to request a delay. While I continued preparing for trial, Professors Gerard Lynch of Columbia and Bruce Green of Fordham agreed to supervise the drafting of our briefs and to argue our responses to the motions we thought North's counsel would file.

Just before midnight on October 10, Sullivan and Simon served us with thirty-five motions supported by a stack of briefs more than a foot thick. We would have less than two weeks to respond. Working long hours and through the weekends, we responded on time to all but one of the motions, for which the deadline was extended by a day. The court then denied Sullivan's request for more time to reply to our responses and set oral argument for November 21.

While we were preparing for the argument, Attorney General Richard Thornburgh startled us by filing a brief in support of North's motion to dismiss the conspiracy count. The attorney general argued that we were trying to criminalize the political give and take between the executive branch and Congress in matters relating to foreign policy, and that we had overextended the concept of conspiracy to defraud. The central element of the alleged conspiratorial acts was deceit, and the thrust of the attorney general's brief was that the administration was entitled to practice deceit. Officials who made specific false statements to Congress might be prosecutable as individuals, he declared, but those who only participated in a plan of action that deceived Congress could not be prosecuted.

The attorney general's brief was counterproductive, arousing Judge Gesell, who characterized it as unprecedented. Indeed it was. It was as though I had been representing a corporate client in court, and the corporation's counsel had filed a memorandum against me and in support of the corporation's opponent. Already smelling a cover-up, Gesell was ahead of me. In September, outraged at having been drawn into stubborn, niggling negotiations by the agencies on one side and North on the other, the judge had exploded in a statement calling on Ronald Reagan to decide whether he wanted this case tried or not.

Gerard Lynch and Bruce Green argued masterfully against the motions to dismiss the indictment. A few days later, Judge Gesell began issuing a series of opinions that denied all the defense motions except a motion to dismiss one count for lack of venue (to which we consented) and a mail-fraud charge that, he thought, too closely duplicated the charge of theft of the proceeds of the arms sales to Iran.

His opinions addressed the issues broadly. He held that the conspiracy count, with its wide scope, was a proper charge of conspiracy to defraud the United States. He scornfully dismissed the attorney general's contention to the contrary. The judge upheld the charge that the diversion of the arms proceeds constituted the theft of government funds. He ruled that lies to Congress, even in informal settings, were prosecutable as false statements and obstruction if the committees were carrying out assigned congressional functions. He held that North's lying to the attorney general during his November 1986 investigation was a prosecutable false statement to a government agency.

By the time Judge Gesell was through, the administration had only one way to block the conspiracy charge that it so feared: denying us the evidence we needed to try the case.

Despite the burden of responding to the defense motions, we had made steady progress in preparing for trial. Since April, we had drafted trial briefs for internal review, winnowed documents for use as exhibits, repeatedly interviewed reluctant witnesses, selected points for possible stipulation, outlined questions for use in jury selection, collected material for cross-examination, identified exculpatory material to be given to the defendant, and drafted requests for the judge's charge to the jury. We had set up witness files and were rapidly filling them with memoranda. On November 1, I calculated that the probable trial date would be January 16, 1989. This left only eight usable weeks, partially discounting the four weeks between Thanksgiving and Christmas, when government personnel would be distracted by holiday demands and activities.

Always present was the question of whether I should try the case. I believed that the Poindexter case could not be tried without North as a witness and that whoever tried North would be exposed to Poindexter's immunized congressional testimony. As delays in John Keker's California case detained him, David Zornow, Michael Bromwich, Chris Mixter, and I divided the responsibilities for the large number of witnesses who would testify. Zornow would examine the financial witnesses, Bromwich the Contra-supply witnesses, and Mixter some of the NSC witnesses. I planned to examine Edwin Meese and Robert McFarlane and a few other witnesses whose testimony would be extensive.

I was concerned that age had slowed my reaction time; even if my hearing and reflexes were only slightly diminished, I would be at a disadvantage in dealing with Brendan Sullivan and the innumerable witnesses we could expect to be hostile. If I had to think for a moment to be sure I understood what was said, I might lose the opportunity to get in the first words of an interchange, or the jury might think I was unsure of myself. I was confident of my effectiveness in making the opening and closing statements to the jury, but I was uneasy about cross-examination, and all the examination of the hostile witnesses would be cross-examination. Moreover, running the office was interfering significantly with my ability to concentrate on trial preparation.

John Keker's return in the fall drew the issue to a head. The views of my team varied. Chris Todd, for example, wanted me to taint myself and supervise the continuing investigation, whereas Herb Stern thought I should try North even if I then became unavailable to try Poindexter. I procrastinated. I wanted to conduct one more complex trial.

Keker and I disagreed on how to handle Robert McFarlane's testimony. As a seasoned criminal lawyer, Keker distrusted McFarlane and felt that a jury would not believe him. Keker would address him outright as a hostile witness. I thought I could protect him on cross-examination and explain him to the jury. We both agreed we needed him as a storytelling witness against North. I did not think McFarlane would deliberately sabotage our case. Keker thought he would.

As Keker became increasingly restive, he concluded that our close teamwork would be jeopardized. In a handwritten note to me, he quoted Napoleon as saying that the only thing worse than one bad general was two good generals. After a night's reflection, I concluded that he was right, that it would be best if he tried the North case and I remained untainted. Keker, Bromwich, and Zornow would take responsibility for trying North, while Mixter and I continued to deal with the problems of declassification.

In June, we had submitted to the judge and to the defendants copies of the documents that we intended to use to prove our case. The interagency group had already decided what parts of the documents had to be redacted. In our meetings with counsel for the agencies, Mixter and I weighed the loss of evidence against the likelihood that the court would reject redactions. We dropped our plans to introduce scores of documents with questionable deletions, reducing the number of our proposed trial exhibits to fewer than three hundred.

North's counsel had been given the unredacted documents so that they could evaluate the materiality of the redacted portions. North's counsel objected to almost every redaction. At first, they declined to supply any basis for the objections. As the court successively rejected their notices, Sullivan and Simon finally complied with the court's requirement that they specify the reasons for their objection so that we and the agencies could respond intelligently. The defense counsel also initially refused to specify the reasons for their objection to the redactions in the exhibits that they wanted to use in the defense case. Judge Gesell held a second ex parte conference with them to resolve those issues.

The career officers of the internal security section of the Justice Department, John Martin and Ed Walsh, with whom I had worked when I was deputy attorney general, had supported us in our controversies with the intelligence agencies over the declassification of documents. But, under CIPA, the responsibility for deciding controversies between prosecutors and the intelligence agencies had been assigned to Edward S. G. Dennis, Jr., the assistant attorney general in charge of the criminal division. Dennis replaced Martin and Walsh with Jim Reynolds, who was sympathetic to the intelligence agencies.

For practical purposes, the working chairman of the interagency group had been William Landers, a quiet-spoken, reasonable, helpful intermediary between us and the agencies. The general counsel for the CIA, Russell Bruemmer, who had followed Director William Webster from the FBI, had a broad-gauged and rational approach to declassification; he did not belittle law enforcement. The State Department's legal advisor, Abraham Sofaer, wanted to force the dismissal of the conspiracy count to avoid the need for the testimony of his principal client, George Shultz. The general counsel to the National Security Agency, Elizabeth Rindskopf, was tough. An attorney trained as an advocate for plaintiffs' class actions, she seemed to us not easily deterred by facts, reason, or appeals to fairness. Her concern was not only the preservation of intelligence sources, but also the protection of her agency from embarrassment. She exaggerated claims of national security risk so grossly that I wondered whether she was bucking for a White House appointment. (After George Bush became president, Rindskopf was promoted to succeed Russell Bruemmer as general counsel of the CIA.)

Lower-ranking lawyers carried out the day-to-day work of declassification. Some were problem-solvers. Others had automatically negative reflexes, developed from opposing numerous Freedom of Information Act requests. A third group comprised those allied, in spirit or in fact, with North. This group was epitomized by Rindskopf's two able assistants, both of them Annapolis graduates. Trained to believe that government officials in a criminal case should not fraternize with defendants, I resented their excessive cordiality to North and his wife in the courtroom.

Gradually, we and the agencies' counsel had narrowed our differences. We agreed, for example, about the need to protect secret intelligence sources, human and electronic, but we unsuccessfully protested the "protection" for foreign hosts of our known intelligence activities and the State Department's insistence that we not antagonize Central American countries by identifying the locations of known Contra-support activities or the foreign officials who participated in them. The agencies stood fast against releasing a dozen categories of information enumerated on a "drop-dead" list. The agencies agreed that they would support each other in refusing to declassify this information even if the court held it to be material to North's defense. If the attorney general supported them, their refusal would force the dismissal of several counts of the indictment.

Finally, on November 30, the hearings on the classified information started. They were handled by Mixter; I was present for continuing discussions with the agencies' counsel. To decide whether the evidence the intelligence agencies refused to make public was relevant and material to North's guilt or innocence, Judge Gesell reviewed, item by item, each of several hundred redactions in the documents we planned to offer into evidence.

On the third day, an unresolvable conflict arose regarding certain intelligence reports from the National Security Agency. The NSA claimed that its capability, as reflected in those documents, was truly secret. We consented to drop the proof from the government's case, but North insisted that it was essential to his defense. Judge Gesell rejected any substitution because he believed that the source of the reports enhanced their credibility and the likelihood that they would have been read by the individuals who had received them. The judge believed that North was entitled to demonstrate that his actions had been known to Poindexter, McFarlane, Caspar Weinberger, and William Casey, even if they could not have legally authorized his actions. This classified evidence dramatically demonstrated that they had known much of what North was doing with respect to the arms sales. The judge said he intended to make sure that North was not a fall guy, but was really the architect of the conspiracy.

The NSA had misled us as to the secrecy of its methods. It had also damaged our credibility with the judge by forcing us to support silly redactions that had angered Gesell. Rindskopf had insisted, for example, that we redact from a PROF note McFarlane sent North the sentence "I hope to daylights that someone has purged the NSA traffic files." She had also insisted that we redact a reference to the agency's former deputy director from another note. When Mixter, with a straight face, attempted to assert the NSA's claim that this disclosure would jeopardize national security, the judge's face had flushed; he had smiled through clenched teeth and peremptorily rejected our position. Under the law, Gesell could not force the declassification of these items. Only the attorney general could do that. But the judge was by now prepared to dismiss the indictment or individual counts to which the withheld evidence was material.

This obviously excessive misuse of the classification power left the judge unsympathetic when we faced a more legitimate problem. North had arranged for the NSA to use its unique intelligence capability to follow the Iranian response to his negotiations. The resulting intelligence reports had been circulated not only to North but also to Poindexter, Weinberger, Casey, and Robert Gates, who had been the deputy director of the CIA and was now the president's deputy national security advisor. We had hoped to introduce these reports as evidence of North's activities. North wanted to introduce the same evidence to show the openness of his activity and to refute our claim of criminal intent. The NSA, claiming that the reports showed a secret capability and could not be exposed, insisted that we use a wholly artificial substitute that concealed the nature of the report and even distorted the substance. When the court ruled the proposed substitute inadequate, the NSA refused to give us a better one. The deputy director simply told us that he did not "feel comfortable" with our expanded proposal. The court ended the matter by holding that the unique nature of the reports dramatized them and made it more likely that they had been followed at cabinet level. On December 12, Judge Gesell issued his fateful order. It required the disclosure of not only the NSA's classified information but also the names of Central American countries and officials as well as CIA installations.

We appealed to Attorney General Thornburgh to overrule the NSA. He referred us to Edward Dennis, the Justice Department official responsible for resolving CIPA disputes. We argued our position orally and supplied an extensive brief supported by a compendium of books and published articles showing that the NSA's capability was not secret. We had amassed numerous clippings to show that the State Department and CIA were preserving not secrets but diplomatic niceties when they insisted on "protecting" the names of already publicized Central American officials, countries, and installations. Our brief urged that our case not be destroyed to preserve diplomatic fictions. We suggested that the independent counsel, as an outsider, was disavowable; if I disclosed the name of a Central American country, it was not as though the secretary of state had done it. Finally, we argued that Iran-Contra activities were no longer covert; the president himself had exposed the U.S. support for the Contras as well as the sale of arms to Iran and the diversion of the proceeds. In his speeches, in his statements and press conferences, and in his communications to Congress, President Reagan had said that he wanted full disclosure.

At the attorney general's request, Colin Powell, the new national security advisor, and his deputy convened the heads of the intelligence agencies or their deputies in the White House situation room on December 21 to discuss the issue. I had offered to attend the meeting but was not invited. The attorney general had to delay the meeting by an hour to absorb the information in our brief. When the group met, the participants agreed to liberalize the classification restraints to some extent, permitting the identification of foreign countries, but not the names of foreign officials or the exposure of the NSA intelligence material required by the court's order. Left unaddressed was the problem of the NSA's unwillingness to permit any disclosure of its high-level participation in North's activities.

William Landers telephoned me after the meeting to say that the attorney general would file an affidavit refusing to produce the evidence ordered by the court. Assistant Attorney General Dennis confirmed this by letter, enclosing a copy of a letter in which Bill Webster, as director of central intelligence, had asserted that national security required the attorney general to retain the classification of the information in controversy.

The deadline for appealing Judge Gesell's order holding verbatim reports of the controversial intelligence reports material to North's defense was December 22. With less than a day to decide our course, Mixter and I hastily collected Keker, Bromwich, and Zornow at the entrance to Keker's office. Mixter wanted to appeal the order. The others urged me to drop the conspiracy and diversion counts and let the other counts go to trial. Earlier that day, during a further CIPA hearing regarding the documents to be used by the defense, Judge Gesell had fixed January 31, 1989, as the date for North's trial to begin. The trial team did not want to lose this starting date. I told Mixter to file a motion for the reconsideration of the December 12 order. The motion would be denied, but it would extend our time to appeal and give us room to think. A few days later, when the judge denied the motion for reconsideration, I was ready to drop the conspiracy and diversion counts and forget about filing an appeal.

Although Judge Gesell's order had deprived us of the most important counts in the indictment, I had no hope that the court of appeals would reverse his order. The standard we would have had to meet was whether Gesell had abused his discretion. An appellate court hardly ever reversed a trial judge's ruling on the materiality of an item of evidence, particularly when the judge was as painstaking and respected as Gesell and in a matter as complicated as ours. In the absence of arbitrary judicial conduct, appellate courts simply do not have time to sift through a long record to evaluate conflicting claims of materiality.

On Wednesday, January 4, I salvaged what I could. What little leverage I possessed derived from the fact that Thornburgh did not want to be the first attorney general to file a court affidavit refusing to produce evidence a court had held material. Also, North had claimed that to prove he had been authorized to do what he had done, he would have to call the president as a witness. The attorney general was preparing his response to North's motion for an order to compel President Reagan's testimony. Narrowing the case by dropping the conspiracy charge would reduce the need for the president's testimony.

Late in the morning, I telephoned Sofaer and his assistant Libby Keefer at the State Department, and they agreed to try to work out a plan for the trial of the remaining counts. Dennis's assistant Stephen A. Saltzburg joined us in my office. Saltzburg, Sofaer, and Keefer agreed in substance to support our other needs for declassification if I would drop the conspiracy and diversion counts without requiring an affidavit from the attorney general defying the court's order. Keker, Mixter, and I met with Thornburgh and his staff in the afternoon. When I offered to drop the conspiracy and diversion counts, Thornburgh assured me of his support in dealing with the intelligence agencies. He said that if we had proceeded with those counts, he would have had to file his affidavit to prevent the use of the information the judge's order required.

At five-thirty that afternoon, I announced my decision to the staff. Like Judge Gesell's decision to sever the original case and try each defendant separately, the administration's support for the intelligence agencies was a major defeat for us. It was also a stunning disavowal of the president's publicly professed desire for full disclosure. To save the case, I had been forced to jettison months of work and the two most important criminal charges. Not only had the administration's tactic freed North from the most serious charges, but it had also left us with a case that amounted to a shell of peripheral charges without a central core. Nevertheless, the conspiracy count had served a key purpose: Like a lightning rod, it had drawn and focused the objections of the administration and the intelligence agencies, and it had enabled me to negotiate an agreement that would ensure a trial for Oliver North.

On January 5, 1989, I filed a motion to dismiss the conspiracy and diversion counts. The judge requested a supporting affidavit from the attorney general, which he reluctantly supplied. On January 30, after the judge dismissed the two counts, we filed a revised indictment. The next day, the court commenced North's trial, and we began selecting the jury.

Less than a month later, I listened bitterly as the author of *The Puzzle Palace*, a book about the National Security Agency, precisely explained on national television the NSA's specific, supposedly secret intelligence capability that had forced the dismissal of the two central counts against Oliver North.

CHAPTER ELEVEN

The Trial of
Oliver North

Eight or nine counsel from the White House, the National Security Council, the State Department, the Central Intelligence Agency, the Defense Department, and the National Security Agency regularly attended the court hearings leading up to Oliver North's trial. Judge Gerhard Gesell, who was fed up with the hovering presence of these lawyers, regarded them as the personification of his classification problems. Apprehensive of their intrusion in his management of the trial, he publicly referred to them as "gurus."

On January 19, 1989, Judge Gesell entered an extensive order explaining his decision to deviate from the Classified Information Procedures Act (CIPA) requirement that he rule before trial on the materiality of each item of classified information that the defense wanted to introduce into evidence. Instead, he grouped the classified information into categories and made general rulings to be used as guides during the trial. Each side was to give the other a day's notice of intent to introduce individual items of classified information. The judge's plan would permit the trial to get underway. He could then decide questions of materiality on the basis of the actual record of the trial instead of relying on pretrial speculation. Brendan Sullivan was satisfied that the court's order gave him enough guidance so that he could outline North's defense in an opening statement to the jury.

The agencies concerned with national security, however, rejected the plan and insisted on doctrinaire, item-by-item compliance with the statute to enable them to decide before trial whether to declassify each of the items of evidence to be offered. To appease the agencies without offending the judge, Chris Mixter and I spent long hours trying unsuccessfully to work out a stipulation for future procedure with them and

Sullivan. Sullivan rejected my first two proposals, and the judge supported him. He angrily denied as unnecessary two motions I made asking him to expand and clarify his January 19 order.

Jury selection began on January 30, but before it could be completed, Attorney General Richard Thornburgh moved to compel rigid adherence to CIPA's statutorily prescribed pretrial procedures. I opposed this motion because the judge's ruling had been a necessary adaptation to make the statute workable in our case. Judge Gesell denied the motion on February 8, and the attorney general appealed. I opposed the appeal. Under the Independent Counsel Act, only I could take an interlocutory appeal. (The attorney general's sole recourse was to file an affidavit refusing to produce classified evidence.) On this basis, both Judge Gesell and the U.S. court of appeals denied the attorney general's applications to stay the trial. Chief Justice William Rehnquist, however, granted a stay until the next conference of the Supreme Court.

On February 10, John Keker finally worked out a solution. Without committing Judge Gesell, Keker and Sullivan agreed to give each other notice before offering classified evidence in the ten categories that remained on the drop-dead list. I committed myself to relay to the agencies any notice we received from Sullivan and to present the agencies' views to the court. I also agreed to submit to the court any affidavit by the attorney general blocking the use of classified information. On February 12, Judge Gesell signed an order approving this procedure, specifying that agency counsel were not to interrupt the trial. The attorney general then dropped his appeal.

As jury selection continued, we undertook extensive negotiations with the agencies and the White House to prevent an impasse over North's requests for the declassification of many documents relating to Ronald Reagan's inducements to Central American heads of state to encourage their tolerance and support of the Contras.

As a compromise, I proposed that instead of releasing documents embarrassing to foreign officials and American diplomats, I would make an admission or stipulation describing the support that President Reagan had agreed to give certain foreign countries in return for their aid to the Contras. The stipulation would be made by me, as a lawyer, solely for the purpose of the trial and was not to be construed as an admission of fact by any government agency. Sullivan drafted a proposed stipulation, and we filed a thirty-six-page counterproposal. Sullivan requested further admissions. Working into the night, the agencies' counsel, Keker, and I expanded our draft to satisfy most of

North's concerns. I adopted some of the language of defense counsel in order to narrow the issues for trial. On February 17, the court accepted our forty-two-page "U.S. Government Stipulation on Quid pro Quos with Other Governments as Part of Contra Operations," which, as a substitute for the classified documents, summarized 107 discussions held or actions taken by our representatives and those of other countries.

Despite the extraordinary measures we had taken to accommodate the conflicting concerns of the defense and the Reagan administration, the trial was interrupted frequently so that we could reconcile an adamant interagency group to the orders of the court. Judge Gesell's irritation was obvious whenever the jury had to leave the courtroom so that he could decide whether the name of a Costa Rican minister was material, for example, or whether private documents had been improperly classified. Stories and commentaries appeared in the press suggesting that the case was untriable. The tension continued until virtually the end of the trial, as the NSA's Elizabeth Rindskopf tried to persuade the attorney general to refuse to comply with the judge's order permitting North to introduce McFarlane's PROF note about purging the NSA traffic files. Throughout these controversies, Thornburgh remained firmly supportive. Once we had agreed on the basic procedures, he kept his side of the bargain.

The trial of Oliver North would be crucial for us: An acquittal could end our investigation. No one else under indictment or likely to be indicted had been involved in the questionable activities to such an extent. This trial would be the first test of our prosecutorial concepts before a trial jury. The trial would also publicly reveal for the first time how much high-level support the Contras had received from the Reagan administration in defiance of the Boland amendments.

During the jury-selection process, Sullivan had objected to the potential jurors who had listened to North's testimony, but by February 21, an all-black jury of nine women and three men had been impaneled. The ages and occupations of the jurors varied; they ranged from a twenty-year-old clerk-typist from the Labor Department to a sixty-four-year-old former messenger and security guard who had worked at the State Department. Under close questioning, all the jurors said that they paid little attention to the national news on television or in magazines or newspapers. They were barely, if at all, aware of North's notoriety or the reasons for it. Judge Gesell did not sequester them.

Confident of John Keker's ability, I stayed away from Judge Gesell's courtroom. Not only was Keker an expert litigator, but unlike most of us in large firms, he had continued to try cases frequently. His reflexes were fine-tuned, his performance almost instinctive. He had assurance, zest, even flamboyance to equal North's. With former prosecutors Michael Bromwich and David Zornow to back him up, I felt that our case was in strong hands—and it had to be. We would have very few allies in court: Most of the witnesses for the prosecution would be eager to help North and undercut us.

On February 21, spectators were in line before five in the morning. In front of a packed courtroom, Keker opened his case by telling the jury that Oliver North had put himself above the law to cover up for crimes he had committed. "When the time came . . . to tell the truth, he lied. When the time came . . . to come clean, he shredded." North had had a "motive to lie to Congress," said Keker. "He considers himself a very patriotic person who knows what's best for our country and our people. But there is no higher patriotism than protecting our system of government . . . [and] there is a difference between keeping secrets and telling lies. You don't have to tell lies to keep secrets." North had lied in 1985 and 1986 to frustrate the House intelligence committee's inquiries into the National Security Council staff's support for the Contras. The lies were in letters drafted by North and submitted to the committee by Robert McFarlane in 1985, and in testimony by North in 1986. North's lies, Keker said, had prevented the committee from operating effectively as the government's watchdog over its spies, eavesdroppers, and covert operators.

Sullivan's opening statement depicted North as a "can-do" officer who had carried out President Reagan's bidding and who had "felt he had a duty to protect the operations he worked in." Neither lawyer gave more than passing reference to the charges related to North's having accepted gratuities or to his having raised funds in violation of the income tax law.

As our first witness, Keker called Representative Lee Hamilton, the chairman of the House intelligence committee. "Does [the committee] need accurate information?" Keker asked him, to establish at the outset the importance of the truth.

"Absolutely," replied Hamilton. "We cannot fulfill our responsibility unless we have accurate information from the executive branch."

On cross-examination, Hamilton acknowledged that the letters and North's testimony, which had been taken in the White House situation room on August 6, 1986, had been "informal." Nonetheless, Hamilton said, they had been "official." Although no transcripts or notes had been kept and the witnesses had not been sworn, the lack of formality had not made the panel's inquiry unofficial or negated its entitlement to honest answers. "On whom can I rely for the truth," asked the congressman, "if I cannot rely on a top advisor to the president of the United States?"

Keker put Adolfo Calero, the silver-haired leader of the United Nicaraguan Opposition, on the witness stand to confirm North's intimate and forbidden involvement with the Contras. Calero also confirmed that he had given North $90,000 in traveler's checks and that they had been intended for North's use in Contra-support activities, although Calero had approved the expenditure of some of the funds for an unsuccessful effort to free Americans in Beirut. He rationalized North's having given $1,000 in traveler's checks to Rob Owen for a wedding present as a proper expense because, as North's courier, Owen had contributed importantly to the Contra cause.

On cross-examination, Calero became a character witness for the defense. "Please tell the jury," Sullivan prompted, "what kind of a guy Colonel North is."

"For us," Calero replied, "he became a sort of savior." Having previously felt "abandoned" by the United States, the resistance fighters "developed a very, a tremendously human relationship" with North. They were "tremendously grateful. . . . [T]he Nicaraguan people have a tremendous appreciation for this man. . . . [T]hey're going to erect a monument for him once we free Nicaragua."

Sullivan also addressed North's misuse of Calero's traveler's checks for his personal expenses. "The prosecution . . . said he stole . . . traveler's checks from you," Sullivan noted. "Is that conceivable?"

"No," said Calero.

Rob Owen took the stand next. We needed his testimony to confirm North's active supervision of his work in supporting the Contras. Owen's activities had included delivering CIA and Defense Department maps and photographs to the Contras, scouting a site for a clandestine airfield, and regularly reporting to North on the Contras' armament needs. In his testimony before Hamilton's committee, North had specifically denied having communicated with the Contras through Owen or even having met with him while the Boland amendments were in effect. Bromwich introduced a chart based on a painstaking examination of North's appointment records, which showed dozens of meetings with

Owen. Owen agreed that the count was fair and accurate, even conservative. Asked to give his own "best estimate" of the number of meetings from mid-1984 to the time North gave his testimony, Owen replied, "Somewhere around one hundred."

On cross-examination, Owen's hero worship of North poured out. "Colonel North," he affirmed, "was always sensitive to the legality of everything he did" and "meticulous" about recording his payments to Owen in a ledger. The marriage gift, handed over at an out-of-town reception following Owen's wedding, had been an exception, he said.

Our subsequent witnesses presented a similar trade-off: After describing on direct examination the details of North's operations to supply the Contras, the witnesses glorified North as a person. He was a "national hero," according to Richard Gadd; a "workaholic . . . a work of art," according to Rafael Quintero; a "wonderful patriotic American," according to Joseph Coors, the beer magnate and Contra donor who, after leaving the witness box, ostentatiously went to the defense table to shake North's hand. As he left the stand, retired major general John K. Singlaub, a staunch Contra supporter, came to attention and saluted North.

An emotional Fawn Hall, whose tears twice required the court to recess, related North's orders and actions in the alteration and destruction of National Security Council documents. She claimed that she had had no qualms about her actions, because she trusted the "very inspirational, tireless . . . , never lazy or self-serving" boss she had served for four years. "He was a man whose character I knew well," she said. "I knew there was a reason why he was doing this." After two days of testimony, she told reporters as she left the courthouse, "Hopefully, the good guy will win." Asked why she had occasionally wept, she replied, "It's tough when people portray you as a witness for the prosecution when you're a witness for the truth."

Other witnesses suffered from having had to tell their story too many times and from having held back in their earlier testimony. When Spitz Channell pleaded guilty to a scheme that had given National Endowment for the Preservation of Liberty (NEPL) contributors illegal tax write-offs for Contra arms, he had pledged full cooperation with our investigation. He kept that promise and gave the jury a detailed description of the presentations that North made to contributors, occasionally arranging meetings with Ronald Reagan—in a walk-on role—to encourage wealthy conservatives to help the Nicaraguan resistance.

But Channell ran into trouble when he described what had transpired at the end of a dinner at the Petroleum Club in Dallas with North and Texas oilman Bunker Hunt, who had later given the NEPL $475,000. Channell said that as they waited for a taxi, Hunt had asked North, "What are you going to do? Do you mind getting in trouble for this?" Channell said that North had replied, "No, I don't care if I have to go to jail for this."

This account varied from Channell's grand jury testimony, in which he had attributed the inflammatory language to Hunt, saying that Hunt had asked, "Ollie, if this policy goes down the drain, are you prepared to go to prison for it . . . ? If you needed to lie before Congress, are you willing to do that?" According to Channell, North had answered "yes" to both questions. "He might have said, 'Hell, yes!' "

The discrepancy, insignificant in substance, allowed Sullivan to tear at the witness on cross-examination. Why had Channell never mentioned the episode to congressional investigators? Out of an "urge to cooperate with the prosecution," Sullivan asked, could the witness have succumbed to "a little danger that you might put words in somebody's mouth . . . ?"

"There is that temptation," Channell admitted.

Openly scornful, Judge Gesell, who increasingly participated in the trial, reminded jurors of their duty to weigh Channell's "credibility."

The testimony of Glenn Robinette drew a similar reaction from Gesell, though not in the jury's hearing. Robinette had admitted having been reimbursed by Richard Secord for installing the security system in North's home. As for the exchange of letters designed to make it appear that North had asked for a bill and been given one, Robinette acknowledged that the correspondence had been fiction. "I had no reason to go to Colonel North" to be paid for the security system, he testified. "I was working for General Secord."

Robinette had surprised Keker, however, by claiming that the idea of backdating the correspondence had been his rather than North's. With the jury out of the courtroom, Keker sought Judge Gesell's permission to cast doubt on Robinette's veracity by introducing the fact that Robinette had initially told flagrant lies to the grand jury, claiming that the letters had been genuine. Gesell refused to allow this evidence to be admitted. Robinette's lies, the judge held, were not North's fault. "It's appropriate for the jury to know this man is a liar," he told Keker. "This man has got a CIA devious mind." He was "a witness who temporarily prevaricated," the judge said. "It happens all the time. He straightened himself out."

These "prevarications" paled beside the testimony of Edwin Meese, former counselor to President Reagan and former attorney general of the United States. Keker called Meese to testify about the false testimony North had given him on Sunday, November 23, 1986, during Meese's fact-finding investigation. These lies formed the basis of one of the charges in North's indictment.

Meese acknowledged that the administration had been in such wide political disarray that its highest officials had discussed President Reagan's possible impeachment. Meese's mission, he said, had been to "get all the facts" and "to make sure that no one, and by that I mean political opponents, could call this a cover-up."

Meese claimed that he had told North that Sunday afternoon that the "worst thing [that] can happen is if someone tries to conceal something to protect themselves or the president or put a good spin on it." Despite this admonition, when North was confronted with his memorandum describing the diversion of Iranian arms proceeds to the Contras, he had falsely asserted that Israel had controlled the excess funds and had determined how much of them to pass on to the Contras. Meese said North had told him that "Israel would decide how much money would go to the resistance, and our involvement, the CIA and the NSC, was none."

To Brendan Sullivan's series of leading questions on cross-examination, Meese obligingly gave short, affirmative replies. He testified that even though "his worst nightmare had come true," being deceived by North had not left him angry.

After all, Sullivan suggested, it had been just "an administrative inquiry."

Meese agreed.

"It was absolutely clear in your mind that you were not conducting a criminal investigation or a formal investigation of any kind. Is that correct?"

"Yes, sir."

The interrogation, Sullivan said, had been "more or less a chat among colleagues . . . almost like coworkers in the administration . . . trying to understand . . . the basic facts."

Meese agreed.

"And your focus," Sullivan continued, "was not really the focus of an attorney general wearing the attorney general's hat, but it was basically to try to gather information to protect the president as best you could and deal with this enormous political problem brewing in the Congress, correct?"

"Yes."

"Are you saying then," Judge Gesell interjected, "that Lieutenant Colonel North had no obligation to answer your questions?"

"He would have had no obligation other than as a loyal member of the administration and a person in the White House," replied Meese.

"In other words," the judge asked, "there was no legal compulsion in the normal sense as there would be perhaps in a criminal investigation? So he could have said, 'I would rather not answer'?"

"He could have said that, yes."

Next on the stand was Robert McFarlane, who had already been sentenced on four misdemeanor counts of withholding information from Congress. He had received a two-year suspended sentence, with a $20,000 fine and a requirement for two hundred hours of community service.

McFarlane acknowledged, as the terms of his plea agreement required, having sent untruthful letters that withheld information requested by Congress. The letters, drafted in part by North and dated September 5 and 12, 1985, had denied "with deep personal conviction" any violation of the Boland amendments by the staff of the National Security Council. The letter to chairman Hamilton of the House intelligence committee had added, "It is equally important to stress what we did not do. We did not solicit funds or other support for military or paramilitary activities either from Americans or third parties. . . ." The letter to Representative Michael Barnes, chairman of the House foreign affairs subcommittee on Western Hemisphere affairs, had said, "We have scrupulously abided by the spirit and the letter of the law. None of us has solicited funds, facilitated contacts for prospective potential donors or otherwise organized or coordinated the military or paramilitary efforts of the resistance."

Those assurances not only had concealed the truth but had been false. McFarlane admitted that he had initiated the discussions with the Saudi Arabian ambassador that had eventually produced $32 million in support for the Contras, but he claimed in his direct examination that the contribution had been "volunteered" rather than "solicited." He had also known of the approaches made to Israel, Taiwan, and South Korea for weapons or cash or both. Additionally, in six different memoranda that had escaped the shredding party, North had advised McFarlane of North's work in guiding the "military or paramilitary" activities of the Contras. One message had sought McFarlane's approval for a scheme to involve South Korea in sinking a Nicaraguan vessel carrying weapons from Taiwan to the Sandinistas. Another had urged rewarding Guatemala for the false end-user certificates its officials had provided to facilitate Secord's arms deliveries to the Contras. Another had reported on military activities, such as cutting Sandinista supply lines, that had been carried out "in response to guidance." This message had also identified arms shipments to the Contras, listing shipments made by Secord separately from those made by others. Another memo reporting the Contras' military progress "in response to guidance" had defined the "delivery of lethal supplies" as a "current activity" that "will be sustained" even after the CIA "take[s] back intelligence gathering and political operations."

On the stand, McFarlane refused to acknowledge that his letters to Representatives Barnes and Hamilton had been lies. "You do not lie to the Congress," said McFarlane, the son of a former congressman from Texas. "It was often the case that congressmen would not always tell us everything on their agenda, and similarly the executive branch didn't always tell everything on its agenda to the Congress. You don't lie. You put your own interpretation on what the truth is."

Keker pressed him. If he hadn't lied, had he perhaps repeated North's lies?

But McFarlane wouldn't concede that North had purposefully misled him. "He was not willfully urging me to lie to anybody. . . . It's my responsibility and not Colonel North's. It's my letter. I believe that I am at fault, not him. He was probably trying to protect me."

Judge Gesell intervened. "You say he was trying to protect you?"

"Yes."

"That suggests he thought that you knew what he knew."

"No, sir," McFarlane responded. "It suggests that if he had told me what he knew that I would have gotten into trouble and perhaps him as well. . . ."

McFarlane also described his hectic efforts to revise North's false chronology of the Iran arms sales. Essentially, McFarlane said, he had depended on North for the details but had tried to delete outright false statements and paper over the omissions.

On cross-examination, McFarlane recalled North's having told him on the morning of November 21, 1986, just as Meese's investigation began, that North "intended to try to protect me and the president." They had been returning from a visit to Ledeen to find out what he would say when questioned. McFarlane said that "at some point in the trip, the fact of documents being shredded was raised, and that seemed to me to be an expression of perhaps trying to protect me from documents which, while explainable, were certainly likely to create criticism and argument."

Sullivan asked, "And you say the documents that he was going to shred would protect you from embarrassment?"

McFarlane replied that North had "said simply that we are going to have a shredding party or something like that, an offhand remark, ... but it was my interpretation that he said it to relieve any fears that I might have in my mind that I was going to be embarrassed by documents."

Sullivan then asked, "And what you had in mind were the documents that you and he had reviewed back in 1985 before you sent those letters to Congress, right?"

"Those," answered McFarlane, "plus probably hundreds of others . . . he didn't specify. I took it not as an act of malice, but just a statement to me that he was going to make sure that I wasn't hurt, . . . a statement of a subordinate trying to be loyal."

The close bond between McFarlane and North was apparent as McFarlane consistently depicted North as having been no more than a good soldier doing his duty. Sometimes McFarlane's language was contorted, his answers evasive. He fended off Keker's questions with his own "interpretation on what the truth is."

The performance exasperated Judge Gesell, who had never reconciled himself to trying North rather than a higher-up. "This man [McFarlane] has told so many stories," the judge observed out of the jurors' hearing, "that there isn't any way to know what he believes or what he knows. He is an intensely unreliable witness in almost every respect of his testimony."

McFarlane not only absorbed responsibility for many of North's acts, but also supported North's claim that those acts had flowed from policies approved at the highest levels. North claimed that his conduct and the secrecy in which he cloaked it had been fully authorized. Although Judge Gesell was skeptical that North's proof of authorization would meet the requirements of a legal defense, he gave Sullivan wide latitude to explore the subject with McFarlane, and Sullivan exploited the opportunity to introduce masses of supporting evidence.

The basis for Sullivan's cross-examination of McFarlane was the forty-two-page quid pro quo concession that we had negotiated with the representatives of the agencies concerned with national security. The document gave a declassified history of once-secret U.S. efforts to enlist foreign support for the Contras from the spring of 1984 through the fall of 1986.

Keker repeatedly tried to narrow Sullivan's use of the concession but failed to persuade Judge Gesell that the facts it conceded were irrelevant to the narrow, surviving charges against North: lying, destroying evidence, and obstructing official inquiries. Consequently, as Sullivan led McFarlane through the extensive stipulation, the public learned of the high-level maneuvers the Reagan administration had undertaken in its commitment to preserve the Contras. Until this information was demanded by North and Poindexter, and ordered produced by Judge Gesell, the Reagan administration had withheld it from Congress as well as from us.

One of the most explosive revelations in McFarlane's testimony dealt with Honduras, Nicaragua's neighbor to the north. Long a sanctuary and staging ground for Contra forces, Honduras had been restive. Under pressure from the Sandinistas, Honduran officials had suggested openly that the Contras should leave and fight from their own soil. A group of high-ranking officials from the NSC, the CIA, the Defense Department, and the State Department had then agreed that President Reagan should write the Honduran president, Roberto Suazo, to urge support for "those who struggle for freedom and democracy" and to hint at rewards for steadfastness.

President Reagan had signed the letter on February 19, 1985. The cover memorandum from McFarlane spoke expressly of "incentives for [Hondurans] to persist in aiding the freedom fighters"—incentives that would be communicated by "an emissary . . . very privately." The emissary had told President Suazo that the United States would release some of the millions in economic assistance funds it had been withholding, would speed up delivery of military aid, and would "enhance . . . existing CIA programs."

President Reagan had quickly approved the policy outlined by McFarlane. Within a month, military supplies had been on their way to Honduras. A few weeks later, the Hondurans had been promised roughly $20 million worth of ground-to-air missiles. Later that spring, McFarlane had recommended freeing $75 million in economic aid for Honduras, thus proposing the use of U.S. funds to stimulate Contra support in violation of the Boland amendments.

The emissary who had personally conveyed the message to President Suazo was George Bush. He had been vice president when he spoke with Suazo; he was president when his role was exposed in Judge Gesell's courtroom. Our stipulation recorded that Bush himself had passed word to Suazo that U.S. aid was on its way and "that the United States would provide from its own military stocks critical security assistance items . . . ordered by Honduran armed forces."

Bush declined comment on the revelation, but two State Department officials who had accompanied him confirmed that both U.S. aid to Honduras and the needs of the Contras had been discussed in the meeting with Suazo. They denied, however, that the two issues had been expressly linked. As Langhorne A. Motley, assistant secretary of state for the region in early 1985, explained, "You don't have to be clairvoyant to understand that you do things to expedite stuff. . . . [Delivering aid] shows good faith, and the guy knows what you are interested in. That's a step back from a quid pro quo."

This high-level interchange confirmed that North had been far from alone in circumventing the Boland amendments. The policy, including the secret use of U.S. funds to encourage aid for the Contras, had been sanctioned and executed by the president, vice president, and key cabinet members.

The secrecy that had shrouded the policy—and ultimately led to deceit—dated back at least to a June 1984 session of the National Security Planning Group, at which Bush, ironically, had cautioned his fellow members of the group against promising U.S. aid as an inducement for other countries to support the Contras. "How can anyone object to the U.S. encouraging third parties to provide help to the anti-Sandinistas?" he had asked rhetorically, seven months before meeting with Suazo. "The only problem that might come up is if the United States were to promise to give these third parties something in return so that some people could interpret this as some kind of an exchange."

As that two-hour session drew to a close, McFarlane had proposed "that there be no authority for anyone to seek third-party support for the anti-Sandinistas until" the attorney general had determined whether such activities would be legal. "I certainly hope," McFarlane had said, "none of this discussion will be made public in any way."

"If such a story gets out," Ronald Reagan had replied, "we'll all be hanging by our thumbs in front of the White House until we find out who did it."

A few days later, Attorney General William French Smith, Meese's predecessor, had given CIA Director William Casey an oral opinion that the administration could ask foreign countries to aid the Contras so long as it did not agree to repay the countries from U.S. funds.

In his testimony at North's trial, McFarlane confirmed President Reagan's personal role in accepting a February 1985 promise from Saudi Arabia's King Fahd to double his monthly contribution to the Contras. McFarlane also testified to an April 1985 telephone call in which President Reagan had asked President Suazo for prompt action to have the Honduran military release a shipment of Chinese surface-to-air missiles purchased by Secord for the Contras. Our stipulation confirmed that Suazo had pledged to get the "ammunition" to the Contras and had "raised the subject of U.S. government aid for his country." The missiles had reached their destination, and more aid for Honduras had soon followed.

As the stipulation disclosed, quid pro quo exchanges had been commonly discussed at policy-making levels and had been almost routinely carried out. Reagan had promised to support trade legislation sought by El Salvador, the distribution point for North's deliveries to the Contras; Guatemala's president had met with Secretary of State George Shultz to propose that "in return for Guatemalan support" for the Contras, the United States "triple military assistance . . . [and] double economic assistance to Guatemala." And President Manuel Noriega of Panama had had a message relayed to North in late August 1986 saying that "in exchange for a promise from the USG [U.S. government] to help clean up Noriega's image and a commitment to lift the USG ban on military sales, Noriega would assassinate the Sandinista leadership for the U.S. government." Alternatively, Noriega's representative had told North, Panamanian agents could perform "many essential things," such as "blowing up a Sandinista arsenal."

Although he had told Noriega's representative that American law "forbade such actions" as assassination, North had reported the proposal to Poindexter, who had thought that Noriega's "assets" inside Nicaragua "could be helpful." Although "involvement" in political killings had been considered beyond the pale, Poindexter had seen "assistance with sabotage [as] another story." He had "recommended that North speak with Noriega directly." After obtaining George Shultz's blessing, North had spoken with Noriega in London in late September 1986. Among other things, they had discussed attacking an oil refinery, an airport, and a harbor facility in Nicaragua. The discussions had ended when the plane carrying Eugene Hasenfus was shot down.

The disclosure of these incidents through McFarlane's testimony deeply implicated Ronald Reagan and George Bush. In the courtroom, Sullivan argued that the "stipulation proved that the executive branch picked Mr. North as the ritual lamb for congressional slaughter, . . . the fall guy for panicking superiors." Judge Gesell, however, was unpersuaded that this top-level support for the Contras constituted a legal defense for North's illegal actions.

Fear of the classified information impasse that had caused the dismissal of the conspiracy and diversion counts also restricted our ability to reconstruct for the jurors the full history of the sale of arms to Iran, but Willard Zucker testified to the flow of funds from Iran through the Swiss bank accounts of Richard Secord and Albert Hakim to the Contras. Zucker also traced some of the funds through Secord to Robinette for North's security fence.

Other witnesses helped depict North as a spinner of falsehoods. Former assistant attorney general Charles Cooper explained that Meese's investigation had been precipitated by the discovery that North's chronology for the congressional testimony of Poindexter and Casey had untruthfully denied U.S. government knowledge of the Israeli Hawk shipment. North had inserted the false statement that for several weeks after the shipment, no one in the United States government had known that the shipment had included missiles. Cooper was followed by the CIA's former general counsel Stanley Sporkin, who described for the jurors the agency's efforts during the week after the shipment to obtain a presidential finding retroactively authorizing the CIA's activity in facilitating the delivery of Israeli weapons to Iran.

After the last of our thirty-two witnesses testified, Brendan Sullivan moved to dismiss the indictment for failure of proof. Judge Gesell denied the motion, ruling that all twelve of our charges should go to the jury. "Giving full play to the right of the jury to determine credibility, weigh the evidence, and draw justifiable inferences of fact," he said, "a reasonable mind might fairly conclude quite beyond a reasonable doubt that the defendant is guilty of each and all of these counts."

The judge had already refused to let North subpoena Ronald Reagan. Nothing in the testimony given over the previous six weeks or in the supporting grand jury record, Gesell held, "remotely supports an authorization claim. . . . Whether or not authorization is a defense, authorization is not established by atmosphere, surmise, or inference. The trial record presently contains no proof that defendant North ever received any authorization from President Reagan to engage in the illegal conduct alleged, either directly or indirectly, orally or in writing."

Denied a living celebrity witness, Oliver North opened his defense on April 3 by summoning the ghost of William Casey to court. The medium was Vincent Cannistraro, a tall, composed CIA official who had been detailed to the National Security Council in December 1984 and had often dealt with North on a range of covert operations. In the spring of 1984, while still at the CIA, Cannistraro had attended a meeting in Casey's office with Adolfo Calero and two officials from the agency's Latin American affairs division. According to Cannistraro, Casey had said that "speaking on behalf of the president of the United States, he wanted to assure the freedom fighters that the United States government would find a way" to keep support coming despite the congressional cutoff. With Reagan's approval, Cannistraro continued, Oliver North had been designated "a principal point of reference" for sustaining the Contras. White House and CIA officials had claimed that "as a member of the National Security Council staff, [North] would not be subject to the restrictions" that barred CIA activity. Cannistraro called it a "handoff."

Judge Gesell asked whether the initial commitment to keep aid flowing had been Casey's "decision or somebody else's."

"At the original meeting at the CIA," Cannistraro replied, "Mr. Casey said he had discussed this with the president of the United States, and . . . it was agreed with the president that this was how it should be handled."

This testimony might have been persuasive had John Keker not demolished Cannistraro the next day. Keker opened his cross-examination by asking Cannistraro when Casey had died.

In 1987, the witness replied.

"You know," Keker continued, "that it's easy to blame things on a dead man, don't you?"

Cannistraro agreed that it was. He also conceded that when he had testified before the grand jury, he had neither mentioned the handoff nor named Casey as the source of North's orders or Reagan as the authority behind Casey. Cannistraro claimed he had not recalled the subject at the time. "It didn't come to my mind," he said.

"When did it come to your mind?" Judge Gesell asked.

"I thought of it yesterday. . . . It was an additional detail that I did not think was relevant in 1987."

Cannistraro's grand jury testimony produced more trouble for North. Inasmuch as Cannistraro was not our witness, we had not been obliged to supply his prior statements to Sullivan. Among the details to which Cannistraro had previously testified was his reaction to North's draft replies for McFarlane to send to Congress. When pressed by Keker at the trial, Cannistraro admitted that when North showed him the drafts, he had responded by extending his hand a foot or more in front of his nose to suggest Pinocchio's nose growing longer as he lied. In court, a reluctant Cannistraro repeated the gesture.

Keker exaggerated the demonstration, stretching his arm as far from his face as it would go. "Like a long nose?" he asked.

"Not *that* long," said Cannistraro.

The courtroom exploded with laughter.

Keker then compelled the witness to acknowledge another passage from his grand jury testimony. "With Colonel North," Cannistraro had said, "you could never be certain that what he was telling you was true or was fantasy or was being told you deliberately to mislead you. So my normal modus operandi when receiving information from Colonel North, as I'm sure it was for most people who knew him for some time, was to take everything with about four grains of salt and try to sort it out from there."

When a second wave of laughter had subsided, Keker asked, "Do you recall those words?"

Cannistraro admitted that he did. The passage, he said, described "the way I came to feel about him during the summer of 1986."

Asked whether the head of the CIA's Latin American division had voiced concern over North's activities in 1986, the witness hesitated.

Again Keker read from Cannistraro's grand jury testimony, quoting his CIA colleague as having said of North, "I don't know what he's doing, but it's probably illegal, and he's going to jail." Did the witness recall that testimony?

"You just refreshed my memory," Cannistraro replied.

Brendan Sullivan tried to resuscitate his witness and his client. Answering a set of softball questions, Cannistraro happily described North as having "a tremendous amount of energy." He was "the first man I would want with me in a foxhole when the first rounds came in."

But, asked Keker on recross, was North also someone "who would lie, cheat, and steal to get the mission accomplished?"

"That is difficult to answer," Cannistraro said. "He did on occasion, in my judgment, put the end above the means."

After two days of testimony, the defense case was not going well. A death in a juror's family gave the court a one-day break and Brendan Sullivan time to consider his options. He decided to present his star witness. On Thursday, April 6, with hundreds of would-be spectators lining the courthouse's second-floor corridor, Oliver Laurence ("with a *u*," he advised the stenographer) North took the oath and the witness stand.

During two days of direct testimony, North admitted most of the activities on which the charges against him were based, but he resolutely denied that any of those actions had been criminal. Saying that he had never operated "without the express permission" of McFarlane or Poindexter or, as a rule, without the "concurrence" of Casey, North depicted himself as having been the administration's ball carrier on the Contra team. "I was not stepping in," he said, "I was brought in. . . . Basically, it was a handoff. You've got the ball, go run with it. Very clearly, I was to be the one to replace the CIA."

To him, the assignment had included fund-raising but not "solicitation." He had made the pitch that resulted in the donation of funds but he had not been present in Channell's final act of solicitation. At Sullivan's request, North repeated for the jury the slide-show presentation given to the likely contributors selected by Channell. North denied that he had actually solicited money himself, explaining that McFarlane had specifically forbidden him to "say to a single person, 'Would you give me money?' " Consequently, North claimed, there had been no instance of "a single donor ever giving money in my presence or . . . [being] asked to give money in my presence. Not one."

He had not disclosed that McFarlane had obtained funds from the Saudis, North said, because he had been "told by McFarlane not to reveal that to anyone. Those were the direct orders of the president. In fact, I was chastised for letting Director Casey know."

Keeping secrets meant deceiving Congress, and North acknowledged that he had drafted a "factually incorrect" response to congressional inquiries and that McFarlane had used two of his paragraphs in replying to Congressmen Hamilton and Barnes. These covert activities had been ones that he "knew it wasn't right to tell the truth about." Similarly, when he had set about revising the texts of his memos to McFarlane, North had seen nothing "unlawful" in the exercise.

"McFarlane gave me a list" of NSC file documents and "said, 'Fix these ... so that they will be consistent with what we told the Congress,' " North testified. "They were his documents. I had written them, but they were memos to him, and therefore his documents."

When Sullivan had North explain his own meeting with the members of the House intelligence committee in August 1986, North dramatically described his reluctance as he tried to avoid the meeting and finally carried it off only because Poindexter had ordered him to do so. "I told him ... there were all kinds of things that could not be revealed. ... He and I both knew what they were. ... [But Poindexter said,] 'You can handle it. ... You can take care of it.' "

"Did you tell them the truth at that meeting on August 6, 1986?" Sullivan asked.

"No," said North. "Almost everything" the members of Congress had wanted to know about, he added, had concerned secret work done "at the direction of the president of the United States." As he had been bound to conceal those activities, not least because of pledges to foreign officials, North said, "I was put in a situation where"—his voice choked as it often had during his congressional testimony—"having been raised to know what the Ten Commandments were, I knew that it would be wrong to [lie], but I didn't think it was unlawful."

"How did you feel," Sullivan asked his client, "about being put in that situation?"

North paused for dramatic effect. His voice shook a second time. "I felt like a pawn in a chess game being played by giants."

Whether pawn or knight errant, Oliver North had been an effective witness in the hands of his own lawyer. To undercut North's credibility, John Keker, opening his cross-examination, quickly went for the weakest spot in North's moral armor: money. Not only had North been casual about Adolfo Calero's traveler's checks and duplicitous about the mock payment for Glenn Robinette's security system, but he apparently had also taken an outright cash payment from Richard Secord and used it to help in purchasing an automobile.

Because proving it would have required Secord's testimony, the transaction was not among the charges we had included in the indictment against North, but our investigators had discovered that North had paid $5,000 down in cash to hold an $8,038 used GMC Suburban van and that Secord's records showed a simultaneous $3,000 cash transfer to North. The dealer remembered that North had made a second cash payment for the $3,038 balance of the purchase price. The coincidence was impossible to overlook.

Keker began by questioning North about his use of Calero's traveler's checks. Referring to a personal expenditure at a supermarket, Keker asked: "You were reimbursing yourself for money that you had spent on Contra or hostage initiatives, is that right?"

"Yes, correct."

"Where did you get [that] money . . . to begin with?"

"It was my money, my cash."

"And where did you get cash?"

"Out of my house."

"Did you have a stash of cash in your house?"

"You call it a stash. I call it a family fund . . . by mid-1985, upwards of fifteen thousand dollars in cash."

That sum, the defendant insisted, had accumulated from spare change emptied from his pocket every Friday night. "I would . . . put [the coins] in that steel box that I'd been issued as a midshipman. That's where it would go, and that's how that fund was built over the course of twenty-plus years."

The implausibility of North's tale could be demonstrated with a simple bit of arithmetic: To accumulate $15,000 in twenty years, making no withdrawals during that time, the weekly deposits of small change would have to have averaged more than $14. Keker did not pursue the issue. Instead, he turned to the purchase of the van. North said he recalled having brought "three thousand dollars or four thousand dollars, something like that, from the fund" to the car dealer in suburban Virginia, eight or ten miles from his home.

"Did you go to General Secord's office that afternoon to get another three thousand dollars for the hostages?"

"I honestly don't remember."

Shown Secord's business records, North still did not remember the transaction. "I got a lot of money from General Secord," he said, "on a lot of occasions."

North agreed that some $10,000 must have remained in "the metal box" after the first car payment. That being the case, Keker asked, why not just go home to get the additional $3,000 that the dealer required? "Because," North said, "I think I had to get to work."

When the purchase was completed three days later, Keker noted, "You hadn't gone to a bank account. You had gone someplace and gotten cash."

"I had gone back to my box that was bolted to the floor of my closet and got the cash, Mr. Keker," North angrily insisted.

Keker turned to the episode of the security fence. North contended that he had always meant to pay for it, but admitted that he had instead engaged in a complicated deception. "He [Robinette] sent me two phony bills," North said, "and I sent him two phony letters back."

"Why didn't you pay those bills?" Keker inquired.

North hesitated. "I don't know," he said. "I guess I had come to the conclusion that, having the system there, having been fairly well trashed by that point, I was kind of angry . . . , so I sent the phony letters in one of the dumber things I've done in my life."

It may have been dumb, but it certainly seemed calculated. In comparing the two letters, we had concluded that North had purposely defaced the typing ball to make the letters appear to have been written months apart. North, however, gave a different explanation: He said that he had typed the two letters on a display typewriter during separate visits to a catalog store near his home. Between the two sessions, another user had apparently damaged the ball. Asked why he had typed the letters in the store, North answered, "Well, one, I don't recall we had a working typewriter at home at the time, and number two, I didn't want to do it at work. I didn't want the Marine Corps, which is where I was, involved in that kind of cover-up. And I went and did it at a store."

But covering up was precisely the activity in which North had regularly engaged at the NSC. Keker went through the whole history of McFarlane's deceit of Congress and North's attempt to alter his embarrassing memos to McFarlane. North blamed McFarlane. The revision had not been "done to protect me," North insisted. "It was done to protect people well above me. . . . I had been led to believe everything I was doing was done at the direction of the president."

Keker pretended astonishment. "You had been told by the president of the United States to destroy documents? Explain how you had come to that conclusion."

North's explanation was circular: "Because, everything I had done that was described in the documents on this list, I had been told was at the direction of the president."

North had misinformed the president's legal counsel Fred F. Fielding that Spitz Channell and Contra backer Barbara Newington had not been raising funds to arm the Contras. Relying on that assurance, Reagan had sent letters of thanks, drafted by North, to both of them. When Keker asked him about these events, North claimed not to remember them.

"Someone," Keker pressed, "was telling the president a flat-out, one-hundred-percent, old-fashioned American lie. Right?"

"I do not recall that," said North. "No."

The most dramatic disclosure of the cross-examination was a true surprise—a telling episode that we had not known about because of our insulation from the congressional hearings.

Questioning North about his false chronology of the November 1985 Israeli Hawk shipment, Keker asked North what he knew about the president's having signed the finding that the CIA had drafted to ratify its assistance in the missile shipment.

Keker asked, "Where's the finding now?"

"I am told it was destroyed totally."

"By?"

"Admiral Poindexter."

"When?"

"I don't know the exact date." North said he thought that it had been November 21, 22, or 23, 1986.

"When did you learn Admiral Poindexter destroyed the finding?"

"I was there," North revealed. "I saw him tear it in two."

Keker showed his surprise. He pushed further. Had the destruction occurred before or after the Meese investigation began?

"It may have been simultaneous."

"Do you remember thinking you were in a den of thieves?"

North was indignant. "I never regarded that I was working in a den of thieves," he declared. "I honestly believed I was working for honorable men doing their level best to make this country a better place, and I was carrying out lawful orders to that end."

North testified that he had believed that the diversion of arms proceeds had been approved by President Reagan.

"You understood that you had the approval of the president to use those monies to undertake operations?"

"I'm absolutely certain . . . that I believed throughout, from early February [1986] when we began the concept or putting in place the concept of using Iranian arms sales monies to aid the Nicaraguan resistance and to do those other things, that I deeply believed that I had the authority of the president to do it."

One of the five witnesses in our brief rebuttal case was Mary Dix, an NSC administrative officer, who portrayed Oliver North as a man routinely strapped for even small amounts of cash. She testified that he had continually importuned her for the immediate reimbursement of his expenses until the middle of 1985, when his urgency had abruptly stopped.

In his summation, Keker hammered less at the venality of North's conduct than at his dishonesty and its effect on government. "Government by deception is not a free government. Government by deception is not a democratic government. Government by deception is not a government under the rule of law. . . . The tragedy of Oliver North is that a man who says he cared so much about freedom and democracy in Nicaragua forgot about the demands of freedom and democracy here at home." Keker charged that North, with McFarlane, had tried to follow "Adolf Hitler's old strategy. He was the one who said, the victor will never be asked if he told the truth. . . . [I]f the lies work, Congress will stop asking questions. . . . By mid-1986, lying had become a habit for Oliver North. . . . [D]uring his testimony in this case, . . . can you believe that this habit has been broken?"

After a lunch break, Brendan Sullivan responded. Seizing on the reference to Hitler, Sullivan stormed that Oliver North "is not Adolf Hitler, and he doesn't do things like Adolf Hitler, and to suggest it indicates the extraordinary drive, the force, the power of this government to put its might on top of Colonel North, to see what they can say is a crime. . . . Everything the government sees this man doing is through a dirty glass, a filthy glass. . . . He throws papers away. Here he is about to leave the office, and he is destroying papers. Why shouldn't he . . . ? The evidence is that he was the covert operations officer for the most secret project in America."

Sullivan belittled North's misleading of Attorney General Meese—"three thoughts" in a "four-hour conversation . . . that they claim Colonel North wasn't candid about"—and North's acceptance of the security system "from a friend, General Secord, after he has been threatened by the world's most dangerous terrorist."

Recalling that Ronald Reagan had telephoned North to call him an "American hero" a few hours after dismissing him, Sullivan drew "the conclusion that the president was using Ollie North as a scapegoat. It doesn't sound like the kind of a thing the president would do unless he knew full well what Ollie North was doing."

Sullivan concluded by reading aloud North's last PROF note to Poindexter. "My prayer," went one sentence, "is that the president is not further damaged by what has transpired and that the hostages will not be harmed as a consequence of what we do now."

"That's Oliver North," said Brendan Sullivan in a voice choked with emotion. "In a sense, he's been a hostage. I ask you to, on the evidence, to set him free."

Sullivan's summation had not stressed the authorization defense he had tried to invoke throughout the trial. And Judge Gesell rejected that defense in his instruction on the law, telling the jury: "Authorization requires clear direct instructions to act at a given time in a given way. Neither the president nor any of the defendant's superiors had the legal authority to order anyone to violate the law."

The jurors listened attentively as Gesell read his ninety-four-page charge to them, making the standard of guilt or innocence clear. For a guilty finding, the jurors would have to decide not only that Oliver North had "acted knowingly, voluntarily, and deliberately," the judge told them, "but that he [had] acted with a bad purpose." The judge then sent the jurors out of the courtroom, telling them not to commence their deliberations yet. Obviously tired, Gesell spent the next several hours ruling on Barry Simon's oral exceptions to the charge, repeating points he had already made in objections to a draft of the charge before it was delivered.

This done, the judge sent for the jurors and told them that they could at last retire and begin their deliberations. They were to be sequestered. Escorted by marshals to help them evade a cordon of reporters, they left the courtroom.

As day followed day without a verdict, the anxiety in our office climbed. I sympathized with the jurors, who were working their way through thirteen hundred pages of exhibits. Judge Gesell had warned us that District of Columbia juries usually read through exhibit after exhibit. He had barred them from consulting transcripts of the testimony, but he did let them use his empty courtroom after they pleaded for space in which to examine the exhibits. Clearly, they took their civic duty seriously.

Finally, after twelve days of deliberations, as three jurors held out for acquittal, they all joined in one juror's simple prayer that they might reach a verdict. On the afternoon of May 4, 1989, the nine women and three men, some of them still wiping away tears of exhaustion, sympathy, and concern, entered Judge Gesell's courtroom for the last time. Denise Anderson, a thirty-four-year-old hospital clerk who had been elected foreperson, handed the completed two-page verdict form to the bailiff, who passed it up to Judge Gesell.

After studying the sheets for about a minute, the judge began to read the verdict for each of the twelve counts. The verdicts on the first five counts were the same: "not guilty." Finally, on count six (aiding and abetting the preparation of the false chronology for the congressional testimony of Casey and Poindexter), the verdict was "guilty." Of the remaining charges, the jury found North guilty on counts nine (destruction of NSC documents) and ten (acceptance of illegal gratuity—the $13,800 security system—from Secord).

Clearly the jurors had given North the benefit of every possible doubt and, ignoring the judge's charge, had accepted the spurious authorization defense. The jury had acquitted North of all the charges related to his own misstatements to the congressional committees and to Meese. It had also brushed aside his pocketing of Contra traveler's checks and the complex charge of conspiring with Spitz Channell and Richard Miller in the scheme to collect funds for the Contras through a tax-exempt foundation.

When Keker telephoned from our small courthouse office to tell me the verdict, I sensed that he was stunned. On the positive side, Oliver North stood a convicted felon. To our disappointment, however, he had persuaded the jurors not to treat his deception of Congress as criminal. The rationale of the verdict was clear. The jurors had held the defendant accountable for the offenses he had clearly committed on his own, and they had forgiven him those crimes that they felt could be traced to orders from his superiors. "He wasn't the boss," the foreperson later told reporters. "Basically, on the counts of 'not guilty,' he was following orders. And there were a lot of people's orders. I think Reagan should stand up and give an accounting for what he did. . . . I think he knew a lot about what was going on."

I was most disappointed that the jury had acquitted North of his own false testimony to the House intelligence committee, while reaching a much more sophisticated verdict that North had aided and abetted the preparation of a false chronology for the testimony of Poindexter and Casey regarding the CIA's participation in the Israeli Hawk shipment. But, I quickly reassured Keker, the critical fact was that the verdict had nailed North as the felon he was. We had skirted the disaster of the congressional hearings and should announce victory. On the courthouse steps, Keker did so in a sober, brief statement that a case that "some even said . . . could not be tried" had ended in a verdict upholding "the principle that no man is above the law."

Brendan Sullivan termed the outcome a "disappointment" and promised to appeal all three convictions. North called for "the support and prayers of the American people" to ensure that "we will be fully vindicated."

The reaction on Capitol Hill varied. Republican Congressman Henry Hyde, who had ostentatiously congratulated North in the courtroom, admitted to feelings of "sorrow" and added, "I'm not sure Oliver North got a fair trial." Senator Warren Rudman called the defendant "a tragic figure" who, "in his dedication to his mission . . . lost sight of the fact that there are rules, and you have to follow the rules." Congressman Lee Hamilton, who claimed to be neither "elated" nor "disappointed"—nor "surprised"—by the verdict, concluded that "President Reagan and President Bush still have some explaining to do. We will be learning about Iran-Contra for a long time to come."

In a presentencing memorandum to the court, we argued that even a brief incarceration would "alert all government officials that activities like North's are indeed unlawful and that if officials engaging in such conduct are caught and convicted, the punishment will be severe." Beyond its effect on those who had not yet told the truth about Iran-Contra, a prison sentence for North would reassure "private citizens . . . that these are serious crimes and that powerful government officials are not accorded special treatment." We urged Judge Gesell not to let North off with "only a slap on the wrist" that "would send exactly the wrong message . . . fifteen years after Watergate." We reminded him of the jail terms imposed on Richard Nixon's lawbreaking aides.

To our regret, the implied parallels did not register as persuasive precedents. Failing to take into account our difficulty in getting North's cooperation against other participants in Iran-Contra, and undoubtedly concerned about the fact that McFarlane had received a minimal sentence and about the prospect of an appellate review of the immunity question, Judge Gesell on July 5, 1989, gave North concurrent suspended sentences of one, two, and three years and issued an order putting him on probation for two years. North was also fined $150,000 and required to perform twelve hundred hours of community service with disadvantaged youngsters in Washington.

The punishment was light. The fine, for instance, represented no more than six standard speaking fees on the conservative lecture circuit, where North had become a well-remunerated folk hero. Explaining the sentence, Judge Gesell—who had responded as many older men did to

North—told him that "jail would only harden [his] misconceptions" and that the "many highly commendable aspects of [his] life" weighed against imprisonment. The deeper motive for leniency, however, was the judge's view of North as someone who had not initiated "this tragic breach of the public trust" but had "responded certainly willingly and sometimes excessively" to orders from above. "I do not think that in this area [of covert operations] you were a leader at all, but really a low-ranking subordinate working to carry out initiatives of a few cynical superiors. You came to be the point man in a very complex power play developed by higher-ups."

Although Judge Gesell had rejected the authorization defense in his jury instructions, it seemed to me that he had forgotten that a con-spirator did not have to be the boss to earn punishment. In determin-ing the sentence, the judge seemed to have accepted North's irrelevant, even if accurate, characterization of himself as a pawn. Although this was a valid factor to consider in sentencing, I was dis-appointed by the complete absence of a term of imprisonment. North could properly have earned leniency by telling the whole truth about his operation and those working with him—rather than telling just enough to defend himself. Looking to our future need for North's tes-timony, we would have found it much easier to deal with someone under a prison sentence than with someone who had nothing to lose by withholding the full truth.

Despite its less than satisfactory outcome, the trial had given us some important new evidence to examine, new leads to pursue, and new reasons to reconsider old conclusions. Of particular significance was the access we had gained to a hoard of data on North's interactions with his colleagues in the CIA and the State and Defense departments. Over the years, North had dutifully kept, in stenographer's pads, exten-sive notes on his work at the NSC, recording his meetings, conversa-tions, and thoughts. Fawn Hall had told us that North had removed his accumulation of notepads from his office credenza on his last evening in the Old Executive Office Building, and that she had seen them in Brendan Sullivan's office soon thereafter. We had tried to sub-poena the notes, arguing that they were official records, but the courts had ruled against us. Not until North took the stand at his own trial had we received the hundreds of photocopied pages. Although there had been too little time for them to play a significant role in Keker's cross-examination, they ultimately led us to other officials and a broadened view of Iran-Contra.

Contra leader Adolfo Calero visits President Ronald Reagan as
Lieutenant Colonel Oliver North looks on, April 4, 1985.

Vice President George Bush with Contra leaders Alfonso Robelo,
Arturo Cruz, and Adolfo Calero, March 6, 1986.

Financier Adnan Khashoggi (left) with Iranian arms broker Manucher
Ghorbanifar in Monaco on December 12, 1986.

Michael Ledeen,
McFarlane's consultant-
intermediary.

David Kimche, director general of the Israeli foreign ministry, who urged Robert McFarlane to deal with Ghorbanifar.

Robert "Bud" McFarlane, President Reagan's national security advisor, 1984–85.

McFarlane reports the failure of his mission to Iran to secure release of hostages immediately after returning from Tehran, May 29, 1986. From left to right, Chief of Staff Donald Regan, President Reagan, Vice President Bush, McFarlane, and Howard Teicher of the National Security Council staff.

A closed National Security Planning Group (the president's senior foreign policy advisors) meeting in the White House situation room, June 16, 1985. From the left, chairman of the Joint Chiefs of Staff John Vessey, Secretary of Defense Caspar Weinberger, Vice President Bush, President Reagan, Secretary of State George Schultz, CIA Director William Casey, and Chief of Staff Donald Regan. National Security Advisor John Poindexter was at the end opposite the president. Meese reported to this group (except General Vessey) on his November 1986 fact-finding investigation.

On November 25, 1986, Attorney General Edwin Meese takes questions regarding the diversion of arms sales proceeds after President Reagan announces in press conference that Admiral Poindexter has resigned and that Lieutenant Colonel North has been reassigned to the Marine Corps.

Vice Admiral John Poindexter, President Reagan's national security advisor in 1986, uses his fifth amendment rights to refuse to answer the House foreign affairs committee's questions on the Iran-Contra affair, December 9, 1986.

Lieutenant Colonel Oliver North takes the oath before appearing before the House foreign affairs committee on Dec. 9, 1986. He refuses to answer questions, claiming his fifth amendment protection.

Retired United States Air Force major general Richard Secord after arraignment on the conspiracy indictment.

Secord's partner, Albert Hakim, who pleads guilty to a misdemeanor charge.

William Casey, director of central intelligence until his fatal illness in 1987.

Clair George, CIA deputy director for operations, arrives at U. S. district court on July 24, 1992, for the first day of his trial. He is subsequently convicted of two felonies.

Duane "Dewey" Clarridge, chief of the CIA's Latin American division until 1984 and then chief of West European division, 1984–87, after indictment on federal felony charges in November 1991.

Alan Fiers, chief of the Central American task force, 1984–87, leaves federal court after pleading guilty to charges of unlawfully withholding information from Congress, July 10, 1991.

Judge George MacKinnon, presiding judge of the panel that appoints me independent counsel.

Judge Walter Mansfield, a member of the appointing panel.

My German shepherd, Bertie, is dubious about being photographed on our
Sunday morning walk after the press learned of my appointment
on December 13, 1986.

The "luxurious" office of the independent counsel: enameled steel, glass partitions, and crowded corridors.

Guy Struve, my closest associate counsel.

Early team leaders in the investigation. From left to right, Bob Schwartz, John Keker, Paul Friedman, and Chris Todd.

RIGHT: Chief Judge Aubrey Robinson, Jr., who impaneled the grand jury and presided over several arraignments.

BELOW: Fawn Hall, who had been our reluctant informant, is sworn in before the congressional Iran-Contra committee on June 8, 1987.

Carl "Spitz" Channell leaves the courthouse on April 30, 1987, after pleading guilty to conspiring with North to violate tax laws in their Contra fundraising.

Richard Miller leaves U. S. district court on May 6, 1987, after pleading guilty to the same crime as Channell.

North, after receiving immunity, testifies before the joint select committees on July 7, 1987, with his lawyer, Brendan Sullivan.

Joint committee leaders take a break during North's immunized testimony, July 10, 1987. Left to right, Arthur Liman, chief Senate counsel; John Nields, Jr., chief House counsel; Senate chairman Daniel Inouye (seated); Senator George Mitchell; Representative Peter Rodino, Jr.; and House chairman Lee Hamilton (seated).

Unsurprisingly, they documented North's extensive contacts with Elliott Abrams and Alan Fiers, as fellow members of the restricted inter-agency group monitoring policy in Central America. Specifically, the notes suggested the degree to which North had revealed to the group his role in funding and supplying the Contras. What he had recorded, once we could decipher his abbreviations and put his notes together with our other information, required us to take another look at Abrams, Fiers, and others in the State Department and the CIA.

CHAPTER TWELVE

Deniability Triumphant

Our top priority after Oliver North was John Poindexter, but the case against Joseph Fernandez, the CIA chief of station in Costa Rica, was speeding toward trial. With North's help, Fernandez had guided and manipulated the Contras on the southern front, the border between Nicaragua and Costa Rica. Linked with the Enterprise's supply network through the National Security Agency's KL-43 communication system, he had kept North informed about what weapons the Contras needed and where Richard Secord's pilots should drop them. When the arms suppliers needed an airstrip in Costa Rica for emergency landings, Fernandez had coordinated Costa Rican officials and Secord's representatives. Unaware that the KL-43 system was recording his calls, Fernandez had telephoned North and Rafael Quintero more than a hundred times.

After North's Iran-Contra activities had been exposed, Fernandez had given false and misleading answers to the CIA's inspector general and to the Tower Commission's staff. The airstrip, Fernandez said, had been a Costa Rican initiative to defend against a Nicaraguan invasion. He claimed not to have known that North had been involved in resupplying the Contras or that the supplies he had obtained from North and Secord had included weapons and ammunition. When the Tower Commission's staff later confronted him with the recorded KL-43 messages, Fernandez conceded the untruthfulness of thirteen of his responses to the inspector general and twelve to the Tower Commission.

On June 20, 1988, the grand jury in the District of Columbia had indicted Fernandez for making some of these false statements, for obstructing both investigations, and for conspiring with North and others to carry out an unauthorized covert action. The case was ill-starred from the outset. The conspiracy charge included acts in the District of Columbia and was properly brought there, but the obstruction and false statements had occurred in Virginia. Those charges could be tried in the District of Columbia only if the defendant did not object. Defense counsel did not raise the question of venue until after Chief Judge Aubrey Robinson had disposed of all the pretrial motions in the District of Columbia, ruling in our favor on most of them.

Once the issue of venue had been raised, we obtained a new indictment in the U.S. district court in Alexandria, Virginia. The indictment was held under seal until April 24, 1989, after the jury in North's trial was sequestered for deliberations. Having consented to the dismissal of the conspiracy charge against North, we did not include it in the new indictment against Fernandez because doing so would have raised similar problems with declassifying evidence and because the agencies had probably interpreted my agreement to drop the conspiracy count from the North case as an agreement not to try it in any case. The new indictment contained only four counts, two for obstructing the investigations of the Tower Commission and the CIA's inspector general and two for the specific false statements Fernandez had made. Only one of the counts was related to the airstrip; the others concerned his denials regarding North and the Contra-supply operation.

I assigned associate counsel Laurence Shtasel and Geoffrey Stewart to try the case for us. Although Shtasel was very young, he had tried several criminal cases as an assistant U.S. attorney in Brooklyn. Stewart, a young litigation partner in the Washington office of the Boston firm of Hale & Dorr, had previously been on the staff of Attorney General William French Smith. Before that, he had worked with me at Davis Polk. Shtasel and Stewart were formidably opposed by defense counsel Thomas Wilson, of Washington's Seaforth firm, who was one of several private lawyers to whom CIA staff regularly referred employees. Experienced, tough, and aggressive, Wilson had been among those suggested by Cole Black, the deputy inspector general to whom Fernandez had lied. A quasi-insider at the CIA, Wilson seemed to have better information about what went on within the agency than we did.

Judge Claude M. Hilton, to whom the case was assigned, was very different from Judge Gerhard Gesell. Born in Virginia's westernmost projection into the Appalachian Mountains, Judge Hilton had studied law at American University in Washington while working as an assistant court clerk in Arlington, Virginia. Then, after a year or two in the commonwealth attorney's local office, he had practiced alone for twenty years until appointed to the federal bench by President Reagan. Experienced in criminal defense, Judge Hilton brought to the Fernandez case a perceptive sympathy and understanding of the needs of a defendant confronted with indisputable evidence. The judge also brought an ardent commitment to expedition.

Known as the "rocket docket," his court was proud of its record for moving its caseload. As we soon learned, neither the CIA nor the federal government, let alone the independent counsel, could persuade Judge Hilton to reconsider a motion once he had ruled. Hardly anyone could be less in sympathy with the hesitant dribbling of the CIA, as it frequently procrastinated before giving up information.

Within a few weeks, Judge Hilton had disposed of all motions except the ones related to classified information. After an ex parte hearing with Wilson, the judge ruled on the remaining classified-information issues over the course of three days of court sessions that were closed to the public. We had so narrowed the charges against Fernandez that we were confident that our indictment would survive the problems of classified evidence. At the last minute, however, the CIA balked. Although it agreed to release information about its station in Costa Rica, the CIA would not release the names and locations of its other stations in Central America or permit us to identify the Ilopango facility, even though it had ultimately consented to the disclosure of this information in North's trial. The CIA's lawyers explained their fear that Fernandez, an agency insider, would be more likely than North to exploit the disclosure in a way that would endanger the continued operation of these facilities.

We distrusted this rationalization. We had been told that at least one of CIA Director William Webster's top assistants had openly insisted that the CIA deliberately withhold classified information to force the dismissal of our case. He argued that because Fernandez had been disciplined by the CIA, he should not be subject to the laws applicable to ordinary persons who lied to government agencies. In his opinion, Fernandez had been a victim of Congress's vacillation.

Other aides had reiterated arguments for the deniability of publicly known facts embarrassing to foreign countries that had accommodated the presence of CIA operatives in our embassies. All of Webster's assistants knew that Fernandez would open a can of worms. He would claim authorization by his superiors and argue that he therefore had not had any reason to lie. No one, so far as we knew, had argued in favor of the rule of law. Apparently, the only argument made for releasing the information had been based on the need to avoid the political embarrassment that would result if an entire case had to be dismissed because of the CIA's refusal to declassify information.

We were able to resolve most of the classification problems, but two remained. Judge Hilton held that, in addition to identifying the CIA station in Costa Rica, Fernandez should be permitted to identify stations in two other countries as well as the CIA's Ilopango facility. The judge also decided that Fernandez should be allowed to expose three ongoing, wholly unrelated CIA activities, which the judge had been persuaded would show a pattern of joint efforts by the United States and Costa Rica to forestall a Nicaraguan invasion of Costa Rica. Fernandez had falsely claimed that the airstrip was part of such an effort.

Judge Hilton announced his decision on July 10, 1989. Two days later, as provided by the Classified Information Procedures Act (CIPA), we presented a CIA-approved substitution for the information Judge Hilton had held material to the defense. Edward Dennis, who was now the acting deputy attorney general, filed an affidavit warning that the three CIA programs and the Central American stations and facilities could not be disclosed without serious injury to national security, but he did not flatly refuse to declassify the information.

These substitute stipulations and subsequent more generous ones that also had been approved by the CIA provoked ever more threatening orders from Judge Hilton. He viewed each proposed substitution as a motion for reargument of the order in which he had held the classified information itself necessary and material. His response was to extend his previous orders. He finally decided to permit Fernandez to introduce evidence that there had been three ongoing operations "set up in the same kind of way as the airstrip, to show how they were done, the purpose for doing them, who instigated them, and for what purposes, and also the magnitude of them." Further, Fernandez could attempt to prove "any and all circumstances of these operations subject only to rulings on relevancy and how much detail he need[ed] to go into." Fernandez would be permitted to testify to whatever he knew about those operations, subject to some limitation on detail. "I am ruling that it is all relevant," declared the judge. "It is all relevant evidence." He peremptorily declined to review the individual documents that described the programs and that would have demonstrated to him their lack of connection with the airstrip.

Exasperated at the very difficulties CIPA had been designed to over-come, and rebelling at the essential elements of the statute, he erupted: "I suppose every prosecutor would like the proposition of being able to put on their live witnesses, and then have a defendant get on the stand and tell his story, and only be able to corroborate it with a brief stipulation. . . . I don't believe that the prosecutor should be permitted to do that. I think the defendant ought to have leeway, in order to have a fair trial, to put on that evidence which is relevant to corroborate his defense."

Vainly, the CIA again expanded its proposed stipulation about the identities and locations of stations and facilities. It agreed to admit that it had maintained facilities and stations in Latin American countries for the collection of intelligence and the management of covert operations and that it had assigned officers and employees in neighboring coun-tries to work on matters involving the Contras, and that some of these individuals had collected intelligence in Nicaragua regarding the mili-tary activities of both sides as well as the lethal aid supplied to the Contras. The CIA agreed to permit Fernandez to refer to persons located in these countries as CIA employees and to permit each chief of station to be identified as "a senior CIA officer." Judge Hilton quickly rejected this proposal and reiterated his holding that, if the case was tried, Fernandez would be able to identify the CIA's Central American stations by name and location.

Although Judge Hilton's orders seemed extreme, arising from Fernandez's utterly false claims, we had decided not to appeal them at this point. I knew that the court of appeals would be reluctant to be drawn into a review of materiality and would be unlikely to reverse a trial judge's decision for exceeding the limits of his discretion. Equally important, if I did ultimately appeal, I wanted the appellate court to consider not just the question of materiality but also, if Judge Hilton dismissed the indictment, the possible excessiveness of the sanction. I did not want to bring two successive appeals—one before dismissal and the second after it. The two points strengthened each other. I wanted them considered together.

We continued to hope that even if the attorney general supported the CIA's refusal to declassify the information, we could persuade the court to penalize us with something less severe than dismissal; he could, for example, impose a broad finding of fact or dismiss some counts and narrow others. The odds weren't in our favor, but I had to exhaust that opportunity.

We spent the remaining week before trial attempting to persuade Attorney General Richard Thornburgh not to file a CIPA affidavit prohibiting the disclosure of the CIA's publicly known Central American stations and facilities. Realizing that we could not successfully urge the declassification of the three ongoing CIA programs in Costa Rica, we intended to drop the charge related to the airstrip to obviate Fernandez's claim that those programs were material to his defense. To deal with the remaining counts, which would necessitate disclosing only the two CIA stations and one facility, we hastily began to assemble proof that this information had already been made public.

Acting Deputy Attorney General Edward Dennis wanted us to take an immediate appeal. I explained to Dennis that we did not want to appeal on the issue of materiality before dismissal and then appeal again after dismissal because of the unnecessary severity of the sanction. I confirmed this view with Gerard Lynch, our appellate lawyer, and then met with Dennis, his two principal advisors, and others from the interagency group. Dennis, whose concern was to get the attorney general off the spot, continued to urge us to take an immediate appeal. Thornburgh did not want to be the first attorney general to kill a case by withholding classified information. Nor did he want to spearhead an effort by George Bush's administration to block our investigation. I again explained our unwillingness to appeal prematurely.

The next day, Dennis sent me a disingenuous, self-serving letter suggesting that I had requested the attorney general to file an affidavit refusing to disclose the ongoing CIA programs. After a single-spaced page of specious recitals, Dennis warned that unless the court modified its order, the attorney general would file a CIPA affidavit that was not limited to the three CIA programs and that he would refuse to disclose any of the classified information in question.

I responded the same day, writing that if Dennis limited the attorney general's refusal to the ongoing CIA programs, we would narrow the charges to avoid those programs. Along with the letter, I sent an extensive collection of news clippings in which the identities and locations of the CIA stations and facilities had previously been revealed. I also warned Dennis that I would seek a broad reevaluation of CIPA standards by Congress if he and the CIA persisted in guarding fictional secrets.

The following day, according to Dennis, President Bush's national security advisor, Brent Scowcroft, convened the heads of the intelligence agencies and either the attorney general or his acting deputy in the White House situation room. The Bush administration then adopted the CIA's position.

On Sunday, July 23, the day before the trial was to start, Bill Webster invited me to his home in Bethesda for one last discussion. When I reached Webster's home, several CIA officials were there, including Richard Kerr, the deputy director of central intelligence; Richard Stolz, the deputy director for operations; George Clark, the acting general counsel; and David Holmes, the CIA lawyer regularly assigned to the interagency group. We were joined by Edward Dennis and his assistant, Ron Noble.

The meeting continued through a light buffet supper into the evening. As we milled around in Webster's living room after eating our sandwiches, I tried without success to persuade the others to my point of view. Dennis, supported by all those present, again urged me to take an immediate appeal. I emphasized the futility of denying public revelation of such well-known secrets. An appellate court would be unsympathetic because it would share Judge Hilton's disbelief that national security would be endangered by the disclosures. Webster and Kerr seemed open-minded and concerned. At one point, they appeared to waver, but then Dick Stolz shook his head grimly and asked rhetorically, "What will they think in Oslo?" Irrelevant as his comment seemed, it brought our progress to a halt. Stolz was concerned that a government disclosure of a foreign facility would shake the trust of other foreign hosts. We talked ourselves out and separated as friends— but with every expectation of disaster. Only a last-minute miracle could save the case.

I saw no way to avoid a dismissal. Judge Hilton was uninterested in fine distinctions. He seemed temperamentally unable to tolerate the CIA's attempt to reduce the argument of motions to a negotiation, giving a little bit here and then a little more there. He did not want to be bothered again by modifications of position, even though a more patient judge might have recognized that the new concessions were significant. Some of his off-the-cuff overstatements sounded like those of a man working toward a predetermined objective. As we tried to narrow the case to avoid the ongoing CIA programs, he kept stretching his assertions of their materiality, expanding his earlier holdings as we tried to satisfy them. I felt like a dog pursuing a sausage held by a stick in front of its head.

I woke up early on the day the trial was to start. A simple solution had come to me: We could give each juror a card identifying each CIA station and facility by a number; the witnesses would be instructed to use only the numbers in testifying, but the jurors would know from their code cards the actual name and location of the station or facility that was being discussed. This would, in form, protect the CIA from embarrassing foreign hosts by making an outright public disclosure. I telephoned David Holmes at the CIA; he referred me to Richard Kerr. Kerr liked the idea and approved it. I caught Larry Shtasel as he was about to leave for court. We thought we had a fighting chance.

In court, however, Judge Hilton was utterly impatient. He thought this kindergarten-like proposal too complicated. He dismissed it as one more belated reargument of a lost motion. He had ruled that the information had to be made public and, despite the Classified Information Procedures Act's express encouragement of substitutions for classified information, he would not alter his ruling.

Although less than sanguine about our prospects, we then intended to proceed as far as we could with the trial. The judge had begun picking the jury, when Ron Noble appeared in the courtroom and moved for a stay of the trial, announcing that the attorney general intended to appeal Judge Hilton's rulings on the materiality of the classified information. I had not agreed to this appeal; in fact, I had told Dennis that I would oppose such an appeal, as I had done in the North case. Shtasel announced to the court that we opposed the stay. The court denied the stay, and the selection of the jury went forward. About an hour later, the clerk of the fourth circuit court of appeals in Richmond telephoned Judge Hilton to say that the court of appeals had, without hearing our views, granted a stay at the attorney general's request. Judge Hilton recessed the trial.

The court of appeals expedited the appeal. A month after the stay was granted, a three-judge panel heard argument; a month later, the court ruled unanimously that the attorney general had no legal authority to take an appeal in a case brought by an independent counsel. The court dismissed the appeal, without considering the question of materiality.

On October 12, as the appellate court was about to return the case to the district court, the attorney general obtained a further delay of thirty days by suggesting that he was considering a petition for a rehearing. On November 9, 1989, without informing me, Brent Scowcroft again convened the agency representatives and the attorney general. After reconfirming the Bush administration's policy,

Thornburgh let the time for filing the petition expire. On November 14, after a loss of three months, the court of appeals returned the case to Judge Hilton for trial.

In early October, I had written to President Bush, forecasting a dismissal of the Fernandez case and asking for an interview to explain the need for different standards and procedures to balance the conflicts between the deniability of diplomatically sensitive information and the enforcement of the law. I warned the president that under the intelligence agencies' current polices, high officials probably could not be prosecuted for crimes that they committed in public office. Agencies responsible for national security would be a protected enclave. Preserving the deniability of publicly known facts would impair a much more important national value: the rule of law. CIPA did not solve this problem; it simply provided a way to expose the problem. Only the president could deal with the agencies of the executive branch if they, on highly subjective bases, refused to make necessary information available to the courts. I asked him to consider some higher level of review for these crucial decisions, either by a member of his personal staff or by a specially appointed presidential body. I told him I believed that concern for national security had been exaggerated to defeat necessary prosecutions of high government officers.

C. Boyden Gray, counsel to the president, responded in a letter saying that it would be inappropriate for President Bush to meet with me, that the president was satisfied with the current procedures—"the president is fully confident with the established procedures to handle the Iran-Contra litigation"—and that I should discuss my problems with the attorney general.

I replied with regret that Gray had belittled the problem; the attorney general had been ineffective and the agencies overprotective. Thornburgh's intrusive delay of our work was not reconcilable with a realistic commitment to prosecute high-ranking national security officials for crimes they had committed in office.

On November 22, without prior notice to us, the attorney general served his CIPA affidavit refusing to produce the classified information ordered by Judge Hilton. It was supported by affidavits from the CIA's director and deputy director as well as the head of another agency who had classified his own name and that of the agency he ran.

On November 24, we unsuccessfully urged the court to dismiss only the count that might require the disclosure of the ongoing CIA programs in Costa Rica. We also offered to make concessions and accept findings of fact binding on the jury to protect the defendant. But Judge Hilton was through with the case: He dismissed it outright. We then appealed. Several months later, the court of appeals affirmed the dismissal.

In September, the House intelligence subcommittee on legislation had invited me to appear at a hearing on the possible inadequacies of CIPA in cases prosecuted by independent counsel. For two hours, I explained the history of the North and Fernandez cases and the classification problems we had encountered. I focused on the issues of fictional secrets and the denial of publicly known facts for diplomatic reasons. I described our efforts to cooperate with the administration and said that our relationship with representatives of the agencies had generally been good. I made no accusations of bad faith, but I criticized the attorney general for taking unauthorized appeals in both cases.

The chairman of the subcommittee was Matthew F. McHugh, a New York Democrat. Having grown up in Brooklyn, he had moved upstate after graduating from law school. Year after year, he had successfully carried a district that stretched through strong Republican country from Ithaca to the Hudson River. Also attending the hearing was the chairman of the full committee, Robert W. Kastenmeier, Jr., a Wisconsin Democrat well versed in the strengths and weaknesses of the intelligence agencies. As I completed my testimony, both men assured me of their recognition of the problem, their desire to solve it for the future, and their availability if I had further problems with the agencies.

Bob Livingston, the ranking Republican member, from Metairie, Louisiana, was hostile but unwittingly helpful. With Louis Dupart, the former CIA assistant counsel who had advised the Central American task force, crouched at his side, Livingston attempted to dramatize the importance of deniability by having me acknowledge that the Ilopango facility had been attacked and burned by hostile leftists. No soft pitch over the middle of the plate could have been more inviting. My argument turned into a home run: If the facility had been attacked despite the CIA's denial of its existence, the CIA would have had little to lose by letting the Fernandez case go forward and admitting that the facility existed.

The committee's staff asked us for specific legislative suggestions, which we made in a second interim report to Congress. The report described our work, detailed the manner in which excessive claims of classification had impeded us, and outlined ways to improve CIPA procedures and standards. The report explained that the procedural weaknesses were twofold. First, no specificity was required in the affidavits of the attorney general and the supporting agencies; and second, the court test of materiality was unsatisfactory and partially subjective.

We proposed that individuals employed by the intelligence agencies be subject to precise, narrowly defined criminal statutes rather than to broad, historically based common-law crimes, which invite extensive litigation on the difficult issue of criminal intent. To violate a criminal ordinance that forbids walking on the grass, for example, it is not necessary that one intend to commit a crime; an intent to walk on the grass is enough. But to be guilty of a common-law crime, such as embezzlement or conspiracy, or the statute based on it, one must have a generalized intent to do something of an unlawful nature and not merely to commit a specified act. Narrowing the issue of the defendant's intent would limit the scope of the evidence that would be material to proving intent. This would reduce the need for broad access to classified information.

At the same time, our report urged that the agency heads who declined to declassify information that had been held material by a criminal court should be required to specify the precise danger it would pose for national security. In the Fernandez case, the affidavits had been extremely general, comprising no more than explanations of the concept of deniability accompanied by conclusions that failure to protect this concept could endanger national security. The affidavits did not, and could not, claim that any single breach in the doctrine would invite calamity, because the shield of deniability had already been breached.

The question has always been one of weighing the embarrassment that accompanies the disclosure or confirmation of a known fact against the objective to be served by such exposure. Even truly secret information and sources has been exposed to serve national purposes—to protect hostages, for example, or to identify terrorists. The decision depends on how critical and immediate the national interest being served is. For a military objective, there might be one test. For a political or diplomatic objective, there might be another. At some point, law enforcement should be entitled to consideration. The president and the agency head should be required to take a stand as to when such consideration should occur.

I explained to the subcommittee both at the hearing and in my report that I had hoped to discuss this with President Bush or his staff representative, but that I had been rebuffed.

I testified later before the full House intelligence committee and before the staff of the Senate intelligence committee. In each case, I received a warm response. David Boren and William Cohen, the Senate committee's chairman and ranking Republican respectively, and others expressed their support, as did Senate Majority Leader George Mitchell.

It was at about this time that President Bush vetoed the one legislative reform to emerge from the Iran-Contra congressional hearings—a bill that would have established time limits within which the president was to notify congressional leaders of new covert actions. The Democratic majority did not have enough votes to override the veto. Legislation to address the tougher problem of setting more specific standards for refusing to declassify information in criminal prosecutions failed to materialize.

Nevertheless, the extended attention paid to the topic by the intelligence committees in both houses of Congress significantly improved the attitudes of the intelligence agencies. After the Fernandez debacle, in which we had to stand by and watch the Bush administration and an inflexible judge let a person avoid trial for admitted false statements, we were never again confronted by an insurmountable problem of declassification. To claim that we had lost a battle but won the war would be extravagant; we had too many other troubles to claim victory. We had, however, moved another half league onward.

CHAPTER THIRTEEN

The Trial of
John Poindexter

On December 19, 1989, our third anniversary passed. Fifteen full-time associates had come and gone; a dozen were still at work. In the interim, we had obtained five guilty pleas and one felony conviction by a jury. One case had been dismissed because of obstruction by the intelligence agencies. We had conducted more than 2,700 interviews of witnesses and examined hundreds of thousands of documents. We had also run up rent, salary, travel, and other expenses of more than $18.5 million, not counting the costs of the offices we had provided for the defendants to work with classified papers. Drafting my final report was to be my principal activity. It would take most of the year, but I hoped to have it ready by the fourth anniversary of my appointment.

I had brought in fresh associate counsel to help me handle the final stages of our work. In August 1989, Dan Webb, a former U.S. attorney in Chicago, had taken over the case against John Poindexter. A protégé of Illinois Governor James Robert Thompson, Webb had run an outstanding prosecutorial office. He had personally led the investigation of corrupt Chicago judges and police and secured their conviction. Fortunately for us, he had been heavily engaged in trial during the congressional hearings and had not heard or read any of Poindexter's immunized testimony. Webb brought with him his partner, Howard Pearl, who had been a former chief assistant U.S. attorney in Chicago. Webb, Pearl, and our National Security Council experts, Chris Mixter and Louise Radin, now constituted the Poindexter team.

In mid-December, Craig Gillen also joined the staff. Despite his youthful looks, he was a hard-driving twelve-year veteran of the U.S. attorney's office in Atlanta. In charge of what we called the continuing or residual investigation, he was to make a final review of the evidence we had rushed to assemble in 1987, before Oliver North had given his immunized congressional testimony. At this point, I did not expect Gillen and his team to uncover any significant new data or grounds for further indictments.

After the indictments of Richard Secord and Albert Hakim had been severed from those of North and Poindexter, we had reindicted the arms dealers for lying to Congress. As senior members of my staff left, I had sought part-time help from former prosecutors Reid Weingarten, a veteran of the Justice Department's public integrity section, and Stuart Abrams, a former assistant U.S. attorney in New York. I had turned these cases over to them. Full-time associate counsel Bill Hassler, Geoff Berman, and Bill Treanor supported them.

Secord faced a dozen felony charges. Three of the counts against him related to planned or actual payoffs to North from the arms sales proceeds, including the installation of the security system for which North had been convicted. The other nine accusations all flowed from Secord's false statements to Congress to conceal his share in the proceeds from the Iranian initiative and to deny that any of the Enterprise's funds had gone "to the benefit of Oliver North."

Less than two weeks before Secord's trial was to begin, he agreed to cooperate with our investigation and to plead guilty to a single felony count—his false denial of the gratuity provided to North. On January 24, 1990, after being sentenced to two years on probation, Secord denounced Ronald Reagan from the courthouse steps, saying, "I think former President Reagan has been hiding out. I think it's cowardly. I believed earlier and I still believe that he was well aware of the general outlines of the so-called Iran-Contra affair. . . . It was my assumption that everyone knew about this all the way to the top."

Albert Hakim had been slippery. He had presented a *Kastigar* problem because he had received immunity from Congress, and his international activities made him the most likely of those indicted to present classified-information difficulties. He also had a potential asset in that he nominally controlled the funds diverted from the arms sales and frozen since December 1986 in Swiss bank accounts. Our indictment charged his Panamanian-registered company, Lake Resources, with the theft of this government property and charged him with supplementing Oliver North's salary by paying for the security system. When Hakim's lawyer indicated that Hakim might consider a corporate plea by Lake Resources and a side agreement to drop his claims to most of the Enterprise funds in Switzerland, I decided to negotiate. By the end of

November 1989, we had a deal. Hakim personally pleaded guilty to a misdemeanor charge of aiding and abetting the effort to corrupt Oliver North; his corporation pleaded guilty to a felony charge of converting U.S. property worth $16.2 million to the benefit of the Contras and others. In February, Judge Gerhard Gesell, in view of Hakim's promise to cooperate, imposed a $5,000 fine and two years of probation on Hakim and ordered Lake Resources dissolved.

In a civil agreement that accompanied his guilty plea, Hakim agreed to waive to the United States his claim to $7.8 million that would remain in Lake Resources accounts after payments to his accountant, Swiss lawyers, and others who had facilitated his dealing with the Iranians. But Hakim went back on his word. After he had avoided a prison sentence, he refused to carry out the agreement. The Justice Department is still pursuing these funds.

The culmination of our efforts, I thought, would be the case against John Poindexter. As President Reagan's national security advisor, he had held the equivalent of cabinet rank. He was the highest official we expected to try. The case had been assigned to Judge Harold Greene in June 1989. After a brief effort to persuade the State Department's legal advisor Abraham Sofaer and Deputy Assistant Attorney General Stephen Saltzberg to permit us to hold on to the conspiracy and diversion counts, I dropped both of them except for a residual conspiracy charge that linked the individual false statement and obstruction charges in a conspiracy to obstruct justice. Sofaer and Saltzberg agreed to this charge and continued their tacit support for the remaining counts. I decided not to add a new charge for the destruction of President Reagan's December 1985 finding, about which we had first learned during the North trial, because a new indictment might raise new immunity problems.

Five charges, listed in reverse order for simplicity's sake, remained against Poindexter: Count five alleged that on November 21, 1986, he had told the Senate intelligence committee that he had not known at the time that Israel, with U.S. approval, had shipped Hawk missiles to Iran in November 1985; count four alleged that he had made the same false statement to the House intelligence committee; count three alleged that he had engaged in the obstruction of a congressional investigation by assisting in the creation of a false chronology to be given to the intelligence committees, by giving the false testimony cited in counts four and five, and by then deleting all the messages sent and received on his National Security Council PROF system; count two alleged that he had engaged in the obstruction of Congress by sending two congressional committees letters falsely denying the actions taken by North in violation of the Boland amendments; and count one alleged that Poindexter had conspired with Oliver North and others in furtherance of these four specific crimes.

Poindexter was represented by Richard Beckler, a partner in the Washington office of the well-known Houston firm Fulbright & Jaworski. Beckler was a pugnacious lawyer, raised in Brooklyn and trained in the office of Frank S. Hogan, who had succeeded Thomas E. Dewey as district attorney of New York County. Frank Hogan had been one of my oldest friends and one of two or three lawyers responsible for my getting a professional start during the depression, despite my mediocre law-school record. When Dewey, planning to run for governor, had not sought reelection, all the political parties nominated Hogan to be his successor. This tribute to Hogan's fairness and ability began the now decades-old tradition of a nonpartisan district attorney in a county that was once the hotbed of vicious partisan politics.

Coincidentally, I owed another of Beckler's sponsors a heavy debt. When Leon Jaworski was president of the American Bar Association, he had supported me as chairman of its standing committee on the federal judiciary in finding two of Richard Nixon's proposed nominees for the Supreme Court "not qualified."

More important to me as a prosecutor, Fulbright & Jaworski were representing Poindexter at no charge, in the best tradition of the bar. A prosecutor receives additional assurance against possible injustice by having a capable opponent. Whereas North had captivated thousands— indeed, fund-raising groups had capitalized on his popularity, placing photographs of North and his wife in advertisements requesting funds—the stolid Poindexter could not match that appeal. Nor would he. Outstanding in his naval career, he could not change from a respected admiral to a fund-raiser. The firm of Fulbright & Jaworski quietly made this unnecessary.

The case bristled with difficulties for both sides. Whereas a score of witnesses, reliable or not, could testify to North's activities, Poindexter had been insulated from these contacts. Only a very few—North, Robert McFarlane, and NSC counsel Paul Thompson—had dealt directly with him. The defense, however, was confronted with an agonizing dilemma. Poindexter could not use an authorization defense without overcoming a lifetime of loyalty to the commander in chief. Could Poindexter testify against the president? Could the defense counsel find some substitute for the president's testimony? Would Ronald Reagan come forward and take responsibility for the deceit of Congress?

The assignment of Judge Harold Greene to the case was a welcome relief, after our tribulations in the Fernandez case. Experienced in many areas of law enforcement, Judge Greene had moved from the District of Columbia U.S. attorney's office to the Justice Department's analytical section, the office of legal counsel, which advises the other departments of the government on their most difficult legal problems. From there he had moved to the department's civil rights division and had become a leader when it took off under Presidents Dwight D. Eisenhower and John F. Kennedy. As a judge, Greene had conducted such extraordinarily complex cases as the breakup of the former AT&T system on antitrust grounds.

Following most of the earlier rulings by Judge Gesell, Judge Greene denied all the defense counsel's motions attacking the indictment. He then held his pretrial *Kastigar* hearing and satisfied himself that Webb and Pearl had not been tainted by exposure to Poindexter's congressional testimony. After moving easily, patiently, calmly, and effectively through the Classified Information Procedures Act problems that had so exasperated his colleagues, Judge Greene tackled the most challenging *Kastigar* problem: our intention to call Oliver North as a witness against Poindexter.

Webb was daring. He gambled on his ability to control the hostile and resourceful witness who had dominated the congressional committees and their counsel. North took the stand in the final pretrial hearing on the immunity issue. The contest began immediately, as the judge evaluated the degree to which we could use North, tainted as he was by having listened to Poindexter's testimony. North unabashedly claimed that he could not distinguish his own memory of his two years of night-and-day activities from his memory of Poindexter's few hours of testimony. Patiently, Webb and the judge identified certain safe areas of the testimony North had given at his own trial—testimony that conflicted with or went beyond Poindexter's. Any notion that North might voluntarily tell the truth evaporated with this performance: He was just another hard-case conspirator lying in court.

Back in the office, as Webb filled me in on North's performance, my mind wandered back to another arrogant liar, Charles "Lucky" Luciano, New York's vice lord in the 1930s. During cross-examination about an earlier arrest for the unlicensed possession of a revolver, Thomas E.

Dewey had asked Luciano why he had the revolver. Luciano had responded that it was for hunting—"to kill peasants."

We faced our next hurdle when Poindexter subpoenaed Ronald Reagan as a trial witness and his diaries as evidence. This was an issue that might require immediate appellate review and delay the trial. We supported Poindexter in opposing the former president's claim of executive privilege, but we agreed with Reagan's claim that his testimony was not material because we did not believe that Poindexter had shown a basis for claiming that the testimony would supply legal authorization for the specific acts charged against him.

On January 30, 1990, Judge Greene denied the former president's claim of executive privilege and ordered him to produce specified extracts from his diaries. Overlooked by those reporting this important legal decision was a startling factual revelation: Facing prosecution, Poindexter had shifted his defense away from what he had said in his congressional testimony. Judge Greene's order recited some of the statements Poindexter's counsel had made in our absence, at an ex parte conference at which they had explained his need for privileged and classified information from Reagan. Among other things, defense counsel had said "that the president knew of and approved [Poindexter's] activities and that his knowledge and authorization will support the defense contention that Poindexter had no reason to conceal these activities from Congress." The activities in question, they said, included the arms sales to Iran and "the alleged diversion of the proceeds of these sales to the Contras." In short, according to the judge, Poindexter's lawyers were now claiming that Reagan had approved the diversion.

When President George Bush supported Reagan's assertion of executive privilege as to Reagan's diaries, Judge Greene bowed to Bush and withheld the diaries, ruling that Reagan's testimony would be enough. A claim by the sitting president received greater deference than that of the former president whose private papers were at stake. We viewed the ruling with relief because it obviated an appeal by the Justice Department that would have delayed the trial for months.

On February 5, after concluding that the former president had "direct and important knowledge that [could] help to exonerate" Poindexter, Judge Greene ordered Reagan to testify. Free access to evidence that might prevent an unjust conviction epitomizes the rule of law. All citizens, the judge held, are obliged "to give evidence that will permit the reaching of a just outcome." It would be "inconceivable," he added, "to exempt Mr. Reagan from [that] duty."

Judge Greene permitted Reagan to give a videotaped deposition in the Los Angeles federal courthouse. The former president testified on Friday and Saturday, February 16 and 17, 1990. With Greene presiding, the testimony was taken in a courtroom closed to the press and the public. A transcript would be released to the news media after being reviewed and redacted to prevent the inadvertent exposure of classified information. The videotapes themselves were to be used at trial and then immediately released to the public. The deposition lasted a total of seven hours.

Despite Reagan's evident desire to help the defense, his performance was less than Poindexter had hoped for. Again and again, the former president's generous impulses were checked by the denials he had signed in his earlier, self-protective, written response to our interrogatories. Repeatedly smiling at Poindexter and winking at him after giving what he may have thought were helpful answers, Reagan displayed not only his bias, but also his helplessness. On more than 120 occasions, he admitted that he did not remember details of the Iran-Contra operation. Astonishingly, he testified that he "had no knowledge then or now" that funds had been diverted to the Contras out of earnings from the sale of missiles to Iran. "No one has proven to me that there was a diversion," he insisted.

Shown by Webb a copy of the March 1987 Tower Commission report that spelled out these facts, the president who had appointed the panel and had accepted its findings declared, "This report, this is the first time that I have ever seen a reference that actually specified there was a diversion. . . . I have to tell you, to my recollection, this is the first time I have ever seen that."

Reagan's memory lapses appeared genuine. The disclosure, four years later, that he suffered from Alzheimer's disease may help to explain his inability to recall events and activities from his time in the White House. Nevertheless, his forgetfulness sharply reduced his ability to bolster Poindexter's case. Although the former president admitted "the Iran-Contra affair" was "a covert action that was taken at my behest," he repeatedly declared that he had told his aides to stay "within the law" in their efforts to aid the Nicaraguan resistance.

Reagan went as far as he could. When defense attorney Richard Beckler showed him the July 1986 letter that Poindexter had sent Congress incorporating McFarlane's false denials of a year earlier, declaring that North had not given improper aid to the Contras, Reagan said that he was "in total agreement" with the message. "If I had written it myself," he added, "I might have used a little profanity."

Cross-examining him the next day, Dan Webb asked about Poindexter's letter, and Reagan admitted that he had not approved the letter at the time it was sent.

"I take it," Webb asked, "as the chief executive and the president of the United States, you did not want your top officials of your administration to provide false information to Congress?"

"That is a fair statement," replied the former president.

"At any time, did you ever approve or give authority to John Poindexter to make any false or misleading statements to any congressional committee regarding events related to the Iran-Contra controversy?"

"No," said Reagan. "And I don't think any false statements were made."

Poindexter's case differed from North's in that false statements were the sole point at issue. All the charges on which Poindexter was to be tried concerned his deception of Congress. But Reagan, in his written responses to our earlier interrogatories, had disclaimed authorizing the false statements by North, Poindexter, or any other person. Reagan now adhered to these answers.

Webb used them effectively to make the witness back away from his implied endorsements of Poindexter. Webb asked Reagan whether he had declared in writing, "I did not authorize or approve of the transfer to the NSC or any of its staff any function or operation performed by CIA with respect to the Nicaraguan Freedom Fighters." Reagan agreed that he had made that statement. Was it still true? Yes, it was.

Webb moved on. Did the former president know that Poindexter's 1986 letters to Congress repeated the falsehoods in letters McFarlane had sent in 1985?

"Well, I simply—no," said Reagan. "I did not have this information, but I have a great deal of confidence in . . . McFarlane. . . . I have never caught him or seen him doing anything that was in any way out of line or dishonest. And so, I was perfectly willing to accept his defense."

Webb pointed out that McFarlane had pleaded guilty to withholding the truth from Congress in the letters that Poindexter had resubmitted. Was the former president aware of that plea?

Reagan said that he was not.

Finally Webb came back to Poindexter's destruction of documents during his last days in office. The former president, on direct examination, had said that he had instructed his assistants at the time not to reveal any information that might endanger the hostages held in

Lebanon. "Secrecy," he contended, "was protecting those individuals' lives."

Webb then produced another interrogatory response. "At no time," said the written statement, "did I authorize or approve of the destruction or alteration of documents, relating to Iranian arms transactions or relating to the Contras."

"Was that answer true in 1987?" Webb asked.

"Yes," Reagan replied.

Was it still true?

Yes, it was.

The former president said that he had not known that North had been secretly helping to arm and advise the Contras while the Boland amendments were in force. Reagan said that he had assured his staff, "We would have to abide by the law."

Webb asked whether the former president had told any member of his administration to act "in a manner that would be illegal."

"I said that we must, whatever we do, that we must continue helping the Contras, but we must do it within the law." Asked whether North was giving the Contras military advice and logistical support, the witness said, "I guess that I have never . . . had any inkling that we were valuing their strategy in any way."

"You, as I understand it," asked Webb, "never after Boland passed ever learned of North's directing and participating in Contra activities?"

"I know that he was very active," replied Reagan, "and that was certainly with my approval, because I yesterday made plain how seriously I felt about the Contra situation and what it meant to all of us here in the Americas. And, so obviously, there were many things that were being done. But again as I say, I was convinced that they were all being done within the law. . . . I repeat that anything that we could do to be of help, but it had to be within the confines of the law, the Boland amendment. And to this day, I assume that that is what he was doing."

Under cross-examination, Reagan repeatedly stated that Poindexter had never told him that he planned to lie to Congress or destroy documents sought by investigators or that he had obstructed or impeded any congressional inquiry.

"At any time, did he ever tell you that he had actually destroyed any records or documents related to the Iran-Contra affair?"

"No."

Reagan admitted that he had supported invitations for donations from foreign governments to help finance the Contras. "There wasn't any restriction on informing others as to how they could help, things of that kind. And that I did approve." Again denying that he had been aware that the proceeds from the arms sales were being diverted to the Contras, he said, "I was only aware finally that we got our twelve million, two [hundred thousand dollars]. . . . May I simply point out that I had no knowledge then or now that there had been a diversion, and I never used that term. And all I knew was that there was some money that came from some place in another account, and that the appearance was that it might have been part of a negotiated sale."

"To the extent that there was in fact a diversion of proceeds," asked Webb, "did you in any way approve or authorize that while you were president of the United States?"

"For heaven's sake, no. And when I was once asked about that extra money and said if it was an added sum to the purchase price, what would I do, I said I would have given it back. No one has proven to me that there was a diversion. To this day, all I know is that some sum of money over and above the twelve-million-two-hundred-thousand-dollar purchase appeared in the Swiss bank account in which it was said that account had been used on other occasions to provide help to the Contras. And to this day, with all of the investigations that had been made, I still have never been given one iota of evidence as to who collected the price, who delivered the final delivery of the weapons . . . , whether there was ever more money in that Swiss account that had been diverted someplace else. I am still waiting to find those things out and have never found them out."

Reagan's lawyers asked Judge Greene to prohibit the news media from broadcasting Reagan's videotaped testimony. Poindexter asked that it be withheld until after the jury was selected for trial to avoid an "incalculable impact on prospective jurors." Accordingly, only the text of President Reagan's videotaped deposition was released on February 22, 1990.

Reagan's counsel filed another motion, asking that the actual videotape be permanently withheld from the public. The Bush administration supported the motion. A brief by the Justice Department said, "Respect for the dignity of the office of the presidency should lead a federal judge to refuse to let any copies be made of the videotape for showing outside the courtroom at the coming trial of . . . Poindexter." The brief went on to say, "It would be ironic and inappropriate if the special precautions taken by this court to acquire the testimony of former President Reagan results in that testimony being subjected to radically broader and more varied uses than the testimony of other witnesses. The deposition was provided in lieu of trial testimony, partly out of respect for the dignity of the office. Similar considerations of respect suggest that the president's deposition be given no greater dissemination than trial testimony."

Judge Greene ruled that "in view of the requirement of openness of criminal proceedings, this segment of the Poindexter criminal trial should not be kept secret. The public is entitled to know now to what the former president testified." Judge Greene ruled that transcript of the testimony was to be made public as soon as it was screened for classified information and that the videotape was to be made available after it was introduced at the trial. C-Span announced a plan to broadcast all seven hours of the testimony as it was made available.

After the transcript was released, the *New York Times* editorialized that "Mr. Reagan's performance was embarrassing. . . . When the video-tape of his pretrial testimony is publicly shown, Mr. Reagan may well convince viewers that he had deceived himself about dealing with terrorists. But that's as far as his credibility can stretch." The *Baltimore Sun* said that "what comes through most clearly in Mr. Reagan's testimony is that once the decision was made to proceed with what is now known as the Iran-Contra affair, Ronald Reagan lost interest—and still is uninterested. There is little evidence of the sort of concern you would expect of a president who has ordered extraordinary actions to be taken." The *Sun* concluded, "The Constitution requires the president to 'take care that laws be faithfully executed.' Ronald Reagan, now by his own admission, didn't."

On March 5, jury selection began. From a pool of more than two hundred potential jurors, twenty-one had qualified for further examination by the end of the first day. The judge held that exposure to Poindexter's congressional testimony would not automatically excuse a juror, but seventy-six potential jurors who had been exposed to his testimony were excused. All but sixteen of the first fifty-four had some familiarity with North's testimony. On March 7, the thirty-five individuals who had survived the first round of jury selection were joined by ten more, forming a pool of forty-five from which the jury was selected.

On March 7, a jury comprising seven women and five men, with six alternates, was impaneled. Judge Greene rejected the defense's sealed motion objecting to North's testimony and citing statements by my office that North, in his own trial, had committed perjury. The judge also denied Poindexter's motion to exclude from North's testimony any reference to Poindexter's having destroyed the presidential finding during Meese's investigation.

The next day, in his opening statement to the jury, Webb charged that Poindexter had directed a cover-up of the Iran-Contra affair and had attempted to rewrite its history by lying in congressional testimony and destroying evidence. Webb described a conspiracy by high government officials to make false statements to Congress, to conceal and misrepresent facts to Congress, and to destroy incriminating documents.

He explained that after President Reagan made repeated assertions and a televised speech denying that the arms sales to Iran had been part of an arms-for-hostages deal, Poindexter, North, and McFarlane had attempted to hide from Congress the nature of those arms sales as well as the provision of military support for the Contras. "But even as [President Reagan] spoke, there existed a document called a presidential finding signed by the president himself that on its face described the November 1985 Hawk shipment as an arms-for-hostage transfer." Its exposure would show that Reagan's televised address had been untrue. To protect Reagan from "gross political embarrassment," Poindexter had ripped up the finding after testifying falsely before two congressional committees.

Webb's opening address lasted nearly two hours. He described in painstaking detail how Poindexter had supervised North's activities. He charged that North had "lied, lied, lied" to Congress. He strode to the defense table and, pointing at Poindexter, said, "Mr. North will tell you that he was getting his authority, his direction, from this man here—John Poindexter."

In the afternoon, Richard Beckler responded. Standing with his jacket open and his hands on his hips, he began his opening statement to the jury. "Despite what the prosecution said, the evidence will show that Mr. Poindexter never lied to Congress. Admiral Poindexter always followed the orders of President Reagan.... Why did he follow those orders? Because the president was his commander in chief.... After thirty years in the Navy, they want to nail him on a five-week mistake and call it obstruction of Congress." Beckler dismissed Webb's charges as "hogwash" and promised to prove that Poindexter had committed "no criminal acts," that he had always told the truth. "He never lied to Congress. There was no criminal conspiracy." Beckler conceded, "Yes, there was a group of people who acted together ... and that group was led by the president of the United States, President Ronald Reagan."

Beckler acknowledged that Poindexter had destroyed the president's finding, but only because it had contained inaccurate information that, if made public, would have embarrassed Reagan. Beckler promised to call George Shultz, Edwin Meese, and Fawn Hall and to use Reagan's videotaped testimony.

After Beckler sat down, Webb told the court and jury that North would be his first witness the next day. In the morning, spectators began lining up outside the courthouse long before it opened. Then they stood quietly outside courtroom number one. At nine forty-five, Judge Greene opened the courtroom, which had six rows of pew-like benches. The first two rows on the left were reserved for the defendant's wife (an ordained Episcopal priest) and their four sons and their wives, as well as neighbors and friends. Most of the remaining seats were taken by the reporters and sketch artists who were to carry the story outside the courtroom. In the last row, a dozen members of the general public squeezed in alongside the intelligence agencies' representatives, who hovered vigilantly waiting to interrupt any unapproved leak of classified information.

If the public felt shut out, so did I. Because of the possibility that I would need to retry North or Poindexter, I had remained untainted by their immunized congressional testimony. Even the press clippings, regularly collected by my staff, were now being withheld from me. Press officer Mary Belcher sent me a memorandum saying that North's testimony so dominated the news stories that I could not read or learn about the trial until I decided to taint myself.

Grouchily, I turned to other matters. To give up my newspaper was like starting the day without coffee. Fortunately, Belcher, who was covering the trial for me, and friendly reporters who knew of my isolation called from time to time not only with reassurance, but also with awe, as they told me in general terms about Dan Webb's examination of Oliver North. More than once, I heard one of my callers describe Webb as the best trial lawyer he or she had ever seen in action. After a few weeks, I decided that I would never personally retry North and Poindexter, which allowed me to taint myself and read the transcript of Webb's examination. Cold print was a poor substitute for the suspense and drama of a living trial, but the transcript was a thrill to read.

There are many kinds of trial lawyers. Some of them go from case to case with little time for preparation, surviving on their instincts and their wits. Many litigation specialists in large firms, however, rarely see juries, because most of their time goes toward refining the issues in complex cases and negotiating settlements or other dispositions. As I read the transcript, I saw that Webb had the perfect combination of experiences. He had kept his personal trial skills intact by regularly trying cases but had long been accustomed to absorbing the careful preparation of his able staff.

The examination of Oliver North was a cross-examination from the beginning. Declaring North a hostile witness, the judge permitted Webb to ask leading questions. Webb skillfully held North in tight rein, confronting him time and again with his testimony before Congress, his testimony at his own trial, and White House documents including many of North's memoranda and prior statements. Facing confrontational witnesses, lawyers who have to rely entirely on previously prepared questions seem like novice drivers in cars with standard transmissions, thinking out each move of their feet and hands as they shift gears, lurching along while trying to watch for oncoming traffic. By contrast, Webb negotiated every twist and turn with effortless precision. Responding seemingly by reflex to North, Webb proceeded inch by inch, each question specifically reciting the facts to be admitted and progressing a word or two beyond the previous question, almost always with a White House document or an excerpt from prior testimony to confront an evasive answer.

There was a fair amount of repetition, as Webb methodically narrowed an issue and moved the witness from one grudging word to the next. Although he recognized the need for what Webb was doing, Judge Greene at times showed mild impatience as he accused Webb of a "belt and suspenders" approach, of being overly exacting in forcing from North the exact word that would express the relevant concept or colorfully portray an event. This rigorous strictness drained North's flamboyance. His husky-voiced histrionics fell flat. Webb emerged before the jury as the person of intense integrity. North intellectually surrendered. Webb's gamble had paid off: North became a prosecution witness.

Since his triumph over the congressional committees some three years earlier, North had changed. Wealth and the adulation of right-wing Republicans and others, including Judge Gesell's probation officer, all had taken their toll. Like a boxer who has lost his fighting edge, the trim marine had been replaced by a patronizing public personality. Addressing Webb as "counselor," North talked down to him as though he—the witness, not the judge—were the officer in authority. Unlike John Keker, Webb did not have to address North's venality. Webb hammered at the central fact: North had lied to Congress, and he had done so with Poindexter's authorization and even at his direction. This fact blanketed the five charges against Poindexter.

North admitted that his normal duties and responsibilities had included keeping McFarlane and Poindexter advised of his Contra-related activities. Claiming that he had not personally accepted funds for the Contras, North acknowledged having participated in the fund-raising activities of Spitz Channell and his organizations. "I certainly kept ... Mr. McFarlane and Admiral Poindexter aware of what I was doing. . . . I certainly did keep them aware that I was doing these things."

"You attempted," asked Webb, "to tell Admiral Poindexter exactly the types of things you were doing by way of private fund-raising?"

"The types of things, yes."

"You did keep them advised of that?"

"Yes." In explaining to Poindexter how the funds had moved, North had given Poindexter a diagram that showed their flow from Channell through U.S. and offshore intermediaries to the Lake Resources account in Switzerland or to Contra accounts in Miami and the Cayman Islands.

Webb then took up the false responses to the letters of inquiry from Congress, beginning with those in 1985 from Representatives Michael Barnes and Lee Hamilton, who had chaired committees with oversight responsibility. Both letters had inquired about recent press reports that National Security Council staff members had been providing advice, fund-raising, and other support for the military activities of the Contras. When the letters reached the White House, North said, he had met with McFarlane and urged him to claim executive privilege and refuse to respond, but McFarlane had said that it would be better to try to answer the letters. North said that he had drafted an accurate letter, from which McFarlane had accepted two paragraphs, and that McFarlane had then drafted a third paragraph that was inaccurate. North had told him that his answer was "totally inconsistent" with the facts. "Basically, having given him a draft of an answer which was factu-ally correct," North testified, "he [McFarlane] then revised the draft, putting in information that was not accurate, that was not correct. It was wrong, and I went in a further meeting with him, pointed out the errors in that, and urged again that he exert—or he go to the president and urge that the president exert—executive privilege. And his advice to me . . . was that he and the president had talked over that approach, that it was too confrontational, and that they had decided that he was going to proceed along the lines that he had drafted the letter, and it is my recollection today that that was the letter that was sent."

"That letter was false?" asked Webb.

"Yes."

After receiving McFarlane's letter, Representative Hamilton had followed up with written questions. McFarlane had assigned the task of answering them to North. McFarlane had then sent North's written answers to Hamilton. In response to Webb's probing, North described several of these answers as having been "absolutely false" and "patently untrue." North testified that when McFarlane's letters went to Congress, Poindexter had received a copy of one of them, and that because North had already told Poindexter the truth about his efforts to aid the Contras, Poindexter had known that the letter was false.

A year later, after Poindexter had replaced McFarlane as the national security advisor, Poindexter had referred Hamilton and Barnes to McFarlane's letters to reiterate the same false statements. During this period, North had continued aiding the Contras and had diverted several million dollars from the proceeds of the Iranian initiative to the Contras. He had kept Poindexter informed. On May 16, 1986, just before the shipment of Hawk parts to Iran, North had sent Poindexter a PROF note listing the assets of his organization for the support of the Contras. North had written that Project Democracy had assets of $6 million, including its airplanes, but that he expected a considerable influx of new funds in a few days (from the sale of the spare parts).

Only a month after North had given this information to Poindexter, President Reagan had been requested to comment on a proposed congressional resolution of inquiry about North. As North explained it, Poindexter had wanted to avoid legislative roadblocks to the pending $100 million appropriation authorizing the CIA to resume its assistance to the Contras. Over North's objection, he said, Poindexter had assigned others on the NSC staff to prepare the reply because North would have raised the issue of executive privilege. In the reply, Poindexter had referred the congressional committees to the misinformation submitted by McFarlane a year earlier. Using leading questions, Webb got North to confirm unequivocally that this information had been false and had continued to be false and that Poindexter had known this because North had regularly informed Poindexter of his activities.

Using North's prior testimony to hold him in check, Webb then led North to explain that in mid-1986, after Poindexter's letter failed to satisfy Representative Hamilton, Poindexter had promised Hamilton that North would meet with the House intelligence committee in the White House situation room. North said he had protested that he would have to reveal things that he could not reveal. Poindexter, according to North, had then told him, "You can handle it" or "You can take care of it." North testified that he had hoped that friendly congressmen would "vector" the conversation away from the difficult areas. He had not intended to lie when he went into the meeting, he said, but he had lied. When asked questions regarding matters that his superiors had told him not to disclose, he had lied. He had not been truthful with the committee about what he had been doing; he had deceived them about the "full measure of his involvement."

North told the jury that after this testimony, Poindexter had sent him a PROF note congratulating him. The note had accompanied a memorandum of his testimony including the false statements North had given the committee: his denials that he had met with General John Singlaub, that he had given Rob Owen guidance, and that he had given the Contras military advice. Webb had North confirm that the memorandum of his testimony had been accurate, and that the denials had been false.

North's testimony lasted four days. Webb then told Judge Greene that the prosecution would complete its case within a week and would not need to call a number of witnesses who had been standing by in case North failed to testify truthfully.

Our next witness was FBI Special Agent Ellen Glasser, who testified that she had interviewed Poindexter at his home two days after his resignation and that he had denied knowing about the destruction of NSC records. He had told her that the Iran-Contra chronologies had been accurate, that he had possessed "no working knowledge" of the shipments of arms to Iran before he had become the national security advisor, and that he had had "no direct knowledge" of the diversion of the proceeds to the Contras.

The NSC's computer expert then took the stand and testified that the computer system's records showed that the day before Poindexter resigned, his computer had contained more than five thousand messages. At four-thirty on the morning of his resignation, Poindexter had turned on his machine; by nine o'clock, no messages remained. It was "fortuitous," the witness said, that the deleted messages had been recovered from the "dump" that preserved duplicates.

On March 15, Stanley Sporkin, who had been the CIA's general counsel and was now a federal judge, testified that he had drafted the arms-for-hostages finding for President Reagan. North had told him that the State Department opposed describing the initiative as a straight arms-for-hostages deal, but Sporkin had felt the description to be necessary to supply authorization for the CIA's activities.

The next day, Ronald Sable, the NSC's legislative affairs director, testified that by using McFarlane's false letters and North's false testimony, Poindexter had succeeded in causing the House of Representatives to abandon its plans to investigate the NSC's secret support of the Contras. Sable described Poindexter as having been "skeptical of the Congress. . . . He indicated he did not trust them."

W. Robert Pearson, who had been the NSC's deputy executive secretary during Poindexter's tenure, took the stand and testified that he had taken notes for Poindexter of North's testimony before the House intelligence committee in the situation room. According to Pearson, North had exuded confidence and self-assurance, performing so well that he had convinced the panel that the allegations about him were untrue. Pearson had not realized that North was lying. After the meeting, Pearson testified, he had sent a computer message to Poindexter describing North's testimony, saying that North had in essence informed the committee members that although he had met with the leaders of the Contras in Central America, he had had nothing to do with arming them: "All that he did was for the purpose of gathering information for the benefit of the president of the United States in carrying out foreign policy." The congressmen, Pearson testified, had accepted this account and had quashed the proposed resolution for an investigation. Pearson thought it notable that the committee members and staff had sat around the long table and in the chairs along the walls, and North had sat in the seat usually reserved for the president.

Pearson was followed by Lee Hamilton, who explained that in November 1986, after the exposure of the arms sales to Iran, Poindexter had promised to provide the House intelligence committee with the "full story," but that his testimony had omitted all of the arms sales to Iran through Israel. In particular, Poindexter had concealed his own contemporaneous knowledge of the November 1985 Israeli shipment of U.S. Hawks to Iran and the CIA's participation in the shipment. Poindexter had told the committee that although Israel had sent the Hawk missiles to Iran in November 1985, the U.S. government had not learned about it until two months later and had then disapproved the sale. He had failed to tell the committee that President Reagan had signed the finding that retroactively authorized the Hawk shipment.

Nor had Poindexter mentioned the diversion of funds from the arms sales to the Contras. Summing up, Hamilton told the jury, "The system simply doesn't work if we lie to each other in government."

Fawn Hall was the next witness. Described by Stanley Meisler of the *Los Angeles Times* as a "thin, very pale, young woman with a bounty of long, blonde hair like that of the medieval princesses in the illustrations for Sir Walter Scott novels," Hall held the attention of every juror. She was less tense and much less distraught than in her appearance in North's trial, but she spoke so rapidly that the judge had to slow her down to let the court reporter catch up. She told of having helped North shred and steal government documents and testified that she had personally delivered North's diversion memorandum to Poindexter.

The prosecution's last witness was a member of the staff of the Senate intelligence committee, Eric Newsom, who testified about Poindexter's briefing of the committee's chairman, David Durenberger, and vice chairman, Patrick Leahy, on November 21, 1986. Newsom said that Poindexter had told the senators that he had not learned of the November 1985 Israeli Hawk shipment until two months after it had occurred.

On March 20, the prosecution rested its case, having called only ten witnesses over the course of some eight days. Beckler rose and moved that the charges be dismissed. Judge Greene denied the motion, holding that the government had shown "that there was a violation under all five counts of the indictment."

The first defense witness was White House assistant counsel Dean McGrath, who attempted to take responsibility for having drafted Poindexter's false letter to Congress. On cross-examination by Louise Radin, McGrath admitted that Paul Thompson had proposed nearly all the original text. McGrath said he had been unaware of the inaccuracies and had not known that anyone on the NSC staff had been aiding the Contras. "I would not have approved [the letter] if I had known it was false," he declared.

"Would you have stopped it?" asked Radin.

"I would have tried to."

On March 21 and 22, Beckler played the tapes of Reagan's deposition for the jury. The tapes had been fast-forwarded to the point where Reagan had taken the oath, so the jury did not see Reagan winking at Poindexter upon entering the room.

The courtroom contained five large television sets in various places for viewing by the jury and spectators, and the judge had a small television set on his bench. At times, one juror or another appeared to doze off; at other times, the jurors smiled or laughed when Reagan relaxed and made whimsical remarks. The jury became alert during Dan Webb's videotaped cross-examination, particularly when he asked questions in rapid-fire fashion:

"Did you . . . give authority to John Poindexter to make any false . . . statements?"

"No."

"Did you ever . . . give authority to John Poindexter to destroy . . . records?"

"No."

"Did John Poindexter ever tell you . . . he planned on destroying any documents?"

"No."

"Did John Poindexter . . . tell you . . . he had learned that Oliver North . . . altered and destroyed records?"

"No."

Copies of the tapes were released immediately after they had been played in court. They were broadcast extensively. For the first time, the country and the world heard a former president of the United States explaining his official conduct under oath. Television critic Tom Shales of the *Washington Post* wrote that "of all Ronald Reagan's television performances, this was the least enjoyable. . . . It wasn't a pretty picture. . . . It wasn't nice to see a beloved former president subjected to this kind of indignity, being questioned by mere lawyers, sitting in a witness stand, even having to spell his name to the court reporter—which Reagan dutifully and cheerfully did. . . . Trapped in that witness stand, Reagan seemed humbled . . . and all for what, the defense of Poindexter? . . . Reagan looked chipper and appeared anxious to be of help. Sometimes the camera would linger on him after a response and his eyes would wander and he'd look a little lost. His camera presence, which has never failed him before, fitfully flickered out."

After the conclusion of the videotapes, Beckler called Edwin Meese to the stand. The former attorney general described his meeting with Poindexter at the outset of the fact-finding investigation. "The purpose of the meeting was to make sure the facts were all accurately portrayed," he said. On direct, Meese denied that there had been any attempt to concoct a false cover story. But on cross-examination, he admitted that

Poindexter had not told him of the diversion of the arms sales proceeds until two days later, after it had been discovered by Meese's assistants. Meese acknowledged that "the political implications and policy implications were critical."

He swore that Reagan had not known of the Hawk shipment until the missiles had already left Israel and that the CIA had not known what the cargo was until after it had been delivered to Iran. When Webb showed Meese a computer message from North to Poindexter advising him in advance of the shipment, Meese said, "I don't know whether Poindexter received it."

Webb asked Meese whether, on learning of the presidential finding ratifying the shipment of weapons, he had become suspicious about North's assertions that there had been no U.S. knowledge of the actual nature of the cargo.

The witness answered elliptically, "No, I was not suspicious of that," because the CIA had learned about the missiles only a week and a half after the delivery. "Yes, there was considerable confusion. Different people had different recollections," because the project had been "highly compartmentalized." Meese admitted that this confusion had become much more problematic after his assistants discovered the diversion memo. "Yes, the political implications and the policy implications were considerable." Nonetheless, said Meese, there had been no deliberate cover-up. "I'm sure nothing like that was ever said in my presence at that meeting [with Poindexter]."

The defense next called Congressman Henry Hyde, a member of the House intelligence committee. Hyde testified that despite McFarlane's views to the contrary, the Boland amendments had not applied to the National Security Council. On cross-examination by Webb, however, Hyde admitted that the chief Republican lawyer for the committee had written in a legal opinion to Hyde that the National Security Council had "clearly" come under the law.

Norman Gardner, Jr., the CIA's congressional liaison, was the fourth defense witness. He described how Senator David Durenberger had "charged right into" Poindexter's office on November 21, 1986, to be briefed. Durenberger had said to Poindexter, "If you're not going to give us all the facts, we're going to get the hell out of here." Gardner testified that to the best of his knowledge, Poindexter had not been involved in obstructing or lying to Congress.

On cross-examination by Chris Mixter, Gardner admitted that he had known of the retroactive presidential finding ratifying the November

1985 Hawk shipment when Poindexter briefed the senators. Gardner said that Poindexter had known about the finding and had been involved in its signing, but that neither he nor Poindexter had mentioned the finding to the senators because "it was not done before the shipment."

Gardner testified that because of North's cover story that the cargo had been oil-drilling parts, the CIA had not learned that its proprietary charter company had flown a cargo of Hawk missiles to Tehran until after the shipment had been completed. This seemed to anger Judge Greene. He eventually began to question Gardner himself. "The CIA shipped something to Iran, to a hostile country that was almost at war with the United States, and the CIA didn't know what was in there?" he asked incredulously.

"That's right," Gardner replied.

"You're saying the CIA didn't know?"

Gardner said the agency had not known until "the pilots and the crew" reported it.

In answering questions from Mixter, Gardner claimed that there had been "a great deal of confusion" and admitted that the CIA had known about the cargo shortly after it was delivered. Gardner persisted in trying to volunteer unresponsive answers, which led the judge to warn him: "You're here as a witness; you're not at some CIA briefing as an expert."

As the trial entered its fourth and final week, the defense called Rodney B. McDaniel, a former Navy captain and former executive secretary of the National Security Council. McDaniel described Poindexter's chaotic fourteen-hour working days and the enormous flow of information that he had had to analyze for the president. McDaniel also disparaged North's credibility, characterizing him as a "gung-ho" staff officer who had "embellished his personal role in things."

On cross-examination by Webb, McDaniel acknowledged that seeing North use a false name on NSC travel vouchers had made him suspicious about North's efforts to support the Contras. When McDaniel had then asked Poindexter if he knew about North's pro-Contra activities, Poindexter had said that he did and that McDaniel need not concern himself about it. According to McDaniel, he had again expressed misgivings to Poindexter after learning that Secord had been involved in the arms deals with Iran. Once more, McDaniel testified, Poindexter had said that he saw no problem.

Perhaps most damaging to Poindexter, McDaniel testified that he had accompanied Poindexter to the Oval Office and had taken notes while Poindexter assured President Reagan that the government had had no connection with Hasenfus's aircraft, which had recently been shot down in Nicaragua. President Reagan, who had learned about the event from television or the newspapers, had asked Poindexter, "What is this all about?" Poindexter had reported that he didn't have all the facts, but that he understood it was not a U.S. government operation.

The defense then called five character witnesses, including an admiral, a senator, a congressman, an Episcopal priest, and a neighbor, to testify to Poindexter's reputation for honesty. Poindexter did not testify, because Webb would have destroyed him. As Nina Totenberg explained on National Public Radio, "The admiral went down with his ship." The defense rested on March 27.

Webb, who knew better than to over-try a case, immediately stated that he would need no rebuttal and that he was ready to submit the case to the jury. Judge Greene scheduled the final arguments for two days later.

On March 30, the summations began. In a two-and-a-half-hour presentation, Webb returned to the theme of his opening address, that Poindexter and North had decided to rewrite history by concealing facts from Congress, lying to Congress, and going on a rampage of document destruction.

Watched by Poindexter's wife, who was wearing her clerical collar and holding the admiral's grandchild, and four of their sons, three of whom were dressed in Navy uniforms, Beckler delivered his summation. Periodically shaking his fists, he blamed President Reagan for Poindexter's predicament. Beckler portrayed Poindexter as a victim of "political bashing" who had stayed within the "spirit and letter of the law." Relying on Reagan's testimony, Beckler argued that this had not been a "grimy little conspiracy. . . . [T]his was the president of the United States; the president of the United States was the driving engine behind his action."

In a fiery rebuttal, Webb ridiculed the defense and President Reagan's faulty memory. He dismissed the former president's claim that he had never traded arms for hostages: Webb charged that this attempted deceit of the public was "a sad day in the history of the United States . . . , when that's exactly what he [Reagan] did." The fact that the president's finding had expressly referred to arms for hostages was the reason that Poindexter had destroyed it. Webb then excoriated Poindexter for having destroyed five thousand computer messages and for having participated in the creation of the false cover story denying official, contemporaneous knowledge of the November 1985 Hawk shipment.

Webb denounced Ronald Reagan without hesitation. "He did not have the slightest clue as to whether John Poindexter did or didn't participate in the crimes charged in this indictment. . . . When people come into court, we expect them to give fair and truthful testimony. When a person is so biased that he turns to a witness and winks, as if to say, 'Did that help you, John?' . . . well, I would have expected more of a former president than that." As for Reagan's testimony that he was in total agreement with Poindexter's letter to Congress but might have added profanity, Webb charged that Reagan "gave that testimony because he didn't have the foggiest idea these were false letters sent to Congress." Webb then mocked the hollowness of the defense. "The reason why Ronald Reagan was called to the stand was in the hopes that if you listened to the testimony of a former president in support of John Poindexter, instead of looking at the facts and evidence, you would assume that just because the president testified, you ought to acquit John Poindexter."

In reporting the summations, journalists contrasted the styles of the two lawyers. According to the *Los Angeles Times*, "Webb spoke softly and precisely, much like a school teacher. . . . Beckler took a much different approach. Raising his voice, slapping his hands, sounding indignant, even truculent, about the accusations against Poindexter."

On April 2, Judge Greene spent less than an hour instructing the jury regarding the law. He charged the jurors not to consider policy questions, because "it's not your function or the court's to decide who was right in particular disputes between Congress and the president, between Democrats and Republicans or between liberals and conservatives. Likewise, it is not your function or the court's to decide whether President Reagan's commitment to assist the Contras in Nicaragua was the correct policy for the United States, or whether his opponents were right in their criticism of that commitment. On the same basis, you are not called upon to decide whether the president's policy toward Iran and the American hostages kept in Lebanon was a wise or unwise policy." The judge also told the jury to give no special weight to the testimony of former President Reagan or to Poindexter's decision not to testify. Judge Greene instructed the jurors that to convict, they needed to be convinced that Poindexter had a "specific intent," which he defined as "intending with a bad purpose either to disobey or disregard the law."

The jury then retired to deliberate the case. After the first day, a reporter telephoned two jurors at home, so Judge Greene sequestered the jury for the remainder of its deliberations. On April 7, the jury reached its verdict. The courtroom was silent as the clerk read the verdict: guilty as charged, on all counts. I issued a statement saying simply, "The trial was exemplary. The verdict speaks for itself."

Webb said the verdict showed that "high men in government office [who] are responsible for [the] national security of this nation ought not to be allowed to commit crimes to pursue their own self-interest."

Later, the jury foreman told reporters, "Mr. Reagan's testimony didn't play any more of an important role than any other testimony. Actually, he didn't give much information." As for Poindexter, the foreman summed it up: "All in all, I think he was very dedicated. But guilty as charged."

CHAPTER FOURTEEN

Reversal and Revival

While Judge Harold Greene was moving the Poindexter case to trial, a powerful band of Republican appointees waited like the strategic reserves of an embattled army. The final evaluation of the immunity Congress had granted Oliver North and John Poindexter would be the work of yet another political force—a force cloaked in the black robes of those dedicated to defining and preserving the rule of law. Although the judiciary is theoretically a neutral arm of government and judges are expected to eschew partisan politics, the underlying political nature of all government institutions was evident when a three-judge panel from the United States Court of Appeals for the District of Columbia Circuit reviewed Oliver North's conviction in 1990.

Appointed for life, federal judges extend the influence of a president far beyond his term of office. This is particularly true in the D.C. circuit. To assure that their nominees will be confirmed, presidents must consider the views of the senators from the states of the districts or circuits in which the prospective judges will serve, but the District of Columbia has no senators. As a result, presidents are relatively free to appoint individuals who have served under them or supported them in their campaigns.

Appointments to the D.C. circuit have also been available for persons who have adhered to principles and concepts of duty unpopular in their home communities. For example, Skelly Wright, a New Orleans district judge who steadfastly enforced the civil rights laws, was appointed to the D.C. circuit because it was obvious that southern senators would have blocked the confirmation of his appointment to the fifth circuit. Thus, the court that would hear North's appeal included many judges who had come from elsewhere and many who had been advocates of political or ideological viewpoints before taking the bench. Moreover, as members of the circuit court most often called upon to review the action of government agencies, these judges were more likely than most to have hardened their viewpoints in politically or ideologically tinged cases.

According to the conventional wisdom, we were in a double bind: The judges appointed by Democratic presidents were supposedly most concerned with protecting the constitutional rights of persons prosecuted for crimes, while most of the other judges owed their appointments to Ronald Reagan or George Bush, who had stated publicly and emphatically that they hoped that North would not be convicted.

Over the years, I had often found such simplistic views to be wrong. Most judges overcome the prejudices and alliances they had when appointed to the federal bench. During my three and one-half years on the federal district court in New York, I had experienced the merging process by which new judges are absorbed into their courts. My hard-line political and professional views had moderated during lunchroom conversations with Learned Hand, Jerome Frank, and Harold Medina and had dissolved after a couple of my decisions had been reversed on appeal.

But I was concerned about the continuing political allegiance of Republican judges as manifested in the Federalist Society. Although the organization was not openly partisan, its dogma was political. It reminded me of the communist front groups of the 1940s and 1950s, whose members were committed to the communist cause and subject to communist direction but were not card-carrying members of the Communist Party. In calling for the narrow construction of constitutional grants of governmental power, the Federalist Society seemed to speak for right-wing Republicans. I was especially troubled that one of White House Counsel Boyden Gray's assistants had openly declared that no one who was not a member of the Federalist Society had received a judicial appointment from President Bush.

These thoughts ran through my mind as I evaluated the panel drawn by lot to hear North's appeal. I was pleased to learn that the presiding judge of the panel would be Abner J. Mikva, a former congressman who had been appointed to the circuit court by President Jimmy Carter. Although Mikva was a staunch protector of the disadvantaged, including criminal defendants, I thought that he would bring a helpful perspective to the panel because he undoubtedly understood the need for honesty on the part of officials from the executive branch who were responding to congressional inquiries.

Next in seniority was Laurence H. Silberman, the judge I had most dreaded having on the panel. He had written the court of appeals opinion holding that the statute authorizing the appointment of independent counsel was unconstitutional (a holding that had been reversed by the Supreme Court); he had been hostile when interrogating my associate counsel in various matters we had had before the court; and at a D.C. circuit conference he had gotten into a shouting match about independent counsel with Judge George MacKinnon, the chief of the panel that had appointed me. Silberman not only had hostile views but seemed to hold them in anger.

With no experience as a trial judge and little as a trial lawyer, Silberman had served under George Shultz as solicitor and then undersecretary of the Labor Department during President Richard Nixon's first term. He had served briefly as deputy attorney general in the early 1970s. I had dealt with him during this period and had tentatively evaluated him as overly bright and cynical. He had next served as ambassador to Yugoslavia under Presidents Nixon and Gerald Ford. After returning to private practice in Washington, Silberman had become an advisor on foreign policy matters to Ronald Reagan's campaign organization. In this capacity, Silberman had been on the fringe of the negotiations to avoid the possibility of an "October surprise"—the pre-election release of the U.S. embassy staff held captive by Iranian radicals. He and Robert McFarlane had represented Reagan in at least one meeting with a person who claimed to have influence with Iranians who might affect the timing of the release of the hostages. Among some career officers in the State Department, he was jokingly referred to as "our ambassador to Khomeini."

Passed over for appointment to head the State Department or the CIA, Silberman had remained in private practice but had served on various government advisory committees dealing with foreign policy; he had also advised George Shultz on matters concerning the Middle East. Even after Reagan appointed him to the court of appeals in 1985, Silberman had continued to give speeches at Federalist Society meetings. He was an obvious prospect for a right-wing appointment to the Supreme Court. I feared that North's appeal would provide him with an opportunity for a virtuoso performance designed to catch the ear of President Bush.

Yet I was reluctant to request that Silberman disqualify himself. Prior government service or political activity did not bar him from serving on the panel. His unfavorable view of independent counsel, if it arose in the course of litigation rather than outside the courtroom, was not a basis for disqualification. Too late, I learned that he had a personal animus: He despised Judge Gerhard Gesell. Indeed, Silberman had stopped having lunch in the judges' lunchroom because of his antipathy for Gesell. Had I known that, the scales certainly would have tipped in favor of my seeking his recusal.

The third member of the panel was Judge David Bryan Sentelle, a recent appointee who was generally well liked by his colleagues and the bar. Proud of his Great Smoky Mountain origins, he had risen through local Republican politics in Charlotte, North Carolina. A supporter of Senator Jesse Helms, Sentelle had served as Republican county chairman and had chaired the North Carolina state Republican convention at the time of Reagan's first presidential nomination. Sentelle had held government office first as an assistant U.S. attorney during the Nixon administration and then as a local state judge. After a period of private practice, he had become a U.S. district judge in western North Carolina. In 1987, shortly after my appointment, President Reagan had elevated Sentelle to the D.C. circuit court of appeals.

I was surprised when Brendan Sullivan asked Judge Mikva to recuse himself on the very slender argument that, as a member of Congress, he had voted for the passage of the Independent Counsel Act. Judge Mikva acceded to the request. Believing that he would have best understood Congress's needs and our effort to bridge the constitutional problem that they created, I was disappointed at losing him.

Luckily for us, he was replaced by Chief Judge Patricia Wald, who had a solid reputation for dedicated ability and hard work. After a career as a litigator for the underprivileged, she had served as the assistant attorney general for legislative affairs during the Carter administration. She had been an active member and ultimately vice president of the American Law Institute, the professional association of judges, law teachers, and practicing lawyers that produces model statutes and publishes scholarly restatements of the law to reconcile differing court interpretations. In her ten years on the court of appeals, she had been noted not only for her scholarly work but also for her rapid, skillful disposition of a heavy workload.

Ordinarily, a court of appeals is not concerned with issues of fact; the verdict of the jury settles those, unless the trial judge has erred in the charge to the jury or in his or her procedures. In the North case, the facts were not in doubt. Except for whether North had possessed the requisite criminal intent, they were virtually conceded. The critical question before the appellate court was whether Congress's need for prompt exposure of a government scandal had been successfully reconciled with the Constitution's Bill of Rights, which protects the accused from being compelled to incriminate himself.

Consequently, I thought that someone who had a detached, scholarly background and had not participated in the trial, in my decision to prosecute, or in our procedures to insulate ourselves from North's congressional testimony would most credibly present the issues and respond to the questions of the court. I was immensely encouraged when Gerard Lynch, who had represented us in opposing North's motions to dismiss the indictment, agreed to represent us again.

On February 6, 1990, the three-judge panel heard the oral arguments by Barry Simon, representing North, and Professor Lynch. Although most of my associate counsel were in the courtroom, I did not attend the session for the same reasons that I had avoided North's trial: I did not want to be unnecessarily tainted or to leave any confusion as to who was in charge. Just as John Keker had been in command during the trial, Gerard Lynch was in command now.

Before Lynch could return from the courthouse, reports began to reach me by telephone. They were uniformly alarming. Those calling said that Lynch had been superb, but that Judge Silberman had been aggressively hostile to us, and that Judge Sentelle had seemed to support Silberman's views. Nina Totenberg of National Public Radio, the first to call, said she believed that a remand for further proceedings would be the best we could hope for. When I met with Lynch in my office, he more or less confirmed Nina's opinion. He did not complain about Silberman's behavior but simply counted him as a vote against us. Although he thought that Sentelle would follow Silberman on the immunity question, Lynch did not know how Chief Judge Wald would vote; she had at least seemed open-minded.

After hearing that Judge Silberman had been overbearing, I decided to read the transcript of the argument. It was redacted to avoid my exposure to the content of North's congressional testimony. As I raced through the pages, my anger surged. Any judge, and particularly an unfair judge, can batter an oral argument. Silberman's bias had been so intrusive that it had almost prevented Lynch, articulate though he had been, from presenting a coherent argument. Lynch had responded expertly to Silberman's questions, but rarely had he reached the fourth sentence in any answer before Silberman interrupted him—not seeking clarification but simply badgering him to make some concession. At times, the judge's sole purpose seemed to have been diversion and obstruction. Finally, after Lynch had exhausted his time in responding to Silberman, Chief Judge Wald had voluntarily given Lynch an additional few minutes to sum up. Before Lynch could begin, Silberman had seized the time to hector him further.

Appellate counsel expect to be questioned. They welcome questions because, if fairly asked, questions invite counsel to explain things that are bothering the judges. Silberman's interrogation had not been of this sort. It had been an overbearing effort to coerce a concession if not just to block a fair statement of our position. His performance had been ugly. I briefly considered sending the transcript—as the product of a temperamentally unfit judge—to Congressmen Peter Rodino and Jack Brooks, the chairman and former chairman of the House judiciary committee, which could review judicial misconduct, but our fate was already in Silberman's hands, and we had enough controversy. The unhappy truth was that I should have swallowed my scruples and moved to disqualify him at the outset.

Oral argument—a coherent oral argument—was to have been particularly important to us in the North case, because the court of appeals had limited the number of pages our appellate brief could contain, and the request for more space had gained us relatively few additional pages. North's counsel had raised so many points in his brief that we had been forced to severely condense each response just to be able to answer them all. Even though some of the points raised by North's counsel had been relatively unimportant, responding to them, even briefly, had consumed several pages of our brief, which had forced us to compress our responses to the major points.

Instead of allowing Lynch to more fully explain the arguments regarding North's immunity, Judge Silberman had chopped much of the oral argument into a dialogue testing Lynch's views on criminal intent and more narrow matters. On the issue of criminal intent with respect to North's destruction of National Security Council records, for example, the response in our brief had been so abbreviated that Silberman could deliberately misread it and—in conjunction with a one-word answer by Lynch to confused multiple questions by the judge—could, in writing his opinion, disingenuously spell out a "concession" by us that we had, in fact, never made.

We had known that we would have a hard time upholding North's conviction on appeal. Congress's grant of immunity had jeopardized

any conviction of North. The difficulty was obvious to everyone familiar with the case, but that only increased the need for a fair argument.
The importance of the issue—the dividing line between Congress and
the courts in the use of key witnesses—merited a fair hearing and a comprehensive resolution. Because the presentation of the basic constitutional point in our brief had been constrained by the need to address
other points, a fair judge would have at least permitted a full exposition
of our position, which was really Congress's position. Only Chief Judge
Wald seemed to have grasped this need, a need that transcended Oliver
North.

While we awaited the outcomes of North's appeal and Poindexter's
trial, we finally gave the residual investigation the concentration it
required. With the sentencing of Albert Hakim and Poindexter's conviction a few weeks later, we had completed the first stage of our work: the
conviction of the central conspirators. The case against Joseph
Fernandez was important as a potential avenue for exposing the crimes
committed by CIA officials, but I had little hope that we would ever be
able to try it. All we could do was wait for the appeal to be heard and the
dismissal affirmed.

Before Poindexter's trial ended, I had decided to taint myself. The
retrial of the North case, even if his conviction was reversed, was too
unlikely and too remote to worry about. But if the retrial happened, the
members of the North team remained untainted; they could handle it.
The same was true of the Poindexter case. Dan Webb and his team
would remain untainted. In any event, to evaluate the need for further
investigation, I had to read the congressional testimony of North and
Poindexter.

Craig Gillen had methodically reviewed our files and found gaps in
the records and witness interviews we had accumulated while racing
with Congress. Working with John Barrett, the last of my original
group, and a newly recruited team of gifted young lawyers, Gillen had
retraced our document assimilation and prepared for a comprehensive
examination of Oliver North, deciphering every line in each of North's
notebooks.

By the end of February, Gillen was reporting that our investigations
of Duane Clarridge, Elliott Abrams, and Colonel James J. Steele, the military group commander at the U.S. embassy in El Salvador during 1985
and 1986, had been incomplete. Abrams appeared particularly vulnerable; Gillen believed him to have been the point man in the cover-up that

had taken place after Eugene Hasenfus's plane was shot down in Nicaragua. Gillen also found that our investigations of Vice President Bush and the cabinet-level members of the National Security Council had been incomplete.

Once North and Poindexter were convicted, we had given them immunity so that they would be available as witnesses against the subjects of our ongoing investigation. In late March, after North testified in Poindexter's trial, we had tried to subpoena him for questioning before the grand jury. North's lawyers refused to accept a grand jury subpoena. We undertook to have one of our FBI agents serve it on North directly, but his ex-marine bodyguards threatened to prevent the service. The FBI agents regrouped and were about to force their way past the bodyguards when Sullivan telephoned me. At his request, we agreed to withhold the subpoena until April, and Sullivan agreed to accept it then.

Once he had received the subpoena, North was polite but mostly uncooperative. Instead of giving narrative answers to Gillen's questions, North provided the most limited and tentative responses possible, frequently halting the grand jury proceedings to consult privately with his lawyers. The questioning dragged on for weeks.

Meanwhile, Gillen's review of CIA documents and the congressional testimony of several witnesses had turned up significant inconsistencies. It was clear that we had not been given many of the documents that were pertinent to our investigations. Our efforts to fill these gaps were hampered by the Bush administration, which was shipping Iran-Contra records to the Reagan Library in California, hoping to bury the scandal. Boyden Gray also delayed us by assigning problems related to Iran-Contra document production to a lawyer in private practice who had no knowledge of the subject and claimed that he needed time to learn about it before he could respond to our document requests. At the same time, members of Gray's staff were consulting with Ronald Reagan's private attorneys regarding possible claims of executive privilege.

In the course of John Barrett's careful review of the notes of State Department officers, he discovered that George Shultz's executive assistant, Charles Hill, and the department's executive secretary, Nicholas Platt, had been very selective in determining relevance when responding to requests for their notes of Shultz's conversations. They had given us only those notes that pertained to the sale of arms to Iran and those that supported Shultz's congressional testimony.

Gillen's team also found that Elliott Abrams had regularly reviewed all the State Department's cables regarding Central America. From

North's notebooks we learned that Abrams had telephoned Venezuelan officials to facilitate the purchase of a C-123 aircraft by Richard Gadd for North's Contra-supply network. If Abrams had known about Gadd, he must have known about North's private benefactors and understood his resupply operation.

Gillen and Barrett concluded that our earlier interrogation of Elliott Abrams had been inadequate. Because we had lacked so many relevant documents, we had too narrowly focused on Abrams's lies regarding a contribution that the sultan of Brunei had made to the Contras. North's notebooks showed North describing his activities to the restricted interagency group that Abrams headed. Although Abrams had denied that Hasenfus had been part of a U.S. operation and had denied knowing who Max Gomez (Felix Rodriguez) was, Abrams and Alan Fiers—and perhaps Fiers's boss, Clair George—had been aware of the truth. We decided to review all the raw notes from the State Department.

Some of our previous document requests had been comprehensive, but others had been piecemeal. The time had come to reformulate them. In view of the gaps in production, we decided to issue subpoenas, rather than less formal document requests. Incongruous though it was, the government's prosecutor had to subpoena the government to get material that should have been turned over long before.

One area we needed to explore was Caspar Weinberger's contemporaneous knowledge of the Defense Department's participation in the November 1985 Hawk shipment to Iran. North's notebooks showed that during the planning of the January 1986 shipment, Weinberger had been concerned with violations of the Arms Export Control Act. An entry that seemed to have reflected advice from CIA director William Casey noted that President Reagan should "just tell Cap to do it."

What we had viewed as a residual investigation was now becoming a third phase of our work. The more we learned, the less Iran-Contra seemed like a rogue operation. We were steadily uncovering information that seriously implicated senior officials from several agencies. References to Fiers, for example, permeated North's notebooks. And reading what Rodriguez, Donald Gregg, Samuel Watson, and James Steele had told Congress and us regarding George Bush's contemporaneous knowledge of Iran-Contra, Gillen concluded that their testimony did not pass the "smell test."

In June, we unearthed valuable material that had been withheld from us. At the Hoover Institution on the campus of California's Stanford

University, to which Shultz had returned after Reagan left office, Louise Radin and John Barrett found a file cabinet filled with Charles Hill's spiral binders. The notes they contained were cryptic but understandable. Moreover, if Shultz's aide had accumulated such a massive volume of notes, surely others must have had similar means of keeping track of their thoughts and activities.

As time passed without a decision on North's appeal, we grew ever more pessimistic. Finally, on July 20, 1990, the court of appeals set aside North's three-count conviction and remanded his case to Judge Gesell for a further hearing to determine whether North's immunized testimony had been used against him. The court reversed the conviction for destroying NSC records, because of perceived errors in Gesell's instructions to the jury. Chief Judge Wald dissented from both rulings and voted to affirm the convictions on all three counts. Differing combinations of judges agreed on the various issues raised on appeal. Because the judges had been so divided, no single judge wrote the majority opinion. Instead, they handed down a per curiam opinion, in which the work of all three had been patched together. Sentelle had been the swing vote between the sharply divergent views of Wald and Silberman. Altogether, the opinions filled 117 pages of the *Federal Reporter*.

The court of appeals held unanimously that the use of immunized testimony to refresh recollection had been an evidentiary use even though the testimony itself had not been introduced as evidence. Wald disagreed with her colleagues about the effect of Gesell's (and our) conceptual error that because North's testimony had merely refreshed a witness's recollection of what he or she had already known, the testimony itself had not become evidence and that, therefore, the witness had not made an "evidentiary use" of it. Wald believed that the trial judge's error had been harmless, because he and we had successfully instructed each witness not to relate anything learned for the first time from the immunized testimony and because the substance of the testimony regarding the three counts on which North had been convicted was the same as the testimony we had presented to the grand jury before North had testified for the congressional committees.

The heart of the controlling opinion was Silberman's rationalization that we had used North's congressional testimony against him simply because we had called witnesses who had heard him testify. It made no difference that my staff had specifically refrained from eliciting the immunized testimony or deliberately using it to refresh a witness's recollection. According to Silberman, backed up by Sentelle, by merely calling a witness who had listened to or reviewed the testimony, we had used the testimony itself.

Silberman and Sentelle briefly acknowledged that my staff and I had successfully insulated ourselves from the testimony. The remainder of their opinion, however, was written to imply that we had deliberately used North's testimony to refresh witnesses' recollections, although the undisputed fact was that we had done no such thing. The opinion contained numerous misleading statements: "If the government uses immunized testimony to refresh the recollection of a witness," for example, and "yet the very purpose of the Fifth Amendment under these circumstances, is to prevent the prosecutor from transmogrifying into the inquisitor, complete with that officers' most pernicious tool—the power of the State to force a person to incriminate himself."

In her dissent, Judge Wald pointed out the unfairness of this ambiguous use of the passive voice to imply that we had deliberately used the immunized testimony. Silberman and Sentelle had written, for instance, that "a central problem in this case is that many grand jury and trial witnesses were thoroughly soaked in North's immunized testimony," when the judges knew from the record that it had been President Reagan's officials, Attorney General Edwin Meese's assistants, and the CIA's counsel—not the prosecutors—who had done the soaking. Ignoring Wald's observation, Silberman and Sentelle let the ambiguity stand.

Silberman and Sentelle focused on Gesell's procedural failure to hold a posttrial evidentiary hearing devoted to the possible effect of the immunized testimony. By collecting and summarizing in an orderly fashion the facts on this subject, such a hearing would have helped the court of appeals and us. Gesell had ordered such a hearing but had then canceled it. Keker and I had decided not to press him for the hearing. Not only had he been angered and exhausted by Barry Simon's obstructive tactics, but the judge also had believed that he had addressed the immunity problem in his rulings and instructions to each witness. Gesell had read all the grand jury testimony and, of course, had heard all the trial testimony. He had found that nothing significant had been added to what had already been known before North gave his congressional testimony. The judge had been satisfied that by furnishing North's counsel with summaries of the grand jury testimony that had been given before North testified in the congressional hearings, the prosecution had met the burden of "going forward" to demonstrate its lack of reliance on the immunized testimony. It had been up to North's counsel, Gesell had ruled, to specify the evidence they believed to have been tainted.

Simon had refused to identify any item in the record as a reflection of North's immunized testimony. Simon had argued that he had no obligation to go forward, and that we would have to prove the negative by calling each witness for examination and cross-examination. Gesell had disagreed, saying that we had met our initial burden by providing the summaries. The hearing had been canceled when Simon refused to restate with specificity his claim that North's testimony had been used.

Chief Judge Wald had undertaken to fill this gap in the record. She had spent weeks going through the transcripts of the grand jury and trial testimony. She had verified Judge Gesell's conclusion that, as to the three counts on which North had been convicted, virtually all the evidence had been known to us and presented to the grand jury before North testified in the congressional hearings. Only two witnesses, testifying to the third of those counts, had testified for the first time after North had given his immunized testimony. One of the witnesses had simply repeated what he had already told the FBI before North testified; the other had reiterated facts to which the other witness had also testified. More significant, neither witness had contradicted North. Their testimony had supported his view of what had happened.

The facts had not been in dispute for two of the counts on which North was convicted. He had admitted having accepted the security system for his home as a gift from Richard Secord and having destroyed NSC records, although he had denied having had the requisite criminal intent. The facts had been in dispute in the third count on which he was convicted—that of assisting in drafting the false chronology for the congressional testimony of John Poindexter and William Casey. North's counsel had objected to the testimony of Robert McFarlane, who had carefully monitored North's congressional testimony. Yet the substance of the testimony of McFarlane and all but two of the other witnesses who had addressed this count had been presented to the grand jury before North had given his immunized testimony. After studying the thousands of pages of transcripts and hundreds of documents produced for the grand jury and trial, Wald had been satisfied "that North received a fair trial—not a perfect one, but a competently managed and a fair one."

Unwilling to rely on the existing record or on Wald's careful review of it, Silberman and Sentelle had postulated a broad rule: Every witness who had heard North's congressional testimony (even those who had testified only to charges on which North had been acquitted) must be examined and cross-examined, if necessary, "line-by-line" and "item-by-item" about the possible effects of North's testimony. Wald noted that such a requirement would play into the hands of witnesses who were hostile to the prosecution, allowing them to claim some undisprovable subjective influence from North's testimony and thereby making it essentially impossible to prosecute anyone who had received congressional immunity.

Under the rule postulated by Silberman and Sentelle, Congress would always be forced to choose between public hearings, which would promptly expose official wrongdoing, and prosecution of the wrongdoers, which would reveal the truth much more slowly. Wald regarded such a choice as unnecessary, at least in this case. She was satisfied that Gesell had dealt with the problem pragmatically and adequately. In refusing to hold a posttrial *Kastigar* hearing, Gesell had found that the defense motion for such a hearing had "raise[d] few new issues" and "[sought] in most instances to re-litigate issues already resolved by the Court." The chief judge concluded that the hearing her colleagues were insisting on would add countless extra weeks or months to the trial to little or no avail. She found that Gesell had actually undertaken a careful analysis and had supplied North with all the constitutional protection to which he was entitled.

Summing up, Chief Judge Wald wrote:

> Of decisive importance, moreover, is the fact that *nearly all of the grand jury witnesses testifying with regard to Counts Six, Nine, and Ten* [the conviction counts] *appeared before North presented his immunized testimony to Congress.* . . . Corroborating this conclusion, the I.C. [independent counsel] represented at oral argument that the testimony relevant to Counts Six, Nine, and Ten was presented before North's immunized testimony. . . . Although North's counsel correctly pointed out that 'many' grand jury witnesses did not appear until after the immunized testimony . . . , he did not dispute the I.C.'s basic characterization of witnesses appearing after North's immunized testimony as irrelevant to the Counts on which he was convicted. And the law in this circuit is clear that even evidence derived from immunized statements does not pose a *Kastigar* problem if it is irrelevant to the prosecution's case. [Italics in original]

The strictures of the majority opinion—and their implications for future prosecutions by independent counsel—dismayed us. The opponents of North's prosecution seized on the opinion as vindication, but the strong dissent by the chief judge softened the blow for us. To fair-minded observers, Wald's careful analysis supplied a fitting explanation and justification for the expense and effort that we had thrown into the prosecution after Congress had jeopardized it.

We were now confronted with the choice of seeking an appeal to the Supreme Court or pursuing the remand to Judge Gesell to try to improve the record. Lynch was not available to represent us in a further appeal, having accepted an appointment as the chief of the criminal division of the U.S. attorney's office in New York. After consulting our new appellate counsel, Andrew Frey, I concluded that the Silberman-Sentelle prescription for a remand proceeding was extreme—almost sardonic. We decided to try to obtain a review on the existing record.

Before petitioning the Supreme Court, however, we had to move for reargument to give Judges Silberman and Sentelle an opportunity to correct the part of their opinion in which they had misread the trial record and erroneously held that Judge Gesell had failed to charge the jury properly on the need for unanimity. After receiving briefs, they acknowledged their mistake and changed the opinion. At the same time, we requested that the decision of the three-judge panel be reviewed by the full court of eleven judges, a form of relief that is rarely granted. Our request was denied, but Judge Ruth Bader Ginsburg (who would later be appointed to the Supreme Court) wrote a dissenting opinion that criticized Silberman's having unfairly claimed that Lynch had made a concession that he had not actually made.

In May 1991, the Supreme Court declined to review the case. We knew that the Court sometimes avoided highly publicized cases as vehicles for pronouncing difficult constitutional rulings. And, technically, the decision of the court of appeals was not a final disposition but merely a remand to permit Judge Gesell to perfect his record. Nevertheless, we had hoped that the issue of congressional immunity was so important that the Court would grant review. We were left with the uninviting prospect of a lengthy remand hearing before Judge Gesell.

The next time a seat on the Supreme Court became available, Boyden Gray included Laurence Silberman's name on a short list of four possible nominees for the president to consider in filling the vacancy. According to published reports, when President Bush received the list, he crossed Silberman's name out. Clarence Thomas received the appointment.

In the late summer of 1990, while the original North team and I were determining how to respond to the reversal of North's conviction, associate counsel Stuart Abrams, Bill Treanor, and Geoff Berman were trying our case against Thomas Clines, Secord's partner and arms purchasing agent, in the U.S. district court in Baltimore, where Clines had filed false income tax returns. On September 18, the jury found him guilty of all four felony charges—two counts of underreporting his gross income to the Internal Revenue Service and two counts for denying in his returns that he possessed foreign bank accounts. Judge Norman P. Ramsey ordered Clines to pay a $40,000 fine and sentenced him to sixteen months in prison. On appeal, his conviction was affirmed. The Supreme Court denied certiorari.

Before the reversal of North's conviction, he had been reluctantly filling in some details, expanding on his hundreds of pages of notes, and backing up some of the assertions he had made to Congress that knowledge of his activities had been widespread among officials in the Reagan administration. North had described his contacts from 1984 to 1986 with the office of Vice President Bush, especially those with Donald Gregg and Felix Rodriguez, who had been Gregg's friend and former CIA subordinate.

After the court of appeals set aside North's conviction, however, North refused to continue testifying, even with immunity, and his counsel filed a motion to quash our grand jury subpoena. Chief Judge Aubrey Robinson denied the motion, but North still refused to testify. Finally, when confronted with a U.S. marshal who was ready to take him to jail, North changed his mind and decided to purge himself of contempt by resuming his reluctant and frequently interrupted grand jury testimony.

During this period, Lewis Tambs, the former U.S. ambassador to Costa Rica, had given us more detailed information about his conversations with Elliott Abrams and other State Department officials about Joseph Fernandez's efforts to open the Contras' southern front in Nicaragua and the embassy's involvement in the building of the secret airstrip in northern Costa Rica.

In the summer, Craig Gillen had begun to subject a few principal witnesses to polygraph examinations to test the truth or falsity of their answers. The process revealed that Donald Gregg had made misstatements about North and Rodriguez to the grand jury and Congress. Gregg had testified that prior to June 1986 he had not known that

North or Rodriguez had any connection with the Contra-supply operation. When James Steele asserted that he had limited his activities to providing humanitarian supplies to the Contras, the polygraph indicated that he was not being truthful. Confronted with the results of the lie-detector test and North's notebook entries, Steele admitted not only his participation in the arms deliveries but also his early discussions of these activities with Donald Gregg and the U.S. ambassador to El Salvador, Edwin G. Corr.

A few members of my staff felt that we had completed our assignment with the conviction of Poindexter, but Dan Webb and Craig Gillen were powerfully convincing that we were obligated to complete our broad assignment, to follow the leads that our new young team was developing, and to address the unsatisfactory responses we were still receiving from too many people. We now had compelling indications that the conspiracy directed by Poindexter and North had been supported by the State Department, the CIA, and the Defense Department. And we got continual reminders that the cabinet-level members of the National Security Council had known more than they had admitted to Congress, the public, and to us.

A note written by Charles Hill on August 7, 1987, could not be disregarded: "Cap [Weinberger] takes notes but never referred to them so never had to cough them up." Weinberger had given us only two pages of notes. Gillen tried to reach him by telephone, but Weinberger would not return his calls. Finally, we issued a subpoena.

The more I thought about it, the more certain I felt that this was no time to quit. I considered making a report to Congress regarding my decision to proceed with the investigation, but I decided instead to announce it at a speaking engagement for the political science department at Washburn University in Topeka, Kansas. In my speech, I addressed the criticism we had received for our expenditure of time and money, and I explained our intention to investigate the agencies that had supported the efforts of Poindexter, North, and Secord, as well as the individuals who had been responsible for supervising them. I estimated that we could complete our investigation in six to nine months. By then, I believed, Poindexter's appeal would be decided, the grand jury testimony of North and Poindexter would be complete, and we would have made our decisions about any further indictments.

CHAPTER FIFTEEN

The CIA Cracks

The reversal of Oliver North's conviction forced us into a new race with Congress, a race for public opinion. I had to outrun a determined political effort by North's supporters, George Bush's administration, and congressional critics to shut down my office. Public support was waning, and many negative editorials and columns appeared as our expenditures approached the $25 million mark in September 1990. The expenses resulting from the delaying tactics employed by North and his counsel, the president and his counsel, and the attorney general were difficult to dramatize for the public, although each day of stalling cost the taxpayers more than $10,000.

Without any political constituency of my own, I depended on the news media to help me reach the public and explain why, after spending so much money only to have the man at the center of the scandal go free, I now planned to expand the scope of my investigation. Fortunately, the most thoughtful commentators continued to back our work, and the expert reporters who had covered it from the beginning retained their interest.

My press officers—Jim Wieghart, followed by Mary Belcher—responded to the day-to-day questions from the media and saw to it that I allotted at least one day each week to interviews with individual reporters. I explained to them that we had discharged our responsibility to investigate and prosecute North and his immediate confederates in the operational conspiracy, but that we could not call our work complete until we had extracted more complete testimony from North and John Poindexter, investigated the agencies that had supported the conspiracy, and evaluated the culpability of the members of the National Security Council who had tolerated the activities of its staff. Without my naming them, the reporters knew I was talking about George Shultz, Caspar Weinberger, and William Casey as well as George Bush and Ronald Reagan.

Our public relations capabilities were minimal compared with those of Congress, the White House, and the agencies we were investigating. But the Washington press corps, perhaps the best group of reporters in the world, regularly published fair and balanced news stories, which offset the virulence of the most hostile editorials against us. This demonstration of the independence and professional standards of our press reaffirmed my faith in its essential importance to the rule of law. Occasional excesses, such as the media frenzy over O. J. Simpson's trial, simply underscore by contrast the excellent day-to-day reporting by Washington's journalists.

Having filed our motion and briefs for review of the court of appeals decision, we concentrated on Craig Gillen's investigation. By now, North had resumed his halting, grudging testimony before the grand jury. Poindexter was also testifying. He had become less unpleasant but was simply denying that he recalled anything that he had not discussed in his congressional testimony.

High-ranking officers continued to lie to us. During October, Gillen and his assistants interviewed Caspar Weinberger twice. In courteous, noncontentious interviews, the former secretary of defense denied having relevant notes or recalling much that had occurred in connection with the arms sales to Iran. As was the case in most of our preliminary interviews, no court reporter was present, but an FBI agent took notes which were then written up as a report, an "FBI form 302." In the event of any controversy over what had been said, the FBI agent could be called as a witness.

Gillen negotiated an agreement with Weinberger's lawyer, William Rogers, who was an old friend of mine, for us to review Weinberger's documents, including his notes, in the presence of Weinberger's secretary at the Library of Congress. As we later learned, the records in the library consisted of two distinct groups, which had been handled differently: The first set, which included memoranda from Weinberger's official files, had gone through the Defense Department's classification procedures; the second set, which comprised Weinberger's private notes and memoranda, had not been reviewed or classified, because Weinberger had kept the material out of the official files. Thinking that the documents we wanted would have been classified, and pointed in that direction by the librarians, two of my associate counsel reviewed the classified material and found little related to Iran-Contra.

In November, we finally got access to Joseph Fernandez. After the court of appeals had affirmed the dismissal of the case against him in September, Attorney General Richard Thornburgh had had a final opportunity to release the classified information that had caused the dismissal. Thornburgh had withheld his decision until the last possible minute, keeping us in the dark for six weeks and preventing us from addressing Fernandez as a witness, because technically he had still been a defendant. Now that the dismissal was final, we were able to give Fernandez immunity and compel his testimony before the grand jury.

Gillen began Fernandez's interrogation by taking him through his KL-43 messages and CIA cables. At first bellicose and defiant, he eventually led us through a word-by-word review of the CIA cables, which had deliberately been written in a manner that would make them difficult for outsiders to understand. Fernandez told us that officials at the CIA's headquarters had known what he was doing. Confirmed by the cables, he described how Alan Fiers had supported him in shifting the leadership of the Contras on the southern front from Eden Pastora to Pedro Chamorro. To keep them fighting inside Nicaragua, Fiers had approved weapons drops in March and April 1986. Fernandez admitted that his denials to the Tower Commission had been false.

While Gillen and his assistants interviewed witnesses about CIA activities, John Barrett focused our attention on the notes that George Shultz had dictated to his executive assistant, Charles Hill. When Barrett and Louise Radin gained access to the notes in George Shultz's office at the Hoover Institution on the Stanford University campus, they had read them in a secure room in Palo Alto. We had then compelled the State Department to have the notes moved to the National Archives. Eventually, copies of the most relevant ones had been brought to our office. After spending nearly a year poring over them, Barrett claimed that they were so hard to read that he had had to have his glasses strengthened three times while he sorted out the truly important notes and compared them with the distorted selection that Hill had originally given us. In the end, we kept copies of a third of the notes Hill had written.

Hill's notes showed that Shultz had more than once told Elliott Abrams to keep an eye on North, because Shultz had needed to know what North was doing. After a captured Eugene Hasenfus had told the Sandinistas that Max Gomez was the CIA's man at Ilopongo, Abrams had told Congress that he did not know who Gomez was. The next day, however, Hill had taken notes as Abrams explained to Shultz that Gomez was actually Felix Rodriguez, who had been sponsored by Vice President Bush's national security advisor, Donald Gregg, and had been part of North's operation in Central America. During that conversation, which had taken place while the State Department officials were en route to El Salvador to inspect earthquake damage, Abrams had told Shultz that Poindexter and North had tried to remove Rodriguez from Ilopongo a year earlier, because he had talked too much and had bragged about his ties to the vice president.

A newly produced set of notes taken by Colonel Stephen Croker when he debriefed his boss, Lieutenant General John Moellering, who had represented the Joint Chiefs of Staff at a critical meeting of the restricted interagency group in the summer of 1986, revealed North's recitation of the details of his activities. The notes showed that Abrams, as chairman of the RIG, had known the structure of North's Contra-supply operation long before Hasenfus's aircraft was shot down.

Apparently uninformed, Shultz had sent messages to all the regional offices of the State Department, declaring that the U.S. government had not been involved in Hasenfus's mission. On October 7, 1986, two days after the shootdown, Shultz told reporters that the aircraft had been hired by private people having no connection with the government. Three days later, he repeated these denials at the Reykjavik summit meeting with President Gorbachev. While Shultz was in El Salvador, Bush had telephoned to ask him to tell President José Napoleón Duarte privately that Bush had met Rodriguez on only two occasions, and that Bush had thought that Rodriguez had merely been helping the Salvadoran air force.

Much of the frustration Shultz had experienced after the exposure of the Iranian arms sales was evident in Hill's notes. They showed, for example, that Shultz had feared that Ronald Reagan's flat denials of having traded arms for hostages meant that he was losing touch with reality. Shultz had also lost confidence in Bush. Believing the vice president's overstated public denial of his connection with Iran-Contra to have been open to easy contradiction, Shultz and his advisors had predicted that my office would try to get Bush through Donald Gregg.

Shultz had worried about how the government would be run. He had become an outsider: Overtures to the Iranians were continuing without the State Department's approval or genuine participation, and the NSC staff had become operational. Shultz had considered asking the president to appoint him to be national security advisor, in addition to secretary of state. After Poindexter's resignation, however, that possibility had been foreclosed by the quick appointment of Frank Carlucci, former deputy director of the CIA and former deputy secretary of defense.

We were not surprised to find that the notes also revealed Shultz's analysis of my work as independent counsel. He had been concerned about the money we were spending and the objectives we were pursuing. In his view, we were attempting to criminalize the political process and expand congressional power. From the notes, we could tell that Shultz and his lawyer, Abraham Sofaer, had been particularly worried about the conspiracy charge in our basic indictment, which would have drawn in Shultz as a witness—a witness who might be cross-examined about the inconsistencies between his congressional testimony and the notes he had dictated to Hill.

When the issue of presidential pardons for North and Poindexter had arisen in 1988, Shultz and Sofaer had initially favored them, but Reagan had resisted granting them, because the pardons would have implied guilt. The administration's internal discussions of the possible pardons had taken place at the very time we were negotiating with the State Department for the release of nonsecret classified information, such as the names of the Central American countries bordering Nicaragua and their officials. One of Hill's notes reported that Sofaer had told Shultz during this period that the State Department was making progress in getting counts dropped in exchange for the declassification of such information. After we were forced to drop the conspiracy count because of the administration's refusal to declassify information that the court had held material to North's defense, Sofaer had advised Shultz to oppose a pardon for North.

Shortly after the conclusion of Poindexter's trial, John Barrett had been looking for information on Elliott Abrams and fortuitously discovered the gaps in the notes Hill had turned over to us. Barrett had realized that the documents we had been given contained virtually nothing about the resupply of the Contras. His subsequent investigation had confirmed that the notes the State Department had produced included only those that supported Shultz's original congressional testimony. After hearing the reports by Barrett and Radin of their first review of Hill's notes, Gillen went to Palo Alto to interview Shultz and

Hill and to determine whether all the notes should be moved to Washington for further review and safekeeping.

On December 10, 1990, Gillen had met with Hill in Shultz's offices at the Hoover Institution. Gillen wanted to know how we had been misled into thinking that the State Department had previously produced all its relevant documents, including notes. Asked for an explanation, Hill arrogantly denied having been told that he had to turn over all the relevant notes. He said that he had been too busy to go through all his notes, and that Abraham Sofaer had told him that he need only supply the notes that he had selected as a basis for Shultz's congressional testimony. (When Gillen and Barrett later questioned Sofaer, he denied that any such limitation had been placed on the production. So did Danny Coulson, the FBI agent who had been in charge of the original investigation.)

Shultz testily asked Gillen whether we were going to indict him and grumbled about our reopening the investigation so late in the game. Gillen listened politely and then began to press Shultz: Had there been a plan to deceive us? Or had Shultz left the document production to others and failed to follow up on it? Shultz said that he had left the task to Sofaer and Hill. When asked about the conflicts between his congressional testimony and the intelligence reports, Shultz said that he had not read the intelligence reports, but had left that to his deputy, Michael Armacost.

When Gillen asked about Caspar Weinberger's role in Iran-Contra, Shultz became protective of the former secretary of defense. From Hill's notes, we knew that Shultz had at least once complained to Hill that Weinberger had been dishonest in his factual statements to President Reagan: "misstates facts—it's tiresome. Wbgr. [Weinberger] dishonest. Says these outrageous things" (about whether the antiballistic missile treaty prohibited deployment). Shultz had complained that Weinberger was either "stupid or dishonest, one or the other." Nevertheless, he insisted to Gillen that Weinberger was honest.

The notes revealed that Shultz and his principal assistants—Charles Hill, Nicholas Platt, Michael Armacost, and John C. Whitehead—had known in advance about the November 1985 Hawk shipment and had known that it had been intended to secure the release of the hostages. Prior to the shipment, Armacost had told Shultz that Robert McFarlane had asked Weinberger how to get Hawk and Phoenix missiles to Iran, and that McFarlane had claimed to have cleared the plan with the president. Hill had ridiculed North's cover story that the weapons had been accidentally discovered in a warehouse en route from Israel to Iran. Hill and Platt had regarded North as untrustworthy. In their notes, their code name for North was "Polecat."

Explaining one of Hill's notes, Shultz acknowledged that he had met with Reagan after his disastrous press conference in November 1986 and that the president had admitted having known about the November 1985 Hawk shipment. Shultz also confirmed that when he later told Attorney General Edwin Meese what the president had said, Meese had replied that the president had not had this knowledge and had not approved the Hawk shipment, and that such a shipment would have been a violation of law.

Although he was generally protective of Elliott Abrams, Shultz was shocked when Gillen handed him a document, written by Abrams's assistant Richard H. Melton, revealing that Abrams had promised to give General John Singlaub a note to the Korean government expressing U.S. pleasure at a possible Korean gift to the Contras. The document also showed that Abrams had participated in discussions with North about Blowpipe weapons for the Contras and had vouched for Richard Gadd to help him obtain an airplane from Venezuela for the Contra-supply operation. Obviously shaken, Shultz said that he would have expected Abrams to report his knowledge of the solicitations of funds from Korea and Taiwan and to report any embassy involvement with the arms shipments.

Shultz claimed not to have known that Abrams had been the chairman of the RIG on Central America. The former secretary of state said that he had not known of the resupply activities or the role played by Felix Rodriguez until after Abrams and Clair George had testified before Congress, following the shootdown of Hasenfus's plane. Shultz said that he had asked Abrams to get the details of the disaster, but that Abrams had relied on false statements by North and the CIA. In denying that he had instructed or authorized Abrams to lie to Congress regarding the solicitation of the sultan of Brunei, Shultz said he had hoped that Abrams could merely give an evasive answer if a committee member asked about the subject.

Responding to questions about other notes Hill had written, Shultz acknowledged having lunched with Bush before the vice president's trip to Israel to meet Amiram Nir in summer 1986. Shultz asserted, however, that they had not discussed the Iranian venture, even though Bush had wanted to go to Syria and bring back a hostage. While minimizing the critical comments about Bush that Hill had reported in his notes,

Shultz confirmed that on hearing Bush's claim that he had been "out of the loop" regarding the arms sales to Iran, he had telephoned Bush's friend Nicholas Brady, then secretary of the Treasury, to say that Bush could not make such a flat denial. Shultz had told Brady that Bush had not only been present at the January 7, 1986, meeting when President Reagan authorized the arms sales, but had also remained silent, thereby tacitly expressing support for the president's plan.

Hill's November 9, 1986, note read: "I said what concerns me is Bush on TV saying it [was] ridiculous to even consider selling arms to Iran. V.P. was part of it." Shultz had warned Brady that the vice president was "getting drawn into a web of lies. Blows his integrity. He's finished then. Should be very careful how he plays the loyal lieutenant role now."

After a November 1986 meeting at which the National Security Planning Group had decided to release a statement supporting the president, Shultz had told Hill that Bush and Weinberger should have supported him in urging Reagan to tell the public the truth. Instead, Shultz had said, they were "taking the president down the drain." Three weeks later, Shultz had observed that Bush "had a thing about wanting to be a hero about hostages. He wanted in [the] Middle East trip to go to Syria. Wanted to have a hostage come back on his plane. There's a superficiality there."

In a series of other comments (based on intelligence-report references whose interpretation we doubted), Shultz had indicated his belief that Bush had been actively collaborating with North and that as a result, Bush would be crushed. According to one of Hill's notes, Shultz had observed that the vice president was "always tempted to lurch to the right. Contra & Iran tempted him."

At our last staff conference in 1990 and again in early 1991, we evaluated the case against Donald Gregg. He had testified to the grand jury and to Congress that he had not known that Felix Rodriguez was helping North supply the Contras until August 1986, when Congress was about to authorize the CIA to take back the responsibility. Gregg had said that he had never told Bush about Rodriguez's role in North's operation. James Steele, however, had admitted to having told Gregg in January 1986 that Rodriguez was busy helping the Contras, and Oliver North had claimed that Gregg had known about his activities as early as 1985. A February 1986 report to Gregg from his assistant, Samuel Watson, on resupplying the Contras was annotated with the phrase "Felix [Rodriguez] agrees," in Gregg's handwriting.

On July 24, 1990, at Gillen's request, the FBI had conducted a polygraph examination of Gregg. The examiner had concluded that the polygraph indicated deception in Gregg's answers to the five most relevant questions he was asked. We knew that while Bush was still vice president, Boyden Gray had interrogated Gregg after discovering a memorandum by his assistant listing one of the topics for a May 1986 meeting between Rodriguez and Bush as "Contra resupply." When we tried to question Gray about the results of this interrogation, President Bush stepped in and asserted his attorney-client privilege to prevent Gray from testifying about what Gregg had told him. Although Gregg had made no claim that Gray was his lawyer, he would probably have done so if we had contested the president's claim.

Our investigation of Gregg retained its vitality because of the results of his polygraph examination, but such results are inadmissible in court, so we could not make a solid case against him without the cooperation of either Felix Rodriguez or Samuel Watson. Rodriguez was a hardened operative, a former CIA agent who consistently protected Gregg, under whom he had served in the CIA. Even though Richard Secord had informed us that Rodriguez's fellow operative Rafael Quintero had told him that Rodriguez had telephoned Gregg every time weapons were delivered, we could not persuade Quintero to testify against Rodriguez. We would have to decide whether it was worth our time and effort to prosecute Rodriguez for denying that he had made the calls, when he was likely to persist in the denials even if convicted and thus would never testify against Gregg.

As for our other potential witness against Donald Gregg, we continued to gather proof that Samuel Watson had known quite early about Rodriguez and about North's Contra-supply activities, but we could not prove beyond a reasonable doubt that Watson had reported this to Gregg and the vice president. Watson's secretary was ready to testify that he had dictated a memorandum specifying "Contra resupply" as a subject to be discussed by Rodriguez and Bush in May 1986. Another secretary corroborated her. Watson denied it. A case against Watson would consist simply of two secretaries' saying that his denials were false. We believed that he had lied, but we did not want to be diverted into a slender case against Watson to try to compel him to talk. Craig Gillen argued against prosecution, saying that he could not see a juror's blood rising over Watson's dispute with his secretaries. "It's a fragment of a day in a larger picture."

Watson declined to make a proffer, and his lawyer would not consent to our subjecting Watson to a polygraph examination. Our only remaining choice was to give him immunity and take whatever testimony we could get before the grand jury. The case against Gregg was still too close to call. We postponed our decision on immunity for Watson.

John Poindexter denied ever having given information to Gregg. Poindexter said that as national security advisor he had dealt directly with the vice president, keeping him informed about the Iranian initiative and sporadically informed about the Contra-supply efforts. The vice president had been present at most of the president's morning briefings. Obviously, Bush knew more than he had acknowledged in his deposition before the trial of Oliver North. We began to accumulate questions for a second, more broadly focused deposition, but now that Bush was president, we could not—as a matter of courtesy and as a political reality—bother him more than once.

By the end of the year, our office had contracted to less than one-third of its original space. Although the office was congested, our spirits were high. Gillen and the younger lawyers worked well and had a lot to give each other. I found myself belatedly agreeing with Chesterfield Smith, one of my predecessors at the American Bar Association, who had insisted that receptions and parties were more successful if held in crowded rooms. Having converted our original conference room to a document-file room, we now held our staff meetings around two tables that had been pushed together in one of our witness rooms. Gillen and I usually sat opposite each other so that we formed a sort of axis for discussion. Ten to twelve of us would crowd around the makeshift conference table for hot, uncomfortable, and sometimes lengthy meetings.

Thinking that we might be able to conclude the investigation soon, Mary Belcher and I intensified our work on the final report, which I regarded as a final internal audit of our possible mistakes and one last chance to correct them. I wanted to be ready to release the report quickly once the investigation was completed.

The new year had begun with a series of personal tragedies affecting various members of the staff: My youngest daughter's best friend had been accidentally asphyxiated by carbon monoxide from a faulty furnace; an associate counsel's wife had miscarried their first child; and Guy Struve's infant daughter, Beverly, had undergone a long, delicate operation, during which her life-support equipment had accidentally become detached, leaving her with injuries that would take her life after weeks of poignant torment for her inconsolable family.

No one talked much about these tragedies. Like a disciplined unit, we simply worked harder. Guy Struve insisted that he not be replaced in litigation that he was handling for us in New York. But, with no urging or suggestion from anyone, the entire Washington staff helped fill the New York church for Beverly's funeral. For one who prided himself on disciplined toughness, I was ashamed to have less control over my emotions than Guy and his wife, Marcia, or their two children. Why were we putting ourselves and our families through the separation, criticism, and strain of this damned investigation?

At this time, former associate counsel Jeffrey Toobin, a young man who had come to us almost fresh out of law school, published a book giving his view of the internal workings of our office, the investigation of Elliott Abrams, and his insight into North's trial, which Toobin had witnessed primarily as a spectator. Never having broken a case, or even tried one, but professing to speak for all "prosecutors," he characterized McFarlane specifically and all accomplices who testified against their confederates as "scumbags." A chapter was devoted to his own shallow investigation of Elliott Abrams, in which Toobin had failed to examine Hill's notes and had reached conclusions fundamentally inconsistent with what we had learned after Barrett took over the job.

We did not try to enjoin the publication, but we asked Toobin to delay it at least until all the appellate proceedings in the North case had been completed and to await my final report before releasing grand-jury-related material, so that the judges who released my report could decide whether such material could be released at all. I was concerned about the possible consequences of Toobin's book because, as the deputy attorney general in 1960, I had seen the convictions of a group of organized-crime leaders, who had assembled in Apalachin, New York, reversed after a young prosecutor had given a self-serving story to *Life* magazine while the case was pending on appeal.

During our negotiations over the timing of the book's publication, Toobin and his publisher surprised us with a preemptive suit to enjoin me from interfering with the publication or punishing Toobin for having copied hundreds of documents, some of them classified, and for exposing privileged information and material related to the grand jury proceedings. I could understand a young lawyer wanting to keep copies of his own work, but not copying material from the general files or the personal files of others.

When the problem had first arisen, the Justice Department had agreed to handle any litigation against Toobin that might be necessary, so that we could avoid any appearance of conflict of interest. After Toobin filed his suit, however, Attorney General Richard Thornburgh personally directed his subordinates to drop out of the case. Struve then pushed me and his grief aside and shaped the case. A New York federal judge denied Toobin an injunction but declared that his conduct had not been unlawful. The judge left open the question of professional discipline. I was unwilling to try to stay publication even during appeal. While we expedited our appeal, the publisher began selling the book. After hearing oral argument, the court of appeals ordered the dismissal of Toobin's complaint as moot, leaving Toobin vulnerable to punishment.

I decided not to pursue Toobin; I did not want to divert any resources. The Justice Department's security officer, however, wanted to recover Toobin's cache of classified documents. After various evasions by Toobin, the security officer found the documents in the wine cellar of the home of one of Toobin's lawyers. Having been torn between a career as a lawyer and one as a writer, Toobin ceased to practice law.

We were hurt less by the book itself than by the erroneous perception that we had tried to block its publication. The litigation probably increased the book's sales. Hostile newspaper editors exulted. One editorial listed all the shops where the book was available.

Toobin did cause problems with some witnesses who had been confiding in us. They may simply have been looking for an excuse to stop cooperating with us, but several of them frankly stated their fears that other members of my staff would follow Toobin's example and expose their conversations with the witnesses.

So far as I know, Toobin was the only member of the staff to undercut the team. There may have been occasional leaks and critical comments, but they were probably inevitable because we dealt with so many highly skilled witnesses, department officials, and reporters. In a way, the anomaly of Toobin's actions demonstrated the remarkable solidarity of our team as it kept its controversies to itself for seven years, despite the ever-changing personnel and many hard-fought disputes.

Meanwhile, Craig Gillen's continuing investigation had been gathering momentum. The careful study of the CIA cables had begun to pay off, revealing the roles played by two outstanding CIA operatives—Duane Clarridge, the architect of the original plan of support for the Contras in the early 1980s, and Alan Fiers, who had replaced Clarridge in 1984 after it became known that the CIA had instigated a blockade of neutral shipping in two of Nicaragua's ports on the Pacific Ocean. The story told by the cables not only detailed the leadership of these individuals but also revealed that the CIA had continued as the agency overseeing U.S. undercover activities in support of the Contras after the Boland amendments were enacted. To be sure, North had been shoved out in front, and North and Secord had organized the logistics of the resupply operation, but the CIA's strategy had determined what North would do.

Clarridge and Fiers had reported directly to William Casey, often bypassing Clair George, their nominal boss. North had also reported to Casey, who had always known what was happening. Poindexter told us that North and Casey had had regular Saturday-morning meetings at the CIA's headquarters in Langley when both were in town. North had reported to Poindexter during the week following each meeting with Casey. Poindexter and Casey had generally agreed about Iran-Contra matters. Poindexter testified that he had been more concerned with Iran, because he had believed it to be strategically more important than Nicaragua, and because the National Security Counsel had had the primary operating responsibility for the Iranian initiative. In Poindexter's view, the NSC's support of the Contras had been simply a stopgap measure until Congress authorized the CIA to resume the operation.

With Casey beyond our reach, we had turned to his principal assistants. Because the Boland amendments had not provided for criminal penalties, and because of our earlier problems with classified information, we looked for any false statements Casey's assistants had made to Congress. Our case against Clarridge would turn on two issues: first, his false denials of having discussed with a foreign country (whose name is still classified) the solicitation of arms for the Contras and financial contributions to the Contras; and second, his false denials of having had contemporaneous knowledge that the November 1985 shipment from Israel to Iran consisted of HAWK missiles, not oil-drilling equipment.

Clarridge had falsely testified to the Senate intelligence committee, the House intelligence committee, the Tower Commission, and the select committees on Iran-Contra that he had first learned that Hawks were being transported only after the delivery had begun and that the realization had developed slowly. He had previously said that he had begun to speculate that arms were the cargo when he received a report of a conversation between the pilots and the foreign officials who were questioning the flight's clearance. On other occasions, he had testified that he had learned about the weapons a couple of days after the delivery or in mid-December, two weeks later. We found his various misstatements farcical: The nature of these relatively large, winged missiles could not have been kept secret from anyone who had handled or delivered them; and forty-eight hours after the shipment, intelligence reports had revealed the Iranians' rage about having been given the outmoded models stenciled with the Star of David.

Having gone to his office at Langley on a Saturday morning specifically to handle the Hawk delivery for North, Clarridge had tried to clear the original Israeli shipment through the European country that was withholding clearance and, at the same time, had set up an alternative delivery by a CIA proprietary via another country. He had known that North was in a bind because the White House was expecting the transaction to result in the release of hostages. Working at a furious pace, Clarridge had had to slip this highly confidential mission past Casey's straitlaced deputy, John McMahon, who had been filling in for the absent CIA director.

Intelligence analyst Charles Allen told us that at North's request, he had driven to Langley to show Clarridge the folder of intelligence material concerning the flight in question. Allen had impressed on Clarridge the sensitivity and importance of the effort. Rather than give him a verbal description of the transaction, Allen had told Clarridge that North wanted him to read the intelligence material. The material had discussed the release of hostages and weapons shipments; it had not mentioned oil-drilling equipment.

After carefully reading through the folder of reports, Clarridge had commented that it was "interesting." Allen had then told him that North had said the cargo was "oil-drilling equipment." This was a typical way of announcing a cover story. It allowed Clarridge and Allen to assert thereafter that this was what they had been told. Indeed, Allen had not detracted from the cover story by anything he *said*. He had merely emphasized the importance of the written material, which had wholly contradicted the oral cover story.

As Gillen's investigation proceeded, Vincent Cannistraro, the CIA operations officer who had been temporarily assigned to the NSC, told us that the true nature of the shipment had been discussed two days in advance in a meeting he had attended with Clarridge and North. Cannistraro remembered that North had telephoned Poindexter to get permission to disclose the transaction to Clarridge. The nature of the shipment had also been specified in cables sent to

Clarridge from the European country where the Israeli shipment had bogged down. The cables had been delivered to Clarridge, but they were now missing. Nevertheless, the individuals who had drafted and sent the cables were ready to testify that they remembered the contents because the cables had been out of the ordinary.

The second area in which Clarridge was vulnerable concerned his activities in the spring of 1984, when he was still supervising the Contras. He had made a trip to a distant country (whose name is still classified) to follow up discussions of a financial contribution for the Contras and a gift to them of 200,000 tons of captured East European weapons. At the last minute, Clarridge had been ordered not to pursue these efforts. In briefing the congressional committees later, he had denied having discussed these proposals within his agency. CIA cables, however, revealed that Clarridge had discussed the proposals with William Casey himself.

Despite the mounting evidence against Clarridge, our strongest developing case was against his successor, Alan Fiers. Appearing before the House intelligence committee, Fiers had confirmed Clair George's statement that the two of them had only had newspaper knowledge of Hasenfus's flight and his cargo. Fiers had added, ". . . and who was behind them we do not know." But the cables showed that Fiers had known that the resupply effort was a cooperative activity carried out by Joseph Fernandez, Oliver North, and Richard Secord. Messages sent through the KL-43 system revealed that Fiers had approved a flight to drop weapons to the Contras in Nicaragua and that he had overseen the development of the southern front by Fernandez, using North's help to deliver weapons.

Meeting with the staff of the House intelligence committee in October 1986, after Hasenfus's capture, Fiers had made three false statements: He had denied having any relevant documents; denied knowing about North's resupply of the Contras; and denied knowing that Max Gomez was Felix Rodriguez.

Although Fiers and Clair George had realized that the truth about Fernandez's operations would ultimately be revealed, they had intended to delay the exposure until Congress had finally passed the $100 million appropriation for the renewal of CIA support for the Contras. The appropriation measure had passed the two houses of Congress in different forms and been locked in conference between the House and Senate.

Our evidence, from a year's painstaking study of CIA cables and documents accumulated by associate counsel Vernon Francis and Mike Vhay and exchanged in successive staff conferences, showed Fiers to have been a strong manager. He had dominated the CIA's Central American task force. He had maintained direct control over cable communications from headquarters to the field, and he had kept his activities largely to himself, holding no staff meetings and eschewing confidants. Handpicked by Casey and allowed direct access to him, Fiers had frequently bypassed Clair George. In spite of his desire to hold Oliver North at arm's length, Fiers had recognized North's influence with Casey, for whom the support of the Contras had become a very high personal priority. With a shrewd instinct for self-preservation and self-promotion, Fiers had tried to avoid back-stabbing by North and yet avoid having the interests of his agency compromised by North's excesses.

When Fiers had taken over, the Contras' southern front in Nicaragua had been in bad shape. To strengthen it, Fiers and Fernandez had pushed out Eden Pastora, the early Contra commander, and had encouraged the anti-Sandinista forces to switch their loyalty to Pedro Chamorro, who had been acceptable to Contra leader Adolfo Calero and responsive to the CIA. To induce Chamorro to cross into Nicaragua from Costa Rica, Fiers and Fernandez had offered him lethal supplies. CIA cables revealed the transmission of flight coordinates and showed Fiers telling Fernandez to get the northern Contras to share their weapons and to make the drop. A KL-43 message from North to Secord in April 1986 showed the need for a weapons drop; subsequent messages reported an abortive effort to make the drop, followed by the ultimate success of the mission.

Fernandez had cabled Fiers that the southern Contras had expected a C-123 aircraft to make the drop, but that Secord had decided to use a larger L-100, which had originally been chartered by the State Department's humanitarian aid program to deliver supplies to Ilopango. Other KL-43 messages showed Fiers and North planning the drop, Fiers expressly concurring with the project, and North informing Secord that Fiers had concurred. A cluster of accompanying meetings that North had omitted from his notebooks had been recorded in his associate Robert Earl's notes, which we had also obtained. Fiers had gone to a Virginia restaurant, for example, to meet with Richard Gadd, who had chartered the L-100 flight, and had then met with North at Langley. By the time Fiers approved the drop, two of the Contras' regional commanders had been on the verge of giving up and returning to Costa Rica. After the successful drop, Chamorro's forces had stayed in the field and denounced Pastora. This had finished Pastora as a leader. We found this episode particularly significant, because it showed that instead of Fiers's having helped North, as we had previously believed, North had used his operatives to achieve a CIA objective for Fiers.

In many ways, North had carried out Fiers's strategy. Fiers had given North the dirty work, but he had followed what North was doing. Fiers had known that Thomas Clines had been running arms through Honduras, that North had helped arrange for the Costa Rican airstrip, and that North had been paying some of the Contras leaders. Fiers had also advised North where to buy Blowpipes in April 1986. Fiers had initially tried to minimize his contacts with the North-Secord operatives but had soon found himself surrounded by them. For more than a year, Fiers had known that Ilopango was the hub of the private benefactors' activity and that North controlled Felix Rodriguez. Fiers's first direct contact with Rodriguez had concerned the weapons drop in the south by the L-100 from Ilopango. Subsequently, Fiers had interceded, with a phone call to North, to prevent Rodriguez from sending an L-100 loaded with weapons into Honduras for the Contras in northern Nicaragua, which would have violated a working agreement with Honduras not to use large aircraft.

Richard Gadd had told us of having explained to Fiers in a face-to-face meeting that Gadd, as directed by North and Secord, was running a full-service operation carrying lethal supplies to the Contras in Nicaragua. In grand jury testimony elicited by Gillen, North confirmed his notebook entries of his conversations with Fiers about the Blowpipes and John Moellering's notes of North's report on his activities at a restricted interagency group meeting that Fiers had attended on August 26, 1986. North testified that he had explained to the RIG what he was doing and had asked whether he should continue. To the grand jury, North confirmed all his KL-43 communications.

In April 1986, both Clair George and Fiers had instructed Fernandez to stop acting as an intermediary between the Contras' representatives and Rafael Quintero, Secord's Central American representative. A few weeks later, at a regional conference of chiefs of station, Fiers had learned from Fernandez that he had continued to deal with these individuals. Again ordered to stop, Fernandez had replied that he could not, because an alternative plan to use a "neutral communicator" between the Contras and Secord's team had failed. Nevertheless, Fiers had later told Congress that the CIA had not dealt with the weapons suppliers.

Fiers had had unusual personal access to Congress: He had not gone through the CIA's congressional liaison office; he had received guidance directly from the White House legislative office. Members of Congress had trusted him. Because of his seeming forthrightness on Central American issues, they had wanted his testimony after Hasenfus's aircraft went down on October 6, 1986. Although Clair George would be the principal witness, Fiers had been expected to accompany him.

Told to prepare George's testimony, Fiers had called in his staff lawyer, Louis Dupart, who had been on leave. Fiers had decided to waffle about the CIA's knowledge of Hasenfus's cargo and to suggest that the flight had belonged to unknown private benefactors. "We have come too far," Fiers had told Dupart, "to commit political suicide on this." Dupart had prepared the testimony for George without knowing about Fernandez's communications with the North-Secord group, the L-100 arms delivery, or the CIA's involvement in the secret airstrip in Costa Rica. Dupart's draft had stated that the CIA had not been involved directly or indirectly in the arms-resupply missions of private individuals supporting the Contras. Fiers had reviewed the statement, made minor changes, and left the misstatements intact.

George and Fiers had then met with Casey to discuss their position. The next morning, George, Fiers, and Elliott Abrams had testified before the congressional committees. In the Senate foreign relations committee, George had read the statement, and Fiers had voiced support for it. He had then briefed the House intelligence committee's staff over beer and pretzels at the CIA's headquarters. Fiers had told the congressional staff that he had had no contacts with the private benefactors and that he had never supplied information to them. He had disavowed knowledge of Rodriguez's activities. On October 14, Fiers, George, and Abrams had repeated their testimony before the Senate intelligence committee.

Later, on learning about Fernandez's contacts with North and Secord, Dupart had told George that he had prepared false testimony. George had just said, "Fix it." Dupart had been forced to wait for approval of his proposed corrections while Fiers and Casey went to Central America. Before the changes had been approved, the diversion of the proceeds from the sale of arms to Iran had been exposed and the resulting alarm had taken precedence over correcting the false testimony. George had entered the hospital for a kidney operation. Dupart had been sent to Miami to get the facts from Fernandez and had prepared a memorandum on December 17, after George returned from the hospital. By then, however, Fiers, despite Dupart's warning, had again testified before Congress and had again lied under oath, saying that there had been no CIA entanglement with the private benefactors. He had denied that Fernandez had had contacts with them. He had denied knowing about Oliver North's specific activities.

To complete our evidence against Fiers, we needed the minutes of the closed hearings held by the House intelligence committee. Charles Tiefer, the Republican associate counsel to the House, delayed us for weeks, insisting that we specify to him in advance the lies we were investigating. To have tried to force the issue by subpoena would have invited litigation regarding the speech-and-debate clause of the Constitution, which Congress claims protects it from having to turn over copies of documents or testimony before its committees for use in the courts. Gillen and I met with Steven R. Ross, the general counsel for the clerk of the House. He arranged a meeting with Speaker Tom Foley and Minority Leader Bob Michel. The meeting in Speaker Foley's office was brief. The congressmen were hurried and reserved, but courteous. When they heard what we wanted, they agreed that we should have the material. Congress authorized the delivery the next day.

In May 1991, in a new and determined assertion that the Iran-Contra problems were behind him, President Bush nominated Robert Gates, his deputy national security advisor and Casey's former deputy, to head the Central Intelligence Agency. Gates had first been nominated in January 1987, while he was serving as the agency's acting director after Casey's resignation, but in the heat of the first exposure of the Iran-Contra scandal he had asked to have his nomination withdrawn. In his story about the new nomination, Lyle Denniston of the *Baltimore Sun* reported: "Mr. Bush, who bristles at the mere mention of the [Iran-Contra] scandal, had made clear he thinks there is nothing further to investigate, including his role."

A few days earlier, Senator David Boren, chairman of the Senate intelligence committee, had telephoned me to ask whether Gates was in danger of indictment. "Probably not," I had told him. The following evening, after discussing our case with Gillen, I explained to the senator that Gates had given answers we did not believe, but that this did not mean he would be indicted. I told the senator that two questions about Gates were troubling: Had he falsely denied knowledge of North's Contra-support activities? Had he falsely postdated his first knowledge of North's diversion of the arms sales proceeds to the Contras? We knew that Charles Allen and his superior, Richard Kerr, had independently informed Gates of Allen's belief that North had diverted funds from the arms sales to the Contras. For each conversation, however, we had only one person's word against Gates's denial of recollection. Therefore, I told the senator that although we doubted Gates's veracity, we were unlikely to prosecute him.

On May 28, 1991, the Supreme Court denied certiorari in the North case, thereby refusing to review the court of appeals decision setting aside the conviction. Having lacked the solicitor general's support, I had entertained only a slim hope that the Supreme Court would review the case. In a brief press release, I expressed our disappointment and stated my intention to proceed with the remand hearing that had been ordered by the court of appeals. To comply with that order, we would have to demonstrate that the eighty-nine witnesses who had testified before the grand jury and the thirty-two witnesses at North's trial had not been affected in their testimony by having heard the immunized testimony of North.

The responses to the Supreme Court's action pointed up the continuing conflict between the political and judicial systems—the very issue that we had hoped the Supreme Court would resolve. According to our appellate counsel, Andrew Frey, the lawyers in the criminal division of the Justice Department liked the decision, welcoming it as a deterrent against future congressional intrusions into criminal prosecutions. By contrast, House select committee chairman Lee Hamilton said that "Congress acted appropriately in moving ahead with the investigation. We understood we were complicating the criminal investigation. But we did not believe the prosecution would be crippled." John Nields, chief counsel of Hamilton's committee, acknowledged that the committee had known that the grant of immunity would create a "big problem," but he said that he nevertheless believed the scandal to have been a political issue rather than a criminal issue.

My decision to proceed with the remand hearing aroused vehement outcries. It was perhaps the single most unpopular decision that I had made. Brendan Sullivan asserted that a "reasonable" prosecutor would determine that "enough is enough." Oliver North expressed a more personal view of me: "I think he's a vindictive wretch who has nothing on his mind other than trying to ruin my family and me."

The day after I announced that we would proceed, Senate Minority Leader Bob Dole asked the attorney general to terminate my appointment: "Each and every workday, Mr. Walsh and his staff report to work at their lavish suite of offices in one of Washington's most expensive buildings. Each and every workday, they continue to add to their thirty-to fifty-million-dollar bill, payable by the United States taxpayers.... Today, I am sending a letter to Attorney General Thornburgh, asking him to request the court to [terminate the office]."

Congressman Bill Broomfield, the ranking Republican on the House foreign affairs committee, supported Dole's request in a letter to the attorney general signed by fourteen other senior Republican congressmen, including Minority Leader Bob Michel, Minority Whip Newt Gingrich, and policy committee chairman Mickey Edwards of Oklahoma City, my home district. The letter concluded by saying, "The time for the Iran-Contra investigation has come and gone; it is time to wrap it up."

Attorney General Richard Thornburgh responded through his press spokesman, saying, "Our understanding is that Walsh is in the process of winding down his operation. Therefore, any action on our part may be unnecessary."

In our press release, I stated that we had an obligation to complete the proceedings against North, Poindexter, and Clines and to pursue our ongoing investigation, which was nearly finished. Privately, I regarded the remand hearing as a sadistic revel of Judge Laurence Silberman, but I felt that I could not simply abandon the case without making any effort to comply with the appellate prescription. I owed respect to the court if not the judge. Although many editors harshly criticized me, a surprising number of commentators urged me to fulfill my responsibility, despite the difficulties that would entail.

My objective was to do what we had to do to get the case back to the Supreme Court—to get to the final judgment that the remand for further hearings had denied us. We now had to decide whether to acknowledge the impossibility of meeting the standards set by the court of appeals or to attempt to meet those standards without much hope of success. The consensus of those I had already consulted was that I could not drop the case without first making an effort to save it.

At a staff conference in April, anticipating the denial of certiorari by the Supreme Court, I had outlined my plan for a truncated hearing that would follow the analysis in Chief Judge Patricia Wald's dissent. We would present our canned material to prove by comparison that the testimony of each witness to the counts on which North had been con-

victed had been the same before and after North had given his immunized testimony. Only those few witnesses who had not been examined
before North testified would have to be questioned at a new hearing
under the standards enunciated by the court of appeals.

If Judge Gerhard Gesell rejected this proposal for a very limited hearing, I would accept the dismissal of the indictment and appeal, arguing
that an additional witness-by-witness inquiry as to subjective reactions
to North's testimony four years after the fact would lack credibility.
Unlike our earlier appeal from the appellate court's order remanding
the case to Judge Gesell, this would be an appeal from a final judgment
of dismissal. It might receive short shrift, but I believed it would discharge our final responsibility.

When I canvassed John Keker, Michael Bromwich, David Zornow,
and Guy Struve, all of them had said that I should not drop the case.
Each had favored a truncated hearing. Our principal concern had been
to avoid being drawn into a quagmire. The North team had agreed to
handle the case if a remand hearing became necessary. I had offered
them the part-time help of two associate counsel. A few days after I
spoke to the team, Bromwich had telephoned to say that the others
wanted him to act for them in handling the remand hearing. He had
expressed his willingness to do so, but wanted to be sure that I would
give him the same free hand I had given Keker. I had agreed.

Once the Supreme Court rejected our case, I twice telephoned
Bromwich, urging him to file a proposed stipulation or concession to
carry out my plan for a truncated hearing, but he wanted to wait and get
a "feel for the proceeding" first. In other words, rather than take a bold
initiative, he understandably wanted to await the first hearing before
Judge Gesell and respond to what the judge had in mind. But, as I had
feared, before Bromwich was ready to act, Judge Gesell took the initiative.

In June, at the first status conference, the judge expressed deep skepticism that the guilty verdicts could be salvaged. He warned that if he
found that any witness had been influenced by hearing or reading
North's congressional testimony, the remaining criminal convictions of
North would be thrown out. "You must realize," the judge said, "that
there is a very slight possibility that the ablest group of lawyers in the
world could meet the standard of the court of appeals. . . . I don't
believe there is anyone I know who could." Summing up, he said, "This
is a pretty big can of worms. . . . If one witness is disqualified under the
standards set by the court of appeals, that is the end of the matter. I
have no obligation to go further." He ordered us to call Robert

McFarlane, our most vulnerable witness, first. The hearing was scheduled for September.

At our staff conference on May 30, I made decisions regarding the ongoing investigation. We would indict Alan Fiers for a felony unless he agreed to plead guilty. We would immunize Samuel Watson and obtain whatever testimony we could from him against Donald Gregg. Before deciding whether to indict the National Security Council's former counsel Paul Thompson, we would wait to see what happened regarding Fiers. For the time being, we would not seek an indictment of Gregg.

That evening, Fiers came to our office with his counsel, Stanley Arkin. We told them that we were in a position to obtain a felony indictment against Fiers. We gave them three weeks to consider a plea of guilty.

On the evening of June 20, Craig Gillen, Vernon Francis, Mike Vhay, and I met with Arkin and his partner, Jeffrey Kaplan, in our witness room. I had known Arkin as an able and forceful lawyer in New York and was impressed by his presentation on behalf of Fiers. Arkin outlined Fiers's prospective testimony. It would support North's testimony and notebook entries showing that Elliott Abrams had known about North's Contra-supply activities. Fiers would confirm that at two restricted interagency group meetings in August and September 1986, when the CIA was expected to take over these activities, North had described them in detail. According to Fiers, Abrams had been present at one of these RIG meetings and his deputies, William Walker and Richard Melton, had represented him at the other. Fiers was also ready to testify that Abrams had known that Max Gomez was Felix Rodriguez and had known what role Rodriguez had played in the Contra-supply operation.

Arkin reported that Fiers would testify that Clair George had knowingly given false testimony in the congressional briefings after Hasenfus was shot down. Before the briefings, Fiers had suggested that George be somewhat more forthright about the mingling of the legal humanitarian cargo with the illicit lethal cargo at Ilopango. George had refused, saying that he did not want to be the first one to "turn a searchlight on the White House." When Fiers told George in the summer of 1986 that North had told him that he had diverted the arms sales proceeds to the Contras, George had simply responded by saying, "You are now one of the very few who know."

The most dramatic disclosure Arkin made during the proffer concerned an incident that had occurred during the May 16, 1986, meeting at which the National Security Planning Group had discussed the Contras' need for stopgap funds until Congress reauthorized the CIA to support them. President Reagan had startled the group in the situation room by asking, "Can't Ollie find funds until we get the hundred million dollars?" According to Fiers, he, North, and the other staff members had been sitting along the wall, behind the principals, and Vice President Bush either had been leaving the meeting or had just left. Donald Regan had abruptly changed the subject, and the minutes of the meeting had not mentioned the president's question. Nonetheless, according to Fiers, the effect of the remark had been to signal North and the others present that Reagan had known what North was doing and had wanted him to keep doing it.

Later that evening, we decided that if Fiers would confirm his counsel's proffer, we were ready to accept a guilty plea to two misdemeanor charges of withholding information from Congress. Such a plea was justified by the late date of the prosecution, by the inevitability of problems under the Classified Information Procedures Act, and by the value of having Fiers as a witness against Clair George and Elliott Abrams. A few days later, after three more hours of negotiation with Arkin, Fiers joined us and agreed that he would plead guilty to the two misdemeanors and would sign an agreement to cooperate with us in our subsequent prosecutions.

We debriefed Fiers extensively before and after his arraignment. He told us that he had taken orders from George and had kept the members of the Central American task force loosely informed. He had also briefed Robert Gates, but not in extensive detail because Gates had usually had a note-taker present. By February 1986, Fiers had known that North was a major influence in the Contras' activities. Twice when he had refused North's requests, Fiers had been quickly overruled by George or, as Fiers put it, he had been "rolled." By early 1986, he had realized that North was dealing directly with Casey.

On July 9, Fiers was arraigned before Chief Judge Aubrey Robinson and pleaded guilty to the two misdemeanor counts of withholding information from Congress. Gillen handled the arraignment and met the press on the courthouse steps. (Nina Totenberg of National Public Radio told me he looked like a "happy camper.") In a public statement to the media, Fiers was neither defensive nor arrogant. He was sober, concerned, and impressive. "In 1986, I was faced with some very difficult decisions. At that time, I did what I thought was in the best interests of the country. Today, I was faced with equally difficult decisions, and today I have done what I think is in the best interests of the country and not only that, but what the Constitution requires of me."

At the arraignment, Gillen had outlined the nature of Fiers's disclosures. The news media immediately speculated that his plea would cause problems for the Senate confirmation of Robert Gates. Some reporters said that this was my first big break. Lars-Erik Nelson, a columnist for the *New York Daily News*, wrote that the pretense that North had run a lone operation had exploded with the plea of Alan Fiers. A Herblock cartoon in the *Washington Post* depicted the White House surrounded by a wall called "Iran-Contra Stonewalling" with "Fiers Testimony" drawn as a crack across it. An editorial in the *New York Times* was titled, "At Last the Stone Wall Cracks." The *Washington Post* editorialized that I needed "to tug at the thread a while longer."

On July 10, Senator David Boren announced that before opening hearings on Gates's nomination, the Senate intelligence committee needed time to consider the information that was emerging from Fiers's guilty plea.

Senate Minority Leader Bob Dole called the Republican members of the intelligence committee to his office to head off a delay of the hearings. "I don't believe it [Gates's nomination] should be withdrawn," said Dole. "Taxpayers, get ready for another multimillion-dollar contribution to futility. I'm convinced that after spending so many millions of dollars, they will still come up with nothing, and if they have anything at all, it should be turned over to the Justice Department."

According to a July 12 report by Walter Pincus and George Lardner, Jr., in the *Washington Post*, "President Bush stated that the committee 'ought to get on with the confirmation. I don't think you can accept some closed-door allegation.' "

In an interview requested by Pincus and Lardner, I explained, "You cannot get a credible investigation of an individual in isolation. You can't go around asking people just about Gates, and not develop the subject matter, and come out with a satisfactory result."

I told David Johnston of the *New York Times*, "The cover-up of a relatively difficult operation doesn't happen accidentally." I reminded him of an anecdote about George Bernard Shaw and H. G. Wells. On a visit to Wells, Shaw had admired a beautiful celestial globe in Wells's home. When Shaw asked who the artist was, Wells had poked fun at Shaw, the atheist. "No one," Wells replied. "It just happened." Speaking to Johnston about Iran-Contra, I said, "Here we have a pretty darn good cover-up. It doesn't just happen because Oliver North doesn't want people to know things."

When reporters reminded me of my earlier prediction that my inquiry would be over by the spring of 1991, I said, "It's not a matter of my judgment anymore as to how long things will go on. I think [Fiers's plea has] really taken the decision out of my hands. It compels a follow-up." I also explained that "criticism for time and expense goes with complex litigation."

On July 12, the Senate intelligence committee postponed indefinitely the hearings on Gates's nomination. Bob Dole said, "I don't think this nomination is in trouble, and I don't believe it should be delayed."

According to the *Los Angeles Times*, President Bush "bristled" at word of the committee's delay, telling reporters that Congress "ought to get on with the confirmation." Bush said that Gates should not be brought down by "rumor and insinuation."

The *Los Angeles Times* also reported that "among those close to Bush, it is clear that the president's anger over the trouble the nomination has run into is directed not so much at the Senate as at Independent Counsel Lawrence E. Walsh, and his [Bush's] office is raising questions about whether the timing of the Fiers case was tied to the scheduled beginning of the Senate committee's formal consideration of the Gates nomination."

According to Pete Yost of the Associated Press, White House counsel Boyden Gray had believed that my investigation was winding down and would not pose a threat. "Gray basically ignored warnings that Walsh could come back to bite them," said Yost's source. "The White House felt it had taken the wind out of his sail."

An angry Bush, meeting journalists as he left his summer home for the golf course, engaged in a fifteen-minute soliloquy, saying that Gates should not be left "twisting in the wind." According to Rita Beamish of the Associated Press, "Bush told reporters at his vacation home that his understanding [was] that Independent Counsel Lawrence Walsh did not have data implicating Gates in the biggest scandal of the Reagan Administration. But, he said, it would be 'extraordinarily helpful,' if Walsh would release any such information, so the Senate can get on with the Gates confirmation hearing. Bush said, 'Let's get to the bottom of it, but let's bring forward these people that are supposedly fingering him. Let's bring them forward and let them stand there before the Senate.' Asked if Walsh should get on with his investigation, Bush said, 'He's been on with it for four years. He ought to get on with it, and off with it, in my view.' Gates's nomination, he said, should not be 'obscured by an investigation that has been going on for four years.

They [the Senate intelligence committee] ought not to panic and run like a covey of quail, and say let's hang it out all over next summer.' He said, 'It seems a little weird' that the Iran-Contra case continues to percolate. 'You shoot down one thing, and somebody raises another.' "

In response to Bush, I explained, "There is no way in which the facts now under investigation as to the cover-up in the CIA, can be completed within a few days or a few weeks. . . . Our investigation has now reached the point of significant breakthrough."

The congressional hearings on Gates's nomination were ultimately set for the third week in September. In an effort to complete our investigation of the CIA before then, we began to assemble every note and minute we could find regarding the November 1986 meetings of CIA officers. The CIA claimed to be unable to produce the notes of Gates's briefings by Fiers. We planned tentatively for an indictment of Clair George on August 28, depending on how our negotiations with his lawyer went.

I recognized that investigating the Bush administration in 1992, an election year, might have political consequences. I told Pete Yost that I hoped we could wrap up our investigation of the CIA by fall. Nina Totenberg reported that I was adding four lawyers to my current five associate counsel to try to complete the inquiry before the Senate held its hearings on Gates. I blamed the CIA's refusal to release classified information for more than a year's delay—a delay that could have been avoided if President Bush had agreed to meet with me. I said that I had planned to tell him that the CIA was prolonging the investigation by withholding information that was public knowledge. "Fifteen months are already lost," I told Nina. "There is nothing he can do now to recover it. But I just think he shouldn't complain about it."

In August, a group of former CIA agents, under the leadership of Dick Stolz, Clair George's successor as the CIA's deputy director for operations, began to raise funds to support those under investigation.

After Labor Day, I met with Craig Gillen, Clair George, and George's counsel, Richard Hibey, to discuss a possible plea disposition. I really liked George. I respected his career of danger and achievement. I urged him as strongly as I could to accept a misdemeanor plea and to cooperate by answering whatever questions might be necessary. The discussion lasted into the evening. He promised that he would consider my proposal overnight, talk with his wife, and let me know in the morning. When our office opened the next day, Hibey told us that the answer was no.

On September 6, 1991, the grand jury indicted George and charged him with ten felonies, including obstructing justice, obstructing a congressional investigation, making false statements, and perjuring himself before congressional committees. With Casey having died and Gates having been involved only tangentially in the illegal activities, we had now reached the highest-ranking CIA officer responsible for executing President Reagan's intertwined covert actions.

CHAPTER SIXTEEN

Roller Coaster

Clair George's indictment mobilized the intelligence community. Support came not only from officials in active service, but also from the CIA's alumni, who were steeped in the agency's traditions and proud of its accomplishments. They keenly felt the irony of the fact that a career officer, who had been trained to protect the secrets of the agency with lies if necessary, was now being indicted for lying to congressional committees to preserve a critical appropriation for a goal the CIA and the president had supported.

One of the cruelest consequences George faced as a result of his indictment was the cost of defending himself. In a lifetime of government service, he had had little chance to amass a fortune. He would have been lucky if he could have looked forward to a modest retirement. Retaining a lawyer with the skill and experience to represent him in a case as complicated as Iran-Contra could well mean financial ruin. Richard Stolz, who had succeeded George as the director of operations and had recently resigned from the CIA, undertook to raise a legal defense fund. The president of the Association of Retired Intelligence Officers, David Whipple, and two former directors of the CIA, Richard Helms and William Colby, pitched in to help Stolz. They quickly raised $40,000—a small part of what George would need, but an impressive showing by donors who were government officials or retirees.

According to the *New York Times*, the rapid response showed "the depth of animosity felt within the intelligence community toward both Mr. Walsh and Alan D. Fiers. . . . It stands as testimony to the traditional instinct inside the agency to circle the wagons during time of trouble. The ferocity of the reaction shows how lasting is the tension between a spy's oath to keep secrecy and the duty to tell the government the truth."

Although George and Fiers had ultimately reached different conclusions about where their duty lay, their backgrounds were similar. Both men had been born in small communities and had volunteered for military service during hostilities. Both had then joined the CIA and devoted themselves to its covert activities, rising through dangerous and difficult posts to the highest echelon of the agency.

Clair George was born in Beaver Falls, Pennsylvania. After his father died, his death hastened by injuries suffered during World War I, George had worked his way through Pennsylvania State University. He had volunteered for service in the Korean War and in 1955 joined the CIA. Admiring colleagues sketched his career for sympathetic reporters. At a time when Africa was in ferment, he had served in Mali. He had then served in India, Beirut, and Athens. His successor in Beirut had been kidnapped and killed. His predecessor in Athens had been killed. In 1978, George had ranked number one among more than a hundred senior operations officers. A colleague described him to a reporter as "an ebullient leader, bright, loud, witty, emotional. . . . You'd exchange views at the top of your lungs. He'd blow up and yell at people and ten minutes later, it's over. He'd argue but respect your views." Others said, "He knows how to keep a secret. That's what he's done all his life. That's what he did in this case, and he did it very well."

In 1983, William Casey had made George his liaison with Congress. Casey's biographer, Joseph E. Persico, quoted Robert Gates as saying, "Once Clair got there, he reinforced all of Casey's worst instincts. Their attitude was 'don't tell Congress anything unless you are driven to the wall.' " A former member of the Senate intelligence committee's staff said that George had "never [been] able to make the adjustment to the idea that somebody from the outside—namely Congress—had a right to know what in fact was going on in the DO [directorate of operations]. He was not able to adjust to the times as they have, in fact, changed."

When George had testified before Congress's select committees on Iran-Contra, he had expressed the resentment felt by agents who had been exposed to danger in the field: "If there is criticism of this country, . . . it's that you can't count on it." He had lashed out at what he viewed as congressional hair-splitting, such as authorizing humanitarian assistance but barring guns and other military equipment, or supplying the Contras with certain kinds of intelligence and certain kinds of communications equipment but prohibiting others. "America looks ridiculous to legalize a war in such detail," George had said. "We make life very tough for ourselves."

Alan Fiers was ten years younger than George. Having grown up in Newark, Ohio, Fiers had set his sights on playing football at Ohio State University under Woody Hayes, the school's fiercely competitive and autocratic football coach. Although Fiers weighed only 195 pounds, he had made the varsity on both offense and defense. After graduation, he had volunteered for active service in the Marine Corps and served in Europe and the Dominican Republic, where he had been promoted, wounded in action, and awarded a Bronze Star. After leaving the Marines, he had sought out a recruiter from the CIA and been hired. Fiers had served undercover in the Middle East and South Asia, then returned to the United States to work in the Middle East section at Langley. His next posts had been as the chief of station in a Middle Eastern country and then back to Langley as chief of the Central American Task Force. Having missed the action in Vietnam, Afghanistan, and Angola, Fiers had welcomed this October 1984 assignment, a posting that would allow him to personally challenge the Brezhnev doctrine that Moscow would not permit a communist takeover to be reversed.

After picking Fiers to run the task force, Casey had invited him to lunch and said, "Alan, you know, the Soviet Union is tremendously overextended, and they're vulnerable. If America challenges the Soviets at every turn and ultimately defeats them in one place, that will shatter the mythology, and it will all start to unravel. Nicaragua is that place."

Fiers had not expected the Contras to secure a military victory, but he had wanted them to inflict enough military and economic damage to force the Sandinistas to participate in the Contadora regional peace process and ultimately to hold free elections. Although wary of Oliver North, Fiers had been fiercely loyal to Casey. To Fiers, Casey had seemed like another Woody Hayes, outstanding and inspirational. It was for Casey that Fiers had worked eighty-hour weeks. After Casey's death, Fiers had felt duty-bound to continue doing what he thought Casey would have wanted him to do.

Fiers had also admired Ronald Reagan. From time to time, Fiers had briefed the president on Central America. Once, as Fiers entered the Oval Office at the tail end of a conversation between the president and Casey, the president had been saying, "Someday we're going to fix it so Americans can be proud to walk in the world, like we were when we were young men."

Having lied to Congress to preserve the $100 million appropriation for Contra support in 1986, having been disciplined within the agency for his untruthfulness, and having been confronted with prosecution, Fiers now acknowledged that his duty to Congress—the elected government of the United States—superseded his loyalty to the CIA. By revealing what he knew about the cover-up, however, he had sacrificed his relationship with his former associates. When it came time for him to testify, they would be in the courtroom, radiating their hostility.

On September 12, 1991, a grim-faced Clair George pleaded not guilty to a ten-count felony indictment for lying to three different congressional panels and a federal grand jury. Judge Royce C. Lamberth made it clear that he intended to move promptly. He soon had the case on track for trial in the early summer of 1992.

George's key role in the administration's cover-up was obvious to anyone who had closely followed our investigation. George had taken over for Casey after the January 1986 meeting in which President Reagan had authorized the direct sale of arms to Iran. George and Tom Twetten had met with Poindexter, North, and Secord in Poindexter's office and put the president's plan into execution. North had then given George a copy of the "notional time line for 'Operation Recovery,'" which George had kept in his private files. As for the Contras, he had told the congressional committees, "starting in 1982, there has probably been no other subject in which more time and energy was spent. I would be less than honest [not] to say that I must have spent a hell of a lot of time on the Contras."

The day after George's arraignment, we turned to Robert Gates. The Senate intelligence committee's hearings on his appointment to head the CIA were scheduled to begin within a few days. Craig Gillen and I met the committee's chairman, David Boren, and ranking minority member, Frank Murkowski, and staff counsel in Boren's office. Reiterating what I had already told Boren, we said that two questions had not been answered satisfactorily: Had Gates falsely denied knowledge of North's Contra-support activities? Had Gates falsely postdated his first knowledge of North's diversion of the arms sales proceeds to the Contras?

We then described what our investigation had turned up about Gates. Fiers had told us that he had kept Gates generally informed of his Contra-support activity, through written reports and regular face-to-face presentations, although his oral reports had been guarded because Gates had always had a note-taker present. The CIA now claimed it could not find the notes of these meetings.

We said that Richard Kerr, the CIA's deputy director for intelligence, had informed Gates in August 1986 of Charles Allen's belief that North had diverted funds from the Iranian arms sales for the benefit of the Contras; Allen himself had told Gates the same thing in early October. Allen had told us that Gates, who had appeared irritated, had told Allen to write a memorandum for Casey and had said that he did not want to hear about North. To us and to the congressional committees, Gates had denied having any recollection of either conversation. Whenever questioned, Gates always claimed that he had first learned of Allen's concern about the diversion on the day after Hasenfus was shot down. Gates said that he and Allen had then reported this to Casey, who told them that he had just received much the same information from another source.

That day, according to North and Gates, Casey had invited North to lunch in his office, which was next to Gates's office. Gates had joined them and, according to North, had heard Casey tell North to clean up the Ilopango operation. North claimed that he had then begun to destroy records. Gates claimed not to remember the discussion of North's Nicaraguan activities. Although he had heard North mention Swiss accounts, Gates said, he had not understood the reference. He claimed to have been in and out of the room. All he remembered, he said, was that North had told him that the CIA was completely clean regarding the Contra-support operation.

We suggested to the senators that they specifically request the notes of Fiers's reports to Gates. We told them that we did not think we had enough corroborating evidence to indict Robert Gates, but that his answers to these questions had been unconvincing. We did not believe that he could have forgotten a warning of North's diversion of the arms sales proceeds to the Contras. The mingling of two covert activities that were of intense personal interest to the president was not something the second-highest officer in the CIA would forget. Moreover, Gates had received the same reliable contemporaneous intelligence reports about North's activities that Charles Allen had. The information suggesting that North had overcharged the Iranians would surely have caught the attention of anyone as astute as Gates.

When, after Eugene Hasenfus's aircraft was shot down, Gates and Allen had told Casey about Allen's concern that North had diverted funds to the Contras, how could Gates have forgotten that Allen and Kerr had warned him about the diversion a few weeks earlier?

The Senate intelligence committee's hearings on George Bush's nomination of Robert Gates to head the CIA began on Monday, September 16, 1991. The hearings were televised. Gates, who had already answered extensive written interrogatories from the committee, was the first witness. In substance, he denied recalling the details of Iran-Contra. He said that he wished he had been more skeptical and that he had asked more questions. Thirty-three times he denied recollection of the facts.

As I watched some of the broadcasts, I was impressed by the strength of the committee's members and by their identification with and sympathy for the national security community. The powerful committee had several respected members, including former secretary of the Navy John Warner and Sam Nunn, both of whom were also on the armed services committee, and Warren Rudman, who had been the ranking Republican on the Senate select committee on Iran-Contra.

Only Democrats Howard M. Metzenbaum of Ohio and Bill Bradley of New Jersey pursued the Iran-Contra connection. I got the impression that most of the senators did not want to hold Iran-Contra against Gates. As associates of the national security fraternity, they might object to venal conduct, but they did not want to rake up the issue of an old nondisclosure. They obviously respected Gates's ability and his stature as Bush's deputy national security advisor; the president clearly was nominating someone he personally knew and trusted.

Senator Rudman openly disparaged the discussion of Iran-Contra: "I might say parenthetically that I hope someday I will never have to talk about this subject again. But I guess it just keeps coming up. It's almost like a typhus epidemic in that anybody within five miles of the germ either died, is infected, or is barely able to survive, so I guess we're back in that mode again."

My prime objective was to avoid a grant of immunity to Clair George or any other likely target of our investigation. I gave up any hope of protecting Fiers from being called as a witness. He was too important to the committee as a source of information about Gates. Fiers had already pleaded guilty, so immunity could not destroy his prosecution. Nevertheless, his being required to testify would jeopardize our ability to prosecute George successfully and would provide George's counsel with not only a preview of Fiers's trial testimony, but also a record that would allow him to impeach Fiers with the trivial inconsistencies that would inevitably crop up from one retelling of his complicated story to the next.

The committee singled out William Casey as the culprit in Iran-Contra and suggested that Gates had been largely bypassed in matters related to it. As Senator Murkowski put it, "What's coming out is a better understanding of the management style of Casey, and the compartmentalization. There are numerous instances where senior CIA officials were bypassed on projects that were worked by the director and his designees solely."

Senator John Chaffee said that Casey had not run a typical bureaucracy: "Bill Casey ran the outfit in a manner that jump-charged the command. . . . Chains of command in diagrams didn't fit with Bill Casey."

This view was contradicted by Thomas Polgar, a decorated former CIA officer and later a Senate committee staff member. Polgar testified that Gates had been Casey's creation and had not been "compartmented" out of sensitive information.

Fiers testified that Gates was an exceptionally gifted operator and that his meteoric rise had aroused jealousy among some older colleagues. Fiers said that Gates was very smart, very capable, although "sort of on the make." According to Fiers, Gates had understood "the universe" of the Contra-supply operation—that it had been run out of the White House, with North as the quarterback—but had not been given extensive operational detail.

Charles Allen told the committee of his efforts to warn Gates about the diversion of the arms sales proceeds to the Contras. After testifying that Gates had appeared irritated, Allen said, "My personal fears were that somehow this initiative had gotten off the track, and that it might have gone even higher to the Oval Office."

Richard Kerr, who was now the deputy director of central intelligence under William Webster, confirmed Allen's story. In addition to relaying the information to Gates, he had told another CIA officer of Allen's concern. As I watched the hearings, I felt certain that Gates would not have brushed off these alarming reports if he had not already known about the diversion. He simply had not wanted to be told by a new witness.

I also disbelieved Gates's testimony about President Reagan's December 5, 1985, retroactive finding purporting to authorize the CIA's facilitation of the November 1985 Hawk shipment to recover the hostages. In the high-level meetings at the CIA a few days after the Hawk shipment, Casey's deputy John McMahon had announced that Reagan had signed the finding. But Gates told the committee that he had forgotten about the finding by November 1986, when he supervised the preparation of Casey's testimony for his appearances before the House and Senate intelligence committees. The CIA's then former general counsel David Doherty, however, told the senators that he had handed Gates a draft of the finding only a day or so before Casey gave his misleading testimony.

The testimony of Charles Allen minimized the likelihood that Gates's failure to remember the president's finding had been accidental. During the preparation of Casey's testimony, said Allen, an agency lawyer had shown him a draft of the finding. Allen had promptly telephoned North. "In an abrupt manner," said Allen, North had "told me emphatically that the finding did not exist and that I was mistaken." Allen had then spoken to George. "I recall with great clarity Mr. Clair George informing me in a blunt and verbally abusive manner that the finding did not exist and that I should 'shut up talking about it.' "

Much of the later testimony in the month-long hearings shifted away from Iran-Contra to the question of whether Gates had slanted intelligence reports to accommodate the political views of Casey or others. At the end of the hearings, Gates was given an opportunity to respond. He directed most of his response to the issue of slanted intelligence reports. By the time the committee voted, eleven to four, to approve Gates's appointment, the testimony regarding Iran-Contra was no longer fresh. The next day, Herblock's cartoon in the *Washington Post* showed the CIA headquarters with a big banner proclaiming, "Now Under Old Management."

In the week before the Gates hearings began, Michael Bromwich and other members of the North team had been in Judge Gerhard Gesell's courtroom for the opening of the remand hearing in the North case. The hearing promised to be a disaster, but if we were to have any hope of persuading the Supreme Court to review the case, we had to establish that we had done our best to accommodate Congress's demand for immunized testimony and to comply with the excessive standards set by the court of appeals. My associates warned me that Robert McFarlane had been fully exposed to North's testimony. McFarlane could not identify any piece of his testimony as having been shaped by North; even after a most careful review, McFarlane did not believe that his recollection had been changed by North. But McFarlane was uncomfortable and might equivocate. A few weeks earlier, he had asked us to drop the remand hearing as a matter of prosecutorial judgment.

I had told Bromwich that I was willing to concede that McFarlane would admit that he had been thoroughly briefed on North's testimony and that, although McFarlane was not conscious of any refreshed recollection, he could not rule out the possibility that the testimony had affected him subconsciously. I was also willing to concede that this would be the best we could expect from other witnesses. The only foolproof assurance we could give the court would be a comparison of the trial testimony with the testimony given to the grand jury before North gave his immunized testimony. By making these concessions, I thought we might get a helpful ruling on two of the conviction counts: the destruction of records and North's acceptance of Richard Secord's gift of the security system for the Norths' home. Bromwich decided against making the concessions at the outset or trying to anticipate Judge Gesell. He planned to have McFarlane testify and make any necessary concessions as the hearing proceeded.

These unattractive alternatives simply showed the desperation of our position. Underlying both was the question of how far we had to go to demonstrate to Congress and the public that we had not abandoned our responsibility in the face of the hostile decision by the court of appeals. Looking back on the dilemma, I believe Bromwich made the right decision. Although an attempt to narrow the controversy by making concessions might have been better for the litigation, the explosive problem of dealing with McFarlane as a witness dramatized for all interested parties and the public the sophistry of the appellate court's remand requirements and the impossibility of salvaging a prosecution after immunized testimony had been nationally broadcast.

The hearing began on Wednesday, September 11. The reports I received from Mary Belcher and some of our lawyers about how the day had gone were even more troubling than I had expected them to be. In opening the hearing, Judge Gesell had characterized the remand as having placed him "in a bucket of feathers." Angered by the unreality of the standards the court of appeals was requiring him to enforce, and perhaps by my unwillingness to concede the hopelessness of our position, he growled, "It certainly isn't fair to Mr. North, who's been dangling around here for years."

McFarlane took the stand. In response to Bromwich's questioning, McFarlane said, "Watching four days of riveting testimony by a man who was like a son to me, how could I not be affected? That my responses were colored by what I heard in Colonel North's testimony, I think was inevitable." Although he admitted that he could not pinpoint any instance where his testimony had been "affected, shaped, or refreshed by North's testimony," McFarlane said that he was sure the testimony had made a powerful impression on him. "My descriptions, my portrayals, my attitudes, my judgments, were, I believe, affected by that testimony. The facts don't change. How I express it is what I am talking about." Writing later about this episode in his book, *Special Trust*, he said, "My intent was to tell the truth, and to attempt to be helpful to Colonel North."

Thursday was worse than Wednesday. McFarlane was going to such lengths to undercut us that Bromwich got the judge's permission to treat McFarlane as a hostile witness and to ask leading questions. McFarlane then began making periodic angry outbursts. We were not only losing, we were being slaughtered.

Because of an intervening matter, the judge recessed the hearing until Monday. After consulting our North team and appellate counsel, Gillen and I telephoned defense counsel Brendan Sullivan and Barry Simon on Friday. Sullivan argued persuasively that our position was untenable. I agreed to review the testimony over the weekend in Oklahoma and to decide whether we would proceed. We were to let the judge know our plans on Sunday afternoon.

It seemed obvious that we were on a downhill slide that could only get steeper. Bromwich agreed. My always slender hope that going through with the hearing might increase the likelihood of the Supreme Court's accepting the case for review had now proved illusory. We had discharged our obligation. On Sunday morning, I telephoned Gillen from Oklahoma City and told him to meet with Sullivan and the judge and tell them that I would move to dismiss the indictment.

On Monday morning, the same day the Gates hearings began, I appeared in court and asked Judge Gesell to dismiss, with prejudice, the remaining counts against North. The session lasted only three minutes. Judge Gesell granted the motion, saying simply, "This ends the case." I thanked him for his enormous commitment to the case and his efforts to keep it viable. Feeling that I had bowed to the inevitable, I congratulated Sullivan and Simon. Then I met with reporters outside the courthouse.

"This, I think, is a very, very serious warning that immunity is not to be granted lightly," I said in response to a question. "Now, I have never criticized Congress. I urged them not to grant immunity, but they have a very broad political responsibility for making a judgment as to whether it's more important that the country hear the facts quickly or that they await prosecution, and that is a matter for the Congress's judgment. But this shows that judgment should not be exercised lightly, that any illusion that immunity can be granted and then a successful prosecution follow is fraught with utmost difficulty."

"This must be a difficult moment for you," a reporter observed.

"Well," I responded, "it's a difficult moment, of course, because an enormous amount of energy has gone into this litigation on both sides, but I don't have any question as to the validity of our decision."

"Do you have any regrets about any decisions you have made along the way?" asked another reporter. "Do you wish you could do anything differently, aside from the congressional problem?"

"Every night when I go to bed, I think of at least one," I replied, "but then in the morning I usually decide we did the right thing."

President Bush also responded to questions that day. Asked if he wished he had done more to get to the bottom of Iran-Contra, the president responded, "I wish the damned thing had never happened. What do you mean 'wished anything done differently'? But what I might have done about it, that's something else. We've spent so much time on it. I must say I was very pleased to see the Ollie North decision today. . . . My basis is, he's been through enough. . . . There was an appeal. He's been let off. Now that—the system of justice—is working, and on a personal basis and for his family, who have been through a lot, I'm very, very pleased." Later, he said, "Listen, why am I going to second-guess the court system? I've stayed out of it. All I'm saying is they've made a statement now, and I think it's a good thing, for the reasons I've given you."

If the president's comments seemed even more inarticulate than usual, one factor might have been his distaste for the whole subject of Iran-Contra. The *Dallas Morning News* had recently reported, for example, that "a senior White House aide said Bush's temperature rises at the mention of Iran-Contra because the Reagan administration's signature scandal refuses to die, rising from the grave like Dracula each time the White House thinks it finally has buried suspicion about high-level knowledge of North's schemes."

The range of opinions about the dismissal of the case was broad. North saw the outcome as vindication, declaring that he had been "totally exonerated." The *New York Times* editorialized that North's claim was a wild overstatement. "The real vindication is for the high value the United States places on protecting citizens from convicting themselves with their own words. The decision marked a serious setback of another objective of the democratic government, promptly to uncover the truth in high-profile cases and to prosecute them when necessary without sacrificing the Constitution's privilege against compelled self-incrimination."

Senate Minority Leader Bob Dole, however, issued a statement attacking the prosecution. "What have American taxpayers received for their fifty million dollars? A lot of press releases, a lot of rumor and innuendo. But little in terms of justice. Every conviction won by Mr. Walsh has been overturned or is likely to be overturned."

House Speaker Tom Foley and Representative Lee Hamilton defended Congress's action. "The hearings were more important than the trial," said Hamilton. "It has always been my view that the policy questions exceeded in importance the question of individual criminal liability, and I do not think Congress made a mistake in granting that immunity. . . . I think the lesson is that Congress, when they grant immunity now, must be very cautious in doing so, because doing so probably defeats any criminal prosecution."

Philip Heyman, a Harvard law professor who had been an assistant attorney general and the principal draftsman of the Classified Information Procedures Act and would later be appointed as deputy attorney general by President Bill Clinton, deplored the outcome of the case. "I think it's a terrible thing for the country. I think that in cases of major national scandal involving the executive branch—and it happens in all administrations—it's very important that Congress be able to get the facts out quickly. And I think it's important that the courts be able to prosecute."

Looking to the future, Howard Phillips of the Conservative Caucus said of North, "He is a great conservative, a great asset to conservative causes, and he will not sit on the sidelines after today. He may or may not get into elective politics. . . . He won't just sit around and rest on the results of today's court action."

A week after the dismissal of his case, North began writing a syndicated newspaper column. Shortly thereafter, his book, *Under Fire*, was published. The book contained little new evidence, but it did provide us with North's insights about what had happened during and after his operations in Iran and Central America. He believed that Ronald Reagan "knew everything about the Iran-Contra scandal." North had no doubt that the president not only had been fully aware of the diversion of the arms sales proceeds to the Contras but also had approved it "enthusiastically." According to the book, North had sent John Poindexter a series of memoranda outlining the diversion. North believed that Poindexter had passed the memoranda on to the president, in accordance with Poindexter's usual practice, but that Reagan did not always remember what he had been told.

North bluntly asserted that Donald Regan, Nancy Reagan, and others close to the president had seized on the diversion to draw public attention away from "what else the president and his top advisors had known about and approved." North believed that either Donald Regan or Nancy Reagan had decided that a blanket cover-up would be impossible; the scandal had to be revealed but attention had to be deflected from the illegal arms sales authorized by President Reagan. North believed that after the president concealed the 1985 arms shipments from the congressional leaders at his first briefing in November 1986, "the president and his senior advisors were committed to this version of events." North concluded that McFarlane had altered North's chronology for the congressional testimony of Casey and Poindexter to conform to the position that had been enunciated by the president.

My staff and I had long ago come to the same general view, except that we believed this maneuver to have been conceived by Donald Regan, Edwin Meese, and William Casey and the position to have been formulated during the numerous meetings and telephone calls that had taken place while Meese was conducting his weekend fact-finding investigation.

In his book, North offered two explanations for why the administration had concealed the bungled November 1985 Hawk shipment. First, the Iranians had been offended, and the American participants had wanted all the blame to fall on the Israelis. Second, acknowledging the shipment would have been politically embarrassing to the president because the first finding had specified its purpose as the delivery of arms for hostages and had said nothing about the broader Iranian initiative later cited as the presidential objective.

North also said that Casey, in testifying before the House intelligence committee, had used North as a scapegoat to shift attention away from the Hawk shipment. Asked about the shipment, Casey had denied knowing anything. He had then voluntarily suggested that "the committees might be fascinated to know what Oliver North has been doing operationally to help the Nicaraguan resistance." Casey had previously told North to expect to be sacrificed if it meant saving the rest of the administration.

North denied that the president had ever asked him to tell "the entire truth," before the commencement of the congressional hearings as the president and his supporters had claimed. "The only message I heard was 'exonerate the president,' " wrote North, who believed that message to be what President Reagan had been trying to convey when he telephoned North after firing him. "Ollie," the president had said, "you have to understand, I just didn't know."

A few weeks later, Reagan had asked the Senate intelligence committee to give immunity to North and Poindexter in the hope that they would exculpate him. The next day, Vice President Bush's military aide had visited North and Brendan Sullivan and suggested that North waive his "Fifth Amendment rights and absolve the president of responsibility." Later, Senator Paul Laxalt, Reagan's close friend, had asked Sullivan to let North exculpate Reagan.

North wrote that he had prepared a "couple of hundred thousand pages of memoranda" and sent them up the chain of command and laterally to the vice president's office. "For someone not to have known I was involved deeply in providing all manner of things to the Nicaraguan resistance, it had to be almost a conscious act of 'I don't want to know.' " North believed that Bush, as vice president, had known in general about the covert operations in Central America. "I don't believe anybody ever said that he wasn't aware of at least a good measure of what was going on." But North did not dispute Bush's claim that he had been unaware of the diversion. North estimated that at least a hundred people in the State Department, Defense Department, CIA, White House, and Congress had known some facets of what he was doing.

In an hour-long interview about his book with Thomas Palmer and Adam Pertman of the *Boston Globe*, North said, "I had dozens of meetings with the vice president. . . . I would put it at scores." Bush had known generally about North's assistance to the Nicaraguan rebels, North said. "He was, from just the meetings he would sit in with the president, they were both aware of what I had been doing down there, back and forth, in terms of the incredible number of trips and meetings."

Two days after the dismissal of the North case, we were ready to interview Elliott Abrams. The five-year statute of limitations was running on the testimony Abrams had given Congress in the fall of 1986. The pressure on my office to complete its work was now acute. I had already gone over the case with Craig Gillen and associate counsel John Barrett and Tom Baker, a young lawyer who had left Covington & Burling to join us the previous summer. We were ready to ask the grand jury to return a felony indictment against Abrams for lying to Congress to protect the $100 million appropriation that had been pending in Congress. He had falsely denied knowing about North's activities and the foreign fund-raising for the Contras.

Abrams had been a lightning rod for the attacks on President Reagan's policy regarding the Contras. Less a diplomat than a political spokesman, he had been a tough and determined proponent of the view that diplomatic efforts to curb the communist infiltration of Central America were essentially worthless without military support for the Contras.

In mid-1985, Abrams had become the assistant secretary of state for inter-American affairs, an assignment that Secretary George Shultz had told Abrams's predecessor chewed up those who held it. Abrams had told associates, "I want to be the first guy to reverse a communist revolution." Able though he was, his strong-willed personality had provoked controversy. He had not hesitated to fire subordinates or to undercut Shultz in his battles with Caspar Weinberger and William Casey over the competing values of diplomacy and paramilitary harassment of the Sandinistas. Abrams had even gone so far as to publicly criticize Admiral William J. Crowe, Jr., then chairman of the Joint Chiefs of Staff, for delaying the 1989 invasion in which Panamanian President Manuel Noriega had been arrested. Although Abrams had been acknowledged as a person of courage and principle, he had been regarded by many members of Congress as a zealot who could not be trusted. Some congressional committees had refused to hear his testimony except under oath.

In a series of lengthy meetings in late September, Gillen, Barrett, Baker, and I discussed a guilty plea with Abrams's lawyer, DeVier Pierson. We then spent an entire Saturday with Pierson and Abrams, who presented their arguments as to why Abrams should not be indicted. Essentially, they claimed that although he had known of North's operation, Abrams had personally avoided participating in it, except for an occasional assist. Shultz had directed him to keep track of what North was doing, because the Contras had been an important element in his area of responsibility.

According to Charles Hill's notes of an early meeting between Shultz and Abrams, Shultz had said, "We don't want to be in the dark. You['re] suppose[d] to be [manager] of overall C.A. [Central America] picture. Contras are integral part of it. So y[ou] need to know how they [are] getting arms. So don't just say go see the W.H. [White House]. It's very risky for W.H." Abrams said that he had given whatever information he received to the State Department, and that his role had fallen somewhere between that of a "message passer" and that of an active participant.

After a long meeting with my staff, I had no doubt that we could prove Abrams guilty beyond a reasonable doubt. He had unquestioningly misled three congressional committees shortly after Hasenfus's aircraft went down in Nicaragua. The only issue was whether the questioning by the congressional committees had been so loose that he could claim that it had been ambiguous and that what he had said, although misleading, had been literally true.

Questioned by chairman Richard Lugar in a closed session of the Senate foreign relations committee, on October 10, 1986, Abrams had conceded that an elaborate supply system existed, but he had claimed that it was independent of the U.S. government. "In the last two years, . . . this system had kept them alive. It is not our supply system . . . we have been kind of careful not to get closely involved with it and to stay away from it. We do not encourage people to do this . . . , we don't have conversations, we don't tell them to do this, we don't ask them to do it. But I think it is quite clear . . . [that] the attitude of the administration is that these people are doing a very good thing. . . . But that is without any encouragement and coordination from us, other than a public speech by the president."

Four days later, Abrams had testified before the House intelligence committee. Chairman Lee Hamilton had asked, "Can anybody assure us that the United States government was not involved, indirectly or directly, in any way in supply of the Contras?"

"I believe we have already done that," Abrams replied. "That is, I think the president has done it, the secretary [of state] has done it, and I have done it."

The chairman had then asked, "So the answer is the United States government was not involved in any way."

"In the supply," Abrams had responded. "Now, again this normal intelligence monitoring is there, but the answer to your question is yes."

Later in the hearing, Hamilton had asked Clair George for a clarification. "Just to be clear, the United States government has not done anything to facilitate the activities of these private groups, is that a fair statement? We have not furnished any money? We have not furnished any arms? We have not furnished any advice? We have not furnished logistics?"

"Mr. Chairman," George had replied, "I cannot speak for the entire United States government."

Hamilton had then turned to the other witness, saying, "Can you, Mr. Abrams?"

"Yes," Abrams had said, "to the extent of my knowledge that I feel to be complete, other than the general public encouragement that we like this kind of activity."

The next day, testifying before the House foreign affairs subcommittee on Western Hemisphere affairs, Abrams had responded to similar questions by Representative Michael Barnes. Abrams had testified that no one in the U.S. government had known who had organized and paid for Hasenfus's flight or similar flights. At the end of a long answer, he had said, "I still don't know—"

Barnes had interrupted him to complete the sentence: "Who organized this and who paid for it?"

"That is correct," Abrams had responded.

Representative Peter Kostmayer followed up: "Do you think there is anyone in the government who does know?"

"No," Abrams had replied, "because we don't track this kind of activity."

When he had been asked about Max Gomez by the Senate foreign relations committee, Abrams had been similarly evasive. When pressed, he had given false answers. He had said that he thought the name was "an alias for an individual who was previously employed by us. But I don't know if that, in fact, is the case. I don't know who he is reporting to."

After Abrams testified before the Senate committee, but before he met with the House committee, the *Washington Post* had identified Max Gomez as Felix Rodriguez, and Vice President Bush had identified him as a counterinsurgency advisor working for the Salvadoran government. When asked about Rodriguez by the House intelligence committee, Abrams had said that there had been "no knowledge . . . at what point he had moved off into doing some other things, which apparently he has done with the resistance."

"That was the extent of your knowledge?" Representative Louis Stokes had then asked.

"That was the extent of it to my knowledge," Abrams had answered. "That is right."

While preparing to testify before the House intelligence committee in October 1986, Abrams had been questioned by reporters and had discussed Rodriguez with Edwin Corr, the U.S. ambassador to El Salvador. From Charles Hill's notes, we knew that the day after telling the committee that he didn't know about Rodriguez's having assisted the Contras, Abrams had explained to Shultz who Rodriguez was. Moreover, Rodriguez had been previously discussed at restricted interagency group meetings attended by Abrams. Notes taken at one such meeting, held the day after Hasenfus was captured, showed the participants' concern about how to handle reporters' inquiries regarding Hasenfus's claim that he had been working for the CIA. Rodriguez had been lying low in Miami. Thinking that the upcoming summit meeting between Ronald Reagan and Mikhail Gorbachev would distract the public, the RIG members had agreed to stall the news media and hope that the interest in Hasenfus would wane.

Abrams had lied in disclaiming knowledge of North's Contrasupport activities. North had outlined these activities in detail at two RIG meetings and had asked for guidance as to whether he should continue helping the Contras until Congress authorized the CIA to resume its support. Abrams had been present at one of these meetings. His principal deputies had attended the other. He had also heard North describe Manuel Noriega's offer to sabotage Sandinista installations in return for $1 million and other favors. North had explained to the RIG that the money would come not from the U.S. government but from Project Democracy, for which he had accumulated funds in Swiss bank accounts. The next day, Abrams had relayed this offer to Charles Hill and Nicholas Platt. The plan had still been under discussion when Hasenfus's aircraft was shot down. Even before the RIG meeting, Abrams had known of North's funding capabilities and had asked him for money to keep the humanitarian assistance flowing until the upcoming appropriation took effect.

Although Shultz had specifically directed Abrams to "monitor Ollie," Abrams had done more than simply monitor North. From time to time, Abrams had given North advice and such concrete assistance as telephoning the Venezuelan officials to facilitate Richard Gadd's aircraft purchase.

In his explanations to the congressional select committees on Iran-Contra, Abrams had claimed that he had relied on North's assurance that he had not done anything illegal. Abrams had also told the committees that he had relied on the false denials in Robert McFarlane's letters to Congress, but this was inconsistent with Abrams's earlier statement that he had not known about the 1985 congressional inquiry to which the letters had responded.

Abrams admitted that he had given false testimony to the House and Senate intelligence committees when he denied having known of the foreign support that had been provided or solicited for the Contras. Before the House committee, he had denied having known about the contributions from Saudi Arabia and "with respect to other governments, as well." To the Senate committee he had stated that "there was no reason to think it was coming from foreign governments" and that he could not remember discussing fund-raising with members of the NSC staff. "We're not—you know, we're not in the fund-raising business." He had assured the senators that he was "fairly confident that there was no foreign government contributing [to the Contras]."

Before giving this testimony, Abrams had been promised a contribution of $10 million for the Nicaraguan insurgents by the sultan of Brunei, and had assured North that the contribution was being delivered. Abrams claimed to have believed that Shultz had directed him not to reveal the anticipated contribution, but Abrams need not have lied. At other points in his testimony, he had stopped the questioning by saying that he needed to consult with the secretary before revealing certain facts. Shultz, in his testimony before the select committees on Iran-Contra, had denied telling Abrams to lie. Shultz said that Abrams had overextended a general instruction to preserve the secrecy of the solicitation.

During the conferences with DeVier Pierson, we rejected several proposals: that Abrams serve a thousand hours of community service, without entering a guilty plea; that he make a plea of nolo contendere, with an acknowledgment that the facts just outlined were true and that they constituted a violation of law; or that he plead guilty to a single misdemeanor. We declined to treat Abrams differently from others who had pleaded guilty under similar circumstances. Finally, with the statute of limitations due to expire in five days, Abrams agreed to plead guilty to two misdemeanors and meet our conditions, which included cooperating with us in our ongoing investigation and prosecutions. On October 6, as we were about to debrief Abrams, he suffered a seizure and was taken to the hospital for observation.

By the next day, Abrams had recovered. He appeared before Chief Judge Aubrey Robinson and pleaded guilty to two misdemeanor counts of withholding information from Congress. Abrams acknowledged his guilt at his arraignment. Afterward, he told the waiting reporters, "I take full responsibility for my actions, for my failure to make full disclosure to Congress in 1986. I am proud to have given twelve years serving the United States government and of the contribution I made in those years. I am very happy to have this entire matter behind me."

In an article in the *Washington Times* a few days later, Abrams wrote that he admired President Reagan but that "he should have stood up to Congress. He should have made his case to the American people for why it was important to stop communism from spreading through Central America and perhaps into Mexico."

On November 15, Abrams was placed on probation for two years and ordered to perform a hundred hours of community service. His agreement to cooperate with us was a condition of the sentence.

On the day Abrams was sentenced, the court of appeals reversed the conviction of John Poindexter. The majority opinion was written by Judge Douglas Ginsburg, who had served in the Reagan administration as the assistant attorney general in charge of the Justice Department's antitrust division, and then in the Office of Management and Budget. Possessed of excellent scholarly credentials, he had been nominated by President Bush for the Supreme Court but had asked to have his nomination withdrawn to avoid controversy about an irrelevant incident. Judge David Bryan Sentelle joined him. Judge Abner J. Mikva dissented. Reasserting the appellate decision in the North case, the court found that we had failed to show—line by line and item by item—that Poindexter's immunized testimony had not been used against him at his trial.

The majority held that the trial court had applied a standard of "use" that was narrower than the standard set by the *North* decision (which was not reached until after Poindexter's trial had ended). Under this standard, if a witness had listened to the immunized testimony, even though his or her trial testimony expanded on it or contradicted it, the possibility remained that the immunized testimony had affected the trial testimony. The trial judge, Harold Greene, had rejected this sweeping view as "absolutist," prior to the North decision.

The most controversial witness at Poindexter's trial had been Oliver North. Judge Greene had carefully examined North and had found him to be lying when he said that he could not distinguish his own recollections from those of Poindexter. The judge had ordered North to testify to the extent that he had testified in his own trial to matters beyond or contrary to the testimony of Poindexter. Judges Ginsburg and Sentelle, however, declined to defer to this factual finding because "whatever the exact contours of the district court's legal standard for 'use' . . . , its view was clearly too narrow to permit us to defer to its ultimate findings on this issue." In his dissenting opinion, Judge Mikva emphasized the need for an appellate court to accept the trial judge's findings of fact unless they were clearly erroneous. Judge Mikva warned that "the Court today tells future defendants that all they need to evade responsibility is a well-timed case of amnesia."

The court of appeals did not remand the case to the district court for a more extensive hearing; mercifully, the majority held that we obviously could not meet its standards. Dissenting from this part of the decision, Judge Mikva wrote that "the decision to prosecute belongs to the prosecutor, and the decision to dismiss belongs to the trial judge, and today this court usurps their authority by denying them the chance to exercise it."

Although the reversal of Poindexter's conviction did not surprise me, I was taken aback that the court, in response to an argument raised by Poindexter's counsel, had also severely narrowed the scope of the section of the United States Code that prohibits individuals from "corruptly" obstructing a congressional investigation. In dismissing the obstruction counts, the court held that the statutory standard "corruptly" was so ambiguous that it could not be applied to a mere false statement; something else—which the court did not define or specify—would be needed. Departing from earlier decisions in other circuits, the court held that making a false statement to Congress was not enough to constitute an obstruction. The opinion strongly implied that it would be necessary for the defendant to have corrupted a third person.

The incipient evil of the opinion was that it left lower courts free to throw out obstruction charges even when the false statements were incidental to broader patterns of obstruction. The trial record actually showed that Poindexter had directed North to give testimony which he knew to be false, but the indictment did not specifically allege this. The preexisting precedents had not required it and the obstruction charge had been drawn before the decision to call North as a witness.

We immediately began working on a petition to the Supreme Court to review the decision. Perhaps the narrowing of the obstruction statute's applicability would invite the Court's attention. We hoped that the solicitor general as well as Congress would support us, because the holding was detrimental not only to us but also to the Justice Department.

The reversal provoked a predictable response from Senate Minority Leader Bob Dole: "Lawrence Walsh's bungling Iran-Contra operation has struck out again. Unfortunately, the American taxpayers continue to be the real losers, watching their tax dollars going down the drain to maintain Mr. Walsh's exercise in futility." Dole urged the Justice Department to shut down the investigation. "Closing the doors on this lavish, fifty-million-dollar waste would be the 'November surprise' the American taxpayers have been waiting for."

As a result of the reversal, Poindexter no longer had any incentive to tell the full truth. Although he had permitted his lawyer to argue during the trial that "the driving engine behind his actions" had been President Reagan, Poindexter himself had never changed his congressional testimony: "The buck stops here."

We next turned to Duane "Dewey" Clarridge, who had played a pivotal role in President Reagan's most incriminating, personal episode of the entire Iran-Contra scandal, and had lied about it to Congress on six occasions, claiming not to have known that the CIA-proprietary aircraft he had helped North charter in November 1985 had carried Hawk missiles and claiming to have believed that the cargo was oil-drilling equipment. Clarridge had told these lies three times in sworn testimony—before the Senate intelligence committee on December 2, 1986, before the House intelligence committee on December 11, 1986, and before the joint select committees on Iran-Contra on August 4, 1987. On three other occasions, his testimony had been unsworn, but he was subject to prosecution for having made false statements to a government agency.

Clarridge's assignment as head of the CIA's Latin American division had capped a thirty-year career of achievement, according to Joseph Persico, Casey's biographer, in 1981, when Clarridge was the CIA's chief in Rome and had caught Casey's eye. Casey had been impressed enough to assign Clarridge to the Latin American division even though he had no background in the region and did not speak Spanish. Persico described Clarridge as "a flamboyant figure who favored Italian silk suits, silk shirts, silk ties, and flashy suspenders; he smoked hand-rolled cigars and dined in the finest restaurants." These superficial characteristics concealed a resourceful operative, a person characterized by others as "a doer" and "a take-charge guy," who, after a career extending from Europe through the Middle East and India, had organized support for the Contra insurgency. Clarridge had awed his subordinates, but he sometimes had alarmed his superiors. By having the Contras mine Nicaraguan harbors with resulting damage to neutral ships, Clarridge had furnished Congress with the excuse it had used to terminate the CIA's support for the Contras.

He had had direct access to Casey, unrestricted by organizational lines of command. Casey had not flinched from Clarridge's bold plan for Nicaragua. After the mining of the harbors was exposed, Casey had simply apologized to the congressional intelligence committees and reassigned Clarridge to head the CIA's Western European division and the agency's counterterrorism unit, the posts he had been holding when North came to him for help with the Hawk shipment. But after Casey fell ill and resigned, his successor had reprimanded and demoted Clarridge because of his misstatements to Congress. He had left the agency and taken on an executive position with the General Dynamics Corporation.

Not only had Clarridge been Oliver North's predecessor as the administration's point man for Contra support, but he had also reportedly been North's role model. After the enactment of the Boland amendments, Clarridge had assembled the Contra forces in a Honduran sanctuary. There, a crisply dressed Clarridge had delivered a military-style farewell speech, then turned the Contras over to North, who had stood beside him in battle fatigues.

We felt confident that we could prove the untruthfulness of Clarridge's claims of ignorance about the true nature of the cargo of Hawk missiles, using the testimony of Charles Allen, who had supplied Clarridge with the intelligence reports explaining the shipment, and the testimony of Vincent Cannistraro, the former CIA officer detailed to the National Security Council staff who had told us about meeting with North and Clarridge at Charlie's Place, a restaurant in Virginia, about a week before the November 1985 Hawk shipment. After telephoning Poindexter for permission to brief Clarridge, North had told Clarridge that the cargo of the shipment would be Hawk missiles. At that time, Clarridge had had to deny knowing about the military cargo in order to slip it past his superiors. A year later, when Clarridge was testifying before Congress, his motive had been to protect the CIA and the president.

Through his lawyer, Clarridge had rejected our invitation to discuss a plea. On November 26, 1991, the grand jury indicted him on seven felony counts—six for making false statements to congressional committees and one for lying to the Tower Commission. He was arraigned before Chief Judge Aubrey Robinson on December 6. As Clarridge left the courtroom, he put on a camouflage jacket that had been given him by the British elite antiterrorist unit, the Special Air Service. He declined to comment on the charges but said, "When you're at battle stations, you might as well be prepared for battle stations." Chief Judge Robinson assigned the case to Judge Harold Greene.

As we completed our investigation of those most closely connected with North, we began carefully reexamining the testimony and conduct of the cabinet officers who had looked the other way while Clarridge tried to cover up the Hawk shipment he had facilitated.

From the beginning, I had felt concern about the fact that my assignment required me to prosecute career officers for having executed the illegal policies of their president. A few of these individuals had personally profited or had acted in furtherance of their professional ambitions, but others, including Clair George, Alan Fiers, and Dewey Clarridge, had acted out of loyalty to William Casey and Ronald Reagan. Having obtained indictments of these three outstanding CIA officers, I welcomed the impulse of the CIA officers and alumni to help their colleagues.

Neither President Bush nor the congressional critics of my investigation expressed much concern for these officers who had carried out Reagan's wishes. Bush was more concerned about our investigation of the former members of his personal staff, who might lead us to him. Dole and other Republicans wanted us to quit before we reached the political upper crust.

PART THREE

Behind the Firewall

CHAPTER SEVENTEEN

What the Secretary
of State Knew

By late 1991, the only remaining subjects of our investigation were former cabinet officers and those who might incriminate them. As we reached higher, the intensity of the political and editorial attacks on me mounted. Having endured steady criticism for spending five years and $30 million on our investigation and prosecutions, I could not ignore our defenses. (Senate Minority Leader Bob Dole, adding in the expenses claimed by all the government departments that had responded to my investigation, computed the government expense at $50 million.) If the attacks became more effective, we might be shut down, despite the provisions of law that seemed to protect our independence.

The attorney general had the power to remove me from office, subject to judicial review. Richard Thornburgh had resigned and his successor, William Barr, was outspokenly hostile toward us. Moreover, some observers speculated that the real attorney general was now White House counsel Boyden Gray, who for so many reasons had hoped to see us go out of business. (Although Gray had perhaps wanted the cabinet post, he might have run into difficulty winning Senate confirmation because of his extravagant views of presidential power; the solution was for George Bush to appoint a subservient substitute. Barr, who had served two years under Thornburgh, was better known as a formidable administrator than as a lawyer.)

I wanted to have at least a rough draft of our final report completed by the time we finished our investigation. I also wanted to be able to file my report promptly if our office was shut down. I gave up my lease on the room at the Watergate Hotel, which in many ways had served as my private office, and worked on the report in Oklahoma City, where I had space within the local office of the FBI. I continued to spend about a third of my time in Washington to follow our ongoing investigation.

The only remaining member of my original staff was Guy Struve, who still gave us 10 percent of his time. John Barrett was next in seniority, having joined the team during the summer of 1987. Except for Craig Gillen, whom I had appointed to serve as my deputy, the other lawyers were young top graduates who had recently finished judicial clerkships. After John Poindexter's trial, the size of the staff hovered around nine or ten full-time lawyers, including Gillen and me.

Clearly, we would have our hands full with the preparation for two major trials and the remaining investigation. We still struggled to gather all the records we had already requested, and newly discovered notes led us to request additional records.

We had initially hoped for a prompt Supreme Court review of the reversal of Poindexter's conviction, but our efforts were blocked by his December 1991 motion for a modification of the court of appeals judgment and for a review by the full court of his claim that the false-statement counts should have been dismissed as a matter of law because the provision of the U.S. Code under which the charges had been brought applied only to administrative matters, not to testimony.

Our appellate counsel told us that the public integrity section of the Justice Department supported our effort to obtain a Supreme Court review of the decision regarding both the effect of congressional immunity and the appellate court's narrowing of the definition of obstruction of Congress. We were also told that the career officers in the solicitor general's office supported us, but that the political appointees at the top of the department were dragging their feet. Although I was skeptical that the solicitor general would ever support an appeal from a reversal that President Bush had welcomed, I felt that we had to continue to give the solicitor general the opportunity to support us, even though it meant that we would have to let our petition wait until the end of the Supreme Court's term—the most unfavorable time at which to ask the justices to take a new case.

In the press interviews that always accompanied the anniversary of my appointment, I stressed my belief that "the cover-up was a very important matter to pursue." I told George Lardner of the *Washington Post* that our work would have a deterrent effect on crime in high office, particularly "national security crime." The deterrence would result from the convictions, regardless of the light sentences. The jury verdicts against Oliver North and John Poindexter had been significant despite the reversals, because "the question was whether arrogant disregard of constitutional and congressional constraints could be brought home to a jury in the District of Columbia. The fact that these convictions had been set aside because Congress saw fit to give immunity to the principal perpetrators by no means reflected adversely on the effectiveness of law enforcement."

Even though several witnesses had lied to us and to Congress, we had decided not to obtain indictments that were peripheral—those that might punish the lies of subordinates, without producing useful witnesses against Ronald Reagan, George Bush, or key officials who had supported or covered up the president's illegal covert actions. A year earlier, we had suspended our investigations of William Walker, who had been Elliott Abrams's principal assistant; Edwin Corr, who had been the U.S. ambassador to El Salvador; Paul Thompson, who had been Poindexter's military assistant and counsel to the National Security Council; and—with considerable misgiving—Donald Gregg and Samuel Watson, who had been members of George Bush's vice presidential staff.

It was at this point that Tom Baker, the newest member of our team, ignored the logical assumption that all the relevant information would have been properly classified. He began looking at Caspar Weinberger's unclassified, supposedly private material in the Library of Congress. Before the year was over, Baker had found, among notes relating to household pets and other family matters, thousands of pages of highly sensitive diary and meeting notes documenting Weinberger's official activities as secretary of defense. These unclassified notes revealed information that, in importance and in national security implications, overshadowed the government secrets related to Iran-Contra. As a condition of their deposit in the Library of Congress, the notes were under the personal control of Weinberger, who was now a private citizen—a supreme irony in view of the administration's fastidious refusal to declassify publicly known information that would have permitted us to prosecute Joseph Fernandez and to try North for the theft of government funds.

Weinberger's notes provided us with an invaluable contemporaneous record of the knowledge and activities of the nation's highest officials regarding the arms sales to Iran. They added a new dimension to our ever-swelling accumulation of notes from State Department officials. Weinberger's notes had already exploded my hope that five years in Washington would be enough when, almost as a postscript in one of our last staff conferences of the year, Barrett mentioned his recollection that "somewhere, someone ha[d] said that Bush began to keep notes in November 1986." Responding to an earlier request for documents, Boyden Gray had told his associate counsel that he believed he had never heard of such notes. I told Barrett to subpoena them if we could not get them by negotiation.

Previously, we had obtained another valuable asset: a diary kept by White House counsel Peter Wallison during November 1986. In addition to giving us the firsthand thoughts, reflections, and discussions of a central player during the scramble to protect Ronald Reagan after the public disclosure of the arms sales to Iran, the diary gave us new insight into Donald Regan, to whom Wallison had reported. It also revealed the tension felt by Wallison, as a concerned White House lawyer who had been caught in the conflict between the national security community and the president's political advisors.

We were also patiently integrating Charles Hill's thousands of pages of notes with those taken by Nicholas Platt, the State Department's executive secretary. In addition, we had obtained the notes of Arnold Raphel, who had been the deputy director of the department's antiterrorism unit; Kenneth Quinn, who had been Platt's deputy; and Christopher Ross, who had been Michael Armacost's deputy.

Our staff conferences in January and February 1992 sparked disagreements as I pressed to wrap up our work and Gillen argued for more time and more staff. He insisted that we were not giving the State Department the same scrutiny that we had given the CIA. With our grand jury due to expire in May, I set March as the deadline for decisions on any further indictments. In the meantime, our dealings with the George Shultz were delayed while a security clearance was obtained for his attorney, Lloyd Cutler, a leading Washington lawyer who had previously served as White House counsel for President Jimmy Carter.

Gillen's investigation now focused on Shultz's misstatements to Congress in November 1986 and July 1987, the roles his aides had played in formulating his misleading testimony, and their failure to produce all their relevant notes. Only after we finally retrieved Hill's original notebooks had we been able to assemble an accurate and complete picture of Shultz's knowledge of the arms shipments to Iran and his awareness of the Contra-supply operation.

From a study of the notes, the pattern of their concealment, and Shultz's testimony, we pieced together the chain of events by which Shultz had come to mislead Congress about his knowledge of the arms shipments. Many details were later confirmed by Shultz's own book, *Turmoil and Triumph*. On November 4, 1986, Shultz had been set to leave for Vienna for a meeting of foreign ministers of the countries sponsoring the Conference on Security and Cooperation in Europe. He had just spoken by telephone with the president, congratulating him on the outcome of the midterm congressional elections, when the Lebanese magazine *Al Shiraa* broke the arms-for-hostages story.

Already late for the Vienna conference, a stunned Shultz had hastily consulted his closest advisors. In addition to Charles Hill and Nicholas Platt, they included Deputy Secretary John C. Whitehead, Undersecretary Michael Armacost, antiterrorism director L. Paul "Jerry" Bremer, and press spokesman Chuck Redman. The contemporaneous notes revealed the explosive frustration of our foremost diplomat, rankled at the disclosure that he had been telling foreign officials one thing while the United States was secretly doing another. His distaste for the questionable characters involved in the transactions, who he believed had been "clearly playing us for suckers," had sharpened his comments. He and his aides had been undercut. While Jerry Bremer was on the road persuading friends and allies not to supply arms to Iran or Iraq and not to reward those who sponsored terrorism, Robert McFarlane, John Poindexter, Oliver North, and Ronald Reagan had been playing a different game.

Shultz had briefly considered following the course of the British foreign secretary who had resigned when his country was surprised by the war over the Falkland Islands. "This could be the kind of thing," Shultz had told his advisors, "where somebody has to resign and take the rap. The hostages keep growing in number. The deal encourages that."

When reporters pursued Chuck Redman for answers, he had referred them to the White House, but presidential spokesman Larry Speakes had apparently been uninformed. The president had been in California, so Poindexter had simply released a vacuous statement: "As long as Iran advocates the use of terrorism, the U.S. arms embargo will continue." Shultz had suspected the beginning of a cover-up.

Late that afternoon, Wednesday, November 4, Shultz's Air Force 707 had taken off for Vienna. Recalling my brief experience as deputy to Ambassador Henry Cabot Lodge during the Paris peace talks on Vietnam, I visualized Shultz's predicament—en route to an international meeting with the world's leading diplomats, out of touch with President Reagan, forced to communicate with him through Poindexter, imprisoned in an aircraft carrying some of the expert reporters who regularly covered the State Department. During the flight, although the secretary and his wife had private quarters in the plane's aft cabin, he would have had to talk with the reporters in the forward compartment. Shultz had surely been immediately embarrassed by questions insinuating that the United States had violated its own antiterrorism policy and that it had, for political purposes, timed the release of a hostage two days before the election.

We knew that Shultz had cabled Poindexter from the plane, saying, "The only way to contain the damage is to give the essential facts to the public as quickly as possible. Get everything out in the open and fast."

Poindexter had responded that this would complicate efforts to secure the release of other hostages and might endanger the opportunity for improving our relationship with Iran as well as the possibilities for an active U.S. role in ending the Iran-Iraq war. "At some point, we will have to lay out all of that, but I do not believe that now is the time to give the facts to the public. . . . I have talked to the vice president, Cap [Weinberger], and Bill Casey. They agree with my approach."

Thinking of my own dawn arrivals in Paris after little sleep, I reflected on Shultz's plight as he disembarked in Vienna, where he would have undoubtedly have met more reporters and photographers. Dismayed by Poindexter's belief that the administration could stonewall the news media, Congress, and the public, Shultz himself would not have had satisfactory answers.

At six-thirty in the morning on Shultz's last day in Vienna, he had been visited by the Irish foreign minister, who had been "hopping mad" because of press reports that forged Irish passports had been used on McFarlane's trip to Tehran. Shultz had suffered the indignity of having to explain that he knew almost nothing of the operation. He had listened in silence as he was told that Ireland's sovereignty had been infringed and America's reputation severely damaged.

During Shultz's stay in Vienna, the State Department had continued to refer questions to the White House. The president's staff had complained that Shultz was "distancing himself." While trying to answer questions about the State Department, Larry Speakes had denied that Shultz had resigned. Speakes had said that Shultz had known about the arms deal with Iran, that he had been involved in it from the start, and that the operation had been handled through normal procedures.

From our interviews with Hill and a study of his notes, we knew that it was during the flight back from Vienna that the critical errors had crept into Shultz's position. Before leaving Washington, Shultz had directed Hill, Platt, and Abraham Sofaer to pull together the record of what he had known and what he had done. But Shultz had been alone with Hill on the way home when, with Hill taking notes, Shultz sketched out what he recalled of his contacts regarding the arms sales. He had relied primarily on his memory of this one disagreeable project out of all his other complex and more constructive activities. With Hill's help, Shultz had developed a three-phase conception of his knowledge about the arms sales: Phase one included contacts that had occurred before December 1985, phase two those that had occurred between December 1985 and May 1986, and phase three those that had occurred after May 1986. Awkward facts were understated or glossed over.

The day after his return, Shultz had begun his battle to recover State Department control of America's dealings with Iran, but Oliver North's operation had continued. According to Shultz, he had soon realized that he was dealing with a "massive, secret White House operation that was totally contrary to the longstanding policy that Ronald Reagan and [he] had constructed to deal with terrorists . . . [to] 'make sure that terrorism does not pay.' "

That afternoon, as Hill took notes, Shultz had analyzed where the administration stood and what it must do. In Shultz's view, the United States had been trapped by terrorists and had become the victim of a "terrorist extortion racket." He had told Hill, "We have assaulted our own Middle East policy. The Arabs counted on us to play a strong and responsible role to contain and eventually bring the Gulf War to an end. Now we seem to be aiding the most radical forces in the region. We have acted directly counter to our own major effort to dry up the war by denying the weapons needed to continue it. The Jordanians—and other moderate Arabs—are appalled at what we have done. And our hopes of getting united allied action against Syria have foundered as the allies see us as doing precisely what we have relentlessly pressured them not to do." The proper course, he had believed, would be a forthright recognition of the damage to major aspects of the president's foreign policy and an agreement that the crisis required immediate action to preserve the president's major achievements.

The illegality of the administration's actions had not escaped Shultz. "We appear to have violated our own laws," he had told Hill. "Certainly we have corrupted ourselves in the eyes of the law. At this moment, others are on trial in U.S. criminal courts for doing what the U.S. government has now revealed itself to be doing."

Shultz had concluded that the president would need to publicly reaffirm his policies on terrorism and the Middle East. Poindexter's operation would have to be terminated, with North returned to the Marine Corps and the responsibility for counterterrorism returned to the State Department. Although he had been prepared to back the president for having undertaken an effort for humanitarian reasons, Shultz had thought that harm would come to "almost every aspect of our foreign policy agenda" unless the president ended the Iranian initiative and let Shultz "clean up the mess."

We never doubted that Shultz had opposed the arms shipments to Iran. Our question was whether Hill's notes had been deliberately withheld to conform with the three-phase approach, which had minimized Shultz's apparent contemporaneous knowledge of the arms transactions.

At our February 4, 1992, staff meeting, Gillen reported that Shultz's testimony before the congressional committees in December 1986 and July 1987 had been inconsistent with the notes kept by Hill and Platt. It looked as though there had been a conscious decision to withhold a number of notes showing the extent of Shultz's knowledge—coordinated action by Platt and Hill, and possibly by Shultz, to create a false picture of almost total ignorance. The evidence seemed stark. The withheld notes were pointed and explicit.

The omissions in the material produced separately by Platt and Hill were parallel, a phenomenon that could not be explained except by their having acted jointly to coordinate the withholding of notes or by Hill's having withheld some of Platt's notes from the FBI. Notes written by each of the two men on the evening before Shultz's congressional testimony, for example, had been withheld from us. Hill's note revealed that he and Platt had considered their knowledge that the arms sales had led to a hostage's release in July 1986 as the "greatest vulnerability" in Shultz's claim that he had been unaware of the activities that had taken place between May and November that year. In his own note, Platt had mentioned this discussion and had gone on to list questions that he thought Shultz might be asked: "What did you think? Why did you avert your gaze?"

Neither Hill nor Platt could explain to us what these notes meant or why they had been withheld. The pair gave divergent explanations for having withheld notes that should have been produced. Platt said that he had intended to give all relevant notes to Sofaer, and that the omissions had been the result of an innocent oversight. Hill claimed that he had never made a comprehensive review of his notes and had never told anyone that he had done so. He had looked only for notes that documented what Shultz had independently remembered in early November 1986. Hill said that he had not been trying to find things that Shultz had not remembered.

In our staff conference, Gillen questioned how, having asked the grand jury to indict Duane Clarridge, we could overlook similar conduct in the State Department. I said I believed that we would face two problems if we sought indictments against Hill, Platt, and Shultz for having withheld the notes.

First, there was some confusion about whether our demand for documents has been absolute. Danny Coulson, the FBI special agent in charge of the investigation begun by Attorney General Edwin Meese, had never released Hill from the obligation to produce every document related to the Iranian initiative, but former associate counsel Geoffrey Stewart had a hazy recollection that, while trying to expedite document production before Congress's grant of immunity to Oliver North, he might have prioritized some categories of documents over others. Hill claimed that he had had an appointment to discuss his notes with Stewart's assistant, Jeffrey Toobin, but that Toobin had canceled it.

Second, we would have difficulty pinpointing criminal responsibility. We had a circumstantial case of collaboration between Hill and Platt to obstruct our investigation and that of Congress. But we would have trouble proving our case, because both men steadfastly disclaimed any intent to withhold evidence, and neither would testify against the other.

To say the least, we had come upon a paradigm of the Washington practice of simplifying the facts to avoid the appearance of uncertainty. As deputy attorney general in the 1950s, I had learned that an equivocal position, which invites questions, can be dangerous in the political give-and-take of Washington. A categorical position, if unimpeachable, terminates questions. In brushing off minor embarrassments or passing harassment, it is tempting to be categorical. In matters of major importance that were not going to go away, however, being too categorical can bring disaster.

Gillen and Barrett showed in detail that Shultz or his immediate advisors had streamlined the evidence to fit an oversimplified picture of his knowledge of the arms sales, to avoid exposing his harsh private criticism of President Reagan and his foreign policy advisors, or to accommodate the administration's unyielding position of nondisclosure. In hindsight, this hasty strategy had conflicted with Shultz's seasoned judgment and his opposition to the cover-up. His acknowledgment that he had continued to receive contemporaneous fragments of information would not have detracted from his unassailable opposition to the arms-for-hostages policy. His heroic record had been jeopardized by this oversimplification.

As Gillen, Barrett, and Baker reported on the evidence, I again reflected on the State Department's determination to force a dismissal of the basic conspiracy count against North. I now saw why Abraham Sofaer had argued so vigorously against the criminalization of the dissembling he viewed as implicit in the political process, and why he had undertaken to have Attorney General Thornburgh support North's motions to dismiss the conspiracy count or, failing that, to kill it by withholding as classified (albeit publicly known) information that would have been necessary to try the count. As Sofaer must have realized, Shultz would have been called as a witness in the trial had the conspiracy count survived. If we had not called him to show his exclusion from the arms sales by the conspirators, Brendan Sullivan would likely have called him to attempt to show his knowledge of North's activities. In either case, Shultz would have been cross-examined about the omissions in his congressional testimony.

Shultz had first given his streamlined account of his knowledge in December 1986, telling a congressional committee that from June to November 1985, he had known arms sales were being debated, but he had not been informed that any had taken place; that from December 1985 to May 1986, he had known the United States was attempting to open a dialogue with Iran, but he had believed the administration to be unwilling to sell arms; and that from May 4 to November 3, 1986, he had received no information about arms transfers.

Contemporaneous notes made by Platt and Hill contradicted this testimony, showing that during the first phase Shultz had known about the transfers of U.S. arms through Israel. The notes confirmed that McFarlane had kept Shultz informed of the early discussions and the first release of a hostage, the Reverend Benjamin Weir. Platt had noted that "Polecat [North] [was] beginning to pay off. Weir has been released . . . other things could happen." Hill had noted that Weir had been taken to the CIA in Virginia for interrogation. Weir's release had been kept secret, Hill had noted, because the operation was ongoing. "McF [McFarlane] & Ollie are getting us into deal where we will have to pay off ISR [Israel]." Platt and Hill had made additional notes after Weir's release became public knowledge.

The U.S. ambassador to Lebanon, Reginald Bartholomew, who had not been informed about what was actually happening, speculated that Weir had been released to deliver a message pressing for the release of prisoners held in Kuwait. In his congressional testimony, Shultz had adopted this erroneous speculation as his own analysis, despite the fact that Hill had warned him that the media were on the track of what had actually occurred. "Bud's [McFarlane's] folly is out," Hill had written.

In addition to the notes taken by Hill and Platt, other evidence contradicted Shultz's testimony. Robert Oakley, who had preceded Jerry Bremer as head of the department's antiterrorism unit and had generally kept Shultz informed through Armacost and Platt, had told us in a 1987 interview that North had claimed that the arms shipments had produced Weir's release. We also knew that when Weir was freed, Shultz, Armacost, and Whitehead had explicitly discussed how to deal with the falsity of the U.S. position vis-à-vis our allies. According to Hill's notes, Shultz had said, "I'm not comfortable, don't know what to do about it."

"Do you think they tell the president?" Whitehead had asked.

"Yes," Shultz had responded, "but he doesn't appreciate the problems with arms sales to Iran."

Shultz had always acknowledged that he had known the November 1985 Hawk shipment had been planned, but he had claimed that his understanding was that it had never been consummated. "Since no hostages were released," he had told the House foreign affairs committee in January 1987, "I assumed that no arms were sent. I later learned . . . that a shipment went from Israel to Iran but was rejected by Iran and presumably sent back; so as of that time, as far as I knew, no arms had been shipped."

McFarlane, however, had told us that at the meeting of the president's senior foreign policy advisors on December 7, 1985, barely a week after the Hawk transaction, he had informed those present, including Shultz, about the delivery of the Hawks. In fact, the delivery and resulting Iranian protests had precipitated the meeting.

Notes taken by Hill and Platt also contradicted Shultz's testimony about his knowledge during the second phase. Shultz had told the congressional committees that from December 1985 until May 1986, he had believed the United States to be unwilling to ship arms to Iran, but the notes showed that Shultz had known that President Reagan had

decided in January 1986 to resume the arms shipments. Platt and Hill
had both taken notes as Shultz complained to Armacost that the
Israelis had been trying to revive the shipments, this time for TOW missiles. Shultz had remarked that this "blows our policy." After unsuccessfully opposing the shipments at the January 7, 1986, meeting with
Reagan, Bush, and the president's senior foreign policy advisors, Shultz
had dictated a brief note to Hill: "P [President Reagan] decided to go
ahead. Only Cap [Weinberger] and I opposed. I won't debf [debrief] anybody about it. (TOWs for hostages)."

When Shultz, Poindexter, Weinberger, and Casey were all in town on
Fridays, they had met for lunch in the family quarters of the White
House. On January 17, Shultz had told Hill about a "family group"
meeting at which he had learned that President Reagan had reauthorized the arms shipments to Iran. Platt had recorded that when Shultz
returned to the State Department and joined his top assistants for
lunch "He half shut his eyes—want it to be recorded as A unwise [and] B
illegal." Thereafter, Shultz had received reports, through Raphel, that
the arms-for-hostages operation had been resumed. Quinn had noted
that Shultz's direction to Armacost had been "Let's stay out. Just keep
informed." Platt had written, "Polecat lives."

On February 11, Shultz had attended another family group lunch,
and—according to Weinberger's notes—the participants had discussed
the planned delivery of a thousand TOW missiles for the release of
additional hostages. The missiles had been delivered between February
15 and 17, 1986, but no hostages had been released. Two weeks later,
after yet another such lunch, Shultz had told Hill and Platt that investigative reporter Jack Anderson had learned of the hostage deal
(although he had not broken the story), that the hostages were supposed to be released that weekend, and that Shultz had pleaded with
Poindexter to shut the operation down if no hostages were delivered.
Shultz had reported that the family group had agreed to respond with
"no comment" to any questions. "We will get crucified," he had
observed.

In April 1986, when Manucher Ghorbanifar visited Washington,
Shultz had commented to Hill and Platt that the Iranian was in town
with money to pay for missiles. Shultz had predicted that if
Ghorbanifar paid up, Poindexter would schedule McFarlane's trip to
Iran. Shultz had reported having told Poindexter, "This all has me horrified. The [Middle East] region [is] petrified that Iran will win and we
are helping them."

Poindexter had argued that TOWs were defensive weapons.

Shultz had replied "So's your old man."

According to Hill's notes from mid-April, Shultz had informed him that the plan was for McFarlane and North to go to Tehran in late April to work on an arms-for-hostages deal and to see Ali Akbar Rafsanjani. Shultz and Hill had been concerned about the danger of the mission. "How much will we pay to get McFarlane back?" Hill had asked.

Shultz had responded by saying that Poindexter had told him that although the Iranians had kept haggling, President Reagan had foreclosed further discussions. He had said, "Here's the deal, and that's it."

McFarlane's trip had actually taken place in May. Notes taken by Hill and Platt showed Shultz discussing the trip with them and with Armacost. They had known that weapons were to be transferred during the trip.

Charles Price, the U.S. ambassador to Great Britain, had heard a leak about McFarlane's mission and had cabled Platt, demanding to know what was going on. Armacost had worried that the arrest of six Israelis in another illegal arms sale to Iran would cause Israel to "blow [the] whistle on Polecat." Poindexter had assured Shultz, who had been in Tokyo for the presidential economic summit at the time, that there was little life in the projects, and that the rumors had been exaggerated. Through May, Shultz had continued trying to persuade Poindexter to halt the operation. Shultz's comments to Poindexter early in the month, recorded by Platt, had been sharp and unequivocal: "This is wrong & illegal & Pres. is way overexposed."

In mid-May, Weinberger had brought an intelligence report to a family group meeting at the White House and had shown it to Shultz. The report had described an arrangement to pay for the Hawk spare parts that the United States was sending to Iran with McFarlane's team. Intelligence reports received by Weinberger had also been seeping from his staff to the State Department officials. On May 27, according to one of Hill's notes, Hill had told Shultz that Poindexter had told Weinberger that "deliveries are being made of our military equipment—may see action today on release." The next day, Hill had recorded the failure of the mission.

Although Shultz had claimed to have received no information during the third phase specified in his congressional testimony, Gillen and Barrett told me that he had actually received foreign intelligence reports on McFarlane's mission. The British antiterrorism counterpart of Robert Oakley's unit had accused the United States of violating its "no concessions to terrorists policy." Oakley had written a formal memorandum to Shultz, reporting that "there was no doubt as to what was going on during the last ten days in May." It had been "a direct, blatant violation of basic hostage policy approved, re-approved, stated, and restated by the president and the secretary of state." Oakley had predicted leaks and embarrassment unless the initiative was stopped. The memorandum had gone to Platt. My staff and I did not believe that Platt would have withheld such a memorandum from Shultz, but we could not prove that Shultz had seen it.

In June, Arnold Raphel had passed a warning to Shultz through Platt's deputy, Kenneth Quinn, that intelligence reports Poindexter had discussed with Weinberger had left no doubt that the Iranian initiative was continuing. Weinberger had been instructed to increase the tilt toward Iran. A report from a friendly third country had disclosed a message from Rafsanjani that the initiative had continued. Fearing that the arms sales would be exposed and the president embarrassed, Raphel had urged that Shultz restate his opposition. According to Hill's notes, this memorandum had reached Shultz.

In a memorandum on July 2, Michael Armacost had added his warning that arms-for-hostages negotiations were continuing and that he expected a further hostage release—and the inevitable public disclosure of a wrongheaded policy. Word had been leaking from Amiram Nir through arms dealers. On the same day, according to Hill's notes, Shultz and Hill had discussed the possibility that hostages might be released; Shultz had complained that Casey had told him the initiative was dead when it was not.

Three weeks later, the Reverend Lawrence Jenco had been released. The notes we had obtained from Barrett's meticulous 1991 review of documents written by State Department officials Hill, Platt, Raphel, Quinn, and Ross mentioned that Jenco's release had been part of an arms deal. North had confirmed this fact to Oakley, and a senior Defense Department intelligence officer had confirmed it to Armacost. Jenco's release had been a hot topic among Shultz's principal assistants. They told us that they had discussed it with each other. Armacost and Platt had engaged in several conversations by secure phone with a vacationing Shultz. The aides agreed it was *likely* that they had told Shultz that they had learned that the release had been part of an arms deal, but none would testify that he had, in fact, told Shultz about it.

The essential flaw in Shultz's congressional testimony had resulted from its dependence on a chronology and a set of documents prepared and assembled by Hill. Hill, who had drafted Shultz's opening state-

ment for the Senate intelligence committee, had later collected his notes
supporting the testimony and had put them in a binder, which he had
eventually given to Sofaer and to FBI Special Agent Danny Coulson,
both of whom had understood the binder to contain all of Hill's relevant notes. Other State Department attorneys who had worked on
Shultz's testimony had apparently had the same erroneous impression.

Cross-checking the notes we were assembling, to make sure that there
were no more omissions, we developed material for extensive and precise examinations of several senior officials of the State Department.
Gillen, Barrett, and Baker questioned these individuals in the office and
before the grand jury. Inconsistencies between the statements of different officials sometimes required repeated examinations. The principal
witnesses had been outstanding career officials. In accordance with the
department's practice, they had alternated tours in Washington with
tours in our embassies abroad. By the time we were ready to question
the group that had served Shultz in Washington, its members had
spread across the globe. Whenever possible, we scheduled their examinations during their trips to Washington.

Dealing with such exceptionally skilled witnesses was a challenge,
particularly if they had gone over their testimony with Shultz's lawyers
before coming to us. Nevertheless, the notes we had obtained left little
room for further deception. Gillen, assisted by the younger lawyers,
questioned most of them. I depended on the interviewers' reports. If we
were not told all the truth, we certainly identified and narrowed the
gaps. In the year since Gillen and Barrett had first questioned Shultz in
Palo Alto, we had confirmed our view that he had not been forthcoming
to Congress. The question was whether his conduct had been criminal.
This had to be resolved by one last examination.

To accommodate Shultz, we deposed him in our office, rather than
call him before the grand jury. Gillen, supported by Barrett and Baker,
conducted the deposition; Shultz was represented by Lloyd Cutler.
Seated at the pushed-together tables in our austere white-walled conference room, with its closed venetian blinds, Shultz and Gillen came head
to head.

The deposition began at nine-thirty on the morning of February 2 and
lasted more than a day and a half. Testy and defiant at the outset, Shultz
realized that he was in trouble before the first morning was over. He initially expressed confidence that Hill had gone through his notebooks
and pulled out everything relevant about the Iranian initiative. Shultz

said that he had not personally participated in the process of reviewing the documents, but that Hill had spent several hours on more than one occasion locating the relevant notes, and that Sofaer had shared the responsibility for complete production. Hill's notebooks had always been available, Shultz argued, and the investigators themselves should have examined them—a disingenuous statement, inasmuch as Hill had never let outsiders examine more than extracts from his notebooks.

Combative about his congressional testimony, despite its apparent inconsistencies with the notes that Hill had withheld, Shultz dismissed some of the notes as "speculative" and suggested that we had misinterpreted others. He split hairs about the November 1985 Hawk missile delivery, claiming that he had been accurate in denying knowledge that the shipment had been "consummated," because the missiles had been rejected by the Iranians. He suggested that Weinberger's notes from the February 11, 1986, family group lunch might have reflected a side conversation between Weinberger and Casey instead of a discussion by the whole group.

Later, Shultz had to admit that many of Hill's notes had been "overlooked," both when Shultz's testimony was being prepared and when they were turned over to the FBI. Becoming ever more contrite, Shultz blamed Hill for his predicament. Shultz denied that he had placed any restraints on Hill as to what notes to produce or which notes to use in preparing his testimony.

In fact, as Gillen's questions made clear, the evidence of Shultz's misstatements went beyond the omitted notes. Information from the intelligence reports about North's activities and the arms sales had, when significant, been relayed to the State Department through its antiterrorism unit and to Shultz himself through Armacost, Platt, and Hill.

Cutler interrupted the deposition to consult with his client, to leave the room on breaks, and even to insert suggested reformulations of Gillen's questions or Shultz's answers—none of which could have happened before a grand jury. Nevertheless, the deposition was probably more productive than formal grand jury testimony would have been. Cutler recognized his client's problem and was wise enough to know that belligerence would not solve it. After returning from lunch, Shultz volunteered that if he had recalled that he had known about the continuing arms shipments, he certainly would have testified to that effect. There had been no reason not to do so, he said. He conceded that he was now "puzzled" about the inconsistency between his testimony and the contemporaneous notes.

Trying to accommodate Shultz's schedule, Gillen continued the deposition late into the afternoon and then broke for the day. When the deposition resumed the next morning, Shultz said that he accepted the accuracy of the notes taken by his staff. The notes had surprised him, he remarked. They no longer refreshed his recollection, he said, but if he had seen them before giving his congressional testimony, he would have testified differently.

In a subsequent meeting with Gillen and me, Cutler pointed out that Shultz's testimony had been essentially accurate, except for the opening summary of the three phases, which had been prepared by Hill.

As it happened, Shultz had been caught up in his battle to halt the Iranian initiative and to regain control over the administration's antiterrorism negotiations, leaving him little time to prepare for his congressional appearance. Preoccupied with protecting Shultz from his enemies within the administration, Hill, Platt, and others who ordinarily would have drafted and reviewed Shultz's testimony had delegated much of the task to two of Abraham Sofaer's assistants, who had not previously been privy to the discussions about the sale of arms to Iran.

As Shultz became increasingly isolated and frustrated with the manner in which the president and the other members of the National Security Planning Group were responding to the growing scandal, Sofaer, who might otherwise have participated more directly in the preparation of Shultz's testimony, had been protesting against the false chronologies that North, McFarlane, and the CIA officials had drafted for use by Poindexter and Casey in their congressional testimony. In the end, Sofaer had alerted Attorney General Edwin Meese and White House counsel Peter Wallison to North's false claim that no one in the U.S. government had had contemporaneous knowledge that Hawk missiles were being flown to Iran to obtain release of the hostages. In a sense, Sofaer's action had forced Donald Regan to enlist Meese in developing a coherent position for the administration.

During the turmoil, Shultz had worked on talking points to persuade President Reagan to discontinue the sales. Shultz's effort had become a preoccupation: He had publicly stated his opposition to any further arms sales to Iran; had admitted on *Face the Nation* that he could not speak for the administration; and, after Reagan's disastrous televised press conference, had tried to disabuse the president of his now hardened conviction that he had never authorized the sale of arms for hostages. Shultz had been nonplussed when Reagan acknowledged that he had known of the November 1985 Hawk shipment but believed it not to have been an arms-for-hostages deal.

On the morning of November 22, the day after Casey and Poindexter gave false testimony to the House and Senate intelligence committees, and while Casey, Weinberger, Nancy Reagan, and the vice president were with varying degrees of intensity considering a movement to displace him, Shultz had held his ground with Meese and told him that President Reagan had recently admitted having known about the Hawk shipment.

Weighing an indictment of Shultz, I thought of his conduct when confronted with the danger of being torn apart by the powerful, resourceful, cornered men who were building the firewall around the president: Shultz had been the sole advisor to tell Reagan not only that the Iranian policy had been a disaster, but also that only honesty could now save the president from his misconception that he had done nothing wrong. While preoccupied with our own political battles, I had to stand back and reflect on what this far more formidable challenge must have meant to someone like Shultz.

Although Shultz had never held elective office, few others in recent history had matched his career of outstanding government service. After a period as dean of the graduate school of business at the University of Chicago, he had joined Richard Nixon's administration as director of the Office of Management and Budget. Shultz had then become secretary of labor and later secretary of the Treasury. After leaving the government, he had served as the president of Bechtel Corporation, a worldwide leader in industrial construction. He had returned to government as the chairman of President Reagan's economic policy advisory board and had later become secretary of state. He was not a whistle-blower. At different times in his career, he had accommodated the rivalries and feuds of academic, industrial, and political strife. Unscathed by the Watergate scandal, he had witnessed it at close range and had learned its primary lesson: that cover-ups are more corrosive than the crimes they would shield. Alone among Reagan's senior advisors, Shultz had foreseen—and warned against—the inevitable and fearful destruction of reputations as subordinates were drawn into lies and other misconduct to protect the false position of the president.

I did not know that while Shultz and his wife were flying back from Vienna, she had asked him whether he would resign. But I realized that day and night, that question had confronted Shultz, not because of his own mistakes but because of the conflict between the loyalty he owed the president and the loyalty he owed the people of the United States. Under these circumstances, could I or anyone else prove beyond a reasonable doubt that the misstatements in Shultz's testimony had been deliberately false? I had to admit that I had no urge to prosecute the one voice of courage and reason among Reagan's senior foreign policy advisors—the one person who had urged him to get the whole truth out to the public promptly.

Hill and Platt had been only slightly less deeply involved in the battle with Poindexter and Casey than Shultz had been. Caught in a political maelstrom, they had responded as would most career foreign service officers. For one brief period in my career, I had worked closely with foreign service officers and admired them. Drawn from a gifted group, expertly trained, they had maintained civilized dialogue with foreign countries, regardless of political fortunes and misfortunes here and abroad. I had found some of these foreign service officers disdainful of the amateurs thrust upon them, amateurs who might shortsightedly disrupt patiently developed relationships by intuitive outbursts. Nonetheless, however understandable within the department, disdain had no place in dealing with Congress or with those who enforced the law.

Although I had seen him only twice, as he took notes of my early interviews with Secretary Shultz, Charles Hill appeared to epitomize these foreign service officers in ability and attitude. I imagined Platt to be much the same. It seemed to me that Hill and Platt had not hesitated to reach a joint decision on which notes to surrender and which to withhold; at the very least, they had decided on the criteria to be applied.

Having decided that Shultz could not be prosecuted, I was again facing the possibility of prosecuting career officers—subordinates—as substitutes. We had prosecuted Alan Fiers, Clair George, and Elliott Abrams for knowingly telling relatively simple lies to avoid the loss of a $100 million appropriation for the CIA. We were now prosecuting Duane Clarridge for lying about his unauthorized participation in a transaction whose very nature he had falsified. Whereas those we prosecuted had also assisted or supervised North in his activities, however, Hill and Platt had been critical bystanders. The misdeeds of Hill and Platt had been part of a complex, intermittent series of discordant activities in which they had been reporters, not central, active players. We had painstakingly investigated their actions. We would fully report our findings. But this time, I decided not to indict the subordinates.

CHAPTER EIGHTEEN

The Note-Taker

While the congressional select committees on Iran-Contra were conducting their hearings, George Shultz had remarked to his executive assistant, Charles Hill, that Caspar Weinberger had taken notes but had "never referred to them," so he had "never had to cough them up." In August 1990, when John Barrett deciphered the note that Hill had made of this conversation, it had been a tantalizing lead.

We had previously surmised that Weinberger, a well-known opponent of the sale of arms to Iran, had been no more than peripherally involved in the illegal activities of Robert McFarlane, John Poindexter, and Oliver North. Although the 1985 arms sales had violated the Arms Export Control Act, we had long since concluded that because the act did not specify criminal sanctions, we could not prosecute anyone under it. Consequently, our principal focus had been on the illegal covert action undertaken by Poindexter and North to supply the Contras without the requisite formal presidential authorization and notice to Congress.

One of Weinberger's close friends, Assistant Secretary of Defense Richard Armitage, had been a member of the restricted interagency group on Central America, which meant that Weinberger had likely been privy to the information discussed by the RIG. Armitage had not, however, been a member of the "RIGLET," the core triumvirate of Oliver North, Alan Fiers, and Elliott Abrams, who had had the most intimate knowledge of the Contra-supply operation.

To assure ourselves that there had been no legal basis for North's having marked up the prices the Iranians had paid for the U.S. weapons, two of my young associate counsel had interviewed Weinberger in April 1988, just after the grand jury indicted Poindexter, North, Secord, and

Hakim. In the course of the interview, the lawyers had asked Weinberger if he had any notes. He had told them that he was in the "habit of making notes on any piece of paper [he] could get [his] hands on," and that his secretaries had kept them for a while but had long ago discontinued the practice. In his first year as secretary of defense, according to Weinberger, he had occasionally made notes on the back of his briefing papers for meetings and had originally given them to his secretary to keep, but he had stopped doing so.

When Weinberger was interviewed by the Tower Commission, he had complained that accurate minutes had not been taken at all the meetings of the National Security Council and National Security Policy Group. Although he had conceded that someone might have taken notes, he had said, "I don't know of any." He had urged the commission to recommend that in the future, accurate records be kept to show "who said what to whom and when."

Caspar Weinberger had been a pillar of the Republican establishment. A native of San Francisco, he had gone east for college and law school. Upon his graduation from the Harvard Law School at the beginning of World War II, he had entered the Army as a private. He had earned a Bronze Star and left the service in 1945 as a captain. After spending six years in the California legislature, he had become vice chairman and later chairman of the California Republican Central Committee. When Ronald Reagan was governor of California, Weinberger had served as chairman of the Committee on California Government Organization and Economics and then as the state's director of finance.

During President Richard Nixon's administration, Weinberger had come to Washington as chairman of the Federal Trade Commission. He had then served as deputy director (under George Shultz) and later director of the Office of Management and Budget, where he had been known as "Cap the Knife." After a brief period as counselor to President Nixon, Weinberger had been appointed secretary of health, education, and welfare. He had left Washington to become general counsel to the Bechtel Corporation and its affiliates; at the time, George Shultz had been Bechtel's president.

After Ronald Reagan was elected president, he had brought Weinberger to Washington as secretary of defense. Weinberger had not only shared Reagan's ideology but had also been devoted to the president. Weinberger had become Reagan's point man in rebuilding the Defense Department and strengthening the U.S. military establishment.

Liked and admired within the department and by Congress, Weinberger had successfully advocated increases in defense appropriations while other parts of the government were being shrunk to permit a tax cut. He had retired as secretary of defense in 1987 and received the presidential Medal of Freedom with distinction as well as a number of high honors from several foreign countries.

After Barrett found Shultz's revelation that Weinberger had taken notes that he had not produced, we had tried to reach Weinberger to arrange an interview and obtain any notes that he might have had, but his secretary had brushed us off repeatedly. Finally, we had issued a grand jury subpoena. Weinberger had avoided being served the subpoena until Mike Foster, our senior FBI agent, caught up with him as he left his office building through the service entrance and threaded his way through barrels of refuse toward a waiting car.

That morning, my friend Bill Rogers telephoned me to ask if we were investigating Weinberger. Bill explained that he was acting for Weinberger because Weinberger was then associated with Bill's firm as counsel. Bill told me that he had to decide whether to get another lawyer for Weinberger. Because of our long relationship, Bill had previously declined to represent subjects of my investigation. (Bill and I had worked closely together in Thomas E. Dewey's district attorney's office and when I had served under Bill while he was attorney general.) I was surprised by the call and thought that he was overreacting to our interest in Weinberger. Bill observed that it would be unjust to pursue a man who had so consistently opposed President Reagan's arms sales to Iran. I assured Bill that I did not think we would want to pursue Weinberger, although we wanted his notes and his help.

Bill told me that he would talk to Weinberger but he was not sure that he had any notes. Later, Bill told Craig Gillen that Weinberger had previously given whatever notes he possessed to the congressional committees or had deposited them in the Library of Congress. As a courtesy, Gillen told Rogers that we had obtained information from two sources that Weinberger had notes that he had not turned over. Following our normal practice, Gillen did not disclose the sources (the comment made by Weinberger in his 1988 interview with my staff and the note George Shultz had dictated to Charles Hill), because we wanted every witness's own full statement, not just the verification of information we already had. In any event, Bill said that Weinberger would voluntarily submit to an interview, so we withdrew the subpoena.

On October 10, 1990, Gillen and his assistant, Tom Bever, interviewed Weinberger, who had come to our office accompanied by Rogers. Mike Foster took notes for an FBI report of the interview. (We customarily did not make verbatim records of preliminary interviews, preferring to give witnesses time to fully refresh their recollections before taking formal depositions or calling them before the grand jury.) Over Foster's protest, Gillen let Rogers and Weinberger read the FBI report of Weinberger's earlier interview, in which he had mentioned his note-taking habit.

Bridling, Weinberger characterized this portion of the report as misleading and said that it incorrectly implied that he habitually took notes, when this was not the case. Repeating what he had said in the 1988 interview, he explained that early in his tenure as secretary of defense, he had taken notes on the backs of pages in his briefing books at meetings, and that his secretaries initially had saved these notes so that he could dictate memoranda. He claimed, however, to have largely discontinued the practice after the first year because he had not had time to consolidate the notes in useful memoranda. Thereafter, he said, he had rarely taken notes at meetings, and few of them had been saved.

He claimed that as a rule, he had not taken notes of meetings with the president or other cabinet members, because it would have been in "bad form." Weinberger said that he specifically recalled not having taken any notes when meeting with the president and other cabinet members to discuss the sale of arms to Iran. Nor, said Weinberger, was he aware of notes having been taken by other participants in these meetings. He said that he had not made records of meetings after returning to his office or when talking on the telephone.

After mentioning that President Reagan had instructed the members of his cabinet to cooperate with the Iran-Contra investigations, Weinberger stated that he had ordered his staff and others at the Defense Department to turn over all notes and documents they had to the various Iran-Contra investigators, Weinberger said that he was not aware that any of his relevant notes regarding Iran-Contra had not been turned over. He maintained that he had not deliberately withheld anything from the congressional investigators or from us.

Without identifying Hill as the source, Gillen told Weinberger that we had a document, written by someone whom Weinberger would consider credible, stating that Weinberger had withheld notes related to

Iran-Contra. Angrily, Weinberger said that he distrusted our unnamed source and questioned his motivation.

Through Rogers, Weinberger consented for us to review his papers in the Library of Congress, but only under the supervision of his longtime secretary, Kay Leisz. Greg Mark, a young associate counsel, went to the library to review the papers. Misled by Weinberger's statement that any surviving notes would be on the back of classified briefing material, Mark was not surprised when the librarian handed him a register that was opened to the classified section. Mark carefully searched the relevant classified portion of the collection but found only a few documents related to Iran-Contra, which was consistent with Weinberger's statement to Gillen. When Mark asked to look through other parts of the collection, Leisz and the librarian told him that he could see only those items that specified Iran or a Central American country in the register. During the second and third day of the search, Mark was joined by fellow associate counsel Mike Vhay. The conditions were the same. Leisz would not even let them examine the file of a country through which an arms delivery had been routed. Accepting Weinberger's statement that he had made few notes, Mark and Vhay did not alert me to this problem.

A year later, in November 1991, recently hired associate counsel Tom Baker went to the Library of Congress with Mike Vhay for another look at Weinberger's notes. Leisz and a different librarian, who was less overbearing, were there. Baker began by reading the entire register that itemized the collection. As he ran through the unclassified section, he found references to hundreds of pages of diary and meeting notes that Weinberger had kept during the period of Iran-Contra activity. Most of the material should have been classified, because it contained some of the country's most sensitive secrets (the most explosive did not relate to Iran-Contra). It would have been obvious even to the uninitiated that these documents did not belong with the unclassified material.

The notes were stacked in boxes. Baker asked for the ones that seemed to be on White House stationery. The first note he picked up was Weinberger's record of Robert McFarlane's report on his December 1985 meeting with Iranian intermediary Manucher Ghorbanifar in London. Baker was familiar with Weinberger's congressional testimony and knew that he had denied having known that the United States was to replace the TOW missiles Israel had shipped to Iran in 1985. Baker was therefore astonished to read in Weinberger's handwriting that the Israeli TOWs were to be replaced by American weapons. Baker next picked up a diary note Weinberger had written in November 1985, as he argued with McFarlane about the illegality of the proposed Hawk shipment and expressed his objection to it, only to be overruled by the president.

Baker then came upon a note in which Weinberger had recorded the November 24, 1986, meeting of Reagan's senior advisors. Baker read with amazement the literal account of the attorney general of the United States telling the group that the president had not known of the Hawk shipment and that if he had authorized it, it would have been illegal.

> *Don Regan*
>   Did we object to Israeli
> sending Hawks shipment
> missiles—to Iran?
>
> *Poindexter—*
>   From July 85 to *Dec 7*
> McFarlane handled this all
> alone—no documentation—
>
> —he went to London—Dec. 7
>
> *EM* [Edwin Meese]:—Israelis told Bud
>   that if we could get big
> weapons supply to Iran we could
> get all hostages out.
>
> — — —
>
> Shultz—he didn't discuss it—
> he told me—
>
> *EM:* Plan was to put
>   Hawks missile into
> [European country] +
> then to Tehran with
> Hawk missiles—
>
> — — —
>
> 18 Hawks—sat at Tehran—
> *returned* later—because Iran
> did not want them.
>
> Not legal because no finding
> president *not* informed.

Having had little experience in criminal investigation, Baker blurted, "My God! Look at this!" Leisz asked what had surprised him. Vhay, fearing the possible destruction of the note, tried to divert the conversation to a technical question of whether we should take copies of notes we already had in our files. Leisz was not deceived. So the conversation quickly came back to reality, as Vhay and Baker made it clear that we would have to have the notes. The librarian's response was that the library's hands were tied; it could not release the notes to us without Weinberger's consent. Vhay and Baker told the librarian that they should have been classified.

Weinberger had regularly taken notes of his activities since high school. As secretary of defense, he had taken enough notes to fill more than seven thousand pages, of which nearly seventeen hundred dated from the Iran-Contra era. In his office, as General Colin Powell and other intimates described it, Weinberger had often stood at a reading desk to relieve his back pain and had written on a five-by-seven-inch government notepad or a leather-jacketed legal pad. He had always kept both on his desk. When a pad was full, he had put it into a desk drawer; when the desk drawer was full, he had moved the pads into the bedroom that was attached to his office.

Weinberger had also taken copious notes at meetings, including White House and cabinet meetings. These notes had sometimes been written on his briefing papers and included drawings, doodles, and slips of paper with comments written by others. His secretaries and military assistants had known about his note-keeping practices. He had frequently given his meeting notes to his secretaries, who had typed his comments. The secretaries had kept some notes and had even labeled and cross-referenced them, but many—including those most important to Iran-Contra—had been retained by Weinberger himself.

After resigning as secretary of defense, he had personally supervised the transfer of his notes to the Library of Congress, with instructions that no one could look at them without his express permission. The library, eager to possess such a historical resource, had not resisted this condition, nor had it questioned the propriety of accepting as Weinberger's personal property notes and records he had made in the course of his official activities.

The notes had been divided into two sets. Set A consisted of original meeting notes, including most of the notes from meetings related to Iran-Contra. These notes had gone directly from Weinberger to the library without being reviewed for possible classification. Set B, which had arrived at the library later, comprised copies of some of

Weinberger's notes, with notations by his secretaries. These notes had been individually indexed for the official files of Weinberger's office and had been reviewed for classification. Many of them had been transferred to the library through the Defense Department's correspondence and directives section, but none of the notes had been in the department's record-keeping system.

After Vhay and Baker warned the librarian that we wanted the notes, further discussions with library officials ensued. Weinberger insisted on reading the notes before turning them over to us. To avoid being delayed by litigation, we agreed to this. But to protect the notes, we sub-poenaed them, which meant that any destruction or alteration of the notes would subject the library staff as well as Weinberger to contempt-of-court and possible felony charges. Weinberger completed his exami-nation of the notes while they were under grand jury subpoena, and they were delivered to us a month after being discovered.

Weinberger's handwriting was difficult to read. Baker and Christina Spaulding, another new associate counsel, spent weeks sifting through all the notes Weinberger had taken while he was secretary of defense and summarizing the relevant ones. Baker and Spaulding found nearly two hundred pages that concerned the sale of arms to Iran. As their work proceeded, our fascination with the disclosures was matched by a deepening realization that Weinberger, hero or not, had deliberately lied to the Tower Commission, to Congress, and to us. The notes con-firmed McFarlane's claim that Weinberger had known in advance that the president had approved the November 1985 Hawk shipment.

In addition to helping us evaluate what other individuals had told us, the notes raised new questions about persons we had not pursued very aggressively. Donald Regan, for example, was revealed as Edwin Meese's foil at the November 24, 1986, meeting in which Meese had warned Reagan's advisors that the president had to be protected from any men-tion that he had known of the Hawk shipment before it took place. We would have to take a new look at Regan.

Colin Powell, Weinberger's senior military assistant from 1983 to 1986, had been mentioned frequently in the notes, so we questioned him. Despite his personal loyalty to Weinberger, Powell confirmed the substance of the notes we asked him to review and also the fact that Weinberger had habitually kept them. Throughout the interview, Powell was responsive and cooperative. He had a commanding pres-ence: Although my staff had seen a long parade of high-ranking wit-nesses come through our office, many of the nonlawyers "snapped to" in admiration as Powell entered. The GSA security guard who sat out-side the office door, sometimes reading a newspaper, actually stood at attention, and others hurried to bring coffee. Everybody respected Powell's accomplishments, but the lawyers recognized that he would make a formidable witness.

We interviewed several Defense Department officials who had been responsible for the production of documents to Congress and my office. These witnesses included the former deputy secretary, William H. Taft IV; the former general counsel, Lawrence Garrett, who had recently been appointed secretary of the Navy; former assistant general counsel Edward J. Shapiro; the former assistant secretary of defense, Richard Armitage; and Weinberger's former personal secretaries, Kay Leisz and Thelma Stubbs Smith.

Once Weinberger's stream of notes had been deciphered, they gave us the equivalent of a reel of motion-picture frames captured by a camera monitoring his office and narrated by his candid, contemporaneous annotations. The resulting depiction of his involvement in Iran-Contra was dramatically at odds with the impression he had created with his congressional testimony. Throughout 1985 and 1986, Weinberger had kept abreast of the illicit arms sales with information supplied by McFarlane and Poindexter, at meetings with the president, and in dis-cussions with individual foreign policy advisors. Like McFarlane, Poindexter, and William Casey, Weinberger had received highly classi-fied intelligence reports contemporaneously revealing the arms-for-hostages negotiations. He had also been given condensed versions of other information that had accumulated at lower levels in the State and Defense departments.

In June 1985, when McFarlane circulated his draft proposal for a new national security directive to improve relations with Iran by providing it with military equipment, Weinberger had rejected the proposal, saying in a marginal note, "This is almost too absurd to comment on—the assumption here is 1) Iran is about to fall; plus, 2) we can deal with them on a rational basis—It's like asking Quadhaffi [sic] to Washington for a cozy chat." Weinberger had sent McFarlane a memorandum opposing any easing of restrictions on arms shipments to Iran and had always begun his congressional testimony by citing the comment he had writ-ten in the margin of McFarlane's proposal.

In mid-July 1985, after the proposal was rejected, McFarlane had informed Weinberger and Shultz that an Israeli emissary claiming to be in contact with Iranian moderates believed that they could secure the release of the seven American hostages if the United States authorized the delivery of a hundred TOW missiles to Iran. The weapons were to be not a ransom but a token of the seriousness with which the United States viewed possible negotiations with Iran. In testifying before the Tower Commission and the congressional committees, Weinberger had referred vaguely to this meeting and emphasized that he had protested against any change in U.S. policy toward Iran.

His prepared testimony had invariably skipped over the next several months; he had claimed that he had been uninformed during this period. Hidden in this gap had been Ronald Reagan's personal participation in the decision to ship arms to Iran through Israel. After the president authorized McFarlane to give Israel the go-ahead to make the transfer of arms, McFarlane had met with Weinberger and Powell at the Pentagon and had told them that the transaction would go forward. Weinberger, according to his notes, had urged McFarlane to insist on the release of all the hostages but had subsequently been informed that only the Reverend Benjamin Weir would be released. Two days later, Weinberger had discussed the matter with McFarlane, Shultz, and Casey at a family group lunch at the White House. By then, Powell had told Weinberger that the Joint Chiefs of Staff had been receiving contemporaneous intelligence reports of the arms-for-hostages negotiations. Weinberger had insisted that he personally receive copies of the reports.

Weir's release in September 1985 had kept alive the hope that a more generous delivery of weapons would result in the release of all the hostages. With this expectation, President Reagan had authorized the Israelis to transfer hundreds of Hawk missiles to the Iranians.

According to Weinberger's notes, on November 19, 1985, just before the president and McFarlane left for Geneva to meet Soviet leader Mikhail Gorbachev, McFarlane had asked Weinberger to supply five hundred Hawk missiles for transfer to Israel to replace those to be sent to Iran. McFarlane had told Weinberger that five hostages were to be released in two days. Weinberger had passed the request to Powell. Working with Noel Koch, Armitage's deputy, Powell had turned to Henry Gaffney, the acting director of the Defense Security Assistance Agency. Gaffney had reported that fewer than two hundred Hawks were available and that they could not be sold to Israel without notice to Congress.

Weinberger's notes revealed that after Powell relayed Gaffney's response, Weinberger had telephoned McFarlane in Geneva to protest the illegality of the sales. McFarlane had brushed Weinberger off, simply thanking him "for the call." The next day, McFarlane had told Weinberger that President Reagan had decided to send 120 of the available Hawks to the Iranians through Israel. A few days later, Weinberger had received intelligence reports confirming that the first shipment of eighteen Hawks had been delivered on November 24, 1985.

After the shipment turned into a debacle, Reagan had arranged to meet with his senior foreign policy advisors on December 7 to discuss North's proposal for renewing arms shipments to Iran. Early that morning, Armitage had briefed Weinberger and Powell as the secretary prepared for the meeting. According to Weinberger's notes, he had "met with Colin Powell & Rich Armitage—re: NSC plan to let Israelis give Iranians 50 HAWKs plus 3,300 TOWs in return for 5 hostages—NSC will present it as a means of helping group that wants to overthrow the gov't—but no assurance that any of this—weapons will go to Iranian army."

At the White House meeting, according to his notes, Weinberger had warned Reagan that the arms sales would violate the U.S. embargo on arms shipments to Iran, and that "washing" an arms transfer through Israel would not make it legal. Weinberger had noted that "Shultz, Don Regan agreed" with him.

The president, however, had dismissed any concerns regarding the illegality of the sales. According to Weinberger's notes, the president had said that "he could answer charges of illegality, but he couldn't answer charge that 'big strong President Reagan passed up a chance to free hostages.'" Shultz's notes confirmed Weinberger's. When the president joked about going to jail, Weinberger had told him he would not be alone.

Congressional committees, questioning all the participants of the meeting, had learned of this exchange, but in his deposition to the select committees on Iran-Contra, Weinberger had denied that the president had ridiculed his concern about the shipment's illegality. Asked whether he recalled saying, "Yes, Mr. President, but the problem is you won't be alone," Weinberger had replied, "No. There wasn't anything of that kind. I made the point that it was—at some point, then or in the January meeting, maybe both—that it was illegal, among other things, but I also talked on the policy aspects of it. I talked on the effects it would have on our friends. I talked on the idea that it wouldn't accomplish what [we wanted] to do in any event because of the kinds of people in Iran.

"The only thing that strikes at all a home chord was that the president at some time, some meeting, said, 'The American people, or no one, could forgive me if I didn't do everything possible to get Americans who are held anywhere released.' But it was not in connection with violating the law or anything like that.... I don't recall anything about the president ever saying anything about violating the law."

On December 10, in the Oval Office, McFarlane had briefed Reagan, Weinberger, Casey, Regan, Poindexter, and North on McFarlane's frustrations in dealing with Manucher Ghorbanifar. McFarlane had advised separating the issue of freeing the hostages from that of improving relations with Iran. President Reagan had said he wanted to try to get the hostages released, even if that meant asking the Israelis to proceed alone. McFarlane had reminded the group that the United States still had to replace the TOWs that Israel had sold to Iran when the first hostage was released. Weinberger had taken two pages of notes on White House stationery and had later written a summary for inclusion with his daily diary notes. After he returned to the Pentagon, he had also scribbled more notes while briefing Colin Powell on the meeting.

When Weinberger testified before the Senate intelligence committee after the exposure of the arms sales, he had made no effort to review his voluminous notes. Instead, he had apparently decided not to refresh his memory but to try to slip through the hearings by following a laudatory outline prepared by Armitage. When asked questions not anticipated by the outline, Weinberger had obviously improvised. He had denied that the group at the December 7 meeting had agreed to send McFarlane to London. He had claimed to have learned about the trip from intelligence sources. He had denied recalling that discussions of arms shipments had continued through December. He had said that he did not remember any discussion with the president between December 7 and January 7, when the president had first discussed a formal finding that would authorize arms sales by the United States to Iran.

Anticipating Weinberger's probable resistance and legal questions about future arms sales through Israel, Oliver North and the CIA's general counsel, Stanley Sporkin, had drafted and redrafted the finding authorizing the CIA to buy the arms and to make the sales without notice to Congress. Attorney General Meese, relying on the president's constitutional responsibility for foreign affairs, had given his opinion that the National Security Act's specific requirement of notice to Congress could be met after the hostages were released. Weinberger had insisted that his own lawyers review the finding.

On January 6, Poindexter had given Reagan the finding, and the president had signed it. The following day, without mentioning that the finding had already been signed, Reagan and Poindexter had discussed with Shultz, Weinberger, Meese, Casey, Regan, and George Bush the proposal for the CIA to sell TOWs to Iran through Israel. Shultz and Weinberger had continued to oppose the arms shipments. Weinberger had again argued that they would violate the Arms Export Control Act. Meese had responded that the Economy Act authorized sales from the Defense Department to the CIA at cost and the National Security Act permitted the CIA to sell arms to the Iranians directly or through an intermediary if the sale had been authorized by a presidential finding.

At this meeting, Weinberger had written a page of notes on White House stationery, recording Shultz's opposition and his own skepticism that the professed arms deal would lead to any moderation of the Iranian government or any significant improvement in the relations between the United States and Iran. When he returned to the Pentagon, he had also made a diary note: "George Shultz & I oppose—Bill Casey, Ed Meese & VP favored—as did Poindexter."

Ten days later, Weinberger had transcribed a meeting with Poindexter, Powell, and Koch at the Pentagon to plan further arms sales. Weinberger had then conferred with Poindexter, Casey, Meese, and Sporkin. Still doubting the legality of the sale of U.S. arms to Iran without notice to Congress, Weinberger had flatly opposed a Defense Department sale under the Arms Export Control Act through Israel. Casey had agreed to have the CIA buy the arms and sell them to the Iranians.

The finding already signed by the president had authorized this transaction, but Sporkin had corrected a technical defect in the language of one paragraph, and Reagan had signed a revised finding on January 17. Weinberger, unaware that any finding had been signed, had questioned the legality of the deal in several complaints to Powell and to Shultz, Casey, and Poindexter. During late January, Weinberger had talked with Powell, then had telephoned Poindexter and read him the statutes. Weinberger had finally given up: His notes reported, "They are going on with it."

To the Senate intelligence committee, Weinberger had denied having had contemporaneous knowledge of the presidential finding. When asked to describe his "participation in the drafting of the finding that was eventually adopted," Weinberger had replied, "Zero. I didn't know there was one." He had said that he had not been shown the finding "until much later." When the chairman expressed surprise that Weinberger would not have been notified of the finding in a timely manner, Weinberger had said, "It was extraordinary to me to find out ten or twelve months later that there had been a finding made that I had not seen."

The day after President Reagan signed the finding, Poindexter and North had promptly commenced operations. Weinberger's diary notes showed that he had regularly followed their progress, with updates almost every other day. He had protested when Poindexter ordered Clair George to give the Iranians U.S. intelligence about the disposition of Iraqi military forces. As the arms shipments proceeded, Weinberger's notes had become less frequent but had recorded his participation in discussions at the White House family group lunches. Weinberger had closely monitored the numbers of weapons shipped and the proposed dates of the shipments. He and Powell had also followed ongoing intelligence reports distributed by the National Security Agency.

On March 4, after two shipments of five hundred TOWs failed to win the release of a single hostage, Weinberger had learned from Poindexter of McFarlane's proposed trip to Iran. Three days later, Weinberger had jotted down notes while expressing exasperation to Powell. On April 10, William Taft had advised Weinberger, who was traveling in Australia, of a new proposal to exchange Hawk spare parts for the hostages. On his return to the United States, Weinberger had confided to Vice Admiral Donald S. Jones, who had just replaced Colin Powell as Weinberger's senior military assistant, that McFarlane's trip was "idiocy." Weinberger had telephoned Poindexter to repeat his opposition at that time and had made another such call on April 18.

In May, Weinberger had alerted Shultz that a recent intelligence report indicated that, contrary to North's assurances, the Iranians had not promised to release any hostages. Weinberger had yet again urged Poindexter to drop the effort. Later that month, while Weinberger was vacationing in Maine, Armitage had telephoned him with the news that McFarlane and his party were en route to Iran. Four days later, Armitage had reported the failure of the mission. The next day, Poindexter had told Weinberger that McFarlane had failed because the Iranians had not discussed the matter in advance with the Shiites who were holding the hostages. Weinberger's diary notes provided us with a running account of all these conversations.

After McFarlane's mission, Weinberger's notes on the arms sales had become sporadic until Father Lawrence Martin Jenco was released in the summer of 1986. The notes showed Weinberger and Shultz arguing with Poindexter that all the hostages should be returned before further arms shipments were delivered. In the month before election day, as plans for the release of David Jacobsen were formulated, Weinberger had again made notes about the arms sales. The Defense Department had been asked to provide five hundred more TOWs for delivery before the expected release. Poindexter had also asked Weinberger to provide military forces to pick up Jacobsen when he was released.

Particularly significant were Weinberger's notes describing the actions President Reagan and his advisors had taken after the public revelation of the arms sales to Iran. Although he had previously joined Shultz in protesting the arms sales, Weinberger had opposed Shultz's efforts to tell the public the truth. In writing up a telephone call to Poindexter on November 5, 1986, Weinberger had disparaged Shultz for having suggested "telling all." According to his notes, Weinberger had "strongly objected. I [said] we should simply say nothing—John [Poindexter] agrees."

Two days later, Weinberger had complained to Poindexter about White House spokesman Larry Speakes's having said that Shultz and Weinberger had known all about the transactions with Iran. On November 9, Weinberger had telephoned Poindexter to say he thought that no congressional hearings on the scandal would be held until after January. The notes, however, showed that Weinberger had immediately begun a self-serving preparation for such hearings, directing Armitage to go over the "chronology of arguments I made to [the] president against [the arms sales]."

The next day, Weinberger had skipped a Marine Corps ceremony to meet with Ronald Reagan and his top foreign policy advisors, including Bush, Shultz, Casey, Regan, Poindexter, and Poindexter's deputy, Alton Keel. Weinberger's extensive handwritten notes of this meeting provided us with much greater detail than had the notes by other participants. At the meeting, Poindexter had described the flow of weapons as though all of them had gone through Israel to Iran beginning after the January 17, 1986, presidential finding. The previous Israeli shipment of five hundred TOW missiles had been portrayed as having occurred without U.S. knowledge.

Casey had sought the group's approval of a proposed public statement that the administration had been trying to improve its contacts with Iran and to end the Iran-Iraq war; that the administration had avoided shipments that could have affected the result of that war; and that, as Weinberger's notes put it, "we have not given in on not paying for hostages—we do need to encourage people who can help [and] we need to pursue dialogue with Iran—president made decision bearing in mind risks."

Reagan had stated that they should "point out in that [statement] that discussion *endangers* sources [and] our plans."

Shultz had commented, "It is [the] responsibility of [government] to look after its citizens, but once you do deal for hostages, you expose everyone to future capture. We don't know, but have to assume [that] the captors *did* get something. Don't emphasize that we only sent small numbers of weapons. [The] Israelis sucked us into this so we couldn't object to their sales to Iran. . . ."

"We shouldn't take any questions after issuing the [statement]," the president had said.

"We are being hung out to dry," Don Regan had complained. "Our credibility is at stake. We'll have to say *enough*."

"We must make it plain we are not doing business with terrorists," Reagan had asserted. "We aren't paying them. We *are* trying to get a better relationship with Iran, [and] we can't add to this [without] endangering people we are dealing with. We are within the law plus our rights."

"We have to bear in mind," Weinberger had warned, "that we can be blackmailed by [the] Iranians plus Israelis."

After the meeting, in which the president had decided not to make a candid disclosure, Weinberger had lunched with an unhappy Shultz, who had complained about the president's acceptance of a public statement proposed by Casey.

Two days later, after President Reagan met with congressional leaders, Weinberger had written a long memorandum about the meeting. Again, Weinberger had been more expansive than had any of the other individuals whose notes we had obtained. He had listened, along with the president, vice president, Shultz, Weinberger, and Meese, as Poindexter briefed Senate Majority Leader Robert Byrd, Senate Minority Leader Bob Dole, Speaker of the House Jim Wright, and House Minority Whip Dick Cheney in the White House situation room. When the meeting began, the president had said that it was important to know what had not been done: The administration had not negotiated with terrorists, and there had been "no bargaining with terrorists." The president had characterized the Iranian initiative as a

covert intelligence operation, not a rogue operation "being run out of
the White House basement." He had described the operation's purpose
as having been "to improve our strategic position in the Middle East.
[This was] important because of Iranian oil and [the] USSR. We also
wanted to get [the] hostages released."

Poindexter had then taken over the briefing. He had read the January
17, 1986, finding and reported that three hostages had been freed. He
had declared that a small amount of arms had been transferred to show
our good faith and to allay suspicion; that we had found out earlier that
the Israelis had been sending arms to Iran in order to get Iranian Jews
out; and that the Israelis wanted the Iran-Iraq war to go on.

"But aren't you trading arms for hostages?" Dole had asked.

"No," the president had replied, "we'd try to open contacts with or
[without] the hostages."

When Byrd asked Shultz if he had not opposed the program, Shultz
had said that he had attended two meetings but that he never discussed
the advice he gave the president. Weinberger had then given the same
answer.

"Weren't contacts initiated before January 1986?" Byrd had asked.

Poindexter had acknowledged that they were. Weinberger's notes
omitted the statement that had followed, but according to Alton Keel's
notes, Poindexter had told Byrd that no weapons had been shipped
until after the January 1986 finding.

The day after this meeting, Weinberger had met with William Casey,
Robert Gates, and William Taft to discuss possible changes in the
speech the president was to give that night. Weinberger had then conferred with Shultz, who had said he did not like the speech because it
was not forthright. Weinberger had next discussed proposed changes
with Keel, one of the principal drafters.

On Friday, November 21, Weinberger had met with Poindexter and
the president in the Oval Office and had urged that everybody stop talking about Iran. According to his notes, the three men had discussed the
testimony Weinberger would give; later, Meese had asked him to "put
together [a] paper covering [the] whole Iran episode."

On Saturday, Weinberger had briefly reviewed his planned testimony
over a secure telephone link with Colin Powell, who was then in
Germany, commanding the U.S. Army V Corps. Weinberger had next
conferred with Armitage and with Admiral William Crowe, chairman of
the Joint Chiefs of Staff, about the congressional testimony Casey had
given the previous day. At a time when Casey and Poindexter were deny-

ing contemporaneous knowledge of the November 1985 Hawk shipment, Weinberger had written a note describing it as a "possible illegal Israeli shipment via CIA carrier last Nov. (before any finding) to Iran."

Prince Bandar, the Saudi ambassador, had visited Weinberger in his office on Sunday to let him know that Nancy Reagan had said that she thought Shultz should go because he had been disloyal to the president. Weinberger had noted Bandar's report that he had recommended to the first lady that Weinberger be named secretary of state—"that I could negotiate an agreement with Soviets because no one could say I was soft on them. She feels that very few are being loyal to president. . . . [She] would like [James] Baker to go in as secretary of defense." On Monday, Weinberger had called his friend William Clark in California and relayed Prince Bandar's comments.

Shocked as we were to read of the Saudi ambassador's maneuvering to select our secretary of state, we were more interested in Weinberger's notes concerning the November 24 White House meeting in which Meese had outlined the false story to be used to cover up President Reagan's illegal authorization of the November 1985 Hawk shipment. There were no official notes because no staff had been present in the situation room. We had Meese's notes, but he had omitted his own comments. (He had been unable to write and talk at the same time). Nor had Shultz's more generalized notes, dictated to Charles Hill after the meeting, provided a literal report of Meese's false proposal. Now, with Weinberger's notes, we finally had a verbatim account of the meeting.

In response to Regan's question of whether the United States had objected to Israel's sending the Hawk shipment to Iran, Poindexter had said that McFarlane had handled the matter on his own, without documentation, between July and early December 1985.

The shipment, Meese had said, had not been legal, because there had been no presidential finding. The president, Meese had asserted, had *not* been informed of the shipment.

After the senior advisors convened again in the Oval Office the next morning, Weinberger had recorded in his diary that Meese had told him, along with Reagan, Bush, Baker, Regan, Shultz, Casey, and Keel, that Israel had charged Iran more for the TOWs than they had cost, and that the balance had been placed in a Swiss bank account for the Contras. Weinberger had then attended the president's meeting with congressional leaders in the cabinet room, where the diversion had been revealed; Weinberger had later returned to the Oval Office, where Shultz had praised the president and offered to support him on Iran.

The notes of these meetings had been followed by notes of Reagan's press conference. After the president's brief public statement announcing Poindexter's resignation and North's return to the Marine Corps, Weinberger had listened to Meese while standing with Reagan, Bush, and Regan in the president's small hideaway office near the press room. When Weinberger returned to the Pentagon, he had telephoned Poindexter to welcome him back to the Navy.

Taking notes as usual, Weinberger had next telephoned his California associates William Clark, Pete Wilson, and William French Smith, all of whom had promised to urge the president to dump Shultz. Weinberger had kept notes on the progress of this campaign. The next day, he had recorded the fact that Senator Dan Quayle had called on him and had expressed displeasure with Shultz. On Thanksgiving Day, Clark had called Weinberger from California to report that William Casey and William French Smith were calling the president and Nancy Reagan to urge changes at the State Department. A day or two later, Casey had written to the president, recommending Shultz's ouster. According to Weinberger's notes, Meese had also concurred. Weinberger had asked Clark not to use his name as a proponent of the dump-Shultz movement.

Our discovery of Weinberger's notes moved the Iranian initiative to the center of our investigation. We had not regarded the arms sales themselves as criminal acts, but if any witnesses had deliberately given false testimony about them, they had committed crimes—and we could not ignore them. Weinberger's notes were our most explicit guide to cabinet-level activities. He had lied to Congress about his activities, and he had lied to conceal his notes. We asked ourselves these questions: Had his motive been to protect his own public image? To protect the president? Or both?

CHAPTER NINETEEN

The Chief of Staff

The public exposure of the arms sales to Iran had instantly thrust Donald Regan, as the White House chief of staff, into the vortex of the political activity needed to assure Ronald Reagan's escape from disgrace and possible impeachment. Regan's participation in the original questionable conduct had been negligible, but his role in coordinating the resources of the presidency to respond to the humiliating revelation of the administration's secret dealings with terrorists had brought him to the fore.

Regan had not been questioned by any congressional committee about his own conduct, but the House and Senate intelligence committees and the Tower Commission had called on him to explain his widely reported disagreement with Robert McFarlane regarding President Reagan's original authorization of the arms sales. McFarlane had claimed that in 1985, while President Reagan was in the Bethesda Naval Hospital recovering from a cancer operation, he had told McFarlane—in Regan's presence—to authorize the Israelis to sell arms to Iran to show goodwill and obtain the return of the Americans held hostage in Lebanon. Regan, however, had denied to reporters that the president had authorized the arms sales in advance. Regan claimed that the president had been surprised by them but had decided not to do anything about them.

During 1987, Regan had been on the periphery of our investigation into the operational conspiracy centered on Oliver North and John Poindexter. Like the president he had served, Regan exuded congeniality. From the moment he entered my office in the spring of 1988, when I was preparing to try Poindexter and North, I had liked him. I had also sensed his shrewdness and directness and had sized him up as someone who would be too smart to lie. And so, to a great extent, I had trusted him.

Regan had grown up in the Irish section of Boston and had been educated at Harvard University. He had joined the Marine Corps a year before the outbreak of World War II and risen to the rank of lieutenant colonel. After the war, he had taken a job at Merrill Lynch, the country's largest stockbroker and underwriter, and had eventually become its chairman and chief executive officer. In 1981, Ronald Reagan had drafted Regan to be secretary of the Treasury. Four years later, Regan had traded jobs with James Baker and had become the president's chief of staff. At the same time, Edwin Meese had left his position as counselor to the president and had become attorney general, and Michael Deaver, who had been Baker's deputy, had returned to the public relations business. This had left Regan, who had had no experience as a politician, to carry the combined responsibilities formerly borne by Baker, Meese, and Deaver.

Despite the power vested in the chief of staff, who in some respects is the second most important official in the executive branch, the post lacks the independence and external trappings of rank that accompany major cabinet positions. Even before Iran-Contra became news, I had wondered why Regan had wanted to switch places with Baker. Regan had said that it was simply something he wanted to do. Both he and Baker had desired the change. Regan had already enjoyed the prestige and earned the respect that went with his cabinet service. He had wanted to take on the work of the presidency.

Once he became an adjunct of the president, his stature had risen and fallen with Reagan's and had depended on the strength of his presidential support. Considering myself fortunate to have served such a straightforward, matter-of-fact administrator as President Dwight D. Eisenhower, I wondered how Regan had found working under Ronald Reagan, who seemed somewhat emotional and dogmatic. Regan had acknowledged that he had also had to contend with intrusions by the first lady, former presidential advisors, and the president's friends.

When I saw the divisions within the cabinet up close during our investigation, my sympathy for Regan increased. As the president's chief of staff, he had been in charge of the White House staff and responsible for liaison between the president and Congress. Almost all the president's personal directives had been transmitted through Regan, their execution had been monitored through him, and—for the most part—

cabinet officers and others had communicated, or arranged to communicate, with the president through Regan. The new chief of staff, however, had soon found himself at odds with the national security advisor.

As McFarlane and Regan both explained it to us, the National Security Council's staff was, in a sense, part of the president's personal staff, arguably subordinate to the chief of staff. President Reagan's first national security advisor, Richard Allen, had reported through Edwin Meese. But Allen's successors had reported directly to the president, and McFarlane had insisted on retaining his independence and his direct line of communication. Although in his dealings with President Reagan McFarlane had claimed the intimacy of a staff officer rather than the somewhat more distant relationship of a cabinet officer, he had not considered himself to be Regan's subordinate. In McFarlane's view, the president had had two staffs—one for foreign affairs and another for everything else. Instead of communicating with the president through Regan, McFarlane had inserted personal messages in the president's briefing books for meetings on foreign affairs. Even though Regan had attended the meetings, the messages had bypassed him; they had gone to the president and no one else.

Both Regan and McFarlane had acknowledged that the ill will between them had begun in a dispute over an office. As usual, space in the west wing of the White House had been tight and highly prized by those competing to influence the president. During President Richard Nixon's administration, National Security Advisor Henry Kissinger had ultimately established himself in an attractive second-floor office, which overlooked Pennsylvania Avenue, a few steps from the Oval Office. Under Ronald Reagan, this had been the office of Edwin Meese. When Regan came to the White House, he had wanted to put his deputy in the office, but McFarlane had claimed it for himself and subsequently for Poindexter, even though the National Security Council's staff had been housed in the Old Executive Office Building, across a courtyard from the White House.

This conflict, trivial though it may seem, had left the president's staff divided as the covert activities that would become Iran-Contra developed. Regan had believed that McFarlane had overstated his authorization to encourage the Israeli arms sales. McFarlane had suspected Regan of personal vindictiveness and of having tried to distance himself and the president from the transactions. When the showdown came in November 1986, secretiveness and distrust between the White House staff and the NSC staff had impaired the ability of the administration and the president to respond effectively. Before turning to Meese to coordinate the administration's response, McFarlane, Poindexter, George Shultz, and William Casey had each maneuvered to guide the president's course. Regan had tried to be an honest broker.

Early in our investigation, we had accepted Regan's claim that he had not kept many notes, although members of his staff had told us conflicting stories about his note-taking habits. According to some staff members, Regan had kept extensive notes during November 1986, after the Iranian initiative was exposed. In his autobiography, Regan had written, "All my life, I have kept detailed notes of my workaday actions and conversations, and I did the same while I worked for the president." As we were intensively preparing for North's trial, we had let this pass. But after the trials of North and Poindexter were concluded and Charles Hill's reservoir of notes about George Shultz's activities was discovered, we had attempted to obtain Regan's notes.

In the summer of 1991, after questioning Shultz and Weinberger about their notes, we had tried to set up an interview with Regan, but his secretary had repeatedly claimed that he was out of town. Once it became clear to me that he was trying to avoid us, we had issued a grand jury subpoena for him and his notes. FBI Special Agent Mike Foster had served him on the golf course near his home. At this point in our investigation, we had simply wanted Regan's cooperation and the information that his notes contained. We had not wanted to prosecute him for having lied about the notes' existence, but I had been ready to put him under oath and prosecute him if he lied again. Instead, he had decided to cooperate.

After we negotiated with his lawyers, he had produced copies of his notes and had permitted us to make copies of those we found relevant. He had claimed to have left the originals in the White House when he resigned, saying that he believed them to have been in a "book file," which we had not been given. We had subpoenaed the original notes, but President George Bush's counsel had asserted that they could not be found, either in the White House or at the Reagan Library in California.

While our negotiations with Regan's lawyers proceeded, we had found Weinberger's unclassified notes. By May 1992, we had completely analyzed the notes of Weinberger, Shultz, and Regan. In addition to supplementing and being consistent with the notes of Weinberger and Shultz, Regan's notes were particularly revealing with regard to the maneuvers within the White House to protect the president from possible impeachment. Regan also supplied us with important testimony in interviews and before the grand jury.

From various appointment calendars, we knew that when President Reagan returned from California three days after the arms sales to Iran had been exposed, he had met with Regan and Meese, who were anticipating a congressional inquiry, but that Meese had not then taken responsibility for coordinating the president's position. The next day, Regan had breakfasted with Poindexter and, according to a PROF note sent by Poindexter to McFarlane, had "agreed that he would keep his mouth shut." Notes taken by Weinberger, Regan, and others described the November 10, 1986, National Security Planning Group meeting at which Poindexter had laid out the false scenario that the arms shipments had not begun until 1986, and that the 1985 Israeli shipments of U.S. weapons had been discovered by accident at a warehouse in Europe.

In May 1992, Regan admitted to the grand jury that he had known Poindexter's claims to be false, but Regan said that he had not corrected Poindexter, because everyone else in the meeting had also known that the statements were false. Regan told the grand jury that at the time, he had thought Poindexter might be trying to distance himself from transactions that had occurred before McFarlane resigned at the end of 1985.

The meeting had been followed by a press statement of support for the president, but—because of Shultz's objection—not support for the president's policy. Regan confirmed that Nancy Reagan, Poindexter, and others had been upset with Shultz because of his unwillingness to support the Iranian initiative.

On November 12, two days after the meeting, Shultz had unloaded his complaints to Regan, just before Poindexter briefed the congressional leaders with a false narrative of the arms sales, concealing the sales through Israel. According to Regan, Shultz had complained that although he had been one of the officials who regularly reviewed covert action findings, he had never seen the presidential finding authorizing direct shipments of arms from the United States to Iran. Shultz had said that he intended to speak to the president because the shipments had undercut our efforts with our allies. According to Regan, Poindexter had later admitted to him that the finding had not been circulated or filed in the usual way; Poindexter had said that the only copy had been kept in his personal file.

Regan's notes also indicated that he had told Shultz, "We [are] getting murdered in [the] press. I want to go public." The president, vice president, and Poindexter, according to the notes, had said that going public would be "too risky," but Shultz had agreed with Regan.

Later that day, as the congressional leaders were being briefed, Regan had noted Poindexter's statement to Senate Majority Leader Robert Byrd that there had been "no transfer of material" in 1985, because it had taken time to assess the contact and to issue a presidential finding. Regan told the grand jury that he had known Poindexter's statement to be wrong but had thought correcting it would be inappropriate.

Nancy Reagan had telephoned Regan before the meeting. According to Regan, she had been very upset because McFarlane had told her that they were going to have to "dump the hostages" to save the president's reputation. Regan had written, "She agreed. Risking presidency." In his grand jury testimony, Regan explained what he had meant: "That, similar to Watergate, he [Reagan] might be impeached; that we were risking the president's tenure in office, his presidency, and his reputation." Regan explained that he had not used the word *impeachment*: "It was a no-no word. . . . You never used the word *impeachment* except to yourself, because that was something no one wanted to even think about, but as chief of staff, I felt I should at least look that beast in the eye to see, you know, were we going up here to another Watergate? What are we doing here?"

When President Reagan made the televised address in which he admitted for the first time that the United States had sold arms to Iran, he had avoided details and had misled his audience about the nature of the weapons shipments. Regan had by then grown concerned that the president seemed to lack factual information that should have come from the National Security Council's staff. By mid-November, Regan and Poindexter had taken over the press briefings, adhering to the false position taken at the November 12 meeting with the congressional leaders. Regan had begun publicly blaming McFarlane for the arms deals.

On November 19, the president had tried to quiet the issue by holding a press conference at which he had made several glaring misstatements. As Regan described it to the grand jury, the president had been "stumbling all over the place and looking very inept and weak and willful during that press conference." Because Regan had previously told some reporters that the shipments had gone through a third country, a reporter had asked the president whether the shipments had gone through Israel, and the president had falsely denied that any third country had been involved. This had necessitated an immediate correction by the White House.

From Charles Hill's notes, we knew that the day after this press conference, Shultz had visited Regan for what Shultz had characterized as
"a very *hard* conversation," in which he had charged that Poindexter had
been telling the president and vice president things that were wrong.
Shultz had told Hill that Regan had seemed subdued. Hill had written
that Regan was "not taking charge" and that the vice president was "dug
in, too. Not taking strong role either."

According to Hill's notes, Shultz and Regan had met with the president in the White House residence late that afternoon. Shultz had outlined the factual misstatements that the president had been given, and
the president had then acknowledged having known about the
November 1985 Hawk shipment but had argued that it had not been a
matter of arms for hostages. Afterward, Shultz had told Hill of having
made little headway: "Hot & heavy. Argued back & forth. I didn't shake
him one bit." Shultz had been frustrated by Reagan's apparent stub-
bornness. "He refuses to see we have a problem. So I never got to what
should be done. Nancy was not there. I had hoped she [would] help." At
that point, according to Regan, Shultz had intended to resign.

Earlier that day, Regan had met with Casey, who had told him that
there had been financial irregularities in the arms transactions. At the
end of the day, Regan had finally obtained a copy of the NSC staff's
draft chronology from Poindexter and had asked the president's counsel, Peter Wallison, to review it.

According to Wallison's diary, which we had obtained in December
1990, he had grown increasingly concerned about the legal problems
that were implicit in the arms sales to Iran. But as Regan dealt with
Meese in ascertaining the facts and evaluating the legal ramifications,
Wallison had first been shunted off to interview Poindexter and then
been excluded from Meese's fact-finding exercise. Wallison had believed
Meese to be an inappropriate choice to head the administration's internal investigation, because Meese had blessed the 1986 decision to sell
arms directly to Iran without notifying Congress, and because Meese
would act as the president's confidant, not as a dispassionate lawyer.

Wallison had protested the president's repeated public statements
that all laws had been complied with. On November 11, after consulting
the CIA's general counsel, David Doherty, Wallison had sent Regan a
legal memorandum. According to his diary, ten days before the congressional hearings were to start, Wallison had flatly told Regan that
"unless the operation could be portrayed as a diplomatic move, it would

have had to have been reported [to Congress] as a covert action in advance." The next day, Regan had told Wallison to speak to Meese. Wallison had found Meese in Poindexter's office, but Poindexter had not permitted Wallison to join the meeting.

Wallison had then become more emphatic, telling Regan that there was an "absolute prohibition" on arms sales to Iran without prior notice to Congress. According to Wallison's diary, he had tried to edit the text of an upcoming presidential speech by deleting the statement that all laws had been complied with, but Poindexter's deputy, Alton Keel, had "exploded."

As conflicts of fact and personal blame intensified, Regan had acted against Wallison's advice and had drawn in President Reagan's longtime trouble-shooter Meese to pull together a coherent administration position. The area of controversy—foreign affairs—had belonged to Poindexter, but Poindexter had been part of the problem. He would have to be consulted, but the president's survival could not be left to him. Consequently, Regan and Meese had been at the hub of the conversations among cabinet officers as the congressional committees demanded explanations for the administration's conduct.

On the morning of November 21, Regan, Meese, and Poindexter had met with President Reagan in the Oval Office to discuss the conflicting versions of the history of the arms sales. "The gist of it was that the thing didn't hang together," Regan told the grand jury. "Every time you seemed to have one piece nailed down, something else popped up and negated that or changed that." According to Regan, he had become angry when Poindexter argued that they should let the matter blow over. Regan said that he had told the president that he wanted the facts "buttoned up once and for all," and that Meese had agreed.

By then, Meese had begun reviewing the relevant contemporaneous intelligence reports gathered by the National Security Agency and distributed to Casey, Poindexter, and Weinberger. Meese had told Regan that these reports revealed that the Iranians were complaining of having been overcharged. Regan testified that these reports had given Meese the first clue that "somebody wasn't telling the straight story. . . . [T]he attorney general was trying to reconcile why would the Iranians be paying a price higher than we were showing that we were getting."

When Regan told Wallison that Meese was starting his investigation, Wallison had once more raised the subject of Meese's conflict of interest. Regan had not responded; he had been concerned with greater dangers. Regan had then given Wallison the chronology he had obtained from Poindexter and had asked Wallison to prepare questions for Regan to ask at the foreign policy advisors' meeting scheduled for Monday, November 24.

That weekend, Casey, Meese, and Regan had talked frequently. They claimed not to remember much of the conversations. No notes of their conversations were ever produced. The parties claimed that none had been taken. With little direct contemporaneous evidence to guide us, we had to piece together the events of the weekend from notes written by other individuals and early statements to the FBI.

According to a note by Charles Hill, Meese had questioned Shultz on Saturday, November 22, at eight in the morning. Shultz had told Meese that President Reagan had known in advance about the Hawk shipment that had taken place before the first finding was drafted. Meese had then interviewed McFarlane and assured himself that the former national security advisor possessed no notes of his conversations with the president. Casey had lunched with North and Poindexter; Meese had lunched with his two top aides, John Richardson and William Bradford Reynolds, who had shown Meese the draft of a memorandum that North had sent to Poindexter, perhaps for the president, in which North had outlined the diversion of the arms proceeds to the Contras.

Regan told us that one of Casey's former clients, who had helped Adnan Khashoggi finance the arms sales, had been complaining to Casey that the Iranians (who had recently discovered that they were being overcharged) had not paid Manucher Ghorbanifar in full for the Hawk spare parts, and that Ghorbanifar had consequently been unable to repay Khashoggi and the others who had put up the bridge loan that had enabled Ghorbanifar to pay the United States in advance for the parts. Regan said that Casey had told him of rumors that some of the arms sales proceeds had been sent to the Contras.

Meese had questioned North for four hours on Sunday and had briefly warned the president and Regan about the diversion early on Monday, November 24. Meese had then told the vice president. That afternoon, the president had met with his senior foreign policy advisors. This was the meeting at which Meese had been scheduled to report on his fact-finding investigation, but he had not revealed the diversion. After Shultz and Poindexter engaged in a prolonged dispute over the continuation of the Iranian initiative, Regan and Meese had embarked on the interchange in which Meese had told the group that the president had not approved the Hawk shipment in advance and that the law might have been violated if he had. In his notes, Regan had described his question and Meese's response. Regan's notes corroborated Weinberger's.

> DTR [Regan] asked about shipment of HAWK missiles to Iran in Nov.... [Meese said] Shultz told in Geneva by Bud [McFarlane] delivery of weapons & maybe hostages out. Didn't approve. Pres only told maybe hostages out in short order. Plane unable to land in Iran. Smaller plane arranged, only 18 missiles aboard—wrong ones. No specific ok for HAWKs. Returned in Feb. from Israeli stocks. Bud told Geo [Shultz] hostages out first, then arms in. Did not take place. May be a violation of law if arms shipped w/o [without] a finding. But Pres did not know—Cap [Weinberger] denies knowing. Israelis may have done this on their own. But it was a low-level contact that did this, probably using Pres' name.

We knew that Regan had not needed to ask whether the president had known about the Hawk shipment before it happened: Regan had been present in Geneva when McFarlane alerted Reagan to it. Regan had told us more than once that he vividly remembered that the conversation had taken place in a child's bedroom in the house in which President Reagan had stayed during his meeting with Mikhail Gorbachev. There had been only one chair. The president had sat in the chair, and Regan had sat on the bed, while McFarlane briefed the president. Our natural suspicion was that Regan had asked the question as part of a planned setup that would allow Meese an opportunity to establish the line that the president's advisors would be expected to follow.

Questioned before the grand jury in May and June 1992, Regan denied that he had agreed in advance with Meese to ask the question. Nevertheless, Regan admitted that Reagan, Bush, Shultz, Poindexter, and probably Casey had known that Meese's statement of the facts was wrong. Asked why no one had spoken up, Regan replied, "I can only describe as best I can the mental attitude of one of them, to wit, myself; why didn't I speak up at that point? First of all, it's a *possible* violation. Wallison had told me a possible violation. We had not had an opinion that, yes, it is a violation for this, this, and this reason. Obviously, we were waiting to be told specifically, is this a violation? That's my attitude now, right or wrong. Second, I was very concerned about the diversion of funds, what is this all about? What new turn is this Iranian arms shipment going to take with diversion of funds? So that was on my mind. Before I start an outburst in this meeting and getting everybody upset, let's get the rest of the facts. Maybe we have found why we had been so puzzled as to why we couldn't get a chronology. So I was waiting for Meese's full explanation to the president before speaking up on that particular subject, that is, the Hawk missiles in eighty-five."

After the foreign policy advisors' meeting and after hearing Meese's full report to the president regarding the diversion, Regan had met with Casey at the CIA's headquarters. In 1992, Regan claimed to be confused about exactly what he had told Casey on that evening in 1986. His recollection was that he had not told Casey precisely what Meese had found out, because he thought that until the attorney general had reached a final conclusion, the less he talked about it the better. Regan said he knew that Meese had been talking with Casey.

Fortunately, we did not have to rely on this hazy recollection, because Regan had been interviewed early in the investigation both by the FBI and by us. In July 1987, when the events were fresher in his mind, he had told us that he had discussed the diversion with Casey on the evening in question. Regan and Casey had agreed that the diversion should be made public even if it would anger the Israelis and others in the Middle East. Casey's view had been that it would not be enough for North to resign, that Poindexter also would have to resign to create a firewall to keep the flames from reaching the president.

Casey's testimony before the House intelligence committee in early December 1986 had partially confirmed Regan's 1987 statement. "Don Regan stopped in to see me on the way home . . . ," Casey had testified. "So that was the first I had any inkling of a diversion."

Meese had told the congressional select committees on Iran-Contra in July 1987 that when he spoke with Casey early on November 25, 1986, Casey had already known of the diversion: "He heard about it, I believe, from Don Regan the previous evening. . . . Well, he had heard from Don Regan that there had been a diversion, and that Poindexter was planning to resign, and that Don Regan felt that Poindexter should resign immediately, and probably—I didn't know whether North was discussed, too, or not."

An undated memorandum entitled "Plan of Action," which Regan said he had written on November 24, called for the resignation of Poindexter, the reassignment of North to the Marine Corps, and the immediate appointment of a special review board to investigate the misuse of the National Security Council's staff. "Tough as it seems, blame must be put at NSC's door—rogue operation, going on without president's knowledge or sanction. When suspicions arose, he took charge, ordered investigation, had meeting of top advisors to get at facts, and find out who knew what. Try to make the best of a sensational story. Anticipate charges of 'out of control,' 'President doesn't know what's going on,' 'Who's in charge?,' 'State Department is right in its suspicions of NSC,' 'secret dealings with nefarious characters,' 'Should break off any contacts with: a) Iranians; b) Contras.' "

Despite his efforts to keep the president above it all, Regan had learned that Reagan had privately telephoned North to impress on him that it was important that the president had not known about North's activities. Regan said he had told Reagan, "Well, I hope you did the right thing."

Regan had taken notes at a December 2, 1986, meeting with the president, vice president, and leading Republicans from Capitol Hill, including Senators Bob Dole, Alan Simpson, and Trent Lott and Representatives Bob Michel and Dick Cheney. After outlining what he called the "Iran situation," the president had read his proposed television statement on the appointment of independent counsel and the appointment of Frank Carlucci to succeed Poindexter as national security advisor. According to Regan's notes, he had asked, "Mr. President, what did you know—when did you know it? That's the question on these fellows' minds. Tell them what you know."

For ten minutes, President Reagan had held forth; he had then been questioned about the arms shipments prior to his January 1986 finding, the lack of support by Shultz and McFarlane, and the revelation of the diversion of the proceeds to the Contras. Reagan had tried to reassure the congressional delegation, but they had emphasized "the magnitude of the issue" and had said that "sweeping changes" would be necessary. "Opponents and press are after the presidency." The appointment of Carlucci would not be enough. Lott, Cheney, and Simpson had said that they needed better answers. President Reagan had denied having known about the diversion and had said that he believed only North and Poindexter had been privy to it. In his notes, Regan had observed, "It is now a domestic political problem, not a foreign policy matter. Maybe a public apology is needed."

Regan's notes of the telephone conversations he and Casey had held during the period when the Senate intelligence committee was beginning its investigation showed that they had tried to use the committee to deflect the focus of the controversy from President Reagan. Although the Republicans had lost their Senate majority in the 1986 elections, they had retained control of the committees for the remainder of the year. Casey had telephoned Regan to say that the intelligence committee's staff director, Robert Bernard McMahon, had said that chairman David Durenberger and most members of the committee wanted to "demolish this molehill." According to Regan's notes, Casey had characterized the message as an "offer of surrender" and had said, "Some senators feel nothing there—'dry hole' in hearings."

Casey had suggested that Regan have the president "announce some morning soon that North violated [the] law on Contras' funding [and] did not tell us" and that Poindexter had known about it and "should have reported it to [the president]." Casey had recommended that North and Poindexter tell their stories on television and then receive presidential pardons. Alongside this note, Regan had written that he would take on the project Casey had outlined and would use "Paul Laxalt as [an] intermediary." Laxalt was a former senator from Nevada and a well-known friend of President Reagan's.

From his diary, we learned that Peter Wallison had, at Regan's direction, invited McMahon to the White House and told him that a presidential pardon was a political "non-starter," but that the president might be willing to endorse immunity for North and Poindexter so that they could testify before Congress. In response, McMahon had said that he thought the committee would resist granting immunity, because it might cause problems for an independent counsel. The following day, Casey had discussed immunity with Wallison. Later, after talking with Regan and attempting without success to reach Meese, Wallison had called Associate Attorney General Steven Trott to discuss immunity.

As Poindexter and North claimed their constitutional privilege against self-incrimination and continued to refuse to answer the Senate intelligence committee's questions, the White House consensus in favor of immunity had solidified. On December 16, President Reagan had issued a public statement calling on the committee to grant immunity to North and Poindexter. On the same day, Regan had testified before the committee. According to his notes, the committee had passed the word to Regan that it planned to lay the responsibility for Iran-Contra on North and would "outline a scam by arms dealers" with government employees who had been "hoodwinked." The committee had not intended to question the president or call him as a witness. The following day, Durenberger and McMahon had secretly—without the knowledge of even the committee members—briefed Reagan, Regan, Keel, and Wallison on the committee's proposed findings. The following day, the chairman and staff director had also briefed Bush and his chief of staff, Craig Fuller.

While struggling to develop President Reagan's public position, Regan had continued his public debate with McFarlane about whether the president had personally authorized the original arms sales by Israel. Both men had been testifying before congressional committees and responding to questions by the press. McFarlane had consistently claimed express authorization; Regan had denied it. In his testimony to the Senate intelligence committee, the Tower Commission, and the select committees on Iran-Contra and before our grand jury in February 1988, Regan had reasserted that the original arms shipment for the release of hostage Benjamin Weir, in September 1985, had surprised the president; that the president had favored a dialogue with Iran but had not authorized an arms shipment; and that after learning that the release had followed an arms shipment by Israel, the president had been angry but had decided to replenish Israel's supply of TOWs, rather than make an issue of it.

This dispute and uncertainty had seriously embarrassed President Reagan himself. In his first interview with the Tower Commission, on January 26, 1987, the president had stated that he had approved the arms shipments before they commenced in August 1985. Surprised as he listened to this statement, Peter Wallison had looked over the president's briefing material after the interview and had found nothing to support the claim that the president had known about the shipment in advance.

According to Wallison's diary, a group including Bush, Regan, and David Abshire (who was then coordinating the administration's responses to the various investigators) had prepared the president for his testimony before the commission, using a chronology prepared by Wallison. Reagan had somehow also picked up the false chronology prepared by North and had, on his own, attempted to supplement it with his diary notes. Because of his faulty memory, the president had depended heavily on the diary notes, which Wallison had later described as "relatively complete." Wallison had been perplexed because North's chronology had said that the president had not known about the shipment in advance, and Wallison had heard the president himself say that he had no recollection of having approved the sales.

Trying to sort out the problem, Wallison, Regan, and Abshire had met with the president again. At first, he had seemed to have no memory of the events at issue. According to Wallison, Regan had then related his own recollection that after learning of the Israeli weapon shipment, the president had said something like "What's done is done." After listening to this, Reagan had said, "You know, he's right."

Joint committee leaders posing with Secretary of Defense Caspar Weinberger, the last committee witness, on August 3, 1987. Left to right, Senate vice chairman Warren Rudman, Senate chairman Inouye, House chairman Hamilton, House vice chairman Dante Fascell, and Republican House member Jim Courter.

Caspar Weinberger fends off the joint committees' inquiries.

On November 18, 1987, I enter the courthouse to project the course of the grand jury's investigation.

United States Judge Gerhard Gesell, in charge of the North trial proceedings.

Accompanied by Mike Bromwich, left, and David Zornow, right, I explain
to reporters the twenty-three-count indictment of Poindexter,
North, Secord, and Hakim, March 16, 1988.

Former judge Abraham Sofaer, legal advisor to the State Department, who negotiated the dismissal of the conspiracy and diversion charges, and the release of classified information for the remaining counts.

Attorney General Richard Thornburgh, who approved the Sofaer compromise.

Followed by press officer Jim Wieghart, I enter the courthouse to accept the dismissal of the conspiracy and the diversion counts, January 1989.

Our North trial team, John Keker (center) with David Zornow (left) and
Mike Bromwich (right), meets reporters after North's conviction
on three felony charges, May 4, 1989.

CIA station chief
Joseph Fernandez out-
side the courthouse after
his arraignment,
June 28, 1988.

Judge Claude M. Hilton, who
dismissed the Fernandez case
because the CIA refused to
release nonsecret classified
information.

President Bush with Director of Central Intelligence William Webster (right)
and Deputy Director Richard Kerr (left). Bush refused to review the
Webster-Kerr decision to withhold nonsecret classified
information required by Judge Claude Hilton.

U. S. District Judge Harold Greene, who presided over the Poindexter trial proceedings.

Associate counsel Dan Webb and our Poindexter trial team meet the press after the jury finds Poindexter guilty as charged, April 7, 1990. From left, Louise Radin, Howard Pearl, Webb, and Chris Mixter .

Vice Admiral John Poindexter, President Reagan's national security advisor in 1986, stands outside the courthouse with his wife after his sentencing for five felonies, June 12, 1990. His convictions are later reversed by the court of appeals because of immunity granted by Congress.

U. S. Court of Appeals Judge
Laurence H. Silberman.

Chief Judge
Patricia Wald,
U. S. Court of Appeals
for the District of
Columbia Circuit.

Assistant Secretary of State Elliot Abrams speaks to reporters on November 15, 1991, after pleading guilty to illegally withholding information from Congress.

Charles Allen, North's liaison with the intelligence community, is one of the first to suspect the illegal diversion. He reports it to CIA Director Gates.

President Bush announces the nomination of Robert Gates to head the CIA, May 14, 1991.

Outside his summer home in July 1991, President Bush criticizes
the continuation of my investigation.

Attorney General
Edwin Meese.

Secretary of State
George Shultz.

Presidential
Chief of Staff
Donald Regan.

Deputy independent
counsel Craig Gillen explains
Caspar Weinberger's indictment,
June 16, 1992. Associate counsel
John Barrett is at his right,
associate counsel Tom
Baker at left.

Weinberger hurriedly leaves
press conference without taking questions, after claiming
that he had been indicted
because he would not give
false testimony against
President Reagan,
June 17, 1992.

Senate Republican
Leader Bob Dole, my
most relentless critic.

Counsel
to the president
Boyden Gray with
President Bush
in 1991.

RUSSELL D. CURTIS/THE RECORDER

Jim Brosnahan takes over
the Weinberger trial.

AP/WIDE WORLD PHOTOS

Judge William Clark, one
of Weinberger's advisors and
President Reagan's former
national security advisor.

William Barr, President Bush's last attorney general.

On Christmas Eve, 1992, Weinberger and his lawyers, Robert Bennett, Carl Rauh, and Roberto Iraola, react after President Bush pardons Weinberger to prevent his case from going to trial.

Free at last: Reporters applaud as Mary Belcher and I leave the press conference after the release of my final report.

Wallison had persuaded the Tower Commission to invite the president for a second interview. To help Reagan, Wallison had drafted a memorandum setting out his understanding of Reagan's recollection. Trying to avoid taking sides between Regan and McFarlane in his second appearance before the committee, however, the president had decided to read from Wallison's memorandum, which said that Reagan had been surprised by the arms shipment and that Regan had a firm recollection that the president had not authorized it in advance. "Unfortunately," as Wallison had noted in his diary, the memorandum had been "written in the second person, and so he flubbed a summary of it. In all, it was a weak performance, and left the unfortunate impression that he might have been influenced to this view against his best recollection." Having had something similar happen with a witness in the first case I tried by myself, I knew how Wallison must have winced when the president picked up the memorandum and announced, "This is what I am supposed to say."

Wallison had then met with the commission's staff to alleviate its concern about the apparent discrepancy. The *Washington Post* and the *Los Angeles Times* had carried stories saying that the Tower Commission was investigating the change of testimony as a possible cover-up.

Finally, on February 20, 1987, President Reagan had written the commission to say, "I'm afraid that I let myself be influenced by others' recollections, not my own. . . . My answer, therefore, and the simple truth is, 'I don't remember—period.' " The Tower Commission had suspected that Regan had deliberately sought to conceal the president's involvement, and that Regan had been trying to shore up the position he had taken in his dispute with McFarlane.

When Reagan's poor performance became public knowledge, Regan had been blamed. Angry about the president's statement that he had allowed himself to be "influenced by others' recollection," Regan had believed Nancy Reagan to have been responsible for the statement and for shifting the blame for the president's problems toward him. Political pressure for the president to fire Regan had built steadily. On February 20, George Bush had confronted Regan about resigning and had pointed to the continuing trouble among the staff and in the press. Regan had agreed that he would leave after the Tower Commission issued its report.

Bush had recorded the results of this confrontation in his diary: "The president was very, very pleased. He thanked me about three times. I gave him a full report. He was concerned that Don would walk in and see us talking, so I left after about fifteen minutes." Bush had written that he and the president had agreed that the discussion would be "a non-conversation."

On February 27, 1987, Regan and Wallison had resigned. Former senator Howard Baker had then replaced Regan as the president's chief of staff.

Having decided not to prosecute Regan after he turned over his notes and began cooperating with us, I was satisfied that his testimony before the grand jury in 1992 had been essentially forthright. Accordingly; we looked to him as a witness, possibly a key witness, against other high officials in the Reagan administration who had persisted in their denials of the November 1986 cover-up. Chief among them were Edwin Meese, who now appeared to have been an architect of the cover-up, and Caspar Weinberger, who had shielded the cover-up by lying to Congress and by repeatedly denying the existence of his own notes.

CHAPTER TWENTY

The President's Protector

The players in the drama that had unfolded in November 1986 included not only the officials who had been responsible for the political decisions of Ronald Reagan's administration but also the lawyers who had been responsible for evaluating the legality of the president's actions. We recognized that the lawyers had faced a difficult task in sorting through the misinformation, conflicting rationalizations, and outright attempts to cover up the facts to protect the president. Nonetheless, we had a duty to carefully examine whether those lawyers—particularly Attorney General Edwin Meese, who had been at center stage during the crucial period—had fulfilled their responsibilities.

Notes taken by some of the participants and information provided in interviews and grand jury testimony painted a dismaying picture of Meese's role in the cover-up.

Edwin Meese had been no ordinary attorney general. He had probably had a closer personal relationship with his president than had any attorney general before him aside from Robert Kennedy and perhaps John Mitchell. Like Mitchell, who had served as Richard Nixon's attorney general, Meese had faced a difficult choice between protecting a willful president and ensuring the administration of justice. Trial lawyers learn to face the facts and realistically evaluate the consequences of illegal conduct, but devotion built on years of close association can sometimes cloud judgment.

Meese had grown up in Oakland, California, and been graduated from Yale University in 1953. After serving in the Army during the Korean War, he had attended the University of California's Boalt Hall in Berkeley and received his law degree in 1958. He had then spent eight years as a deputy district attorney in Alameda County. He had worked on Ronald Reagan's campaigns for the governorship of California and had served on his personal staff as secretary on clemency and extradition for four years and then as executive assistant and chief of staff for four years. After other brief ventures, Meese had become a law professor and had been an important advisor in Reagan's 1980 presidential campaign.

When Reagan came to Washington, he had considered making Meese the White House chief of staff, but doubts about Meese's administrative ability had led the president to appoint James Baker to the position instead. Meese had become the president's counselor, a newly created post that had entailed serving as the president's lawyer and overseeing important policy matters. Other presidential counsel, particularly the first, Sam Rosenman, had held such responsibilities, but the title change had given the office parity with that of the chief of staff.

After President Reagan's reelection, Meese had been appointed attorney general. By then, he had served as an advisor to Ronald Reagan for more than a dozen years. At first, Meese had made relatively few changes in the Justice Department other than promoting William Bradford Reynolds, the ultraconservative head of the civil rights division, to counselor to the department. Charles Cooper, a young lawyer who had been Reynold's deputy in the civil rights division, had been put in charge of the office of legal counsel. Cooper had hardly finished serving as a Supreme Court law clerk when he became Reynolds's deputy; a mere four years later, Cooper had been advising the attorney general as well as supervising the Justice Department lawyers who guided the federal agencies in many of their most difficult problems. Another of Meese's intimate assistants had been John Richardson, his personal chief of staff. Richardson's responsibilities had primarily been administrative rather than investigative or prosecutorial.

The Justice Department's production of documents had been slow but excessive. The most critical evidence had been buried among eighteen thousand largely irrelevant documents. Nonetheless, we had quickly found the personal notes of Meese, Cooper, and Richardson.

In January 1986, Meese had approved the presidential finding that had authorized the sale of arms to Iran without immediate notice to Congress. After the sales were exposed ten months later, no one at the Justice Department had moved to investigate the possibility of criminal conduct. On November 8, as John Poindexter looked ahead to briefing the president's foreign policy advisors, the congressional leaders, and congressional committees, he had asked Meese for advice about the legality of the sale of U.S. arms to Iran. Meese had turned the assignment over to Charles Cooper, who would later testify before our grand jury, and had instructed him to proceed with one trusted assistant.

On November 10, Meese had attended the meeting of the National Security Planning Group at which Poindexter had denied that any arms had been shipped before the president signed the finding. On November 12, Meese had heard Reagan and Poindexter tell the congressional leaders that there had been no arms sales before the finding was signed. That day, without awaiting Cooper's conclusions, Meese had advised the president to assert that no U.S. laws or policy had been violated.

The next day, Cooper—who had not known about the prior shipments through the Israelis—had given Meese a memorandum justifying the arms shipments that had taken place after the finding went into effect. Cooper concluded that because the finding had complied with the National Security Act, the shipments had not been subject to the Arms Export Control Act.

Meanwhile, White House counsel Peter Wallison had been less certain. Wallison had feared that Reagan's failure to notify Congress about even the 1986 shipments had made them illegal. Wallison, however, could not match Meese's influence with Reagan's inner circle. At a White House meeting of staff members reviewing the address that the president would deliver that evening, Wallison had objected to the statement that no federal laws had been broken. According to Wallison's diary, Alton Keel had lashed out at him, saying "that this is what the president wanted, this is what the AG [attorney general] wants, and this is what the National Security Advisor wants; that the [president] had already said as much earlier in the week; that this statute was the AG's to interpret, and [Wallison] should not go around expressing disagreement with the AG's conclusion."

Still concerned, Wallison had attempted to reach the attorney general and had finally heard from him by telephone late in the afternoon. Meese had then had Cooper phone and explain his theory that the shipments had been legal because the January 1986 finding had authorized them as covert actions under the National Security Act. Cooper had also suggested that the president had an inherent constitutional power to ship arms without notifying Congress. Cooper had claimed that the preamble of the National Security Act, in general terms, acknowledged the president's broad power in foreign affairs. Wallison had pointed out that whether legal or not, the shipment would "provoke a constitutional confrontation that we have tried to avoid." Cooper had acknowledged having had only one day to review the question. As Wallison had noted in his diary, "It thus appear[ed] that the [president] was going to state in his speech that no laws had been violated, but the Justice [Department], which supposedly had given him that advice, had not even begun to research the question in any depth."

In his nationally televised address that evening, November 13, President Reagan had admitted the "transfer of small amounts of defensive weapons and spare parts for defensive systems to Iran" and had stated that no federal laws had been broken. This assurance had not quieted the media. Under pressure to provide more detailed information, Reagan had scheduled the press conference of November 19.

At a meeting called by Wallison the day before the press conference, Paul Thompson from the National Security Council, Abraham Sofaer from the State Department, Lawrence Garrett from the Defense Department, and David Doherty from the CIA had listened as Cooper laid out the reasons he believed the 1986 shipments to have been legal. Cooper had said that there were precedents for the delay of notification to Congress. Wallison had questioned this claim, but the others had accepted it.

According to Cooper's notes, Thompson had told the group that Israel had shipped TOWs to Iran when Benjamin Weir was released in September 1985, but that the United States had not replenished Israel's stocks until after the president signed the finding in January 1986. Sofaer told us that Cooper had relied on a chronology drafted by the NSC staff to indicate that the United States had had no advance knowledge of the TOW shipment. Cooper had expressed concern to the group that the shipments prior to the president's finding might have violated the Arms Export Control Act. Wallison had asked Cooper whether Meese had known of the 1985 shipments when he rendered his opinion that the shipments had been legal. Cooper had agreed to ask Meese about the matter.

According to notes taken by Wallison and by Charles Hill, who had debriefed Sofaer, the meeting's participants had complained to Thompson that the NSC staff was "stiffing everybody." Sofaer and Wallison had said that they could not advise their clients without knowing the facts, and that the administration would have to rely on Meese as its sole authority on the legal issues. This had opened a fissure more dangerous than the conflict over what to say at the press conference.

Although Meese, as attorney general, had more authority than all the other lawyers, he could not have quieted any public disagreement among the senior lawyers by pulling rank.

After the meeting, Sofaer had told Hill that Thompson's secretiveness about the facts had created two problems. First, the latest arms transfer had occurred after the Arms Export Control Act was amended to "*absolutely* prohibit shipments to Iran." Second and more serious, the September 1985 transfer of arms to Iran had been subject to the Arms Export Control Act because there had been no presidential finding. According to Hill's notes, Sofaer had expressed profound skepticism, inferring that this conduct had reflected not confusion, but a cover-up: "If [the administration] claims we did *not* approve September '85 transfer plus it can be proved we *did*, it's a Watergate-style theme." Interviewed by my staff in 1992, Sofaer explained that he had harbored "suspicions" about people "trying to hide the facts," and that he had been concerned that Poindexter and Meese were shutting him out because they had already set their legal arguments and had not wanted him to be involved.

At the November 19 press conference, the president had erroneously denied that any sales had been carried out through Israel. The White House had then had to issue a correction. Although Meese had not participated in preparing Reagan for the press conference, he had authorized Wallison to tell those responsible for the preparation that the president had relied on Meese's advice that all the shipments had been legal. Just before the press conference, George Shultz had warned the president to avoid flatly denying that the arms had been sold for the release of hostages. Meese and the other lawyers had known nothing of this meeting or the one that had taken place the following day, during which Shultz and Donald Regan had reminded the president of his prior knowledge of the November 1985 Hawk shipment and the president had admitted that he had known about it.

On November 20, the attorney general had met for two hours with Charles Cooper, William Casey, Robert Gates, John Poindexter, Paul Thompson, and Oliver North in Poindexter's White House office to prepare for Casey's congressional testimony and Poindexter's congressional briefing. A month later, Meese had described this discussion to the Senate intelligence committee as having been dominated by legal issues. He had testified that he had attended the meeting to ensure that the January 1986 findings would be properly discussed in the chronology. "We discussed the nature of the findings, the legal theories that were involved," he had told the committee, "and it was that, more than any factual basis," that had constituted the core of the meeting. In June 1987, Poindexter had told the select committees on Iran-Contra that Meese had identified the 1985 shipments as the key legal problem. Poindexter had claimed that Meese had told the group that "it would make a difference whether the president approved it ahead of time or afterwards, or words to that effect."

In December 1987, scarcely a year after his Senate testimony, however, Meese had testified before our grand jury and set the pattern for his future testimony: He had sworn that he could not remember. Inexplicably, he had claimed not to remember having discussed any legal questions at the November 20, 1986, meeting, but he had said that the group might have talked about the Arms Export Control Act.

Cooper told the grand jury that during the meeting, North had claimed that the Hawks had been returned to Israel not because of the Iranians' dissatisfaction with them but because the United States had complained to Israel about the shipment. Cooper said that he had accepted North's version and that the other participants had also relied heavily on North as the one person who seemed to know the facts. North, however, had told the select committees that the participants had known his statement to be false: "They had a darn good reason for not putting the straight story out, and their reasons might have been the same as mine."

While Poindexter's White House meeting was in progress, Sofaer and Hill had been preparing Armacost for his testimony. For the first time, Sofaer had learned from Hill's notes of Shultz's knowledge of the Hawk shipment. He had then received a draft of Casey's proposed testimony stating that the CIA had not learned that its proprietary had delivered Hawks to Iran until two months after the shipment. Sofaer had realized at once that he would have to tell Meese and Wallison of his disbelief.

Unable to reach Meese, who was at the White House, Sofaer had spoken to the deputy attorney general, Arnold Burns. Sofaer had said that he did not believe Casey's proposed testimony, because Shultz had contemporaneous notes showing that Robert McFarlane had informed Shultz of the shipment beforehand. Burns, who had known nothing about the subject, had said that he would talk to the attorney general. When Burns called back later, he had told Sofaer that Meese had spent the afternoon with Poindexter and Casey and "was fully aware of the facts [Sofaer] mentioned." According to Sofaer's notes, Burns had added that the attorney general "knew of certain facts that explained all these matters and that laid to rest all the problems [Sofaer] might perceive." Burns, who had not understood the cryptic message, had characterized it to Sofaer as a "mysterious assurance."

When Sofaer phoned Wallison to alert him to the problem with the Hawk shipment, Cooper had been with Wallison. Sofaer later reported to Hill that when Cooper told Meese the substance of Hill's notes, Meese had assured Cooper that when he asked Reagan about it, Reagan had replied, "I didn't know about that. I never approved it." Yet Meese had consistently testified that he had not discussed the matter with the president.

Because Meese had left town for a speaking engagement at West Point, Cooper had been unable to reach him until ten-thirty that night to advise him that Casey was about to give false testimony. Meese had told Cooper to have David Doherty at the CIA make the necessary changes in Casey's testimony. After first calling Poindexter, Cooper had telephoned Doherty, who had assured him that the change had already been made.

Meese had canceled a speaking engagement at Harvard University and returned to Washington the next morning, November 21. In testifying before the select committees on July 8, 1987, Meese had said that Cooper's information had prompted his early return by presenting "a whole new area of information that was beyond what I had assumed, . . . because it went beyond the corrections that we had made in the testimony in Mr. Poindexter's office."

It was after this discovery of the efforts by North, Poindexter, and Casey to mislead the congressional intelligence committees—and Meese himself—that Meese had undertaken his effort to develop a coherent overview of the administration's position. As a former prosecutor, a rough-and-tumble politician, and a very shrewd lawyer, Meese must have known that he had been told a skein of lies that had undercut the validity of his legal advice and jeopardized the president. To the select committees, however, he had excused the outrageous misstatements made by Poindexter, Casey, and North as the result of "compartmentalization" of the facts. But as Meese well knew, tough agency heads like Casey and Poindexter had rarely been "compartmented out" by their subordinates unless they had wanted to be compartmented out—unless they had not wanted to know the truth or to reveal the truth.

Cooper told the grand jury that when Meese returned to Washington on November 21, he had met with Cooper, Reynolds, and Richardson. The group had been concerned about the possibility that criminal acts had been committed. "Any legal problems?" Cooper had written that

morning. "Are there any other facts that would raise criminal problems?" By this time, Cooper testified, he had come to believe that North
and Poindexter had known the true nature of the cargo when the Hawk
delivery was made, that their statements to the contrary had been knowingly false, and that they had deliberately attempted to mislead Meese
and Cooper when discussing the proposed statements that Casey and
Poindexter would make to the congressional committees.

John Richardson's grand jury testimony was more general than
Cooper's. "The big problem for us," said Richardson, "was what laws
might have been kicked into focus or violated by the administration by
shipping these arms in 'eighty-five, before there was a finding in
'eighty-six. And that was the entire focus—whether the U.S. government
knew about it and authorized it."

Meese, however, denied to us that the legality of the November 1985
Hawk shipment had been at issue in his investigation. When deposed by
Gillen in May 1992, the former attorney general said that he had undertaken his investigation on the "assumption that everything was legal,"
and he claimed not to have believed that there had been any question of
illegality "until the memorandum was found regarding the diversion."

On Friday, November 21, Meese had joined Donald Regan in a morning meeting with the president and Poindexter. According to Meese's
testimony to the select committees, he had explained to the president
that "because of the highly compartmentalized nature of the whole initiative, . . . people had not talked to each other, you did not have the
normal documentation and reporting, and . . . therefore there was a
great deal of confusion. . . ." Meese had said that he had told the president that it was "absolutely necessary" that "someone look into the
matter . . . to develop a coherent overview of the facts." The president
had accepted Meese's offer to undertake the mission and had asked him
to report at the senior advisors' meeting set for the following Monday.

At this point, the obvious legal tasks had been twofold: to find out
whether the conduct of the president and the administration had violated the various statutes Congress had enacted to control U.S. covert
involvement in foreign military and paramilitary operations; and to prevent administration officials from committing new crimes, primarily
lying to Congress, to cover up any violations that had occurred.

Although the applicable statutes had acknowledged the president's
constitutional powers with regard to foreign policy, the administration
had been required to promptly notify Congress of foreign covert
actions. If an action was too sensitive to permit its disclosure to the

entire Congress, the administration had been bound to report it to the leaders of the House and Senate and the chairmen and ranking minority members of the intelligence and foreign relations committees—who were known as the "gang of eight." The CIA could have undertaken a covert action only if it was pursuant to a written finding signed by the president, with notice to the gang of eight. No other government agency could have undertaken a foreign covert action without the president's written approval and explanation of why he had selected an agency other than the CIA. Any agency that had undertaken such intelligence activity would have been required to report it to Congress.

As the embarrassing details of the arms sales came to light, it was Peter Wallison who, in his singleness of concern for the president, had waded into the legal quagmire in which the president had become trapped. While the president's foreign policy advisors scurried for cover, argued about policy, and struggled to refurbish U.S. prestige abroad, Wallison had assessed the president's legal vulnerabilities and had addressed the policy confrontation that might expose him to impeachment. Wallison had been chiefly concerned that the president not be drawn into the kind of cover-up that had disgraced the Nixon administration.

Wallison had found an able ally in Abraham Sofaer, one of the most skilled of the government lawyers to have dealt with Iran-Contra. Although primarily concerned for his own client, George Shultz, Sofaer had recognized that a presidential debacle would doom any federal official who had been involved, no matter how reluctantly, in the policy of trading arms for hostages. Moreover, in the best tradition of the profession, Sofaer had been unwilling to be a party to a cover-up.

Wallison and Sofaer had been accustomed to working with Cooper, their usual liaison in the Justice Department. Together, the three lawyers had succeeded in identifying and deleting the specific false claims that Casey and Poindexter had planned to include in their prepared statements, but Poindexter and Casey had reinserted the lies in extemporaneous responses to questions. Later, the attorney general had overriden the efforts Wallison and Sofaer had made on behalf of truthfulness. Meese's four-day effort to develop a coherent overview had resulted in a simple, false denial that the president had known of the November 1985 Hawk shipment in advance.

In reporting on his investigation to the president's senior foreign policy advisors on November 24, Meese had not been speculating or giving an offhand view of the facts. He had been reporting on a mission, a critical mission, for the president and the administration. Meese had told the vice president, the secretaries of state and defense, the director of the CIA, the White House chief of staff, the national security advisor, and the president himself what Meese had concluded they should say when questioned by Congress. He had not expressly told them what to do, but he had told them what would have to be said to protect the president.

It was my duty to examine whether Meese's conduct would have been proper if the diversion of the arms sales proceeds to the Contras had never been discovered and had not deflected official scrutiny from the Iranian initiative. I then had to examine Meese's handling of the investigation of the diversion.

Meese had consistently claimed that he had been acting not as an attorney general conducting an investigation but simply as a cabinet member and friend compiling a factual overview for the president. Although Cooper's notes had designated the president's knowledge as an important aspect of the investigation, Meese told us in 1992 that he had never got around to asking the president what he had known, because the concerns about the November 1985 Hawk shipment had been superseded by the concerns about the diversion. Meese's 1986 notes, however, revealed that he had not listed the president among the officials to be interviewed.

The notes of both Meese and Cooper concerning Meese's fact-finding exercise revealed a plan to identify and isolate the possible evidence against the president. The individuals slated to be pinned down had included George Bush, Caspar Weinberger, George Shultz, Robert McFarlane, Oliver North, Paul Thompson, and John Poindexter. From Hill's notes and testimony, we knew that Meese had been concerned about what written evidence existed and what Shultz had actually given or shown Reagan. Next to Poindexter's name, Meese had written a reminder to obtain every document, including telephone logs. He had personally telephoned Poindexter to find out what he possessed. It was then that Poindexter had met with North and directed Thompson to pull together all the documents related to the sale of arms to Iran. When Thompson came into Poindexter's office with the December 1985 finding, Poindexter had destroyed it. Meanwhile, North had begun shredding his own files and altering NSC documents.

The top officials at the State Department had distrusted Meese. When Cooper asked for all the department's information regarding the

November 1985 Hawk shipment, for example, Hill had been reluctant to entrust his critical notes to Cooper or the Justice Department. Sofaer had nevertheless insisted that Hill comply with Cooper's request. One of the notes that Hill had not turned over expressed his concern that Meese would try to have Shultz "finger" McFarlane for something "that could get him prison."

When Cooper and Meese interviewed McFarlane on the afternoon of Friday, November 21, 1986, they had assured themselves that he possessed no written notes. McFarlane had falsely told them he had learned of the November 1985 Hawk shipment nine months after the event, while preparing for his own trip to Tehran. He had denied remembering his conversation with Shultz in Geneva. As Cooper and Meese were leaving, McFarlane had drawn Meese aside to tell him that whatever had been done was something that the president had generally favored. Questioned about this exchange during his appearance before the select committees, Meese had claimed that he had told McFarlane not to try to protect the president but to "tell exactly what happened." Meese had acknowledged that he might have also said, "If the president knew earlier, it might even be helpful as a legal matter." Cooper's notes contained nothing to suggest that Meese had asked McFarlane whether he had told the president about the November 1985 Hawk shipment. Meese told Gillen in 1992 that "what the president knew was not an issue at that time."

This conflicted with a computer note McFarlane had sent Poindexter immediately after being interviewed by Meese. According to the note, Meese had suggested to McFarlane that if the president had made "a mental finding" in advance of the transfers, that fact would have been helpful. "Well, on that score," McFarlane had added, "we ought to be OK because he was all for letting the Israelis do anything they wanted at the very first briefing at the hospital. Ed [Meese] seemed relieved at that." Confronted with McFarlane's account by the select committees, Meese had denied any recollection of discussing an oral or mental finding with McFarlane.

On Saturday, November 22, Hill had written a note expressing his suspicion that Meese, who was scheduled to interview Shultz that morning, was trying to get Shultz to support a claim that the president had been misled. Shultz had told Hill that "when [the matter is] dug into—[it] will be shown that [the president] pushed these people."

The interview had begun at eight in the morning. Shultz had told Meese that the president had admitted two days earlier that he had known about the Hawk shipment. Meese had responded that the president had not taken notes, and that he had trouble remembering meetings. According to Hill, Meese had then asked Shultz, "As of November 1985, did [you] know of any contact by McFarlane with the president?" Shultz had replied that he did not. Meese had then told Shultz that the law might have been violated, and that the president had not known about the Hawk shipment. According to Hill's notes, Meese had said that if the Hawks had been shipped to Iran and the president had not reported it to Congress, it would have been "a violation." Cooper had omitted this remark in his notes, but otherwise they generally supported Hill's account.

Immediately after Meese left the State Department, Shultz had consulted Abraham Sofaer, Michael Armacost, John Whitehead, and Nicholas Platt. Shultz had asked Sofaer whether he was serving the secretary of state or the president. According to Hill's notes, Sofaer had said that he felt he could serve both, but he had added that if the information indicated that someone had broken the law, as in the case of Watergate, he could not simply step away from the evidence. Shultz, Sofaer had advised, could not do so either "just because you are a nice guy." Shultz had been ready to be open, but he had had reservations about dealing with the White House. Believing that Poindexter had been supplying the president's advisors with false information, Shultz had cautioned Sofaer about providing information to the White House.

According to Platt's notes, Sofaer had felt that "the president is in the hands of people who are lying." According to Hill's notes, Shultz had believed that the president had sent the attorney general to find out whether people had been telling him things that were untrue. Hill had predicted that the president would find his way out of the scandal by claiming to have been misled.

After leaving Shultz, Meese had again interviewed McFarlane, then had lunched with Cooper, Reynolds, and Richardson. Reynolds and Richardson had told the attorney general that they had discovered Oliver North's memorandum describing the diversion of the arms sales proceeds to the Contras. That afternoon, while Reynolds and Richardson returned to North's office and resumed searching his surviving files, Meese and Cooper had continued their investigation of the November 1985 Hawk delivery. From Stanley Sporkin, the CIA's former general counsel, Meese and Cooper had learned of the president's December 1985 finding retroactively approving the Hawk shipment. Sporkin had claimed to have been told that the Hawk shipment had been an arms-for-hostages trade, and to have drafted the finding to reflect that fact. He had also revealed that CIA officials had known that the cargo being transported consisted of Hawk missiles.

Cooper had spent the evening interviewing other officials at the CIA. His assistant, John McGinniss, had spent the entire night reading the summaries of the National Security Agency's intelligence reports on the arms-for-hostages negotiations—summaries that had been regularly distributed to Poindexter, North, Casey, Robert Gates, and Caspar Weinberger. The summaries had revealed, among other things, the Iranians' complaints that they had been overcharged. After completing his review, McGinniss had prepared a set of questions to be asked of North. Meese, Cooper, Richardson, and Reynolds had questioned North for nearly four hours on Sunday afternoon but failed to ask him any of the five questions McGinniss had raised regarding the president's knowledge.

According to Richardson's notes, North had claimed to have been told by Israelis that the shipment had contained oil-related equipment but to have learned shortly afterward that it had contained missiles. He had said that he had alerted the compromised CIA officials to this fact. North had denied having known about the December 1985 finding, and Meese had not asked him whether a retroactive finding had been signed. North had told Meese that President Reagan had been motivated not by any desire to improve America's strategic relationship with Iran but by the fact that he "wanted the hostages." Meese had unsuccessfully pressed North to try to get him to say that Reagan had talked about both.

Although North had admitted that funds from the arms sales had been directed to the Contras, he had attributed the scheme to the Israelis. He had claimed that he, Poindexter, and McFarlane had been the only government officials who had known about it. North had told Meese that any legal problems arising from his activities were limited to the diversion and the November 1985 Hawk shipment.

On Monday, November 24, Meese had questioned McFarlane for the third time, before meeting with the president and Donald Regan. Meese had then conferred with George Bush. To the select committees, Meese had stated that he had informed Bush of the diversion that morning but that he was uncertain whether he had told Reagan about it then or had simply alerted him to an important development that they would need to discuss later. Bush had denied prior knowledge of the diversion.

At two that afternoon, President Reagan had met with senior foreign policy advisors Bush, Shultz, Weinberger, Meese, Casey, Regan, and Poindexter in the situation room. George Cave had summarized the arms transactions, then left the meeting. Regan, for whom Wallison had prepared a series of questions, had asked whether "we objected to" the November 1985 Hawk shipment, providing the opening for Meese to say that McFarlane had outlined the proposed shipment to Shultz in Geneva in November 1985, but that President Reagan had been told only that the hostages might soon be released.

Meese had explained that the shipment had misfired, and that the Hawks had been returned to Israel in February 1986. According to Weinberger's notes, Meese had advised the group that the shipment was "not legal because [there was] no finding" and that the "president [had] *not* [been] informed." According to Regan's notes, Meese had said that there might have been "a violation of law if arms [were] shipped [without] a finding. But the [president] did not know." Regan had noted that Weinberger had denied knowing about the shipment. Meese then added that the "Israelis may have done this . . . probably using [the] president's name. . . . [The] president [was] only told maybe [the] hostages [would be] out in short order." No one at the meeting had contradicted Meese, although everyone else—including the president—had actually been informed of the Hawk shipment in advance.

Cooper told the grand jury that he had not attended the meeting but had concluded that Reagan had known in advance of the Hawk shipment and might have approved it. Cooper claimed not to have discussed his views with Meese or to have reviewed Meese's presentation to the meeting, rationalizing that because Cooper and Meese had talked with the same informants, Meese knew what Cooper knew.

After the meeting, Shultz had returned to the State Department and told Hill, "They may lay all this off on Bud [McFarlane]. That won't be enough." Shultz had complained that he had expected Meese to report fully on his weekend investigation. Instead, Meese's presentation had been brief, and Poindexter had used up most of the time arguing for a continuation of the Iranian initiative. Shultz had described President Reagan as "very hot under the collar [and] determined he was totally right."

On November 25, when Poindexter resigned and North was fired, Meese had taken over the presidential press conference and reiterated the false story that the president had not learned of the November 1985 Hawk shipment until February 1986. Meese had also declared that all shipments had been legal.

In 1992, Gillen questioned Shultz about the conversation in which he had told Meese that the president had known about the shipment in advance. Appearing unperturbed by Meese's contradiction, Shultz said that he had assumed that Meese might have had more information. Charles Hill was more direct: He had thought that Meese was trying to make Shultz back off. Hill described Meese's style of questioning as "leading" and said that Meese had stood over Shultz during the interview in a "back-on-your-heels" manner.

Gillen deposed the former attorney general in May 1992. Meese appeared voluntarily and came to our office without an attorney. Although the interrogation was thorough, it was not particularly confrontational. Gillen hoped to get as much as he could from Meese as an informant. Too much time had passed for an effective prosecution based on new lies, and Meese had—by claiming not to recall events—avoided telling prosecutable lies in the past. The interrogation was lengthy and broken periodically by recesses, as Meese retreated to the men's room to think before answering some of the questions.

Gillen was surprised when Meese unexpectedly agreed that Shultz had told him that the president had admitted that he had known about the November 1985 Hawk shipment. This set up an inevitable series of difficulties for Meese as Gillen led him through note after note.

"Did you express a concern to Mr. Shultz," asked Gillen, "that it was important that the president not know about the 'eighty-five shipments because they could potentially be a violation of law?'"

"No," Meese replied. "I'm positive I didn't say that."

Gillen then read from Hill's note: " 'Certain things could be violation of a law. President didn't know about Hawks in November. If it happened and president didn't report it to Congress, it's a violation.' Do you remember making such a statement to Mr. Shultz?"

"No, I don't," Meese replied. "I don't remember that about violation of law and that sort of thing. . . . I don't know whether he misunderstood me or what I was trying to say there."

Meese next denied having said that the president had not known of the Hawk shipment and denied having said that it could have been a violation of law. "I'm sure I would not have said that. It seems strange to have me saying that. I'm not sure what that means." He then claimed to have no recollection of this portion of his conversation with Shultz.

As the subject of the deposition turned to the November 24, 1986, meeting of the president's senior advisors, Meese asked for more recesses. Each time he returned, he claimed not to recall having felt or expressed any concern about the legality of the November 1985 Hawk shipment. Confronted with the notes in which Regan and Weinberger had stated that Meese had told the meeting's participants that the president had not known about the Hawk shipment, Meese claimed not to recall it. He said that he could not have made the statement because Shultz had told him two days earlier that the president had admitted knowing of the Hawk shipment. When Gillen pressed him, Meese said, "I can't explain it."

Gillen then confronted him with the statement he had made at the press conference the day after the meeting—that the president had not known of the Hawk shipment.

"I'm confused now," said Meese.

In 1987, when associate counsel Judith Hetherton first questioned Meese, our chief interest in him had concerned the delays in his fact-finding investigation and his earlier intrusions—at the request of Poindexter and North—into collateral Justice Department investigations of gunrunning in Central America. Our primary goal then had been to have him testify against North. Neither we nor the congressional committees had adequately questioned Meese about his effort to cover up Ronald Reagan's advance knowledge of the November 1985 Hawk shipment.

If we had been able to question Meese about the notes of Charles Hill, Caspar Weinberger, and Donald Regan in 1987, his dubious lack of recollection and his flat denial of having said what those at the November 24 meeting heard him say would have led to a more extensive investigation and a probable prosecution. By 1992, however, to have asked the grand jury to indict Meese for a false statement made to us five years after the event would have invited the plausible defense that the delay, in itself, created a reasonable doubt that the misstatement had been deliberate rather than a faded and erroneous recollection.

The basic cause for our failure to proceed further against Meese had been the delay in the production of notes. Perhaps more than any other single failure, it drove home to me some of the major mistakes I had made: my initial underestimation of the scope of my job; my consistent understaffing; my reliance on document requests rather than subpoenas; and my drastic narrowing of our early investigation in an unsuccessful effort to escape the consequences of the congressional grants of immunity to Poindexter and North. While making my task infinitely more difficult, the cover-up had saved its chief architect from suffering the fate of President Nixon's attorney general John Mitchell and following further in his footsteps—perhaps all the way to prison.

CHAPTER TWENTY-ONE

Like Brushing
His Teeth

Robert McFarlane once observed, "I did not have any Hawk missiles in my basement." The man who had controlled the arsenal of the United States was the secretary of defense, Caspar "Cap" Weinberger. His acquiescence had been necessary to assure the Israelis of replacements for the weapons they sold to the Iranians. For this reason, even though Weinberger had opposed the arms sales, McFarlane had kept him informed about the progress of the arms-for-hostages efforts. We had to discover what Weinberger had known about those efforts and the cover-up that had occurred when news of the arms sales became public.

That Weinberger had opposed the arms shipments was irrefutable, but he had not merely simplified his testimony, he had flatly lied. Weinberger had misinformed Congress about his knowledge of the 1985 Israeli arms shipments to Iran. He had denied having known in advance of the November 1985 Hawk shipment, and he had denied having known that the Israelis expected the United States to replace the arms that Israel had shipped. Both denials had concerned his official responsibilities. Both had concealed Ronald Reagan's violation of the Arms Export Control Act.

On July 31, 1987, Neil Eggleston, the deputy chief counsel of the House select committee on Iran-Contra, had asked Weinberger about the Hawk shipment, saying, "The committee has also received testimony that on the weekend of November 23 and November 24 there was a shipment of eighteen Hawk missiles from Israel to Iran. . . . Did you have any knowledge that that transfer was to take place?"

"No," Weinberger had responded, "I did not."

His notes, however, revealed a series of conversations with McFarlane for two weeks before the shipment, beginning with Weinberger's protests against the policy. The notes literally documented McFarlane's request for five hundred Hawk missiles, Weinberger's discussions with his top military aide, and his response to McFarlane. "Colin Powell in office re: data on Hawks—can't be given to Israel or Iran [without congressional] notification," Weinberger had written in one note. "Breaking them up into several packages of 28 Hawks to keep each package under $14 million is a clear violation." He had then recorded his warning to the national security advisor: "Called McFarlane in Geneva—re above—he 'thanks me for call.'"

When questioned by Craig Gillen, Powell had explained to us that this was McFarlane's way of dismissing a subject: "So, whereas Mr. Weinberger was calling back to Mr. McFarlane to tell him, 'This is illegal; it's a bad idea; you shouldn't be doing this,' he was getting back from Mr. McFarlane something along the lines [of] 'thanks for the call,' rather than 'I agree' or 'I don't agree.'" The day after this call, Weinberger had written on his five-by-seven-inch notepad that McFarlane had called from Geneva and that Weinberger had "told him we shouldn't pay Iranians anything—he [said] president has decided to do it thru Israelis." Weinberger noted that "Bud McFarlane . . . [is] working on broad agreement language—Israelis will sell 120 Hawks older models to Iranians—Friday release." Weinberger had added that he had "called Colin Powell re above." Later, Weinberger had received intelligence reports that eighteen Hawks had been delivered.

Two weeks after the arms sales were exposed, Weinberger had met with the Senate intelligence committee in a closed session and had been asked by Senator William Cohen, "So, to the best of your recollection, there was no discussion about the Israelis transferring arms and us possibly resupplying them?"

"Not in my presence," Weinberger had responded. "No. I heard about that only much later after these things started to come out, and as I say I heard—only heard that statements were being made, not that that had actually happened."

We could not prosecute Weinberger for this lie to the Senate intelligence committee, because the five-year statute of limitations had run. But he had repeated the false denial eight months later before the select committees on Iran-Contra, a crime that had occurred within the statutory period.

"In addition," he had been asked during the later hearings, "there are various documents, which are in evidence before the committee [and] which refer to the Israeli desire and need for replenishment of weapons, that the Israelis were sending to you. Did you know that replenishment was an issue?"

"No," Weinberger had replied, "I have no memory of that."

McFarlane had told the select committees that he had informed Weinberger in the summer of 1985 that the president had agreed to replenish the Israelis' stockpile of weapons. McFarlane had reminded Weinberger, as well as the president, of this commitment on December 10, 1985. Notes taken by Weinberger that day included the following sentence: "We still must replace 500 TOWs to Israel." A month later, Weinberger had learned that the Israelis had agreed to postpone the replenishment until after the hostages had been released. The TOWs sent by Israel in September 1985 had been replaced by the Defense Department in May 1986, when the Hawk spare parts were sold to Iran.

When we told McFarlane of the existence of Weinberger's notes, McFarlane became angry. To a certain extent, he had been victimized by the effort Edwin Meese and Donald Regan had undertaken to shield the president. If McFarlane had had access to the notes, his early testimony before the congressional intelligence committees might have been more emphatic. He could also have been more authoritative in his public disputes with Donald Regan. McFarlane told us that he specifically remembered having been asked by Weinberger, "Are you sure the president approved of it [the Hawks shipment]?" and having answered in the affirmative. McFarlane said that he had urged Weinberger to speak to the president. McFarlane was also certain that he had told Weinberger and the president's advisors that replenishment of the Israeli stockpile was necessary.

One of Weinberger's principal concerns had been maintaining good relations with Saudi Arabia, a pivotal ally in the Middle East and a recipient of sophisticated weapons from the United States. Consequently, Weinberger's relationship with the Saudi ambassador, Prince Bandar, had been of utmost importance. The Reagan administration's most flagrant defiance of Congress's effort to control policy through appropriations had been McFarlane's suggestion to Prince Bandar that Saudi money replace the funds Congress had refused for the covert action in Nicaragua.

Weinberger's false statements had consistently shielded not only the president but also Prince Bandar. On September 4, 1986, for example, Weinberger had dissembled in his response to a letter of inquiry from Congressman Dante Fascell, chairman of the House foreign affairs committee. Asked about a public report of a fund—said to have been created from the sale of airborne warning and control system (AWACS) aircraft to the Saudis—that was being used to support the Contras, Weinberger had written that he "regarded the allegations of Saudi funding of U.S. assistance to anti-government forces in Nicaragua as so outlandish as to be unworthy of comment from this department."

On December 17, 1986, six weeks after the arms sales to Iran and the diversion of funds to the Contras had been exposed, Weinberger had testified at a closed session of the Senate intelligence committee and had falsely denied having known about the Saudi funding of the Contras.

"Have you been in any meetings . . . in the last two years," Senator Bill Bradley had asked Weinberger, "that discussed the funding of the Contras outside of a direct congressional act?"

"No," Weinberger had replied. "I did spend a lot of time trying to persuade various members of the Senate and House that the hundred million dollars was required and—"

"But outside of—"

"Not outside. No sir, no."

"You have had no discussions with any third party about provision of equipment or money to the Contras?"

"No sir."

"You've been in no meeting where it was discussed?"

"To get—from outside assistance?"

"Uh-huh."

"No," Weinberger had said. "I don't have any recollection of that. I know there were a lot of attempts to get aid to the Contras, but my efforts were concentrated entirely on trying to get the hundred-million-dollar bill passed."

"But prior to that, in 1985 or early 1986, you had no discussions with anyone about providing funds or equipment to the Contras?"

"I have no recollection of anything of that kind at all, senator. No. I concentrated, as I said, entirely on trying to get the Congress to approve the hundred-million-dollar appropriation, which I thought then and think now was very necessary."

"You were in no meeting in which this was discussed?"

"I don't have any recollection of it, senator. I really don't. No."

Seven months later, Weinberger had taken the same stance before the select committees on Iran-Contra. In the course of being deposed by the staff of the House select committee, he had been asked, "Do you recall learning at some point that the Saudis or some people connected with the Saudis provided funds for the Contras?"

"No," he had responded. "I don't have any memory of any Contra funding or anything connected with the Saudis that I can remember now."

On July 31, 1987, Weinberger had appeared before the select committees in a joint hearing and had been questioned about a memorandum prepared by William Casey's deputy, John McMahon, based on a conversation between Weinberger and Casey at one of their weekly breakfast meetings. According to McMahon's memorandum, Weinberger had reported that Prince Bandar had earmarked $25 million for the Contras in $5 million increments. When confronted with this memorandum at the hearing, Weinberger had said, "Well, I don't really . . . remember saying it, but I did frequently joke with Mr. Casey to the effect that I frequently picked up things from his rival intelligence agency, which was one of the morning radio stations, and I may very well, simply have been passing on that kind of a report. I don't have any specific memory of it, but John McMahon is a good reporter, so he probably heard the statement made. . . ."

"But you don't have any recollection of being advised by Mr. McFarlane or—"

"No."

"—the president or anyone else that there had been such a large contribution from [Saudi Arabia]?"

"No. The reason I am quite sure about it is that we were all making major efforts at that time to get funding for the Contras from the Congress."

Having lied shortly after the first public exposure of the Saudi contribution in December 1986, Weinberger had been forced to maintain that position later, but this had required him to also deny the existence of his notes, which would have revealed that on May 20, 1984, the day after Prince Bandar informed McFarlane that the Saudis would provide $1 million a month to the Contras, Bandar had visited Weinberger in his office. Weinberger had informed McFarlane of the visit and had talked with him about U.S. officials' soliciting foreign countries for aid to Central America.

Several months after Bandar's visit, General John "Jack" Vessey, who had replaced Admiral William Crowe as the chairman of the Joint Chiefs of Staff, had told Weinberger that Bandar had given $25 million to the Contras. Weinberger had telephoned McFarlane and made diary notes of both conversations. The next morning, Weinberger had told Casey, McMahon, and William Taft about the contribution at the breakfast meeting described in McMahon's memorandum.

Interviewed in 1992 by my associate counsel Tom Baker, Vessey said that Bandar had twice told him of the contribution, and that he had passed the information along to Weinberger both times. According to Vessey, Weinberger had simply replied that he did not want the issue to become public. Vessey said he believed that one of his conversations with Weinberger about the contribution had taken place during a White House meeting with McFarlane on May 25, 1984, concerning an AWACS sale to the Saudis. Questioned by Baker, McFarlane confirmed this meeting as well as Weinberger's earlier telephone report about Bandar's gift to the Contras.

After the investigations began, Vessey had warned Weinberger that he had just told an FBI agent about his conversations with Prince Bandar and with Weinberger. Weinberger had made the following diary note: "Jack Vessey in office—he remembers telling McFarlane about Saudi. Claimed they had sent funds to Contras." By this time, Weinberger had already committed himself to the cover-up.

Weinberger's diary notes documented his assiduous attention to relations with Saudi Arabia and his concern about Nicaragua. During the three years of the administration's illegal secret efforts to support the Contras, Weinberger had noted at least sixty-four contacts with Prince Bandar, including sixteen meetings at the Pentagon. Weinberger's public denials of knowledge of the Saudi contributions had supported Bandar's denials, including an October 21, 1986, press release in which the prince had stated, "Saudi Arabia is not and has not been involved either directly or indirectly in any military or other support activity of any kind for or in connection with any group or groups concerned with Nicaragua."

We had no doubt whatsoever that Weinberger's note-taking had been a purposeful, deliberate, and important part of his daily routine. Nor did we doubt that he had knowingly concealed the notes' existence. We had documented five separate investigative requests for Weinberger's handwritten notes, logs, and diaries.

On April 4, 1987, the Senate select committee had requested that the Defense Department produce all documents relating to the Iranian initiative, including "notes, . . . diaries, . . . or other such records, of attendance at, recollection of, or participation in, . . . any meetings, discussions, conferences, or events pertaining to the committee's inquiry, prepared by or in the possession of" several individuals, including Weinberger. Ten days later, the House select committee had made a similar request for documents, including "calendars, logs, diaries, appointment books, records of meetings, and handwritten notes kept by or on behalf of" certain individuals, including Weinberger. Weinberger had instructed the Defense Department's general counsel, Lawrence Garrett, to produce all the documents requested by the committees, but Weinberger himself had withheld virtually all his notes.

This had been no oversight. Before serving the Defense Department with the document request, Arthur Liman, the Senate committee's chief counsel, had met with Weinberger personally and inquired about his notes. According to Liman's memorandum summarizing the meeting, Weinberger had responded, "I have the deepest sympathy for the president's memory problems. . . . I should have done what Henry Kissinger did after every meeting. He would dictate a thorough memo of what transpired, which was used in writing his memoirs. For me, after I finish a meeting, I go off to another meeting." After Liman left, Weinberger had picked up a five-by-seven pad and noted, "2 Senate staff of special Iran committee in office—with Larry Garrett—re my recollections of Iran events."

The Defense Department's general counsel had relayed to Weinberger the committee's formal request for documents in a series of memoranda. We knew that at least one of these memoranda had reached Weinberger, because it was stamped "SEC DEF HAS SEEN April 20, 1987." Garrett had also sent Weinberger a personal memorandum that specified the request for notes and diaries and added, "I know you understand the nature of the obligations placed upon us by this request. I understand that these materials, if any such exist, are highly personal and sensitive. Accordingly, I would, of course, insist that any provision of these materials to the committees, be conducted in as discreet and limited a manner as you wish."

Weinberger had returned the memo with a note that said, "Larry— let's have a meeting after you hear what others are doing." Four days later, Garrett had conferred with Weinberger, who had memorialized the meeting in a note that said: "Larry Garrett in office—re demands by Sen-House Committees for briefings on black programs—plus their demand for my diary."

At a White House meeting, Garrett and other general counsel had discussed President Reagan's plan to permit a review of excerpts of his personal diary. Garrett had reported this to William Taft, warning him that the Senate committee had asked whether Weinberger kept a diary. Garrett had written, "I do not know whether the secretary keeps a diary, but it is obviously necessary to pursue this." Taft had told Garrett that Weinberger had regularly kept notes during Richard Nixon's administration. Taft had advised Garrett to ask Weinberger and his secretary to be sure that everything had been produced. That day, Weinberger had written in his diary, "Larry Garrett in office re preparation for Senate, House staff interview on Iran [hearings]—also re papers to be turned over."

The next day, Garrett's assistant, Edward J. Shapiro, had told Liman's executive assistant, Mark A. Belnick, that Weinberger's office staff had informed him that Weinberger had "entries in his diaries responsive to requests 'but not many.' " Later, a House committee lawyer had written Garrett that the committee had received a few documents from Weinberger, but not Weinberger's "diaries, appointment books, records of meetings, and handwritten notes." The lawyer had specified that the committee's request was "inclusive of personal diary entries made from October 1984 through 1987, pertaining to the Boland Amendment, Iran, Nicaragua, and the Contras." On June 10, the lawyer had followed up with another letter. Two days later, Weinberger had noted that he had been consulted about "data on my calendar to be turned over to Iran committee." Weinberger had then produced his official calendars and activity logs but none of his diary notes and only one of his meeting notes.

On June 17, the House select committee's chief counsel, John Nields, and an associate had taken Weinberger's deposition in his office at the Pentagon. Weinberger had sat at a conference table, facing his huge desk, whose drawers were filled with his notes. After discussing a number of meetings, the counsel had asked, "Is there any way you have of making a record of the highlights of meetings of this nature?"

"Now?" Weinberger had asked.

"No," counsel had said, "then."

"No," Weinberger had replied. "There wasn't. I did dictate a memorandum on this particular one [the November 10, 1986, National Security Planning Group meeting], but I've often said that I understand that Henry Kissinger made a memo of every meeting he ever attended, and that enabled him to write his book rapidly. I wish I had done that with day one of the administration. I am usually getting ready for the next meeting, and don't have time to write these memorandums. I took notes about this one and dictated this memorandum, because it seemed to be important."

"Do you ever take notes that are not dictated?" counsel had asked. "Or make jottings when you get back?"

"Yes," Weinberger had said, looking at his desk, "occasionally, but comparatively rarely. I don't know if we kept those in any formal way. I don't think they have been filed or labeled. My handwriting is notoriously bad. I have trouble even reading it myself. [I] occasionally take a few notes, but not really very often."

"If there is any chance there are—"

"I think we made this examination, and whatever there is, is in our so-called C and D, correspondence and directives. They have been asked to plow through everything."

Later in the deposition, Weinberger had been asked, "Are you aware of any other potential source of . . . a record that might supplement your memory of some of these meetings?"

"Well," he had replied, "I don't really think of anything. We could plow through everything again; we have done that, I think pretty well."

When the congressional lawyers left, Weinberger had picked up a five-by-seven pad and written, "Gave deposition to Senate plus House staff members on joint Iran investigation.—10:35 AM–1:10 PM. Larry Garrett & Mr. Shapiro there." He had then opened a desk drawer and deposited this notepad with the others.

Weinberger had never produced his daily notes or additional meeting notes to any congressional committee. When he resigned as secretary of defense in 1987, shortly after the conclusion of the select committee's hearings, he had boxed up his notes himself. As he packed them, he had allowed a photographer to take pictures of the notes for a possible magazine profile. The photographer and Weinberger had briefly discussed the fact that they both kept diaries. His counsel later argued to us that this showed Weinberger to be innocent, that it proved his lack of intent to lie. To me, it showed a total lack of concern for the truth, if it got in his way.

The fact was that Weinberger knew his notes conflicted with the positions taken by President Reagan and Vice President Bush as well as by himself and other cabinet officers. He kept them secret until after the Iran-Contra select committees concluded their hearings. He then tried to conceal them from me.

When I read Tom Baker's summary of the notes Weinberger had concealed, my instincts told me that we should charge him with having participated in a continuing cover-up of Ronald Reagan's illegal actions and a massive obstruction of the investigation of Iran-Contra. Weinberger's misconduct had been part of a broader pattern of obstruction by the Reagan administration that had begun on November 10, 1986, and had entailed withholding information from congressional leaders; blocking our work by overclassifying documents; lying to Congress, the Tower Commission, the grand jury, and my staff; and withholding Weinberger's notes, those dictated by George Shultz to Charles Hill, and those taken by other high-ranking officials, including Edwin Corr, Nicholas Platt, and Donald Regan. To put together such a broad case, however, would take months. Each individual episode would be a mini-trial, and the statute of limitations was running out. A more limited alternative that would allow us to investigate and expose the cover-up of the illegal 1985 arms transactions would be to prosecute Weinberger alone for perjury and obstruction of a congressional investigation.

On April 14, 1992, my legal staff and I held our first meeting to discuss our options regarding Weinberger. Craig Gillen, Tom Baker, Christina Spaulding, and John Barrett summarized the notes and the charges to be considered.

Weinberger's congressional testimony seemed to have been prepared without the least concern for his notes. He had always begun his testimony by noting his criticism of McFarlane's proposal to open the arms trade with Iran. He had then moved to the December 1985 meetings, pausing only briefly to mention his vague recollection of the August 1985 meeting in which the Israeli arms deliveries had first been discussed by the president and his senior foreign policy advisors. Weinberger had next moved on to the January 1986 discussion of the presidential finding, under which the Defense Department would provide arms to the CIA for shipment to Iran. Sometimes Weinberger had claimed not to have been told that the president had signed the finding. At other times he had acknowledged having sent William Taft to the White House in April 1986 to read the finding and make certain that it provided adequate authority for the Defense Department to sell the Hawk missile parts that McFarlane would take to Iran.

Weinberger had consistently denied having known about the 1985 shipments through Israel, their linkage to the release of Benjamin Weir, the U.S. commitment to replace the TOWs shipped by Israel, and the November 1985 Hawk shipment. Throughout his congressional testimony, Weinberger had tried to portray the president and himself as having had no responsibility for the arms sales, while characterizing McFarlane and the National Security Council's staff as rogue agents who had misled the president.

The core of Weinberger's false position, as his notes revealed, had been his deep concern about the illegality of the 1985 shipments. He had obviously believed that the president's authorization of these shipments without notice to Congress might have been an impeachable offense. His lies to Congress had been intended to shield the president. Weinberger's own possible complicity had further motivated his testimony. Once he had lied, he had had no choice but to deny the existence of his vivid notes, because they contradicted his testimony.

At the conclusion of our staff meeting, one associate counsel questioned whether our investigation was still a sufficiently live issue. Gillen suggested that we not make an immediate decision, but await further testimony. I agreed, but I told the staff that my tentative decision was to proceed against Weinberger. In my view, a president might occasionally use his power in furtherance of some questionable policy, but if he was caught, he had to tell the truth, and so did his subordinates. I was glad to see our focus shifting back to the actions of the president and his highest advisors, after being diverted to the pursuit of subordinates and the supposed runaway conspiracy.

Furthermore, when a witness lied to us as arrogantly as Weinberger had done, we had to react. Mike Foster's FBI report of Weinberger's interview was good and would support a prosecution. In my judgment, we had been exceptionally courteous to Bill Rogers and had given Weinberger a chance to come in and tell us the full truth. If he had done so, we would have had a difficult decision to make. But Weinberger had chosen to continue lying. I did not see how we could look the other way.

As our investigation progressed, I anticipated a political counterattack. I began to prepare a defense against criticism of Gillen and me for not having moved our homes to Washington and for our travel and lodging expenses. I had Phil Rooney, our finance officer, allocate our general office expenses among the various investigations and trials. I doubted that our expenses for Oliver North's trial had exceeded the expenses for his defense. I also believed that the expenses of the congressional investigation would prove greater than ours, at least during the period we had overlapped. Rooney was prepared to show the sharp decline in our expenses after North's trial. We also worked steadily on our final report, so that it would be ready if we were closed down.

On April 16, from ten o'clock until noon, Gillen, Barrett, Baker, and I conferred with Weinberger's new lawyers, Robert Bennett, Carl Rauh, and Roberto Iraola. This meeting was one of twelve we held with

Weinberger's lawyers within a six-week period in the spring of 1992. Gillen had already met with Robert Bennett and had warned me that he was "a piece of work." The antithesis of Brendan Sullivan, the rotund Bennett radiated joviality and informality. With his coat off, the collar of his brightly striped shirt open, and a dazzling tie hanging loosely between cheerful suspenders, he beamed pleasantly through oversized glasses and ran his hand through his thick dark hair. He was regarded as one of the most effective white-collar criminal lawyers in Washington (he would later defend President Bill Clinton in a private lawsuit), and I hoped he would be candid, realistic, and professional.

Carl Rauh, a former U.S. attorney for the District of Columbia, the son of the archliberal Joseph Rauh, was tall and slender. He usually kept quiet, but he was ready to speak up when the conversation turned to litigation. Roberto Iraola, a former assistant U.S. attorney, was obviously responsible for keeping track of the details of the case. The team seemed not only able but affable as well.

Bennett suggested that we had a common problem: how to reach a just solution that would end Weinberger's current embarrassment. Contrasting himself with Brendan Sullivan, Bennett said that he eschewed the practice of inundating the opposition with motions. Then, although he knew that I was a friend and former colleague of Bill Rogers, Bennett said that it had been Bill's failure to review the files in preparing Weinberger for his interview with us that had resulted in Weinberger's misstatements. I said nothing, but I considered this a cheap shot. I felt certain that Weinberger had misled Bill. Moreover, Weinberger had made the same misstatements to Congress more than three years before making them to us.

Bennett's most memorable argument was that Weinberger's denials of having taken notes had been innocent mistakes. He had simply forgotten that he took notes. His note-taking was so habitual that it was "like brushing his teeth"; it left no impression on his memory; he forgot it. I listened with a straight face, but the story convulsed my fellow lawyers when we shared it after the meeting was over. Even though we might forget actually brushing our teeth, we would hardly deny ever having brushed them.

Bennett went on to say that Weinberger had turned over to us all his notes, and that there had been no concealment. Our failure to obtain Weinberger's notes in a timely manner, Bennett said, had resulted from the negligence of my staff. I listened in stunned silence as Bennett pulled out and read from a copy of the unclassified register of the

Library of Congress's Weinberger collection: Item after item was clearly related to Iran-Contra. I had not realized that the register was so detailed. No one had told me, because no one wanted to embarrass the first lawyer we had sent to review the collection.

After they left, that lawyer explained that Weinberger's secretary and two members of the library's staff had given him the impression that his access was restricted to the classified section of the depository. Always more than fair, he acknowledged that he might have misunderstood them, but the search he had undertaken had been consistent with what Weinberger had told us. In view of the administration's tendency to overclassify potentially embarrassing documents, he had assumed that significant Iran-Contra documents would have been classified (and, according to the standards applied to the information we had sought, most of them should have been). When the librarian had tendered the index to him, it had been opened to the classified section; the unclassified section that preceded it had been closed. Furthermore, Weinberger had repeatedly said that he had taken only a few notes, a claim that had seemed borne out by the small number our lawyer had found in the unclassified section.

Hearing this explanation, I could picture what had happened. This lawyer was an outstanding scholar who respected librarians, particularly those at the Library of Congress. He had probably been led into a sterile part of the collection without anyone's having made express misstatements. Although I was chagrined about the incident, I did not berate him. There was no need. He knew that he had been too sure of himself in assuming that Weinberger's notes would have been properly classified. The incident had simply confirmed my longstanding observation that no matter how strong the case, in complex litigation something always goes wrong. That is why trials are rarely dull. At the same time, I could not let embarrassment affect a prosecutorial decision. That had to be made on the merits.

In a staff conference in late April, I played devil's advocate and argued the case for Weinberger. Many of the questions put to him by the congressional committees and their counsel had been imprecise. Excessively deferential, the questioners had permitted Weinberger to give rambling answers. I asked my staff whether we would prosecute Weinberger if he had told the truth to us in 1990. The staff expressed uncertainty. Some members said that they would have been reluctant to bring a case based solely on his lies to Congress, because so much time had passed since he told them. And yet, the prosecutability of his lies to

us might have been lessened by his having subsequently authorized us
to examine the material he had deposited in the Library of Congress.

After weighing the arguments in Weinberger's favor, I examined
those against him. On balance, I concluded that the library register
would hurt Weinberger. Placing highly sensitive, classifiable material
among unclassified personal records was, in itself, evidence of an intent
to conceal. The misfiling had delayed the discovery of the damaging
notes long enough to protect Weinberger from prosecution for at least
some of the crimes he had committed.

Viewing Weinberger's actions in the context of the Reagan
appointees' widespread practice of hiding notes, I concluded that the
concealment lay at the heart of our investigation. We could not prosecute everyone who had hidden his notes, because most had turned over
enough material to allow them to claim that the withholding had
resulted from accidental oversight. But we could prosecute one of these
individuals. As the highest-ranking and most arrogant member of the
lot, Weinberger was the obvious choice.

Word reached us that six or seven lawyers working for Robert Bennett
had been collecting affidavits from potential witnesses. This seemed a
dubious litigation tactic to us. If a witness is friendly, getting an affidavit too early in the process is usually a mistake. A witness's recollection improves as a case gets closer to trial and the lawyers have a clearer
view of what happened. An inaccurate or incomplete affidavit could easily be used by an opponent for cross-examination. If a witness is hostile,
an early affidavit might be valuable. In this case, however, I did not
believe that any witnesses—except possibly McFarlane—were hostile to
Weinberger.

It was important to show that Weinberger had not been forthcoming
and that we had been led to believe that there were no relevant notes.
Weinberger had not produced any of the material until we had subpoenaed and interviewed him. Before we interviewed Weinberger in 1990,
his secretary Kay Leisz had given us a memorandum that essentially
denied the existence of her boss's notes, but when we tried to question
her in 1992, she asserted her privilege against self-incrimination. It then
became clear that we would have to pin Bill Rogers down on his recollection of Weinberger's 1990 interview and the discussions of records
Rogers had had with Craig Gillen beforehand.

When we requested an interview with Rogers, he protested, citing his
position as a former lawyer for Weinberger, but finally agreed to a depo-

sition. Although Gillen remained polite throughout the process, Rogers was furious. He frequently refused to give responsive answers and insisted on making hostile speeches, accusing us of seeking to indict Weinberger to offset our record of failure.

Bill had written me asking for a meeting. I had referred him to Gillen because, ironically, I was not ready to indict Weinberger and I did not want to complicate a possible decision not to indict by our longstanding friendship. But I could not explain this to Rogers. In hardball prosecutions, as in hard-driving business, friendships suffer. One can only hope that in time they will be restored.

Near the end of April, Gillen, Barrett, Baker, and I had a long meeting with Bennett, Rauh, and two of their associates for a final review of the facts. The next day, Gillen and I met with Bennett and Rauh for an hour and a half to discuss a possible plea and proffer. We inquired about individuals, including President Reagan, but we did not specify any individual as a target. We said that we wanted a truthful statement from Weinberger about the activities of those involved in covering up the November 1985 Hawk shipment and other material facts. Bennett and Rauh did not say no, but they indicated that Weinberger was still adamantly opposed to pleading guilty to any charge. They agreed to discuss our invitation with him.

While we were carrying on these discussions with Bennett, he had persuaded Senators Daniel Inouye and Warren Rudman to write a letter saying that Weinberger's knowledge of the 1985 shipments through Israel had not been material to the select committees' inquiry. The senators claimed that they had been responsible for framing the issues for the hearings. When Congressman Lee Hamilton, who had chaired the House select committee, learned of the letter, he was angry. He disagreed with the senators' conclusions, which had belittled the importance of Weinberger's knowledge of the Israeli shipments and had ignored the cover-up of the president's illegal actions as well as Weinberger's deliberate concealment of his notes. The letter was inconsistent with the select committees' report, which both senators had signed.

Bennett's next move was to give us a report by a "memory expert," who asserted that Weinberger had innocently denied the existence of his notes because the note-taking had been so "routine, compulsive, and habitual" that it had not been "stored in memory for easy retrieval," and that the questioning of Weinberger by Congress and by us had lacked "sufficient specificity" to trigger any recollection. The expert had not reviewed the Defense Department's internal memoranda about the need to produce the notes.

Bennett also produced a polygraph examiner's report saying that no deception had been indicated by the polygraph when Weinberger denied that he had deliberately misled or lied to Iran-Contra investigators about his diary notes and when he denied that he had misled investigators about his knowledge of arms transfers to Iran.

On receiving this material, I wondered what tack Bennett was taking. All three documents showed a superficial view of Weinberger's misconduct and the prospective trial. The memory expert's testimony would be laughable. The lie-detector test would be inadmissible, and the significance of Weinberger's denials was weakened by the qualifying adverbs the interrogator had used in his questions; he had not simply asked Weinberger if he had lied. The letter from the senators revealed their own lack of interest in the administration's cover-up of President Reagan's deliberate violation of the law.

I found it appalling that the two senior leaders of the Senate select committee on Iran-Contra would have allowed themselves to be sucked into signing such a silly letter without at least talking to me first, but Inouye and Rudman had always wanted to stop at North and Poindexter. I knew that if the senators were to testify as witnesses for Weinberger, we would demolish them on cross-examination. Their letter, which seemed to me to be nothing more than politicians circling the wagons, helped convince me that Weinberger presented a true test of the applicability of the rule of law to the political upper crust.

If Weinberger's counsel thought that he was giving me reasons to back away from a prosecution, he was mistaken. What I failed to appreciate, however, was that Bennett was not thinking just about me or even just about the trial; he was building a record, shallow though it was, for a political defense or a political solution.

A week after receiving this material from Bennett, I showed a very able former colleague a memorandum detailing Weinberger's false statements to Congress and my staff. My friend's evaluation was that "with a small amount of perjury," Weinberger could escape conviction. The congressional interrogators had been too deferential and imprecise. Weinberger's 1990 interview with my staff had not yielded a question-and-answer transcript, as a deposition would have, but had merely provided an FBI agent's report of what had been said.

These observations did not convince me to drop the pursuit of Weinberger, but they confirmed my view that we should not prosecute

Weinberger just for his individual lies to Congress. Instead, we would have to make a broad case of obstruction of a congressional investigation.

The court of appeals, in reversing Pondexter's conviction, had recently narrowed the applicability of the obstruction statute. To prevail, we would have to show more than false statements; we would have to show that a defendant had actively concealed information and, perhaps, that he had corrupted others. Weinberger and those closest to him knew that he had taken notes and that he had not produced them. Although we had no evidence that these individuals had expressly conspired to withhold the notes, they had tacitly acquiesced in Weinberger's failure to produce them. When questioned by the select committees in 1987, for example, Colin Powell and Richard Armitage had given incomplete answers that avoided revealing the notes' existence. Regardless of whether the activities of Weinberger's associates had been criminal, the activities seemed corrupt enough to meet the new, poorly defined test of obstruction.

I spent the ten days leading up to May 14, when the grand jury would expire, going through the testimony by Weinberger and his associates, the transcripts of his notes, and the documents related to his failure to produce them. To build our case against Weinberger, we would have to confront Donald Regan and Edwin Meese, who would be openly hostile to us.

To confirm my judgment, I sought the opinion of Dan Webb, who had tried Poindexter. I spoke several times with Webb while he was trying a long case in Tucson, Arizona. He said that he thought our case against Weinberger was stronger than the case we had presented against Poindexter. Webb said that subject to the approval of his partners, he would be glad to try the case for us.

At a staff conference on May 5, we agreed that an indictment of Weinberger was likely. Gillen, Barrett, and Baker had already completed a draft of the indictment. From Weinberger's notes and our investigation, we knew that the sale of arms to Iran had been no runaway activity; it had been approved by the president and supported by his administration. Weinberger and Casey had aided it. Shultz had dissented, but only to the degree appropriate to a disagreement over policy. None had told the full story to Congress. Casey was dead, and Shultz had escaped prosecution by cooperating, if grudgingly, with our investigation. But Weinberger had remained dishonest and defiant.

After this conference, Gillen and I again met with Bennett, Rauh, and their associates. For two more hours, we tried to persuade them that

Weinberger should take a plea and make a proffer of his testimony against those who had participated in the cover-up. Later that day, Gillen told me that Donald Regan's testimony before the grand jury had gone well. What Regan had said would make him a useful prosecution witness in any case involving the events of November 1986.

Gillen, Barrett, Baker, and I spent the next day, a Saturday, going over every item in the case. The notes belied any claim that presidential authorization for the Israeli shipments had been lacking. They could have refreshed President Reagan's recollection for his testimony before the Tower Commission. Weinberger's notes provided support for McFarlane's early testimony before the standing committees of Congress as well as his later testimony before the select committees on Iran-Contra. The notes confirmed Shultz's congressional testimony that President Reagan had known the Hawk transaction to be illegal, and they rebutted Weinberger's denial that the president had acknowledged the transaction's illegality.

We possessed overwhelming evidence that Weinberger's denials that he had notes had been deliberate and false. Despite the imprecision of the questions he had been asked, the fact that Weinberger had consistently tried to divert his interrogators by giving rambling answers merely reinforced the documentary evidence that he had been deliberately deceitful.

The events of which Weinberger had denied knowledge had been dramatic and unforgettable. He had denied having known that McFarlane was traveling to Iran, but the notes described a meeting in which Weinberger and Taft had discussed the Hawk parts that would be sent with McFarlane. An intelligence report had informed Weinberger that payment in full had been made for the Hawk parts so that they would be available for delivery by McFarlane's party in Iran. Weinberger had noted that Shultz was "appalled" at the plan to send McFarlane to Iran. Later, Weinberger and Poindexter had discussed the failure of McFarlane's mission.

Weinberger had denied having known of the Hawk shipment that had taken place on November 24, 1985, but his notes showed that he had discussed the matter with McFarlane on November 9, 10, 19, 20, 22, and 23. McFarlane had corroborated this evidence. Other notes showed that Weinberger had monitored the possibility that hostages would be released that weekend, and that he had discussed the mission with Admiral William Crowe the day after it failed. We knew from National Security Agency documents that Weinberger had received a November

25 intelligence report that the negotiators were requesting a response from Iran for the delivery and were informing the Iranians that eighty new items would be added to those already delivered. In statements to the staff of the select committee, Weinberger had denied that he had personally received these actual reports. Nevertheless, Powell, Armitage, and other witnesses contradicted Weinberger and described how, at his own vigorous insistence, he had been given the basic reports as well as summaries of them.

In denying to the Senate intelligence committee and the select committees on Iran-Contra that he had known that the United States was obligated to replenish Israel's stockpile for the TOWs it had delivered to Iran, Weinberger had lied about his own direct responsibility and that of the Defense Department. He had gone along with a transaction he had believed to be illegal.

On May 10, Gillen and I spent an hour and a half with Bennett and Rauh. By then, I had boiled the case down to two major issues: Weinberger had consistently denied knowledge of the 1985 transactions; and he had repeatedly denied the existence of his notes. I told Bennett and Rauh there were four possibilities. One, we could drop the prosecution because of lack of proof beyond a reasonable doubt or as a matter of policy; two, Weinberger could give us a proffer so valuable that we would drop the case against him; three, we could arrange a plea disposition coupled with a proffer; or four, we could indict Weinberger for multiple felonies and go to trial.

I explained that I had just about ruled out the first possibility. Consequently, any decision to drop the case would depend on Weinberger's proffer or a proffer combined with a plea. We would not ask him to plead guilty to any charge without showing him our proof.

We considered our case strong because Weinberger had had such a powerful motive. He had lied to protect the president, who—Weinberger believed—had committed an unlawful act. Once having lied, he had been forced to conceal the existence of the notes that would have exposed him as a liar. I felt that the evidence of the materiality of his lies and notes would be persuasive to a jury.

Bennett and Rauh asked us to let Weinberger make a personal presentation, to state his case in his own words, and we agreed to meet with him on Tuesday, May 12.

On Monday, we held a brief staff conference to discuss the presentation we expected Weinberger to make. Weinberger's counsel had suggested that to eliminate any concern for the expiration of the grand jury on May 14, Weinberger would waive an indictment and let us proceed by information. Although a prosecutor may charge a misdemeanor by filing an information, a felony charge requires an indictment by a grand jury. A prospective defendant may, however, consent to a felony prosecution by information. Bennett wanted a delay, but Gillen and I wanted a grand jury indictment, which would more impressively formalize the charges for a trial jury.

The next day, Weinberger gave his presentation, stating his view of the facts, explaining his position, and making his proffer of testimony. Except to ask broad questions for discussion, we let him have the floor. He conceded most of what he knew we could prove. He volunteered that his notes were accurate. He said that McFarlane had told him that the president intended to ship Hawks through the Israelis and that the sole purpose of the shipment had been to get the hostages back. In Weinberger's view, the shipments made through the Israelis had been illegal, and he said that he had stated this opinion at the time. He also offered to testify to his belief that President Reagan, at the January 7, 1986, meeting, had deliberately deceived his advisors by concealing the fact that he had already signed a finding authorizing the resumption of arms sales to Iran. But Weinberger would not acknowledge that a cover-up to protect the president had been planned in November 1986. Nor would he plead guilty, not even to a single misdemeanor.

As I watched Weinberger make his presentation, I had the impression that he had testified countless times about complicated matters that he had necessarily simplified. Over the years, in the process of facilitating his explanations, he had apparently begun to alter the underlying facts to support his policy arguments and to avoid lengthy detours that might distract the audience from his message. I sensed a poker-face quality to his performance, a dismissing of questions rather than an earnest openness of discussion. Nonetheless, I found him personable. He was pleasant and appealing. At all times, without his mentioning it, we were sensitive to his extraordinary contribution to the country.

We never pressed Weinberger to testify against President Reagan or any other individual. We did not cross-examine him, although we asked a few questions. In response to one query, Weinberger said that President Reagan had not felt that he needed to cover anything up and had been adamant that he had done nothing wrong. This observation impressed me as an accurate and candid perception. It confirmed Shultz's notes.

That evening, after a long discussion with Bennett and Rauh, I agreed to wait two weeks before seeking an indictment against Weinberger. They agreed that if they became convinced that Weinberger had intentionally withheld information, they would recommend a plea disposition.

On May 14, I appeared before the grand jury, thanked the jurors for responding to the pressure to complete the investigation of Weinberger, and explained that we would not request them to take any action. If we were unable to work out a disposition of the charges with Weinberger, we would ask another grand jury to indict him, presenting a streamlined case based largely on evidence already adduced before the grand jury that had expired.

We continued to concentrate on accumulating evidence of Weinberger's motive for having concealed the existence of his notes. Our most promising case would be to prove beyond a reasonable doubt that his intention had been to protect the president. A less dramatic motive, such as protecting Weinberger's personal reputation, might not be enough to satisfy a trial jury. Would the testimony and notes about the November 24, 1986, meeting bring the motive for the cover-up into focus for a jury?

McFarlane would confirm Weinberger's notes that McFarlane had told him in 1985 that the president had approved the shipment before it took place. Although their conversations had occurred a year before the pivotal meeting in the situation room (which had coincidentally taken place on the anniversary of the Hawk shipment), the discussions had been intense and unforgettable. A secretary of defense is hardly likely to forget his repeated challenge of the legality of a president's action. Would Weinberger's notes and McFarlane's testimony be enough to prove beyond a reasonable doubt that Weinberger had realized not only that Meese had misstated the facts when he said that the president had not known about the shipment but also that Meese had been concocting a false cover-up for President Reagan? Could we connect proof of Meese's purpose with a case against Weinberger?

Fortunately, the case against Weinberger would not be limited to that one meeting, because he had also denied any knowledge of the Israeli shipments. His silent acquiescence in Meese's misstatement had been simply one incident in a broad pattern of false accommodations designed to protect President Reagan from possible impeachment. As the administration concentrated on disassociating itself from the 1985 Israeli shipments in preparing for congressional testimony in late 1986,

Weinberger's denials of his own knowledge had been neither inadvertent nor accidental.

Our final decision about indicting Weinberger was to be made at a staff conference on May 26. That morning, I woke up at four o'clock. I concluded that we had a strong obstruction case and a passable perjury case against Weinberger. I now felt certain that his motive had been rooted in a tacit agreement to cover up for the president. We could never prove that an express agreement had been made. Nonetheless, each person in the situation room on November 24 had known Meese's statement to be wrong. Each had received the signal from Meese that the coherent position he had developed for the administration was that Reagan had not known about the November 1985 Hawk shipment. Each had been left to make a personal decision about how to trim his own testimony.

Of course, if Meese was called to testify, he would undoubtedly deny that he had reached a conclusion about the shipment's illegality. Trapped between Charles Hill's notes (which showed that Shultz had told Meese about the president's advance knowledge of the shipment) and the notes taken by Regan and Weinberger at the meeting (which showed that Meese had indeed declared the president to have been unaware of the shipment until later), Meese might be brazen enough to lie, rather than admit to what he had done. But his cross-examination would be a circus.

Despite the narrowing of the obstruction statute in the *Poindexter* decision, I was satisfied that we would be able to present a comprehensive and unifying obstruction charge, with pendant perjury and false-statement counts, and to prove the motive for the obstruction and perjury. I therefore concluded that we should proceed with an indictment of Weinberger.

I also concluded that Webb, rather than Gillen, should try the case. This would minimize the damage from our having failed to discover Weinberger's notes in the Library of Congress on the first attempt and would permit Gillen to testify if Bill Rogers claimed that Weinberger had disclosed the existence of notes to Gillen. The perjury charges and false statements would have to be measured against a defense that Weinberger, despite his reputed computerlike memory, had remembered only those things that had fallen within the Defense Department's purview. Our response would be that the Defense Department had been responsible for supplying the replacement Hawks and TOWs to Israel.

At our staff conference, I argued in favor of bringing an obstruction charge and against bringing most of the possible perjury charges. I was concerned, I said, about the imprecision in the questions and answers on which the perjury charges would be based. In addition, the amount of time that had elapsed between the events and the lies Weinberger had told about them, as well as the time that had elapsed between the lies and the trial, might raise a reasonable doubt in the mind of at least one juror.

Gillen said that he was pessimistic about an obstruction case, because it would depend on Lawrence Garrett's testimony about the discussions he had held with Weinberger while attempting to obtain his notes. (We did not yet have Garrett's contemporaneous memorandum to Weinberger explaining the need to produce his notes, because Defense Department counsel were still concealing it from us.) Although the spirit of the case was clearly obstruction, and that was the way the case would be tried, even if it was limited to the perjury and false-statement charges, Gillen was concerned about the *Poindexter* opinion. He did not want us to have another big case that triggered appellate review. It would be lengthy and costly, he pointed out, and the likelihood of drawing a hostile panel on the court of appeals was considerable. Gillen argued that we should try Weinberger on the perjury charges, proving his obstruction of the congressional investigation as evidence of his motive and his deliberate intent to perjure himself.

I responded that the facts of the perjury had been thirteen months old when Weinberger first testified before the Senate intelligence committee. In the fall of 1985, he had been concerned about things other than the Hawk shipments. He had opposed the basic arms-control position taken by President Reagan and Shultz at Geneva, for example. I believed that the concealment of Weinberger's records had entailed sufficient corruption to satisfy the *Poindexter* opinion's narrow interpretation of the provision prohibiting the obstruction of a congressional investigation. The big advantage of an obstruction case was that it would not be hurt by the passage of time; Weinberger had continued to deny the existence of his notes until Baker found them.

Our last question was whether to allege Weinberger's false denials of keeping notes as false statements to Congress in addition to referring to them in the obstruction charge. In Poindexter's indictment, we had supported each obstruction charge with a false-statement charge. I believed that the parallel charges had contributed to the dismissal of the obstruction counts. I decided to rely exclusively on the obstruction charge and not to complicate our problem with parallel false-statement charges. If I was proved wrong and the obstruction charge was dismissed, we planned to ask the grand jury for a supplemental indictment to replace the obstruction charge with false-statement charges based on Weinberger's denial that he kept notes. We believed that such a technical change could be made even after the statute of limitations had run.

On June 12, Gillen, Barrett, Baker, and I had our last conference with Bennett, Rauh, and their associates. They told us that there would be no plea or further proffer. After two additional hours of discussion, I told them that we would seek an indictment from the new grand jury.

As they left, Bennett shook my hand. Smiling, he looked at me and said, "Of course, you know this means nuclear war."

PART FOUR

Political
Counterattack

CHAPTER TWENTY-TWO

Nuclear War

In the spring of 1992, we hired three new full-time associate counsel, bringing the total to nine; in July we hired a young lawyer who had not yet been admitted to the bar. Craig Gillen and three associate counsel were preparing to try the case against Clair George, the CIA's former director of operations. Two lawyers were preparing for the trial of Duane Clarridge, the CIA official who had preceded Oliver North as the administration's liaison with the Contras. Three other lawyers were gathering the remaining evidence against Caspar Weinberger and, in the course of their work, completing the investigation of Edwin Meese.

After noticing the number of current and former Defense Department employees coming and going from our grand jury room during this period, reporters had begun focusing on Caspar Weinberger. They reviewed his congressional testimony. Fed information by Weinberger's attorney, Robert Bennett, and George Shultz's lawyer, Lloyd Cutler, the news media reported that we were trying to determine why Weinberger's notes had not been given to us sooner. Friends and associates of Weinberger and Shultz expressed "exasperation ... that the two most vigorous opponents of the arms sales should come under questioning when 'the people who did wrong' have had their convictions reversed."

On May 13, the day before the grand jury was scheduled to expire, we had the interagency group of lawyers review a draft indictment to be sure it did not contain classified information. Someone in the White House promptly gave columnist Rowland Evans a "scoop" by flatly predicting that Weinberger would be indicted the next day. Evans reported the story on the Cable News Network evening news. When May 14 passed without an indictment, Evans suggested that it had been sealed. Two days later, CNN retracted the story. "On Thursday," Evans explained, "the White House was informed by high Bush administration officials that the indictment would be returned by Saturday. Judge Walsh, clearly acting within his authority, has now decided differently."

The day Evans withdrew his story, George Lardner and Walter Pincus of the *Washington Post* reported that "special prosecutors have told former Defense Secretary Caspar W. Weinberger that he might face indictment on felony charges in the Iran-Contra scandal, unless he provided them with evidence they believe he has against former President Reagan." The story, attributed to "sources familiar with the investigation," had been fed to the reporters by Weinberger, Bennett, or someone very close to them. When we postponed our decision to indict Weinberger in the hope that he would agree to cooperate with us, I had known that Bennett might use the extra time to prepare a counterattack, but I had not expected such flat-footed misstatements.

"The dramatic attempt to get a former cabinet officer to turn on his commander-in-chief," wrote Lardner and Pincus, "occurred a few days ago as Independent Counsel Lawrence E. Walsh tried to conclude his five and one-half year investigation of the affair. Weinberger so far has rejected the overture, insisting that he did nothing wrong, and that he had no information that would show Reagan took part in covering up the scandal."

Bennett was also the source of stories written by David Johnston of the *New York Times* and Pete Yost of the Associated Press. Bennett told Yost that "the prosecutor's theory is that . . . the Reagan White House decided to . . . conceal the most troubling of the Iran arms deals." Yost's wire story suggested that we were focusing on the November 24, 1986, meeting of the National Security Planning Group.

In May, Bennett announced that Weinberger had passed a lie-detector test. Bennett also told the press that Senators Daniel Inouye and Warren Rudman had given him a letter denying that Weinberger's statements had been material and asserting, "It is inconceivable to us that [Weinberger] would intentionally mislead or lie to Congress." In an interview, Rudman belittled Weinberger's deception. Criminalizing the misleading of Congress was always questionable, Rudman said, and it was particularly dubious in the case of Weinberger. "If he didn't fully answer every question I asked him, . . . it was a matter of omission, not commission." It was not important that Weinberger's recollection might have been "imperfect."

Shortly after Rowland Evans retracted his prediction, he and his associate, Robert Novak, wrote a column implying that George Bush himself, or his press office, had been the source of Evans's erroneous report on CNN. "So sure and so alarmed were administration officials late last week that they told the White House to inform President Bush that an indictment of former Defense Secretary Caspar Weinberger in the Iran-Contra affair would be handed down Friday or Saturday. . . . What made them alarmed was fear of a sensational trial of a prominent Reagan cabinet official during a presidential election campaign."

A Pentagon spokesman told Pete Yost that "in recent weeks, Bennett has obtained a dozen affidavits supportive of Weinberger including one from Joint Chiefs of Staff Chairman Colin Powell [who had succeeded Jack Vessey] and other current and former government officials." Bennett told David Johnston that he had given us copies of these statements, which had been intended to show that Weinberger had not treated his notes in a secretive manner. Bennett also told Johnston, "To the best of my recollection, he did not know that [the November 1985 Hawk shipment] had actually been carried out until long after."

In an interview with Ron Ostrow and Doyle McManus of the *Los Angeles Times*, Bennett suggested that Gillen and I were divided, and that Gillen was pressing me to accuse Weinberger of lies. "On another level for Walsh," wrote Ostrow and McManus, "there are historic and personal considerations that are more nebulous but perhaps significant, and Weinberger's lengthy record of public service . . . could influence Walsh, who is six years older than Weinberger, has a similar record of public service and, like Weinberger, is a lifelong Republican. . . . Among those waiting and watching is Weinberger's first lawyer, William P. Rogers, who was U.S. Attorney General when Walsh, earlier in his career, left the federal bench to work for Rogers as Deputy Attorney General."

On June 16, 1992, the grand jury indicted Weinberger, charging him with five felonies, including one count of obstructing a congressional investigation, two counts of making false statements, and two charges of perjury. The obstruction charge was based on his concealment of diary notes and other memoranda requested by Congress. Although Weinberger had lied to counsel for the select committees in denying that he had notes, I did not include specific charges for these individual false statements because of the rambling nature of the questions and answers and because I did not want to detract from the obstruction charge by suggesting that it duplicated other charges. The false statements for which Weinberger was charged included his telling the staff of the House select committee on Iran-Contra that he had not known about the Saudis' having funded the Contras and his telling us that he had not taken notes. The perjury charges arose from his testimony before the joint select committees, in which he had denied having known in advance about the November 1985 Hawk shipment and having known that the weapons shipped by Israel in 1985 were to be replaced by the United States.

Weinberger responded to the indictment by calling a press conference at his attorney's office. Reading a prepared statement, Weinberger said, "In order to avoid this indictment, I was not willing to accept an offer by the independent counsel to plead to a misdemeanor offense of which I was not guilty, nor was I willing to give them statements which were not true about myself or others. I would not give false testimony, nor would I enter a false plea. Because of this refusal, which to me is a simple matter of conscience, I have now been charged with multiple felonies."

When Weinberger finished reading, a reporter addressed a question to Robert Bennett, saying, "Your client has made a very serious allegation: that someone in the special prosecutor's—independent counsel's—office tried to get him to lie. Who tried to get him to lie?"

"We'll stand by Mr. Weinberger's statement," replied Bennett.

"Well, Mr. Bennett," asked another reporter, "is Mr. Weinberger suggesting that the special counsel tried to get him to make statements about President Reagan?"

"The statement speaks for itself."

"No, it doesn't," said a third reporter. "It leaves us—"

Bennett cut the reporter off, saying, "All right, thank you very much," and he and Weinberger walked out.

"It is a very serious charge to make that allegation," the reporter shouted after them.

Neither Bennett nor Weinberger responded to this reporter or to another who shouted, "Do you think the special prosecutor is out to get the president, Mr. Bennett?"

As CNN commentator Lou Waters observed, "Precious little [was] said at what was billed as a press conference."

Weinberger's insinuation that we had conditioned a plea bargain on a false accusation was a brazen lie. We had asked in a general way about various information he might have, but we had neither asked him to give false testimony nor specified the testimony he would be required to give. We had merely wanted him, like every other potential witness, to tell the truth—the whole truth. Specifying before a plea bargain that a witness is to provide specific testimony or to testify against a particular person is a tactical mistake in most cases and would have been a mistake in this one. Such deals are inevitably exposed when the witnesses are cross-examined at trial. Inasmuch as Weinberger would not even discuss a plea, we had never seriously negotiated a possible proffer of testimony.

Weinberger's lies about his indictment were a crucial part of the political counterattack engineered by his attorney, and Republicans in Congress reacted heatedly. Senate Minority Leader Robert Dole opened the attack. Speaking in the empty Senate chamber late on the day of the indictment, Dole broadened the assault with a hardened statement of Weinberger's false claims: "Mr. Walsh and his highly paid assassins saw Mr. Weinberger as a way to get at their ultimate target—President Reagan. They threatened Mr. Weinberger that unless he testified that President Reagan violated the law, they would see that he was indicted. To his credit, Mr. Weinberger refused to buckle under to this blackmail."

We were "criminalizing policy differences," according to Senator Orrin Hatch. "To do this to Cap Weinberger . . . two days before the statute of limitations has expired—is criminal in and of itself. . . . We're going to wreck this country if we keep allowing these politically oriented and politically motivated young [sic] prosecutors to run amok without anybody having any control over them."

To me, Dole seemed ever more sinister: He had no concern about using his office to intrude in a matter before the courts. He had become a Bennett-Weinberger advocate, using his high office to broadcast whatever they fed him. Hatch didn't seem venal, but he certainly was blind; from the beginning, he had seen no crime by anyone—not even Oliver North.

Editorial comment about Weinberger's indictment was mixed. The *New York Times* said that the case should be tried and the proof fairly assessed. The *Philadelphia Inquirer* observed, "It may seem like overkill. . . . But then, it may be Mr. Weinberger's obfuscation—and that of many others—that has caused the independent counsel's probe to take so long. There is a larger issue here, too, for the American people: It is whether they believe that, on occasion, it is all right to have a government of men, not laws. Or to suspend checks and balances. Or to shelve, in moments of rough decision making, the Constitution."

USA Today expressed a similar viewpoint: "Whether or not the indictment proves warranted, the post-Watergate skepticism that led to it—an unwillingness to turn suspicion away from the powerful—is an asset. . . . That kind of vigilance is much needed today. . . . If anything's been learned in the years since Watergate, it is that no reputation or ideology is worth subverting the laws officials pledge to uphold."

"Echoes of Watergate are discernable," the *Baltimore Sun* declared. "The Weinberger notes may even be the equivalent of the Nixon tapes. They may reveal in rich detail that some familiar 'attractive, well-intentioned' individuals considered themselves above the law and contemptuous of the Constitution's division of powers. If so, Congress, courts, and the public should respond harshly. But if the Weinberger notes turn out to be flimsy or ambiguous as evidence against him, then a guilty verdict should be, as critics have suggested, against the independent counsel."

"When he was indicted," wrote syndicated columnist Mary McGrory, "Weinberger gave a little glimpse of the knife he has always carried with him during his long career—and not just to cut welfare budgets. He has always been an alley fighter, and he showed it again with his savage strike at Walsh. . . . He accused his venerable nemesis of trying to force him to lie and to turn in Reagan. It was breathtaking and poisonous, but not totally out of character. Weinberger's way with those who oppose him is viperish. Congressmen who objected to the trillion dollar defense buildup were dismissed as deficient in concern for the national security. . . . The gentlemanly Walsh is an unlikely villain but an easy target for the outraged. . . . If Walsh had [had] Weinberger's notes, the inquiry would not have taken five years. We might even have had the truth by now."

Bennett continued to feed information to reporters in an effort to shape public opinion. In an interview with Walter Pincus and George Lardner, for example, Bennett trivialized his client's crimes: Weinberger's daily jotting of notes, most of them about personal events, was so habitual that he had forgotten the events they described; his note-taking was so routine that he had not linked his notes to any requests for Iran-Contra material; he had turned over to Pentagon lawyers the responsibility for fulfilling requests for documents and had given them the authority to produce whatever was required; and the lawyers were the ones who should have determined whether the "daily jottings" should have been produced.

On June 19, Weinberger was arraigned before Judge Thomas F. Hogan, a native Washingtonian and a graduate of Georgetown University and George Washington University Law School. Bennett asked for a speedy trial, and the judge scheduled it to begin on November 2, the day before election day. Bennett also declared that he would require Gillen as a witness and would ask the court to disqualify him as prosecutor. Having foreseen this possibility, I had already tentatively arranged for Dan Webb, who had tried John Poindexter, to try Weinberger.

The arraignment provoked another attack by Senator Dole. He urged the Justice Department to close my inquiry, saying, "Yes, Mr. Walsh's crowd browbeat two people into guilty pleas, threatening to ruin them financially if they didn't roll over. . . . But when it comes to major cases, Mr. Walsh's batting average is zero. And with the indictment of Mr. Weinberger, his credibility is now at zero as well."

The next day, on the CNN program *Newsmaker Saturday*, Secretary of State James Baker denounced us. "To see a man like [Weinberger] hounded and chased five or six years after the events in question, I think it's a tragic situation."

To show Weinberger's motive for concealing his records, the indictment had set out an extensive discussion of the background of the false statements. Reading this discussion, reporters spotted information that might prove embarrassing to President Bush. Although Bush had denied having known that Shultz and Weinberger had opposed the sale of arms to Iran, for example, the indictment revealed that the vice president had attended the January 7, 1986, White House meeting in which President Reagan had overridden Shultz and Weinberger and authorized the sale of missiles to Iran.

Walter Pincus observed in the *Washington Post* that some of Weinberger's "notes may include mention of President Bush, because the prosecution's case is designed to try to show that a White House cover-up was discussed during two November 1986 meetings attended by Bush, who was then vice president."

Laurie Asseo of the Associated Press wrote, "Caspar Weinberger's indictment again raises the question of what President Bush knew about the Iran-Contra affair because, as vice president, Bush attended two meetings at which prosecutors say the arms sales were discussed."

On the evening of Weinberger's arraignment, June 19, I appeared on the ABC program *Nightline*. Host Ted Koppel asked me whether I had prosecuted Weinberger because he would not incriminate Reagan. I replied that I had not. I explained that we had never specified a target for a proffer of testimony. We had asked for the truth. The critical test was that we be satisfied that we would receive essentially complete testimony. I added that I had been very reluctant to prosecute Weinberger because of his distinguished career, but that there was no way in which I could avoid a prosecution for such flagrant lies. We had offered to accept a guilty plea to a single misdemeanor, a generous offer that we had not extended to anyone else. Because Weinberger had refused to plead guilty to anything, we had never engaged in any serious discussions about his possible testimony.

In late June, I filed my third interim report. The report's purpose was to inform Congress of the status of my investigation, but my goal was to stave off the political attacks and to assure the public that the final phase of the investigation was to determine whether officials at the highest level of government had sought to obstruct official inquiries. In the report, I explained that we had concentrated on the crimes of lying to Congress and withholding and destroying documents, because we had been denied the classified information that would have allowed us to prosecute individuals for the other crimes they had committed. "This was not merely a clean-up chore," I wrote. "It has provided a significant shift in our understanding of which administration officials had knowledge of Iran-Contra, who participated in its cover-up, and which areas required far more scrutiny than we previously believed." I reported that I expected the investigation to be completed by the end of summer.

At the time of Weinberger's indictment, we were badly overextended and needed to wind up our investigation. We had decided give the remaining subjects one last chance to tell the truth. Among these subjects were former president Ronald Reagan and President George Bush. We requested Bush's diary and we needed a specification of which national security briefings he had attended, but we had agreed with White House counsel to defer Bush's examination until after election day. In the meantime, we would go ahead and interview Reagan.

I decided to take the former president's deposition myself. John Barrett, Christina Spaulding, and I flew to California and met with Reagan in his Los Angeles office on July 24. He was cordial and offered everybody licorice jelly beans, but he remembered almost nothing. Groping desperately for things he *could* remember, he told us anecdotes about his days in office. He recalled talking with Mikhail Gorbachev in Geneva about a second summit meeting, for example. At Reagan's suggestion, he and Gorbachev had gone off by themselves and sat in front of a fireplace. They had worked out the arrangements by themselves and then informed their assistants. Reagan also remembered a conversation with Margaret Thatcher when she was leader of the Conservative Party, before she became prime minister. But these were simply fragments of memory that had no connection to Iran-Contra.

I was saddened to discover that the former president didn't remember such basic facts as that Michael Deaver had come to Washington with him from California or that John Poindexter had resigned. When asked to confirm his contemporaneous reactions to Iran-Contra developments, as recorded in his diary and in the notes of Weinberger and Shultz, Reagan most often responded that what I had read to him sounded like what he would have said, that the notes reflected the way he would have felt.

During a break, he took me to the window overlooking the city of Los Angeles and identified points of interest with pride and affection. It had been a long time since anyone had captivated me so completely. I knew that I was dealing with an actor but, after sixty years of examining witnesses, I was ready to stake my reputation that this was no act. This was Ronald Reagan—disabled, to be sure, but still enormously appealing.

By the time the meeting had ended, it was as obvious to the former president's counsel as it was to us that we were not going to prosecute Reagan. Nevertheless, two days later, the *Washington Post* carried a story by Walter Pincus saying that Reagan might be indicted. According to the article, "The sources say that Walsh's office is focusing . . . on whether Reagan and his former aides tried to conceal the White House role in the deliveries of 508 TOW anti-tank missiles and 18 Hawk anti-aircraft missiles from Israel to Iran in 1985."

CNN picked up the story and ran it all day. After trying unsuccessfully to get through to CNN with a denial, our press officer Mary Belcher drafted a statement and filed it with the Associated Press, hoping to get the word to CNN via the wire service. At six o'clock, CNN finally stopped airing the story. Meanwhile, viewers were being told that I would decide within ten days whether to start moves that could lead to an indictment of the former president and several of his close advisors, charging them with having participated in a criminal conspiracy to hide Reagan's role in the arms-for-hostages shipments through Israel.

In my statement, I discounted the report as "speculation by defense lawyers." President Reagan's spokeswoman told reporters, "We have been assured by the independent counsel that President Reagan is not a target of that investigation."

I knew that Pincus, one of the best of the reporters covering us, would not have written such a story on speculation—even though he had been among the first to see through the White House's strategy to use Oliver North's diversion of funds to deflect public and congressional attention from the president. But who was Pincus's source? I did not think it was

Ted Olson, Reagan's lawyer. When Olson telephoned me about the story, he seemed genuinely distressed. He said that Nancy Reagan was in tears as the story was carried throughout the world.

I doubted that the White House's participation in the inaccurate, premature report of Weinberger's indictment two months earlier had been coincidental. I was aware that the lawyers representing Reagan, Bush, Weinberger, Shultz, and Donald Regan were keeping each other informed. My visit to Los Angeles would have been discussed. Bennett later bragged about his use of the press. And Bush's counsel, Boyden Gray, had been known to float stories through persons close to the publisher of the *Washington Post*; Pincus had sometimes been asked to write these stories. I suspected that Gray or someone in the White House had played a role in disseminating the misinformation, but I had no proof.

Of all the sideswipes we suffered during this period, the false report that we were considering indicting the nation's still admired former president hurt us the most. It infuriated the congressional Republicans, even some of the moderate ones.

Meanwhile, President Reagan had been invited to speak at the Republican National Convention in Houston. He gave a rousing speech, one of his best. (With cue cards, he did not need to depend on his memory.) Fans could be seen waving blue-and-white signs that proclaimed, "Reagan '96." The backs of the posters—supplied by the Council for Inter-American Security, a conservative, pro-defense group that claimed 83,000 members—were used for an attack on me: "Ollie North, Caspar Weinberger, Ed Meese, Is Reagan Next??? Help Me Stop the Biggest Witch Hunt in America Since Salem." Hoping to send a message to George Bush, the council issued a special Western Union number that individuals could use to ask the president to support the Republican congressmen who were pushing for a Justice Department investigation of my office.

On July 29, Lyle Denniston of the *Baltimore Sun* reported, "Congress is moving forward with an angry demand—initiated by Republicans, but not resisted by Democrats—for a report by the end of the year from its auditing agency, the General Accounting Office, on exactly how much Mr. Walsh has spent. . . . Senate Republican Leader Bob Dole . . . persuaded the Senate to endorse the GAO report idea unanimously on Monday after complaining of the 'never ending Iran-Contra investigation' and of Mr. Walsh's 'inability to understand the simple fact that it is time to leave Iran-Contra to the history books.' " The article continued: "As much as the time and money spent riles the Walsh critics, they also fret openly that Mr. Walsh constantly retains the opportunity to stir up anxiety about new indictments. The latest flurry of excitement over the Walsh probe came last weekend when the *Washington Post* reported that Mr. Reagan and three of his former top aides ... might face criminal charges."

A few days after the *Washington Post* article appeared, I sent a letter to Reagan's lawyers formally stating that the former president was no longer a subject of my investigation. Having been lambasted after the false report that I planned to prosecute the former president, I now faced criticism of another sort. An op-ed piece in the *New York Times* declared that because I had decided *not* to prosecute Reagan, I had become a prosecutor without a purpose: "He has missed the political forest for the prosecutorial trees. By spending years prosecuting these perjuries, Mr. Walsh has muddled the basic democratic purpose of his task. For most Americans, Iran-Contra stands for a legal morass. Prosecutors look for certainty beyond a reasonable doubt, and when they win a case, they've got it. But in politics, wrongdoing is frequently a murky enterprise, a mixture of mendacity and idealism. Judging the perceived wrong is ultimately a task for voters, not jurors. Reagan's drop in the polls shows we did the job ourselves. There is no reason for Mr. Walsh, despite his dedication, to serve as our St. George. We already did the job ourselves."

A Reuters article by Deborah Zabarenko noted that the "scandal that began with a bang nearly six years ago may end with a whimper ... for the more than $32 million ... spent ... [the independent counsel has] relatively little to show and never managed to touch former President Reagan. ... After nearly six years, the world is not watching so closely. ... The last U.S. hostages were freed last year, democratic elections have been held in Nicaragua, and the threat of world communist domination seems remote after the collapse of the Soviet Union in December."

While the political attacks on us mounted, Craig Gillen was in Judge Royce C. Lamberth's courtroom, prosecuting Clair George for having lied to three congressional panels and a federal grand jury. At the outset, Gillen had been forced to explain to the judge the belated delivery to defense counsel of copies of two thousand CIA documents, some of them relevant, that we had just found under the desk of the CIA custodian of documents during an interview. The material had not been part of any CIA records system.

After the opening statements, Gillen called his first witness, Senator John Kerry of Massachusetts, to the stand. Kerry testified that George's false statements to the Senate intelligence committee had been material to the committee's inquiry. Kerry was followed by witnesses who introduced declassified CIA cables, testimony transcripts, and other documents.

On July 28, Alan Fiers began his testimony. He described the frantic efforts to prepare George's congressional testimony about the downing of Eugene Hasenfus's plane in Nicaragua. Relating how George had made him rewrite the testimony, Fiers likened his situation to that of a racecar driver trying to steer between two cars that had crashed and burst into flames. Fiers had wanted to explain the shipment of military supplies as an operation that had grown from a humanitarian-aid program authorized by Congress, but George had overruled him: "He said, 'No, I don't want that . . . . It puts the spotlight on the White House, Ollie North, or the administration. . . . I don't want to be the first person to do that.' "

To get to the witness stand, Fiers had been forced to run a gantlet of former CIA officials. "Spies in the first row, spies in the second row, spies sprinkled throughout the courtroom," as the *Washington Post* put it. "They have come to see their former leader and a former colleague face off in what has become the hottest ticket in town for the intelligence community. . . . One, a lawyer, even sits at the defense table. They call themselves the 'readers' and have spent the last half year culling through millions of classified documents that were turned over to George's lawyers by the government, trying to find material that will bolster his defense. . . . There was palpable tension in the courtroom when [Fiers] appeared Tuesday to testify against George and again yesterday when Fiers broke down in tears on the stand." The tears had come when Fiers was asked to read commendations of him written by George.

The first whisper of a personal attack against me had come just before Weinberger's indictment. A career officer in the independent Office of Government Ethics had alerted me that there were unanswered questions about my annual financial disclosure reports, which were intended to show all my income and property. In preparing the reports, my accountant had made minor errors and inconsistent entries. Our office manager, who was also our ethics officer, had failed to respond to OGE's questions or even to inform me of the problem. Chagrined at being left vulnerable by my own employee, I had replaced the office manager with Carol McCreary-Maddox, my executive assistant. Phil Rooney, our financial officer, became our ethics officer. My financial disclosure reports were promptly corrected.

On July 29, the general counsel of the Administrative Office of the United States Courts telephoned my office to alert me that Representative Gerald Solomon of Glen Falls, New York, the ranking Republican on the House rules committee, had obtained the administrative office's records for my personal travel and subsistence in Washington. Inasmuch as Oliver North had obtained some of this information under the Freedom of Information Act, I was not surprised at the news of Solomon's interest in the subject. North had been born in his district. Nor was I unprepared for the political skirmish his actions presaged.

Back in 1991, I had awakened in the middle of the night with the realization that perhaps the most embarrassing item of our expenses would be the cost of my personal travel. Like all my predecessors, I had treated the appointment as independent counsel in the same way I would have treated a retainer by any new client: I had maintained my office and home in Oklahoma City even though much of my work would probably take place in Washington. I had left all the details to my Washington office manager, who had turned for advice to the courts' administrative office, which—for 3 percent of the total—had handled the expenditures of each previous independent counsel. The administrative office had approved my lease from the Watergate Hotel (which took into account the fact that other part-time members of my staff and witnesses would sometimes stay there, as well), and I itemized all my other expenditures and paid personally for any that exceeded the government limits. When I totaled my travel expenses in 1991, however, I realized that they might stagger the public. It was after this that I had asked Philip Rooney to conduct an internal audit, which would help us to be prepared for any attacks.

The administrative office's general counsel, William Burchill, and his deputy, George Weiskopf, explained to me that my office probably was not subject to executive-branch limits on expenses. The Senate had attempted to impose such limits in 1987, but they had been rejected in conference with the House. My authorization to incur expense was broad and general. The statute directed that my investigation be prompt, responsible, cost-effective, and conducted without undue delay. The test for validity was whether I deemed an expenditure necessary. The temporary nature and unpredictable length of service, as well as my statutory per diem status, had justified my keeping my home base. All prior independent counsel had kept their homes and continued to work out of their private offices in their home cities. Unlike my predecessors' work, however, mine had stretched over years.

After returning from Burchill's office, I set Steve Ellis, our youngest lawyer, to sorting out the arcane restrictions on government expenses for travel and subsistence. Phil Rooney developed an analysis of our expenses to show the relative insignificance of our travel expenses, our ratio of administrative expenses, and the high proportion (more than 20 percent) of direct expenses we had incurred for maintaining the security of classified documents.

On the evening of July 30, after Fiers began his testimony, Congressman Solomon took to the floor of the House and assailed Gillen and me for our travel and subsistence expenses. A provision tucked away in an appropriation act required that the General Accounting Office audit all independent counsel every six months. Solomon revealed that the GAO had never done so. Minority Leader Bob Michel joined him on the floor and called for an immediate audit. I felt confident that the audit would turn up no irregularities.

Another charge by Gerald Solomon, however, was a most unpleasant surprise: It was that Gillen and I owed the District of Columbia for taxes on our compensation as independent counsel. We had instead paid taxes to the states in which we lived and in which I practiced. The law, however, required us to pay D.C. taxes for any year in which we spent more than 182 nights in Washington. As it happened, both Gillen and I had fallen into that category one year. Our accountants, who had been unaware of the problem, quickly prepared our D.C. returns. We promptly paid the taxes and interest without penalties, then sought partial reimbursement from our home states.

Solomon criticized us both for failing to move to Washington. By statute, I was a part-time per diem employee. We had allowed Gillen to keep his home in Atlanta because his job had always been temporary. His fiancée was permanently employed there. We had always expected that his job would end within another six to nine months; as it stretched out, the projections of continuing work had never extended beyond a year. Nonetheless, Solomon charged Gillen and me with a possible crime of making false statements to a government agency in support of Gillen's reimbursement for expenses.

Ordinarily, I favored making a quick and clean public response to attacks, but with Clair George's trial in progress, Gillen and I feared that a detailed reply might build up the story and draw the interest of the mainstream press, which had so far ignored it. Gillen and I agreed to issue a generalized statement: "We believe we are in compliance with federal law. Reimbursement requirements are rigid. The administrative office oversees our expenses. We have always expected an audit and governed ourselves accordingly."

The next morning, August 4, the *Washington Times* printed a first-page article under a two-column headline: GOP QUESTIONS WALSH SPENDING. According to the article, Congressman Solomon would ask the Justice Department to investigate whether Gillen and I had violated federal laws regarding personal expenditures. Other Republican members of the Senate and House were expected to support the request. Representative John J. "Jimmy" Duncan, Jr., claimed to have twenty signatures on a letter addressed to the General Accounting Office asking for an audit of my office. The other newspapers continued to ignore the story.

That morning, the CIA contingent at George's trial carried copies of the *Washington Times* and sat in the first two rows, holding the papers with the dramatic headline tipped down so that the jury could read it. The judge, after taking the bench and seeing the problem, instructed the jury to ignore the newspapers.

Later that day, while I was working on my final report in Oklahoma City, a new bombshell hit. My security officer telephoned to tell me that the document specialist whom I had brought to Los Angeles and to whom I had entrusted President Reagan's responses to our interrogatories and the accompanying exhibits had lost them. Despite my having emphasized the material's sensitivity, the specialist (who, as our file clerk, had become familiar with the documents) had placed the material in a suitcase that he then checked with the airline. After arriving at Washington's Dulles International Airport, he had not waited for the suitcase at the baggage carousel until he had picked up his car. When he returned to retrieve the suitcase, it was gone. The document specialist had been extremely reliable. He had worked for me while I was in private practice as well as during all of the Iran-Contra investigation. I was unbelieving. Like me, he had apparently assumed that these documents had been declassified in Poindexter's trial, but a single document had not.

I was properly vulnerable. At the last minute, as I left the office for my trip to question President Reagan, I had picked up the exhibits to his interrogatory answers, thinking that they had all been declassified. In fact, they should never have been taken out of the office except by our security officer or an armed FBI agent. Understandably angered about the loss of this material, the Justice Department had the FBI launch an investigation. Ultimately, I was twice interviewed by the FBI, and the document specialist was polygraphed. The embarrassing matter was dropped but subsequently leaked to the press.

A couple of days after I learned about the missing documents, another crisis struck. Judge Hogan's law clerk telephoned John Barrett to say that Robert Bennett's partner, Carl Rauh, was in the judge's chambers asking him to postpone Weinberger's trial. Rauh told the judge that he needed the postponement to permit an October trial of another client, former secretary of defense Clark Clifford, who suffered from a serious, chronic heart condition. Despite Rauh's discourtesy in having failed to give us notice, I probably would have consented to delaying Weinberger's trial if Clifford's health had been the real concern, but there was no evidence of any change in Clifford's health that would necessitate his being tried in October rather than a few months later. The postponement was a mere strategic maneuver: Clifford and his partner, Robert A. Altman, had been indicted in the District of Columbia and were about to be indicted in New York; the defendants preferred to be tried first in Washington because the D.C. case was narrower than the New York case.

I did not believe that Bennett and Rauh would really be ready to defend Clifford in October. Moreover, Weinberger's early trial date had been fixed at Bennett's urgent request. To prepare for the trial, we had curtailed other investigations and had hired an additional lawyer. With expenses of more than $10,000 a day, we could not afford unnecessary delays. I directed Barrett to oppose the postponement; if the postponement was granted, Barrett was to seek a day certain, with an order preventing further postponements to accommodate counsel's schedule.

When Barrett reached the judge's chambers, Rauh was still there. Judge Hogan said that he had already talked with the judge presiding in Clifford's case and had decided to postpone Weinberger's trial. Judge Hogan permitted Barrett to make a record—to state our opposition and give our reasons for opposing the postponement—but the judge had already made up his mind. He did agree to our request that the trial go forward on the new date, January 5, 1993, regardless of any other commitments counsel might have.

Thus, having generated favorable publicity by demanding an early trial for Weinberger, Bennett had quietly backed away from his commitment and positioned his client to apply for a postelection presidential pardon. I found myself wondering why Judge Hogan had given us so little consideration. As an outsider, I had always worried about the close-knit fraternity of Washington lawyers. Clifford had been a leading Washington lawyer. Hogan and Bennett had served at the same time as law clerks to District of Columbia district judges, and Rauh had then been an assistant U.S. attorney in the same courthouse.

The Independent Counsel Act, which had to be reauthorized every five years, was due for renewal in 1992. The public hearings gave the Bush administration and Congress numerous opportunities to disparage us. Attorney General William Barr said, for example, "I don't think [the act] adequately provides for a selection process that appoints individuals who understand the prosecution function and the standards and policies used by the Department of Justice. I don't think the statute provides any accountability or adequate supervision of independent counsel."

Senator Dole said, "In far too many instances, the investigations conducted by independent counsels have turned out to be partisan political fishing expeditions—expeditions which have accomplished nothing more than wasting millions of tax dollars." Dole, who opposed the act's renewal, singled me out as "the most egregious example."

In response to the congressional demands, the General Accounting Office assigned ten full-time accountants, plus part-time support staff, to examine all our expenditures. My lease at the Watergate Hotel was reviewed by the Office of Government Ethics. Margaret Harris, the head of the GAO audit team, and David Clarke, the associate controller general who was to have overall responsibility for the audit, visited our office on August 6. As they looked at the spare, overcrowded, bustling space, Clarke's first comment was "This doesn't look luxurious to me." My impression was that the auditors would accept our view that there were no precise rules and regulations and that we, like previous independent counsel, had voluntarily adapted to the government limitations for employees of the judicial branch of government service. There might be some question of reasonableness, but hardly of illegality.

A few days later, seventy-five Republican congressmen signed a letter requesting the attorney general to investigate my spending practices and to remove me if I had violated the law. The letter also requested that Barr consider investigating Gillen and me for making false statements in connection with our travel expenses. The letter was signed by the

Republican House leadership, including Minority Leader Bob Michel, Minority Whip Newt Gingrich (who signed twice), and others in the GOP caucus.

The *Washington Times* Sunday magazine published a long story, "The Most Expensive Special Counsel," based largely on a reporter's conversation with Gerald Solomon's investigator. By contrast, the major newspapers each noted the charges in a small item placed at the end of a news story on our other activities. Although the jurors in George's trial had been instructed not to read anything about Iran-Contra, they had not been sequestered. I was concerned that some jurors might disobey the judge's order and form a negative opinion about the prosecution based on the *Washington Times* reports of our expenditures.

During August, the controversy over the renewal of the Independent Counsel Act kept the public's attention on the political dispute. In testimony before the Senate oversight committee, former Watergate congressional counsel Sam Dash, who supported the act's renewal, suggested that the attacks on me were coming from the targets of my prosecutions. "The more important questions," Dash said, "are whether the office has honestly and competently tried to carry out [the independent counsel's] responsibilities, and whether it has acted objectively, without personal or political bias. I believe both questions must be answered in the affirmative." Dash proposed that our expenditures be compared with what the Justice Department spent to prosecute Manuel Noriega.

Michigan's Senator Carl Levin, chairman of the Senate committee on government oversight, inserted a similar statement in the *Congressional Record*: "Judge Walsh is doing what he was asked to do. He is carrying out the task to which he was assigned. I cannot help noticing some of the most specific critics of the independent counsel are also past targets of independent counsel investigation."

Common Cause president Fred Wertheimer argued that my work provided a "clear lesson" on the need for the law. Government agencies had resisted cooperating and had slowed the investigation's progress. "Under such circumstances," said Wertheimer, "it would have been especially difficult for the Department of Justice to conduct a credible investigation into this matter."

The opponents of extending the Independent Counsel Act were equally vocal. Attorney General William Barr threatened to recommend that President Bush veto the legislation unless it held independent counsel "more accountable" for their spending, including prosecutorial decisions. "There is no one to determine whether or not time is being wasted, ... whether individuals are being singled out and treated unfairly, whether an exorbitant amount of money is being spent."

Barr's deputy, George Terwilliger, complained that it was an "affront to the integrity of the dedicated men and women of the department who toiled daily in the pursuit of justice" to suggest that the department could not investigate high-ranking officials accused of wrongdoing.

Senator William Cohen, the ranking Republican on the Senate oversight committee, disagreed with the deputy attorney general. There would always be a "cloud of suspicion," argued Cohen, when an attorney general investigated a high-ranking official in the same administration. As to the expense of our investigation and prosecutions, Cohen scoffed that "the Justice Department [had] spent nineteen million dollars to prosecute Noriega in a much less complex case."

While the various controversies roiled, stirred up by our opponents at both ends of Pennsylvania Avenue, Clair George's trial continued. Alan Fiers testified that North's activities had been an open secret: "If you could imagine Oliver North as a luminescent paintbrush, if you turned out all the lights in Washington, you would be stunned at how many people had luminescent paint on them from brushing up against him."

Richard Secord, who was the next major witness, established the falsity of George's denial of having known him. Secord said that he had sat within a few feet of George at a White House meeting to which Poindexter had invited Secord so that the others would know "who the third party was"—who, in other words, was serving as the cutout between the United States and the Iranians. Secord also said that George had questioned the president's decision not to notify Congress of the arms shipments.

Former CIA agent George Cave then testified that Clair George had expressed concern about Secord's participation in the arms sales. The last prosecution witness was former Senator Thomas F. Eagleton, who testified that George had misled the Senate intelligence committee. Eagleton described George as a "founding father of the whole sordid mess."

The first defense witness, David Gries, who had succeeded George as the CIA's congressional liaison officer, suggested that George had been the victim of confusion and compartmentalization. George then took the stand and conceded that there had been errors in his previous testimony, but he stated that he had not lied. Within acceptable limits, he said, he had been protecting secret information and denying CIA involvement. "I made the decision to stay away from [North's private supply network] no matter what." George said that Fiers had had regular access to William Casey, and that George had relied on Fiers to keep the CIA within the law. Although he denied having told Fiers not to identify Max Gomez as Felix Rodriguez, George did not directly contradict Fier's other testimony. As for many of the events that had led to his indictment, George claimed not to recall them.

Cross-examined by Gillen, George became testy. When asked about his relations with Congress, he replied, "I would say that when I left the congressional job, I was disliked by many members of Congress and their staff." Aid to the Contras had been "the most controversial issue in the mid-1980s." Frequently clashing with Gillen, George protested the use of documents to establish his earlier statements and knowledge that he now claimed to have forgotten. He admitted that his denial of having met Secord had been misleading, but he claimed not to have lied: "One doesn't lie when they know the truth is going to come out absolutely." He asserted that he had been literally correct when he said of Secord, "I do not know the man." Finally, shouting that he had been charged with Iran-Contra crimes because a hypocritical Congress "wanted to set somebody up," George pounded the witness stand.

At times, George became so loud that he could be heard in the hallway outside the courtroom. After warning George several times not to interrupt Gillen, Judge Lamberth eventually slammed down his gavel, sent the jury out, and warned George that he was in danger of being cited for contempt of court. George apologized but remained explosive.

"Goddamn it," he said on his second day of cross-examination. "It's hypocrisy. I am sitting around seven years later being accused of being a criminal, and that's criminal." He claimed that Congress had known about North's supply operation. "Congress knew. Congress wanted to set somebody up, . . . and I walked right into it. They were waiting for me to say the wrong thing."

After being confronted with yet another piece of evidence, George complained: "Mr. Gillen, you are going to go through these documents one by one for the next X number of days and nitpick me to death about these things I said six years ago. It's just not fair."

In the course of his testimony, George confirmed the familiarity his directorate had had with Vice President Bush's office. After Hasenfus had been shot down, Bush's national security advisor, Donald Gregg (who had recommended Felix Rodriguez to the officials of El Salvador), had handed out buttons lampooning Rodriguez's pseudonym. The buttons, which had been passed around the CIA, had said, "Who is Max Gomez?" and "I am Maximo Gomez." George said that his people had accepted the buttons because they were funny and had come from the White House.

In his summation, Gillen argued that George had tried to hide "the dirty little secret that the people in the administration knew and that people in Congress suspected but could not get confirmation."

Defense counsel Richard Hibey responded that forgetting was human: "If George had been charged with murder, would you believe Fiers?"

The jury received the case on August 20. On the fifth day of deliberation, the jurors reported to Judge Lamberth that they could not reach a verdict. The judge asked them to try again. The next day, August 26, he declared a mistrial and set October 19 for a retrial.

Jury foreman Steven Kirk told reporters that "there was never a point in our deliberations where a majority found the defendant guilty. . . . Some jurors did feel he could have been more forthcoming, but from a criminal perspective, we did not find that Clair George told false statements to Congress."

Hibey said of the jurors that they had not been "prepared to convict anybody based on questions which contained ambiguous phrases."

Robert Bennett, who had no connection with the case, took the opportunity to launch another jibe at my office: "The fundamental flaw in Walsh's cases is that he is pursuing decent, honorable Americans for a highly questionable crime."

In analyzing the appropriateness of a retrial, I took into account the attacks by Dole and Solomon and the fact that the jury had seen the *Washington Times* headline. Also, Gillen had made a mistake during jury selection by accepting Steven Kirk, who had turned out to be an advocate for the defense. Kirk's answers to the juror questionnaire showed that he was a law school dropout, a public relations operator, and a sole proprietor who depended on the government's goodwill to get funding for his charitable clients. With more attention to jury selection, we stood a good chance of winning a conviction. Furthermore, the case was important. I decided that Clair George should be retried.

CHAPTER TWENTY-THREE

An Unusual Proposal

In August 1992, while the jury was still deliberating in the Clair George case, William Clark came to see me. Clark, who was Caspar Weinberger's friend and Ronald Reagan's former national security advisor, said that Weinberger faced near ruin from the cost of defending himself. He would have to sell his summer home, which was important to him and his wife, both of whom were in poor health. If we would drop the case, Clark said, he would arrange to have us supported and praised in Congress "on both sides of the aisle."

After Clark left, I discussed the matter with Craig Gillen, who had joined the meeting halfway through. Reasoning that sympathy for Weinberger's plight could not justify ignoring his bald-faced lies, Gillen and I agreed that we should not drop the charges.

A few days later, Clark telephoned me in Oklahoma City to say that he was "of counsel" to Weinberger and that Robert Bennett, who was on vacation at his Montana ranch, had authorized Clark to speak for him. Bennett's bill was already $800,000, said Clark, and would reach $3 million after a four-week trial. Clark told me that Weinberger was unwilling to plead guilty but that he would give a "carefully crafted" apology to the government, the court, and the independent counsel. Bennett had promised Clark that his own response would also be gracious.

Clark felt that they could assure me that "Congress and the president and other interested people" would "accept" a resolution that did not include a trial. "Cap [Weinberger] and Bob [Bennett] would respond graciously to any disposition short of trial, in public and by correspondence." Clark repeated that he was confident, although he had discussed it only with Bennett and Weinberger, that congressional reaction would be most favorable if we moved to dismiss the charges in the interest of justice. Clark and Bennett could work with the House and Senate leadership and with former senators Howard Baker and Paul Laxalt to prepare the appropriate public commendation. No response would be needed from me.

Clark may have intended to reassure me with this information, but it actually had a disturbing effect: I surmised that he, Bennett, and Weinberger might have been using Baker and Laxalt to orchestrate the public attacks on me by the Republican leadership in the Senate and perhaps the House.

Clark explained that Weinberger's public relations advisors had planned a reception to express support for Weinberger that would be cohosted by former presidents Ronald Reagan, Gerald Ford, and Richard Nixon. Clark, Bennett, and Weinberger would like to cancel the reception and could do so if we dropped the charges against Weinberger.

I told Clark that even though our investigation had probably been damaged by the negative publicity developed against us by Weinberger's political supporters, we had enough evidence to win a felony conviction of Weinberger. I said that I would be willing to accept a guilty plea to a misdemeanor in exchange for Weinberger's cooperation, and that I considered this to be the best outcome for all concerned. Nonetheless, I said, I would explore Clark's proposal with my associates.

Clark replied that unless I told him it was hopeless, he would like to pursue a resolution short of a plea. He said that there was enough goodwill at the highest level, toward both Weinberger and me, that such a disposition would be well received. Clark reiterated that Weinberger would go a long way in his acknowledgment and apology to the government and to me, and that he had a great deal of humility. Although Weinberger would not admit to having committed any crimes, he would make a full confession of what had occurred. He would acknowledge having withheld information from Congress and my office, but he would deny having intended to mislead anyone for an improper purpose. In view of the time that had passed, my sympathy for Weinberger and his wife, and my desire to conclude my work, I considered the proposal. But I could not forget that Clair George and Alan Fiers had not been let off so easily.

I suggested that Clark convene Weinberger's advisors to consider a misdemeanor plea. By the end of the conversation, I believed that Clark was maneuvering toward a nolo contendere plea, but neither of us mentioned it. (Such a plea does not acknowledge guilt but subjects the defendant to punishment as though he had pleaded guilty. Spiro Agnew, for

example, pleaded nolo contendere to a charge of federal income tax evasion, which led him to resign the vice presidency in disgrace.)

Two days later, Clark made an appointment for himself and Bennett
to meet me in my Oklahoma City independent counsel's office. I asked
associate counsel Rick Ford to join us so that I would have my own witness to the conversation. The meeting began at quarter to ten on the
Sunday morning before Labor Day. Clark opened with a long recitation
of Weinberger's background and then described the plan for the reception, which was slated to take place on September 23, with more than a
thousand people in attendance.

Bennett addressed the strength of Weinberger's case and the statements he and Weinberger were willing to make if I moved to dismiss the
charges. Bennett said that in his proposed statement he would correct
Weinberger's misstatement that I had asked him to give false testimony.

I responded that we had large areas of agreement, but that I would
not dismiss the case. We could not just walk away from the prosecution.
I asked Bennett, as an expert in such matters, to suggest a range of possibilities for a disposition. He outlined four options: a guilty plea; a nolo
contendere plea; an Allen plea (which acknowledges the facts but not
the crime); or a dismissal. Bennett said that Weinberger would never
plead guilty.

Bennett had to leave at twelve-thirty to catch a plane. I left Ford with
Clark and accompanied Bennett outside. As we waited for his taxi to
arrive, he spoke highly of Judge Thomas F. Hogan and invited me to
consider trying the case without a jury. This could be done only if we
both consented. I expressed doubt that I would agree to forgo a jury, but
promised to think it over.

After I returned to my office, Clark reviewed the indictment to identify
a possible charge to which Weinberger might be willing to plead nolo
contendere. Clark took a copy of the indictment with him when he left.

On Labor Day, Clark telephoned me to say that he, personally, was
thinking about a nolo contendere plea, but that he did not speak for
Weinberger. Bennett was against it and felt confident that he could win an
acquittal if the case went to trial; Clark was not so sure. I promised Clark
that I would take the matter up with my staff. When Gillen and I met with
associate counsel the following day, we discussed the possibility of
Weinberger's making a nolo contendere plea. We did not rule out accepting such a disposition, but we decided to wait for Clark's next move.

A few days later, Bennett filed pretrial motions to dismiss the basic
obstruction count; to disqualify Gillen from trying the case because of

his being a necessary witness; to dismiss the counts based on lies to Congress as falling beyond the scope of my prosecutorial authority; to dismiss the count charging lies to my office; to obtain a bill of particulars; and to strike surplusage (irrelevant and superfluous matter) from the indictment.

The most important motion was the one to dismiss the count charging Weinberger with obstruction of a congressional investigation by corruptly withholding his notes from Congress. This count supplied a coherent background for the individual false statements charged in the other counts. In reversing John Poindexter's conviction, the court of appeals had held that the statutory requirement that the obstruction be done "corruptly" was so ambiguous that it had to be limited to its narrowest meaning: obstruction by the corruption of a third person.

At the hearing in Judge Hogan's courtroom, associate counsel Ken Parsigian argued that Weinberger had corrupted Defense Department officials to conceal his notes from Congress; that our charge was within the scope of the statute, even as narrowed by the court of appeals; and that other precedents not overruled in the *Poindexter* decision supported it.

I argued against the motion to disqualify Gillen. This was my first opportunity to observe Judge Hogan and the defense counsel in court. Carl Rauh argued the most important motions, while Bennett, who did not participate, sprawled at the back corner of his counsel table, his girth protruding through his open coat and both arms extended along the rail that separated the well of the court from the spectators—a possessive posture that reminded me of the nineteenth-century Thomas Nast cartoons of Boss Tweed.

John Barrett argued our response to the claim that the indictment contained prejudicial surplusage. At one point, when Judge Hogan asked a question about the relevance of the notes of Prince Bandar's statement that he had recommended Weinberger to be secretary of state, Bennett—who was still lounging against the rail—interrupted Barrett to say derisively that this conversation was not criminal and that Weinberger had just whispered to him that he had never wanted to be secretary of state. The reporters in the courtroom laughed, and Judge Hogan laughed with them.

It was a small thing, but I was disappointed with Judge Hogan's reaction. The background allegations of the indictment were important to explain the materiality of Weinberger's lies. Bennett's interruption was the sort of cheap shot that a young lawyer soon learns to survive, but Barrett had not argued many motions and was for a brief moment disconcerted as he resumed his argument. Gerhard Gesell and other judges who ran tight ships would surely have reprimanded Bennett. He was not an active participant in the argument or any of the proceedings that day; he was just a heckler.

As a lawyer who did not frequently practice in Washington, I had to be alert to the relationship between Judge Hogan, a Reagan appointee, and my opponents. When I was prosecuting felony cases before the Tammany judges of the old court of general sessions in New York, I learned to be sensitive to problems that arose when a judge seemed to accept familiarity by a defendant or defense counsel as if he or she were "one of the neighbors' children." I disliked Bennett's ostentatious familiarity with the judge.

Later that day, after I returned to our office, Dan Webb telephoned me with more bad news: The managing committee of his firm had split over whether he should try Weinberger. Some members of the committee strongly opposed it. Webb was the chairman of his firm's litigation group and a business-getter. He had been away in Tucson for five months and had a case for an important client coming up in Cleveland. I asked to meet with the committee, but Webb telephoned back to say that they did not want to meet; they did not want to exacerbate the division. I had planned to send John Barrett and Christina Spaulding to Chicago to work with Webb to minimize his absence from the firm, but Webb did not want to provoke a rift in the firm by pressing the matter with the partners who opposed his taking the case.

As the Weinberger motions were playing out, we completed our investigation of Edwin Meese. No evidence turned up that would significantly strengthen a prosecution for a five-year-old crime or a lie about five-year-old facts. Under political attack and with three major trials coming up, we had all the work we could manage. On September 17, I declared an end to our investigation. In letters to the attorney general and George MacKinnon, the presiding judge of the court that had appointed me, I wrote that unless something new developed during one of our pending trials, the investigation was over.

Reaction to this news varied. Some observers praised our work. According to Representative Lee Hamilton, who had headed the House select committee on Iran-Contra, "It has reinforced the principle that all Americans, regardless of their position, regardless of their objectives, have to be held accountable under the law for their actions."

Professor Paul Rothstein of Georgetown University Law School agreed, saying that "the probe was well worth the monumental effort if for no other reason than it will help preserve the Constitution's crucial checks and balances."

Others criticized me for having taken so long. "I think what happened is that the investigation just went on much too long," said Arthur Liman, who had been the chief counsel to the Senate select committee. "The attention span of the public is very short. If an independent counsel is to retain the confidence of the public, he must proceed with an investigation much more promptly, as if he is operating with a shorter statute of limitations."

The *New York Times* editorialized: "Even after six years of investigation, the information remains maddeningly incomplete. But . . . there is nonetheless enough information available to pass judgment on some basic points about this monumental crisis in constitutional government."

In press interviews, I responded to my critics by saying, "It's always a question of judgment whether an investigation is too expensive. I made the decision that we were going to do a comprehensive investigation—not grab a small, runaway conspiracy." More than eight hundred spontaneous letters from around the country urged me to continue the investigation.

Because it would take several weeks to complete the final report, noted Lyle Denniston of the *Baltimore Sun*, President George Bush would escape public criticism before election. A *USA Today*-CNN–Gallup poll revealed that 55 percent of the respondents were not satisfied with Bush's explanation of his involvement, 36 percent were satisfied, and 9 percent had no opinion.

As Congress prepared to adjourn, a Republican threat of a filibuster killed the bill to renew the Independent Counsel Act. This did not directly affect me, as a previously appointed independent counsel, but it showed Minority Leader Bob Dole's hostility and power. When Senators Carl Levin and William Cohen attempted to bring the issue to a vote, Dole objected. He read from a letter signed by twenty-eight Republican senators: "With the disgraceful indictment of Caspar Weinberger and the subsequent announcement of the end to Lawrence Walsh's five-year multimillion-dollar investigation, this hardly seems the time for Congress hurriedly to consider reauthorization of such pernicious legislation." Supporters of the bill had the sixty votes necessary to limit debate, but without the unanimous consent of the Senate, other delaying tactics would prevent the bill from being considered before the date fixed for adjournment.

On September 23, the reception for Weinberger filled the ballroom at the Mayflower Hotel. The honorary cochairmen, the three Republican past presidents, were not in attendance. Presiding over the event were the actual cochairmen, including Paul Laxalt, President Bush's current national security advisor Frank Carlucci, and former national security advisors William Clark and Henry Kissinger. The organizing committee numbered eighty well-known individuals, including Edwin Meese and Elliott Abrams.

Letters of praise for Weinberger from Richard Nixon and Ronald Reagan were followed by speeches of support by would-be Republican presidential nominee Jack Kemp and former ambassador to the United Nations Jeane Kirkpatrick. The indictment drew the wrath of numerous speakers. Senator Alan Simpson, the Republican whip, aroused a wild ovation as he declaimed, "This is the rottenest, son-of-a-bitchin'est thing that ever happened." Navy Secretary John Lehman called me "a sleazy bounty hunter." Meese averred that he was "absolutely outraged." Senator Steve Symms of Idaho said, "The American people should rise up in righteous indignation." Senator Malcolm Wallop of Wyoming called the indictment "the revenge of a petty, small-minded man, trying to find something to salvage his career."

A more serious public relations assault on me was timed to coincide with Weinberger's reception. That day, the *Washington Times* carried a false story that Gillen and I had been fined for nonpayment of D.C. taxes. Editorials in the *Wall Street Journal* and the *Daily Oklahoman* repeated several libelous statements from the article: that Gillen and I were guilty of "tax evasion"; that we had been "fined"; that we had been subject to "civil penalty"; that we had "padded expenses"; that I had accepted an unethical gift of a low-rent lease from the Watergate Hotel; and that we were guilty of a felony (making a false statement to a government agency regarding the anticipated temporary nature of Gillen's work).

Because the mainline press largely ignored these wild attacks, we did not feed the story by responding to them. Except on two occasions when one newspaper picked up a false editorial from another, I avoided replying to editorials, believing that publishers have the right to say what they believe—right or wrong—and that responses simply invite more savage attacks.

In a preliminary meeting at the end of September, the auditors from the General Accounting Office told me that they would probably conclude that my office was subject to the executive branch regulations regarding expenditures rather than the judicial branch regulations that we and previous independent counsels had used as guidelines. If applied immediately, the GAO's interpretation—which contradicted the position of the Administrative Office of the United States Courts and the legislative history of the Independent Counsel Act—would disallow travel and subsistence reimbursement for Gillen and me while we were away from our homes. Despite the precedents set by previous independent counsel, the auditors said that they believed the Independent Counsel Act to be defective because it contained no specific authorization for travel expenses; they considered its generalized authorization for me to commit government funds inadequate.

Counsel to the administrative office suggested that we stand our ground because the problem was not a true question of audit but one of law—the interpretation of the statute. Although we believed our view would prevail, we had to solve the problem or face the loss of Gillen's services just as he was preparing to retry Clair George. Gillen could not support two homes and could not move to Washington, because his wife's work prevented her from leaving Atlanta.

On September 29, Judge Hogan issued his rulings on Weinberger's motions. The judge granted the motion to dismiss the basic obstruction count of the indictment. He took under advisement the motions to disqualify Gillen and to strike surplusage from the indictment. The judge denied the other motions. In short, he ruled in our favor only when we had precedents directly on point. He decided against us or deferred his decisions on motions that required him to analyze the issues or exercise his discretion. The taking of important motions under advisement, which required us to prepare for trial without knowing what the ultimate rulings would be, was as bad as an adverse ruling. I took his action as a forecast of his conduct of the trial. I had to assume that he was going to rule against us on any close question of law.

Particularly troubling was Judge Hogan's dismissal of the count that accused Weinberger of obstructing a congressional investigation. The judge stated that the count dealt "solely with alleged lying" and did not assert that Weinberger had caused somebody to act corruptly; withholding the notes was "no more and no less than passive lying to Congress." Judge Hogan concluded that we had failed to meet the *Poindexter* test, which he believed required us to show that Weinberger had corruptly caused other Pentagon officials to knowingly violate a legal duty to turn over his diaries. "If the indictment alleged that Mr. Weinberger informed the general counsel of the DOD [Department of Defense] that Mr. Weinberger had notes but that the DOD should not give the notes to congressional staffs, Mr. Weinberger would be properly charged with corruptly obstructing the investigation. In this case, there is no allegation that DOD or any individual acted in a manner that is consistent with the *Poindexter* definition of 'corruptly.'"

When the indictment was drafted, we had not yet learned of the memorandum that would have enabled us to fill the gap perceived by the judge. In the memorandum, the Defense Department's general counsel, Lawrence Garrett, had specifically warned Weinberger that Congress had requested his notes; Weinberger's handwritten response had been "Larry, let's discuss this." In grand jury testimony before the indictment, Garrett had denied asking Weinberger specifically about his notes, and we had not had this memorandum for cross-examination because the Defense Department's counsel had withheld the document from us until after the original indictment had been drafted and filed—and after the statute of limitations had run.

To attempt to add new facts in a new indictment after the statute of limitations had run would probably have been unsuccessful, and inasmuch as the judge had ruled that we had really charged false statements, we decided to do that—in express terms—and to argue that the new indictment was only a restatement of facts already charged.

The gravity of Judge Hogan's decision was obvious. As David Johnston of the *New York Times* observed, "Without this central charge, prosecutors are left with a narrower case based on charges of piecemeal perjury and a making of false statements."

After the judge issued his rulings, Clark called me to say that Weinberger's physical condition had deteriorated, as well as his wife's, and that there was no possibility of his making any plea other than not guilty. The outcome Clark proposed was a motion for dismissal "orchestrated" in the interest of justice and because of newly discovered evidence—the shallow affidavits Bennett had been distributing to the press. Clark believed a dismissal would be acceptable on Capitol Hill, and that both Republicans and Democrats would "laud" me, Weinberger, and the process. Clark said he was making one last prayer for dismissal.

I replied that I didn't see how we could bring Weinberger to a position where he would accept what we could give.

Clark said that Bennett wanted to do what was best for Weinberger but had suggested no solution other than a "charitable" dismissal. Clark said he knew that I would not be deflected from the merits by a concern for the news media; nevertheless, he said, the press was a factor. A carefully prepared motion and concurrence for dismissal would be good for all of us. Clark would help craft a disposition. Weinberger would refrain from declaring victory. He realized that he had made uncharitable remarks about me and my staff at the time of the indictment. He would retract those statements. He had the highest regard for me.

In the end, did this proposal boil down to dismissing the case in exchange for political acclaim? I could remember only once being offered a personal reward for dropping criminal charges: When I was deputy assistant district attorney in New York, a defense counsel was so enthused by my decision to dismiss a case (because of reasonable doubt) that he tried to send me to his tailor for a suit of clothes. I had brushed the offer aside, viewing it as having arisen from the exuberance of the moment.

The Clark-Bennett proposal had a different ring. When I mentioned it to a colleague later, he laughed and told me that I was out of date; this was the way cases were fixed in Washington. Indeed, Bennett publicly projected himself as one who could "jolly along prosecutors in the crucial pre-indictment phase of a case and end up with a good deal." This was more than jollying me along. By backing their offer with political force and implying that the alternative was a return to the onslaughts by Senator Dole and his Republican colleagues, plus counterinvestigations by various government agencies, the proposed deal smelled to me like Tammany Hall in its heyday, when a party assembly district leader could talk this way to a Tammany-elected district attorney. I didn't want that kind of political commendation.

Actually, the counterinvestigations were reassuring. Although politicians had initiated them, they were conducted by career officers of integrity and courage. The seasoned officials who investigated my operation stood up to the political pressure exerted on them by the staffs of House Minority Leader Bob Michel and Representative Gerald Solomon, and even by the staff of the president himself. Late in the afternoon of October 2, I spent nearly three hours presenting my arguments to a high-level group of auditors, associate counsel, and directors at the General Accounting Office. My interrogators were gracious and well prepared, having obviously considered the memorandum of law I had submitted. They recognized our good faith and accepted our position that Gillen and all our part-time lawyers were eligible to be reimbursed for travel and subsistence expenses "when actually employed" in the work of the independent counsel's office.

I, however, posed a problem because the group did not consider an "agency head" to be in the same category as his or her employees; the group had difficulty squaring my operating from Oklahoma City when the preponderance of my work was in Washington, even though the statute described me as a "per diem" employee with compensation limited to prevent full-time work. Because of the lack of guidance in the statute, they suggested that the comptroller general grant us a waiver until Congress could address the question. I welcomed the waiver, but we undertook to conform our practices to executive branch regulations in the future.

During this period, I found out that a career officer in the District of Columbia finance department had been subjected to pressure from the Republican Party and his supervisor because he had refused to recommend penalties against Gillen and me. (Like other taxpayers who voluntarily disclosed errors, we had been charged simple interest but no penalties had been imposed on us.)

A week later, Mary Belcher reported that an official in the Bush administration had told reporters about the loss of Ronald Reagan's interrogatory answers and exhibits and had characterized the loss as a flagrant violation of security. The official who had leaked the story admitted to the reporter he had done so in the hope of embarrassing me.

On October 9, Gillen, assisted by Barrett and Spaulding, represented our office at a status conference in Weinberger's case. Although I had told him that I would not consent, Robert Bennett had at the last minute moved for a trial without a jury. Gillen declined to waive the jury. Under the law, Judge Hogan had no choice but to deny Bennett's request, but the motion gave Bennett favorable press headlines. A trial without a jury would have exposed Judge Hogan, if he decided to convict, to the political retaliation I was receiving. One of the beauties of the American system of justice is that factual and legal decisions are made by different entities: Leaving the decision to a jury protects not only unpopular defendants, but also unpopular prosecutions of popular and politically entrenched defendants.

Gillen informed the court that he would withdraw from the case and be replaced by another lawyer. Gillen said that we would seek a superseding indictment to replace count one, which Hogan had dismissed. The judge then set the pretrial schedule. Bennett would have fourteen days to respond to the new indictment and would have until November 16 to file a notice specifying the classified information he needed. We were to file the response of the intelligence agencies to this notice before November 23. The hearing on classified information was set for December 7. Trial was to start January 5. Implicit in the schedule was the expectation that we would file our supplemental indictment by November 2 to give Bennett fourteen days to prepare his demand for classified information. To enable Bennett to meet this schedule, Gillen committed us to obtaining the new indictment before the end of October.

That afternoon, I telephoned James Brosnahan, whom John Keker had recommended as the "best criminal trial lawyer in San Francisco." Brosnahan was controversial because he was outspoken and had testified against the confirmation of Chief Justice William Rehnquist, but he was highly regarded as a courageous and able advocate. Having found Brosnahan on Cape Cod about to start a vacation, I asked him to take over Weinberger's trial. We talked again that evening; the next day, Brosnahan agreed to try the case.

His catch-up problems would be formidable. We were about to file our list of potential trial witnesses and specify the excerpts from Weinberger's prior testimony that were to be introduced as part of our case in chief. I anticipated having difficulty in admitting evidence. In view of Judge Hogan's past performance, I expected him to hold us to a narrow view of relevance and materiality and to protect his record on appeal by leaning against us on evidentiary questions. (As the prosecution, we would be unable to appeal from an acquittal.) Fortunately, Brosnahan was not afraid of judges; he had demonstrated the ability to succeed with juries in spite of judicial partiality.

The retrial of Clair George began on October 19, with jurors who had been exposed to media coverage of the political attacks on us. This trial proceeded much as the first one had. Alan Fiers gave the same testimony as he had given before, and George used essentially the same defense. Unlike the first trial, however, this one generated relatively little public interest. Most of the time the courtroom was only half filled.

For some reason, the room was cold. George's loyal supporters continued to attend, some of them wearing gloves and scarves and some draping blankets over their laps. To a *New York Times* reporter, they looked like "a bunch of wealthy alumni in the stands in a homecoming football game."

George's successor Dick Stolz, however, characterized the group as "seething with indignation." Said Stolz: "An effort to break down the organization brings people together. . . . Our active operation may be over, but I don't think security should be breached." Essentially, Stolz regarded the exposure of lies to Congress as a breach of security.

A new witness for the prosecution was a pilot known as CIA Officer Number Seven, who had worked for Richard Gadd in Oliver North's Contra-supply operation and had later been hired by the CIA. The witness's name was classified because he was still employed in undercover work for the agency. He testified that he had reported to one of George's aides. When Eugene Hasenfus's plane was shot down, CIA Officer Number Seven had advised his superiors; and Norman Gardner, one of George's two executive assistants, had traveled to Pennsylvania to tell him not to talk to the press. The officer had given Gardner a full description of North's operation just before Gardner and George appeared before the House intelligence committee—in the session at which George had denied knowledge of the individuals who had been responsible for Hasenfus's flight.

The trial lasted four weeks. Like the jurors who had judged Oliver North, these jurors showed a capacity to methodically sort out the various charges. On December 9, after eleven days of deliberation, the jury returned its verdict, finding George guilty of two felony counts of lying to Congress and acquitting him of the other five counts. The first count on which he was convicted was based on his October 14, 1986, statement to the House intelligence committee that he had not known Felix Rodriguez had been involved in North's operation—a statement that had been refuted during the trial by CIA Officer Number Seven. The second count on which George was convicted was based on his December 3, 1986, statement to the Senate intelligence committee that he had not known what role Richard Secord had played in resupplying the Contras. The counts on which George was acquitted had relied on the testimony of Alan Fiers, a co-conspirator, whom the jurors had apparently found inadequately corroborated.

On the courthouse steps, Gillen said, "This marks the first time that a senior CIA official was convicted of felony offenses for crimes committed while he was in his position at the CIA. Congress expects and deserves full and truthful answers from the intelligence agencies." Gillen went on to say, "Make no mistake about it, we are very pleased with this verdict. Word has gone out to senior officials in the intelligence agencies that they cannot use the secrets of our nation to hide."

In a press release, I characterized the verdict as a "significant victory" and said, "It will be an important deterrent to protect the

Congress and the public from cover-ups by high-level national security officials."

Writing in the *New York Times*, Neil A. Lewis observed that "the most lasting impact of the verdict . . . may be on the fractious and distrustful relationships between Congress and the intelligence agencies. Intelligence officials may now find testifying before Congress a far more perilous business than they have in the past. In essence, the jurors found that Mr. George gave crafty and misleading answers in the final months of 1986 to two congressional committees."

While Gillen was retrying George, Paul Ware of Boston had agreed to try Duane Clarridge. Ware was well known for his trial work. Two associates from his office, Ken Parsigian and Sam Wilkins, were already on my staff, and he brought one more. It was late; some pretrial motions had already been argued. Shortly after Ware arrived, the defense counsel persuaded the judge to set the trial for the spring of 1993, which meant that we wouldn't have to try Weinberger and Clarridge simultaneously.

On October 21, James Brosnahan made his first appearance before Judge Hogan at a status conference in the Weinberger case. Robert Bennett pressed Brosnahan to file our superseding indictment against Weinberger. Bennett understandably insisted that he had to have the new indictment in order to prepare his request for classified information in accordance with the schedule fixed by the court. Brosnahan requested a week's postponement of the court's pretrial schedule, but the judge denied the request.

Under Brosnahan's direction, John Barrett drafted a supplemental indictment to be presented to the grand jury. Following the strictures set out by Judge Hogan, Barrett converted the obstruction count to a false-statements charge and substituted quotations from Weinberger's notes for the paraphrased references that had been in the original indictment.

Preoccupied with my determination to have my final report ready by the end of Clarridge's trial in March, I had not thought it necessary to go to Washington simply to review a superseding indictment. All of us agreed about what it should charge. The case was Brosnahan's, and I was in the doghouse for having insisted on omitting the false-statements charge from the original indictment. On the evening of October 28, two days before its due date, Barrett faxed me a copy. As I reviewed the draft in Oklahoma, I thought that the long series of quotations would be difficult to read to a jury. I had opposed using them in the original indictment. When Barrett called me the next afternoon, October 29, I expressed this concern and asked him if everyone on the trial team wanted to use quotations; he said that they did. He reminded me that Weinberger's counsel had objected to our use of paraphrases in the first draft as having been inaccurate and unfair. More important, said Barrett, exact quotations were the essence of a false-statement case. I agreed.

An hour later, Brosnahan called to make sure that I had no objection, because of the presidential campaign, to including a quotation of Weinberger's note about having met on January 7, 1986, with Ronald Reagan, George Bush, George Shultz, William Casey, Edwin Meese, and John Poindexter in the Oval Office. In his note, Weinberger had written that the "president decided to go with Israeli-Iranian offer to release our 5 hostages in return for sale of 4,000 TOWs to Iran by Israel. George Shultz and I opposed—Bill Casey, Ed Meese and VP favored—as did Poindexter."

I was unwilling to weaken any part of the indictment by eliminating a note that was material. I told Brosnahan that the substance of the note was already public knowledge. Poindexter had described the meeting in his congressional testimony. I told Brosnahan I did not think the quotation would be newsworthy, despite its reference to President Bush.

The next day, October 30, the grand jury voted to approve the indictment, and it was filed in court. That evening, I stayed at the office past dinnertime, working on the final report. When I came home, my wife said, "You were all over the news."

"What news?" I replied. "We didn't do anything newsworthy today. We simply filed a superseding indictment."

"There isn't any question," she answered, "it was about the Weinberger case." I tuned in to CNN's *Headline News*.

Although the January 7 meeting had been frequently raised during the presidential campaign to contradict Bush's claim that he had not known how strongly Shultz and Weinberger had opposed the arms sales, the note quoted in the superseding indictment had supplied the first documentary evidence that such a meeting had occurred and that Bush had supported the arms sales. Bill Clinton's campaign officials had seized on the note as confirmation that Bush had lied in denying that he had supported the sale of arms for hostages. In a few words, the published note had ended years of equivocation.

I then watched *Larry King Live* and saw George Bush grapple with questions about the note. He was tired. What he was saying was accurate, but his delivery was uncertain. Then King took a question from George Stephanopoulos, Clinton's press officer. Bush's replies seemed defensive, unresponsive, and unpersuasive.

Old, forgotten campaign reflexes surfaced. Although I was not a Bush partisan, I did not want him hurt unfairly. I actually started to reach for the phone to call the White House or Bush's campaign headquarters to get the message through that the president needed a better briefing. He should have had two or three succinct, forceful sentences, like those Clinton had used when questioned in the presidential debate about his draft status. Bush should have been told to say, one, that the attorney general of the United States had been at this meeting and had approved the proposed activity as legal; two, that the story of the meeting was not new, inasmuch as Poindexter had mentioned Bush's participation to the congressional committees in 1988; three, that it had already been extensively discussed during the campaign (the president's position had been explained by him and by his counsel); and four, that although Weinberger might have characterized the transaction as arms for hostages, that was not how President Reagan had viewed it.

I did not place the call. An independent counsel must remain independent. But I was chagrined at the realization that I had been oblivious to the dramatic effect the quotation would have once it became public. Even if I had foreseen the outcome, it would not have affected my action; I would not have modified an indictment for political reasons. But I didn't like being surprised. As I sat with my wife watching the president falter on national television, incredibly I found myself thinking of Tolstoy's classic narration of the events leading up to the battle of Borodino, which emphasized the role of happenstance in massive operations and a turning point of history. Was it possible that, after six years of contentious, costly, and painstaking effort, the independent counsel could affect the outcome of a presidential election through sheer inadvertence?

Unknown to me, my associate counsel in Washington had thoroughly discussed the political consequences of the quotation. Although he was on the team preparing to try Duane Clarridge, Ken Parsigian had increasingly assumed responsibility as my counselor in defending us from political attacks. On hearing that Brosnahan's team had decided to use quotations and to include the one referring to George Bush, Parsigian and others in the office had protested that it would be regarded as a political intrusion into the presidential campaign and would give new emphasis to the political attacks against us. Brosnahan, Barrett, and Spaulding had vigorously responded that they had reached their decision solely in the interest of what was best for the case and that Parsigian was bringing a political factor into their decision.

Parsigian had been so alarmed that he had gone to see Craig Gillen, who had been at the courthouse for George's retrial. Gillen had characterized the quote as a "nuclear bomb" but had said that he did not want to intrude in Brosnahan's case. Nor had he or Parsigian wanted to go over Brosnahan's head and protest to me. Brosnahan and Barrett had not told me of the dissent. It would not have affected my decision, but I would have been less surprised by the explosion that followed.

CHAPTER TWENTY-FOUR

Boomerang:
The Character Issue

In view of the compromises, the fund-raising, and the corrosive competition a politician must engage in to win the presidency, I have often wondered why any presidential candidate would make character a campaign issue. Lawyers know to avoid introducing the subject of character at trial unless their clients are invulnerable, because doing so invites possibly devastating attacks based on otherwise inadmissible incidents. But in 1992, George Bush was better situated than most candidates. With his inherited wealth, an extremely popular first lady, and a photogenic family, Bush seemed secure. Moreover, Bush had narrowly missed death as a hero of World War II, whereas his young opponent had not only opposed the Vietnam War but had also gone to some effort to avoid serving in it. Bill Clinton, who depended on his own relatively meager earnings, had fashioned a seat-of-the-pants career in politics and had been forced to explain away charges of marital infidelity and marijuana use. On the character issue, the balance seemed to fall in Bush's favor.

Bush's Achilles' heel, however, was his split-second instinct to categorically deny anything that might be politically embarrassing. His repeated statement that he had been "out of the loop" regarding Ronald Reagan's secret effort to sell arms to free the hostages was one such blanket—and false—denial. The phrase had been too vivid; it would stick to him forever. Over the years since he had first uttered it, Bush and his aides had struggled to explain and rationalize statements and facts to bridge the gap between this memorable denial and the unfolding truth. But the Washington political reporters and those covering Iran-Contra were too able and too well prepared to be deceived.

The task of extricating Bush from the problems that arose from his various statements about Iran-Contra fell to White House counsel

Boyden Gray, who had served Bush for twelve years and was intensely loyal to him. Having been the vice president's counsel while Bush was involved in Iran-Contra activities, Gray had spearheaded Bush's defense of these activities after he became president. It was Gray who had shrugged off my complaints about the CIA's abuse of its classification power to force the dismissal of Joseph Fernandez's indictment. It was Gray who had delayed the production of White House and vice presidential material, including Bush's diary. And it was Gray to whom other agencies had reported significant activities by my office.

Although it was well known that, through Donald Gregg, Bush's office had to some extent been tied to North's Contra-supply operation Bush had never revealed the extent of his involvement in the sale of arms for hostages. At different times in two presidential campaigns, he had admitted knowledge of some aspects and denied knowledge of others, sometimes contradicting his own previous statements. Bush's most consistent contentions were that he had not been aware that the transactions with Iran had been a matter of arms for hostages, and that he would have objected to the operation if he had known that George Shultz and Caspar Weinberger strongly opposed it. On December 3, 1986, for example, Bush had stated in a Washington speech to the American Enterprise Institute that Ronald Reagan was absolutely convinced that he had not swapped arms for hostages. "And I am not aware of," Bush had continued, "and I oppose . . . any ransom payments or any circumvention of the will of Congress and the law of the United States." On several occasions, Bush had claimed not to have realized that the United States had been trading arms for hostages until Senator David Durenberger briefed him on the Senate intelligence committee's hearings in late 1986.

Weinberger and Shultz had strenuously protested the sales of arms to Iran at meetings in early August 1985, when McFarlane first proposed the sales; on December 7, 1985, after the disastrous Israeli Hawk shipment; and on January 7, 1986, when President Reagan authorized the continuation of sales to Iran directly from the United States. Although Bush had missed the second meeting, he had attended the first and third. When he claimed to have been "out of the loop," he had been focusing on the second meeting, at which Weinberger and Shultz had spoken most emphatically and had appeared to have stopped the sales. Bush had later qualified the statement, but he had never really come clean. He had not mentioned, for example, that he had been regularly briefed by John Poindexter on the arms sales and the efforts to free the hostages. Poindexter had brought Bush up to date whenever he missed one of the president's daily intelligence briefings.

In January 1988, Bush had told syndicated columnist Mary McGrory that he had "said over and over again that the original proposal was not presented as an arms-for-hostages swap." According to Bush, he had not been "at meetings in 1985, especially the December 7, 1985, meeting when objections were apparently forcefully stated. Records indicate I probably attended an *ad hoc* meeting on January 7, 1986, which was not an NSC meeting, but I do not recall any strenuous objection."

In his 1988 autobiography, *Looking Forward,* Bush claimed to have had misgivings about the arms sales to Iran. "As it turned out," he wrote, "George Shultz and Cap Weinberger had serious doubts, too. If I had known that and asked the president to call a meeting of the NSC, we might have seen the project in a different light, as a gamble doomed to fail."

In August 1987, shortly after the close of the hearings by the congressional select committees on Iran-Contra, Bush had spoken with the *Washington Post's* David Broder and had said, "If I had sat there and heard George Shultz and Cap [Weinberger] express [their opposition] strongly, maybe I would have had a stronger view. But when you don't know something, it is hard to react."

After reading Broder's article, a startled Weinberger had telephoned an equally astonished Shultz, who had later dictated a note of their conversation: "VP [Bush] in papers [yesterday said] he [was] not exposed to Cap [Weinberger] or my arguments on Iran arms. Cap called me [and said] that's terrible. He [Bush] was on the other side. It's on the record. Why did he say that?"

On August 25, 1992, we had quoted this note in a footnote to our brief responding to one of Weinberger's motions. Reporters had spotted it and written stories about it. David Broder reported that he had asked Bush three times whether he had really been unaware that Weinberger and Shultz opposed the arms sales. Each time, Bush had said he had not been aware of their objections, because he had not attended the December 7, 1985, meeting when they had protested most strongly. This claim was clearly disingenuous, inasmuch as Weinberger and Shultz had vigorously reiterated their opposition in Bush's presence on January 7, 1986. Indeed, Shultz had told the select committees in July 1987 that at the January 7, 1986, meeting, "I expressed myself as forcefully as I could. . . . That is, I didn't just sort of rattle these arguments off, I was intent." The State Department chronology introduced at the time recited, "Shultz and Weinberger argue strongly against Iran proposal, but everyone else favors going forward."

Questioned about Shultz's note at a press conference on August 26, Bush had said, "No, I don't know about that. I've told very openly everything I have to say about it. I don't know about that memo. And I find nothing—you know, I see no reason to contradict myself at all. I think what I have done is give the facts as I have seen them. So I don't—I saw a story on it, and to be honest with you, I didn't read it."

By September, the presidential campaign had turned ugly, with each candidate assailing the other's character. Bush had disparaged Clinton's explanation of his draft deferment; Clinton had targeted Bush's evasions about Iran-Contra. On Labor Day, vice presidential candidate Al Gore had cited Shultz's note as evidence of what Gore called Bush's "credibility canyon." At a speech to the United Steelworkers of America, in Pittsburgh, Gore had said, "We have some hard reasons to wonder about the story George Bush has told. . . . So who's not telling the truth? The former vice president, who tells us he never had a chance to know that his good friends Shultz and Weinberger were strongly opposed to the sale of weapons to Iran? Or the former secretary of defense, who was talking candidly—and he thought privately—to his colleague, the secretary of state? There were a lot of people running for cover when the arms sales to Iran were revealed, now it appears George Bush was one of them. He's still running."

Gore had told the steelworkers, "What he didn't know was that somebody made a record of conversations that took place at the time. He said he didn't know what was going on, and he is still saying that he knew nothing about one of the most controversial policies of the Reagan administration."

When reporters questioned Bill Clinton about his draft status in early September, the irritated candidate had protested that reporters had made no similar effort to query Bush regarding Iran-Contra. Clinton had suggested that Shultz's note indicated that Bush might have demonstrated "support for illegal conduct." Compared to this, Clinton had said, the actions of the individuals who had helped him obtain his draft deferment did not amount to "a hill of beans." Clinton continued, "There is a memorandum of a conversation between two cabinet members who were—unlike these guys who were not my political friends—in the Reagan-Bush cabinet, which, if true, would call into question not only the president's veracity but his support for illegal conduct, which you all don't even ask him about."

On September 6, Bush had been interviewed by Tom Brokaw on a Sunday-night NBC program. When Brokaw asked if Bush was claiming that Shultz and Weinberger had not told the truth in the conversation recorded in Shultz's note, Bush had replied, "I'm not saying that at all. I don't think they've said that I'm not telling the truth. . . . This seems to me to be just a late smoke screen out of that dead old saw out there. And I have nothing to explain."

That morning, on NBC's *Meet the Press*, David Broder had asked National Security Advisor Brent Scowcroft whether Bush was telling the truth in his denial of having been aware that Shultz and Weinberger had opposed the arms sales to Iran.

Scowcroft had answered artfully: "I think it's quite possible it was a truthful statement."

The Clinton campaign had disagreed. Spokesman George Stephanopoulos had told the press, "I think George Bush has a big credibility problem."

Democrats on Capitol Hill had weighed in with their opinions. Senate Majority Leader George Mitchell, for example, had observed, "There still remain many unanswered questions. Our time frame [for investigation] was clearly inadequate." When Mitchell was later questioned by reporters, he had said that "at the very least, [Shultz's note] raises questions about the completeness, accuracy, and credibility of the president's entire statement."

Thomas Polgar, who had served on the staff of the Senate select committee on Iran-Contra, had told Sam Meddis of *USA Today*, "There was no smoking gun to confront Bush, but I think that memo [Shultz's note] would have done it. It would have been inevitable [for the congressional committees] to call Bush and have him questioned under oath."

Reporters had become increasingly interested in the topic. In his column in the *New York Times* on September 11, Anthony Lewis had returned to a statement Shultz had made in the hearings of the select committees about the January 7, 1986, meeting: "It was clear to me that the president, the vice president, and others still favored the operation." Lewis had also cited a February 1987 PROF note from Poindexter to McFarlane stating that the "president and vice president are solid in taking the position that we have to try."

Against these facts, Lewis had reviewed the unforgettable climax of the 1988 Iowa primary campaign: When Dan Rather had tried to pin Bush down on Iran-Contra, the candidate had blustered, said that it was old stuff, and accused Rather of unfairness. Bush's campaign telephone banks had then stimulated calls to CBS-affiliated stations complaining about Rather. As Lewis noted, "It was a carefully prepared gambit and it worked. Through the rest of the 1988 campaign, reporters hardly raised the Iran question. It is still working. President Bush brushes off questions on the subject as dated, unfair, silly. He makes the press feel uncomfortable for asking. . . . But this was the worst government scandal in years, a true violation of the Constitution that damaged the national interest. It matters whether Mr. Bush is telling the truth about his part in it."

Several reporters had contrasted the statements by other participants in the arms sales to Iran with Bush's claims that he had been "excluded from key meetings" and that he would have opposed the deal if he had known "what was going on." On September 21, *Time* had reported that Bush had been regularly briefed by Poindexter and that there had even been some "discussion in the White House about sending Bush to meet the Iranians personally." The next day, numerous articles pointed out that Richard Secord had credited Bush with the renewal of the arms sales in the summer of 1986, after his visit to Israeli counterterrorism expert Amiram Nir. According to Secord, "Nir's briefing must have been a doozy, moving Bush from note-taker to advocate."

Howard Teicher, a former senior member of the National Security Council's staff, had been interviewed by Ted Koppel on ABC's *Nightline* and then by David Johnston of the *New York Times*. Teicher had told Johnston that he and Oliver North had briefed Bush on the failure of McFarlane's mission just before Bush went to Israel in May 1986. Teicher had commented, "This was not complex. We're not talking about quantum mechanics. What really stunned me was how all these principals suddenly knew nothing about what was going on."

The *Washington Post* had editorialized that Bush's credibility on Iran-Contra had become a central issue of the campaign:

> He's in a squeeze. If he maintains his denials, there will be sharpened challenges to his credibility when he's made trust a principal issue of his attack on Clinton, but if he changes his story, he opens himself up to a whole range of charges bearing on personal integrity and conceivable culpability. . . . So what? some say—it was a tough situation and

another day. But Iran-Contra was not just a little failed stunt. It was, in practical consequence, a major diplomatic and political disaster; in its wielding of secret executive powers, an assault on the constitutional government, and in its demands on involved officials, a far-reaching test of judgment and integrity. In short, few other experiences could be more relevant to the measuring of presidential capacity. Not just for the president, but for the country, it is embarrassing to have questions raised about a chief executive's stand. But a full and honest accounting is due.

In a radio interview on September 24, Bush had said, "I've leveled with the American people, and I've nothing to add to it." Three weeks later, however, he had added a mouthful. During a televised tour of the White House, NBC reporter Katie Couric had asked Bush whether he had known about the sale of arms for hostages, and he had replied, "I have testified four hundred and fifty times, under oath some of them. . . . What was challenged, I think—will help you with the question. What . . . was asked was whether I knew that Caspar Weinberger and George Shultz, how strongly they opposed it. And I said to that, there were two key meetings where they almost got into a shouting match, I'm told, that I did not attend. But I said all along that I knew about the arms going, and I supported the president."

"You knew about the arms for hostages?" Couric had asked.

"Yes," Bush had replied. "I've said so all along, given speeches on it."

This had reopened one of the major points in dispute: When had Bush first realized that the Reagan administration was trading arms for hostages rather than for diplomatic advantage? Reporters had asked Bush to explain the contradiction between his most recent statement and his earlier claims on the subject. Bush had disparaged the questions as "a desperate attempt to level it with the failure [of Clinton] to tell the truth" about his draft status. "I think we're totally different. . . . It's a crazy thing to try to equate this with telling the truth on the draft."

Meanwhile, the Clinton-Gore campaign had charged that Bush's statements "just don't add up." Stephanopoulos had called on Bush to make public his deposition to my office and the notes of his interview by the Tower Commission. "Bush either told the American people one thing in public and told the investigators another in private," Stephanopoulos had said, "or misled both."

In response, Boyden Gray had said that Bush had misspoken: "I think he misinterpreted the question."

A White House press spokesperson, Walter Kansteiner, had also "clarified" Bush's remarks: He had misunderstood the questions; Bush had known that arms were being shipped to Iran and that hostages were being released, but he had never regarded the events as two elements of a ransom deal until after they became public in late 1986.

In a follow-up letter to the *Washington Post*, Boyden Gray had claimed that Bush had always acknowledged having attended the key January meeting. "Moreover, the president's comments did not alter his stated recollection that he did not fully recognize that the Iran initiative had deteriorated into straight trading of 'arms for hostages' until December 1986. . . . Katie Couric asked if he 'knew about the arms for hostages.' The president thought her question referred to his knowledge of the Iran initiative, and reiterated his previous answer: 'Yes, and I've said so all along, given speeches on it.' "

Bush's running mate, however, had muddied the water. Dan Quayle had told reporters that Bush had been aware "all along" of arms-for-hostage deals with Iran. "That's no news," Quayle had said. To a question about paying ransom for hostages, he had replied, "Look, on hindsight, this was not a good deal. The president said that. It was not well handled, but he has always said, of course, he knew about the policy." Quayle's remarks had led to further stories contrasting Bush's various statements.

On October 19, the *New York Times* had editorialized that the White House's clarification had added "something incomprehensible to what had previously been merely incredible. . . . If George Bush, as vice president, did not know that the Reagan-Bush administration was dealing in arms to ransom Iranian-held American hostages, he was negligently ignorant. If he did know, he was derelict in failing to protect the president and his country from a scandalous mistake." The editorial had observed, "The burden has long since shifted to Mr. Bush to prove his difficult-to-believe assertions of ignorance."

The next day, reporters had contrasted a cable in which John Poindexter had named Bush as one of those who favored a "closed-mouth policy" with Bush's early public call to "let the chips fall where they may. We want the truth. The president wants it. I want it. And the American people have a right to it. If the truth hurts, so be it. We've got to take our lumps and move ahead."

In his October 30 column for the *New York Times*, Anthony Lewis had written, "At the end of what has seemed an interminable campaign, we are left with a question of character: How does George Bush live with the knowledge of his disregard for truth in politics? . . . Surely there is a level of brazen falsehood that they should be ashamed to breach." According to Lewis, Bush had passed that point in his August 1987 interview with David Broder, by denying knowledge of Weinberger's and Shultz's opposition to the sale of arms to Iran. After discussing the evidence of how much Bush had actually known about Iran-Contra, Lewis had observed that "cynicism has characterized Mr. Bush's career in politics for a long time."

On the day Lewis's column appeared, we had filed the superseding supplemental indictment against Caspar Weinberger. In a brief press release accompanying the indictment, we had explained that the new indictment had resulted from the dismissal of the original obstruction charge, and we had mentioned our promise to the court that we would seek a second indictment before the end of the month. The release had not quoted Weinberger's notes. We had not pointed the press to any quotation. Nevertheless, the news media had seized on the indictment's recital of Weinberger's notes, particularly the note concerning the January 7, 1986, meeting.

The full text of the note had become a lead story in the evening news on television and radio. It was widely published and its implications spelled out. The Associated Press, for example, reported that the indictment contradicted "George Bush's denials that he knew of arms-for-hostages swaps in the Iran-Contra affair and that two cabinet officers opposed them. . . . In Weinberger's handwritten notes, the indictment described a . . . meeting at which President Reagan and his top aides discussed a straight swap of arms for hostages. . . . The indictment also indicated that Bush knew of the opposition of Shultz and Weinberger."

When asked about Weinberger's note, White House spokesman Marlin Fitzwater, who was traveling with the president, claimed to be unaware of it. "I figure there is no such thing as a new document or memo that hasn't been looked at."

Speaking for Clinton, George Stephanopoulos pounced on the opportunity: "It is never pretty to see a defense secretary question a commander in chief, but this is conclusive evidence once and for all that George Bush was as deep in the loop as you can get on Iran-Contra. This is the smoking gun." Candidates Clinton and Gore declared that the note impeached Bush's claims about his knowledge of the arms sales.

Bush's aides dismissed Weinberger's note as containing nothing new and charged that its release shortly before the election had been politically motivated to stop the momentum that had recently been building for Bush. Boyden Gray tried to narrow the question by saying that Bush had "never said he didn't know there was opposition," but that "he didn't know how strong it was expressed and didn't know there was a raging fight."

Bush called the Iran-Contra probe a "big witch-hunt" and said, "People are tired of this, and I think they know I've told the truth."

On November 1, just after being told that the CNN-Gallup-*USA Today* poll showed a widening of Clinton's lead from 3 percent to 7 percent, Bush appeared on the CNN program *Newsmaker Sunday*. Tired, sagging, and somewhat irritable, he said, "I didn't know ... how strongly they [Shultz and Weinberger] felt about it, that there was a kind of ravaging fight going on, and I did know [sic], and I have said that, and I testified to that." Holding the unopened report of the select congressional committees in his hand, he ineffectively waved it as he contended that there was nothing new in the recent stories. As for their effect on his campaign, he said, "The headlines don't help, but I don't think people believe this."

From Bush's campaign train in Wisconsin, however, Maureen Dowd of the *New York Times* reported that Bush had been "told that the new poll numbers indicated that his surge had flattened after a day of news reports suggesting that he was more in the loop on the Iran-Contra scandal than he had yet allowed. . . . Mr. Bush did not hide his vexation. He took off his baseball cap and tossed it on the table, and he and Mrs. Bush quizzed [an aide] about what the numbers meant." Bush walked to the back of the train for a rally and went into the campaign mode his friends called "jet propulsion. . . . The words tumbled out in a bracing, breathless aria of insults about Bill Clinton: 'The waffle man, . . . governor of taxes, . . . the ozone man. . . .'"

In the final days of the campaign, Dowd observed "all the contradictory sides of George Bush . . . his elation at bashing freaks and rivals, and fatigue and frustration at having to justify his actions as president—and now as vice president—when he feels he has done a good job and is . . . a superior candidate. As he began one more day racing around the country, Mr. Bush sounded listless and sour in a CNN interview this morning, saying that the press coverage of this campaign had been the worst ever and refusing to explain why his account of his role in the

Iran-Contra affair was at such variance with [Weinberger's] contemporaneous notes."

On the eve of the election, the *New York Times* editorialized that
George Bush had been "caught in a loop" by Weinberger's note, which
"clearly aligns him with Mr. Reagan's decision to seek release of five
hostage 'in return for' selling 4,000 antitank missiles.... Despite his
complaint about the timing of these charges, it's never too late to seek
Mr. Bush's full accounting."

Anthony Lewis's column that day focused on Bush's character. "More
than any incumbent president in memory, [Bush] has been a candidate
without shame. Lies, hate, vulgarity; nothing has been too shameful for
George Bush.... The big lie that has now been definitely exposed is ...
a powerful example of the need for an independent counsel on such
politically charged matters.... George Bush's falsehoods have none of
the justifications sometimes offered for lying. They are not white lies, to
save hurt feelings. They are not lies to serve some great cause. They are
only lies, small and large, to serve George Bush's ambition.... The foul
words and falsehoods that have spewed out from Mr. Bush in the last
days of the campaign show us a man in a frenzy for something—anything—that might work. They show us a man without the inner values
that restrain human conduct: a man without a core."

Also in the *New York Times* that day was an essay by syndicated
columnist William Safire, who made five suggestions to avoid "late
hits and last minute maneuvers that we can do without next time
around." The final suggestion was "Independent Counsel Restraint. In
handing up his second indictment of Cap Weinberger, Judge Walsh
supplied more evidence that blew away Bush protestations of having
been out of the arms for hostages 'loop.' ... Was Vice President Bush
in the Casey-Poindexter ransom camp? Yes; his denials ring ever more
false. Was the Independent Counsel right to drop the bombshell four
days before the election? No; the indictment should have been handed
up weeks earlier, or sealed—special prosecutors should stay outside
politics."

The polls were inconclusive as to what effect Weinberger's second
indictment had actually had on the campaign. There was no question
that until one week before election day and four days before the
indictment was filed, Bush had improved his standing. The two polls
most favorable to Bush showed the outcome as being too close to
call; but a day or two before the new indictment was filed, Bush's

position had seemed to stabilize. Other polls showed a wider margin between the two candidates. Clinton's poll-taker, Stan Greenberg, announced that a national survey of twelve hundred individuals and a state-by-state survey of ten thousand showed that the race between Bush and Clinton had stabilized on October 28 and 29—before the superseding indictment against Weinberger was filed—and that Clinton had retained a 7 percent lead. Most polls showed that Clinton had widened his lead after the second indictment was filed but that Bush's progress in catching up with Clinton had slowed or stopped before then.

When all the ballots were counted, Clinton had received nearly 44 percent of the vote, while Bush and Ross Perot wound up with roughly 38 percent and 19 percent, respectively. An exit poll conducted by the *Los Angeles Times* on election day showed that although voters considered the Iran-Contra affair an important issue in their decision, the late revelations had not substantially increased the damage to Bush. Postmortems conducted by political analysts suggested many other reasons for failure.

Many observers condemned the campaign itself. Disorganized management, lack of message, and narrowness of appeal were but a few of the criticisms from well-placed Republicans. *New York Times* reporter Michael Wines concluded that, "crippled by chaos and lack of strategy," George Bush had "stumbled to defeat." Wines described Bush's campaign as a "thoroughly snake-bit enterprise" from the nominating convention, which had alienated millions of voters with its right-wing oratory.

Bush partisans, however, blamed me for their candidate's loss. The day before the election, officials from Bush's campaign had charged that the timing of my release of the second indictment of Weinberger had been calculated to harm Bush's campaign. Boyden Gray, who had been assured by Deputy Attorney General George Terwilliger that my investigation was over and that my final report would not harm Bush, was nonplussed by the reference to Bush in the superseding indictment. Gray told reporters that he believed I had deliberately intruded in the presidential campaign, and he implied that President Bush took the same view.

During his October 30 appearance on *Larry King Live*, Bush had denied that he was accusing me of being politically motivated. He had said he was just asking, "Isn't it strange?" and claimed that he was "not implying anything." By Sunday, November 1, Bush had become more outspoken. Asked whether he would fire me, Bush declined to say, but he characterized my investigation as "a big witch-hunt out there, when you see a decent man like Cap Weinberger going through all kinds of hell."

Others were even more direct. One senior official, for example, had told Ann Devroy and Walter Pincus of the *Washington Post* that the inclusion of Weinberger's note in the indictment had been "an incredibly low blow by a mean, political hack. . . . This was the lowest of the low. It amounts to a dirty trick."

Another official quoted by Devroy and Pincus had predicted that "this could change the dynamic in play, it could stall us out if he spends the next two days being asked about this."

An election-night party for Dan Quayle at Indianapolis was described by Michael Abramowitz of the *Washington Post* as "akin to an Irish wake." One of Quayle's advisors had told him, "Nobody's crying. Most people saw it coming." Another top aide told reporters that the vice president had "seen the election as winnable" and had believed that attacks on Clinton's character had been "really cutting against" him, but that the disclosure of Weinberger's note had "blunted" the Republicans' momentum.

Quayle himself told the reporters, "You could feel this thing slipping away in the last days of the campaign." The reindictment of Weinberger had been "the last nail in the coffin," Quayle said, "a travesty of justice" that had halted Bush's comeback and "smell[ed] of politics." Flying back to Washington with reporters, however, Quayle blamed the failure of the campaign to develop a domestic agenda.

Aides told reporters that the president believed the filing of the superseding indictment and the release of the notes had eliminated any chance he might have had of winning reelection. According to the *Washington Post*, Bush was also "said to believe that Weinberger is 'an innocent victim of Walsh's drive to get [Bush]' and that 'it is a travesty overall.' " Bush was described as bitter about the superseding indictment.

The *Post* quoted one presidential assistant as saying, "Many of us will go to our graves believing there was political motivation in the timing of this by Walsh and that any dim hope we had of catching Clinton died when we spent the last two days of the campaign on the defense over Iran-Contra."

Some members of the news media agreed with Bush and his supporters. According to Weinberger's colleague Malcolm S. Forbes, Jr., editor in chief of *Forbes* magazine, "What stopped President Bush's last-minute comeback dead in its tracks was Special Prosecutor Lawrence Walsh's Friday-before-the-election new indictment of Caspar Weinberger, which made reference to a memo purporting to show that Bush was lying about his Iran-Contra role. . . . Talk about a brazen—but successful—attempt to manipulate a national election. . . . Even though Walsh's record is one of unrelieved failure, he ultimately got what he wanted all along—the scalp of the president of the United States."

For my part, I would have been glad to accept credit for ridding the country of a cover-up administration, but only if I had earned it through appropriate investigative action. As it happened, the culminating event had been accidental. The fact was that my investigation had never been effectively directed against George Bush. He had not been questioned by Congress; he had therefore not lied to its committees. He had not been in the chain of command, and he had been well insulated by witnesses loyal to him. The deposition we had taken was primarily to eliminate him as a witness for North. Whether Bush had lied to the public would not have been an issue for my investigation unless the lying had constituted a crime.

Even after finding Caspar Weinberger's notes, we had not targeted Bush. We had been engrossed by the task of proving Weinberger's guilt beyond a reasonable doubt and had been exerting our full effort to win motions and to prepare for trial. It was our most important case, not only because it would be devastating to lose, but also because some of the facts about Iran-Contra would be publicly revealed for the first time during the trial. Every move we had made in that litigation had been narrowly motivated and, in my judgment, necessary. I would not have limited our proof or changed our tactics in the case against Weinberger to accommodate a lying president or candidate. The exposure of Weinberger's note hurt George Bush not as a prosecution target by showing that he had done something criminal, but politically by showing that he had lied to the public about what he had done.

Writing in the *New York Times* editorial notebook on November 9, John P. MacKenzie observed that I would have to answer the question of whether quoting Weinberger's note in the superseding indictment had been "a political cheap shot or a legitimate prosecutorial action," but that "the reverse question also needs attention: Would it have been proper to suppress the information and release it only after the election?" The effect of the disclosure was debatable, wrote MacKenzie. "But the news plainly rattled the president in his public appearances over the campaign's final weekend." MacKenzie then analyzed the issues:

Timing, and its implications for the prosecutor's motivation, are the significant questions. No one disputes that the prosecutor may use any and all of Mr. Weinberger's notes as evidence at the trial. The note in question serves the additional function of suggesting to the jury a motive for falsely denying the notes' existence: They were explosive, damning. Was it necessary to quote from the notes in the indictment itself? No; that was the prosecutor's option. It's clearly proper and quite common to quote evidence, especially in perjury-type cases. Could Mr. Walsh have postponed the indictment past the election? Yes, but his office had promised it by the end of October under a demanding court timetable. Could he have sealed it until after the election? Perhaps, but that would have had political consequences too, and sparing candidates' embarrassment is not one of the customary reasons for sealing an indictment. [In fact, there was no statutory basis for filing the indictment under seal, unless the defendant was at large, which was not the case with Weinberger, who had already been released on his own recognizance.] So the question becomes: What should an independent prosecutor, appointed to guard against politically tainted justice, do when his decision—either way—might affect a national election? Here's a rough first answer: If Lawrence Walsh had suppressed this information, the public would be justifiably angry. Angry enough to wonder why we bothered to have an independent counsel.

Several other observers also came to my defense. *The New Republic* published an article by Simon Lazarus, who blamed the Republicans for having failed to be more alert to the superseding indictment, particularly in view of its public forecast. "It would be a delicious irony if Bush's defeat could be laid at Walsh's door. The Reagan and Bush administrations, along with their allies in Congress and their appointees on the federal bench, had waged an unrelenting—and quite successful—war to undermine the institution of the independent counsel and the Iran-Contra investigation in particular. . . . But though Walsh is a convenient scapegoat, he was just doing his job. On Iran-Contra, as with other problem issues, the president and his aides chose to look the other way until it was too late to save themselves."

New York Daily News columnist Lars-Erik Nelson expressed similar views: "If the belated Iran-Contra indictment of Caspar Weinberger really cost George Bush reelection, you can't accuse the prosecutors of playing politics. This wasn't politics. It was poetry. Poetic justice. . . . Out came the damaging evidence on the Saturday before election. . . .

Bush had ducked this incriminating evidence for six years. . . . Had he chosen, he could have controlled the damage by setting the record straight at a more favorable opportunity. . . . Instead, he blustered. The devastating evidence then hit him at his most vulnerable possible moment. . . . But he has no grounds to blame the special prosecutor for a late hit. The only reason the investigation has taken so long, and cost so much, is that Bush and his friends were so good at covering up the evidence."

CHAPTER TWENTY-FIVE

Bob Dole, Pardon Advocate

George Bush's loss to Bill Clinton in the 1992 presidential election left Senate Minority Leader Bob Dole as the Republican Party's senior spokesman. He had already captured a great deal of public attention with his successful efforts to prevent Congress from overriding President Bush's thirty-one legislative vetoes. By various procedural manipulations and threats of filibuster, Dole had also managed to block much of the legislation proposed by the Democrats, despite their status as the majority party on Capitol Hill. In addition, he had marshaled Senate support for Bush's income tax hike and the soaring spending deficits the United States ran up during the administrations of Bush and Ronald Reagan.

Dole had been an outspoken opponent of our investigation since Robert Gates's nomination to head the Central Intelligence Agency ran into difficulty because of his role in Iran-Contra. But after Caspar Weinberger's indictment in June 1992, Dole harshened his rhetoric and political maneuvering in an effort to shut down my office. In these attacks, he found an easy opportunity to win public attention and to make sardonic comments without the risk of offending any organized political constituency.

More significantly, Dole's assaults reflected the resentment felt by many Republicans, primarily those from the party's right wing, of what they perceived to have been my interference with the presidential campaign. As the *New York Times* put it four days after the election, "In the finger-pointing ambiance of the post-election White House, the Walsh-as-saboteur theory has already risen to the status of received wisdom. . . . Some Bush loyalists suggested that Mr. Walsh had finally achieved by negative publicity what he had failed to accomplish in the courts: driving a high Reagan administration official from office over the affair."

Ironically, I had once felt a certain kinship with Dole as a fellow mainstream Republican. My wife and I had favored him against George Bush in the Oklahoma primary election in 1988. My wife had voted for him; I had not done so, but only because I had unexpectedly been called back to Washington and had missed the vote. I respected him for the courage he had shown in surmounting his war wounds and resuming his education to become a lawyer and for his hard-fought political career. I agreed with his 1988 campaign claim that, as President Reagan's principal congressional ally, he had been more important than Vice President Bush.

Although I was a transplanted easterner, my wife and I felt strong ties to Kansas. My legal work for the Kansas Gas and Electric Company had brought me in contact with the business leaders of Wichita and other communities in the state. My wife's most important financial investment was in a Kansas company, and our youngest daughter was a graduate of Washburn University, Dole's alma mater. In fact, my wife's family was as deeply rooted in Kansas as Dole's family. She was born in Arkansas City, just north of the intersection of the Arkansas River and the Oklahoma state line. Her mother had taught school there and in Hutchison after growing up in Newton, where her family had lived since before the Civil War. My wife's father had come to Kansas from West Virginia during the 1920s to explore for oil. A staunch Republican, he had been a friend of Governor Alf Landon. By the long stretch of coincidence, my first work for the Republican Party had been in support of Governor Landon's presidential run; I had been a New York election-district captain in 1936, when Dole was in the eighth grade.

Perhaps because of my previous favorable impression of Dole, I was doubly shocked that he would so openly intrude in a federal prosecution and would permit himself to be used by Caspar Weinberger's attorneys. This type of influence-peddling is generally left to party functionaries, who are important within a political organization itself but are not usually public leaders. Although I had sometimes seen state or local officials engage in such conduct, it was surprising to me that a Senate leader—especially one who seriously aspired to the presidency—would use the power of his Senate office directly or indirectly to influence the outcome of a criminal case being prosecuted by the federal government. Never during my service at the Justice Department, the district attorney's office, or the governor's office had I encountered one instance of a U.S. senator's trying to influence the disposition of a pending case. Neither straitlaced senators like Robert Taft nor freewheeling senators like Lyndon Johnson, Everett Dirksen, and Styles Bridges—who sometimes protected individuals in other arenas—had ever intruded in federal court cases.

I knew that concern for Bush did not motivate Dole, who had told my press officer Jim Wieghart at a chance meeting several months after the 1988 campaign that Bush had been in the center of the Iran-Contra activities. Dole had urged Wieghart to have me "dig into it."

George Bush was vulnerable to appeals for Weinberger. He sympathized with Weinberger and was furious at me. The day after the election, the *Los Angeles Times* described the president as having been "clearly angered by the release of" Weinberger's note and having "declined to rule out firing Walsh." Pete Yost of the Associated Press compared my situation to that of Watergate independent counsel Archibald Cox, who was thrown out of office during the infamous Saturday Night Massacre, after he subpoenaed Richard Nixon's records.

Although firing me might give Bush a measure of satisfaction, the prosecution would continue under my successor. If Craig Gillen or James Brosnahan succeeded me, new embarrassing disclosures would be inevitable when Weinberger's case went to trial. The full extent of Bush's guidance of President Reagan had not yet been adequately explored—by me or by Congress. Bush's failure to produce his own diary was indefensible, as were his various conflicting contentions regarding his Iran-Contra contacts. The only way for him to avoid the revelations that would emerge at Weinberger's trial would be to pardon Weinberger before the case went to trial. Inasmuch as I had already stated that new indictments were unlikely, all that was necessary was to eliminate the pending indictments. But granting pardons of persons about to go to trial would be scandalous in itself.

Under the Constitution, the president's pardon power is absolute and unreviewable. In the early years of the Republic, pardons had sometimes been granted before trial to induce witnesses to testify for the prosecution, but pardons had never been granted to prevent the exposure of embarrassing facts that would come out at trial. Once immunity statutes were enacted, pardons had been granted only as acts of mercy after individuals were convicted. There was no precedent for granting a pardon to block the trial of an indicted person—let alone the trial of a president's colleague or a trial at which the president might be called to testify. Other presidents embarrassed by scandals had refused to use the pardon power as a cover.

To overcome these hurdles and soften public resistance to a pardon, Bush, Weinberger, and their lawyers needed to batter the Weinberger case, my office, and me without getting their own hands bloody. As Robert Bennett afterward explained on *Larry King Live*, Washington is a mean town. If you represent a public figure in litigation, Bennett said, you have to use the media to beat your opponent. He pointed to his own activities on Weinberger's behalf as examples of his skill.

The election-eve timing of the reindictment, which Bennett had forced, had given Bennett and his colleagues the opening they had been looking for, and Dole became their hatchet man. With a sardonic ruthlessness reminiscent of Joseph McCarthy, Dole hurled a continuous barrage of unsubstantiated charges at us.

Anyone who accepts appointment as independent counsel must expect ample criticism, but I did not like being attacked by the leader of my own political party. More important, I did not want our case against Weinberger to be pounded to pieces by an untouchable spokesman on the eve of trial. While my hands were tied by the restraints on pretrial comments by prosecutors, Dole was like a professional boxer who had jumped out of the ring to beat up a hostile reporter.

On November 8, the first Sunday after Bush's defeat, Dole began his attack during the CBS program *Face the Nation*. Calling my office "a hotbed of Democratic activist lawyers," he demanded that a special prosecutor be appointed by the Justice Department to determine "whether or not politics played any part" in the superseding indictment of Weinberger. Dole argued that the fact that the Clinton campaign's press release regarding Weinberger's note had been dated October 29, the day before the indictment was filed, proved that we had given Clinton's staff advance notice of the indictment's allegations. Dole singled out James Brosnahan as the culprit solely because he was a Democrat who, before joining my staff, had contributed $500 to Clinton's primary campaign; his law firm, one of San Francisco's largest, had given the campaign $20,000.

In an Associated Press interview, I denied that we had revealed the superseding indictment to anyone other than the interagency group of intelligence officers who had reviewed it to screen out any classified information. I dismissed as irrelevant any question about political contributions before appointment to office, whether by Brosnahan to Democrats or by me to Republicans.

Clinton's spokesman, George Stephanopoulos, told reporters that he had learned about the superseding indictment from a Reuter News Service story at about one in the afternoon on October 30, and that his rapid-response group had prepared and issued the press release within the next two hours or so. In their haste to get it out to the candidates, they had simply misdated the release. Stephanopoulos categorically denied having had any contact with me or my staff prior to the indictment.

Having learned from an Atlanta friend that Craig Gillen had strong Republican credentials, Dole centered his attack on Brosnahan. But Brosnahan's political affiliation had nothing to do with either his appointment or the handling of the superseding indictment. By the time he joined my staff, we had already decided what charges the indictment would contain, had notified the court of our intentions, and had committed ourselves to the deadline for returning the indictment. Brosnahan had personally double-checked the controversial quote with me to be sure that I wanted to include it. Moreover, because of his late assignment to the case, he had asked Judge Thomas Hogan to set the pretrial schedule back by a week, which would have eased the need to file the indictment before the election. The court had denied his request.

On November 9, Dole sent me a letter—with copies released to the news media—asking that I fire Brosnahan because of the contributions he and his law firm had made to Clinton's campaign before Brosnahan was appointed to my staff. Dole wrote that he understood Brosnahan to have been involved in Democratic activities for some time. Dole also mentioned that Brosnahan had testified against the confirmation of Chief Justice William Rehnquist and had defended the *Sacramento Bee* in a libel suit filed by Senator Paul Laxalt, who had been chairman of the Reagan-Bush reelection campaign at the time. "Accordingly," Dole concluded, "it is my opinion that the credibility of your office is severely compromised by the employment of Mr. Brosnahan. . . . While I do not know Mr. Brosnahan personally, I have strong reservations over the ability of such an individual to function independently of what would appear [to be] a strong political bias."

In my reply, I emphasized the effect of public controversy on a case that was about to go to trial. "I can recall no case where a Senate leader has so directly intruded in a pending lawsuit," I wrote. "There is no truth to the suggestion that James Brosnahan . . . gave the Clinton campaign advance warning of the new indictment." Although I had assumed Brosnahan was a Democrat, I told Dole, I had never asked the political affiliation of any appointee. What I had seen in Brosnahan was "a courageous lawyer . . . willing to expose himself to unpopularity in order to carry out his responsibilities." I reaffirmed my confidence in Brosnahan's ability, impartiality, and fairness. I explained that the advance notice of the indictment was given not to the Clinton-Gore campaign, but to the intelligence agencies of the Bush administration. After informing Dole that before my own appointment I had made contributions to Republican candidates, I concluded by saying, "The significant point is that neither [Brosnahan nor I have] made any contributions since undertaking to work as an independent counsel."

Dole's spokesman, Walt Riker, disparaged my letter, saying that it did "not address the active, liberal agenda of Mr. Brosnahan and, obviously, it is politics at its worst. . . . The letter fails to address the most basic questions of appearance of impropriety and outright partisanship. This will not go away. We will continue to pursue this vigorously. . . . If Mr. Walsh does not think that contributions to the Clinton campaign from his top aide are relevant, then that, in and of itself, is an indictment—not of the Bush administration, but of Mr. Walsh and his entire operation."

On November 11, four Republican members of the Senate judiciary committee carried out Dole's request that they petition Attorney General William Barr to seek the court appointment of an independent counsel to determine whether I had timed the superseding indictment of Weinberger so as to embarrass Bush. "We have questions whether or not improper political considerations went into the timing of the indictment," the senators wrote, ". . . and whether improper disclosure of the indictment was made to the Clinton-Gore campaign." The letter was signed by Senators Alan Simpson, Strom Thurmond, Hank Brown, and Charles Grassley. Republicans Arlen Specter and Orrin Hatch, who were also on the committee, did not sign the letter.

In an accompanying letter, Dole—as the Senate minority leader—added his own views: "The entire Walsh operation appears to have been seriously compromised by recent developments, including strong indications of partisanship and election year manipulation. . . . It is time to clear the air. . . . I believe Mr. Walsh would welcome this opportunity to defend the independence of the independent counsel's office. The American people deserve no less." Without urging the appointment of a new independent counsel, Dole called on the Justice Department to investigate whether politics lay behind Weinberger's second indictment. He again described my office as a "hotbed of Democratic activist lawyers."

Speaking for the White House, Marlin Fitzwater said, "The Dole idea of a special prosecutor [to investigate Walsh] is something that the Congress can do themselves. You don't have to have us involved." According to the *Washington Times*, however, President Bush supported "an investigation into special prosecutor Lawrence Walsh's probe of the [Iran-Contra] affair."

George Stephanopoulos called the proposal to appoint a special prosecutor to investigate the independent counsel "the silliest thing I ever heard. There was absolutely no contact between Judge Walsh and our campaign."

Reporters were inviting me for interviews, and it was galling not to be able to express my opinion that Dole was simply being used by Weinberger's counsel to smear my office so that the public would more readily accept a presidential pardon for Caspar Weinberger or so that prospective jurors would view us unfavorably. But I could not make such an accusation without drawing Weinberger into the discussion, and such an attack by a prosecutor so close to trial would invite severe action by Judge Hogan. Brosnahan suspected that Bennett might be deliberately trying to provoke a response that he could attack in court. Brosnahan believed that pressure for a pardon was gathering force, although most of us doubted that Bush would grant one. Brosnahan wanted me to at least explain the process prosecutors follow in reaching indictments. We considered making an interim report to Congress, but the press was already explaining the facts, and I questioned the wisdom of reporting to Congress on an extraneous political matter.

In addition to absorbing Dole's onslaughts, we had to deal with old charges that had been revived, apparently by the Justice Department. The FBI reinterviewed me regarding the loss of Reagan's interrogatory answers and exhibits. The FBI asked the General Accounting Office for copies of the material I had submitted in support of our contention that our travel and subsistence expenditures had been legal. We surmised that the bureau was acting for the public integrity section of the Justice Department's criminal division.

Gillen felt certain that the professionals reviewing the material would act responsibly, but he regarded the inquiry as "major league and serious." I saw the review as more likely a reluctant deference to the demands of Senator Dole's office and perhaps Boyden Gray. I felt confident of our legal position: I thought there was little chance that the inquiry would result in a criminal proceeding against us. My chief concern was that the loss of Reagan's exhibits could lead to a reprimand and perhaps new restrictions on our use of classified information. Because Senate Majority Leader George Mitchell strongly supported our work, I doubted that Congress would hold hearings.

On November 20, Dole and Strom Thurmond, the ranking minority member of the Senate judiciary committee, sent a letter to the attorney general. "In connection with the review by the Department of Justice of the possible occurrence of any illegal, improper, or unethical activities within the office of independent counsel Lawrence Walsh," the senators wrote, "we take this opportunity to bring to your attention certain federal criminal statutes and rules which we believe warrant your consideration." The enumeration of the provisions they believed would have been violated if we had given the Clinton campaign advance notice of the superseding indictment suggested involvement with the Weinberger defense team:

> (a) 18 U.S.C. 595 which . . . relates to government employees using their official capacity to interfere with or affect the election of any candidate for president; (b) 10 U.S.C. 241 which relates to a conspiracy to deprive an individual of his or her constitutionally protected rights. We have concerns whether improper considerations, including political considerations, went into the decision to bring the indictment against Caspar Weinberger on October 30, 1992; Rule 6(e) . . . prohibits the disclosure of matters occurring before the grand jury. Press reports indicate that the Clinton-Gore presidential campaign released a press release dated October 29, 1992, commenting in detail on the indictment which was handed out one day later on October 30, 1992. . . . This list . . . reflects certain matters which we believe should be reviewed by the Department of Justice.

Because the attorney general had the power to remove me for cause, my staff and I discussed what would happen if that came to pass. I could apply to the district court for a stay of the action pending the court's review of the attorney general's claim that he had cause for removing me. If the court declined to stay the removal, it would take effect immediately. The office would not close, however. My duties would pass to Gillen until the special division of the court of appeals replaced me with an acting or permanent appointee.

In any event, I felt sure that the attorney general had no cause to remove me. Contrary to Dole's allegations, we had gone to exceptional lengths not to intrude in the campaign. We had left the investigation of

Bush incomplete and had deferred his interrogation until after the election. I had simply wanted to finish my job. Deliberately provoking the president of the United States was not something I had had any desire to do. Although I considered responding publicly to the Dole-Thurmond letter by explaining how Weinberger's notes disclosed the November 1986 cover-up and Bush's acquiescence in it, I decided not to respond. Not only did I feel that it would be unseemly to discuss a case that my office was about to try, but I also preferred that we demonstrate the high-level cover-up in the course of Brosnahan's cross-examination of Weinberger during the trial.

Throughout the fall, as Dole's attacks accelerated, I continued to rely on the advice of press aides Jim Wieghart and Mary Belcher. So long as Dole's only media support came from the unabashedly biased *Washington Times*, they did not want me to make any comments that would draw the mainstream press into covering the spurious attacks. We were also reluctant to volunteer our views about a possible pardon, but we decided that we should be prepared to provide a full report if Bush requested it.

While Senator Dole executed his public attacks, Robert Bennett and William Clark privately pressed their advocacy on White House counsel Boyden Gray. They stressed claims of the poor health of their client and his wife as well as the specter of their financial ruin from the high cost of his legal defense. Bennett, who was in a delicate position because his demands for a prompt superseding indictment had been responsible for its timing, argued that the specific quotation referring to President Bush had been superfluous, something he could not have foreseen.

Gray had been stung by the sudden recurrence of Bush's Iran-Contra problem and was worried about what might emerge at Weinberger's trial. Bennett apparently had no difficulty persuading Gray that pardoning Weinberger would solve many of Bush's problems. To nudge the president, Bennett announced in a court hearing that under certain circumstances, he might have to call Bush as a defense witness, and Clark passed a false message through the Defense Department's public relations officer to the president's office that Bush would be called as a government witness. Regardless of which side called him, the president would not have welcomed the prospect of being cross-examined as a hostile witness by Brosnahan, whose skill was unquestioned.

The *New York Times* reported that some of Weinberger's friends were "beginning an effort to persuade President Bush to pardon the former defense secretary. . . . One former Reagan administration official said today that the idea was gaining credence, with the support of old associates like former Attorney General Edwin Meese III and California friends of Mr. Weinberger like William P. Clark. . . . A lot of people think that Bush, having destroyed himself, ought to do something nice for the party by closing up this matter."

The *Washington Times* suggested that Bush would be a "wimp" if he didn't use his pardon power to close down our investigation. In one column, Terry Eastland, a former aide to Meese, wrote that "if a weak-kneed President Bush . . . fails to pardon at least Mr. Weinberger, . . . then President Clinton ought to, as soon as he takes office."

In a way, President Bush was being presented with a variation on the proposal that Bennett and Clark had presented to me: praise for doing what they wanted, personal exposure and embarrassment for failing to do so.

Despite the fact that Bush's aides and many of his Republican colleagues were advising him to pardon Weinberger and the other Iran-Contra defendants, the president seemed disinclined to follow that course. On November 10, the *Washington Times* reported that "one senior administration official said of a pardon, 'It's not going to happen.' Another said, 'We don't rule it out, but it's unlikely.' "

On Capitol Hill, even Senate Minority Whip Alan Simpson, who had denounced the indictment, cautioned against pardons. Senate Majority Leader George Mitchell was more emphatic, saying that a pardon would be "an abuse of power," and that pardons would make it appear that Bush was trying to prevent any further investigation of his own role in the scandal.

As for the public, a *USA Today* poll showed that 59 percent of those interviewed thought Bush should not pardon Weinberger, 27 percent supported a pardon, and 14 percent had no opinion. Most newspapers opposed pardons for the individuals who had participated in Iran-Contra or covered it up. Pardoning Weinberger, wrote David Johnston in the *New York Times*, "would leave the impression that [Bush] was rewarding a colleague's refusal to cooperate with the independent prosecutors." In the *Washington Post*, Jim Hoagland wrote, "Too much is at stake for American Democracy for investigations into the Iran-Contra Scandal . . . to be turned off by pardons or other whitewash."

Saying that a pardon would be "unforgivable," the *New York Times* editorialized that "the Republicans urging George Bush to pardon former Defense Secretary Caspar Weinberger do not have the president's interests in mind, much less the nation's. To pardon any of the defendants accused by the Iran-Contra special prosecutor would ensnare Mr. Bush forever in a scandal in which he was probably only a peripheral figure." The editorial described the president's dilemma: "Mr. Bush is now beyond the voters' further discipline but not beyond their wrath, or history's judgment. Mr. Ford, after all, wasn't implicated in Watergate when he absolved Mr. Nixon of any legal liability for his crimes. By contrast, a pardon now would prompt widespread suspicion that Mr. Bush was shielding himself as well as others. Already, despite his denials, he is shown in Mr. Weinberger's notes to have been a witting participant in the Iran arms decision. . . . But he did stay out of the day-to-day operational loop. To issue pardons now would put him, for all time, into the thick of the plot."

Overshadowed by developments in Weinberger's case, Duane Clarridge's case was proceeding. It would turn on the issue of whether Clarridge had known that the CIA proprietary aircraft was carrying Hawk missiles rather than oil-drilling equipment. Associate counsel Paul Ware, who was now in charge of the case, believed that the proof would be strong. I was concerned only about the lateness of the trial date, March 15, 1993.

On November 16, Judge George MacKinnon told me that Chief Justice Rehnquist had replaced him with Judge David Bryan Sentelle as the presiding judge of the U.S. court of appeals division that appointed independent counsels. This meant that we could no longer count on the division's support. Having sided against us in the *North* and *Poindexter* cases, having actively badgered our lawyer in the *Poindexter* oral argument, and having voted to narrow the interpretation of the statute that prohibited the obstruction of congressional investigations, Judge Sentelle had to be presumed hostile.

At a long staff conference that day, Brosnahan said he believed that Judge Thomas Hogan was well regarded but that he would be hard to predict because of his friendship with Bennett. Brosnahan expected to be treated as an outsider. Nevertheless, he expressed confidence in his ability to convict Weinberger. In Brosnahan's view, Weinberger had withheld his notes because he had seen other officials, including Bush, making statements that were contradicted by the notes. Looking at the case as a newcomer, Brosnahan believed that any prosecutor would have sought an indictment and that we should no longer be willing to accept a misdemeanor plea. With John Barrett, Christina Spaulding, and George Harris, an impressive lawyer whom Brosnahan had brought from his office, Brosnahan had an able trial team, but jury selection would be critical.

I was concerned that Judge Hogan would dismiss the new first count because, in deference to his view that the essence of the crime we had originally charged in the first count was "false statements" rather than "obstruction," we had relabeled the charge and alleged a violation of a different section of the law. Although the statute of limitations had run before the second indictment, a mere formal correction of an indictment that still alleged the same facts was a permitted exception to the statute. Brosnahan believed that even if the judge dismissed count one, we could introduce all the necessary evidence, because the concealment of the notes was a necessary part of our proof of Weinberger's motive and the materiality of the misstatements charged in the other counts.

Weinberger was arraigned on the new indictment on November 24. At the arraignment, Bennett's partner Carl Rauh complained to the judge that although Weinberger had been receiving "full cooperation from the Pentagon until October 13," our office had directed the Defense Department to cease its cooperation. Brosnahan explained that we were counsel to the government, and that Weinberger had been improperly bypassing us and getting special access from Secretary Dick Cheney to government files. In fact, Brosnahan said, Weinberger had even been given copies of all the documents we had requested from the department. This was contrary to Defense Department regulations. The judge rejected Rauh's complaint.

After the arraignment, Weinberger spoke to reporters, saying, "It is unfortunate that my family has to go through this terrible ordeal not because of anything I have done, but rather because I have become a pawn in the clearly political game, as is shown by the return of the indictment only days before the presidential election."

Dole backed him up: "It is time for Mr. Walsh and his staff to plead guilty to playing politics with their taxpayer-funded inquisition. . . . As of August, Walsh had billed taxpayers for more than $5.6 million for office space, $881,000 for incidental expenses, $401,000 for maintenance, $698,000 for contractual services, and a whopping $655,000 for per diem and subsistence, including $300,000 for personal living expenses and an estimated $65,000 in room-service meals."

On November 22, Dole appeared on CNN's *Newsmaker Sunday* and griped that the mainstream press had not been covering his complaints: "I can't believe we almost have a news blackout on . . . our allegations about Mr. Walsh. You never read anything in the *New York Times* or the

Washington Post, never see anything on the network news. You know, we're the minority party now. If we ever needed help from the media, it's now." Attacking Brosnahan, Dole said, "He's a very active liberal Democrat. He's been engaged in a number of activities to try to derail Republicans."

On November 20, Dole had written chairman Joseph Biden, of the Senate judiciary committee requesting that he hold hearings on whether I had colluded with the Clinton campaign. Dole had charged that "the recent hiring of Mr. James Brosnahan, an individual widely known to have strong ties to the Democratic Party and politics, to handle the Weinberger indictment, would seem to further undermine the impartiality of the office, and the legitimacy of its actions." During his CNN appearance, Dole mentioned his request for hearings but minimized the likelihood that they would take place. "There is a double standard here," he said, "and I am just asking anybody to help us. You think Joe Biden's going to investigate Democrats? Certainly not."

Dole now specifically urged that all those implicated in the Iran-Contra scandal be pardoned. "I'm not suggesting what [the president] should do, unless there's politics involved. Now, if there's politics involved, then I think it changes everything. But how do we find out if nobody will investigate?"

The next day, Senator Biden rejected Dole's request for immediate hearings. Biden left open the possibility of holding hearings later, after the attorney general decided whether to conduct an investigation. "I am not aware of any facts indicating that immediate intervention in the matter by Congress is necessary," wrote Biden.

Dole's spokesman responded by saying, "We will continue to press the issue. It's a fairness issue. The independent counsel is unfair. Slowly, the story is getting out that if the American people knew what was going on with the Walsh investigation, there would be a demand for hearings. It is an outrage."

On November 25, Dole released a copy of a letter he had sent to Attorney General William Barr asking him to obtain a list of my employees, "to see if they had been involved in any partisan 'hanky panky.' . . . We already know that the man handling the Cap Weinberger case, James Brosnahan, is a longtime liberal activist who along with his law firm has contributed $22,000 to the Clinton campaign. Now what about all the others who have been helping Mr. Walsh during his six-year, taxpayer-funded crusade to nail Republicans? . . . Mr. Walsh seemed both unaware of and unconcerned with Mr. Brosnahan's political endeavors—even to the extent such activities clearly compromise the ability of the office to appear non-partisan in the fulfillment of its responsibilities."

Later that month, ABC Radio journalist Beverley Lumpkin, one of the most accurate and diligent of the reporters who covered our work, summarized an investigation she had made into the release of the superseding indictment. She found that the first report had come from the Reuter News Service shortly before two o'clock on the afternoon of the indictment. By midafternoon, other news organizations had picked up the story. The White House had responded that the indictment contained nothing new, but the Clinton campaign had put out a press release saying that one note showed that Bush had "flatly lied" about his role. This release had been followed by vice presidential candidate Al Gore's calling the note "a true smoking gun." That evening, all three network news shows had begun their broadcasts with the story, reporting that at a time when Bush was assailing Clinton's character, the president's own truthfulness was in question.

Lumpkin said that although a number of Republican leaders claimed that the superseding indictment had halted the Bush campaign's momentum and might even have cost Bush the election, "most pollsters said the issue had little impact on the electorate, for whom the main issues were the economy, the deficit, and health care." Lumpkin credited Stephanopoulos's denial of any contacts with us and his acceptance of responsibility for the inadvertent misdating of the press release: "His office began sending the release out at 3:30, . . . shortly after the first wire reports ran. Most news organizations had received the press release by five in the evening, by which time they had had the indictment itself for several hours."

Not every journalist was willing to let us off the hook, however. Writing for *Legal Times*, Stuart Taylor, Jr., called my wounds "self-inflicted":

> Republican partisans have been spewing vitriol for so long at Lawrence Walsh . . . that it's tempting to brush off the current claims that Walsh played a dirty election-eve trick on President George Bush as more right-wing ranting. But this time, Walsh's critics have a point, though a more modest one than they claim. . . . Brosnahan is a terrific trial lawyer with a reputation for integrity, but he is also a Democratic activist and a Clinton campaign contributor. In choosing someone with so much baggage, Walsh shot himself in the foot and presented

an irresistible target to those who already suspected his staff of political animus. . . . There is no evidence, however, that anyone in Walsh's office committed a crime, and thus no legal basis for the request by Senate Republicans that another independent counsel be named to investigate Walsh's office . . . nor does the evidence come close to proving that either Walsh or Brosnahan acted with an improper political motive. . . . In short, while Walsh did not apparently intend to arm Clinton with an October surprise, he did not take enough care to avoid doing so.

On December 2, Dole asked me for a list of my employees during the past six years "so that further questions as to the impartiality of your office can be resolved. . . . Indeed, I would think it important that in the hiring of your employees—particularly those responsible for decisions that relate to the indictment and prosecution of former members of the Reagan administration—that you would be concerned about *anything* that would compromise or appear to compromise an employee's objectivity and impartiality." Dole concluded his letter by saying, "Because you and I differ on this issue, and because you are both unaware of and unconcerned with prior activities of your staff that may compromise the actions of your office, I urge you to release a list of anyone who has worked for your office and to further review these important matters on your own."

Inasmuch as Dole was writing as an individual senator without authorization by any committee or by the Senate itself, I initially refused to provide the information he was seeking. "I find your request inappropriate," I wrote. "It is declined. Each lawyer appointed to this office, including myself, underwent thorough investigation as to their personal integrity and professional qualifications. You can be sure I was more than satisfied. I am proud of their exceptionally high qualifications. Let me make it very clear that I regard a political test for service in this office as abusive and inappropriate. Your public charges of political motivation for decisions of this office consistently appear to be without foundation, but they constitute an intrusion into pending court proceedings."

A few days later, after experts on the Freedom of Information Act convinced me that any person was entitled to know who my employees were, I gave Dole the list he had asked for. In response to a further request from Dole, I sent him a list that showed my employees' titles and their dates of employment.

On December 6, Dole asked for information about the salary I had received during each of the past six years; Brosnahan's current salary; our "fringe benefits," including reimbursable meals and accommodations; and the total payroll of my office for the past six years. A week later, again following Freedom of Information Act standards, I supplied this information, explaining that Brosnahan and I, as per diem employees, did not receive fringe benefits, and that the reimbursement for meals and accommodations was in fact less than the cost we had actually incurred.

I was tempted to ask Dole to disclose any relationship he had with Bennett's law firm. To avoid the appearance of attacking Weinberger on the eve of trial, however, I decided not to ask Dole for any disclosures.

On the day that Dole asked for information about my salary, Defense Secretary Dick Cheney appeared on the NBC program *Meet the Press* and denounced Weinberger's indictment as "a travesty." Said Cheney, "I was the senior House Republican on the committee that investigated the Iran-Contra matter. . . . The fact that now—six years after the fact—the special prosecutor, who has yet really to nail anybody, and has spent millions of dollars, is out trying to prosecute, I think is an outrage."

The next day was a busy one. As the newspapers reported Cheney's statements, the prospective jurors in Weinberger's case were receiving notices telling them when to report to the courthouse. As a result, anything we said publicly could be seized by the defense as prejudicial to a fair trial, so we could neither respond to Cheney's remarks nor take any public preemptive action to head off a pardon by President Bush.

Also that day, the Supreme Court denied certiorari in the *Poindexter* case. Dole seized the opportunity to say, "Lawrence Walsh's bungling investigation is an ongoing embarrassment. Most tax-funded officials in his position would recognize the futility of it all by packing it in and giving the taxpayers a break."

An editorial in the *New York Times*, however, decried the Supreme Court's action and criticized Solicitor General Kenneth Starr for having failed to support our petition.

Meanwhile, as a forerunner to calling George Bush and Ronald Reagan as witnesses, Weinberger's lawyers requested access to the sworn testimony we had taken from them.

On December 11, Judge Hogan dismissed our supplemental indictment, which had superseded the first count of the original indictment. The judge ruled that it had violated the five-year statute of limitations by charging a different crime from the count it had replaced. The decision was unprecedented and clearly appealable, but an appeal would delay the trial.

Bennett applauded the ruling, telling reporters, "It knocks out the heart and soul of their case, and all that's left are some minor capillaries."

Once again, Dole backed him up: "This is the latest failure of Lawrence Walsh's high-cost, low-result crusade against Republicans. It's incredible to me that the independent counsel continues to bumble along trying to get an indictment right. . . . This is the same indictment that was so important to have handed up four days before the presidential election, . . . the same indictment in which it was so important to directly quote Mr. Weinberger's notes to implicate President Bush. . . . With the election over, maybe the Walsh political operatives will decide to pack it in; the only mischief left for them is more humiliating courtroom defeats."

By now, Dole's attacks had become repetitious and predictable. Carl Stern of NBC told me during an interview that Dole's staff had said that he liked to attack me because he got "a lot of one-liners out of it."

From reporters, however, we had learned that Dole was linked to Weinberger's attorneys by more than their mutual disdain for me. Robert Lighthizer, now a partner of Bennett's, had served for several years as Dole's chief of staff and as the vice chairman of his 1988 presidential campaign. John G. McMillan, counsel to Dole as the Senate minority leader, had recently been an associate of Bennett's firm. Several of the firm's partners had over the years made modest campaign contributions through a political action committee, and their principal beneficiary had been Bob Dole. He had received $8,000 for his most recent Senate campaign, more than the political action committee had contributed to any other candidate. To me, this epitomized Dole's hypocrisy in his professed concern about Brosnahan's contributions before he joined my office.

On December 11, the Associated Press reported that Dole had received $13,000 in campaign contributions since 1987 from members of Bennett's law firm. Dole dismissed questions about the contributions, saying, "I am not part of a prosecuting team. . . . I think there is a vast difference." Dole denied having discussed Iran-Contra with Robert Lighthizer. His claim that he had not known Bennett and Rauh were members of the same firm as Lighthizer seemed incredible in light of the fact that the Washington papers had more than once traced Bennett's professional history.

On the same day, Attorney General Barr turned down the four Republican senators' request for an independent counsel to investigate my office. Instead, Barr referred the complaint to the Justice Department's criminal division.

John McMillan, who had left Bennett's law firm to become Dole's counsel, told reporters that he hoped the criminal division would undertake the inquiry. He released a list of campaign contributions to Democratic candidates and organizations previously made over the years by members of my staff. Brosnahan's contributions, before his appointment to my staff, totaled $17,000, and the recipients included the presidential campaigns of Walter Mondale and Michael Dukakis as well as the senatorial campaigns of Howard Metzenbaum and Dianne Feinstein. Two of my associate counsel had each contributed $250 to Bill Clinton's campaign. Former associate counsel had also contributed to Democrats, but not while on my staff. John Keker had given $12,450 to Democratic candidates, including Senator-elect Barbara Boxer and Senator Paul Tsongas, as well as the Democratic Senatorial Campaign Committee. David Zornow, who was now a partner of Bennett's, had given $2,000 in contributions, including a $500 donation to Clinton.

Dole renewed his demand that I fire Brosnahan. "There is either impropriety or the appearance of impropriety, and it ought to be investigated. . . . It's time for Mr. Walsh and his staff to plead guilty to partisan politics with their taxpayer-funded inquisition. The taxpayers have gotten a lot of politics and not much justice for the $41 million Walsh has wasted in his lavish operation."

When a reporter questioned Dole's press secretary, Walt Riker, about McMillan's former relationship with Bennett's firm, Riker snapped, "What does that have to do with anything? I just don't get it. That is a pathetic smear that will not wash."

In mid-December, a *Washington Post* editorial entitled "Dole v. Walsh" took account of Dole's charges that my investigation was politically tainted. The editorial concluded that "if Senate Republicans can prove that Mr. Walsh's operation did not meet this high standard [lack of partisanship]—and it is important to remember they have not done so—the new version of the [independent counsel] statute can set guidelines and incorporate safeguards."

I was now very concerned that the publicity would taint the potential jurors who had already received their notices to report for Weinberger's trial. In preparation for jury selection, Brosnahan conducted a mock trial of the case before thirty-six persons selected from the Washington area by an organization that assists lawyers in such exercises. Mock trials, in which surrogate jurors representing cross sections of their communities are hired to observe abbreviated dry runs of cases, are frequently conducted by defense counsel. The procedure is rarely used by the government, because local prosecutors usually have had extensive experience with the jurors of their communities. Knowing that San Franciscan Brosnahan would be at a disadvantage in selecting District of Columbia jurors, however, I approved the expenditure, which totaled $52,600.

Brosnahan argued the case for the prosecution. Another lawyer acting as Bennett argued for Weinberger. Others acted as witnesses and were examined and cross-examined. The jurors were then divided into three groups to deliberate separately. Two of the mock juries found Weinberger guilty on all four counts; the third found him guilty on three of the counts. The jurors' discussions were videotaped for future analysis by our trial team.

One of the mock jurors disclosed the activity to the *Washington Post*, which published an article about it. The story provoked a fresh attack by Dole, as he released his written complaint to the comptroller general regarding the expense. "Their 'mock trial' is a mockery of the taxpayer, and is the latest arrogance from Lawrence Walsh's outrageous . . . political persecution of Republicans." Dole declared that the mock trial was a waste of federal funds, and he urged me to resign. Dole said that the Justice Department had told him that it did not engage in mock trials.

We responded with a statement by Mary Belcher, saying, "This is an important case, and we have an obligation to be fully prepared."

In an interview with Associated Press writer James Rowley, New York University professor Steven Gillers, an authority on legal ethics, defended the use of mock juries. "It helps a lawyer to understand what the jury is interested in. It's unusual for the government to do it, and I have never heard of it being done in criminal cases. But I am not offended by it." Robert Bennett, however, complained to Rowley that our action was "unseemly," and that our use of mock trial showed we were "hellbent on convicting" Weinberger.

On December 15, House Minority Leader Bob Michel asked the General Accounting Office to conduct weekly audits of my office. On December 22, the Administrative Office of the United States Courts informed me that in awarding a sole-source contract for the mock trial, we had not complied with federal requirements. The letter urged us to pay attention to these matters in the future. Nevertheless, to avoid interference with our work, the office retroactively authorized the contract.

When Dole learned of the administrative office's action, he said that the contract had shown "a troubling pattern of taxpayer-funded irregularities, mismanagement, and malfeasance. If [the independent counsel] can get away with this kind of disregard for procedures designed to protect the American taxpayer, its no wonder he's kept his office in business for more than six years in his relentless, partisan political pursuit."

On December 16, Brosnahan moved to compel production of Weinberger's early diaries to show the habitual nature of his note-taking. Bennett protested that our request constituted harassment. Two days later, Bennett moved in court to cross-examine our lawyers and FBI agents, using an affidavit in which the husband of one of Weinberger's secretaries who claimed that his wife's statements had been misrepresented by an associate counsel in a presentation to the court. That evening, Bennett told reporters that the husband's allegations were true and that we had engaged in highly improper conduct. We denied this in a court motion to strike the affidavit as scurrilous.

On December 17, outgoing attorney general William Barr said in an interview that he believed some of our defendants should not have been prosecuted. "I think people in the Iran-Contra matter have been treated very unfairly, many of them," he said. He declined to say whether he recommended pardons, but he expressed contempt for the prosecutions. "People in this Iran-Contra matter have been prosecuted for the kind of crimes that would not have been criminal or prosecutable by the Department of Justice, applying standards that we have applied for decades to every citizen." Barr took particular exception to the case against Clair George, saying that George's character, past record, and the seriousness of the offense seemed not to have been "given much weight in that case."

At a court hearing the next day, Brosnahan criticized the attorney general for having made such statements, especially at this time. Brosnahan asked that Judge Hogan try to prevent Barr's statements from prejudicing our case and that he inquire of potential jurors whether they were aware of Barr's remarks. "I would have thought," said Brosnahan, "that the attorney general of the United States . . . would be concerned about the effect he might have as the nation's top law-enforcement officer . . . on a jury [to be] selected two and a half weeks after he gave an extensive interview."

In the course of the hearing, Judge Hogan ruled that the polygraph test Bennett had arranged for Weinberger was inadmissible. The judge also denied the defense request for the records of the mock trial, an exercise the judge called "classical pretrial preparation, although of a rather extravagant nature." Judge Hogan said he was concerned about the possible publication of the mock trial's results. He said that he would add questions for the examination of prospective jurors to deal with any prejudice arising from the mock trial and possibly from Attorney General Barr's remarks. The judge expressed disappointment that both sides were engaging in ad hominem attacks. The evenhandedness of this criticism reminded me of an old World War I joke: An army cook admits having added horse meat to his rabbit stew; when asked for his recipe, he says, "fifty-fifty—one horse, one rabbit."

At the hearing, Bennett notified the court that he might try to call George Bush and Ronald Reagan as defense witnesses, particularly if Judge Hogan permitted the prosecutors to present evidence that Weinberger's lies had been in furtherance of a cover-up to conceal Reagan's involvement in the Iran-Contra affair. Bennett said that he might also need to call George Shultz and Edwin Meese.

A week later, at the next status hearing, Brosnahan declared our intent to prove that Weinberger had made seven additional false statements. The statute of limitations barred us from charging these statements as crimes, but proof of the statements would be admissible as evidence to prove that Weinberger's false statements concealing his notes had been part of a common plan and scheme. The additional statements had been made in appearances before the Senate and House intelligence committees on December 17 and 18, 1986: Weinberger had repeatedly denied that he had been present at any discussion about Israeli transfers of arms to Iran, or that the Israeli stockpile was to be replenished by the United States. Each false statement was contradicted by a note Weinberger had written.

With Christmas approaching, writer Fred Barnes summarized the pardon prospects in *The New Republic*. He quoted an unnamed senior official as having said, "The generous view . . . is that Walsh was only seeking to strengthen his position against Weinberger at trial. . . . The 'ungenerous' view is that Walsh sought to hurt Bush's chances of reelection. Bush takes the ungenerous view."

According to Barnes, Bush was "being prodded from four directions to issue the pardon." The first source of pressure was Bob Dole, who had "raised the issue on every TV interview show on which he [had] appeared since the election." The second source was Robert Bennett. "The day after the election, [Dan] Quayle ... called the case against Weinberger 'a travesty.' Within two hours, Bennett was on the phone to Quayle's office. He also talked to White House aides, various Reaganites, and members of Congress." The third source of pressure came from administration officials. William Kristol, the vice president's chief of staff, was said to be "an active proponent of a pardon." The attorney general was described as "sympathetic." The fourth source was William Clark, who had "written Reagan urging him to press Bush to pardon Weinberger" and was "also organizing other Reaganites."

Barnes then described Bush's own incentives for granting a pardon. "Beyond sparing Weinberger, who's a friend, Bush has a personal interest in a pardon. It would avert a highly public trial at which Weinberger and ... Shultz might give testimony contradicting Bush." Barnes reported that the president didn't "want to be accused of a blatant cover-up. So an arrangement is being discussed. Bush would pardon Weinberger and others. ... In return, Dole would withdraw his demand for an investigation of Walsh's operation. And to counter accusations of a cover-up, Bush would waive his right to keep his deposition or other information secret and would urge others to do the same. Unfavorable evidence might become public, but it would draw less attention than at a trial."

On November 4, 1986, George Bush had begun keeping a diary, which consisted of observations dictated to his secretary at the end of each day. These observations had been typed and stored in Bush's Houston office. Bush had continued the diary through his 1988 campaign but had kept its existence secret from most of his staff. In September 1992, Bush's secretary had raised with Bush the need to produce the notes after receiving a memorandum from Boyden Gray's office regarding material we had requested. Bush had told her to turn them over to Boyden Gray for his decision. Boyden Gray had held them until after the election.

We were first told about the diary on December 11, 1992, by Paul Beach, one of Boyden Gray's assistants. Beach turned over some of the notes that day, and Gillen set about reviewing them. On December 23, he told me that the diary notes would have been relevant—though not necessarily dramatic—in 1987. In one note, Bush had written of his amazement that George Shultz had given the select committees and us copies of two hundred pages of notes; Bush had written that he himself would not have done so.

The production of Bush's notes had clearly been delayed until after I announced the end of my investigation and after the election. Had their delay also been related to a decision on pardons?

CHAPTER TWENTY-SIX

The Last Card in
the Cover-up

Christmas Eve was always a long day for me, beginning with Crowe &
Dunlevy's traditional holiday breakfast, which was held at seven-thirty
so that everyone would be back on the job as usual when the firm
opened for business. The breakfast had been established by V.I.P. "Vip"
Crowe, a hard-driving manager whose success as a prosecutor and a trial
lawyer stretched back to the days when Bonnie and Clyde and other
free-spirited bank robbers sometimes took refuge in Oklahoma. The
tradition had continued long after Vip was gone. Members of the firm
took pride in the unusual time of its holiday celebration. Lawyers from
the firm's offices in Norman and Tulsa duly left home in the dark of
night to be on time for the breakfast, which was held at the Oklahoma
City Golf and Country Club. Living only a few hundred yards from the
country club, I would have been ashamed to miss the occasion.

Accordingly, the morning of December 24, 1992, found me sitting
next to the guest speaker, Oklahoma's Chief Justice Marian Opala. As
we finished our coffee, we drifted into a discussion of Caspar
Weinberger. I said that I was concerned about the possibility of a pardon, but I was betting against it. Chief Justice Opala said he thought
that George Bush would pardon Weinberger before leaving office.

When confronted with scandals in their cabinets, Presidents Ulysses
S. Grant, Warren G. Harding, and Calvin Coolidge had eschewed pardons. Richard Nixon had not been under indictment when Gerald
Ford pardoned him to expedite his departure from the White House.
Even Ronald Reagan, whose popularity might have enabled him to get
away with pardoning those who had acted illegally in support of his
policies, had left office without issuing any pardons to Iran-Contra figures. I did not think that George Bush, who seemed to pride himself on

490

his character, would be the first president to use his pardon powers in a cover-up.

Nevertheless, as Christmas approached, news stories had quoted unnamed White House sources as saying that the president was seriously considering pardons for Weinberger and other Iran-Contra figures. Bush was said to have received briefing papers as well as summaries of the relevant legal and historical precedents. Reportedly, he was particularly keen to pardon Weinberger but feared that doing so would trigger a widespread negative reaction. Although White House counsel Boyden Gray and others advocated such a pardon, some advisors were said to have warned that it might taint Bush's place in history. To blunt the impression that the pardon stemmed from his desire to avoid the embarrassing disclosures about himself that might emerge in a trial of Weinberger, aides recommended that Bush also pardon Elliott Abrams, Duane Clarridge, Alan Fiers, Clair George, and perhaps Robert McFarlane.

According to the *Washington Post*, White House officials had informally queried reporters about how the news media would react if Weinberger was pardoned. At the same time, Senate Minority Leader Bob Dole had been lobbying high-ranking Democrats on Capitol Hill, asking them to refrain from protesting if the president issued the pardons. According to conservative columnists Rowland Evans and Robert Novak, some Democrats had "promised they would not make a fuss."

Evans and Novak dismissed as an "outrageous canard" the notion that Bush's motive for pardoning Weinberger would be to protect himself. "Bush will never again run for office. Politically, he is untouchable. . . . It is taken as an article of faith in the Bush inner circle that [the timing of the superseding indictment] broke the president's momentum in trying to catch Bill Clinton. . . . If injustice to Cap Weinberger did not melt Bush's heart, the rabbit punch to his political career stirred his fighting juices."

Having witnessed at close hand the defeats of presidential candidates Thomas Dewey and Richard Nixon, I understood the immeasurable strain of running for the presidency and the crushing aftermath of losing. The demands and dimensions of a presidential election dwarfed all other candidacies. Nonetheless, I did not think Bush would demean himself by granting a lame-duck pardon to retaliate against an independent counsel, even if he believed I had contributed to his defeat. He had been a world leader of some distinction. I felt certain that he would be more interested in assuring his place in history than in receiving the applause of a handful of defeated party leaders, many of whom would be largely forgotten once he left office.

After the Crowe & Dunlevy breakfast, I returned home for a conference call with James Brosnahan, Craig Gillen, John Barrett, and Mary Belcher to discuss what I would say if Bush did pardon Weinberger. Belcher had drafted a powerful statement for me, and I had changed it slightly. We discussed the contents of the statement, but did not waste much time debating the likelihood of a pardon. We decided that if it came to pass, I would react strongly. As we talked, a journalist passed word to Belcher that reporters had been alerted that the White House would issue a press release on Iran-Contra at noon. This could mean only one thing. My muscles tightened and my heartbeat jumped, but I felt cold and unflustered, the way I always felt when something threatening but not wholly surprising occurred in a trial.

With noon scarcely more than half an hour away, there was no time for comment. I was in the wrong place. This was a Washington story. The reporters who had covered us for six years were all in Washington. Belcher and I had to move quickly. We decided that Belcher would release my statement in Washington to coincide with a press conference by me in Oklahoma City. To ensure that my comments would move through the wire services simultaneously with the White House story, my press conference had to take place as soon as possible after the White House issued its release.

My administrative assistant, Brenda Carman, began searching for a site for the conference because my Oklahoma independent counsel's office was too small to accommodate a large group of reporters, photographers, and broadcasting personnel with all their equipment. The local FBI office might have been a good bet, but it had closed for Christmas Eve. Finally, Crowe & Dunlevy came to the rescue and offered me the firm's largest conference room. We scheduled the press conference for one o'clock, Oklahoma time.

Having changed into casual clothes after returning home, I now had to change back into a suit. As I was dressing, the phone rang. Mary answered it, then called out that the White House was trying to reach me. With a necktie in one hand, I picked up the phone with the other. It was Boyden Gray. Half-laughing, he said he had just learned that no one had told me the president was going to pardon Weinberger and the "nonprofit defendants."

I asked which defendants he meant. He could not recall all their names offhand, so I listed those who seemed most likely, and he confirmed them. Those to be pardoned included Caspar Weinberger and Duane Clarridge, who had not yet been tried, as well as Elliott Abrams, Alan Fiers, Clair George, and Robert McFarlane, all of whom had been convicted of withholding information from Congress. I thanked Gray for letting me know, told him I had a lot to do, and hung up.

I told Mary what Gray had said. We knew each other too well to have to talk. If I had had time to outline to her what I planned to say, as I often did before a speech or argument, I would have done so, but I did not yet have any words ready. I simply knew that I was going to go all out and that the words would come when I needed them.

I drove to my independent counsel's office for a few minutes to think. I read aloud the statement prepared by Belcher and had Carman enter my changes in her computer and print a clean copy, which would be easier for me to read. I then talked out some of the points I would make in response to questions. This relaxed my voice and collected my responses at the tip of my tongue so that I could say them emphatically and without hesitation. I usually did not speak from notes but I often talked out some of the things I planned to say. The words always seemed to flow better if I had said them aloud beforehand.

At Crowe & Dunlevy, the conference room was packed with representatives of all the major television networks and the wire services, as well as Oklahoma City reporters for all the major news sources. I stood at the end of the conference table, with a painting of wild horses as a backdrop, and read my statement. I then took questions for about half an hour. According to the *Daily Oklahoman*, I was "calm in voice but angry with [my] choice of words" and "in no holiday mood."

CNN covered part of the conference live, after broadcasting Bill Clinton's reaction to the pardons from Little Rock. "I am concerned about any action," the president-elect had said, "which sends a signal that if you work for the government, you are above the law, or that not telling the truth to Congress under oath is somehow less serious than not telling the truth to some other body under oath."

My first point was that the pardon of Weinberger undermined the principle that no one is above the law. "It demonstrates that powerful people with powerful allies can commit serious crimes in high office—deliberately abusing the public trust—without consequence.... Although pardons are the president's prerogative, it is every American's right that the criminal justice system be administered fairly, regardless of a person's rank and connection. . . . Weinberger's early and deliberate decision to conceal and withhold extensive contemporaneous notes of the Iran-Contra matter radically altered the official investigations and possibly forestalled timely impeachment proceedings against President Reagan and other officials." These notes evidenced "a conspiracy among the highest-ranking Reagan administration officials to lie to Congress and the American public. Because the notes were withheld from investigators for years, many of the leads were impossible to follow, key witnesses had purportedly forgotten what was said and done, and statutes of limitation had expired. . . . Weinberger's concealment of notes was a part of a disturbing pattern of deception and obstruction that permeated the highest levels of the Reagan and Bush administrations."

I then disclosed that President Bush had concealed his own "highly relevant contemporaneous notes," which had been "revealed to us only two weeks ago, in spite of repeated requests for them." I announced that "the production of these notes is still ongoing and will lead to appropriate action. In the light of President Bush's own misconduct, we are gravely concerned by his decision to pardon others who lied to Congress and obstructed official investigations."

After reading my statement, I addressed the contents of the three-page executive order in which the president had explained his granting of the pardons. Bush had described Weinberger as "a true patriot" who had "rendered long and extraordinary service." Weinberger, according to the president, had given up "a lucrative career in private life" and had earned a Bronze Star for bravery during World War II. "I am pardoning him not just out of compassion or to spare a 75-year-old patriot the torment of a lengthy and costly legal proceeding, but to make it possible for him to receive the honor he deserved. . . . Some may argue that this will prevent full disclosure of some new key facts to the American people. That is not true. The matter has been investigated exhaustively."

Describing my investigation as "politically inspired," Bush had written, "The prosecution of the individuals I am pardoning represents what I believe is a profoundly troubling development in the political and legal climate of our country. The proper target is the president, not his subordinates. The proper forum is the voting booth, not the courtroom. In recent years, the use of criminal processes in policy disputes has become all too common. It is my hope that the action I am taking today will begin to restore these disputes to the battleground where they properly belong."

Bush had attempted to analogize his action to grants of amnesty, such as those bestowed on Confederate officers and soldiers after the Civil War. "Now the Cold War is over. When earlier wars have ended, presidents have historically used their power to pardon, to put bitterness behind us and look to the future."

I told the reporters that amnesty for brave soldiers should not be equated with pardons for criminals who were the president's colleagues. Bush had explained the rationale for selecting those to be pardoned. "First, the common denominator of their motivation—whether their actions were right or wrong—was patriotism. Second, they did not profit or seek to profit from their conduct. Third, each has a record of long and distinguished service to his country."

As for his own culpability, Bush had claimed, "While no impartial person has seriously suggested that my own role in this matter is legally questionable, I have . . . requested that the independent counsel provide me with a copy of my sworn testimony to his office, which I am prepared to release immediately."

In response, I told the reporters gathered at my press conference that "a lie to Congress is not a matter of political controversy. It is a crime. When those implicated appeared before congressional committees investigating the matter, they had three options. They could tell the truth, they could refuse to answer, or they could lie. The third option is criminal, not political. The Iran-Contra cover-up, which has continued for more than six years, has now been completed with the pardon of Caspar Weinberger."

The reporters' questions focused on the significance of the president's action to my investigation and to the country: What had we accomplished? The questions gave me an opening to demonstrate the hypocrisy of Bush's professed concern for presidential subordinates who had been prosecuted for carrying out a presidential policy. Why had he acted only to prevent the trial of his close friend Weinberger? Why had he waited until after his reelection bid failed? Where was his concern when Clair George was being dragged through two trials?

Invited to speculate on the president's motives, I declined to choose among an array of possibilities. Instead, I decried the waste of prolonging our investigation and litigation if Bush had truly felt the pardons to be warranted.

I strongly criticized the unprecedented use of the pardon power to block a public trial. I distinguished the Nixon pardon as an act of statesmanship to get him out of the White House. Also, he had not been indicted and was not on the eve of trial. But when asked if I recommended curtailment of the president's power to pardon, I said that I did not. I explained that pardons, as acts of mercy, had been necessary when many felonies were punishable by death. It was an ancient power, I said, a constitutional power. The circumstances of every pardon cannot be foreseen. "It's a matter for the conscience of the president and the judgment of the president as reviewed by the public after that judgment is exercised."

Near the end, one reporter asked, "Is the message here if you work for the government, you're above the law?" I answered, "That depends on the president you work for."

When the pardons were released, the president was at Camp David, unavailable to reporters. Syndicated columnist Rick Horowitz later reflected, "On the TV, there was footage of Gerald Ford pardoning Richard Nixon for Watergate. There'll be no footage of George Bush pardoning Caspar Weinberger and the rest for Iran-Contra—just a written statement as the president left town, words sent aloft as the news hole shut down for Christmas weekend. Almost as if it happened on its own. Almost as if George Bush was—how to say this—out of the loop on the pardon too."

Back at the White House on Christmas Eve, press secretary Marlin Fitzwater refused to take questions. It was left to Weinberger to try to justify the pardons. He claimed innocence and described my investigation as "dismal" and "a mockery of law enforcement and of justice."

I replied through Mary Belcher, saying that Weinberger was "a biased observer who had intensified his efforts to obtain a pardon as the trial date approached, which suggested that he did not regard the charges as frivolous."

Most of the Democratic leaders on Capitol Hill condemned the pardons. "The president unfortunately has left the impression," said Senate Majority Leader George Mitchell, "that the alleged felonies of perjury and the making of false statements to Congress are not to be taken seriously." According to Mitchell, the pardons showed "contempt for democratic processes and the rule of law. Our system of government cannot function effectively if the legislative branch has no assurance of the truthfulness of the officials of the executive branch [who] come before it."

House Majority Leader Richard Gephardt said, "The pardon maintains the appearance of an Iran-Contra cover-up, suggests presidential approval of violations of law, and condones ill-founded foreign policy decisions that never would have been made in the light of day."

Senator Carl Levin, who headed the committee that oversaw my activities, said that Bush's action "undermines the American system of justice."

To no one's surprise, Bob Dole praised the pardons as "a Christmas Eve act of courage and compassion" and renewed his attack on my office: "Lawrence Walsh and his desperate henchmen would have stopped at nothing to validate their reckless thirty-five-million-dollar inquisition, even if it meant twisting justice to fit their partisan schemes."

Bush's predecessors in the White House disagreed about the step he had taken to end the Iran-Contra prosecutions. A statement issued through a spokesman declared that Reagan "was pleased to hear the news of the pardons." Jimmy Carter, however, said, "I thought it was a travesty of justice and an insult to the integrity of the White House." Calling Bush's actions "unprecedented," Carter said he was troubled by Bush's personal stake in shutting down Weinberger's trial: "I consider [it] to be the concealment of evidence."

Returning home from the press conference in mid-afternoon, I felt let down: It had been a good fight but a losing one. Although Mary and I talked briefly, she was considerate and refrained from asking a lot of questions. The day was far from over: I had agreed to appear that evening on the Public Broadcasting System's *MacNeil-Lehrer News Hour* and then on ABC's *Nightline*. Mary Belcher and I spoke by phone and agreed that we were satisfied with our responses. She said that the reporters at the courthouse in Washington had reached for the statement as she delivered it. She warned me that a CNN team was in Oklahoma City on another story and would be looking for me.

I took a shower, changed clothes, and at dusk set off in my car. The drive to the local PBS studio was cold and lonely, taking me past homes ablaze with Christmas lights and then down deserted two-lane roads through farmlands to the outskirts of the city, where the broadcasting buildings with their slender aerial masts stood desolate watch. I thought of them transmitting the dismal farewell of an administration that had briefly sparkled in mobilizing the world for Desert Storm but had chosen a political cover-up as its last significant presidential act.

As I drove, the usually magnificent Oklahoma sky was a foreboding deep blue. It seemed to close in on me. There was just enough light to see the outlines of leafless trees against the deserted fields. The parking lot was bleak and empty.

When I entered the PBS building, the reception room was momentarily unattended. While I stood there waiting, CNN special correspondent Steve Emerson and his cameraman came in. Emerson asked to interview me, and I agreed but said he would have to wait until I was finished with *MacNeil-Lehrer* and *Nightline*. Although he was helpful and considerate, having one more person to deal with added to the strain and fatigue I already felt.

Presently, I was escorted into the barnlike studio. A friendly technician wired me for sound and had me sit in a chair before a camera. There was no monitor for me to watch, so—although Robert MacNeil and the audience would be able to see me—I would be talking to the proverbial blank wall. Shortly before five o'clock, MacNeil's voice came through my earpiece. I had always admired him and regularly watched his program. In a gentle and friendly way, he complimented me on my news conference. I felt a lift as he told me that he understood I was from Nova Scotia, and that he had grown up in Halifax. I suggested that it would be a cold night for a swim in the Northwest Arm of Halifax Harbor.

I then waited while, in accordance with the program's normal format, MacNeil and Lehrer covered the news of the day. The pardon was the first story, and there were generous extracts from Weinberger's news conference—not defending his innocence or explaining why he had withheld his notes, but attacking me for having used the power and resources of my office to prosecute him. In response to reporters' questions, he claimed that his trial would not have harmed Bush's reputation because "none of the evidence that [the prosecution] had had anything to do with it. He attended some meetings, as I did, and I don't think anything that was there would have hurt him in any way."

Asked to put in "the clearest words possible what you think the motive of Mr. Walsh was," he answered, "Well, I really don't know. You'll have to ask him. . . . He seemed determined to get somebody. . . . He seemed to feel that he was going to be . . . judged on the number of convictions he got that withstood appellate review. . . . I cooperated fully with him and gave him all these notes."

Without realizing it, Weinberger had given me a new lift. My fatigue vanished. Criminal lawyers have an adage: If the law is against you, talk about the facts; if the facts are against you, talk about the law; if the law and the facts are against you, attack the prosecutor. Weinberger's ridiculous claim that he had "given" us his notes and his jibes revealed him once more as the unabashed deadpan liar that he was. Now all that was left for me to do was to refrain from reacting with anger: The prosecutor who has been assailed has it made if he can impress the jury—or the television audience—with his fairness while demonstrating the guilt of the defendant.

MacNeil began our interview by inviting me to respond to Weinberger's accusations. Weinberger was no longer my principal opponent; President Bush had taken his place, and I did not want to be long diverted. I simply said, "Well, all I can say is that it shows that Mr. Weinberger lies as well in . . . media interviews as he does when he testified before Congress." I explained that for two months we had delayed the indictment to give him every opportunity to show why his deliberate lies to Congress and to our office should not be prosecuted, and that we had not wanted to hurt a person with so distinguished a career. His notes, however, showed him to have been not a bystander but an actor in the Iranian arms sales. Although he had opposed the sales, he had recorded every step of the process in his notes, and he had been sitting only four feet away from his desk—its drawers full of those notes—when he told the counsel to the House and Senate select committees on Iran-Contra that he did not have any notes. He had lied because he knew that his notes would show that President Reagan had deliberately violated the laws that prohibited his selling arms to Iran, had ignored his own stated policy against dealing with terrorists, and, most important, had secretly defied Congress by failing to give it legally required notice of these transactions.

MacNeil then gave me the opportunity to explain the statement we had released in Washington. He first focused on my charge that Weinberger's concealment of his notes had "forestalled a timely impeachment of President Reagan."

"Those could be the grounds," I said. "The president [Reagan] had a head-on confrontation with Congress. His own counsel was concerned . . . . , and the most valuable part of the notes show the November 1986 cover-up by high-ranking Reagan appointees to prevent Congress [from] learning that the president had deliberately defied the Arms Export Control Act. . . . It was a deliberate defiance of Congress, and Congress's remedy . . . is to consider impeachment. It's unlikely that they would have impeached him, but that was for them to decide. It wasn't to be hidden from them by Secretary Weinberger or anyone else, by lying to them."

I then explained that Weinberger's claim that the notes had been publicly available in the Library of Congress was false. They had been intentionally concealed among unclassified material about his family. His failure to produce them in a timely manner had been deliberate and had radically altered our investigation by delaying it for five years, at which point claims of faulty memory could not be prosecuted because they had become plausible.

MacNeil next turned to Bush's statement that "no impartial person has seriously suggested that my own role . . . is legally questionable." He asked whether I was suggesting that it was.

"I am suggesting that he [Bush] did—he withheld notes from us," I said. "There's no question that until December 11, 1992, President Bush withheld notes that should have been available to Congress in the spring of 1987 and to my office at the same time. . . . [T]hey're highly relevant. . . . We still don't have all his notes."

MacNeil continued to press me about the phrase "in the light of President Bush's own misconduct," which had appeared in my statement.

I explained that Bush was pardoning someone who had committed some of the same illegal acts that he himself had committed. "It's the same type of misconduct that President Bush is trying to gloss over. His suggestion that lying to Congress is a political crime is rubbish. It's a phony statement. . . . The official can either tell the truth, or he can claim executive privilege . . . , but he is not privileged to lie to Congress to cover up President Reagan or to cover up President Bush or to cover up himself or his friends."

"You say the production of Mr. Bush's notes 'will lead to appropriate action,'" said MacNeil. "What are the alternatives for action open to you?"

I said that we would follow "the natural stream of activity that flows from the discovery of illegally withheld documents."

MacNeil asked whether it was "remotely conceivable there could be a prosecution of President Bush."

"I could not comment on that," I answered. "He's a subject now of our investigation."

As for Bush's belated claim that "the proper target is the president, not his subordinates," I commented that "the president of the United States is entitled to an area of tolerance. . . . The problems that he has are greater in scale, immensely greater, than any other government official. . . . A prosecutor should be very slow before he picks at a president, but that does not protect the secretary of defense . . . or anyone else who carries out a policy by illegal means or tries to cover up a policy by illegal means."

"In short," MacNeil asked, as he prepared to conclude our interview, "do you think this pardon is part of a continued cover-up of Mr. Bush himself?"

"I think it's the last card in the cover-up. He's played the final card."

The next segment of the program consisted of analyses by Tom Blanton, the National Security Archives' executive director, who had written extensively on Iran-Contra, and Richard Perle, who had been an assistant secretary of defense under Weinberger. Perle characterized my prosecutions of Abrams and Weinberger as "malicious." Blanton then corrected Perle's misstatements.

When MacNeil asked about the pardon, Blanton said, "I think it's a sad day for government accountability. I think that most of the people of America will . . . say, 'Aha! This is the way Washington insiders work: You keep your mouth shut, you hide your notes, you go along with the president, and the president will take care of you.'"

Perle expressed concern that officials "simply won't keep any notes. . . . That is what happened in the McCarthy period. Nobody kept any records. This business of criminalizing policy judgments, particularly complicated policy judgments, can only have the effect of paralysis and eventually the destruction of any significant paper trail of the decision-making process."

After the interview was over, Steve Emerson volunteered to drive me to the ABC studio for my interview with Ted Koppel, which was not scheduled to begin until more than an hour later. I had considered returning home but decided against it because I did not want to be interrupted by telephone calls or conversations. I really just wanted a place to rest, relax, and think. I accepted Emerson's offer but warned him that I needed a chance to contemplate for a little while. We didn't talk much on the trip. I was somewhat wrung out by the interview; Emerson and his cameraman were occupied with trying to find their way through unfamiliar territory guided by street signs that were barely visible in the darkness.

The ABC studio was somewhat more active than the PBS studio had been. The local news programs were just finishing, and a dozen people were moving about. Someone offered me some pizza, but I settled for a Coke. As time passed and I felt more relaxed, I suggested that we begin the CNN interview, so long as no one else would hear it until after my interview on ABC. Answering Emerson's questions helped me warm up for *Nightline*, although we had not finished before I was summoned into the broadcast studio.

Once again, technicians posed me in a chair looking at a camera in a cable-cluttered room, then adjusted the lights and sound. The camera-man and I chatted about Iran-Contra as we waited for the interview to begin. When Ted Koppel spoke to me from his Washington studio, I found him extraordinarily reassuring. He led me through what apparently was an effective interview (perhaps my best, judging from the flood of letters we later received). Koppel's treatment of the subject matter was comprehensive but pointed and appropriately accentuated. In its evenhandedness, it was devastating to President Bush.

As Koppel began, he said it all in two dozen words: "But if Cap Weinberger and the five others are off the hook tonight, it appears that George Bush has moved right to the center of the bull's-eye." Koppel reported that according to an informed source, "the president's initial instinct ... was not to issue a pardon. His national security advisor, Brent Scowcroft, agreed, but Vice President Quayle, Senate Minority Leader Bob Dole, and White House counsel Boyden Gray all lobbied the president to issue the pardons."

Koppel reminded his listeners that during the 1988 Iowa primary, Bush had been asked to turn over his notes and had claimed to have produced everything he had been asked for. Koppel quoted my statement that the notes had been held back for five years—until after Bush's election defeat.

Koppel's first questions dealt with Caspar Weinberger's claim that he had turned over his notes and with my response that his consistent tactic had been to lie; that the notes had been turned over too late to be useful.

Asked for a simple statement of my accusation against Weinberger, I said that he had lied to Congress, lied to their counsel, lied to my office. He had been looking at his desk full of notes when he denied having any. He had later concealed his notes by separating them from his defense department records, squirreling them away in the unclassified section of the Library of Congress, where nobody could see them without his permission. "So it is a deliberate scheme ... in order to protect himself, in order to protect President Reagan, and in order to protect others in the cabinet."

I agreed that I was charging President Bush with similar conduct but explained that I did not yet fully understand the circumstances of Bush's failure to turn over his notes. I mentioned that months of notes were missing from the material Bush had finally turned over to us.

Asked to explain why the White House would withhold the notes, I said, "Well, my first cynical thought was 'It's after election.'" I added that Bush "knows there's going to be no forthcoming Weinberger trial which could add to the exposure of the cover-up and that perhaps this is the time in which it could be done with minimum damage to him."

Koppel asked whether I thought Bush had just held the notes back until the statute of limitations had run.

I acknowledged that if that was his intention, he had succeeded with regard to the underlying substantive crime, but I pointed out that a new false statement would in itself be prosecutable. "Action will certainly be taken to learn the facts," I said. "Then we'll see where the action leads."

Asked whether I thought President Bush and President Reagan had engaged in a cover-up, I said that President Reagan thought he had done the proper thing, but his advisors had been afraid for him, which had been the reason for the cover-up. I declined further comment about Bush except to say that we would issue a grand jury subpoena if he did not promptly produce the notes that were still missing.

I said that the pardons had had the effect of shutting down our prosecutions, which made them comparable to President Richard Nixon's firing of Archibald Cox in the Saturday Night Massacre. As for history's judgment, I said, "I think it will prove to be an imprudent move. . . . He has shown an arrogant disdain for the rule of law. There was no excuse for pardoning these persons. . . . They were prosecuted for covering up a crime, for lying to Congress, to keep Congress from finding out what happened. . . . They were deliberate lies, and I think that President Bush's sugarcoating is going to become increasingly transparent, and the American public is, in the end, a very perceptive body of people."

After the *Nightline* interview, I answered more questions for Emerson. He and his cameraman then drove me back to my car, and I went home.

By now, Christmas Eve was waning. All I really wanted was something to eat and a good night's sleep, but the telephone calls kept coming in. Dan Webb, for example, called to say, "You hurt him."

I had wanted to hurt Bush in the sense that I wanted to drive home to him and to the audience the infamy of his action—the blatant political favoritism of sparing Weinberger (and himself) after having allowed heroic career officer Clair George to endure two trials.

Christmas was nearly as busy as Christmas Eve had been. Carl Stern of NBC arranged to have a local reporter interview me at home, and other Washington reporters interviewed me by phone. Then, as we sat down to our turkey, who should turn up but Steve Emerson and his cameraman. We shared our meal with them, but Emerson was primarily interested in resuming our interview, so we adjourned to my library. Reporters continued to telephone and visit for the next few days.

As a result of my press conference and interviews, the pardon story dominated the Christmas news broadcasts on television and radio, with our side receiving fair and usually favorable treatment. CNN and other networks carried it hour after hour through the weekend, and Steve Emerson was repeatedly asked to comment on the air. Anyone who tuned in to the news even momentarily during that period was exposed to the story of the pardons and my condemnation of the president's action.

The newspapers provided balanced first-page coverage, with large photographs of a grinning Weinberger as well as extensive reports of my statements. The New York Times reported that "for the first time, the prosecutor charged that Mr. Weinberger's notes about the secret decision to sell arms to Iran ... included 'evidence of a conspiracy among the highest-ranking Reagan administration officials to lie to Congress and the American public.'"

The Los Angeles Times said that "in an angry statement, ... Walsh accused Bush of 'misconduct' and declared that the pardon was part of the cover-up that 'had continued for more than six years.' And in a potentially explosive revelation, he said it was recently discovered that Bush himself had kept personal notes on aspects of the arms-for-hostages affair."

Politicians routinely attempt to limit the effectiveness of news coverage of shameful decisions by announcing them at times when the public is paying less attention than usual, and polls showed that most Americans, on Christmas Eve, had not followed the news reports of the pardons. A fourth of those surveyed, however, had followed the story carefully enough to evaluate it: They opposed the pardons by a ratio of four to one.

Robert Bennett later claimed to have won a public relations victory, saying that the coverage of the pardon had lasted only two days. Not only did he misstate the extent of the coverage, but the nature of the coverage was primarily negative for Bush. In the days following the announcement of the pardons, I received hundreds of thoughtful letters, nearly all of them favorable. Even old adversaries wrote warm letters of encouragement, and for weeks afterward, strangers came up to me in airports to offer their thanks and commendations.

Bush's attempt to justify the pardons failed utterly. According to a CNN-USA Today-Gallup poll, half of those who had followed the news coverage thought that Bush's real motive in granting the pardons had been "to protect himself from legal difficulties or embarrassment resulting from his own role in Iran-Contra."

In the process of weighing Bush's unconvincing rationalizations, journalists also came to ask whether the president had granted the pardons to protect himself. He might have won more support if he had limited his rationale to sympathy for Weinberger, but by asserting that no real crimes had occurred, he had shifted the focus from Weinberger to himself.

Having inserted himself as the ultimate actor in the cover-up, Bush now became the target for the appraisal of the nation's editorial writers. According to the *New York Times*, for example, "If Mr. Bush had rested his pardon of Mr. Weinberger on the former defense secretary's health alone, he might deserve credit for compassion. But he went on to lecture Lawrence Walsh, the independent prosecutor, against what he called 'the criminalization of policy differences.' That's a bogus complaint. Mr. Weinberger was charged with lying to Congress *because* of policy differences; lying to Congress for any reason is criminal conduct. When Congress calls the highest executive officials to testify, as it did in probing Iran-Contra, it is entitled to truthful testimony under pain of prosecution for telling falsehoods."

The *Washington Post* opined that "the 'unpardonable aspect' of what happened yesterday was that Mr. Bush couldn't bring himself to say at the same time that what they did or were accused of doing was wrong, and pardons matter less than the self-serving, see-no-evil gloss put on them."

Other thoughtful observers expounded on the crassness of the president's clumsy effort to justify the pardons. In an op-ed piece for the *Los Angeles Times*, CNN political analyst William Schneider concluded that Bush had broken every rule. "All the examples Bush cited had to do with wars . . . , and pardons were granted to people on the other side—an act of generosity, in the spirit of Abraham Lincoln's second inaugural address . . . . It's hard to see how pardoning your former enemy justifies pardoning your former colleagues—and possible co-conspirators. . . . Not only did he pardon his political allies, he pardoned them for illegal activities in which he himself may have been implicated."

"Exit smelling," wrote Molly Ivins in a scathing article for the *Houston Post.* "By what insane logic is misguided 'patriotism' an excuse for perverting the entire premise of a government of the people, by the people and for the people?"

With heavy sarcasm, a column by Henry Gay in the *Seattle Post Intelligencer* concluded, "All those involved in Iran-Contra are patriots of the highest order. They are experts in covert government, trained and dedicated liars and lawbreakers who persevere—despite the strictures of the United States Constitution—in the cause of Democracy. It is unfortunate President Bush did not pardon them all. Many were called but few were chosen to receive the blessing of their conscientious leader acting for their grateful fellow countrymen."

Aggressive journalists uncovered information about the extraordinary efforts Weinberger's supporters had made to pave the way for the pardons. They had managed to silence Colin Powell, House Speaker Tom Foley, and Congressman Lew Aspin, who chaired the House armed services committee. Bob Dole, Boyden Gray, and Dan Quayle had been instrumental in pressing the case for the pardons. Secretary of State James Baker, Attorney General William Barr, and National Security Advisor Brent Scowcroft had recommended that Bush promise to make public his own notes and the transcript of his deposition, in an attempt to deflect the hostile reaction they expected the pardons to generate.

Apparently none of the president's advisors had considered inviting me to provide a report on the pardon issue before the decision was made. Acting without the benefit of my viewpoint was a tactical mistake for Bush: The Justice Department did not know the facts; Bennett was an advocate for Weinberger, not Bush. For his own protection, regardless of his opinion of me, the president should have taken the trouble to find out about the powerful evidence of the intentional nature and material consequences of Weinberger's lies, instead of leaving me free to assail his ignorance and autocratic arrogance.

"It's hard to find an adjective strong enough," I told *Newsweek* reporter Bob Cohn, "to characterize a president who has such a contempt for honesty and such a lack of sensitivity to the picture of a president protecting a cabinet officer who lies to Congress. Using the pardon power to help a friend and other associates from the Reagan administration shows a disdainful disregard for the rule of law. It gives the impression that people in high office with strong political connections can get favored treatment. . . . It makes one wonder if the president understood the magnitude or the gravity or the horror of it."

Apparently, he did not. In the White House Rose Garden before leaving to spend New Year's Day with U.S. armed forces in Somalia, he was asked whether he was "sending a signal that big shots live by different rules." In response, Bush said, "No, it should not give any such appearance. Nobody is above the law, and I believe when people break the law that's a bad thing. I have read some stupid commentary to the contrary."

In granting the pardons on Christmas Eve to minimize the attention that would be paid to them, Bush was still the politician thinking of the present. He should have realized that history—and his place in it—could not be fooled by the tricky timing of a press release.

"He hopes to be remembered as the victor of Kuwait," wrote R. W. Apple, Jr., in the *New York Times*, "and as the man, even in his hour of defeat, who planned a humanitarian mission to Somalia, sought an end to the strife in Bosnia, and pressed for reductions in nuclear weapons. But will he, in fact, be remembered instead, or at least in part, as the president who, in effect, pardoned himself?"

Apple contrasted Bush's action with Gerald Ford's pardon of Richard Nixon. The difference, wrote Apple, was that Ford had "acted before his campaign for a full term . . . in the full knowledge that it could cost him the presidency," whereas Bush had "waited until after the election. . . . That deprived his action of the aura of selflessness that clung to Mr. Ford's pardon, all the more so since it was clear that Mr. Ford had no role in the Watergate scandal that drove Mr. Nixon from office. Caspar Weinberger and Robert McFarlane will soon be forgotten by all but the experts. . . . But George Bush will be remembered . . . and he will be judged and rejudged after years go by, not only for what he did, but also for the standards he demanded of those around him."

In a commentary for the *Los Angeles Times* on January 10, investigative reporter Carl Bernstein wrote, "The escalating criminality of the Bush-Reagan era . . . refused to go away, like some dark stain on the national conscience. In pardoning Caspar W. Weinberger and some old friends from CIA days, Bush ensured that the stain will not be removed. With the stroke of his pen and the disingenuousness of his words, Bush forced the issue of his own culpability. He has also made stunningly clear the pattern and purposes of serious criminality in his and Reagan's administrations. To hold office at any price."

Academic leaders took similar views of what Bush had lost by granting the pardons. Laurence Tribe, professor of constitutional law at the Harvard Law School, said that "the verdict of history will not be a kind one for the president." As Tribe put it, "the framers [of the Constitution] did not intend the power to pardon to enable a president to cover his own tracks." After saying that he was unaware of any precedent for Bush's action, Tribe observed, "This definitely represents a significant abuse of presidential power, but not the kind of abuse our system has provided any remedy for. It's just a disgrace. That's all."

Professor Gerald Gunther of Stanford University Law School explained the value of special prosecutors, then said, "As a president who obviously cares about his place in history, [Bush has] just smeared himself with it. He's gotten a blot on himself that will be hard to erase when the historians come to look at him."

Even academicians who supported the pardons said that the president had acted on the wrong grounds. Professor Steven L. Carter of Yale University, for example, believed the Independent Counsel Act to be unconstitutional, but he dismissed as "nonsense" Bush's claim that policy disputes had been criminalized. Professor Walter Dellinger of Duke University, who asserted that the president's power to pardon in advance of conviction was well established, cautioned that "pre-conviction pardons are always troublesome, because the public will never know the full story that might have been brought out at trial."

Although the pardon story continued to dominate the Sunday-morning news broadcasts into January, I declined invitations for further interviews, because I still had a possible prosecutorial role. Fortunately, articulate supporters were available: Senators George Mitchell and Carl Levin and Congressman Lee Hamilton defended my position from the attacks of Senators Warren Rudman and Bob Dole on *Face the Nation, Meet the Press*, and *This Week with David Brinkley*.

Hamilton, who had chaired the House intelligence committee during Iran-Contra, said, "I think what really disturbs me about the president's statement this week is really not so much the pardons as his—just unwillingness to acknowledge that crimes were committed, that misdeeds and misconduct took place, that Congress was lied to, that Congress was misled. There is no recognition of wrongdoing, it seems to me, in the president's statement, and I think that disturbed me far more than the fact of the pardon."

"I would agree with Lee on that point," said Rudman. "I do agree with that point." Nonetheless, Rudman said that I had unnecessarily extended my investigation.

Dole charged that I was guilty of contempt of court because I had discussed Bush's protection of his own vulnerability. According to Dole, I was "totally out of control and ought to resign immediately." Later, he charged that because of this conduct I should be disbarred. Although I had long since lost all respect for Dole and his statements, I had to wonder how any lawyer who had used his Senate office to interfere in a case pending in the courts could be so blind to his own contempt while accusing others of it.

Rudman said he did not agree with Dole's comments, and Levin pointed out that of fourteen indictments, we had won convictions on eleven, and two had been pending at the time of the pardons. Levin also reminded the audience that many powerful individuals had "helped to thwart the investigation of themselves, and now claim there has been a long delay." He went on to say that the attorney general could remove me if he could show that such action was warranted.

For me, a high point of these Sunday-morning broadcasts occurred on December 27, when ABC's Sam Donaldson cross-examined Weinberger on *This Week with David Brinkley.*

"So you made misstatements," asked Donaldson, "but you did not intend to deceive?"

"Well," replied Weinberger, "misstatements and some inaccuracies. I misplaced myself at one meeting, or something, or got a date wrong, but bear in mind that this was 1987, and I was testifying about events [that had taken place] in 1985, and now this is 1992."

"Well, it comes up, sir, because some people are suggesting that the president pardoned you in order to cover his own tracks in this story which they don't believe, the one he's told today."

"Well, I think that's totally wrong," said Weinberger, defending Bush. "He knew these discussions were going on. He said so. But again, whether or not it was arms for hostages was basically a matter of opinion."

"Then [Bush] knew [Reagan] was trading arms for hostages. . . ."

"Well, [Reagan] had mixed motives on it. . . . He said he wanted to get a better relationship with Iran. I didn't believe that."

"I understand, Mr. Secretary, but you just said that his [Reagan's] compassion for the hostages—you made that clear."

"Yes," replied Weinberger, "that was certainly part of his motive, without any question, but—"

"But he denied that, when it all came out," said Donaldson.

"No, he said it many times, Sam, that's one of the things that motivated him. . . ."

"Now," said Donaldson, "back to the special prosecutor's assertions. They claim they talked to you on October 10, 1990, and that you denied to them that you had any notes. They claim that you said to them, it was not your habit, as it was George Shultz's, not your habit to make notes throughout the—"

"That's exactly wrong," interrupted Weinberger, "because in September—"

"So you didn't say that to them?"

"In September," said Weinberger, "my attorney . . . telephoned them and told them that whatever papers they wanted . . . are all out at the Library of Congress, and you are all free to go out there and look at them. . . ."

"So then you did not."

"It's not the act of a man who's [in] a conspiracy."

"You did not, as they claim, deny to them on October 10 that you had notes?"

"I had a different understanding of what they meant by notes," said Weinberger. "They were talking, I thought—"

"Notes are notes," Donaldson persisted.

"Well, I thought they were talking about notes or minutes that you keep at a meeting, and I kept a few of those and had given them all to the Defense Department files. . . ."

"So you didn't realize they were talking about a personal diary?" asked Donaldson.

"That is correct, I did not. . . ."

"All right," said Donaldson. "The day before the pardon came down, the prosecutors claim that, in court, your lawyer said they might have to call President Bush during the trial, as a witness. . . . Now did President Bush know this, that they'd said that?"

"No. . . . In that meeting in court, the point came up as to what kind of evidence and who the prosecution was going to call, and in response to some of their refusals to be completely clear about what they were going to do, our counsel said that 'it might be necessary, if you're going to do that, for us to call President Reagan or President Bush. . . .' So there's no—ever—any decision and, of course, though, the president's decision—"

"Does President Bush know about that conversation?"

"Well," said Weinberger, "I don't know. I assume not, because there was never any decision to call him. But . . . the important thing is, Sam, that . . . the president would not have been called as our witness. But if it was necessary to refute some of the things that the prosecutor was doing, then we would have had to call him. But that was widely known."

During the week between Christmas and New Year's, I met with my staff to decide the course of our investigation. George Harris, James

Brosnahan's partner, reported that governors had been prosecuted for taking bribes for pardons, but that we had no evidence that Bush had been criminally induced to issue the pardons. Advocacy, even by politicians like Bob Dole, however questionable, was not criminal unless there was a provable connection between a political contribution and the pardon. Bush's failure to produce his notes was a more likely basis for investigation.

At a minimum, we had to be certain that we had all of Bush's relevant notes, which were still being delivered piecemeal. We had been relying on Boyden Gray, but I now wanted verification from other sources or from the obvious continuity of the notes themselves. Further, the late delivery required explanation: Who had actually been holding back the notes? Was it Bush, his personal secretary, or Gray? In addition, we needed to question Bush about the relevant information that we had accumulated since his deposition in January 1988.

Also, now that Weinberger and Clarridge had been pardoned, they could be questioned. We discussed whether to use a grand jury to compel their testimony if they refused to give us voluntary depositions.

The strong consensus of my staff was that we would not be able to develop any further criminal cases, and that it would be a mistake to increase public expectation by presenting evidence to a grand jury. The statute of limitations had run on virtually all the underlying activities. Brosnahan felt that we should cut off the investigation promptly, thereby freeing ourselves to participate in the public discussion of the pardon. Craig Gillen wanted to avoid the appearance of vindictiveness. Guy Struve observed that even if we did use the grand jury, the witnesses would probably claim not to remember the crucial facts or would only confirm what the records already proved, a phenomenon known as "half spills." Accordingly, we decided to seek voluntary interviews of Bush, Gray, and Gray's assistant, John P. Schmitz. If they refused to be interviewed, we would simply report the refusals to Congress.

In a sense, Bush's notes had an exculpatory quality. Except for a few that were relevant to our investigation of Donald Gregg, the notes would have been valuable primarily as an aid to questioning others about the development of the Reagan administration's positions. Although we recognized that Bush may have written his notes as self-serving protection for his position, they credibly showed the problems he had experienced in trying to keep up with the administration's ongoing activities, when—as the vice president—he was not in the line of command. Important decisions had been made in his absence. Sometimes he had been able to participate in policy discussions only because he had happened to be in the Oval Office at the time the president made his decision.

Gillen and Barrett undertook an investigation into the delay in the production of Bush's notes. We had first requested the notes in February 1987 and had renewed the request in June 1992. Gillen and Barrett learned that Bush's secretary, Patti Presock, had found the diary notes in September, more than a month before election day. She had thought the notes should be given to us; Bush had disagreed. They had handed Boyden Gray the responsibility for deciding whether to produce the notes or not. He had withheld them until December 11. When the notes were given to Gray's assistants, they had been told that Bush had claimed not to have been aware of our requests for his notes.

Bush had begun dictating notes on November 5, 1986, the day the arms sales to Iran were exposed—apparently when he foresaw, as a presidential candidate, the need to document his personal trail through the desperate maneuvers about to begin. "On the news at this time is the question of the hostages," he had dictated. "I'm one of the few people that know fully the details."

On November 10, the day John Poindexter briefed the National Security Planning Group, Bush had warned President Reagan that George Shultz was worried "about a Watergate syndrome."

On November 13, Bush had noted, "I remember Watergate. And I remember the way things oozed out. It is important to level, to be honest. . . . Everybody's making judgments based on erroneous information and it is the wrong fact coming up. It really is hemorrhaging."

The next day, he had confided to his diary, "I keep urging total disclosure, and not making statements that are not accurate."

On November 19, he had reported having had "interesting meetings with the president this morning—all alone, encouraging him to iron out the difficulties with Shultz and the White House. . . . My gut instinct is to rise to Reagan's defense and jump in the fray. But you don't want to shout into a hurricane."

Thursday, November 20, had been "a tough day in the White House," according to Bush's notes. "The president tells me that at lunch 'I really had a shocker. Don Regan has just told me that George Shultz has told him Poindexter has to go or he goes.'"

The next day, Edwin Meese had begun his fact-finding investigation. "I walked into Don Regan's at lunch today and he said, 'Well, here's a new bombshell.' Ed Meese, Poindexter, and Regan, excluding me, had a meeting in the White House about it. I am a statutory member [of the National Security Council]. I am the one guy that can give the president objective advice, and I have felt a twinge as to why the hell they didn't include me, but, on the other hand, you wind up not dragged into the mess."

"Ed Meese came to see me," Bush had noted on November 22. "He laid a real bombshell on me that Ollie North had taken the money and put it in a Swiss bank account . . . to be used for the Contras. They're going to blow [this] into a major thing. . . . And I told him that in my view, the president should ask me if I knew anything about it. I told him absolutely not. . . . It's going to be a major flap. The president has got to move fast. I've decided to take a 'no comment' posture. The president has asked us to shut up, and that is exactly what is happening."

If Bush had dictated anything to his diary on November 24, the day Meese reported to the NSPG on his investigation, it was not turned over to us.

"The big day," Bush had written of Tuesday, November 25. "It started out with the 9:00 meeting and Meese came in. . . . The president and Don Regan and I were there—Meese and Don outlining to the president that Poindexter had agreed to resign. . . . Ollie North was resigning. The president seemed troubled. . . . He didn't quite see that there was anything wrong." Bush had written that Poindexter had come in and "the president had a nice, frank discussion with him. He told him that he was sorry that it had worked out this way, . . . though he had done the right thing. And, then he left. And then, a little later, in came Shultz, and Cap [Weinberger] and [William] Casey. The president broke the news to them. I don't think any of them had known this—maybe Casey had been tipped off." Bush had noted that the group "went on to meet with the members of Congress. They were shocked. . . . I, later in the day, went in and told the president that I really felt that Regan should go, Shultz should go. . . . The administration is in disarray—foreign policy in disarray—cover-up—who knew what when? . . . I called the president early in the morning and made a suggestion to him that I head the investigatory panel."

In view of Bush's efforts to impede my work, I had to laugh when I read what he had dictated on November 30: "My own judgment at this point is that they ought to go the special prosecutor route."

"I was with the president," Bush had noted on December 11, "frustrated that we can't get Poindexter and Ollie to get the truth out. The president seems more relaxed about it than I. But I really think—before

Christmas—it will help him if North and Poindexter would say that the president did not know!"

A week later, Bush had written that his military aide "Terry Mattke talked with North. He knows that North would like to do this, and I am convinced both North and Poindexter will. But it is hard to get them to take action when their lawyers are diametrically opposed."

On Christmas Eve 1986, Bush had noted, "One good thing that will affect politics is that Felix Rodriguez . . . is going to come up and testify to the special prosecutor. He's willing to give a statement . . . as to my and Don Gregg's role."

On New Year's Day 1987, Bush had observed that "the irony is that on many of these key meetings, I was not there. The irony is that everyone says that the vice president has no power, and yet I'm the one damaged. . . . The truth of the matter is: The president makes his decision in very oblique ways. I'm not in the decision process, . . . not on personnel and not on major decision matters—unless I'm sitting in at the time the president makes the decision, and I can speak up."

According to the note, Bush had not remembered the presidential findings authorizing the sale of U.S. arms to Iran. "I have got to see them to believe that they were even signed by the president, frankly. But sometimes there are meetings over in the White House with Shultz, NSC guy, Casey, and Weinberger, and they make some decisions that the president signs off on. I'm not trying to jump sideways on this, but I think it is important to have the facts. And the facts are that the vice president is not in the decision-making loop. He does not have to sign off on decisions, it's sometimes overlooked, although not on purpose by the NSC bureaucracy."

More and more, the prospect of a continuing investigation of Bush and additional possible aspects of Iran-Contra seemed anticlimactic. The notes arguably showed the evolution of Bush's position from his having known all the details and recommending candor to his having been "out of the loop," but the notes were not incriminating. Even though the pardon had made Weinberger and Clarridge available for further grand jury testimony, it had come too late for the development of new cases. Moreover, the pardon itself was the ultimate proof of the cover-up. How could we top that? What could we produce that would be as shocking and revealing?

We had to formalize our position. This we could accomplish with an interim report to Congress. The report, filed on February 4, had two purposes: to reveal the evidence that would have been introduced at Weinberger's trial, including a complete appendix of his relevant notes about Iran-Contra; and to provide for Congress and the public, as a matter of record, a fair and comprehensive explanation of the nature of Bush's decision to issue the pardons, the decision's unwarranted nature, and its place in history as the final step in the cover-up. I briefly considered adding a chapter on Senator Dole's intrusion into our case against Weinberger, but I did not want to divert attention from the importance of the case itself and Bush's pardon.

After filing the interim report, we continued investigating how Bush's notes came to be withheld and what role he had played in the 1986 cover-up. We planned to begin interviewing witnesses after Bush left office on January 20. Gillen was ready to depose Bush and Gray. Griffin Bell, a former attorney general who was now Bush's counsel, asked me to announce that Bush was no longer a subject of our investigation. I, of course, refused.

In February, we began negotiating with Bush about his submitting to another deposition. The negotiations culminated in a letter from Bell's partner saying that Bush would agree to be deposed but only on the topic of the nonproduction of the notes. His agreement was also subject to other conditions, such as time limitations.

My immediate instinct was to use the grand jury and subpoena Bush; he was no longer in a position to set the terms for his deposition. In this I was alone. The staff unanimously opposed the use of the grand jury, arguing that to do so would exaggerate public expectations and would appear retaliatory. Underlying this position was the legal question of whether there was a sufficient likelihood of indictable criminal conduct to supply an appropriate basis for a grand jury proceeding. I gave up. We would not depose Bush.

We then turned our full attention to our final report. On August 4, I filed my report with the special division of the court of appeals that had appointed me. My investigation was over. For the next six months, I fought off efforts by Ronald Reagan, Oliver North, Edwin Meese, and others to suppress my report. It was finally released on January 18, 1994.

In the postmortems, we received more praise than criticism. *Newsday* columnist Robert Parry, for example, had this to say: "Undeterred by persistent attacks against him and his investigation, Walsh has dragged out more truth about the scandal than anyone else. . . . Without Walsh and his small band of prosecutors, . . . the scandal would have been blamed largely on the late CIA director, William Casey, and a few overzealous underlings. . . . Thanks to Walsh, we now know that the earlier Iran-Contra investigation missed the bigger picture—the direct participation of Reagan and Bush in the key decisions, as well as the brazen dishonesty that concealed their actions once the scandal finally broke in the fall of 1986."

Syndicated columnist Joseph Speer was generous: "My belief is that most of Lawrence Walsh's critics couldn't carry his briefcase, and my fervent prayer is that when the next constitutional crisis comes, someone with his rectitude and courage will be here to carry the public's banner."

The New Yorker offered a novel but perceptive view. "An ironic beneficiary of the pardons may well be the independent counsel, Lawrence Walsh, who has conducted the investigation too slowly and too haltingly. . . . Apparently, Mr. Bush believed that the defendants awaiting trial would be convicted, but by issuing the pardons, he has let Mr. Walsh off the hook and has bestowed on him a form of martyrdom. Mr. Walsh no longer has to prove anything."

REFLECTIONS

Occasionally, when I think back on my experience as an independent counsel, I am reminded of *The Old Man and the Sea*, Ernest Hemingway's tale of a fisherman who struggles for two days and nights to capture a giant marlin. Finally victorious, he lashes the marlin to the side of his skiff and begins the long trip back to shore. Suddenly, sharks attack. Alone, the man cannot fend off all the sharks, and they eventually strip every bit of flesh from the marlin. Worn out from the ordeal, the man collapses after reaching shore, leaving his fellow fishermen to marvel at the size of the skeleton he has beached. As the independent counsel, I sometimes felt like the old man; more often, I felt like the marlin.

In the years since my service ended, I have given many lectures, speeches, and interviews about Iran-Contra. This has provided me with innumerable occasions to rethink my decisions and mistakes as well as my basic notions about government.

Perhaps the most fundamental concept guiding my approach was respect for the rule of law, a long-established principle of Anglo-American political philosophy. The rule of law stands for several things. George Bush cited it repeatedly in stating our objectives in the Persian Gulf, using the phrase to mean the opposite of arbitrary action imposed by force and violence in international affairs. The rule of law is more commonly viewed as the antithesis of autocracy, restraining government officials, including the president, from unauthorized conduct toward individuals. Since at least the thirteenth century, English kings have been regarded as subject to the law. Under our constitutional scheme, the rule of law also connotes the balance of power among the three branches of government.

Procedural due process—which is intended to ensure that the government treats individuals fairly—is a cherished element of our rule of law, although it and other constitutional protections substantially increase the difficulties of enforcing the rule of law. In an effort to prevent injustice, we have developed a very elaborate, expensive, and time-consuming legal system. Despite their justified complaints about cost, delay, and uncertainty, few Americans would sacrifice the safeguards.

Reforms emanating from the decisions of the Supreme Court since 1940 have invited extensive and possibly excessive use of court procedures. Many of these changes, which I as deputy attorney general defended before the judiciary committees of Congress, occurred during a period when, in many states, the administration of justice was corrupted by racial discrimination. Nevertheless, the result has been to create a field day for lawyers—some of whom charge their clients $500 an hour. Although corporate defendants, persons whose fees are paid by corporations, and wealthy individuals can meet these demands, middle-class individuals can be destroyed by just the threat of litigation. Ironically, reforms that were intended to protect the impoverished now exaggerate the differences in the treatment of the wealthy and the middle class.

This problem is particularly acute for career government officials. Although some law firms adjust or eliminate their fees to ameliorate this problem, others insist that reducing their usual fees could be misconstrued as gifts to a public official—an extreme view in the light of centuries of flexibility in legal fees. This in turn leads to raising legal defense funds from private contributors, which, in the case of a continuing officeholder, seems much more questionable and nationally embarrassing than moderating a high fee. The Independent Counsel Act provides for government reimbursement of legal fees of those investigated but not indicted but not of those who have been indicted.

Crimes at high levels of government raise even more complex questions. Can our system be effectively employed in dealing with crimes committed by high-ranking officials? In dealing with officials of the various agencies concerned with national security? In cases where the motivation is political rather than personal? Are there better means to address high-level misdeeds? Can anything aside from the stigma of criminal prosecution deter presidentially tainted crime? If there is no substitute for prosecution, can it be accomplished by some less expensive means than the appointment of independent counsel?

In my view, the answer is probably yes to the first three but no to the remaining questions. Our experience showed that jurors will convict high-ranking officials for politically motivated crimes in the national security arena—but only at great cost. The alternatives to prosecution that are available to Congress cannot deal with criminal misconduct at staff levels. And if there are to be criminal prosecutions at the highest levels of government—levels at which the Department of Justice, not just the attorney general, is disqualified—independent counsel will be necessary, despite the expense, to avoid the appearance of conflict of interest. This is particularly true when the gravity of the crime affects the president and the basic relationship between Congress and the president.

The nature of executive misconduct has changed because the executive branch has changed. Since the New Deal and World War II, the size and number of executive agencies have grown dramatically. Andrew Jackson's "kitchen cabinet" has evolved into today's tangle of presidential councils and advisory boards, particularly the president's personal staffs, including those of the White House and the National Security Council.

Headed by men and women who are unelected and, in many cases, not subject to the confirmation process, these entities exist outside the traditional cabinet departments. Their work may shadow that of the departments, but the presidential advisors differ from the departments in that the advisors respond solely to the president's interests. Furthermore, they may be motivated less by the need to comply with congressionally enacted laws than by the desire to implement presidential policy.

As I learned during my term as counsel to the governor of New York, a chief executive's personal assistants exercise the power of the unitary executive. In Iran-Contra, the assistants exercised the power of the president of the United States. Regardless of whether he was being truthful when he said it (and he said it many times), Oliver North was able to accomplish numerous feats by saying, "This is what the president wants. I've talked with the president, and he approves." Such words are not taken as idle talk; they are often accepted as government commands.

The president's expanded personal staffs simultaneously present fertile ground for politically motivated misconduct and repel efforts to combat it. Assume, for example, that the president has set an important policy objective. He can expressly or tacitly encourage his subordinates to implement it by any means, whether legal or illegal. Suppose he merely sets the policy, and zealous subordinates take it upon themselves to employ illicit methods to promote it. Or suppose that the subordinates are the de facto policy-makers, which is inevitable with regard to at least some of the vast responsibilities that must be carried out by the president. The greater the number of people responsible for wielding executive power, the greater the chances that the power will be abused.

Ironically, the very size of the executive staffs diminishes the traditional means of deterring misconduct. Harry Truman's maxim "The buck stops here" may be legally and constitutionally correct, but as a practical matter the American people are not prepared to impeach a president for having failed to rein in an advisor who has acted improperly. Although presidents routinely say that they accept full responsibility for the actions of their subordinates, the misdeeds are usually portrayed as remote and isolated incidents, and no one is truly held politically accountable.

The Iran-Contra affair illustrates both the forces that propel high-level officials to engage in illegal activities and the barriers to full disclosure once the illegal activities have been exposed.

President Ronald Reagan deeply believed in the need for U.S. support of the Contras' military and paramilitary activities. When Congress withheld appropriations and then prohibited the intelligence agencies from providing that support, the administration was solidly behind the president's decision to continue providing it anyway. All his foreign policy advisors approved of using funds from foreign allies to replace the U.S. funds that Congress had expressly denied. Although the use of Saudi funds to carry out a policy that Congress had rejected was not in itself criminal, it reflected a contempt for the rule of law more shocking than the precise illegalities of North's conduct.

Organizing, funding, and directing the resupply of the Contras were illegal activities for a member of the National Security Council's staff, but North had the tacit support of the president and the administration, even though relatively few of the details were known by the small group of high-ranking officials who were aware of the project. Witnesses from executive agencies lied or dissembled to Congress to conceal those activities and to protect the expected $100 million appropriation for renewed CIA support of the Contras.

Once the arms-for-hostages transactions were exposed, no one—not even the cabinet members who had opposed the deals—told the full truth about them. The initial stonewall of denial was followed by the disclosure of only those arms sales that had taken place after the

January 1986 presidential finding and finally by the assignment of the blame to Robert McFarlane, John Poindexter, and Oliver North. Although we found no evidence that the president had specifically authorized or directed members of his administration to lie to Congress, their false testimony was an obvious result of his secretive policy. The officers called to testify had been left with a dilemma: They could not both tell the truth and protect the president. Some, like George Shultz, dissembled and gave incomplete testimony. Others, like Caspar Weinberger and Duane Clarridge, chose to lie.

Truth can be elusive. Four hundred years ago, Francis Bacon, a staunch defender of royal prerogative and one of the most intellectual of lawyers, opened his essay on truth with Pontius Pilate's memorable question: " 'What is truth?' said jesting Pilate, and would not stay for an answer." Distinguishing truth in theology and philosophy from truth in "civil business," however, Bacon wrote that "there is no vice that doth so cover a man with shame as to be found false and perfidious." A decade after publishing these words, he was exposed for corruption in the exercise of his office as lord chancellor to King James I. Rather than lie, Bacon confessed, accepted the loss of his office, endured brief imprisonment in the Tower of London, and nearly forfeited his noble rank.

Some observers have argued that actions that violate the criminal statues against fraud, obstruction, or perjury should—if undertaken by members of the executive branch—be viewed merely as political rough-housing, or playing hardball. These observers have argued that criminal prosecution, and the so-called criminalization of disputes between the legislative and executive branches, might prevent officials in the executive branch from representing the president's interests vigorously, particularly when interacting with Congress in dealing with questions inspired by partisan politics. But dishonesty seems a poor substitute for thoughtful analysis and forthright advocacy. Otherwise, we are left to conclude that certain people, because of their proximity to the president, are above the law.

There are several approaches to ensuring honesty in responses to congressional inquiries. One of the advantages of having Congress review politically motivated misdeeds is that the political judgment of our highest elected public officers comes into play. This very advantage, however, deprives congressional reviews of the credibility enjoyed by the courts, whose processes are supposedly free of politics. Nonetheless,

Congress can control how questionable conduct will be investigated and prosecuted: Congress can compel disclosures in private hearings; it can compel exposure in open hearings, subjecting miscreants to public criticism and the resulting broad political consequences; it can retaliate legislatively through the denial of appropriations and politically through oversight; and it can remove wrongdoers from office.

Public hearings can be of significant value both to the workings of government and to the education of the polity, but they can be difficult to focus. If they are not effectively focused, public hearings are likely to have relatively little lasting effect as deterrents to misconduct by the executive branch. Even if they are properly prepared and conducted, such hearings are an enormous drain on the energies of Congress.

After exposing the facts in public hearings, Congress can wait for voters to "throw the rascals out." However, an active citizenry and responsive and open government would be necessary to make this approach feasible. Furthermore, most officials in the executive branch are not vulnerable to the electorate. Because the president and vice president are the only elected members of the executive branch, only they can be directly thrown out by dissatisfied voters.

Nor do voters ordinarily use elections to police specific acts of misconduct. To be sure, some people in some elections vote on the basis of single issues, perhaps even issues of misconduct, but such behavior is unusual. An administration's misdeeds can and do go into the mix of reasons for voting behavior, but the function of elections is not—and ought not be—primarily to police misconduct.

Congress has sometimes used its ability to retaliate against the misdeeds of the executive branch by withholding appropriations or blocking legislation. The drawback to this approach is that it may restrict programs that are beneficial to the country.

Congress has rarely resorted to its power of impeachment, which is the most legalistic of the traditional responses to misconduct by the executive branch. Under the Constitution, the House of Representatives is charged with collecting the evidence of "high crimes and misdemeanors." If the evidence is deemed sufficient to warrant removing a "civil officer" from his government post, the House can send articles of impeachment to the Senate for trial. The Senate deliberates and decides the issue. The convicted officer's penalty is to be removed and permanently barred from federal office.

There are important limitations to impeachment, however. Sometimes, for example, sanctions heavier than the loss of office are necessary. Moreover, although arguably any civil officer can be impeached, it would be impractical for the Congress to consider every instance of executive misconduct. To avoid legislative paralysis, Congress must continue its current practice of impeaching only the very highest officials. Thus, impeachment cannot serve as a direct deterrent for subordinates.

What happens if the investigation and prosecution are left to the judicial system? Even in cases that do not entail such problems as congressional grants of immunity, criminal prosecution is a stiff and clumsy procedure, particularly in dealing with sophisticated, politically motivated misconduct. The broader, subtler, and more policylike the misconduct, the greater the difficulty in prosecuting it. Even where the underlying facts are essentially undisputed, questions of criminal intent may be formidable. Prosecutors must often choose between proving conspiracy and proving narrower, more specific, statutorily defined crimes. When the misconduct in question has flowed from a presidential directive or policy, the ordinary difficulties of prosecution are magnified by the constitutional responsibilities and accompanying protections of the presidency, particularly if the motivation for much of the conduct under investigation has been political rather than venal.

Prosecution can produce a very unsatisfactory and incomplete result when a president has directed a group or an agency to undertake an activity from which there is no honest and politically safe way out if Congress decides to ask questions. Executive privilege may protect the president, but it might not shield his subordinates when they are compelled to respond to a congressional inquiry. If they lie to avoid the political disaster that would result from telling the truth or openly refusing to answer, they run the risk of being prosecuted for obstructing the congressional investigation and making false statements. Nor will their individual virtues be taken into account as they would in isolated prosecutions. When their testimony is necessary to a complete investigation of the president and other high officials, candor is their only currency. The criminal justice system can deal with these officials, but unless they are willing to incriminate the president, it cannot reach him—even when it was loyalty to his policy that led to their indictment.

If a prompt congressional hearing requires the testimony of an immunized witness, the appellate decision in the *North* case seems to have eliminated the possibility that the hearing could be followed by a successful prosecution of the immunized witness's wrongdoing. This holding was based on the constitutional privilege against self-incrimination. To overcome it, therefore, would require reconsideration by the courts or a constitutional amendment. In the past, similar problems were addressed in several state constitutions; the usual remedy was to require the discharge of any government employee who claimed his privilege against self-incrimination. When the excesses of the House committee on un-American activities in the early 1950s led witnesses to assert this privilege regarding matters unrelated to their official duties, the Supreme Court held these state provisions unconstitutional.

The threat of dismissal would have been ineffective for North and Poindexter, who had already resigned. Requiring certain officials to irrevocably waive their privilege against self-incrimination as a condition of appointment seems an extreme measure; it would have to be enforced by contempt proceedings. Any such waiver should be limited to questions related to an official's conduct in office.

This might require an amendment to the federal Constitution. Unlike state constitutions, which frequently include a host of detail, the U.S. Constitution retains its original beauty and simplicity. Amendment should be a last recourse.

The investigation and prosecution of individuals employed by the federal agencies concerned with national security present special problems. In Iran-Contra, the chief problem aside from the congressional grants of immunity was the overclassification of documents. The problems caused by the arbitrary nature of the classification process could be curbed by statute. Greater specificity should be required to support agencies' claims of threats to national security. At the same time, the materiality of the classified information could be narrowed by statutes that explicitly defined criminal misconduct in the field of national security. The more precise the statute, the narrower the issues of criminal intent and the more limited the amount of classified material that would need to be exposed. Such a statute could, for example, provide criminal penalties for activities taken in furtherance of a policy that Congress has expressly rejected by denying appropriations for it.

A neutral arbiter could resolve disagreements when the agency classifying the documents is the agency under investigation and the attorney general is disqualified. Retired Supreme Court justices, former members of the Joint Chiefs of Staff, and persons of similar stature come to mind as those who might be called on to serve as arbiters.

Where criminal investigation and prosecution are appropriate, a special problem arises in applying the rule of law to a president and those around him: how to deal with obvious conflicts of interest that involve the attorney general and senior officials in the Justice Department. In the Iran-Contra affair, for example, it was Attorney General Edwin Meese who advised the president that prompt notice of the Iran arms sales need not be given Congress, despite provisions of the National Security Act and the Arms Export Control Act to the contrary. As information about the arms deals with Iran began to leak, it was the attorney general who supervised the gathering of facts in order to evaluate the president's vulnerability. In this role, the attorney general was not representing the United States as a prosecutor; he was acting to protect the president.

Could the Justice Department have handled the Iran-Contra prosecutions? For example, even if the attorney general had personally disqualified himself, would there have been a perception of conflict of interest? If someone in the Justice Department had decided not to prosecute Edwin Meese, would the public have accepted the determination as valid?

The conflict-of-interest concerns are even more pronounced when the potential offenses under investigation occur in the context of national security matters. In such matters, particularly those involving clandestine operations, the executive branch alone determines what, if any, information about its actions is produced or publicly disseminated. Some secrecy is clearly necessary, but secrecy can be employed to mask political mistakes, unwise decisions, or abuses of authority. It can also be used to mask crimes.

Although the current independent counsel statute leaves the attorney general as the only judge of the legitimacy of the insistence on secrecy, an independent counsel can at least raise the issue to congressional and public notice. The combination of the executive branch's control of national security information and the natural reluctance of even fair-minded intelligence officials to release such information makes a truly independent prosecutor necessary if highly placed national security officials are to be brought to justice for engaging in criminal activities related to their duties.

Although the taxpayers incur heavy costs when misconduct by high-ranking officials of the executive branch is investigated or prosecuted, both Congress and the public pay a price for eschewing criminal prosecution in cases of executive malfeasance. The issue then becomes whether we are willing to shoulder the enormous expense of an independent prosecution, as well as the cost of setting up separate secure facilities for each indicted defendant, to attempt to ensure that no one—not even the president—is above the impartial application of the law.

The independent counsel statute has been controversial since it was enacted as part of the Ethics in Government Act of 1978. Some commentators have argued that the statute unfairly burdens the operations of the executive branch and subjects a small class of potential suspects to disproportionate expense and abuse. The use of the statute, however, is initially a question for the attorney general. Unless the attorney general determines that an independent counsel is necessary and asks the court to appoint one, the statute does not come into play. The attorney general's decision is not reviewable.

(Except in a few cases specified by the statute, the attorney general may avoid a conflict of interest by appointing an independent counsel of his or her own choosing. Requesting a court-appointed independent counsel simply adds an additional layer of insulation for the attorney general.)

Some observers have complained that the standard for triggering an independent counsel request—"reasonable grounds to believe that further investigation is warranted"—is too low. Some appointments seem to have been unnecessary. Perhaps the attorney general should be required to make an additional finding that prompt investigation by an independent counsel is necessary in the public interest. A high-level federal official's alleged conduct prior to taking his or her oath of office, for example, ordinarily should not justify the expense of an independent counsel. Instead, prosecution for that conduct might be deferred during his federal service by an appropriate exception to the statute of limitations; after the official left office, the Justice Department could undertake the prosecution.

There are and should be significant restraints against abuses of discretion by independent counsel. In most cases, they are obligated to comply with the applicable policies of the Justice Department and to report their activities and findings to the appointing court and to Congress. They are subject to removal for cause by the attorney general. These measures, in addition to the appointing court's limitations on the scope of the investigations, should provide effective checks on an independent counsel's abuse of authority.

Some critics of the concept of independent counsel complain that appointees drawn from private practice lack the values of those who make prosecutorial decisions every day in a steady flow of cases. This criticism is less valid when, as is usually true, the appointee has previously held prosecutorial responsibilities. In the case of Iran-Contra, for example, I had served as special assistant attorney general of the state of New York for two years, as deputy assistant district attorney of New York County for four years, and as deputy attorney general of the United States for three years. Thus, my prosecutorial experience matched or exceeded that of most individuals serving as regularly appointed or elected prosecutors. My deputy, Craig Gillen, came to us straight from twelve years as an assistant U.S. attorney in Atlanta. That alone should have exempted our team from any such criticism.

What some critics do not realize, however, is that the judgments that must be made in pursuing complex conspiracies by governmental officials, as in pursuing complex fraud or racketeering cases, require the use of standards somewhat different from those employed in dealing with run-of-the-mill crimes. The independent counsel statute provides that independent counsel may depart from the guidelines of the Department of Justice when necessary to their missions. In trying to break through a cover-up, whether in a racket or in government, a guiding concern is to get subordinates to testify against those higher up in the leadership of the illegal enterprise. To achieve this result, it is sometimes necessary to forgo the exclusive consideration of the virtues and vices of lower-ranking individuals who have made themselves vulnerable by lying to Congress or government agencies. The controlling consideration becomes whether they persist in withholding the truth.

In reenacting the independent counsel statute, Congress would be unwise to hamper the counsel's all-out efforts with petty restrictions. Nor should Congress require independent counsel to move their personal offices and residences to undertake work that is likely to be temporary. Otherwise, lawyers who lived beyond commuting range of the principal forum of activity would be excluded from serving as independent counsel. This result would be particularly undesirable if it limited most appointments to District of Columbia lawyers, who are far more likely than lawyers elsewhere to have conflicts of interest because their firms handle so many matters that involve the government and to some extent depend on the government's goodwill.

Independent counsel should not be deprived of their rights and responsibilities to issue interim reports to Congress. These reports are the independent counsel's most effective defense against political intrusion and attack. The statute should also continue the requirement for a full final report explaining why, if the attorney general thought independent counsel necessary, no action was taken as to the subjects he investigated.

I believe that the independent counsel system has been integrated successfully into our constitutional framework. The statute must be renewed every five years, which provides regular opportunities for amendments. But, inasmuch as the Supreme Court upheld the statute in *Morrison v. Olson*, it would be regrettable to endanger the statute's constitutionality by any radical change.

The concepts of the superiority of law and equality before the law were not developed solely by courts and lawyers. They were developed and have survived with the support of persons who possessed political power. When the U.S. Constitution was drafted, the restraints on potentially autocratic presidents were not left to lawyers alone; the founding fathers provided for checks and balances within the political structure of the country, so that the political forces could counteract excesses by one another. In a sense, the judicial system and congressional oversight serve as dual alarm systems, intended to be mutually supportive in halting misconduct.

Unfortunately, the alarm systems can conflict. If you had two alarm systems for your home, one that sent a secret message to the police department so that a burglar could be arrested and a second that blew a shrill whistle to scare the burglar off, they would work at cross-purposes. At times, congressional oversight is like the whistle: It makes a lot of noise, but it permits lawbreakers to go unpunished.

If Congress pushes aside criminal prosecutions by granting immunity, it must act with the same degree of discipline and thoroughness as prosecutors would employ. There should then be no arbitrary fixed time limits for completing investigations.

The select committees on Iran-Contra apparently accepted John Poindexter's testimony that he had not told Ronald Reagan of the diversion, that he had had no need to do so because he had known that the president would have approved it, and that he had wanted to preserve the president's deniability. The committee did not question Reagan, although it seemed unbelievable that he would have permitted the arms shipments to continue without the return of a single hostage for months at a time unless he understood that in some way the shipments were benefiting the Contras. By adopting the administration's characterization of Iran-Contra as a runaway conspiracy, the select committees not only misled the American people but also measurably increased the difficulty of prosecuting those responsible for the breach of law and the defiance of congressional control.

The committees also did the nation a disservice by establishing Oliver North as a folk hero. He nearly became a senator from the Commonwealth of Virginia. For a time, he even seemed about to become a possible president-maker, as Republican presidential hopefuls—including former high-ranking officials from the Bush administration—sent funds or made the pilgrimage to Virginia to ingratiate themselves with North. This was a matter of national concern, not that of Virginians or Republicans alone.

Legitimate oversight is an important power of Congress. All that can be hoped for is that the congressional committees will exercise restraint when granting immunity regarding possibly criminal conduct. In hearings conducted after Iran-Contra, Congress has shown consideration for the independent counsel, withholding grants of immunity from subjects of investigation about misconduct at the Department of Housing and Urban Affairs, about the Whitewater matter, and in the confirmation of Robert Gates as director of central intelligence.

Spurious congressional oversight is another matter altogether. More pernicious than any error in judgment made by me or the select committees on Iran-Contra was the censorious oversight conducted by partisan members of Congress, most notably Bob Dole. His carping denunciations of our efforts to enforce the law and his use of his congressional leadership post to harass a federal prosecution (not in debate and not pursuant to any congressional resolution or the work of any congressional committee) constituted arrogant misuses of his office. Dole's mean-minded model, Joe McCarthy, at least had the support of a committee, and he never spoke as the Republican leader of the Senate. Dole's contempt for the rule of law was clear when he kept up his public attack on our case against Weinberger even after the jury panel had been notified to report for the trial.

Although the House Republicans' attack on my travel expenses played on the ambiguity of the independent counsel statute, the massive nature of the attack reflected the congressmen's misplaced fear that Ronald Reagan was in danger. An inflated story about my expenses intruded in the trial of Clair George and caused the judge to instruct the jurors to disregard the *Washington Times* headlines they had seen. I believe the attack led to the mistrial and made it necessary to try the case a second time.

The ducking stool has long been abolished as the treatment for common scolds, so there may be no remedy for oversight by denunciation. Occasional legislators may continue to become special pleaders, but judicial proceedings should not be overshadowed by congressional disparagement. If the houses of Congress fail to restrain members' comments about ongoing court cases, at least at time of trial, then congressional watchdogs like Common Cause as well as law school faculty members and bar associations must focus public attention on the misconduct.

Certainly, prosecutors must not be deterred by partisan attacks. The brand of personal defamation spread by Bob Dole is frequently aimed at individuals engaged in high-visibility work in Washington. Nonetheless, prosecutors cannot acknowledge personal concern; their concern must be only for the public duty that is being hampered. Their obligation is to apply law enforcement evenly to high officials as well as low and to go as far as is possible and fair. When these efforts are blocked by partisan politics, independent counsel must publicly expose the derogation of the rule of law.

The most cynical aspect of the spurious congressional oversight was its role in laying the groundwork for the unprecedented pardon of Weinberger before trial. The pardon power was never intended to be used to block the trial of an indicted defendant or to prevent the public exposure of facts. Under the applicable rules of the Justice Department, ordinary persons cannot even apply for a pardon until seven years after conviction.

The reason George Bush gave for his action did not hold water. In claiming that I was criminalizing a political dispute, he disregarded the law and ignored the history of prosecutions under it. Lying to Congress had been a crime for decades, and lying to a government agency, including independent counsel, was also a crime of long standing. Bush did not try to explain why he pardoned Weinberger before trial but let the other defendants charged with similar crimes stand trial or plead guilty before being considered for pardons.

In taking the Weinberger case away from the court and jury, Bush blocked the equal application of the law to political appointees in high office. Lying to Congress goes to the heart of Congress's power of oversight, which is essential to constitutional checks and balances. Protecting cabinet-level and presidential deceit in such matters can hardly be justified as preserving the political process. Contrary to Bush's view, lying to conceal the autocratic action of a president and the evasion of congressional restraints calls out for punishment to a greater extent than most other lies to Congress or the courts.

Whatever the intentions, the effects of the political intrusions—legitimate and illegitimate—were to prolong the Iran-Contra investigation, to increase its costs, and to frustrate the prosecution of those who had helped conceal President Reagan's willful disregard of constitutional restraints on his power.

But if Congress made my work more difficult, the root of the problem was the executive branch's strategy. Ronald Reagan's advisors succeeded in creating a firewall around him. He escaped meaningful interrogation until it was no longer of use, and he escaped prosecution altogether, while subordinates suffered. The delay in producing government records and the concealment of personal notes were crucial to the strategy. George Bush's misuse of the pardon power made the cover-up complete.

What set Iran-Contra apart from previous political scandals was the fact that a cover-up engineered in the White House of one president and completed by his successor prevented the rule of law from being applied to the perpetrators of criminal activity of constitutional dimension.

INDEX

Abramowitz, Michael, 463
Abrams, Elliott:
    congressional testimony of, 269, 280, 304-9
    Contra aid supported by, 80, 106, 153, 254-55, 261, 285, 286, 305
    cover-up by, 253-54
    North and, 104, 153, 209, 255, 265-66, 285, 305, 308
    pardon for, 490-510
    plea bargain for, 305, 309-10
    as RIG member, 77, 112, 336
    Rodriguez and, 285, 307-8
    Shultz and, 265-66, 267, 269, 305, 307-8, 309
    Walsh's investigation of, 265-69, 273, 335
    Weinberger supported by, 440
Abrams, Stuart, 223, 261
Abshire, David, 56, 69, 70, 78, 368
Agnew, Spiro, 435-36
airborne warning and control system (AWACS), 390, 392
al-Da'wa al-Islamiya (Islamic Call), 123
Alexander, Gail, 57, 73
Allen, Charles, 42, 53-54, 100, 101-2, 112, 276, 282, 295-96, 297, 298, 313
Allen, Richard, 357
Al Shiraa, 7-8, 22, 47, 112, 321
Altman, Robert A., 428
Amalgamated Commercial Enterprises, Inc. (ACE), 57
American Bar Association (ABA), 88, 141-43, 146, 225
American Law Institute, 250
Amtrak, 91
Anderson, Denise, 205
Anderson, Jack, 328
Apple, R. W., Jr., 507
Arkin, Stanley, 285-86
Armacost, Michael, 106, 112, 268, 321, 327, 328, 329, 330, 376, 382
Armitage, Richard, 53, 77, 336, 344, 346, 347, 349, 350, 352, 403, 405
Arms Export Control Act, x, 3, 6, 13, 45, 65, 255, 336, 348, 373, 374, 375, 376, 387, 499, 525
Aspin, Lew, 506
Asseo, Laurie, 419
Associated Press, 421, 459, 470, 483

Bacon, Francis, 521
Baker, Howard, 78, 370, 435
Baker, James, 68, 353, 356, 372, 419, 506
Baker, Tom, 304, 319, 326, 331, 340-42, 343, 395, 396, 397, 403, 404, 409, 410
Baltimore Sun, 232, 418
Bandar bin Sultan, 19, 353, 389, 391-92, 437
Barbadoro, Paul, 63
Barnes, Fred, 487-88
Barnes, Michael, 190, 191, 199, 236, 237, 307

Barr, William, 317, 429, 430-31, 472, 479, 484, 486, 487, 506
Barrett, John, 253-56, 265, 267, 268, 273, 304, 305, 318-20, 325, 326, 329-31, 336, 338, 396, 397, 403, 404, 410, 420, 428, 437-38, 447-48, 450, 477, 492, 512
Bartholomew, Reginald, 327
"B. Button" fund, 61-62, 98, 122-23, 133-34, 149-50, 223
Beach, Paul, 488
Beamish, Rita, 288
Bechtel Corporation, 334, 337
Beckler, Richard, 164, 166, 225, 228, 233-34, 240, 241, 244, 245
Been, Vicki, 66, 147
Belcher, Mary, 234, 263, 272, 299, 421, 444, 475, 485, 492, 493, 496, 497
Bell, Griffin, 515
Bellows, Randy, 55, 66
Belnick, Mark A., 394
Bennett, Robert, 397-407, 413-18, 422, 428-29, 433-38, 442-43, 444, 447, 470, 473, 475, 476, 482-88, 504
Berman, Geoff, 223, 261
Bermúdez, Enrique, 107
Bernstein, Carl, 507
Bever, Tom, 339
Biden, Joseph, 479
Black, Cole, 211
Blanton, Tom, 501
Boland, Edward P., 18, 85
Boland amendments, 18, 19, 20, 60, 61, 65, 67, 75, 78, 102, 103, 104, 113, 114, 116, 117, 120, 121, 128, 132, 151, 154, 155, 156, 184, 186, 190, 193, 194, 225, 230, 242, 275, 313, 394
Boren, David, 88, 221, 281-82, 287, 294
Bork, Robert, 69
Boxer, Barbara, 484
Bradley, Bill, 296, 390
Brady, Nicholas, 270
Bramble Bush, The (Llewellyn), 48n
Bremer, L. Paul "Jerry," 321, 327
Brezhnev, Leonid, 293
Bridges, Styles, 469
Broder, David, 453, 455, 459
Brokaw, Tom, 455
Bromwich, Michael, 55, 61, 66, 74, 81, 128, 148, 167, 174, 175, 179, 185, 186, 284, 298, 299, 300
Brooks, Jack, 252
Broomfield, Bill, 283
Brosnahan, James, 445, 447, 448, 449, 450, 469, 470-72, 475, 477-87, 492, 511
Brower, Charles, 56, 69-70
Brown, Hank, 472
Bruemmer, Russell, 171, 176
Brunei, Sultan of, 255, 269, 309
Buckley, William, 4, 36, 39, 43

Burchill, William, 425, 426
Burns, Arnold, 376-77
Bush, Barbara, 451, 460
Bush, George:
  character of, 451, 454, 458-59, 463, 480, 490-91
  classified information as viewed by, 215-16, 217, 218, 220, 221
  Contra arms supplies and, 80, 93, 105-6, 155, 193-94, 196, 266, 271, 272, 286, 307, 432
  covert action bill vetoed by, 221
  credibility of, 454, 455, 456-57
  denials by, 451, 456-57, 458, 459, 461, 464
  deposition of, 155, 272, 464, 488
  diary of, 8, 420, 452, 488-89, 512-14
  disclosure as viewed by, 215-16, 217, 218, 220, 221, 301, 363, 367, 458, 512-14
  historical analysis of, 491-92, 507
  Iran arms sales as viewed by, 8, 28, 47, 111, 155, 269-70, 301, 363, 367, 447-66, 512
  judicial appointments by, 248, 260
  McFarlane's relationship with, 155
  media coverage of, 451, 453, 455-61, 470-71, 475-77, 492-510
  Meese's investigation and, 383, 512-13
  North's relationship with, 155, 261, 304, 456
  notes of, 319-20, 456, 488-89, 494, 500, 502-3, 506, 511-15
  as NSPG member, 3, 14, 41, 286, 453
  as "out of the loop," 451, 460, 461
  pardons for North and Poindexter opposed by, 159
  pardons granted by, 429, 469-70, 475-77, 479, 482, 486, 487-88, 489, 490-510, 511, 514, 515, 516, 530-31
  Poindexter's relationship with, 452-53, 455, 456, 458
  Reagan's relationship with, 227, 231, 369-70, 500, 502, 512, 513-14
  Regan's notes and, 358
  Regan's resignation and, 369-70
  responsibility of, 28, 90, 155, 207, 254, 255, 266, 281, 304, 439, 447-50, 516
  Shultz's relationship with, 266, 269-70, 334
  Silberman and, 249
  Suazo's meeting with, 193-94
  vetoes of, 221, 431-32, 467
  Walsh's investigation of, 264, 289, 474-75, 500-503, 510-15
  Walsh's investigation opposed by, 254, 263, 287, 288-89, 301, 314, 317, 318, 460, 462-63, 469, 473, 499, 513
  Walsh's letter to, 218
  Weinberger indictments and, 414-15, 419, 447-50, 459-68, 494
  as witness, 464, 475, 482, 487, 510
Byrd, Robert, 10, 351, 352, 360

Cable News Network (CNN), 413, 414-15, 419, 421, 439, 448, 460, 493, 497, 498, 501, 504
Calero Portocarrero, Adolfo, 15, 17, 20, 57, 80, 82, 98, 102-3, 107, 122, 145, 153, 186, 197, 200, 278
"canning," 90, 97, 125, 130, 283-84
Cannistraro, Vincent N., 102-3, 197-99, 276-77, 313
Carlucci, Frank, 266, 366, 440
Carman, Brenda, 492, 493
Carter, Jimmy, 16, 17, 248, 497
Carter, Steven L., 508
Casey, William:
  congressional testimony of, 11, 12, 54, 67, 112, 152, 196, 206, 258, 298, 303, 334, 352-53, 365, 375, 376, 377, 378, 379
  Contra aid supported by, 19, 53, 101, 105, 119, 120, 195, 199, 277, 295, 297, 513
  death of, 132, 145, 197, 290
  disclosure opposed by, 350-51, 366-67
  George and, 45, 292, 294, 432
  hospitalization of, 28, 35
  Iran arms deal supported by, 5, 8, 40, 41, 43, 54, 255, 297, 403
  North's relationship with, 105, 107, 132, 153, 197, 199, 275, 286, 295-96
  as NSPG member, 3, 14, 38, 41

Reagan's relationship with, 24, 105, 144, 293
Regan and, 361, 363, 365
responsibility of, 297, 314, 515-16
Shultz's relationship with, 13, 305, 322, 328, 330, 335, 354
Walsh's investigation of, 264
Weinberger and, 344, 345, 391
Cave, George, 84-85, 101, 109, 123, 383-84, 431
Central Intelligence Agency (CIA):
  Contra operations of, ix, x, 18-22, 67, 74, 75, 79, 100-105, 108, 121, 132, 191, 196, 197, 199, 212-19, 229, 237, 274-81, 286
  directorate of intelligence of, 153
  directorate of operations (covert action) of, 153, 292
  files of, 55, 67-68, 69, 94, 112, 147-49, 165, 170, 178, 212-19, 254, 274-75, 278, 289, 295, 452
  in Iran arms sales, xi, 5-7, 12, 14, 36, 40-45, 90-91, 111, 140-41, 150, 152-54, 206, 238-44, 297-98, 347-53, 383, 388
  legal staff of, 51, 78, 147
  presidential finding for, 12, 40-41, 44-45, 90-91, 140-41, 152-53, 196, 203, 224, 233, 234, 238-44, 297-98, 347-53, 355, 359, 360, 363, 366, 380, 514
  Walsh's investigation of, 145, 147-48, 149, 152-54, 165, 253, 262, 265, 287-90, 320
Chaffee, John, 297
Chamorro, Pedro Joaquín "Blackie," 16, 104, 265, 278, 279
Chamorro, Violeta, 17
Chancellor, John, 137
Channell, Carl R. "Spitz," 60, 66, 74, 81, 82, 92-93, 95, 103, 153, 187-88, 199, 202, 206, 236
Cheney, Dick, 48, 49, 50, 63, 117, 351, 366, 478, 482
Chien, Fred, 103
CIA Officer Number Seven, 446
Civil War, 143
Clark, George, 216
Clark, William, 159, 353, 354, 434-36, 440, 442-43, 475, 476, 488
Clarke, David, 429
Clarridge, Duane "Dewey," 18, 19, 40, 102, 253
  congressional testimony of, 275-76, 312, 313, 521
  Contra activities of, 274-75, 312-13
  indictment of, 313-14, 325, 335
  Iran arms sales and, 275-77, 312, 313, 477
  pardon of, 490-510
  planned trial of, 413, 447, 449, 477
  as witness, 511, 514
Classified Information Procedures Act (CIPA), 157, 169, 176, 178, 179, 182-84, 213-21, 226, 286, 302
Clifford, Clark, 428
Clines, Thomas, 63, 74, 81, 93, 104, 105, 108, 118, 150, 151, 261, 279
Clinton, Bill, 302, 398, 448, 449, 451, 454-55, 457, 459, 460, 467, 470-71, 472, 474, 476, 479, 480, 481, 484, 491, 493
Cohen, William S., 32, 117, 127, 221, 388, 431, 439
Cohn, Bob, 506
Colby, William, 291
Common Cause, 530
Compagnie de Services Fiduciaires (CSF), 56, 146
Conference on Security and Cooperation in Europe, 321-22
Congressional Record, 430
Conrad, Daniel, 82
Conservative Democratic Party (Nicaragua), 17
Contadora peace process, 293
Contras, Nicaraguan:
  air drops for, 20-22, 57, 74-75, 76, 79, 93, 103-6, 210, 213, 265, 277, 278-79, 280
  anti-Sandinista activities of, 191, 193, 194, 195-96, 265, 278, 312, 313
  CIA support for, ix, x, 18-22, 67, 74, 75, 79, 100-105, 108, 121, 132, 191, 196, 197, 199, 212-19, 229, 237, 274-81, 286
  comanderos of, 104
  congressional ban on aid to, ix-x, 19-20, 74, 108, 116, 117, 132-33, 134, 292-93, 312, 520
  congressional support for, 17-19, 21, 108, 277, 286, 391
  fund-raising operation for, 60-61, 65, 81-83, 92-93, 99,

102-3, 107, 109, 122, 131, 132, 151, 153, 158, 187-88,
    190, 199, 202-3, 230-31, 236, 277, 309
humanitarian supplies to, 76, 79, 103-4, 106, 262, 278,
    292
leadership of, 278-79
organizations of, 17, 19, 104
see also Iran-Contra affair
Coolidge, Calvin, 490
Cooper, Charles, 196, 372, 373-74, 377-78, 379, 380-81,
    382, 384
Cooper, William, 79
Coors, Joseph, 92-93, 187
Corporate Air Services, 21, 57, 74-75
Corr, Edwin G., 80, 106, 262, 307, 319, 396
Costa Rica, 104, 210, 218-19, 278
Coulson, Danny, 32-33, 51, 61, 128, 268, 325, 331
Council for Inter-American Security, 422
Couric, Katie, 457-58
Cox, Archibald, 69, 469, 503
Crédit Suisse, 107
Croker, Stephen, 266
Crowe, V.I.P., 490
Crowe, William J., Jr., 305, 352, 391, 404
Cruz, Arturo J., 17
C-Span, 232
Cuba, ix, 17, 18
Culvahouse, A. V., Jr., 78
Customs Service, U.S., 73
Cutler, Lloyd, 320, 331, 333, 413
"cutout," 152

Daily Oklahoman, 440, 493
Dallas Morning News, 301
Dash, Sam, 430
Davis Polk & Wardwell, 26, 27, 28, 60, 164
Deaver, Michael, 69, 70, 356, 421
Defense Department, U.S., 51, 53, 75, 100, 111, 153, 165,
    255, 262, 264, 337-38, 348, 350, 392-93, 396, 405,
    408, 442, 478
Defex, Inc., 74, 80
Defex S.A., 81, 150
DeGaray, Edward T., 57, 74-75
deGraffenreid, Kenneth, 78, 90-91
Dellinger, Walter, 508
Dennis, Edward S. G., 176, 178, 179, 213, 215, 216, 217
Denniston, Lyle, 281, 422-23, 439
Devroy, Ann, 463
Dewey, Thomas E., 61, 225, 226-27, 338, 491
Díaz, Adolfo, 16
Dirksen, Everett, 469
Divers, Neil, 51
Dix, Mary, 203-4
Doherty, David, 298, 361, 374, 377
Dole, Bob, 288, 302, 311-12, 314, 317, 351, 352, 366
    pardons supported by, 479, 487-88, 491, 497, 502, 506,
        511
    Walsh's investigation criticized by, 282-83, 287, 422, 429,
        467-69, 470-75, 478-86, 488, 497, 508-9, 530
    Weinberger indictments and, 417, 419, 422, 429, 433, 439,
        443, 468-69, 515, 529
Donaldson, Sam, 509-10
Douglass, John, 29, 55, 58, 59, 60, 62, 67, 81, 125, 136, 139,
    141
Dowd, Maureen, 460-61
"drop-dead" list, 177, 183
Duarte, José Napoleón, 266
Duemling, Robert, 106
Dukakis, Michael, 484
Duncan, John J. "Jimmy," 427
Dupart, Louis, 219, 280-81
Durenberger, David, 240, 242, 367, 452
Dutton, Robert C., 75, 79

Eagleton, Thomas F., 431
Earl, Robert, 83, 91, 92, 99-100, 278
Eastland, Terry, 476
Economy Act, 348
Edwards, Mickey, 283

Eggleston, Neil, 59, 387
Eisenhower, Dwight D., 28, 148, 226, 356
Ellis, Steve, 426
El Salvador, ix, 17, 18, 93, 195, 266
Emerson, Steve, 498, 501, 503-4
Energy Resources, 80
Enterprise, 108, 109, 119, 123, 125, 132, 150, 151, 153, 210, 223
Erria, 81, 153
Ethics in Government Act, 526
Evans, Rowland, 413-15, 491

Face the Nation, 333, 470, 508
Fahd bin Abdul Aziz, King of Saudi Arabia, 195
Fascell, Dante, 389-90
Federal Bureau of Investigation (FBI), 23, 32-35, 51-54, 63,
    97, 103, 113, 124, 136, 144
    Walsh aided by, 29, 32-33, 51-54, 60, 66, 73, 80, 264, 428
Federalist Society, 248, 249
Federal Office for Police Matters, 147
Federal Reporter, 256
Feinstein, Dianne, 484
Ferch, John, 106
Fernandez, Joseph, 76, 80, 91, 104, 105, 128, 153-54, 253,
    277-81
    trial of, 210-21, 226, 265, 319, 452
Fielding, Fred F., 202
Fiers, Alan, 77, 80, 102, 104, 106, 147, 153, 255, 335, 336
    congressional testimony of, 277, 279-81, 294
    Contra activities of, 209, 265, 274-75, 277-81, 285, 293
    Gates and, 287, 288, 289, 294-95
    George and, 279, 280-81, 286, 291, 292, 424, 431, 432,
        433, 445, 447
    pardon of, 490-510
    plea bargain for, 285-87, 288, 314, 435
    as witness, 294, 296-97, 424, 431, 432, 433, 445, 447
Fifth Amendment, 30, 88, 107, 157, 257, 304
Fischer, David, 93
Fiske, Robert, 26, 27-28
Fitzwater, Marlin, 459, 473, 496
Foley, Thomas P., 48, 124, 281, 302, 506
Forbes, Malcolm S., Jr., 463-64
Ford, Gerald R., 25, 249, 435, 477, 490, 496, 507
Ford, Rick, 29, 57, 436
Fortier, Donald, 44
Foster, Mike, 338, 358, 397
Francis, Vernon, 278, 285
Frank, Jerome, 248
Freedom of Information Act, 164, 176, 425, 481, 482
Frey, Andrew, 260, 282
Fried, Charles, 160
Friedman, Paul, 54, 66
Fulbright & Jaworski, 225
Fuller, Craig, 367
Furmark, Roy, 37, 101

Gadd, Richard, 75, 79, 91, 187, 255, 269, 278, 279, 308,
    446
Gaffney, Henry, 345
"gang of eight," 379
Gannon, Robert I., 142
Gardner, Norman, Jr., 242-43, 446
Garrett, Lawrence, 344, 374, 393, 394, 395, 409, 442
Garwood, Ellen, 82
Gates, Robert, 54, 68, 101-2, 178, 286, 290, 292
    confirmation hearings of, 281-82, 287, 288, 289, 294-98,
        466, 529
Gay, Henry, 506
General Accounting Office (GAO), 422, 426, 427, 429,
    440-41, 443-44, 473, 485-86
General Services Administration (GSA), 34, 57, 73
George, Clair, 68, 105, 113, 147, 153
    background of, 292
    Casey and, 45, 292, 294, 432
    classified documents and, 423-24, 432
    congressional testimony of, 269, 285, 292-93, 294, 306,
        423-24, 431-32, 446, 447
    Contra operations and, 255, 275, 277, 279, 280, 292-93,
        292-93, 294, 431-33

George, Clair, (continued)
  conviction of, 446-47
  Fiers and, 279, 280-81, 286, 291, 292, 424, 431, 432, 433, 445, 447
  indictment of, 289-92, 294, 296, 314, 335
  Iran arms sales and, 100, 101, 349
  national security community's support for, 291, 424, 427, 445-47
  North and, 45, 68, 100, 101, 294
  pardon for, 490-510
  plea bargain for, 289-90
  Poindexter and, 45, 349, 431
  retrial of, 433, 440, 441, 445-47, 450, 530
  Secord and, 431, 432, 446
  trial of, 413, 423-24, 427, 430, 431-33, 435, 486, 529-30
Gephardt, Richard, 496-97
Gesell, Gerhard, 164-74, 176, 177-80, 182, 183, 211, 224, 226, 235, 250, 284-85, 438
  in North trial, 188, 190, 191, 192, 193, 194, 196-97, 205-8, 257-58, 259, 260, 298, 299
Ghorbanifar, Manucher:
  as arms broker, 5, 6, 7, 36-38, 39, 41-42, 43, 45, 46, 47, 53-54, 84, 100, 101, 109-11, 113, 152, 328, 340, 347
  background of, 36-37
  financial records of, 147
  payments to and from, 81, 101, 109, 110-11, 363
Gillen, Craig, 222-23, 253-55, 261, 262, 264, 265, 271, 272, 274, 281, 285-89, 294, 300, 305, 318, 378, 385-86, 469, 471, 474, 488, 492, 511, 512, 527
  expense reimbursement of, 426-27, 429, 440, 441, 443-44
  in George trials, 413, 423-24, 427, 432, 433, 440, 446-47
  in Shultz investigation, 267-70, 320, 324, 325, 326, 329, 331, 332, 333, 384-85
  in Weinberger investigation, 338, 339, 340, 388, 396, 397, 400-406, 409, 410, 418-19, 434, 436-37, 441, 444, 445, 450
Gillers, Steven, 485
Gingrich, Newt, 283, 430
Ginsburg, Douglas, 310
Ginsburg, Ruth Bader, 260
Giuliani, Rudolph, 29, 55
Glasser, Ellen, 238
Gomez, Frank, 82
Gomez, Max, see Rodriguez, Felix
Gorbachev, Mikhail, 12, 39, 84, 266, 308, 345, 364, 420
Gore, Al, 454, 459, 480
Grant, Ulysses S., 490
Grassley, Charles, 472
Gray, C. Boyden, 218, 248, 254, 260, 271, 288, 317, 320, 422, 451-52, 457, 458, 460, 462, 473, 475, 488, 491, 492-93, 502, 506, 511, 512, 514
"graymail," 170
Green, Bruce, 172
Green, Tom, 62, 83, 164, 166
Greenberg, Stan, 462
Greene, Harold, 314
  in Poindexter trial, 224, 226, 227-28, 231, 232-33, 234, 235, 238, 240, 243, 244, 245, 246, 247, 310
Gregg, Donald, 22, 93, 105, 106, 255, 261-62, 266, 270-71, 272, 285, 319, 432-33, 452, 511, 514
Gries, David, 431
Guatemala, 191, 195
Gulf War, 517
Gunther, Gerard, 508

Hakim, Albert:
  background of, 53
  congressional testimony of, 122-24, 168
  conspiracy charge against, 158
  Contra funds managed by, 20, 45, 49-50, 223
  in Europe, 35
  immunity for, 60, 63, 89, 91-92, 98, 122, 126, 140, 149, 168, 223
  indictment of, 145
  Iran arms sales and, 45, 54, 123, 223
  North's relationship with, 76, 123-24, 149, 150, 153
  North's trust fund established by, 61-62, 149-50, 223

  plea bargain for, 223-24, 253
  profiteering by, 151, 152
  as Secord's partner, 52-53, 81, 107, 108, 118, 119, 122, 126, 146, 150, 153
  Swiss bank account of, 49-50, 56-57, 60, 63, 81, 89, 91, 92, 119, 125, 126, 146-47, 149, 196, 223
  Walsh's investigation of, 49-50, 56-57, 97
  as witness, 98, 150
Hall, Fawn, 12, 58-59, 62, 75, 76, 78, 81, 83, 87, 99-100, 122, 124-25, 131, 187, 208, 234, 240
Hamilton, Lee H., 48, 49, 50, 59, 63, 86, 117, 185-86, 190, 191, 199, 207, 236, 237, 238, 239-40, 282, 302, 306-7, 401, 438, 508
Hand, Learned, 248
Harding, Warren G., 490
harmless error doctrine, 139-40
Harris, George, 477, 510-11
Harris, Lowell Gordon, 141
Harris, Margaret, 429
Hasenfus, Eugene, 21, 79, 80, 101, 108, 123, 196, 244, 254, 255, 266, 269, 277, 280, 285, 295, 306, 307, 424, 432, 446
Hassler, Bill, 66, 98, 223
Hatch, Orrin, 67, 134, 417, 472
Hawk missiles, 5, 9-15, 39-40, 46-47, 54, 71, 99-102, 108-21, 132-55, 196, 203, 206, 224, 233, 237-45, 255, 268, 269, 275-76, 297, 303, 312, 313, 327-34, 341-46, 353, 361-65, 375-89, 396-408, 415, 452
Hayes, Woody, 293
Headline News, 448
Helms, Jesse, 250
Helms, Richard, 291
Hemingway, Ernest, 517
Herblock, 287, 298
Hetherton, Judith, 66, 141, 386
Heyman, Philip, 302
Hezbollah, x, 4, 7, 36
Hibey, Richard, 289-90, 433
Hill, Charles, 321, 374, 375, 377, 384
  notes taken by, 14, 112, 254, 255-56, 262, 265-70, 273, 305, 307-8, 320, 322-33, 335, 336, 338, 339-40, 346, 353, 358, 361, 363, 376, 380-86, 396, 406, 421, 453, 454, 455, 488-89, 509
Hilton, Claude M., 211-19, 221
Hitler, Adolf, 204
Hogan, Frank S., 225
Hogan, Thomas F., 418, 428, 436, 437-38, 441-42, 444, 445, 447, 471, 473, 477, 478, 482, 486, 487
Holmes, David, 216, 217
Honduras, 120, 193-94, 279, 313
Hoover, J. Edgar, 114
Hoover Institution, 255-56, 265
Horowitz, Rick, 496
hostages, U.S.:
  execution of, 6, 36, 42, 43
  kidnapping of, 4, 7, 36, 39, 111
  Reagan's views on, 4, 6, 42, 84-85, 120, 143, 229-30, 245, 352, 383, 509, 528
  release of, 5, 6, 7, 10, 14, 38, 39, 43, 46-47, 81, 84, 110, 111-12, 122, 123, 131, 144, 155, 268, 269, 270, 276, 322, 324, 327, 328, 330, 345, 347, 349-50, 352, 368, 375, 384, 389, 396, 423
  Shultz's views on, 321, 322, 324, 350, 351
  U.S.-Iran arms deal for, x, 12, 36-47, 98, 110, 111, 123-24, 152-53, 156, 236-37, 268-69, 324-30, 345, 347, 349-50, 352, 355, 375, 389, 396, 451-66
House committee on un-American activities, 524
House foreign affairs committee, 152
House intelligence committee:
  hearings scheduled by, 11, 12
  North's testimony before, 151-52, 185-86, 237-38, 239
  Poindexter's testimony before, 239-40
House intelligence subcommittee on legislation, 219-21
House select committee on Iran-Contra:
  documents requested by, 393-95
  hearings scheduled by, 48-51
  immunity granted by, 50, 58, 59, 63, 67, 86, 89
  information shared by, 49-50

North's testimony before, 85, 89
Poindexter's testimony before, 85, 89
Walsh's meetings with, 48–51, 85–86, 93, 219–21
see also Joint hearings of select committees on Iran-Contra
Hunt, Bunker, 82–83, 92, 188
Hutton, Deborah J., 105
Hyde, Henry, 117, 207, 242
Hyde Park account, 80

Iceland Saga, 81
Ilopango air base, 20, 21, 76, 79, 80, 93, 105, 106, 153, 213, 219, 266, 278, 279, 285, 295
Independent Counsel Act, 68–70, 160, 183, 249, 250, 429–31, 439, 441, 508, 518–20
Inouye, Daniel, 48, 72, 86, 88, 117, 133, 401, 402, 414
Internal Revenue Code, 158
Internal Revenue Service (IRS), 66, 67–68, 73, 80, 95, 261
International Business Communications (IBC), 82
Iran:
  Islamic revolution in, 4, 84
  U.S. arms embargo against, 6, 120, 321, 346
  U.S. arms shipments to, 5–8, 11, 38–40, 45–47, 53–54, 65–66, 71, 108–12
  U.S. relations with, 4, 6, 10, 13, 36, 266–67, 344, 351, 383, 509
Iran-Contra affair:
  arms prices inflated in, 7, 45, 46, 53–54, 99, 100, 101, 109, 111, 118, 155, 156, 295, 336, 353, 362, 363, 383
  chronology of, 11, 64–65, 116, 152, 191, 196, 203, 206, 303, 359, 361, 362–64, 368–69, 374, 375
  classified information in, 146, 147–48, 210–21, 264–65, 267, 273, 274, 319, 342, 396, 398–99, 400, 452, 473–74, 524
  compartmentalization in, 377, 378, 431
  congressional investigation of, 10–11, 12, 30–32, 199–200, 251, 366–67, 494, 495, 496–97, 521–24, 528–31
  congressional notification and, 9, 12–13, 30, 41, 44–45, 156, 191, 193, 199–200, 237, 239, 345, 347, 348, 361–62, 373–74, 378–79, 499, 525
  as conspiracy, 15, 23–25, 65, 70–71, 97, 98–99, 113–15, 127, 128, 151, 154–58, 208, 210–11, 220, 226, 233, 244, 262, 263, 267, 355, 365, 396, 397, 439, 494, 504, 510, 515–16, 527, 529
  constitutional issues in, ix, 13, 30, 65–66, 85, 98, 117, 119, 134, 142, 159–60, 169, 171, 232, 248–53, 260, 281, 287, 302, 347, 373–74, 378, 417, 418, 456, 469, 496, 506–8, 516, 520, 522, 524, 528, 531
  cover-up in, 62, 74, 76, 132, 185, 189, 202, 204, 233, 241–42, 268, 287, 289, 294, 303–4, 321, 326, 333, 334, 369, 370, 375, 379, 386, 392–96, 401–8, 464, 466, 475, 488, 495–504, 514, 527, 531
  deniability in, 212–13, 219, 220
  disclosure in, 8–15, 28, 69–70, 112, 178–80, 194, 215–21, 229–30, 301, 321–26, 333–35, 339, 350–55, 359–71, 386, 458, 512–14, 525
  foreign policy and, 25, 158, 245, 323–24, 328
  funds diverted in, 13, 14, 15, 20–25, 46, 49, 53, 65–66, 75, 80–84, 92, 97–102, 107, 116, 118, 134–36, 144, 145, 150–56, 171, 189, 196, 227–31, 240, 242, 280–85, 295–97, 302–4, 353, 363–66, 380–83, 390, 421, 528–29
  illegality of, x, 3, 5, 6, 10–14, 49, 65–66, 75, 87, 93, 127, 141–43, 152, 171, 185, 199, 204, 220, 228–33, 267, 323, 325, 328, 341, 345–47, 354, 364, 371–79, 382–88, 397, 402–7, 452, 493–99, 503–7, 517–25, 529, 531
  immunity in, 30–31, 35, 56–59, 60, 75, 79, 91–92, 99, 104, 165–68, 252–60, 300–304, 523–24
  media coverage of, 7–9, 20–25, 30, 35, 43, 47, 112, 135–36, 281, 286–89, 298, 307, 318–19, 322, 328, 360, 369, 374, 430–31, 478–79, 492–510
  national security and, 47, 51, 54, 55, 67–68, 116, 146, 158, 165, 170, 171–72, 175–82, 192–93, 210–22, 246, 289, 291–92, 296, 314, 318, 418, 420, 424–27, 445–47, 518–19
  obstruction of justice in, 65, 67, 99, 128, 129, 145, 151–52, 158, 229–30, 244–45

pardons in, 158–59, 267, 367, 429, 469–70, 475–77, 479, 482, 486, 487–88, 489, 490–510, 511, 514, 515, 516, 530–31
  political impact of, 27, 30, 31, 70–71, 72, 85–86, 88, 90, 114, 242, 267, 300, 303, 447–50, 461–68
  "private benefactors" in, 105, 106, 154, 255
  profiteering in, 98, 105, 113, 118, 122–23, 126, 146, 151, 152
  Swiss bank accounts in, x, 15, 20, 49–50, 56–65, 74, 80–82, 91, 92, 95, 101, 107, 108, 113, 119, 125–30, 146–51, 231, 295, 308, 353, 513
  tax violations in, 151, 158
  U.S. public opinion on, 9–10, 24, 31, 68, 95, 504–5
  see also Contras, Nicaraguan; Iran
Iran-Iraq war, x, 4–5, 37, 110, 120, 322, 323, 328, 349, 350–51, 352
Iraola, Roberto, 397, 398
Israel:
  information provided by, 56, 64–65, 74, 80
  Iran arms deal and, x, 6, 9, 13, 14, 15, 36, 37–46, 92, 109, 120, 140, 189, 190, 196, 224, 239, 240, 276, 277, 326, 328, 341, 345, 347, 351–55, 360, 364, 368, 375, 383, 387, 388–89, 396, 407–8
Ivins, Molly, 505

Jackson, Andrew, 519
Jacobsen, David P., 111–12, 350
James I, King of England, 521
Janis, Richard, 126, 164, 166
Jaworski, Leon, 225
Jenco, Lawrence Martin, 111, 330, 349–50
Johnson, Lyndon B., 469
Johnston, David, 287, 414, 415, 442, 456, 476
Joint Chiefs of Staff, U.S., 77, 345
Joint hearings of select committees on Iran-Contra:
  hearings scheduled by, 49
  immunity granted by, 95, 97, 125–26, 138–39, 142
  preparations for, 96–97
  public reaction to, 96, 116, 118–19, 124–25, 126
  report of, 154
  Republicans on, 116, 117, 134
  schedule for, 115–16, 127, 130
  televised proceedings of, 96–97, 115, 116, 118–19, 122, 124–25, 136, 137, 138–39
  see also House select committee on Iran-Contra; Senate select committee on Iran-Contra
Jones, Donald S., 349
Justice Department, U.S., 49, 78, 113, 148, 164, 224, 227, 231–32, 274, 282, 287, 312, 318, 372, 374, 419, 422, 428, 431, 470, 472, 473, 474, 506, 519, 525, 526, 527

Kagan, Robert, 107
Kansas Gas and Electric Company (KGE), 25–26, 89, 468
Kansteiner, Walter, 458
Kaplan, Jeffrey, 285
Kastenmeier, Robert W., Jr., 219
Kastigar decision, 58, 139, 143, 157, 160, 223, 226, 259
Keefer, Elizabeth "Libby," 180
Keel, Alton, 350, 352, 362, 373
Keker, John, 29, 55, 61, 66, 73, 77, 86, 128, 129, 148, 284, 445, 484
  North prosecuted by, 174–75, 179, 180, 183, 185, 188, 189, 191, 192, 193, 197, 198, 200–203, 204, 206, 208, 235, 251, 257
Kemp, Jack, 440
Kennedy, John F., 226, 371
Kennedy, Robert F., 371
Kerr, Richard, 101–2, 216, 217, 282, 295, 296, 297
Kerry, John, 424
Khashoggi, Adnan, 37, 47, 81, 109, 363
Khomeini, Ayatollah Ruhollah, 4, 10, 36, 118, 249
Kimche, David, 37, 38, 39, 41, 64
Kirk, Steven, 433
Kirkpatrick, Jeane, 13, 120, 440
Kissinger, Henry, 52, 357, 393, 394, 440
KL-43 encryption devices, 76, 104, 105, 154, 210, 265, 277, 278, 279

Koch, Noel, 345
Koppel, Ted, 419, 456, 501-3
Kostmayer, Peter, 307
Kristol, William, 488
Kuwait, 123

Lake Resources, 40, 80, 82, 92-93, 109, 223-24
Lamberth, Royce C., 294, 423, 432, 433
Landers, William, 171, 176, 179
Landon, Alf, 468
Lardner, George, Jr., 287, 318, 414, 418
Larry King Live, 448-49, 462, 470
Laxalt, Paul, 13, 304, 367, 435, 440, 471
Lazarus, Simon, 465
Leahy, Patrick, 240
Lebanon, x, 36
Ledeen, Michael, 37, 39, 42-43, 191
Lee, Robert E., 143
Lehman, John, 440
Leisz, Kay, 340, 341-42, 344, 400
Levin, Carl, 430, 439, 497, 508, 509
Lewis, Anthony, 95, 455-56, 458-59, 461
Library of Congress, 264-65, 319, 338, 340-42, 343, 398-99,
    400, 408, 499-500, 502, 510
Life, 273
Lighthizer, Robert, 483
Liman, Arthur, 57-58, 63, 67, 86, 88-89, 92, 118-19, 122,
    123, 126, 132, 133, 393, 394, 439
Lincoln, Abraham, 505
Livingston, Bob, 219
Llewellyn, Karl N., 48*n*
Lodge, Henry Cabot, 321
Looking Forward (Bush), 453
Los Angeles Times, 23, 67, 245, 288, 369, 462, 469, 504, 505
Lott, Trent, 366
Luciano, Charles "Lucky," 226-27
Lumpkin, Beverley, 480
Lynch, Gerard, 172, 215, 251-52, 260

McCarthy, Joseph, 115. 470, 501, 529
McCollum, Bill, 134
McCreary-Maddox, Carol, 424-25
McDaniel, Rodney B., 243-44
McFarlane, Robert C. "Bud":
    attempted suicide of, 77
    background of, 52
    Bush's relationship with, 155
    congressional testimony of, 28, 35, 83, 116, 117, 119-21,
        151, 157, 185, 199-200, 368, 404
    Contra funding arranged by, x, 19, 20, 21, 83, 235-36
    FBI investigation of, 52
    indictment of, 145
    information withheld by, 157, 190, 199-200, 202, 229
    Iran arms deal negotiated by, 4-5, 7-8, 10, 13, 14, 38-39,
        41-47, 109-10, 112, 113, 340, 341, 347, 353, 357, 360,
        364, 366, 387, 452
    letters drafted by, 190-91, 192, 198, 199-200, 228-29,
        236-37, 239, 240, 245, 308
    Meese's views on, 363, 382, 383, 384
    as national security advisor, 52, 85, 237, 357-58
    North's relationship with, 77, 83-84, 103, 118, 120-21,
        131, 132, 146, 151, 172, 190-92, 199-200, 202, 236,
        303
    in North trial, 174, 175, 190-96, 258, 273, 284-85,
        298-300
    obstruction of Congress by, 151, 191
    pardon for, 490-510
    plea bargain for, 156-57, 190, 207, 229
    PROF notes of, 177, 184
    Reagan's relationship with, 157, 229, 249, 347, 364, 381,
        396
    Regan's relationship with, 8, 35, 355, 357. 360, 368, 369,
        389
    resignation of, 77, 359
    responsibility of, 23, 24, 70, 77, 151, 191, 235-36, 521
    Shultz and, 326-27, 341, 344, 364, 376, 381, 382, 384, 404
    Tehran mission of, 7-8, 45-47, 84, 101, 109-10, 112, 121,
        144, 152, 322, 328, 329, 349, 381, 404, 456

Walsh's investigation of, 75-78, 97
Weinberger's relationship with, 268, 336, 340, 344-46,
    387-88, 391-92, 396, 400, 404, 406, 407
as witness, 77-78, 146, 157, 175
McGinniss, John, 383
McGrath, Dean, 240
McGrory, Mary, 418, 453
McHugh, Matthew F., 219
MacKenzie, John P., 464
MacKinnon, George, 26, 27, 249, 438, 477
McLaughlin, Jane, 60
McMahon, John, 6, 40-41, 276, 297, 391
McMahon, Robert Bernard, 367
McManus, Doyle, 415
McMillan, John G., 483, 484
MacNeil, Robert, 498, 499-501
MacNeil-Lehrer Newshour, 497-501
Mansfield, Walter, 26-27
Mark, Greg, 340
Martin, John, 176
Mattke, Terry, 514
Meddis, Sam, 455
Medina, Harold, 248
Meese, Edwin, 371-86
    as attorney general, 146, 356, 371, 372, 373, 375
    background of, 371-72
    conflict-of-interest of, 362, 525
    congressional testimony of, 136, 137, 375-76, 377, 386
    deposition of, 378, 385-86
    disclosure as viewed by, 352, 353, 354, 359, 362-65, 370,
        371, 386
    grand jury testimony of, 376
    investigation by, 12-15, 23, 31, 33, 34, 53, 54, 55, 62, 78,
        83, 99, 112-13, 135, 137, 189-90, 191, 196, 203, 204,
        241-42, 269, 325, 333, 334, 358, 361, 362-65,
        380-85, 408, 512-13, 525
    Iran arms sales and, 341, 343, 348, 361, 373-86
    McFarlane's role as viewed by, 363, 382, 383, 384
    North's role as viewed by, 24-25, 189-90, 363, 380, 383
    in North trial, 174, 189-90
    notes of, 148, 372, 380, 386
    as NSPG member, 3, 4, 373
    perjury charge against, 377, 386
    Poindexter's relationship with, 372-73, 375, 376, 380,
        382
    in Poindexter trial, 234, 241-42
    presidential finding and, 347, 372, 373, 374, 375, 379,
        380, 381, 382-83, 384
    Reagan's relationship with, 371, 373, 377, 378, 379-86,
        407
    Regan and, 361-65, 378
    responsibility of, 112-13, 370, 386
    Walsh's investigation of, 371-86, 413, 438
    Weinberger and, 440, 476
    as witness, 386, 403, 408, 487
Meet the Press, 455, 482, 508
Meisler, Stanley, 240
Melton, Richard H., 269, 285
Merchant, Bryan, 91
Metzenbaum, Howard M., 296, 484
Miami Herald, 20
Michel, Robert H., 48, 49, 281, 283, 366, 426, 430, 443, 485
Mikva, Abner J., 248, 250, 310-11
Miller, Richard R., 60, 66, 81, 82, 92-93, 95, 153, 206
Mitchell, George J., 32, 126, 127, 133, 221, 455, 474, 476,
    496, 508
Mitchell, John, 371, 386
Mixter, Chris, 66, 77-78, 113, 141, 174, 175, 177, 179, 180,
    182, 222, 242, 243
Moe, Dick, 48
Moellering, John, 266, 279
Mohammed Reza Shah Pahlavi, 4, 36, 46, 107
Mondale, Walter, 484
Morrison, Alexia, 159-60
Morrison v. Olson, 528
Moses, 142
Motley, Langhorne A., 194
Murkowski, Frank, 294, 297

National Endowment for the Preservation of Liberty (NEPL), 60, 82–83, 107, 151, 187–88
National Security Act, 3, 13, 347, 348, 373, 525
National Security Agency (NSA), 8, 76, 100, 104, 165, 176, 177–78, 179, 181, 184, 210, 349, 362, 383, 404–5
National Security Council (NSC):
  blame shifted to, 14–15, 70–71, 365–66
  computer system of, 63–64
  Contra activities of, 19, 21, 70, 102, 119–20, 128, 185, 229, 236, 240, 242, 275
  files of, 8, 12, 35–36, 53, 67, 78, 91, 94, 148, 165, 170
  Iran arms sales and, 152–53, 267, 275, 346, 365–66, 374, 396
  staff of, 58, 78, 357–58, 360, 365, 374, 396, 514, 519, 520
  Walsh's investigation of, 145, 147–48, 165, 254, 262, 263–64
  see also National Security Planning Group (NSPG)
National Security Decision Directive, 36
National Security Planning Group (NSPG):
  Bush in, 3, 14, 41, 286, 453
  Casey in, 3, 14, 38, 41
  Meese in, 3, 4, 373
  meetings of, 3–4, 8–9, 13–14, 19, 38, 41, 53, 194, 270, 285–86
  Poindexter in, 3–4
  presidential finding and, 44–45
  Regan in, 3, 4, 14, 38, 286, 359
  Shultz in, 3–4, 14, 38, 41, 333
  Weinberger in, 3, 38, 41, 337, 394, 414
Nelson, Lars-Erik, 287, 465–66
Newington, Barbara, 202
Newsmaker Saturday, 419, 460
Newsmaker Sunday, 478
Newsom, Eric, 240
New Yorker, 516
New York Times, 232, 287, 291–92, 301–2, 417, 423, 439, 445, 447, 458, 461, 467–68, 475–77, 478, 482, 504, 505
Nicaragua:
  Cuban arms transfers in, ix, 17, 18
  elections in, 423
  Sandinista movement in, 16–17, 18, 104, 116, 191, 193, 194, 195–96, 265, 278, 293, 312, 318
  U.S. relations with, 16–17
  see also Contras, Nicaraguan
Nicaraguan Democratic Force (FDN), 17, 19
Nicaraguan Humanitarian Assistance Office, 106
Nields, John W., Jr., 59, 63, 68, 89, 91–92, 98, 118, 282, 394–95
Nightline, 419, 456, 497, 498, 501–3
Nimrodi, Yaacov, 37, 38, 39, 41
Nir, Amiram, 42, 47, 109, 111, 155, 269, 330, 456
Nixon, Richard M., 69, 115, 207, 225, 249, 334, 337, 357, 371, 379, 386, 394, 418, 435, 440, 469, 477, 490, 491, 495–96, 507
Noble, Ron, 216, 217
nolo contendere plea, 435–36
Noriega, Manuel, 195–96, 305, 308, 430, 431
North, Betsy, 62, 91, 98, 122–23, 135, 149–50
North, Oliver L.:
  Abrams and, 104, 153, 209, 255, 265–66, 285, 305, 308
  appointment records of, 186–87
  authorization for, 132, 145, 154, 155, 157, 172, 177, 180, 192, 196–97, 199, 200, 205, 206, 208, 233, 236, 302–4
  background of, 51–52
  bodyguards of, 254
  Bush's relationship with, 155, 261, 304, 456
  car payments of, 200–202
  Casey's relationship with, 105, 107, 132, 153, 197, 199, 275, 286, 295–96
  character of, 117, 120–22, 186, 187, 198
  conflict-of-interest of, 153
  congressional testimony of, 28, 30, 83, 85, 88–89, 90, 97, 114, 126–35, 138, 139, 145, 146, 151–52, 157, 159, 160, 165–68, 184–85, 200, 206, 223, 235–39, 251–60, 298–300, 303–4, 311, 377, 529
  Contra support directed by, x, 13, 14, 19–21, 74–77, 81–83, 103–7, 131–34, 153, 155, 171, 236–37, 243, 275, 279, 367, 383, 431, 432

credibility of, 117, 127, 200, 243
criminal intent of, 127–29, 145, 250–51, 252, 258
dismissal of, 15, 100, 204, 354, 365, 366, 384, 524
documents altered by, 62, 78, 98, 124–25, 132, 187, 199–200, 241, 380
documents destroyed by, 8, 23, 58–60, 62, 67, 72, 75, 83, 87, 90, 93, 98, 99, 124, 127, 185, 187, 191–92, 202, 204, 206, 240, 241, 244, 252, 256, 258, 295, 299, 380
encryption used by, 76, 93, 104, 105, 154, 278, 279
false statement accusation against, 99, 127, 128, 131, 151–52, 158, 233, 236, 237–38, 239
FBI investigation of, 35, 51–52, 63
George and, 45, 68, 100, 101, 294
grand jury testimony of, 254, 261, 262, 279
Hakim's relationship with, 76, 123–24, 149, 150, 153
"honorable disposition" for, 158
immunity for, 63, 67, 88, 90, 126, 127, 129, 130, 138, 140, 146, 157, 165–68, 247, 252–60, 282, 300–302, 304, 325, 367, 386, 523–24
Independent Counsel Act challenged by, 68–69
indictment of, 59–60, 89–90, 98–99, 113–14, 127–31, 134, 145, 155–59, 166, 172, 177, 178, 179–81, 184, 196, 284
Iran arms sale directed by, xi, 5, 7–8, 39, 40, 41, 42, 45–47, 152–53, 171, 236–37, 268–69, 378
McFarlane's relationship with, 77, 83–84, 103, 118, 120–21, 131, 132, 146, 151, 172, 190–92, 199–200, 202, 236, 303
Meese's views on, 24–25, 189–90, 363, 380, 383
memoranda of, 54, 75, 83–84, 136, 151, 189, 190–91, 202, 235, 238, 240, 302–3, 304, 382
Noriega's meeting with, 195–96
notebooks of, 43, 63, 208–9, 253, 255, 262, 278, 279, 285
pardon for, 158–59, 267, 367
patriotism of, 122, 131–34, 158, 185
Poindexter's relationship with, 77, 83–84, 103, 131–32, 136, 172, 199, 200, 233, 236, 238, 276, 302–3
in Poindexter trial, 226–27, 232–38, 310
"Polecat" codename for, 269, 326, 328, 329
power abused by, 98, 123–24
profiteering by, 98, 122–23, 127, 133–34, 145, 149–50, 151, 152, 171, 186–88, 202–4, 206
PROF notes of, 63–64, 67, 75, 76, 77, 98, 120–21, 127, 204, 237
public opinion on, 97, 126, 133, 135, 138, 141, 142–43, 207–8, 225, 302, 529
Reagan's relationship with, 23, 84–85, 100, 103, 118, 121–24, 131, 144, 154, 155, 180, 185, 191, 193, 199, 200, 202–3, 204, 206, 286, 302–4, 366, 513–14, 519
responsibility of, 23–25, 82–83, 115, 521
at RIG meetings, 77, 106, 112, 255, 266, 285, 308, 336
as scapegoat, 15, 23–25, 99, 196, 204, 303
Secord's relationship with, 107–8, 113, 118, 123, 146, 201
security system of, 94–95, 98, 127, 133–34, 145, 151, 158, 188, 200, 202, 204, 206, 223, 258, 299
Shultz's relationship with, 265–66, 308
subpoena received by, 254, 261
Swiss bank account for, 56, 62, 98, 101, 149–50, 155, 513
Tehran mission of, 7–8, 45–47, 84–85, 101, 110, 121, 329
trust fund for, 61–62, 98, 122–23, 133–34, 149–50, 223
Walsh's investigation of, 28–29, 31, 32, 35, 55, 59–61, 72, 75–76, 97–100, 127–31
as witness, 74, 97–98, 127, 145–46, 174, 199–203, 208, 254, 261, 262, 263
North, Oliver L., trial of, 182–209
  appeal for, 180, 207, 247, 248, 249, 250–53, 256–61, 263, 273, 282, 283, 301, 310, 477, 523–24
  appellate brief for, 252
  classified documents in, 149, 157, 165, 168–72, 175–84, 196, 212, 219, 284, 319, 326
  conspiracy charge in, 155–56, 158, 167, 171, 172, 173, 174, 176, 177, 179–81, 196, 211, 326, 355
  defense team in, 163–64, 397
  discovery in, 164–65, 170, 171, 172
  dismissal in, 300–302, 304, 318–19
  diversion charge in, 155, 171, 172, 173, 179–80, 181, 196
  evidentiary hearing for, 257–58

North, Oliver L., trial of, *(continued)*
  ex parte conferences in, 169–71, 176
  false statement charge in, 158, 171, 173–74, 185–86, 191,
    193, 198–99, 204, 229, 232
  Gesell as judge in, 188, 190, 191, 192, 193, 194, 196–97,
    205–8, 257–58, 259, 260, 298, 299
  jury for, 174, 181, 183, 184, 188, 192, 196, 199, 205–6, 211,
    260
  Keker as prosecutor in, 174–75, 179, 180, 183, 185, 188,
    189, 191, 192, 193, 197, 198, 200–203, 204, 206, 208,
    235, 251, 257
  McFarlane's testimony in, 174, 175, 190–96, 258, 273,
    284–85, 298–300
  media coverage of, 158, 159, 184, 205, 251, 300–302
  Meese's testimony in, 174, 189–90
  North's testimony in, 199–203
  obstruction of justice charge in, 158, 193
  pretrial proceedings for, 163–81, 182
  prosecution team in, 149, 164, 174–75, 185
  quid pro quo stipulation in, 183–84, 192–93, 195, 196
  remand hearing for, 251, 256, 258–59, 260, 282–85,
    298–302
  Republican reaction to, 247, 248
  sentencing in, 207–8
  severance in, 156, 166–68, 223
  Sullivan as defense lawyer in, 157–58, 164, 166, 172–73,
    174, 175, 182–83, 184, 185, 188, 189, 192, 193, 196,
    198, 199, 200, 204–5, 207, 300, 326
  summaries of grand jury testimony provided in,
    257–58
  summations in, 204–5
  Supreme Court rejection of, 260, 282, 283, 284, 298, 300
  tax violations in, 151, 158
  trial date for, 168, 172
  verdict in, 205–7, 318–19
  witnesses in, 165, 166, 168, 174–75, 185–204, 253, 256–59,
    282, 284, 310
Novak, Robert, 414–15, 491
Nunn, Sam, 296

Oakley, Robert, 327, 329–30
Office of Government Ethics (OGE), 424–25, 429
Old Man and the Sea, The (Hemingway), 517
Olson, Ted, 421–22
O'Neill, Thomas P. "Tip," 48
Opala, Marian, 490
Operation Recovery, 45, 294
Operation Staunch, 4
Ortega, Daniel, 17, 18
Ostrow, Ron, 415
Owen, Robert, 91, 104, 106, 121–22, 186–87, 238

Palestine Liberation Organization (PLO), 39
Palmer, Thomas, 304
Parry, Robert, 515–16
Parsigian, Ken, 437, 447, 449–50
Passage, David, 106
Pastora, Eden, 17, 18, 104, 265, 278, 279
Pearl, Howard, 222, 226
Pearson, W. Robert, 239
per curiam opinions, 256
Peres, Shimon, 37, 42, 111, 155
Perle, Richard, 501
Perot, Ross, 46
Persico, Joseph E., 292, 312
Pertman, Adam, 304
Petroleum Club (Dallas), 188
Philadelphia Inquirer, 417
Phillips, Howard, 302
Pierson, DeVier, 305, 309
Pincus, Walter, 287, 414, 418, 419, 421–22, 463
"Plan of Action," 14–15, 365–66
Platt, Nicholas, 254, 268, 269, 308, 320, 321, 323–30, 335,
    382, 396
Poindexter, John:
  authorization for, 154, 155, 225–26
  background of, 52
  Bush's relationship with, 452–53, 455, 456, 458

congressional testimony of, 11, 28, 30, 83, 85, 88–90, 97,
    126, 127, 130, 135–41, 151, 152, 160, 165–68, 174,
    196, 206, 222, 224–27, 232, 233, 239–40, 258, 303,
    310–12, 334, 352–53, 359, 372–79, 448, 449
  Contra support approved by, 20, 131–32, 144, 195,
    235–36, 243–44, 272, 275, 367
  credibility of, 136
  disclosure opposed by, 8, 9, 10–11, 112
  documents destroyed by, 229–30, 233, 238, 241, 244, 380
  FBI investigation of, 23, 52, 97
  George and, 45, 349, 431
  grand jury testimony of, 262, 264
  immunity for, 67, 88, 90, 97, 130, 140, 165–66, 167, 168,
    224, 247, 254, 304, 310, 367, 386
  indictment of, 89–90, 127, 145, 224–25, 240, 409
  Iran arms sales negotiated by, 5, 6–7, 8, 39, 40, 41, 42, 44,
    46, 118, 140–41, 144, 233, 237, 245, 275, 341, 352,
    353, 378, 384
  Meese's relationship with, 372–73, 375, 376, 380, 382
  as national security advisor, 224, 237, 272, 373
  North's relationship with, 77, 83–84, 103, 131–32, 136,
    172, 199, 200, 233, 236, 238, 276, 302–3
  as NSPG member, 3–4
  pardon for, 158–59, 267, 367
  PROF notes of, 64, 224–25, 238, 245, 359, 455
  public opinion on, 136
  Reagan's relationship with, 144, 145, 154, 155, 225–26,
    228–30, 240–41, 244, 245, 312, 348, 361, 513–14, 528
  Regan and, 359, 513
  resignation of, 15, 238, 267, 354, 365, 366, 384, 421, 513,
    524
  responsibility of, 15, 23, 24, 70, 115, 135–36, 521
  Shultz's relationship with, 321, 322, 328–29, 335, 359,
    363, 382, 512
  Walsh's investigation of, 29, 31, 32, 35, 75–76, 97, 262
  Weinberger's relationship with, 328, 330, 336, 344, 404
  as witness, 74, 146, 254, 262, 263, 264, 275
Poindexter, John, trial of, 222–46
  appeal for, 247, 262, 310–12, 409, 437, 477
  authorization defense in, 225–26, 227, 229, 241
  Beckler as defense lawyer in, 225, 228, 233–34, 240, 241,
    244, 245
  classified documents in, 149, 157, 165, 226, 234, 427
  conspiracy charge in, 158, 167, 224, 355
  defense team in, 164
  discovery in, 164–65, 170
  diversion charge in, 131–32, 224, 231
  Greene as judge in, 224, 226, 227–28, 231, 232–33, 234,
    235, 238, 240, 243, 244, 245, 246, 247, 310
  jury in, 231, 232, 235, 240, 241, 245–46
  media coverage of, 228, 231, 234, 240, 241, 244, 245, 246
  Meese's testimony in, 234, 241–42
  North's testimony in, 226–27, 232–38, 310
  obstruction of justice charges in, 158, 224, 225, 229–30, 233,
    244–45, 311, 403, 408, 409, 437, 441, 442
  perjury charge in, 151, 158, 224–25, 228–29, 230, 233
  pretrial proceedings for, 163–68, 210
  Reagan's testimony in, 227–32, 234, 240–41, 245, 246
  reversal in, 310–12, 318–19, 403, 437
  severance in, 156, 166–68, 233
  "specific intent" in, 245
  summations in, 244–45
  Supreme Court decision on, 311, 318, 482
  verdict in, 246, 253
  Webb as prosecutor in, 222, 226, 228, 229–31, 233,
    234–38, 240, 244–45, 246, 253
  witnesses in, 165, 166, 168, 225, 232–44, 310
Polgar, Thomas, 297, 455
Powell, Colin, 179, 342, 343–44, 346, 347, 348, 349, 352, 388,
    403, 405, 415, 506
Powell, Lewis, 143, 146
Prensa, La, 16, 17
presidential elections:
  of 1976, 25
  of 1980, 372
  of 1984, 19
  of 1988, 32, 72, 87, 155, 452, 468
  of 1992, 415, 439, 448–50, 451, 452, 454–68, 478, 502

Presock, Patti, 512
Price, Charles, 329
Project Democracy, 20–21, 77, 108, 109, 128, 237, 308
Puzzle Palace, The (Bamford), 181

Quayle, Dan, 354, 458, 463, 448, 502, 506
"queen for a day" arrangement, 94
quid pro quo agreement, 183–84, 192–93, 195, 196, 213,
    214, 217
Quinn, Kenneth, 320, 330
Quintero, Rafael, 104, 187, 210, 271, 279

Rabin, Yitzhak, 39
Radin, Louise, 66, 113, 222, 240, 256, 265, 267
Rafsanjani, Ali Akbar, 7, 45–46, 47, 329, 330
Ramsey, Norman P., 261
Raphel, Arnold, 320, 328, 330
Rather, Dan, 455, 456
Rauh, Carl, 397, 398, 401, 403, 405, 407, 410, 428, 437, 478,
    483
Rawlinson, Lord, 146
Read, Donald, 142
Reagan, Nancy, 303, 334, 353, 354, 356, 359, 360, 361, 369,
    422
Reagan, Ronald:
    Bible inscribed by, 85
    briefing books of, 85, 357
    Bush's pardons supported by, 488, 497
    Bush's relationship with, 227, 231, 369–70, 500, 502, 512,
        513–14
    Casey's relationship with, 24, 105, 144, 293
    chronology used by, 368–69
    Contra aid supported by, ix–x, 46, 60–61, 76, 93, 119–20,
        131–32, 144, 179, 183, 187, 193–94, 195, 196–97,
        199, 227, 230–31, 245, 520, 528–29
    credibility of, 231–32
    deposition of, 420–21, 427–28, 444, 473–74
    diary of, 9–10, 227, 368, 393–94
    disclosure as viewed by, 56, 69–70, 180, 339, 350–54
    executive privilege of, 227, 236–37, 254, 523
    foreign policy of, 25, 158, 245, 323–24, 328
    as governor, 372
    hostages as viewed by, 4, 6, 42, 84–85, 120, 143, 229–30,
        245, 352, 383, 509, 528
    impeachment as danger for, xi, 3, 9, 24, 72, 189, 355,
        358–59, 360, 379, 397, 407, 494, 499, 520, 522–23
    interrogatories submitted to, 154–55, 228, 229–30,
        420–21, 427–28, 444, 473–74
    Iran arms sales supported by, x, 3, 6–7, 11–15, 38, 40–45,
        71, 110, 111, 118, 120, 137, 143–44, 152, 179, 227,
        228, 242, 269, 270, 303, 327–29, 343, 345, 350–54,
        360–64, 375–76, 379, 384–87, 396–97, 449, 452, 461,
        499
    isolation of, xi, 14–15, 23–25, 71, 83, 100, 119, 135, 354,
        365–66, 500, 502, 513–14, 520–21, 531
    judicial appointments by, 248
    McFarlane's relationship with, 157, 229, 249, 347, 364,
        381, 396
    Meese's relationship with, 371, 373, 377, 378, 379–86, 407
    memory lapses of, 228, 393, 420–21, 422
    North's relationship with, 23, 84–85, 100, 103, 118,
        121–24, 131, 144, 154, 155, 180, 185, 191, 193, 199,
        200, 202–3, 204, 206, 286, 302–4, 366, 513–14, 519
    pardons considered by, 158–59, 267, 367, 490
    Poindexter's relationship with, 144, 145, 154, 155,
        225–26, 228–30, 240–41, 244, 245, 312, 348, 361,
        513–14, 528
    in Poindexter's trial, 227–32, 234, 240–41, 245, 246
    presidential finding signed by, 12, 40–41, 44–45, 90–91,
        140–41, 152–53, 196, 203, 224, 233, 234, 238–44,
        297–98, 347–53, 355, 359, 360, 363, 366, 380, 514
    press conference of, 269, 333, 354, 374, 375
    Regan's relationship with, 356, 358–61, 365–66, 368–70,
        375, 378
    responsibility of, 71, 83, 90, 95, 112, 113, 116, 135, 136,
        143–45, 154–55, 206, 207, 223, 227, 228–31, 244,
        245, 266, 286, 302–4, 310, 312, 314, 396, 516, 519–20,
        521, 528–29, 531

    Shultz's relationship with, 266, 268, 269, 321, 323–24,
        327–28, 329, 333–34, 335, 346, 353, 361, 375, 379,
        381–82, 386
    tape recording system used by, 148
    television addresses of, 11, 143–44, 233, 360, 374
    terrorist negotiations opposed by, x, 3, 4, 10, 123, 322,
        323, 329–30, 351, 499
    Walsh's investigation of, 264, 401, 414, 416, 417, 418,
        420–23, 531
    Walsh's views on, 25, 420–21
    Weinberger reception and, 435, 440
    Weinberger's relationship with, 337–38, 346–47, 354, 405,
        406, 407, 435, 440
    as witness, 180, 196–97, 482, 487, 510
Reagan Library, 254, 358
Redman, Chuck, 321
Regan, Donald, 355–70
    autobiography of, 358
    background of, 356
    Casey and, 361, 363, 365
    as chief of staff, 356–58, 360
    congressional testimony of, 136, 137, 355, 367, 368
    Contra aid and, 286
    disclosure as viewed by, 8, 9, 13–15, 28, 333, 351, 355,
        359–60, 364–66, 367, 368
    FBI investigation of, 144
    grand jury testimony of, 359–60, 362, 364, 370, 404
    interviews of, 358, 363, 365
    Iran arms sales and, 13–15, 71, 341, 343, 361, 377, 384,
        451
    McFarlane's relationship with, 8, 35, 355, 357, 360, 368,
        369, 389
    Meese and, 361–65, 378
    notes of, 358–60, 364, 367, 370, 384, 385–86, 396, 408
    as NSPG member, 3, 4, 14, 38, 286, 359
    "Plan of Action" memorandum of, 14–15, 365–66
    Poindexter and, 359, 513
    Reagan's relationship with, 356, 358–61, 365–66, 368–70,
        375, 378
    resignation of, 78, 369–70
    responsibility of, 28, 97, 303
    Shultz and, 359–60, 361
    subpoena for, 358
    Walsh's investigation of, 355–70
    as witness, 370, 403
Reger, Brenda, 62, 99
Rehnquist, William, 183, 445, 471, 477
restricted interagency group (RIG), 77, 80, 106, 112, 255,
    266, 269, 285, 308, 336
Reuter News Service, 471, 480
Reynolds, Jim, 176
Reynolds, William Bradford, 99, 363, 372, 382, 383
Richardson, Elliot, 69
Richardson, John, 99, 112, 363, 372, 378, 382
RIGLET, 336
Riker, Walt, 472, 484
Rindskopf, Elizabeth, 176, 177, 184
Robelo Callejas, Alfonso, 17, 104
Robinette, Glenn, 94–95, 98, 127, 134, 188, 196, 200, 202
Robinson, Audrey, 58, 157, 160, 211, 261, 286, 309, 313,
    314
Rockefeller, Nelson, 96
Rodino, Peter, 252
Rodriguez, Felix, 21–22, 80, 93, 105–6, 255, 261–62,
    266, 269, 271, 277, 279, 280, 285, 307–8, 432–33, 446,
    514
Rogers, William P., 264, 338, 340, 397, 398, 400–401, 408,
    415
Rooney, Phil, 397, 425, 426
Rosenman, Sam, 372
Ross, Christopher, 320
Ross, Steven R., 281
Rothstein, Paul, 439
Rowley, James, 485
Rubenstein, Eli, 64
Ruckelshaus, William, 69
Rudman, Warren, 72, 88, 90, 93, 117, 119, 124–25, 126, 134,
    137, 207, 296, 401, 402, 414, 508, 509

Sable, Ronald, 239
Safire, William, 461
Saltzburg, Stephen A., 180, 224
Sandino, Augusto César, 16
"Saturday Night Massacre," 69, 469, 503
Saudi Arabia, x, 19, 20, 74, 80, 107, 153, 190, 195, 199, 309, 353, 389–92, 415, 520
Sawyer, Wallace, 79
Schmitz, John P., 511
Schneider, William, 505
Schwimmer, Adolf "Al," 37, 38, 39, 40, 41
Sciaronni, Bretton G., 78, 103
Scowcroft, Brent, 215–16, 217, 455, 502, 506
Secord, Richard, 107–12
    background of, 52–53
    congressional testimony of, 107, 116, 117, 118–19
    conspiracy charge against, 158
    Contra support directed by, 7, 19–21, 45, 49–50, 63, 66, 74, 79, 80, 81, 83, 107–9, 191, 275, 278, 279
    encryption used by, 76, 104, 278
    FBI investigation of, 35, 52–53
    George and, 431, 432, 446
    as government agent, 113, 152
    as Hakim's partner, 52–53, 81, 107, 108, 118, 119, 122, 126, 146, 150, 153
    immunity for, 166
    indictment of, 145
    Iran arms sales directed by, 11, 40, 44, 45, 54, 100, 108–12, 113, 118, 146
    North's relationship with, 107–8, 113, 118, 123, 146, 201
    North's security system financed by, 95, 98, 133–34, 188, 200, 204, 206, 223, 258, 299
    plea bargain for, 223
    profiteering by, 105, 126, 146, 151, 152
    staff of, 60
    Swiss bank account of, 49–50, 81, 107, 108, 119, 125, 146, 196
    trial of, 164, 223
    Walsh's investigation of, 49–50, 97
    as witness, 94, 107–12, 116, 146, 150
secure compartmented information facility (SCIF), 165
Senate intelligence committee:
    hearings scheduled by, 11, 28, 30
    immunity granted by, 58, 59, 67
    Walsh's meetings with, 220–21
Senate select committee on Iran-Contra:
    documents requested by, 392–94
    hearings scheduled by, 49
    immunity granted by, 86–89
    Walsh's meetings with, 86–89, 93
    see also Joint hearings of select committees on Iran-Contra
Sentelle, David Bryan, 250, 251, 256–60, 310, 477
Seymour, Whitney North, Jr., 69
Shackley, Theodore, 36
Shales, Tom, 241
Shapiro, Edward J., 344, 394, 395
Shaw, George Bernard, 287
Shenon, Philip, 27
Shtasel, Laurence, 211, 217
Shultz, George P., 320–35
    Abrams, 265–66, 267, 269, 305, 307–8, 309
    background of, 334
    Bush's relationship with, 266, 269–70, 334
    Casey's relationship with, 13, 305, 322, 328, 330, 335, 354
    chronology used by, 323, 324–26, 330, 333
    congressional testimony of, 11, 136–37, 267, 268, 309, 320–21, 324, 326, 327–28, 329, 330–35, 404, 453–54, 521
    Contra aid and, 195, 267, 320
    deposition of, 331–33, 384–85
    disclosure supported by, 8, 9, 321–26, 333–34, 335, 350–54, 359–60, 512
    at family group meetings, 328, 329, 332, 345
    Gillen's interview with, 267–70
    Hill's notes for, 14, 112, 254, 255–56, 262, 265–70, 273, 305, 307–8, 320, 322–33, 335, 336, 338, 339–40, 346, 353, 358, 361, 363, 376, 380–86, 396, 406, 421, 453, 454, 455, 488–89, 509

hostages as viewed by, 321, 322, 324, 350, 351
Iran arms deal opposed by, x, 3, 4, 5, 11, 14, 28, 38, 39, 41, 44, 84, 120, 136–37, 144, 266–67, 320–34, 348,   350, 352, 359, 366, 376, 403, 413, 419, 448, 452–54, 457, 459, 460
    McFarlane and, 326–27, 341, 344, 364, 376, 381, 382, 384, 404
    Meese's investigation and, 269, 363, 381–82, 384–85, 408
    North's relationship with, 265–66, 308
    as NSPG member, 3–4, 14, 38, 41, 333
    Platt's notes for, 320, 324, 325, 326–27, 328, 329, 335, 382, 396
    Poindexter's relationship with, 321, 322, 328–29, 335, 359, 363, 382, 512
    presidential finding and, 359
    Reagan's relationship with, 266, 268, 269, 321, 323–24, 327–28, 329, 333–34, 335, 346, 353, 361, 375, 379, 381–82, 386
    Regan and, 359–60, 361
    resignation considered by, 3, 13, 321, 322, 334–35, 353, 354, 361
    responsibility of, 325, 334–35
    Silberman and, 249
    Walsh's investigation of, 264, 265–70, 320–35
    Weinberger's relationship with, 268, 270, 305, 322, 328, 329, 334, 337, 338, 349, 350, 351, 352
    as witness, 176, 234, 267, 326, 487, 488
Shwartz, Robert, 55, 60, 61, 65, 66, 73–74, 80, 91, 98, 126, 128, 149, 150
Sigler, Ralph, 148
Sigur, Gaston, 103, 121
Silberman, Laurence H., 70, 159–60, 249–50, 251–52, 256–60, 283
Silverman, Leon, 28
Simon, Barry, 164, 172, 173, 175, 205, 251, 257, 258, 300
Simpson, Alan, 366, 440, 472, 476
Simpson, Natasha, 133–34
Simpson, O. J., 264
Singlaub, John K., 187, 238, 269
Sirica, John, 74
Smith, Chesterfield, 272
Smith, Thelma Stubbs, 344
Smith, William French, 195, 354
Sofaer, Abraham, 51, 112, 176, 180, 224, 267, 268, 323, 324, 326, 331, 332, 333, 374, 375, 376–77, 379, 382
Solomon, Gerald, 425, 426, 427, 430, 433, 443
Somoza Debayle, Anastasio, 16–17
Somoza García, Anastasio, 16
Southern Air Transport, 53, 74, 76, 81
South Korea, 20, 190, 191, 269
Spaulding, Christina, 343, 396, 420, 438, 444, 450, 477
Speakes, Larry, 321, 322
Special National Intelligence Estimate, 36
Special Trust (McFarlane), 300
Specter, Arlen, 472
Speer, Joseph, 516
Sporkin, Stanley, 40–41, 44, 196, 238–39, 347, 348, 382–83
Stanford Trading Technology International, 52–53
Starr, Kenneth, 482
State Department, U.S.:
    Contra activities of, 21, 22, 76, 79, 106–7, 153, 254, 305–6
    files of, 165, 170, 178, 255, 265, 267, 268
    Iran arms sales and, 46, 239, 323
    Meese's investigation and, 380–81
    North's trial and, 176, 177, 326
    Walsh's investigation of, 64, 145, 165, 262, 320, 325
Steele, James J., 253, 255, 262, 270
Steffens, Lincoln, 92
Stephanopoulos, George, 449, 455, 457, 459, 471, 473, 480
Stern, Carl, 483, 503
Stern, Herbert, 160, 175
Stewart, Geoffrey, 211, 325
Stokes, Louis, 307
Stolz, Richard, 216, 289, 291, 445–46
Strauss, Audrey, 75, 125, 128
Struve, Beverly, 272–73, 318
Struve, Guy Miller, 28, 48, 50, 51, 54, 58, 59, 65, 86, 88–89, 98, 128, 129, 130, 148, 272–73, 284, 511

Struve, Marcia, 273
Suazo, Roberto, 120, 193-94, 195
Sullivan, Brendan, 59, 68-69, 98, 126-27, 129, 131, 133, 208, 250, 254, 282, 304, 398
  in North trial, 157-58, 164, 166, 172-73, 174, 175, 182-83, 184, 185, 188, 189, 192, 193, 196, 198, 199, 200, 204-5, 207, 300, 326
Supreme Court, U.S., 58, 69, 70, 139, 143, 160, 183, 225, 249, 260, 261, 518, 524, 528
  North trial and, 260, 282, 283, 284, 298, 300
  Poindexter trial and, 311, 318, 482
surplusage, 437, 441
Symms, Steve, 440

Taft, Robert, 469
Taft, William H., IV, 344, 349, 394, 396, 404
Taiwan, 20, 190, 191, 269
Tambs, Lewis, 77, 104, 261
Tayacan Manual, 18-19
Taylor, Stuart, Jr., 480-81
Teicher, Howard, 83, 109, 456
Terwilliger, George, 431, 462
Thatcher, Margaret, 103, 420
This Week with David Brinkley, 508, 509
Thomas, Clarence, 260
Thomas, Eugene, 142
Thompson, Paul, 62, 78, 91, 92, 99, 112, 140-41, 152, 240, 285, 319, 374, 375
Thornburgh, Richard, 146, 173, 178-79, 180, 181, 183, 184, 215, 217-18, 219, 265, 274, 283, 317, 326
Thurmond, Strom, 472, 474, 475
Tiefer, Charles, 281
Time, 130, 456
Todd, Chris, 66, 128, 175
Toobin, Jeffrey, 273-74, 325
Totenberg, Nina, 27, 244, 251, 286, 289
Tower, John, 30, 55-56
Tower Commission, xii, 30, 35, 43, 56, 64, 67, 70-78, 84, 85, 115, 117, 119, 137, 154, 210, 211, 228, 265, 275, 313, 337, 343, 345, 355, 368-70, 396, 404, 457
TOW missiles, 5, 7, 38-39, 44, 45, 46, 47, 99, 109, 111, 118, 120, 328-29, 341, 345, 346, 347, 348, 349, 350, 353, 368, 374, 389, 396, 405, 408, 421
transactional immunity, 139
Trans World Arms, 80
Treanor, Bill, 223, 261
Treaty for Mutual Assistance in Criminal Matters, 151
Tribe, Laurence, 160, 507
Trible, Paul S., Jr., 87
Trott, Steven, 367
Truman, Harry S., 520
Tsongas, Paul, 484
Turmoil and Triumph (Shultz), 321
Twetten, Thomas, 45, 100-101, 153, 294
Tyler, Harold, 26, 27

Under Fire (North), 302-4
United Nicaraguan Opposition (UNO), 19, 104
United States Code, 311, 318
United States Court of Appeals for the District of Columbia Circuit, 247-53, 256-60
United States v. Lee, 143
USA Today, 417, 439, 476, 504
U.S. News & World Report, 136

Vessey, John "Jack," 391, 392, 415
Vhay, Mike, 278, 285, 340, 341-42, 343
Vietnam War, 451

Wald, Patricia, 250, 251, 252, 253, 256-60, 283
Walker, William, 285, 319
Wallison, Peter, 71, 78, 112, 320, 333, 361-63, 364, 367, 368, 369, 370, 373-74, 375, 376, 377, 379, 384
Wallop, Malcolm, 440
Wall Street Journal, 159, 440
Walsh, Ed, 176
Walsh, Elizabeth, 135
Walsh, Lawrence E.:
  ABA speech of, 141-43
  appointment of, 26-33
  audits of, 422, 424-27, 429, 440-41, 443-44, 485-86
  background of, 25-26
  Bush's pardons criticized by, 490-510
  congressional investigations and, 30-32, 47, 48-51, 55, 58, 70-71, 85-96, 116-17, 122, 125-26, 130, 131, 138-41, 259, 260, 263, 282, 300-302, 311, 367
  continuing or residual investigation by, 222-23, 253-56, 274, 283
  credibility of, 163, 419
  depositories of, 90, 97, 125, 130, 283-84
  document requests of, 29, 35-36, 55, 67-68, 73, 77, 78, 87, 90, 92, 93, 94, 97, 102, 112, 125, 130, 147-49, 170-71, 222, 254-56, 281, 325, 372, 386, 427-28, 444
  end of investigation by, 438-39, 489, 511, 514-16
  evidence evaluated by, 49, 59, 66-67, 90-91, 97, 113-14, 125, 128-29, 130, 140, 166, 175, 208, 222-23
  expenses of, 164, 165, 168, 222, 260, 262, 263, 267, 283, 287, 302, 311-12, 317, 397, 422-31, 439, 440-44, 473, 478, 482, 485-86, 497, 525-26, 529-30, 531
  FBI briefing book for, 33, 34
  FBI clearance for, 27, 87
  FBI cooperation with, 29, 32-33, 51-54, 60, 66, 73, 80, 264, 428
  final report of, 222, 272, 317, 447, 462, 515
  financial disclosure reports of, 424-25
  grand jury proceedings and, 49, 56-58, 69, 73, 74, 94, 113, 125, 129, 130, 139, 163, 188, 196-97, 198, 210-11, 254-59, 273, 282, 290, 299, 304, 313, 320, 331, 336-37, 386, 403, 406, 407, 410, 413, 448, 511, 515
  immunity granted by, 56, 57, 58-59, 60, 75, 79, 91-92, 99, 104
  independence of, 27, 35, 70, 138, 264, 317, 449, 472
  as independent counsel, xi, 26-33, 68-70, 85-86, 93, 94, 159-60, 163, 178-79, 183, 212, 217, 249, 267, 282-83, 317-18, 367, 417, 419, 425-31, 438-44, 449, 461-84, 491, 505, 508-9, 513-20, 524-31
  information shared by, 49-50, 56, 58, 68
  interagency group of lawyers and, 165, 171-72, 175-77, 182, 184, 192-93, 215, 413
  interim reports of, 93-94, 95, 420, 473, 514-15, 527-28
  interrogatories served by, 147, 154-55, 228, 229-30
  as lawyer, 25-26, 89, 163-64, 174, 183
  legal strategy of, xi, 28-29, 32, 43-44, 47, 54-55, 58, 65-67, 72, 95, 127-31, 140
  mandate of, 26-27, 31, 48, 75, 88, 90, 262, 282-83
  media coverage of, 27, 57, 73, 87, 95, 130, 142, 143, 159, 163, 164, 263-64, 283, 318-19, 430-31, 433, 439, 440, 443, 470, 473, 475, 478-79, 492-508
  national security community and, 47, 51, 54, 55, 67-68, 146, 165, 171-82, 192-93, 215-18, 222, 289, 291-92, 296, 314, 424-27, 445-47
  office of, 72-73, 283
  "one-way-street" approach by, 58
  open discovery provided by, 164-65
  polygraph test of assistant taken, 428
  polygraph used by, 261-62
  press conference of, 492-96
  public opinion and, 126, 138, 141-43, 263
  Reagan as viewed by, 25, 420-21
  Reagan's support for, 56, 69-70
  Republican criticism of, 87, 93, 282-83, 287, 422-23, 429-31, 467-86, 529-30
  reputation of, 157
  security for, 27, 33, 34, 73, 427-28, 444
  staff of, 27-28, 29, 32, 51, 54-55, 57, 59, 60, 61, 66, 73, 87, 96, 138, 145, 155-56, 163, 167, 175, 222, 262, 272-74, 318, 320, 481-82
  tainted information avoided by, 116-17, 122, 125-26, 135-36, 138-41, 154, 157, 160, 166, 175, 226, 234, 251, 253
  television interviews of, 497-504
  time limitations of, 55, 87-89, 93, 97, 130, 138
  travel expenses of, 425, 426, 429, 440-41, 443-44, 473
  Washburn University speech of, 262
  Watergate Hotel residence of, 34, 163, 425, 429

Walsh, Lawrence E. *(continued)*
    witnesses interviewed by, 57, 65, 74–75, 76, 78, 88, 90–91, 94–95, 99, 102, 129, 139–40, 163, 165, 222, 253, 274, 425, 511
Walsh, Mary, 25, 26, 27, 135, 468, 492, 493, 497
Walsh, Sara, 135
Ware, Paul, 447, 477
Warner, John, 296
Washburn University, 262, 468
Washington Post, 135–36, 287, 298, 307, 369, 421, 422, 423, 424, 456–57, 458, 463, 479, 484, 485, 491
Washington Times, 427, 430, 433, 440, 473, 475, 476, 530
Watergate scandal:
    congressional hearings for, 115
    cover-up in, 379, 386
    immunity granted in, 58
    impeachment in, 360
    Iran-Contra affair compared with, 10, 11, 30, 57, 136, 360, 375, 382, 386, 417–18, 469, 512
    Nixon pardon in, 477, 490, 495–96, 507
    Nixon tapes in, 418
    "Saturday Night Massacre" in, 69, 469, 503
    special prosecutor in, 69
    trials in, 74, 207
Waters, Lou, 416
Watson, Samuel J., III, 105, 106, 255, 270, 271–72, 285, 319
Webb, Dan, 262, 403, 419, 438, 503
    in Poindexter trial, 222, 226, 228, 229–31, 233, 234–38, 240, 244–45, 246, 253
Webster, William, 102, 148, 171, 176, 179, 212, 216
Weinberger, Caspar W., 336–54, 387–410, 413–50
    arraignment of, 418–20
    background of, 337–38
    Casey and, 344, 345, 391
    chronology used by, 350
    Clark's proposal for, 434–36, 442–43, 476
    classified information for, 413, 444–45, 447, 499–500, 502
    congressional testimony of, 136–37, 340, 343, 344, 346–49, 352, 354, 370, 387–91, 396, 397, 399–402, 403, 407–8, 409, 413, 437, 502, 505, 521, 530–31
    Contra aid supported by, 120, 389–92
    as defense secretary, 337–38, 418
    defense team of, 397–407
    deposition of, 394–95
    diaries of, 319, 340–41, 349, 353, 391–92, 393, 394, 395, 486, 510
    disclosure opposed by, 8, 350–54
    Donaldson's interview with, 509–10
    false statements by, 415, 434, 442, 447–50, 478, 487
    in family group meetings, 328, 329, 332, 345, 349
    health of, 434, 442, 475, 505
    indictment of, 395–410, 413–44, 499
    Inouye-Rudman letter on, 401, 402, 414
    interviews of, 336–40, 397, 402
    Iran arms deal as viewed by, x, 4, 5, 14, 28, 38, 41, 44, 45, 53, 84, 120, 136–37, 144, 255, 268, 328, 336–40, 344–53, 364, 387–89, 403–5, 413, 419, 448, 452–60, 487
    legal expenses of, 434
    McFarlane's relationship with, 268, 336, 340, 344–46, 387–88, 391–92, 396, 400, 404, 406, 407
    media coverage of, 413–18, 419, 421–23, 443, 478, 482, 484, 485, 492–510
    Meese and, 440, 476
    memoranda of, 339, 394, 415
    memory lapses of, 398, 401–2
    mock trial for, 484–86, 487
    motive of, 408, 419
    notes of, 112, 262, 264–65, 319, 328, 332, 336–54, 358, 364, 370, 384–410, 413, 415, 418, 419, 421, 437, 442, 447, 459–66, 477, 478, 480, 486, 498–500, 502, 509–10
    as NSPG member, 3, 38, 41, 337, 394, 414
    obstruction charge against, 395–97, 403, 404–5, 407–10, 415–16, 436, 437, 441–42, 447, 459, 478
    pardon for, 429, 470, 475–77, 482, 490–510, 511, 514, 515, 530–31
    perjury charge against, 343, 354, 388, 402–3, 404, 405, 408–10, 415, 416, 437, 442
    plea bargain for, 401, 403, 405–7, 410, 416–17, 419–20, 434–36
    Poindexter's relationship with, 328, 330, 336, 344, 404
    polygraph test for, 402, 414, 487
    presentation by, 405–7
    presidential finding and, 347–49, 396, 404, 406
    press conferences of, 416–17, 498–99
    pretrial motions for, 436–38, 441–42, 444–45, 447, 471
    public opinion on, 418
    Reagan's relationship with, 337–38, 346–47, 354, 405, 406, 407, 435, 440
    reception for, 435, 436, 440
    Republican support for, 417, 419, 420, 422–23, 429–31, 433, 439, 440, 443, 467
    responsibility of, 347–49, 370, 395–97, 404–5
    Saudi deal known by, 353, 389–92, 415
    Shultz's relationship with, 268, 270, 305, 322, 328, 329, 334, 337, 338, 349, 350, 351, 352
    subpoenas received by, 262, 338, 343
    supplemental indictment for, 445, 447–50, 459–71, 472, 474–75, 477–78, 480, 482–83, 487, 491, 494
    trial date for, 418, 428–29, 496
    Walsh's investigation of, 264–65, 336–54, 370, 387–410
    as witness, 406, 511, 514
    witness for, 400
Weingarten, Reid, 223
Weir, Benjamin, 10, 39, 46, 326–27, 345, 368, 374, 396
Weiskopf, George, 425
Wells, H. G., 287
Wertheimer, Fred, 431
Whipple, David, 291
Whitehead, John C., 268, 321, 327, 382
Whitewater affair, 529
Wieghart, Jim, 263, 469, 475
Wilkins, Sam, 447
Williams & Connally, 164
Wilson, Thomas, 211, 212
Wilson, Pete, 354
Wines, Michael, 462
World Court, 18
Wright, Jim, 48, 49, 351
Wright, Skelly, 247
writ of certiorari, 160, 261, 282, 283, 482

Yannett, Bruce, 65, 66
Yost, Pete, 288, 289, 414, 415, 469

Zabarenko, Deborah, 423
Zhang Wang, 103
Zornow, David, 55, 61, 66, 81, 128, 167, 174, 175, 179, 185, 284, 484
Zucker, Willard I., 56, 61–62, 81, 91, 98, 113, 122, 126, 128, 129, 146, 149, 151, 153, 155, 196